The Eastern Shawnee Tribe of Oklahoma

The Eastern Shawnee Tribe of Oklahoma
Resilience through Adversity

Edited by Stephen Warren

In collaboration with the Eastern Shawnee Tribe of Oklahoma

UNIVERSITY OF OKLAHOMA PRESS : NORMAN

This book was made possible by funding from the Administration for Native Americans.

Library of Congress Cataloging-in-Publication Data

Names: Warren, Stephen, 1970– editor of compilation.
Title: The Eastern Shawnee Tribe of Oklahoma : resilience through adversity / edited by Stephen
    Warren in collaboration with the Eastern Shawnee Tribe of Oklahoma.
Description: First edition. | Norman, OK : University of Oklahoma Press, [2017] | Includes
    bibliographical references and index.
Identifiers: LCCN 2017001724 | ISBN 978-0-8061-5744-3 (hardcover) ISBN 978-0-8061-9220-8 (paper)
Subjects: LCSH: Eastern Shawnee Tribe of Oklahoma—History. | Eastern Shawnee Tribe of
    Oklahoma—Government relations. | Eastern Shawnee Tribe of Oklahoma—Biography.
Classification: LCC E99.S35 E37 2017 | DDC 976.6/03—dc23
LC record available at https://lccn.loc.gov/2017001724

Contents

Illustrations

FIGURES

MAPS

TABLE

Acknowledgments

Ambitious projects such as the grant "A Search for Eastern Shawnee History," from which this book derives, involve the work of many hands. Having said that, Glenna Wallace, the first female chief of the Eastern Shawnee Tribe, made it all possible. Nearly four decades of work as a college professor, administrator, and global traveler certainly contributed to her visionary leadership. But it has been Wallace's intrinsic confidence in her people and the project team that has made the difference between success and failure.

The Administration for Native Americans funded "A Search for Eastern Shawnee History," and tribal citizen-scholars have used the money to travel all over the country in an attempt to repatriate their history. These individuals include Chief Glenna Wallace, Lola Hampton Purvis, Leslie Miller, Robert Miller, Renée Gokey, and Eric Wensman (Shawnee).[1] Team members joined forces with the tribe's director of cultural preservation, Robin Dushane, and several non-Native allies, including me and my friend and colleague John Bowes. Together and separately, we gathered research materials in the National Archives in both Washington, D.C., and Fort Worth, Texas, as well as Chicago's Newberry Library, the Ohio History Connection in Columbus, and the Great Lakes and Ohio Valley Ethnohistory Collection in Indiana University Bloomington's Glenn A. Black Laboratory of Archaeology. Our project team would like to thank archivists at each of these institutions, particularly Martha Briggs at the Newberry, Meg Hacker at the National Archives at Fort Worth, and April Sievert at the Glenn Black Laboratory.

Students at Augustana College and the University of Iowa, including Paul Landahl, Thom Johnson, Maxwell Moyer, Stephanie Grossnickle-Batterton, Jason Sprague, and Stacey Moultry, digitized thousands of documents. Eric Wensman, along with several other Eastern Shawnee citizens, including Karlee Gibson, Maliah Silverhorn, Shawnee Mayner, Michael Koch, Kenny Glass, and Rachel Worley, added metadata to the archival materials. Karlee Gibson also transcribed the bulk of the oral histories included in this volume. The marvelous staff at the Ohio History Connection, including Jillian Carney and Phil Sager, helped convert our research to the Eastern Shawnee Tribe of Oklahoma digital collection that is now available on the *Ohio Memory* website.[2] It is the tribe's hope that *Ohio Memory* will become the hub of this digital repatriation effort.

It has been a privilege to work on this grant because it has brought people from the Eastern Shawnee Tribe together with a handful of universities and a premier historical society in the Ohio History Connection (OHC). Stacia Kuceyeski, Sohayla Pagano, and Carmen Derrick from the OHC worked with the project team to create an online teaching manual derived from this book with the hope of returning our research to Ohio educators and their students, two communities that continue to struggle with the legacy of Indian removal in a state—Ohio—that has been so profoundly impacted by ethnic cleansing.[3]

Our grant coordinator, Michael Lowery, worked tirelessly to keep all of the grant "deliverables" moving forward, even after health problems and myriad other issues threatened our progress. Michael spent countless hours with me, working through the innumerable challenges to fulfill the objectives of this ambitious grant.

Sadly, one of our foremost contributors, William Rice (United Keetoowah Band, Cherokee), a professor of law at the University of Tulsa, passed away before his work could be included in this volume. Bill's tireless work on behalf of Oklahoma's Native peoples and his signature achievements, including being part of the working group that resulted in the United Nations Declaration of the Rights of Indigenous People, will never be forgotten.

Tami Lowery, Michael's wife, is an extraordinary grant writer who successfully integrated the Eastern Shawnee Tribe's particular needs into the work of non-Native scholars such as myself. This is no small feat. But Tami was able to translate these competing interests into a successful grant application for "A Search for Eastern Shawnee History," one of the finest, most comprehensive proposals I have ever read. Thank you, Tami.

The tribe's Cultural Advisory Council helped with many things, including the choice of subjects, the challenge of cultural privacy, and the determination of which tribal citizens we should interview. Advisory council members who have served at one time or another include Norman Amos, Patty Amos, Justin Barrett, Ben Bingham, Ben Dixon, Larry Dushane, Tammy Gibson, Shawn King, Lamont Laird, Sue Rendell, Roy Ross, Carrie Silverhorn, Maliah Silverhorn, and Chance Wallace. Others working on the grant in attendance during the advisory council meetings were Melanie Allen, Audrey Dixon, Robin Dushane, Karlee Gibson, Tami Lowery, Lola H. Purvis, Glenna Wallace, and Eric Wensman. Audrey Gardner Dixon (Eastern Shawnee) the tribe's in-house counsel, helped us manage the project on many different occasions. Marti Chaatsmith (Comanche/Choctaw), associate director of the Newark Earthworks Center, worked closely with the project team and helped devise a cultural preservation plan that will guide the efforts of the Eastern Shawnee Tribe for years to come.

As director of the Eastern Shawnee Cultural Preservation Department, Robin Dushane helped to organize the annual history summits, held every September from 2014 to 2016.[4] She and her husband, Larry (Eastern Shawnee), helped to welcome scholars and, more importantly, tribal citizens and their allies as we shared our research findings. In fact, Larry presided over the blanket ceremony that ended the history summit in 2014 and 2015, and Larry, Travis Patton, Chance Wallace, and Talon Silverhorn performed the same duty in 2016. Being wrapped in a Pendleton blanket provided our many contributors with a gift and a memory that will last a lifetime.

Over the last three years, hundreds of people have attended these summits, asked questions, and improved the quality of our work. Amid the many academically oriented papers, George Blanchard (Absentee Shawnee) and Kathleen Moore (Eastern Shawnee) worked with Eastern Shawnee children on a series of language performances showcasing the tribe's efforts to ensure that Shawnee remains a living language for future generations. Lora Nuckolls (Seneca-Cayuga), working from the tribal library, helped to promote these summits. Lora also helped us scan the many images that grace this volume. Dr. Sandra Garner of Miami University and her students assisted with research, as did Sharon Dean and Angela O'Neal.

Renée Gokey (Eastern Shawnee/Sac and Fox/Miami) took time from her work at the National Museum of the American Indian to assist us as we gathered documents at the National Archives. Meanwhile, Renée joined forces with artist Carrie Silverhorn-Boyd (Eastern Shawnee) to create yet another element of this grant: a stunning children's book entitled *The Story of Our Corn*. Based on a story given to anthropologist Erminie Wheeler-Voegelin by Nancy Skye (White Oak/Loyal Shawnee) in 1934, *The Story of Our Corn* showcases an adaptation of the team's archival research for the benefit of future generations of Shawnee children.

We would like to thank Lola Purvis, who served as the research manager of "A Search for Eastern Shawnee History" for the first and second years of the grant. Mrs. Purvis, whose personal area of interest is tribal genealogy, holds a master's degree and certificate of advanced studies in library and information science with a specialty in archival studies. For thirteen years prior to working for the tribe she was employed with the Veteran's Administration as chief medical librarian.

Our editor, Alessandra Jacobi Tamulevich, and the anonymous reviewers at the University of Oklahoma Press understood that we have designed this book for the use and benefit of Eastern Shawnee tribal citizens. It is our belief that Native scholar-activists should be included in this volume whenever possible and that, concomitantly, tribally funded research should meet the bar of peer-reviewed scholarship. We have been very grateful to the University of Oklahoma Press for understanding these dual imperatives and for helping to create a book that is designed to be of lasting benefit to the Eastern Shawnee people.

It is our hope that *The Eastern Shawnee Tribe of Oklahoma: Resilience through Adversity* initiates a new round of research and discovery of the tribe's history.

Stephen Warren

NOTES

1. Individuals' tribal citizenships follow their names in parentheses throughout this book.

2. The Eastern Shawnee Tribe of Oklahoma digital collection is available at www.ohiomemory.org /cdm/landingpage/collection/p16007coll27.

3. This book's online teaching manual can be accessed at http://educatorsguide.estoo-nsn.gov/.

4. The Eastern Shawnee Tribe History Summit is described at http://history.estoo-nsn.gov/.

The Eastern Shawnee Tribe of Oklahoma

Introduction

The Eastern Shawnees and the Repatriation of Their History

STEPHEN WARREN

From a rise above Lost Creek, the Indigo Sky Casino in Wyandotte, Oklahoma, towers over the town of Seneca, Missouri, just over the state line. On most evenings its parking lot tells an economic success story, filling with patrons from Oklahoma, Arkansas, Kansas, and Missouri who enter the sovereign territory of the Eastern Shawnee Tribe of Oklahoma to try their luck. With nearly six hundred employees, the tribe's premiere casino has become a dominant player in the regional economy. Only 2,300 people live in Seneca and about 300 in Wyandotte, so there are often more people inside the casino's walls than in either town. The Eastern Shawnees have used this success to vastly increase and diversify the tribe's finances and to provide many social services as well as educational scholarships to its people. The tribe now owns a majority share of the local bank, People's Bank of Seneca, and employs nearly 950 people in its various operations, from gaming to recycling.[1] By 2015 the tribe has grown its net assets to almost $153 million with no debt.[2]

It has not always been this way. Fifty years ago the tribe owned literally nothing but dirt. Eastern Shawnee tribal citizen Larry Kropp guessed that his grandfather, Chief Thomas A. Captain, "probably never had over a hundred dollars in the bank at one time in his life." Similarly, Chief Glenna Wallace and Norma Kraus earned their first wages as migrant farmworkers in Oregon and California. In the years following World War II most Americans enjoyed an economic boom, but the suffering of the Eastern Shawnees continued. Tribal citizens recall a time in the early 1970s when the entire tribal budget averaged fifty dollars per year. Their chronic poverty was the result of the United States government's systematic effort to deprive the Eastern Shawnees of their land. By treaty the tribe owned 60,000 acres in 1832; a century later their reservation in the four-corners region—where Oklahoma meets Kansas, Missouri, and Arkansas—had been reduced to a mere 58.19 acres, and the tribe had no assets. Landless Shawnees found work in nearby lead and zinc mines and supplemented meager salaries by planting extensive gardens, canning what they could to make it through the winter.[3] The tribe's land, in a location that gamblers find so convenient today, was a source of heartache through much of its history. Indian Territory was supposed to be free from whites, with only government officials and registered missionaries allowed in, and the sale of alcohol was illegal there. But these rules were unenforceable along the porous frontier, making border towns such as Seneca particularly dangerous. Tribal members were regularly swindled and harassed by con men, ruffians, and proponents of slavery, experiences that taught them to be wary of non-Natives, and local officials in particular.[4]

Native people can recall a litany of violence and discrimination throughout the late nineteenth and twentieth centuries. In 1879 a young Modoc man named Shepalina was shot and killed by a non-Native shop owner because he couldn't pay his store debt for a pair of boots. The store owner was later acquitted of his murder.[5]

No one was immune. The Eastern Shawnees' longtime chief Thomas A. Captain, who lived from 1884 to 1990, never forgot being beaten by a local sheriff. Larry Kropp—the tribe's first council and Captain's grandson—proudly recalls how the aging Captain told the tale, ending with how he got revenge by kicking out the lawman's teeth.[6] In the chapters that follow, various authors describe how state-sponsored violence and discrimination directly led to the taking of tribal land, the denial of access to education, and other impediments to the success of future generations.

Eastern Shawnee history confirms the "white possessive" idea, which Aboriginal scholar Aileen Moreton-Robinson has described in her analysis of Australian history. The racial logic structuring wealth, power, and what passed for democratic participation in Oklahoma was plainly evident to the Eastern Shawnees by the time they lost almost all their land. Historian David A. Chang has described how Oklahoma's Native Americans fell victim to a kind of "racial nationalism," which applied to African Americans, as Oklahoma's founders used their whiteness as a weapon, creating the Dawes allotment rolls, black codes, and other laws to control people of color. "Ensuring that a person's race was legally fixed and unchanging was crucial to the making of a capitalist order in eastern Oklahoma," he explains.[7]

The federal government established a record of every Native person's blood quantum, usually at the time of land allotment on reservations, and some Eastern Shawnees lied about their family trees, knowing that full-blooded Indians were seldom declared competent enough to lead their lives free from the guidance of government agents. However, this worked against them as well; because of U.S. government policy, children with less than one-quarter blood quantum lost the right to enroll in boarding schools. Many Eastern Shawnees fell victim to this policy, including Elsie Mae Hoevet, who is featured in this volume.

The rules left the Eastern Shawnees with very few Native spaces in Ottawa County. They had the Captain Grocery, the Seneca Indian Boarding School, the Quapaw Powwow, and the Seneca-Cayuga Cowskin Ceremonial Ground, but not much else. Between the passage of the Indian Removal Act in 1830 and the close of World War II in 1945, non-Natives gained possession of almost all tribal lands. United States surveyor Henry Goddard described the unfolding tragedy in 1904: "Whites in the Indian Territory outnumbered the Indians many times over, making a situation fraught with great peril for the Indians."[8]

The dispossession extended to the tribe's very identity, as many of the records defining the Eastern Shawnees were created by whites for their own purposes. In 2013 the tribe sought to reverse the course of this history, obtaining a 1.3-million-dollar grant from the Administration for Native Americans (or ANA, a branch of the Department of Health and Human Services) to fund "a search for Eastern Shawnee history." The tribe's grant writer, Tami Lowery, explained that the money will enable tribal citizens and their allies to collect, organize, and repatriate the tribe's history during a vast, critically important but little-known period of their history, from the end of the War of 1812 to the conclusion of World War II.

Eastern Shawnee tribal citizens chose 1813 because that is the year in which Tecumseh, their most famous warrior, was killed at the Battle of Thames. Non-Indians have amassed a robust archival and scholarly record surrounding Tecumseh, his brother, Tenskwatawa, and earlier Shawnee leaders of revitalization and reform such as Blue Jacket. Indeed, thanks to decades of research conducted on the era between the French and Indian War and the War of 1812, we now know much more about the Shawnees and their allies, including their Miami, Delaware, Wyandotte, Seneca-Cayuga, Ottawa, Potawatomi, and Sac and Fox kinsmen. Their efforts to save their midwestern homelands from land-hungry Americans are now an integral component of early American history.[9]

The same cannot be said of their descendants. Judging by the small number of scholarly articles and books on these same tribes after 1813, one could reasonably assume that their survivors died with Tecumseh. Scholarly indifference toward them becomes even more acute after the Civil War. In fact, seven of the ten federally recognized tribes now resident in Ottawa County have not been systematically investigated. These tribes are the Eastern Shawnees, Miamis, Peorias, Ottawas, Modocs, Wyandottes, and Seneca-Cayugas. Their postremoval histories remain largely unknown and therefore are poorly integrated into larger histories of both American Indian history and American history more generally.[10] Notable exceptions to the rule of ignorance are the Cherokees, and to a lesser extent, the Quapaws.[11]

Most of the thirty-nine federally recognized tribes in Oklahoma suffer from various forms of historical neglect. Unlike the Cherokees, Creeks, Chickasaws, Choctaws, and Seminoles, who have robust archival records, the smaller tribes that were removed to Indian Territory are much harder to research. For example, in 1875, 150 citizens of the Modoc Tribe arrived on cattle cars, in chains, as survivors of a genocidal war in northern California and Oregon. In contrast, at the same time, the Cherokees numbered more than 15,000 people. They arrived with their own syllabary, their own newspaper, and their own form of constitutional government. Similar processes in nation building, including the adoption of constitutional governments, did not take place until 1936, with the federal adoption of the Oklahoma Indian Welfare Act.

On a local level, the smaller tribes of northeastern Oklahoma live in close proximity, and so separating out their intersecting lives is more than difficult. Rather, it does violence to the lived experience of Native peoples in this area. In 2014 the Seneca-Cayuga ceremonial chief, Charles Diebold, reminded me, "For as long as anyone can remember, Shawnees and Seneca-Cayugas have been helping each other prepare for each other's ceremonies."[12] A similar ethic informs the relationship between the Miamis and Peorias and between the Wyandottes and Eastern Shawnees. Teasing out the differences between these Native nations may seem like a fool's errand.

Why, then, do we need a new generation of tribal histories? Scholars recall the wave of tribal histories written primarily by non-Native historians in the 1970s, at a time when American Indian history had just emerged as an academic specialization. These tribal histories tended to be strictly chronological, based almost entirely on the written record. Importantly, they shed light on the horrors of colonialism, introducing non-Native readers to a radically new, and more difficult, interpretation of American history. Even so, these authors viewed American Indian history almost exclusively in relation to colonial forces. And so their histories often closed with the last, tragic battle with American settlers. These tribal histories, then, serve as a kind of requiem for the vanishing Indian interpretation of American history.[13]

The Eastern Shawnee Tribe of Oklahoma: Resilience through Adversity offers a new brand of tribal history. This book came about because of important shifts in both tribal and scholarly communities within the Eastern Shawnee Tribe and throughout the United States. First, a new generation of tribal leaders and indigenous scholars began pursuing their own sovereign interests as never before. Spurred on by the Native American Graves Protection and Repatriation Act (1990) as well as the Indian Gaming Regulatory Act (1988), tribal communities began to sponsor their own systematic investigations of their history. Today many tribes finance their own research centers and coordinate everything from language preservation to the repatriation of indigenous artifacts, customs, and knowledge.[14] Secondly, the digital age has made it possible for these same communities to partner with academics and other related institutions. A "new ecology of learning" has emerged, one that emphasizes deeply collaborative, project-based learning experiences for tribal citizens and students alike. Non-Native scholars have become interested in sharing their work, and in many cases, in designing their research interests around the questions and concerns that are of central importance to Native communities.[15]

These new tribal histories, then, focus on questions and concerns that are of vital importance to Native communities. When speaking publicly, Eastern Shawnee chief Glenna Wallace likes to contrast her audience's knowledge of American presidents to that of Eastern Shawnee chiefs. She challenges her audience to Google "chiefs of the Eastern Shawnee Tribe" and watches as crest-fallen members of the audience slowly come to grips with the relationship between power and knowledge. Before they rise to the challenge, however, she assures them that they "won't find much. . . . From the time of our arrival in Indian Territory in 1832 until our modern reorganization in 1939, it is close to a blank slate."[16] For the Eastern Shawnees, filling that slate has meant traveling back to Ohio and Indiana to protect sacred sites, reclaim human remains, and examine historical records, not with the dispassionate view of non-Native scholars, but with the zeal of people researching their own genealogies.

Glenna Wallace has been a driving force behind this effort, along with second chief Benjamin Barnes and Roy Baldridge, both citizens of the neighboring Shawnee Tribe.[17] In July 2009, Sharon Dean, the former director of collections at the Ohio Historical Society (now the Ohio History Connection), described meeting Chief Wallace for the first time. Wallace had taken her people on a bus tour of Ohio, and one of their first stops was Wapakoneta, which had been the largest Shawnee village in Ohio before removal. In conversation with Dean, Wallace explained that "although she loved Oklahoma and called the state home, she had a responsibility to instill pride and reconnect her people to the place where their ancestors once lived."[18]

Ohio, like many midwestern states, has a problematic history with Native peoples. In 1953 Sharon Dean's predecessors at the Ohio State Museum established an "organization for the study of the historic Indian." Erminie Wheeler-Voegelin, a professor of history and folklore at Indiana University, took up the charge and became the society's first president. Their organization later became the American Society for Ethnohistory, one of the premiere outlets for the study of the American Indian. Even so, most of its founders, including Erminie Wheeler-Voegelin, were deeply involved in the work of the Indian Claims Commission. These scholars were tasked with assisting the United States government in resolving disputed treaties and, ultimately, in terminating the United States government's relationship with Native nations.[19] Small wonder that Wallace had tried, and initially failed, to meet with state officials in an attempt to protect her ancestors' remains and holy places and to remind her people of their Ohio homeland. Thankfully, a new generation of state leaders, at the Ohio History Connection in particular, promises to bring about some reconciliation.

As the Shawnee experience in Ohio makes clear, the questions and concerns of colonizers have dominated the central themes of American Indian history for far too long. Neither the Eastern Shawnees nor their non-Native neighbors know very much about the long peace that followed the War of 1812 and the various ways in which both the United States government and American settlers deprived the Eastern Shawnees of their homeland in the Ohio River valley long before they took away their new homes in Oklahoma, too.

The Eastern Shawnee case is particularly egregious because their founding leader, Quatawapea (or Captain Lewis), fought for the United States, and against Tecumseh, during the War of 1812. After the war, when territorial governor of Michigan Lewis Cass embraced the goal of removing Native peoples from the Old Northwest, Captain Lewis, and later Tecumseh's own brother, Tenskwatawa, became advocates for removal, arguing that their people would be better off somewhere far from the white vigilantes who were constantly harassing them.

Most Shawnees disagreed, making Lewis a pariah among his own people. Historian R. David Edmunds describes how John Johnston, the subagent in Piqua, Ohio, played a large role in unfairly defining Captain Lewis. His carefully researched essay reminds us to view the archival record with a degree of skepticism, and always with corroborating evidence, noting that other U.S. officials, including Indian agent and territorial governor William Clark and Secretary of War John Calhoun, showed a much more nuanced understanding of Captain Lewis. Even so, the criticism directed at Quatawapea had consequences: he died in 1826 on the Shawnees' new reservation, in what is now Kansas, estranged from the town that bears his name.

The 258 residents of Lewistown (in modern-day Logan County, Ohio) who ultimately signed the 1831 removal treaty were Shawnees and Senecas who had believed that the best way forward was a life among Americans, in a racially and ethnically pluralistic Ohio. Historical anthropologist Sami Lakomäki describes how, when they finally conceded to removal, the Shawnees made the difficult decision to stay with their Seneca neighbors from Sandusky and Lewistown, rather than their Shawnee kinspeople. While the Wapakoneta and Hog Creek Shawnees started over on a reservation in what is now Johnson County, Kansas, the Lewistown Shawnees moved with their Seneca neighbors to a reservation in modern-day Ottawa County, Oklahoma. Ohio's Native peoples lost more than their homelands in the 1830s and 1840s. They also lost a unique, multiethnic, indigenous world in which commerce, culture, and intermarriage easily intermingled.

Eastern Shawnee tribal citizens know very little about who their leaders were during this critical period. Indeed, there are so many unanswered questions, so many lines of inquiry to pursue, that this time and place offers a Pandora's box of discovery for tribal citizens and scholars alike. Eastern Shawnees do know that they owe a great debt to their ancestors, to the people who struggled to rebuild their communities after removal, and then again after the Civil War, when their people rebuilt destroyed farms even as the United States compelled them to share their land with five more tribes from Kansas and California. Glenna Wallace likes to remind her people, "We will die, but our tribe, our people, will live on."[20]

The United States government's relentless campaign of ethnic cleansing and dispossession was truly continental in scope. After the Eastern Shawnees' treaty of 1831 led to their expulsion from Ohio, they became one of thirty-one federally recognized tribes that arrived in Oklahoma between 1830 and 1877, most coming from eastern states embracing the Indian Removal Act. Ultimately, nine tribes were removed to what is now Ottawa County, Oklahoma. The Senecas, the Mixed Band of Senecas and Shawnees, and the Quapaws, arrived in the 1830s. The Ottawas, Shawnees, Miamis, Peorias, Wyandottes, and Modocs arrived in the aftermath of the Civil War. All nine had traveled very far from the lands they knew.[21]

For these tribes, some of the most significant events in their history followed soon after their arrival. The Eastern Shawnees adapted to life on a reservation they shared with Seneca Indians who had lived among them in Lewistown, Ohio. As Lakomäki points out, their removal agent, James B. Gardiner, might have pushed them to the limits of their tolerance. He forced them to begin their journey to Indian Territory in late September 1832, and they arrived days before Christmas. They were sick, they lacked provisions, and they discovered that their land lacked the improvements promised them in the 1831 treaty. Even in their weakened state, they stood firm, refusing to accept a reservation west of the Neosho River on marginal lands that would have increased their suffering. Instead, on the advice of other Seneca Indians from Ohio who had already arrived, they held out for better land between the foothills of the Ozark Mountains and the eastern reaches of the southern plains, a region described by C. A. Harris, the commissioner of Indian Affairs, as "high, healthy, well-watered, and timbered country, the soil rich and productive."[22] The Eastern Shawnees made a life for themselves in this section of Indian Territory, raising wheat, corn, and "considerable herds" of horses, cattle, and pigs. They lived well in log cabins, despite their distance from markets and the cash economy that they had thrived in for generations before then.[23]

The Eastern Shawnees signed eleven treaties that were ultimately ratified by the United States between 1795 (the Treaty of Greenville) and 1871, when Congress ended treaty making with Native peoples. Legal scholar and tribal citizen Robert J. Miller makes a powerful case for the political sovereignty of his people in his analysis of these treaties. Today some American Indians, like many of their non-Native neighbors, subscribe to the vanishing Indian thesis. In fact, the United States government continues to trace the blood quantum of its Native peoples under the false assumption that tribal identity can be revealed by one's phenotype or genome. Miller demonstrates a deeper and more multifaceted understanding of sovereignty, noting, "Through political and contract-like negotiations, tribes [have] reserved rights they already owned and traded other rights with the United States." In 1994 the Eastern Shawnee Tribe of Oklahoma amended its original constitution, which had been approved on November 7, 1939, to reflect this understanding. Their preamble states that the tribe's "inherent sovereignty has existed since historic times," and as a result, their "inherent powers of self-government . . . have not been extinguished by Congress."[24] Native American identities, therefore, are multifaceted and can't be captured by phenotype or by a fixed idea of their precolonial culture. Miller reminds readers that they are sovereign nations whose existence predates the founding of the United States and continues today.

By the 1870s the Eastern Shawnees were living among citizens of nine different federally recognized tribes, ranging from the Modocs of Northern California to the Quapaws of Arkansas. Between 1888 and 1902, Eastern Shawnee lands were allotted to individuals, and under the auspices of the 1898 Curtis Act all tribal governments were dissolved. Boarding schools and other government-funded programs aimed at assimilating Native peoples reached their apex during these decades. Then, in 1936 the United States government changed course again with the Oklahoma Indian Welfare Act, which decreed that tribes had to adopt constitutional governments modeled after the United States. All of these transformative events continue to impact contemporary tribal citizens.

Even before these sweeping changes, government agents pursued a relentless campaign to lease Indian lands to non-Native peoples. Historian John Bowes chronicles this story of dispossession as an essential prelude to allotment. He shows how leasing effectively meant that the Eastern Shawnees lost control of their land and had to find work elsewhere. Between the Civil War and World War II their diaspora extended to Tulsa, Oklahoma; Wichita, Kansas; and as far away as Oregon and California.

The Eastern Shawnees and their neighbors fought back, in part by drawing together for mutual support. Historian Amy Bergseth describes how the Eastern Shawnees developed alliances with their Indian neighbors to make up for their small population. Even before their removal from Ohio, the Eastern Shawnees lived on a reservation held in common with the Seneca-Cayugas. During the Civil War their principal spokesman, Lewis Davis, was both Shawnee and Seneca. Then in 1870 the Eastern Shawnees traveled to Okmulgee, the capital of the Creek Nation, where they joined in the Okmulgee Constitution. As Captain Lewis had done a half-century earlier, they were creating an Indian state out of tribes struggling to survive.

Tribal historic preservation officer Robin Dushane uses family papers and oral interviews to showcase the boarding school era that coincided with the allotment of Indian lands. Through the memories of Sarah Longbone and Robert BlueJacket, among others, Eastern Shawnees share memories of Seneca Indian Boarding School and other boarding schools, such as Haskell, Chilocco, and Carlisle. Their firsthand experiences with assimilation give depth and weight to the historic changes described in this book.

Nevertheless, out-migration from Oklahoma gathered momentum during the infamous Dust Bowl years. In the late 1930s and early 1940s good-paying jobs in Oregon and California lured Eastern Shawnees away. Elsie Mae Hoevet and Catherine Osborne-Gowey help readers imagine the push and pull of this diaspora. While Hoevet found work in the shipyards of Portland, others, including Norma Kraus and Glenna Wallace, worked as migrant farmworkers following the harvest in Oregon and California. Wallace ultimately returned to the Oklahoma of her girlhood, but her relatives, including Norma Kraus, stayed behind and made lives for themselves in the Pacific Northwest. Osborne-Gowey uses her family history, and the Eastern Shawnee oral histories she spent years gathering in Oregon, to reflect on the long-term consequences of this diaspora. That she continues to work for the Eastern Shawnee Tribe tells another story, one of resilience and connection in spite of the geographic distance created by this out-migration.

Second chief Ben Barnes of the neighboring Shawnee Tribe then returns the focus of the book to Ohio in order to address the ongoing legacy of Indian removal. He shares a surprisingly long series of attempts by Shawnee people to return to their homeland. Absentee Shawnee Thomas Wildcat Alford initiated these efforts in 1931, one hundred years after the Eastern Shawnees signed their removal treaty. Upon his return, Alford found himself thrust into a nationalistic display designed by white supremacists interested in justifying the conquest of Native peoples. Today, Wallace and Barnes have initiated a new conversation, one they hope is based on mutual respect and a spirit of equanimity.

Against all odds, Shawnees remained in Oklahoma. They worked under desperate circumstances in the lead and zinc mines, farmed what little remained of their land, and in some cases, developed successful careers in the government, the military, and other professions after attending boarding schools such as Seneca, Chilocco, and Haskell. The oral histories of Larry Kropp, Glenna Wallace, and Shawn King describe a tenacious commitment to their land, their people, and life itself.

The Eastern Shawnee Tribe of Oklahoma: Resilience through Adversity is only a beginning. The tribe continues to strive to learn more about the epic disaster that the Civil War visited upon its people. Unfortunately, in the course of writing this book, noted legal scholar G. William Rice, professor of law at the University of Tulsa, passed away before he could help the tribe fully understand the origins of their tribal constitution. Bill was a longtime champion of Native rights; he successfully argued for the Sac and Fox Nation in *Oklahoma Tax Commission v. Sac and Fox Nation* (1993) and he served on the working group that ultimately passed the United Nations General Assembly's *Declaration on the Rights of Indigenous Peoples*.[25]

The repatriation of knowledge is a critical first step in rediscovering Eastern Shawnee history. In partnership with the Ohio History Connection, the Eastern Shawnee Tribe is collecting and digitizing material from many archives and personal collections, including the National Archives (in Washington, D.C., and Fort Worth, Texas), the Newberry Library, the Ohio History Connection, the Kansas State Historical Society, the Oklahoma Historical Society, the Western History Collections (at the University of Oklahoma), the Randolph Noe Collection, Stephen Warren's personal archive, and many other collections we have visited over the last three years. Once collected, digitized, and labeled, these documents will be permanently stored in *Ohio Memory*, a digital archive run by the Ohio History Connection.[26]

The transmission of the archival material to tribal citizens is a central outcome of this grant. Over the past three years the Eastern Shawnee Tribe has hosted history summits, inviting scholars and tribal citizens to present subjects related to either the archival material we have collected or the time period in question. The first, on September 21, 2014, was a smashing success, with more than 260 people from twenty different states and representing twelve Native nations.

Tribal citizens have decided to disseminate their history through this volume and many other related efforts. Accordingly, this book is tailored for the specific needs and concerns of the Eastern Shawnee people, 40 percent of whom live in and around northeastern Oklahoma. Because so little is known about this period in Eastern Shawnee history, we encouraged authors to provide as much context as possible when explaining past events. This book is very much engaged in the scholarship of discovery. It is our hope that this work will inspire future historians to take up the history of the Eastern Shawnee Tribe, their Absentee Shawnee and Shawnee neighbors, and the rich multiethnic heritage of eastern Oklahoma more generally. Under the auspices of the ANA grant, the Eastern Shawnee Tribe will share this book with the 3,300 Eastern Shawnee tribal citizens.

NOTES

1. "Eastern Shawnee Tribe: Business Committee Minutes," *The Shooting Star* 3 (March 2016): 29–31.

2. Glenna Wallace, e-mail to Stephen Warren, March 13, 2016.

3. Larry Kropp, interview with Stephen Warren and Eric Wensman, this volume.

4. Norma Kraus, interview with Stephen Warren and Eric Wensman, this volume; Larry Kropp interview.

5. Robert E. Smith, "A Life for a Pair of Boots: The Murder of Shepalina," *Chronicles of Oklahoma* 71 (Spring 1991).

6. Larry Kropp interview.

7. Aileen Moreton-Robinson, *The White Possessive: Property, Power, and Indigenous Sovereignty* (Minneapolis: University of Minnesota Press, 2015); David A. Chang, *The Color of the Land: Race, Nation, and the Politics of Land Ownership in Oklahoma, 1832–1929* (Chapel Hill: University of North Carolina Press, 2010), 110.

8. Henry Gannett, "A Gazetteer of Indian Territory," United States Geological Survey, Bulletin No. 248, (Washington, D.C.: Government Printing Office, 1905), 7–8.

9. For example, see Gregory Evans Dowd, *War under Heaven: Pontiac, the Indian Nations, and the British Empire* (Baltimore: Johns Hopkins University Press, 2004); see also the numerous books of Colin Calloway, including *The Shawnees and the War for America* (New York: Viking, 2008); R. David Edmunds, ed., *Enduring Nations: Native Americans in the Midwest* (Urbana: University of Illinois Press, 2008); and, of course, John Sugden, *Blue Jacket: Warrior of the Shawnees* (Lincoln: University of Nebraska Press, 2000); and *Tecumseh: A Life* (New York: Holt, 1997).

10. Anthropologists who have studied Northeastern Oklahoma have argued that, as a result of pan-Indianism, there is little reason to study individual tribal communities. For examples, see James H. Howard, "Pan-Indian Culture of Oklahoma," *Scientific Monthly* 18, no. 5 (November 1955): 215–20; James F. Hamill, *Going Indian* (Urbana: University of Illinois Press, 2006). Scholars who have taken exception to the pan-Indian thesis include Jason Baird Jackson, "The Opposite of Powwow: Ignoring and Incorporating the Intertribal War Dance in the Oklahoma Stomp Dance Community," *Plains Anthropologist* 48 (2003): 237–53; Stephen Warren, *The Worlds the Shawnees Made: Migration and Violence in Early America* (Chapel Hill: University of North Carolina Press, 2014), esp. chap. 1. General histories of Oklahoma's removed tribes include Linda Parker, "Indian Colonization in Northeastern and Central Indian Territory," in *America's Exiles: Indian Colonization in Oklahoma*, ed. Arrell Morgan Gibson (Oklahoma City: Oklahoma Historical Society Press, 1976); David LaVere, *Contrary Neighbors: Southern Plains and Removed Indians in Indian Territory* (Norman: University of Oklahoma Press, 2001). More recently, scholars have become interested in stitching together pre- and postremoval histories. However, these scholars tend to emphasize the transition from Ohio to what is now Kansas, therefore bypassing Northeastern Oklahoma. See, for example, Stephen Warren, *The Shawnees and Their Neighbors, 1795–1870* (Urbana: University of Illinois Press, 2007); John P. Bowes, *Exiles and Pioneers: Eastern Indians in the Trans-Mississippi West* (New York: Cambridge University Press, 2007); Sami Lakomäki, *Gathering Together: The Shawnee People through Diaspora and Nationhood, 1600–1870* (New Haven, Conn.: Yale University Press, 2014); Brian Joseph Gilley, *A Longhouse Fragmented: Ohio Iroquois Autonomy in the Nineteenth Century* (Albany: State University of New York Press, 2015).

11. W. David Baird, *The Quapaw Indians: A History of the Downstream People* (Norman: University of Oklahoma Press, 1979); Tiya Miles, *The House on Diamond Hill: A Cherokee Plantation Story* (Chapel Hill: University of North Carolina Press, 2010); Theda Perdue, *Nations Remembered: An Oral History of the Cherokee, Chickasaws, Creeks, and Seminoles in Oklahoma, 1865–1907* (Norman: University

of Oklahoma Press, 1993); Andrew Denson, *Demanding the Cherokee Nation: Indian Autonomy and American Culture, 1830–1900* (Lincoln: University of Nebraska Press, 2004).

12. Michael D. Green, "Small Indian Tracts in Northeastern Indian Territory," in *Historical Atlas of Oklahoma*, ed. Charles Robert Goins and Danney Goble (Norman: University of Oklahoma Press, 2006), 110–11; Jon S. Blackman, *Oklahoma's Indian New Deal* (Norman: University of Oklahoma Press, 2013), 4; Diebold quoted in Warren, *The Worlds the Shawnees Made*, 9.

13. The trope of the vanishing Indian has a long history in American culture. See, for example, James Earle Fraser, *The End of the Trail* (sculpture), 1915, National Cowboy and Western Heritage Museum, Oklahoma City, Oklahoma. For an analysis of the evolution of the field, see R. David Edmunds, "Native Americans, New Voices: American Indian History, 1895–1995," *American Historical Review* 100, no. 3 (June 1995): 735.

14. Examples of these initiatives are too numerous to list. However, a prominent example from a Great Lakes tribe is the Myaamia Center (MyaamiaCenter.org). Food sovereignty initiatives have become an important site of decolonizing knowledge. See, for example, the White Earth Land Recovery Project (WELRP.org), and Oneida Community Integrated Food Systems (www.OneidaNation.org /tsyunhehkwa/).

15. For the "new ecology of learning," see Randy Bass, "Disrupting Ourselves: The Problem of Learning in Higher Education," *Educause Review* 47, no. 2 (March/April 2012). For recent examples of engaged scholarship, see Sergei Kan, ed., *Sharing Our Knowledge: The Tlingit and Their Coastal Neighbors* (Lincoln: University of Nebraska Press, 2015); Elizabeth Hoover, "Cultural and Health Implications of Fish Advisories in a Native American Community," *Ecological Processes* 2, no. 4 (2013); Gerald Vizenor and Jill Doerfler, *The White Earth Nation: Ratification of a Native Democratic Constitution* (Lincoln: University of Nebraska Press, 2012); Keith Thor Carlson, *The Power of Place, the Problem of Time: Aboriginal Identity and Historical Consciousness in the Cauldron of Colonialism* (Toronto: University of Toronto Press, 2011).

16. Glenna Wallace, "Did Ja Know?" *The Shooting Star* (2015); Glenna Wallace, "Current Native American Perspectives on the Earthworks and World Heritage Status," speech delivered at National Endowment for the Humanities Landmarks Workshop, "Following in Ancient Footsteps: The Hopewell in Ohio," July 17, 2015, Ohio History Connection, Columbus, Ohio.

17. There are three federally recognized Shawnee tribes in Oklahoma: the Absentee Shawnee Tribe of Oklahoma, headquartered in Shawnee, Oklahoma; the Shawnee Tribe of Oklahoma, headquartered in Miami, Oklahoma; and the Eastern Shawnee Tribe of Oklahoma, headquartered in Wyandotte, Oklahoma. These are the only federally recognized Shawnee tribes in the United States.

18. Sharon Dean, e-mail to Stephen Warren, February 29, 2016.

19. "Minutes of a Committee Meeting for the Purpose of Establishing an Organization for the Study of the Historic Indian," July 10, 1953, American Society for Ethnohstory, Box 1, Meeting Correspondence, 1953, National Anthropological Archives, Smithsonian Institution, Washington, D.C. For termination, see Kenneth R. Philp, "Termination: A Legacy of the New Deal," *Western Historical Quarterly* 14, no. 2 (April 1983).

20. Glenna Wallace, interview with Stephen Warren and Eric Wensman, this volume.

21. After the separation between the Senecas and Shawnees, Senecas originally from Lewistown merged with the Sandusky Senecas. Thereafter, members of the Cayuga Tribe, who had not previously been recognized, finally received recognition. Thereafter, the tribe became known as the Seneca-Cayuga Tribe of Oklahoma.

22. Report of the Principal Disbursing Agent for the Western Territory, Annual Report of the Commissioner of Indian Affairs, 1836–37, 585, Documents Relating to Indian Affairs, History Collection, University of Wisconsin Digital Collections.

23. Ibid.

24. The tribe's 1939 constitution may be found at www.loc.gov/law/help/american-indian-consts /PDF/40029055.pdf. Their 1994 constitution may be found at www.estoo-nsn.gov/wp-content/up loads/2011/06/Government-Constitution.pdf.

25. For Rice's obituary, see "University of Tulsa College of Law's Tribute to Bill Rice," https://turtle talk.wordpress.com/2016/02/16/university-of-tulsa-college-of-laws-tribute-to-bill-rice/. *Oklahoma Tax Commission v. Sac and Fox Nation*, 508 U.S. 114.

26. OhioMemory.org.

PART I
EASTERN SHAWNEE HISTORY
An Introduction

Over the last three years, the Eastern Shawnee Tribe has drawn on the work of a great many non-Native historians to learn more about their history. John P. Bowes and R. David Edmunds worked with research team members when they conducted research at the National Archives in Fort Worth, Texas. I (Stephen Warren) worked with research team members in Washington, D.C. Sami Lakomäki and Amy Bergseth have spoken at the Eastern Shawnee tribal headquarters and assisted the tribe in other ways in years past. Robin Dushane is married to Laurence Dushane, an Eastern Shawnee tribal citizen, and she directs the tribe's Cultural Preservation Department.

Each of these historians has engaged in the scholarship of discovery about topics that are of fundamental importance to the Eastern Shawnee Tribe. Captain Lewis, or Quatawapea, for whom the Lewistown Shawnee community was named, offers a kind of origin story for the tribe. Removal, allotment, and the intertribal alliance systems that enabled the Eastern Shawnees to survive the forces of assimilation are no less important. All tribal citizens have either personal or familial history with boarding schools. As such, Robin Dushane, Sarah Longbone, and Robert "Bobby" BlueJacket recover some of their voices.

We hope that the following chapters inspire still more research on the Eastern Shawnee Tribe during its long nineteenth century.

1

A Patriot Defamed

Captain Lewis, Shawnee Chief

R. DAVID EDMUNDS

The days were dark. His heart was heavy. On a dreary, rainy morning in early November 1825, an aging Shawnee man huddled beside a smoldering campfire amid a cluster of makeshift canvas shelters on the eastern bank of the Mississippi, near the southern end of the American Bottom floodplain in southwestern Illinois. Short of food and facing a long, cold winter, Quatawapea (the Man Who Swims Below and Above the Water), known to white Americans as Captain (or Colonel) John Lewis, sat reflecting upon a recent series of events that bore down heavily upon him. For the past four years he had journeyed back and forth between Ohio and the White River country in southern Missouri and northern Arkansas, meeting with Shawnee, Cherokee, and Delaware leaders in an attempt to establish a new intertribal homeland in the southern Ozarks. In addition he had conferred with federal officials in Saint Louis, Ohio, and even Washington, D.C., securing what he had believed to be their support for the relocation of eastern tribes onto the Missouri-Arkansas border.[1]

But it all had been for naught. His plans for the removal of Shawnee, Seneca, Wyandotte, and Delaware tribesmen from Ohio and Indiana, which had been praised by federal officials in Saint Louis and Washington, had subsequently been sabotaged by Indian agents and white traders in Ohio. Moreover, other Shawnee leaders, his own people, jealous of Lewis's assumption of leadership and fearful that federal annuities might be paid to Shawnees in Missouri rather than to their villages in Ohio, had also undercut his efforts. He knew his heart was good. He had tried. As a village chief among the Shawnees in Ohio, he had spent the past three decades laboring to provide his people with economic security, a home of their own, and an opportunity to control their own lives amid the changes that swirled around them. But now, as a chilly wind drove a scattering of rain in off the Mississippi, Quatawapea felt that he had failed. He also believed that he had been betrayed.

Political unity has never been easy for the Shawnee people. Although the tribe traces its origins back to the Ohio heartland, during much of their recorded history the Shawnees have been fragmented into separate villages and scattered across the eastern United States. In the seventeenth century, when the Iroquois invaded the Ohio country, some Shawnees fled westward into Illinois, while others sought safety in the South, erecting new villages along the Savannah River in Georgia and South Carolina. As the Iroquois threat diminished, many of these former refugees journeyed to southern Pennsylvania, where they settled near the Delawares, but during the 1740s they quarreled with the British, and part of the tribe again fled to the South, seeking sanctuary among the Creeks. Others moved westward, forming villages on the upper Ohio River, downstream from its origins at modern Pittsburgh. In the decades that followed (1740–70), Shawnees residing in the South rejoined their kinsmen in Ohio, and new villages were erected along the Scioto and Muskingum Rivers. The Shawnees were home. Yet the tribal coalescence in Ohio during the third quarter of the eighteenth century did not rekindle the fires of political harmony. Although tribespeople living in the separate villages shared a common language and culture, and all strongly identified as "Shawnee," they often disagreed over what path to follow in regard to outsiders. No one who knows the Shawnee people has ever accused them of compliant acquiescence.[2]

Quatawapea emerged from this maelstrom of Shawnee migration. Like many Shawnee people born in Ohio during the middle decades of the eighteenth century, the events surrounding his birth and early life seem shrouded in the mists of those rivers which lace their homeland. Based upon the oral traditions of Shawnee people in the late nineteenth century, the sketchy investigation of local white historians and antiquarians from those years, and some very limited documentary evidence, it would seem that Quatawapea, or Captain Lewis, was born in about 1760 at a Shawnee village near the banks of the Scioto River on the Pickaway Plains, south of modern Circleville, Ohio. Evidently a member of the Piqua division of the tribe, he participated as an adolescent in the Battle of Point Pleasant (1774), and during the American Revolution he accompanied Shawnee war parties on their raids against frontier settlements in Kentucky and Virginia.[3] In the early 1790s he resided at one of the three Shawnee villages near the juncture of the Auglaize and Maumee Rivers in northwestern Ohio; from there he joined in the inter-tribal warfare against American settlement in southern Ohio and Kentucky. Although he fought against American military expeditions at St. Clair's Defeat (1791) and Fallen Timbers (1794), he did not play a leading role in these battles.[4] Lewis was probably among the 143 Shawnees from the Auglaize who attended the speeches and ceremonies surrounding the Treaty of Greenville (1795), but he is not mentioned in the treaty minutes, nor did he sign the document.[5]

If Lewis' role in the border warfare against the Long Knives (the Shawnees' name for white Americans) had been limited, he did achieve considerable success in providing for his extended family. By 1795 he was highly regarded as a hunter and as a younger village chief whose common sense, practical knowledge, and ability to mediate disputes attracted growing numbers of Shawnees, Mingoes, and Senecas to his village. During the mid-1780s he had married Polly Kaizer, a white captive taken as a girl near Lexington, Kentucky, who had later been adopted into the Shawnee tribe. The union produced two children, a boy and a girl, who both survived to adulthood. A second marriage to Mary Succopanus, a woman of Shawnee-Mingo descent, evidently produced no children.[6]

Sometime in 1796 or 1797 Lewis and his followers established a new village, Lewistown, just north of the Greenville Treaty Line, near the Great Miami River in modern Logan County, Ohio.[7] Other Shawnees settled nearby, forming villages at Wapakoneta and Hog Creek. The Shawnees expected the government to honor its promises of "domestic animals and implements of husbandry" stipulated by the Treaty of Greenville, and during the first decade of the nineteenth century villagers from all three communities attempted "to walk the white man's road." But that road was rocky and full of pitfalls. Federal assistance and annuities that had been promised to the Shawnees were delivered to Fort Wayne or Detroit, not to Ohio. At Fort Wayne acting Indian agent William Wells, the adopted son of Miami chief Little Turtle, funneled the lion's share of such merchandise to the Miamis, while in Michigan annuity goods deposited for the Shawnees were pilfered by local merchants.[8]

Angered, late in December 1801 Lewis joined with a party of seven Shawnees and five Delawares led by Black Hoof, the Shawnee chief from Wapakoneta, and journeyed to Washington to meet with federal officials. Interestingly, while in the capital, Lewis and several of the other Shawnees were inoculated against smallpox. On February 5, 1802, the Shawnees met with both President Thomas Jefferson and Secretary of War Henry Dearborn. Black Hoof spoke for the delegation, complaining about William Wells and denouncing white hunters who poached game on Indian land, but more importantly, he also requested that federal officials provide the Shawnees and Delawares with federal deeds to specific tracts of land in western Ohio and

1.1. Quatawapea, or Captain Lewis, a staunch ally of the Americans during the War of 1812. Captain Lewis later championed Shawnee removal to lands in the West. Thomas Loraine McKenney, *Qua-Ta-Wa-Pea, a Shawanoe Chief*, 1872–74, lithograph with applied watercolor. Amon Carter Museum, Fort Worth, Texas, 2004.19.48.

eastern Indiana. Black Hoof argued that such documents would enable these tribes to secure a permanent homeland against the claims of other people, both Indian and white. In response Dearborn assured the Shawnees that officials in Washington would try to distribute the annuity goods nearer to the Shawnee villages. Poachers would be punished, but ominously, the Shawnees' request for a deed to specific lands was flatly refused. According to Dearborn, "Your Father, the President," could not "divide the Lands of his red children." Such "division and grants" could only be made by "the great Chiefs and Sachems of your several nations."[9]

Lewis and the other Shawnees left Washington on February 16. En route back to Ohio they passed through Philadelphia, where they met with Quakers who were much impressed by the Indians' desire to adopt white agricultural practices. The Quakers treated the tribesmen well, and some of the Shawnees lingered in Philadelphia until mid-March, when Lewis and his kinsmen eventually returned to Ohio.[10]

The meeting with the Quakers proved fortuitous. In 1804 the Quakers founded a mission among Miami villages near Fort Wayne, but Quaker missionary William Kirk quarreled with William Wells over the distribution of federal "civilization funds," and in June 1807 the Quakers transferred their efforts from Fort Wayne to the Shawnee villages in western Ohio.[11] Initially the Quakers established a mission among Black Hoof's people at Wapakoneta, but Kirk's influence soon spread to neighboring Shawnee villages, including Lewistown. Like Black Hoof, Captain Lewis also embraced the Quakers' acculturation program, and by 1808 Shawnee villagers at Lewistown and Hog Creek had built "comfortable cabins of hewn logs with chimneys." They also planted orchards and cultivated modest fields of corn, squash, potatoes, and cabbages.

1.2. Black Hoof, a village chief from Wapakoneta, during the first quarter of the nineteenth century. Black Hoof was the most prominent pro-American Shawnee chief in Ohio. He opposed Shawnee removal to the West. Thomas Loraine McKenney, *Ca-Ta-He-Cas-Sa-Black Hoof, Principal Chief of the Shawanoes*, 1872–74, lithograph with applied watercolor. Amon Carter Museum, Fort Worth, Texas, 2004.19.40.

Several raised hogs, and a few even pastured small herds of cattle. By frontier standards, the Shawnees at Lewistown fared well, and Captain Lewis personally prospered. White observers commented upon his expensive clothing, fine horses, and "costly . . . equipment, rifle, and side arms." Meanwhile, Kirk hired a blacksmith, began the construction of both grist- and sawmills, and made plans to expand his endeavors to the Delawares and Wyandottes. At Lewistown, Lewis and his followers believed that good times, like the rapids in the Maumee River, seemed destined to keep flowing.[12]

They were wrong. Trouble, like the Great Serpent who haunts the waters of Shawnee nightmares, loomed on the horizon. In this case, the serpent had two heads. First, despite his success among the Shawnees, Kirk ran afoul of the federal bureaucracy. From Fort Wayne, Wells conducted a poison-pen campaign of character assassination against him. Meanwhile, Kirk contributed to his own problems through poor bookkeeping and by overspending some of his accounts. In retrospect it seems that the missionary did spend more than his allotted funds, but such extravagance, if any, was expended in support of the Shawnees, not himself. But in the end it mattered little. Late in December 1808 Dearborn dismissed Kirk from his post among the Shawnees. In response, Lewis, Black Hoof, and other Shawnee chiefs wrote to the president asking him to reconsider, but their letters were ignored. In April 1809 Kirk left Ohio. Lewis and many other Shawnees remained committed to adopting many of the white man's ways, but without Kirk's guidance, the acculturation process faltered.[13]

The second head of the serpent posed a much more serious threat. In 1805 Lalawethika (the Noise-Maker), a ne'er-do-well younger brother of Tecumseh—an up-and-coming but culturally

1.3. Tenskwatawa, or the Shawnee Prophet. The younger brother of Tecumseh, Tenskwatawa opposed the Americans and threatened both Captain Lewis and Black Hoof. Thomas Loraine McKenney, *Tens-Kwau-Ta-Waw, the Prophet*, 1872–74, lithograph with applied watercolor. Amon Carter Museum, Fort Worth, Texas, 2004.19.6.

conservative young Shawnee war and village chief residing in eastern Indiana—experienced a vision. This traumatic experience transformed Lalawethika, a former alcoholic, into Tenskwatawa (the Open Door), or the Shawnee Prophet, whose new doctrine stated that the Americans were the "Spawn of the Great Serpent," and that all Indians who emulated them were guilty of witchcraft. Obviously, such denunciations threatened Lewis and other proponents of acculturation. In 1806 the menace increased. In March the Prophet's disciples among the Delawares burned four of their more acculturated kinsmen at the stake. Three months later Tenskwatawa's successful prediction of a solar eclipse brought an influx of new converts to Tecumseh's village near Greenville, Ohio, substantially increasing the number of tribespeople who were potentially dangerous to Lewis and his followers.[14]

One year later, in 1807, the two Shawnee camps almost came to blows. In June, Black Hoof accused the Prophet and his followers of murdering two Shawnee hunters from Wapakoneta. The Prophet disavowed any responsibility for the deaths, but when several white settlers were also killed by unknown assailants, Governor Edward Tiffin of Ohio demanded that Shawnees from both camps meet with state officials at Springfield, on the Mad River. At the meeting both Tecumseh and Black Hoof blamed each other, and the two almost came to blows, but cooler heads prevailed. Further investigations indicated that the attack upon the settlers had been made by a party of Potawatomis.[15]

Although Lewis must have been interested in the outcome of these meetings, there is little evidence that he attended either conference. Most certainly, in 1807 he remained on the periphery of the growing rift within the Shawnee Nation, content to remain a member of Black Hoof's party, but obviously deeply concerned by the growing host of potentially hostile tribesmen who continued to flock to the Prophet's camp. But during the following months things changed. In the spring of 1808 Tecumseh and the Shawnee Prophet moved their village from Greenville, less than fifty miles from Lewistown, to Prophetstown, a new village in western Indiana. Obviously the departure of the militant Shawnee brothers from Ohio encouraged many Shawnees who remained in the state to more closely ally with the pro-American camp. In response, during late November 1808 Lewis and Black Hoof led a small party of Shawnees to Detroit, where they and chiefs from the Chippewas, Potawatomis, Ottawas, and Wyandottes met with Governor William Hull and agreed to cede a right-of-way for a federal road across northwestern Ohio, connecting the Maumee River valley and Lower Sandusky. Lewis and Black Hoof were the only Shawnee chiefs who signed this land cession.[16]

Tecumseh dismissed the cession of the roadway as unimportant, but he was incensed by the Treaty of Fort Wayne. Signed in September 1809 by delegates from the Potawatomis, Miamis, and Delawares, the treaty ceded more than three million acres of Indiana to the Long Knives. In the months preceding the treaty, Tecumseh had believed that those tribal chiefs who opposed his efforts were too intimidated to cede additional lands to the government. The treaty proved him wrong, but his angry response only strengthened the ties between Lewis and the United States. Neither Lewis nor any of the Ohio Shawnee village chiefs had participated in the treaty, but Tecumseh charged that they supported the pact and threatened to kill any tribal leaders who cooperated with the government.[17]

In the spring of 1810 Tecumseh journeyed to Wapakoneta, but both Black Hoof and Lewis refused to meet with him. When Stephen Ruddell, a former white captive who had been adopted into the Shawnee tribe, showed Tecumseh a recently arrived letter from Governor William Henry Harrison of Indiana Territory, the Shawnee war chief seized the document and threw it into a council fire. Tecumseh found few new followers among the Shawnee villages, but other members of his movement who rode on to the Wyandottes were more successful. In June they also denounced chiefs who were friendly to the government and convinced some of the Wyandottes to burn three of these individuals, including the elderly Leatherlips, as witches.[18]

Tecumseh's travels among the Ohio Shawnee villages and the death of Leatherlips alarmed both Captain Lewis and Black Hoof. It also shocked federal officials and white settlers. In Michigan, Shawnee chiefs such as George BlueJacket and Logan met with Governor William Hull, while in Ohio, Lewis, Black Hoof, and more than three hundred of their followers traveled to Fort Wayne, where in October they received their annuities, complained about the Prophet's followers, and urged federal officials to establish a military post on the Tippecanoe River to counter the Shawnee brothers' growing influence.[19]

During the following winter tensions eased in Ohio, but hostilities flared in Illinois. Led by the irascible old Potawatomi war chief Main Poc, war parties of Potawatomis, Sacs, and Kickapoos raided the road between Vincennes and Saint Louis, then spilled over into Missouri. Governor Ninian Edwards of Illinois complained to Governor Harrison in Indiana that the forays into Illinois and Missouri had originated at Prophetstown and asked Harrison to intervene. In response Harrison decided to attack the hostile village. He was aware that Tecumseh was in the South, and in his absence Harrison hoped to destroy Prophetstown and disperse the Prophet's followers. Meanwhile, Harrison instructed Indian agents at Fort Wayne and in Ohio to assure friendly tribesmen that his expedition up the Wabash was aimed at Prophetstown, not their villages.[20]

In Ohio federal officials took pains to keep the Loyal Shawnees attached to the government. John Shaw, an Indian agent now living at Wapakoneta, assured local settlers that the neighboring Shawnees were friendly, and late in August, John Johnston, the Indian agent from Fort Wayne, assembled Shawnees from Lewiston, Wapakoneta, and Hog Creek at Piqua, where he requested formal pledges of their allegiance. Captain Lewis spoke first and stated that all the Shawnees, Mingoes, Delawares, and Ottawas residing in the region wanted peace. He declared his good wishes toward the United States and promised to abide by the terms of recently signed treaties. Black Hoof delivered a longer speech and also pledged his loyalty to the government. He blamed the Prophet for "all the mischief" that recently had occurred, then assured Johnston that, although the Shawnees wished to remain neutral, if war broke out between the Long Knives and the Redcoats they would warn the Americans if they heard of "any mischief coming your way."[21]

But mischief arrived on its own. Harrison's victory at Tippecanoe in November 1811 dispersed the Prophet's followers from Prophetstown, but some of them scattered back up the Wabash Valley into western Ohio. Horses were stolen, livestock was butchered, and other depredations occurred. The new attacks caused Lewis considerable concern. Late in November, Lewis and Black Hoof journeyed to Fort Wayne, where they reassured officials that their people remained loyal and were not responsible for the attacks; then in December they met with several groups of settlers on the Mad River, again professing their friendship to the United States.[22] The "Indian alarm" temporarily diminished, but in the spring of 1812 rumors reached Ohio that the Prophet planned to move back to Greenville, and Lewis grew more apprehensive. So did his white neighbors. After four settlers were found dead in the forest and another was murdered on Greenville Creek about thirty miles from Lewistown, settlers in western Ohio sent numerous petitions to state and federal officials asking for protection. In response, the War Department established a new Indian agency at Piqua and appointed John Johnston as the agent at that post. Secretary of War William Eustis also ordered federal troops to strengthen Fort Loramie, on Loramie Creek, about midway between the Shawnee villages and Greenville.[23]

In May, Captain William Perry, the American commander at Fort Loramie, summoned Lewis and several other Shawnee chiefs to the post. Lewis and the other Shawnee chiefs reiterated that they only wished to remain at peace and even volunteered to furnish two young men to scout for the army and to assist them in patrolling the Greenville Treaty Line. The Shawnee chiefs then journeyed on to Piqua, where they met with Johnston and repeated their professions of friendship, but also expressed their alarm over recent attacks by local militia upon friendly Indians. As the Shawnees pointed out, just three days previously frontier militia units from Greenville had murdered two friendly Potawatomi hunters, stolen all their property, and made prisoners of their wives and children. They asked for the attacks to stop. Following the conference Captain Lewis returned to his village, where relatives informed him that the same militia unit also had seized a small hunting party of Shawnees from his village. Fortunately, Johnston interceded and the Shawnee captives were returned to Lewistown, but Johnston admitted that frontier whites were "out in all directions breathing destruction against Indians indiscriminately." As a consequence, William Perry, the commander at Fort Loramie, sent his two Shawnee scouts back to Wapakoneta, since he feared they might "be killed by some of the [local] Inhabitants."[24]

In June 1812, even before news of the declaration of war against Great Britain officially reached Ohio, General William Hull had assembled an army in Cincinnati, then marched north, determined to protect Detroit from the British. En route he stopped in Urbana, where Governor Return J. Meigs gathered friendly Wyandottes, led by Tarhe (the Crane), and Shawnees and Senecas from Wapakoneta, Lewistown, and Hog Creek. He assured the assembled Indians that Hull's army would not attack their villages and secured their permission for Hull to cross their lands. The Shawnees also agreed to permit the army to construct several small blockhouses to protect a new road from the Greenville Treaty Line to the Maumee rapids. Following pro-American speeches by Tarhe and Black Hoof, Lewis spoke briefly for the Shawnees and Senecas at Lewistown, stating that he "was but a stripling in comparison with my aged father [Black Hoof] who spoke before me," but assuring Meigs that he agreed with the older chief, commenting, "Although the Heavens should fall asunder and the earth open beneath," he would remember the promises he made in Washington to Jefferson and Dearborn in 1802. As a sign of their fidelity, Lewis and several of the other chiefs at the council agreed to serve as scouts and interpreters for Hull's army as it marched toward Michigan.[25]

Honoring their promises, Lewis and his kinsmen accompanied Hull's army across northwestern Ohio to Detroit. The march north proved uneventful, and Hull and the Shawnee scouts reached Detroit on July 6, 1812. Six days later Hull crossed the Detroit River to Sandwich, intending to march south and seize Fort Malden, a British post on the eastern bank of the Detroit River, about twenty miles south of Detroit. Yet the expedition failed. In mid-July, British and Indian defenders repelled Hull's forces at the Canard River, and the Americans retreated, first back to Sandwich, then across the river to Michigan.[26]

Lewis took no part in these skirmishes. While the Americans and British exchanged fire in Canada, he met with tribal leaders from several tribes at Brownstown, a Wyandotte village south of Detroit. There he joined with Black Hoof and Tarhe, attempting to persuade delegations of Ottawas, Chippewas, Potawatomis, Delawares, Kickapoos, Sacs, and even some Iroquois to remain neutral in the conflict. Lewis and Black Hoof "made great exertion to detach the Indians from the British standards." They argued that twice before, after the American Revolution and following Fallen Timbers, the British had deserted their Indian allies. The Redcoats could not be trusted. The tribes should not become involved. Let the Redcoats and the Long Knives fight their own battles. If the tribesmen remained neutral, they argued, their Great Father would care for his red children. The conference ended on July 20, and Hull ordered Lewis and his companions to return to Piqua, where American officials were planning a similar meeting designed to ensure the loyalty of these Indians remaining in Indiana and Ohio.[27]

The meeting at Piqua did not go as planned. Federal officials had hoped to meet with tribal leaders in early August, but logistical problems caused them to postpone the meeting until August 15. Yet by that date both the officials and the tribes in Ohio learned that British and Indian forces led by Tecumseh had defeated the American reinforcement attempting to reach Detroit, and that Hull had retreated from Canada back into Michigan. Many of the Indians who previously had agreed to attend the Piqua conference now joined the British. On August 16, when Lewis and other pro-American tribespeople assembled at Piqua, they found that they numbered only 750. John Johnston and other officials who had planned for the conference had anticipated three thousand. Moreover, while the conference was in progress, Lewis, Black Hoof, and other chiefs learned that Hull had surrendered Detroit and that the British now controlled all of eastern Michigan. John Johnston, Thomas Worthington, and other officials at Piqua extended the conference throughout the last two weeks of August, awaiting an army raised by William Henry Harrison, which planned to march through Piqua en route to the Maumee valley. Lewis did not speak formally at the meeting, but Black Hoof gave the usual assurances of Shawnee loyalty while the Loyal Shawnees waited for Harrison and his army to arrive.[28]

Meanwhile, the news from northern Ohio was bad. As the tide of battle in Michigan had turned in the British Army's favor, many of the tribes in the Detroit region and south along the upper Maumee had transferred their loyalty to Tecumseh and the British. Parties of Tecumseh's followers now infiltrated the Maumee valley, and in late August the Potawatomis in northeastern Indiana first attacked, then besieged, Fort Wayne. Rumors also reached Piqua that other Potawatomis in northern Illinois had attacked and killed most of the garrison at Fort Dearborn. Aware that their villages were also now vulnerable to attack by hostile war parties, Lewis, Black Hoof, and other Loyal Shawnees pondered the wisdom of their friendship with the Americans. Perhaps the Long Knives were too frightened. Perhaps Tecumseh and the Redcoats had gained the ascendancy.[29]

But things soon changed. On September 2 Harrison and an army of two thousand men arrived in Piqua, and Harrison was breathing fire and brimstone. He assured the Shawnees that those Indians who fought against the United States "should not long be known among us," and in a veiled insult to William Hull's surrender of Detroit, he warned that "the American army will no longer be commanded by an old woman." Harrison's spirit gave the Shawnees heart, and when he marched from Piqua toward the Maumee, Captain Lewis and a handful of other Shawnee warriors, including Logan, Captain Johnny, Bright Horn, and the Wolf, rode with him. Harrison's arrival at Fort Wayne broke the Potawatomi siege, and after his army was reinforced by a contingent of Kentucky militia led by Brigadier General James Winchester, Harrison returned to Ohio to organize logistical support for a larger campaign to recapture Detroit.[30]

Informed of the Potawatomi siege, Tecumseh and Major Adam Muir had left Fort Malden on September 14 with about one thousand British troops and Indians, intending to assist the Potawatomis, but when Muir learned of Harrison's arrival, he retreated back toward Canada. In response, Winchester's militia, assisted by Lewis and the Shawnee scouts, followed in Muir's wake, hoping to engage the fleeing British. In contrast to Muir, many of the British-allied Indians who had accompanied him remained along the Maumee, and on October 8, 1812, Lewis and a handful of Shawnee scouts, who were advancing in front of Winchester's column, encountered a war party of Potawatomis led by their infamous war chief Main Poc. Both sides exchanged musket fire and yelled insults at each other from a distance, but the Potawatomis fled when they realized that Winchester's troops were following in Lewis's wake. During the next two months Lewis and his companions continued to range up the Maumee valley and into southern Michigan, spying on hostile Indians and British troop movements. It was hazardous work. In November they skirmished again with a war party of Potawatomis and Ottawas. Lewis remained unscathed, but in the aftermath Logan, Captain Johnny, and Bright Horn were captured. They escaped, killing three of their captors, but in the struggle Logan was killed and Bright Horn wounded. And British-allied Indians were not the only threat. The scouts also were at risk from ill-disciplined American militia who considered all Indians to be friends with the British and thus fair game. In December 1812 the scouts returned to their villages.[31]

They arrived none too soon. In his absence, Lewis learned, white settlers had pilfered Shawnee livestock, and in October a Seneca man residing in Lewistown was shot by a local settler whom he encountered near Piqua. In 1813 white resentment against the Shawnees increased. In January word reached Ohio that the British and Indians had defeated Winchester at the Battle of Frenchtown in southern Michigan, and in the aftermath dozens of wounded American captives had been "massacred" by British-allied Indians. Although Lewis and his followers had no part in the Frenchtown affair, many local white Ohioans were incensed. They burned a dozen Shawnee and Wyandotte cabins and stole additional livestock.[32]

To defuse the hostility, Captain Lewis, Black Hoof, and several of the Shawnee scouts "reenlisted" with Brigadier General Edwin Tupper and a force of militia en route to reinforce Harrison, who had earlier returned to the rapids of the Maumee. The Shawnees joined Tupper's force at McArthur's blockhouse, near modern Kenton, Ohio, but on the evening of January 25 the militia's suspicion of all Indians (both friendly and hostile) exploded. While Lewis and Black Hoof were meeting with Tupper in the blockhouse, an unknown militiaman fired a pistol through a chink in the logs, striking Black Hoof in the face. Although the wound was not fatal, Black Hoof was forced to return to Wapakoneta. Tupper was enraged, but the assailant was never captured. In the aftermath Lewis led the remainder of the disillusioned scouts on to the Maumee.[33]

In February 1813, while Lewis and the scouts again patrolled along the Maumee valley, Harrison constructed Fort Meigs, a new American post, just below the rapids on the east bank of the Maumee River. Meanwhile, Tecumseh had spent the winter back on the Tippecanoe River recruiting additional warriors, and when he returned to Detroit in late April, he and Colonel Henry Procter, the British commander at Amherstburg, led nearly twelve hundred Indians and one thousand British troops, accompanied by several pieces of artillery, up the Maumee valley, determined to either capture or destroy the new American fortress. Outnumbered, Harrison took refuge behind the heavy log walls of the fort, and although the British had artillery, Harrison excavated a series of earth traverses within the fort, which effectively limited the impact of the cannons. Lewis and the other Shawnee scouts took shelter with the Americans in the fort, where they joined with American marksmen, periodically firing at the Redcoats. Meanwhile, Captain Lewis and his comrades repeatedly assured the Americans that Tecumseh and the hostile warriors would eventually become bored and just go away.[34]

Other Shawnees became involved. Intent upon reinforcing Harrison's command, General Green Clay and a force of about twelve hundred Kentuckians also marched north across Ohio toward the Maumee. Unfamiliar with the terrain, they requested Shawnee scouts as they passed through Piqua, but since all of the experienced scouts were already on the Maumee with Harrison, Indian agents at Piqua coerced a group of other Shawnees from Wapakoneta to accompany them. Led by Black Fish, the son of the Shawnee chief who had led the attacks on Kentucky during the American Revolution, these Shawnees had preferred to remain neutral and wanted no part of the warfare. Moreover, they generally disliked the Kentuckians, and their service to Clay's militia was half-hearted at best. On May 4 these reluctant scouts and some of the Kentuckians, led by Lieutenant Colonel William Dudley, surprised part of the British besiegers and overran a British artillery emplacement, but when the British counterattacked, Black Fish and his Shawnee companions promptly surrendered. As a result, the Redcoats and their Indian allies quickly gained the upper hand. Of the eight hundred men who had formed Clay's command, only about 150 reached Fort Meigs safely. In the aftermath, Potawatomis led by Main Poc again killed some of the American prisoners. The British finally abandoned the siege, but Black Fish (now a British captive) claimed that all the Shawnees still resident in Ohio had helped the Americans only because they had been coerced and that villagers at Wapakoneta and Lewistown were virtual prisoners in their own lodges. According to Black Fish, if given a chance, all the Ohio Shawnees (even Captain Lewis, Black Hoof, and the loyal scouts) would much prefer to serve the British. In response, British commander Procter offered to exchange the prisoners he had taken at Fort Meigs if Harrison would allow the Ohio Shawnees to remove to Canada.[35]

Lewis denounced Black Fish as a liar, and although Harrison did not doubt the loyalty of Lewis, Black Hoof, Captain Johnny, and the other scouts who had so faithfully served the Americans, other Ohioans were not so sure. Late in May, after Procter and Tecumseh had abandoned the siege and withdrawn to Amherstburg, Captain Lewis and the other Shawnee scouts returned to their villages. Again, Lewis did not like what he found. In his absence, word of Dudley's Defeat had reached the American settlements, and in response frontier mobs and militia units had stolen Shawnee horses, cut down Shawnee cornfields, and killed a friendly Shawnee warrior near Fort Loramie. Johnston attempted to intercede in the Shawnees' behalf, but his efforts were undercut by local officials.[36] Lewis conferred with Black Hoof, attempting to formulate a strategy to stop the violence, but even Harrison had been influenced by Black Fish's declarations. On July 21 he met with a large delegation of Shawnees, Delawares, Wyandottes, and Senecas at Franklin, where he was organizing logistical support for his coming invasion of Canada. Harrison privately admitted that he did not doubt the fidelity of Captain Lewis and the Shawnee scouts, but he questioned the pledges of friendship by some of the other Shawnees and Wyandottes. They must choose, he informed the warriors, either to accompany him in the upcoming invasion of Canada or to take their families and move south of the Greenville Treaty Line, where they would be closely guarded by either federal troops or local militia units. The assembled warriors "unanimously agreed, and observed that they had long been anxious . . . to fight for the Americans." Harrison then instructed them to return to their villages and await a summons "when he should want their services." Following the conference, Lewis returned to Lewistown.[37]

They did not wait long. During the first week of August the summons arrived, and Captain Lewis, accompanied by Black Snake and more than two hundred friendly Shawnee and Delaware warriors, again rode north to rendezvous with Harrison at Sandusky. Harrison believed he needed their assistance. During his absence from northern Ohio, the British had launched another siege of Fort Meigs then attacked Fort Stephenson, a small American post on the lower Sandusky River. Both attacks failed, however, and after joining with Harrison at Upper Sandusky, Lewis and his kinsmen rode to Fort Meigs then pursued the retreating British and their Indian allies up the Maumee valley. During the next three weeks they patrolled the lower Maumee region, capturing British stragglers, seizing abandoned British equipment, and meeting with Wyandottes from Brownstown. Led by the vacillating chief Walk-in-the-Water, these Wyandottes' loyalty to the British was tenuous at best, and Lewis informed them that the tide of battle had turned and that they also should join with the Americans.[38]

On September 27, 1813, when Harrison invaded Canada, Captain Lewis and the Shawnee scouts were in the vanguard. Even the aging Black Hoof, who had partially recovered from his gunshot wound, had journeyed to Michigan to join Harrison's forces. Although age and infirmities limited him from taking an active role in the campaign, Black Hoof added his authority and moral support. Captain Lewis took a more active role. Attached to Lieutenant Colonel James V. Ball's regiment of American dragoons, Lewis and Black Snake led parties of Shawnee and Seneca warriors who served as scouts and skirmishers as the Americans followed the fleeing British up the Thames valley toward Kingston (Toronto). Early on the morning of October 5, Lewis informed Harrison that Tecumseh and Procter had decided to stand and fight about two miles west of Moraviantown, a Delaware village on the banks of the Thames. There the road followed the north bank of the Thames and passed between the river and a swampy, low-lying thicket. According to the scouts, Tecumseh and his followers had taken defensive positions in the thicket, while the British, supported by two pieces of artillery, were deployed in two lines across the road.[39]

Harrison approached the British position in midafternoon. He ordered his infantry to engage Tecumseh and the Indians in the thicket, while he planned to lead his cavalry against the British center. Meanwhile he instructed Ball and Captain Lewis to lead the Shawnee scouts and other friendly tribesmen along the river, below the bank, and to secretly gain access to a position behind the British regulars, where the Shawnees would then open fire upon the British rear. Harrison believed that if the Indians surprised the British from behind, Procter would believe he had been betrayed by some of Tecumseh's followers and would be forced to redeploy part of his regulars, pulling them from the ranks of those troops that faced the American cavalry.[40]

Following Harrison's orders, Lewis led the Shawnees below the riverbank and began to move quietly upstream below the British field of vision. But they never fired a shot. Before they could infiltrate the British lines, Harrison's cavalry charged, and after firing two volleys, the British turned and fled toward Moraviantown. The cavalry then turned and attacked Tecumseh and the Indians in the thickets, and Ball ordered Lewis and the Shawnees to remain along the riverbank, afraid that they might be mistaken for hostiles. After about an hour Tecumseh was killed and his followers disengaged. Thus the Battle of the Thames ended.[41]

Following the battle, Lewis led the Shawnee scouts back to Detroit, where they rendezvoused with Black Hoof then journeyed to their villages in Ohio. For Lewis, the return to his home again was bittersweet, at best. He learned that late in August, while he and other warriors were absent from Lewistown fighting for the United States, local militia leaders had threatened to kill all the Shawnees and Delawares remaining in Ohio; then a mob of frontier whites had attacked his village, burned many of the cabins, and cut down the remaining Shawnee cornfields. Johnston had again interceded, and the violence had subsided, but Lewis and his people now faced a long winter. With the well-armed Shawnee warriors now back at their village, the white "irregulars" no longer dared to attack Lewistown, but the Shawnees and Senecas were short of food. Johnston sent flour and other supplies from Piqua, and they made it through the winter, but sometimes the Shawnees went hungry.[42]

Yet the war continued. In February 1814 Lewis, Black Hoof, and other Shawnee leaders met with officials in Dayton, where they requested additional food and assured Governor Meigs that they would continue to serve as scouts for the Americans. The officials welcomed their support, but informed them that, prior to any new campaigns, the government planned to meet with delegates from all the western tribes at Greenville, where they would ask their chiefs (both allies and former enemies) to sign a treaty affirming (or reaffirming) their allegiance to the United States and pledging to assist the Americans against the British. Both Lewis and Black Hoof advised against such a meeting, since they believed many of the hostile tribes remained loyal to the British and would not honor such a pledge, even if they signed it. Moreover, they knew that some of the pro-British tribesmen harbored deep grudges against them, and they feared for their own personal safety. Discounting the Shawnees' warnings, on July 8, 1814, Harrison, Johnston, and Lewis Cass, assembled the Shawnees and nine other tribes, including formerly hostile Miamis, Potawatomis, Kickapoos, and Ottawas, at Greenville. Interrupted by rainstorms, the treaty proceedings dragged on for two weeks. Although Lewis, Black Hoof, the Wolf, and other prominent Shawnee leaders attended the conference, they watched in silence; they made no formal speeches. In reply to requests by Harrison and Cass for pledges of allegiance and assistance against the Redcoats, the pro-British chiefs remained ominously silent, and only after considerable coaxing did Charley, a Miami chief, rise and castigate the United States. Other Miami and Ottawa chiefs, though more guarded in their rhetoric, also championed a position of neutrality, not a pledge of allegiance to the Long Knives. When Tarhe, the pro-American Wyandotte chief from Sandusky, attempted to defend the Americans' request, he was rudely interrupted by pro-British Indians. Finally Harrison was able to coerce grudging pledges of loyalty and assistance from the former hostiles. On July 22, 1814, Captain Lewis signed the treaty, but he doubted the former hostiles' sincerity.[43]

Lewis's doubts were confirmed. Following the conference, the Potawatomis, Ottawas, and Miamis returned to northern Indiana and Michigan, where they promptly informed hostile tribesmen still living in the region that the Long Knives were planning a campaign against their villages. Even the Wyandottes, who had previously supported the United States, now refused to cooperate since they were irate over frontiersmen who were illegally settling on their lands near Sandusky. In contrast, a small party of Shawnees from Wapakoneta escorted Lewis Cass back to Detroit then scouted westward across Michigan, where they learned that the Potawatomi villages to be targeted by American military expeditions were well defended and could rely upon additional support from warriors in Illinois and Wisconsin. They delivered such intelligence to officials at Fort Wayne then returned to Ohio.[44]

Colonel Duncan McArthur had originally intended to strike the Potawatomi villages near modern South Bend, Indiana, but upon learning that his plans had been exposed, he turned his attention toward Canada. In October he mustered about 650 men, mostly mounted Kentucky militia, then rode north toward Detroit. Accompanying him were sixty-five Shawnees from Lewistown and Wapakoneta led by Captain Lewis, the Wolf, Captain Johnny, and Anthony Shane. They arrived at Detroit, and on October 23 crossed over into Canada north of Lake Saint Clair, then passed unnoticed into Ontario. Led by Lewis, the warriors accompanying McArthur rode with the Americans across Upper Canada, destroying mills and storehouses full of the recent harvest. They hoped to reach Burlington, but on November 6, 1814, they were turned back by Canadian militia and British-allied Iroquois at Malcolm's Mills, on the Grand River. They then returned to Detroit. The Shawnees fought well. In their official reports, American officers singled out Captain Lewis, the Wolf, Civil John, and Anthony Shane for their honorable deportment and valiant service. Among McArthur's men there were one killed and six wounded, but the Shawnees were unscathed.[45]

In late November Lewis returned to Lewistown, where he again found his followers short of food. In addition, McArthur had promised to pay the scouts for their recent service in Canada, but funds for such wages failed to reach Ohio. As in the past, Johnston provided some foodstuffs, and they made it through the winter, but by the spring of 1815 the Shawnee villages of Lewistown and Wapakoneta, once model villages of frontier prosperity, had deteriorated into communities of tribespeople huddled around fires in barren cabins. Most of their livestock had been killed or stolen, and their fields lay fallow. Why plant corn when it was destroyed before the harvest? When news of the Treaty of Ghent reached Lewistown in March 1815, Lewis was gladdened, but he also worried about an uncertain future.[46]

Seeking answers, Lewis journeyed to Chillicothe, where he met with McArthur. He requested that McArthur use his influence to pry loose funds for the Shawnee scouts' back pay, which had been sent to Fort Wayne, but which had not been forthcoming to the Shawnees. Lewis informed McArthur that because he and his men had been absent from Lewistown, first attending the conference at Greenville, then accompanying Cass to Detroit, and finally participating in McArthur's raid into Ontario, they had not had an opportunity to plant and cultivate crops for their families. They wished to continue the programs initiated by the Quakers, and they wished to grow crops; they did not want to "be compelled to hunt for a subsistence." Indeed, after several meetings among themselves, they had decided to "put a number of their children out to learn trades." Lewis also asked that the president "send them suitable persons to teach their children to read and keep their accounts." Meanwhile, Black Hoof met with Johnston at Piqua and sought similar assistance, requesting another gristmill and blacksmith, so that all Shawnees in western Ohio could "live upon their own resources."[47]

Yet the Shawnees' requests for Quakers, teachers, gristmills, and blacksmiths were initially ignored. By the summer of 1815 federal officials had focused all their efforts on a formal peace treaty to be negotiated with all the midwestern tribes. Scheduled for early August at Spring Wells, a location adjacent to Detroit, the meeting was plagued by problems. During the summer an influenza-like epidemic swept through the upper Midwest, infecting both whites and Indians, and the meeting was postponed until August 31. Lewis attended the conference, but he arrived late because he had contracted the illness. Neither Lewis, Black Hoof, nor any of the Shawnees from western Ohio spoke formally. Tarhe again spoke for the American-allied Indians, and after ceremonially opening the proceedings, the old Wyandotte chief urged all the tribes in attendance to forget their former differences and live together in peace. Harrison spoke for the United States and gave the usual assurances of the government's good intentions. The Shawnee Prophet, lured by hopes of reestablishing himself as a prominent village chief back in Indiana, also attended the proceedings. At first he seemed both remorseful and cooperative, but both Lewis and Black Hoof opposed his return to Prophetstown, and when Harrison informed the holy man that he could only return to the United States if he resided under Black Hoof's authority at Wapakoneta, he became infuriated and returned to Canada. On September 8, 1815, Captain Lewis, Black Hoof, and the other Shawnee chiefs signed the Treaty of Spring Wells. For the Shawnees and other tribes, the bloodshed officially associated with the War of 1812 was over.[48]

Yet for tribal people north of the Ohio River, many of the same old problems continued. Lewis had cast his lot with the Long Knives, but he, like other Shawnees, was wary of their greed for tribal land. And he should have been. The Treaty of Spring Wells guaranteed that the Shawnees and other tribes still owned the lands awarded to them at the Treaty of Greenville. But it did not guarantee that they could keep them. American demands for Indian lands were intense. Between 1810 and 1820 the non-Indian population of Ohio doubled from 230,000 to 581,000, and much of it spilled northward onto lands supposedly belonging to tribespeople.[49]

Lewis, the aging Black Hoof, and other Shawnee chiefs were aware of the encroachment, but they initially believed that their service to the government and their strides in accultura- tion would protect them. They also sought renewed assistance from the Quakers. The latter responded, sending James Ellicott and Philip Thomas to Ohio during the summer of 1816. On August 1, 1816, after visiting Lewistown, the Quakers stated that the village contained approxi- mately four hundred Shawnees and Senecas, or about half the population of Wapakoneta. Under Lewis's leadership, however, the Indians at Lewistown had made "considerable advances toward civilization." According to Ellicott and Thomas, Lewis's followers had cleared and enclosed at least five hundred acres with split-rail fences, planted more than two hundred acres of corn, cultivated large gardens full of vegetables, and were tending "some cattle and hogs and a very sufficient stock of horses." The Quakers particularly praised Lewis for his efforts to prohibit liquor in his village and reported that, before they left Lewistown, the chief personally pleaded with them for Quaker missionaries to reside in his village. He also asked the Quakers to build grist- and sawmills at Lewistown.[50]

Lewis's requests for assistance reflected his desire to build a strong economic base as a hedge against mounting local and federal pressure for the acquisition of Indian lands. Like Black Hoof, Lewis believed that permanently settled Shawnee villagers who combined some tradi- tional hunting and fishing with the white man's yeoman agriculture would be able to maintain their residency in Ohio. What concerned him, however, was the Shawnees' nebulous title to their homeland. From the government's perspective, they held their lands through the broadly defined terms of the Treaty of Greenville: the lands had been jointly granted to all the tribes who signed the treaty, and the Shawnees held the lands near their villages only in joint owner- ship. Within the American legal system, they shared in the ownership, but they did not exercise exclusive hegemony or control over the lands. As Lewis was well aware, land ownership for the Americans was based upon specific written deeds, which clearly defined the acreage under the control of an entity (that is, an individual, a tribe, a county, or a state). Consequently, the Shaw- nees' claim to their lands, while both moral and just, was legally weak.[51]

The Treaty of Fort Meigs seemed to offer a solution. As white settlement poured into Ohio, the state's demands for Indian lands increased. Envisioning any new land cession as an oppor- tunity to secure a more definitive title to their lands, the Shawnee chiefs initially supported the government's efforts. During the summer of 1817, Captain Lewis, Black Hoof, and several other Shawnee chiefs traveled to neighboring Wyandotte, Seneca, Miami, Ottawa, and Delaware vil- lages, promoting the upcoming negotiations and urging the tribes to attend.[52]

The Shawnees were successful. Held in September 1817, the conference for the Treaty of Fort Meigs, which ceded northwestern Ohio to the United States, was attended by delegates from the Shawnees, Senecas, Delawares, Ottawas, Wyandottes, Miamis, Potawatomis, and Chippe- was. All the tribes in attendance received either cash payments or increased annuities. More important, however, were the reservations set aside for the Shawnees, Senecas, Wyandottes, and Delawares. These tracts, carefully delineated in terms of acreages and exterior borders, were specifically awarded to the different tribal village communities. For example, the federal govern- ment agreed to grant, "by patent, in fee simple, to Quatawape or Captain Lewis" and other chiefs of "the Shawanese tribe of Indians residing at Lewistown, . . . and to the Seneca Chiefs residing at Lewistown . . . a tract of land to contain forty eight square miles," which was then carefully laid out to surround their village. Yet even more important was the government's agreement to divide these lands among individual Shawnees. Similar to the provisions awarding lands to Shawnee villagers at Wapakoneta and Hog Creek, a separate schedule was attached to the treaty, listing the heads of families among the Shawnee and Seneca villagers at Lewistown who should receive individual tracts. The treaty also indicated that Lewis and other Lewistown chiefs were authorized to divide the reservation into separate acreages and then award them to these heads of families.[53]

The treaty immediately encountered opposition in the U.S. Senate. Objecting to the concept of tribal leaders holding lands "in fee simple," the Senate refused to ratify the agreement unless the treaty was altered so that the reservations would be held "in a like manner as has been practiced in other cases." Moreover, the senators were unwilling to allow Lewis and the other chiefs to gain control of lands that they could regulate without government supervision. In consequence, Lewis Cass and Duncan McArthur were instructed to renegotiate the treaty so that the Shawnees and other tribes would not have complete control of the properties. They would hold them at the pleasure of the government, and if they sold them, they could sell them only to the United States. In September 1818 Cass and McArthur once again met with the Shawnees, Senecas, Wyandottes, and Ottawas and negotiated a supplemental treaty. As part of the revised agreement, the Shawnees at both Lewistown and Wapakoneta received additional acreages to their reservations, but they were forced to agree that they held the reservations only at the pleasure of the federal government. If they surrendered reservation land, it could only be sold to the United States. Lewis signed both treaties, but the second one must have left him somewhat discouraged. His reservation at Lewistown had been enlarged, but after the second treaty it also remained more tenuous.[54]

Meanwhile, they began walking the white man's road at an increased pace. Encouraged both by Shawnee requests and by government support, the Quakers enlarged their missions in western Ohio. At Lewistown the Shawnees and Senecas enlarged their fields and planted corn, cabbages, and potatoes. They also set out orchards of peaches and apples. Women still did much of the farming, but additional livestock was purchased, and Shawnee men sold surplus hogs or cattle to nearby whites or drove them to Cincinnati. Shawnee hunters still sought game in the forests, but as the deer population plummeted, they relied more on their domestic animals and on wildfowl harvested during the spring and fall migrations. In addition, some children periodically enrolled in a Quaker school at Wapakoneta.[55]

Yet all did not go well. The large tracts of good agricultural lands occupied by the Shawnees were coveted by their neighbors. White settlers continued to poach Shawnee livestock, and although the Quakers still interceded on their behalf, former Kentuckians, now spilling over onto lands recently sold at the Treaty of Fort Meigs, discounted such intercession as "meddling." And John Johnston, their agent at Piqua, seemed ineffective. As the tide of political opinion in Washington moved inexorably toward Indian removal, Johnston's superiors opposed his commitment to honoring past treaties that protected the Shawnees in Ohio. Fallen from favor, Johnston attempted to defend reservation boundaries, but his efforts were often undercut or ignored. Again, Lewis, Black Hoof, and other Shawnees found that their Great Father, who had welcomed their assistance against the British, now was eager to take his red children's land. He was also reluctant to protect them from their white neighbors.[56]

Bewildered, Captain Lewis and Black Hoof remembered when Indian agents in the West had seemed unwilling or unable to remedy their problems twenty years earlier. They had journeyed to Washington, and assisted by the Quakers, they had met with Jefferson and Secretary of War Dearborn. Neither the president, nor the secretary of war had solved all their problems, but they had listened attentively, and following the meeting, conditions in Ohio had, at least temporarily, improved.

At first Johnston opposed such a trip, but Lewis and Black Hoof badgered him relentlessly, and he finally agreed. On March 21, 1820, Lewis, his wife, Black Hoof, the Wolf, John Perry, two other Shawnees—James McPherson (a subagent from Lewistown) and Francis Duchoquet (an interpreter)—all bedecked in new clothing for the journey, left Wapakoneta for the nation's capital. En route they passed through Baltimore, where they sought help from leading Quakers in scheduling a meeting with Secretary of War John C. Calhoun.[57]

They met with Calhoun in April, but the meeting did not go well. Attempts by Lewis, Black Hoof, and other Shawnee spokesmen to secure patents in fee simple to small tracts of land within their reservations were denied. Disappointed, Lewis seemed to reassess his struggle to stay in Ohio. Perhaps the only chance for the Shawnees to retain any autonomy and cohesion as a community was to migrate to the West, where they could reestablish themselves among other villages of their tribe and among other tribes who also chose to live apart from the Long Knives.[58]

In retrospect, the trip to Washington served as a watershed. It seemed to convince Lewis that removal to lands west of the Mississippi was inevitable. He knew that Black Hoof opposed such a move, but the subject had been discussed among the Ohio Shawnees for some time, and Lewis believed that removal had considerable support.[59] He also knew that there were many friends and relatives who would welcome them in the West. Large numbers of Shawnees had migrated into eastern Missouri during the American Revolution, and in the subsequent decades additional Shawnees had followed. Most resided in the Cape Girardeau region, but in the decade following the War of 1812 some had migrated farther southwest, establishing new villages along the White River, in southwestern Missouri and northwestern Arkansas. All of these Shawnee villages had attracted other tribesmen: Delawares, Kickapoos, and members of the old Illinois Confederacy. By the 1820s they had joined with Cherokees from Arkansas intermittently to war against the Osages. Obviously, they would welcome new Shawnee emigrants from Ohio, seasoned warriors who had recently fought in the War of 1812.[60]

Lewis's decision to go west must have come after considerable reflection, but events in Missouri strengthened his determination. In 1821 he learned that most of the Shawnees and Delawares previously residing near Cape Girardeau had left their homes to form new villages on the James and White Rivers in southwestern Missouri. Shawnees from these villages arrived in Ohio, informing Lewis that the Cherokees welcomed the newcomers and had joined them in new attacks against the Osages, attempting to drive the latter from the rich buffalo lands just west of the modern Missouri border. William Clark, Richard Graham, and other Indian agents in Saint Louis had attempted to stop the bloodshed, but they had little control over the hinterland in the southwestern Ozarks. Moreover, these agents knew that the former Shawnee and Delaware lands in eastern Missouri were being overrun by white settlers, and they encouraged the Missouri Shawnees to move farther west. Lewis also learned that these agents would welcome the Ohio Shawnees to the growing community of emigrant Indians in southwestern Missouri.[61]

The decision was made. In the spring of 1822 Lewis, his family, and a small party of his closest followers left Lewistown and journeyed west, first crossing the Mississippi River near the old Shawnee tract at Cape Girardeau, then traveling on to the Ozarks region. Meanwhile, in 1821 William Clark had arbitrarily assigned tracts of land in southwestern Missouri to the Delawares, Kickapoos, and Shawnees, but villages of Peorias, Weas, and Piankashaws also were scattered across the secluded valleys of the region. To the south, Cherokee villages dotted northern Arkansas as far south as the Arkansas River. The lands assigned to the Shawnees encompassed more than 1,250 square miles on the headwaters of the north fork of the White River, but Lewis took his followers into northern Arkansas, establishing a new village on more fertile lands closer to the Cherokees, near the site of modern Yellville.[62]

Lewis found the region in a state of flux. Although American officials had tried to broker a peace between the emigrant Indians and the Osages, their efforts had failed. Meanwhile, whites continued to infringe on the eastern borders of Cherokee, Delaware, and Kickapoo lands in Arkansas and Missouri. In response, Cherokee leaders such as Tahlonteskee, John Jolly, and Takatoka met with the Delawares, Shawnees, and Kickapoos, proposing a new confederacy of emigrant Indians to defend their lands against both the Osages and intruding whites. Lewis readily enlisted in this movement, and within a few months he had emerged as one of its leading spokesmen. In February 1823 delegates from the Cherokees, Shawnees, Kickapoos, Delawares,

Piankashaws, Weas, and Peorias assembled in council in northwestern Arkansas and made plans to form a formal confederacy. The council was dominated by the Cherokee chief Takatoka and by Captain Lewis, who was appointed to carry wampum back to the Shawnee villages in Ohio and to invite his kinsmen at Lewistown, Wapakoneta, and Hog Creek to join the confederacy in southern Missouri.[63]

Late in August 1823 Lewis left his village on the White River to travel back to Ohio. En route he passed through Saint Louis, where he met with William Clark and explained the purpose of the proposed confederacy. According to Lewis, the emigrant Indians wished to form an autonomous state, or haven, for the Indians still residing in Indiana, Ohio, or New York: a new homeland, where tribal people would be free from illegal intruders, whiskey peddlers, and other problems that had plagued them in the past. They also planned to establish an intertribal council to govern the region, and to strongly encourage the pursuit of an agricultural lifestyle, which they were "extremely anxious to exchange for that of the hunters," which was "precarious . . . and so little to be depended upon." Unlike traditional tribal councils, the proposed council would have coercive powers to enforce its decisions. And finally, the new intertribal government would welcome "teachers and husbandmen" to instruct the Indians in the "blessings" of industry and agriculture, which were enjoyed "by the white man." Captain Lewis also informed Clark that he intended to carry his message to Wapakoneta and that a delegation of Cherokees led by Takatoka would join him in Ohio to assure the Shawnees that they would be welcome in the West and then travel with him to Washington, where they would ask the president to support their plans.[64]

Clark was so favorably impressed with Lewis's proposal that he immediately wrote to Calhoun, urging him to support the scheme. He instructed Indian Agent Richard Graham to accompany Lewis to Ohio to assure the Shawnees that the government favored the project. Clark also instructed Graham to assist Lewis in preparing for the arrival of the Cherokees and to help him recruit other tribes (such as Miamis, Ottawas, and Wyandottes). But then a series of setbacks occurred that eventually ended in disaster. Lewis and Graham expected the Cherokee delegation to appear at Wapakoneta in October, but they failed to arrive. Renewed trouble with the Osages delayed the Cherokees' departure from Arkansas, and they did not reach Saint Louis until December, at which time Clark advised them that the season was too late and that they should return to Arkansas. He persuaded them, however, to return in the spring and meet with the Shawnees at Wapakoneta in May. Yet, once again, skirmishes with the Osages intervened, and the Cherokees were forced to postpone their journey to Ohio.[65]

Lewis's optimism slowly eroded. In the fall of 1823, when he had returned to the Shawnee villages in Ohio, many of the Shawnees and Senecas had embraced his proposal. Black Hoof remained resolutely opposed, but Lewis was hopeful about the plan's success. The Cherokees' failure to arrive in October somewhat dampened his spirits, but he was encouraged by the Shawnees' positive response to news that Takatoka and other prominent Cherokees would visit Wapakoneta in the spring. But the second failure of the Cherokee envoys played into the hands of Black Hoof and other Shawnees who were opposed to removal, and rumors spread through the Shawnee villages that Captain Lewis had deceived them. According to the rumormongers, Lewis only wanted to recruit additional followers for his village in Arkansas; the Cherokees had issued no invitations.[66]

Wondering if they had been hoodwinked, the Shawnees sent riders to Saint Louis, where Clark assured them that the Cherokee invitation was genuine and that the Cherokees now planned to journey to Kaskaskia in southern Illinois in October. There the Cherokees would meet with delegates from all the Ohio, Indiana, and Illinois tribes to explain the proposal, and then the Cherokees would join the delegates in a trip to Washington. Clark informed them that the Cherokees would assist the northern tribesmen in negotiating the sale of their lands and in making preparations for removal to southern Missouri. Indeed, the Cherokee delegation would be led by Takatoka, the tribe's "Great Beloved Man," and he would be accompanied by other Cherokee dignitaries, including Spring Frog, the Tassel, and Young Glass. Reassured, the Shawnee messengers returned to Ohio, and Lewis's hopes were renewed. Accusations against him declined and interest in removal seemed to be rekindled. In October, when the Cherokee delegation arrived at Kaskaskia, Captain Lewis and several of his kinsmen were there to meet them.[67]

But another setback occurred. Takatoka and the Cherokees reached Kaskaskia on October 24, but within twenty-four hours, the Cherokee Great Beloved Man became violently ill and died. On his deathbed he urged the Indians in attendance to continue on to Washington, but Takatoka's death cast an aura of shadows over the assembled tribesmen. Loyal to Takatoka, the other Cherokees had supported the proposal, but only Lewis, among all the other Indians in attendance, had worked assiduously for its implementation. Assuming the mantle of leadership, Lewis watched in dismay as some of the Cherokees departed back to Arkansas. Alarmed, he led the remainder of the Cherokees, accompanied by a few Shawnees and a lone Wyandotte, on to Saint Louis, where he persuaded Clark that the mission to Washington should continue.

Clark instructed Indian Agent Pierre Menard to accompany Lewis back to Wapakoneta, where news of Takatoka's death and the apparent failure of the Kaskaskia council had preceded them. In December, Lewis and Menard met in council with the Shawnees and Senecas, attempting to convince them that plans for the autonomous Indian state had not died with Takatoka. He pointed out that William Clark still strongly supported the proposal, and the agent had assured both Lewis and the tribesmen who had accompanied him to Saint Louis that President James Monroe also favored the plan. Some of the Shawnees and Senecas still seemed to favor removal, but Black Hoof and his followers remained opposed. Others seemed noncommittal. What would happen to their annuities in the West? If they moved to Missouri, would they be forced to share the annuities they now received in Ohio with other Indians?[68]

In early February 1825 Lewis, Menard, six Cherokees, and nine other Shawnees and Senecas (including Kiscallawa, Mayesweskaka, and Petecaussa, western Shawnee chiefs from Missouri) left Lewistown for Washington, arriving in the capital on February 19. They were unaware that three weeks earlier, while they were preparing to leave Ohio, President Monroe had sent a message to the U.S. Senate, proposing a new policy regarding Indian removal in the West. Under pressure from politicians in Missouri and Arkansas, Monroe urged that no more tribespeople be removed to those states and that those tribes already resident there be removed farther west. He did recommend, however, that once settled in the West, the tribes be granted considerable political autonomy. The policy was strongly supported by both Secretary of War Calhoun and Senator Thomas Hart Benton of Missouri, who suggested that the government purchase lands in modern Kansas and Oklahoma from the Osages to serve as a new homeland for all the tribes currently residing in Arkansas and Missouri.[69]

Lewis and his companions remained in Washington for about one month, meeting with Calhoun, Monroe, and other officials. Although the Cherokees were reluctant to exchange their lands in Arkansas, Lewis and the Shawnees were more willing to accept a new home farther west. Lewis still favored a Cherokee alliance, but he had no close ties to the lands in Arkansas or Missouri, and he was eager to embrace any federal policy that would enable the Shawnees to be free of whiskey peddlers, dishonest traders, and hostile settlers in Ohio. He believed that the Shawnees in Ohio would agree to the new policy and asked Calhoun to send federal commissioners to Wapakoneta so that his kinsmen might negotiate a treaty exchanging their remaining lands for a new homeland in the West. Calhoun willingly agreed, lavishly praised Lewis, and informed him that he would appoint Governor Lewis Cass of Michigan Territory to meet with the Shawnees, Senecas, Wyandottes, and other tribes at Wapakoneta. Late in March, Lewis, the Shawnees, and several of the Cherokee delegates returned to Ohio.[70]

The setbacks continued. In Lewis's absence both Black Hoof and John Johnston had worked steadily to sabotage the removal. Obviously, Black Hoof was jealous of the attention that Clark, Calhoun, and even Monroe seemed to be paying to Lewis, and he resented the latter's role in initiating the latest removal proposal. Moreover, Black Hoof relished his role as a government chief. He still exercised considerable control over the distribution of federal annuities at Wapakoneta and in western Ohio. He feared he would lose command over such funds in Missouri or Kansas. In addition, by 1825 Black Hoof was an old man in frail health, and he had no desire to move west of the Mississippi. Like many elderly people, he did not embrace change. He had lived his entire adult life in Ohio and had vowed "never to leave it, but to live upon it as long as the high spirit should permit" and "to lay my bones in its earth when I left the world." Accordingly, he counseled the Shawnees, Senecas, and even the Wyandottes against Lewis's proposal.[71]

At least Black Hoof's opposition was open and aboveboard. Johnston's was more insidious. Like Black Hoof, Johnston was also angry that he had not been consulted in formulating plans to remove the Shawnees from Ohio, and he described the entire proposal as "money thrown away"; it would "produce no benefit to the government or the Indians." In addition, Johnston spread rumors that Lewis was an ambitious man, interested only in his own advancement, and that he had kept annuity funds for his personal use. After insulting the Cherokee delegates and refusing to provide them with any provisions, he warned the Shawnees, Wyandottes, and other Indians that the Cherokee tribe only wanted to use them and would treat them harshly after they arrived in the West. According to Johnston, if the Shawnees moved west, they would "no more be a people" and would "be gone forever as a nation"; essentially they would fade from history. Johnston also wrote to Cass, denouncing Lewis as no longer a chief and as exceedingly unpopular among the Shawnees still at Lewistown. Attempting to hide his own duplicity, Johnston informed Cass that, although he supported the government's removal policies, he would not attend the upcoming conference because he was obligated to attend "other matters of importance." Johnston was assisted in his campaign by several local merchants who were eager to retain the profits from overpriced trade goods and from illegal whiskey that they bartered to the Indians and who informed the Shawnees that the lands in the West held no game and were rocky and barren.[72]

At Lewistown, Captain Lewis labored mightily to dispel these rumors, but it was an uphill battle. The council was scheduled to take place in May at Wapakoneta, where a special open-sided shelter had been constructed and covered with tree boughs. Black Hoof remained implacable, and his messengers to the Wyandottes, Miamis, and other tribes discouraged most of those tribesmen from attending the meeting. Cass arrived at Wapakoneta in mid-May, but to add insult to injury, he was accompanied by Tenskwatawa, the Shawnee Prophet, who previously had been living in exile in Canada. Unknown to Lewis, Cass had met with the Prophet at Detroit, and in return for promises of amnesty, the Prophet had agreed to accompany Cass to Wapakoneta to promote the removal of the Ohio Shawnees. Since both Lewis and Black Hoof had fought against Tecumseh and the Prophet during the War of 1812, Cass's decision to invite him to the conference at first seems bizarre, but Cass believed that the Shawnee holy man still possessed some influence among the Ohio villages and that his powers of persuasion would facilitate the removal process. Events would prove Cass to be correct. The Prophet's participation in the conference eventually worked to the government's advantage; it did not assist Captain Lewis.[73]

On May 18 Cass formally presented the proposal for removal. He informed the Shawnees that the government would purchase their lands in Ohio and provide them with a much larger reservation in the West, where they could live free from the destructive influence of whiskey peddlers and other evil white men. Lewis promptly supported the proposal, even if it no longer contained the possibility of an autonomous Indian state, but Black Hoof and most of the other Shawnees sat sullen and said very little, then asked for several days to formulate a response.

In the meantime, the Shawnee Prophet learned that Black Hoof was jealous of Lewis and had personally vowed that he would never leave Ohio, but that many other Shawnees who were now under Black Hoof's influence might be willing to remove at a future date. He promptly relayed such information to Cass. Hoping to salvage some advantage from the conference, Cass then informed the Shawnees that they would eventually have to remove, and that he had offered them a fair price, but if they refused, he would meet with them again "a year or two hence."

Black Hoof was encouraged by Cass's obvious equivocation. On August 23 he gave the Shawnees' formal reply. Speaking for the majority of the Shawnees in attendance, Black Hoof informed Cass that they wished to remain in Ohio. The acrimonious old chief then chided Lewis for promoting a removal proposal without first consulting with the Shawnees at Wapakoneta, adding, "We could have done this on our own accord, if we had been disposed to remove, and we did not want any other person to do [so] for us. It is impossible for us to think of getting up and removing away in this hurried manner."[74]

Cass's offer of another removal "a year or two hence" took Lewis completely by surprise. In contrast to Black Hoof, Lewis found the governor's willingness to accept a postponement disastrous. All his efforts during the past three years had come to nothing. Lewis's disappointment was evident in his reply. He addressed his assembled kinsmen and sadly informed them that he once had hoped to live all his life on the reservation at Lewistown, but his people were now surrounded by whites, and they could not sustain themselves. Instead, the Shawnees now had an opportunity for new lands in the West, which promised "an abundance of room" for themselves and their children. He pointed out that the invitation had been offered not only by the Cherokees but also by fellow Shawnees as well as Delawares, Weas, Piankashaws, and Kaskaskias who also lived beyond the Mississippi. They were all eager to welcome the Ohio Shawnees to a new home. Lewis stated he was sorry that, after such a generous offer of hospitality and safe haven, many of his brothers at Wapakoneta had rejected their invitation. As for himself, he planned to sell his lands near Lewistown and take his people to new lands in the West.[75]

Ever an opportunist, the Shawnee Prophet proposed a compromise as the Wapakoneta council came to an end. He believed that many of the Shawnees would eventually remove, but they were hesitant to question Black Hoof's leadership and feared they might not receive their annuities in the West. He suggested that those Shawnees who wished to emigrate should join with Lewis and move to new lands beyond the Mississippi. Others who preferred to follow Black Hoof should remain in Ohio. Carefully hedging his bets, the Prophet then privately informed Cass that if he and his followers would be permitted to return to Ohio from Canada, he would undercut the elderly Black Hoof's influence and actively promote the removal of all Shawnees to the West.[76]

Following the council at Wapakoneta, Lewis and his Cherokee companions returned to the Lewistown reservation, where Lewis spent the summer meeting with the Shawnees and Senecas who lived there, attempting to persuade them to accompany him to the new lands in the West. He was partially successful. In the fall he led a party of 255 Lewistown Shawnees and a handful of Senecas westward across Indiana and Illinois, where they encamped on the east bank of the Mississippi, just above the mouth of the Kaskaskia River. In November, Lewis attended the treaty negotiations at Saint Louis at which the Missouri Shawnees ceded all their lands near Cape Girardeau to the United States in exchange for a tract of land in eastern Kansas. Although he served as a witness to the treaty, he did not sign it as a chief or head man of the Missouri Shawnees, leaders whose people held legitimate claims to the Cape Girardeau lands.[77]

Three days after the treaty was signed, Lewis also met with William Clark and informed him that he and his people would remain encamped north of Kaskaskia until they could move to "a new land in the hope that it will be to our benefit." He asked Clark for corn and for lead and powder so his people could hunt during the winter and fill their cooking pots. He also requested that his followers be paid for their cabins, fences, and other improvements that they had left behind and that the annuities due to the Shawnees and Senecas at Lewistown now be paid through Clark in Saint Louis. He assured Clark that he believed that the other Ohio Shawnees eventually would follow them to the West, but as far as his people were concerned, they were eager "to avoid the destruction that threatens us remaining amidst the White People from the introduction of whiskey." And finally, he assured Clark that he and his party "shall move over the Mississippi, for my people now with me will not return to Ohio."[78]

Following the meeting with Clark, Captain Lewis rapidly faded from recorded history. Evidence suggests that he and his party remained near Kaskaskia or in the Cape Girardeau region until early spring, then traveled on to Arkansas and joined the Shawnees from Lewistown who previously had settled near modern Yellville. William Clark's diary indicates that Lewis and eight other Shawnees arrived in Saint Louis via steamboat on July 13, 1826, but departed in early August, so he did not participate in the formal negotiations that led to a tenuous peace treaty between the Shawnees, other emigrant Indians, and the Osages, which were held in that city during the following September. Accounts of his death are sketchy, but he seems to have died of natural causes sometime during the autumn of 1826, either in northern Arkansas or perhaps in Kansas.[79]

In many ways Quatawapea, or Captain Lewis, is an admirable but tragic figure. He played an important role in both Shawnee and American history during the first quarter of the nineteenth century, but his image was badly tarnished by the brief biographical sketch accompanying his portrait in the McKenney-Hall portfolio (a famed three-volume collection of Native American portraits and biographies).[80] The primary damage to Captain Lewis's reputation has emerged from the biographical sketch accompanying his painting. James Hall, a Cincinnati lawyer who coauthored the McKenney-Hall portfolio, used notes compiled by McKenney, but he also seems to have been heavily influenced by John Johnston. Ironically, Johnston had been very supportive of Lewis until 1823, when Lewis attempted to champion the removal of the Shawnees from Piqua, an emigration that seemed to challenge Johnston's authority and threaten the agent's position. Attempting to thwart the 1825 removal, Johnston defamed Lewis, charging that he had defrauded the government, had no influence among the Shawnees, and was generally disliked by his tribe. Johnston offered no proof for his charges, but Black Hoof's opposition to the removal added kindling to this fire. Of course, all of these accusations were forwarded to McKenney, who only one year earlier (1824) had been appointed as commissioner of Indian affairs, and who had no previous relationship with the chief. Since information regarding Lewis was quite limited, when Hall wrote the biographical sketch to accompany Captain Lewis's portrait, he relied almost entirely upon McKenney's notes and opinions, both collected or formed in conjunction with the failed treaty and removal of 1825. All of Lewis's previous service to the United States and his leadership during the War of 1812 were either unknown by McKenney (and Hall) or ignored.[81]

That service was considerable. With the possible exception of Black Hoof, no other Shawnee leader had so steadfastly assisted the United States during the first two decades of the nineteenth century. In the years preceding the War of 1812, Captain Lewis had championed cultural patterns and agricultural programs promoted by both the Quakers and the federal government, and he had labored assiduously to limit the influence of Tecumseh and the Shawnee Prophet. During the war Lewis had led many of the Shawnee scouts who supported the American campaigns against the Redcoats, and in his absences his people had been harassed by frontier riffraff who had stolen their livestock, cut down their cornfields, and even burned their cabins. Still, Lewis had ridden with McArthur on his raid into Ontario, and in the postwar years he had cooperated with federal officials, again promoting agriculture and Shawnee self-sufficiency on his reservation at Lewistown. Obviously, Lewis had usually deferred to Black Hoof's leadership, since the chief from Wapakoneta had more experience and a larger following, but in 1820, when Lewis became convinced that removal to the West was the Shawnees' only hope, he broke with the elderly chief. Yet even in his ill-fated attempt to promote Shawnee removal, Lewis had readily conferred with federal officials and had received both the blessing and praise of Secretary of War John C. Calhoun, and Indian Agents William Clark, Richard Graham, and Pierre Menard. His loyalty to the United States and his service to the government remained undeterred. Indeed, with the possible exception of Black Hoof, the name of no other Loyal Shawnee leader is praised as often in the thousands of letters, reports, or other federal documents that fill the National Archives from this period.[82]

In the end, his loyalty to the United States also contributed to his downfall. Like many other Native American leaders, he failed to understand that promises made in the West were not always honored in Washington. Although William Clark supported the creation of a semiautonomous multitribal confederacy with hegemony over lands along the Arkansas-Missouri border, such a coalition frightened officials in Washington since it smacked of Tecumseh's efforts before the War of 1812—a venture that had seriously threatened the American republic. Meanwhile, politicians in Arkansas and Missouri also adamantly opposed such an entity, and they used their influence in Washington to demand that the Shawnees, Cherokees, and other Indians be removed beyond the borders of these states, into either Kansas or Indian Territory. Consequently, while Lewis, Takatoka, and other Cherokees labored to finalize their plan and to recruit the Shawnees and other tribes to the White River Country, Monroe, Calhoun, and McKenney had already changed their minds and authorized Clark to purchase lands from the Osages and remove the Missouri and Arkansas tribes farther west. Cass was aware of this change in policy when he arrived at Wapakoneta, and the tribesmen who attended the council in May 1825 sensed that Cass's promotion of Lewis and Takatoka's removal plan was half-hearted at best.[83]

Other factors also contributed to Captain Lewis's downfall. As scholars such as Stephen Warren and Sami Lakomäki have pointed out, Shawnee politics had always been characterized by fluidity: both fragmentation and centralization. The Shawnees, like the Kickapoos, Potawatomis, and several other Algonquian tribes, have rarely been unified as a centralized political unity, and Lewis's attempts to bring Shawnees from many separate villages located in different states together in a more unified political entity in southern Missouri and Arkansas ran counter to much of the Shawnees' political tradition. Even today, the modern Shawnee people, while proudly sharing many tribal cultural patterns and a rich tradition, remain divided into several separate political entities, tribal governments, or bands. Lewis's efforts in the mid-1820s may have been doomed from the start, but like Tecumseh, he too had a noble objective; and he too believed that he was working in behalf of his people.[84]

NOTES

1. The location of Captain Lewis's winter camp can be found in William Clark, "Report of a Council with the Cherokees of Arkansas and the Shawnees," 1825, Richard Graham Papers, Missouri Historical Society, St. Louis (hereafter cited as Graham Papers).

2. For excellent discussions and analyses of Shawnee migrations and the nature and evolution of Shawnee political structure, see Stephen Warren, *The Shawnees and Their Neighbors, 1795–1870* (Urbana: University of Illinois Press, 2005); Stephen Warren, *The Worlds the Shawnees Made: Migration and Violence in Early America* (Chapel Hill: University of North Carolina Press, 2014); Sami Lakomäki, *Gathering Together: The Shawnee People through Diaspora and Nationhood, 1600–1870* (New Haven, Conn.: Yale University Press, 2014).

3. "Qua-Ta-Wa-Pea, or Col. Lewis, a Shawnee Chief," in Thomas L. McKenney and James Hall, *History of the Indian Tribes of North America, with Biographical Sketches and Anecdotes of the Principal Chiefs*, reprint of 1855 edition (Edinburgh: John Grant, 1933), 1:168–71. See also "Lewis, John—Capt. Lewis—Col. Lewis—Quatawepay—Kaitwawypie," *The United Tribe of Shawnee and Delaware Indians*, at http://www.angelfire.com/ok3/utsdi/UTSDINEXUS.html (hereafter cited as UTSDI website).

4. For a description of the Shawnee towns in northwest Ohio prior to the Treaty of Greenville, see Helen Hornbeck Tanner, "The Glaize in 1792: A Composite Indian Community," in Peter C. Mancall and James H. Merrell, eds., *American Encounters: Natives and Newcomers from European Contact to Indian Removal, 1500–1850* (New York: Routledge, 2000), 405–10. See also UTSDI website.

5. Minutes of a Treaty with the Indians, June–August 1795, in *American State Papers: Documents, Legislative and Executive, of the Congress of the United States*, Class II, *Indian Affairs*, ed. Walter Lowrie, Matthew St. Clair Clarke, and Walter S. Franklin (Washington: Gales and Seaton, 1832–34), 1:564–82 (hereafter cited as *American State Papers*); "A Treaty of Peace between the United States of America and the Tribes of Indians," August 3, 1795, in Charles J. Kappler, comp. ed., *Indian Treaties, 1778–1883* (New York: Ameron House, 1972), 39–45.

6. W. H. Perrin and J. H. Both, *History of Logan County and Ohio* (Chicago: O. L. Baskin, 1880), 206; McKenney and Hall, *History of the Indian Tribes*, 168–71; UTSDI website. See also Henry Clay Alder, *A History of Jonathan Alder: His Life and Captivity among the Indians* (Akron: University of Akron Press, 2002), 45–48.

7. William Henry Harrison to the Secretary of War, March 22, 1814, in Logan Esarey, ed., *Messages and Letters of William Henry Harrison* (New York: Arno Press, 1975), 2:636–41 (hereafter cited as Esarey, *Harrison Papers*). See also Helen Hornbeck Tanner, *Atlas of Great Lakes Indian History* (Norman: University of Oklahoma Press, 1987), 98–99, 101; and Lakomäki, *Gathering Together*, 134.

8. Harvey Lewis Carter, *The Life and Times of Little Turtle* (Urbana: University of Illinois Press, 1987), 158, 162. Wells served as the unofficial, or "Temporary Resident," Indian agent at Ft. Wayne from 1796 to 1801. On January 1, 1802, Henry Dearborn appointed him as the official Indian agent at Ft. Wayne. See also speech by Black Hoof, February 5, 1802, in Barbara B. Oberg et al., eds., *The Papers of Thomas Jefferson* (Princeton, N.J.: Princeton University Press, 1950–2012), 36:517–22.

9. Speech by Black Hoof, February 5, 1802, in Oberg, *Papers of Thomas Jefferson*, 36:517–22; Thomas Jefferson to Shawnees and Delawares, February 10, 1802, in ibid., 36:522–23; Henry Dearborn to the Shawnees and Delawares, February 1, 1802, in ibid., 36:523–25.

10. "Conference with Black Hoof: Editorial Note," in ibid., 36:516. See also "Some Account of the Religious Society of Friends toward the Indian Tribes . . . ," 1802, in Shawnee File, Great Lakes and Ohio Valley Ethnohistory Collection, Glenn A. Black Laboratory of Archaeology, Indiana University, Bloomington (hereafter cited as GLOVEC).

11. Carter, *Little Turtle*, 163, 197–200. See also R. David Edmunds, "'Evil Men Who Add to Our Difficulties': Shawnees, Quakers, and William Wells, 1807–1808," *American Indian Culture and Research Journal* 14, no. 4, (1990): 1–4.

12. Edmunds, "'Evil Men,'" 4–7; "Qua-Ta-Wa-Pea," in McKenney and Hall, *History of the Indian Tribes*, 168–69. See also Quatawapeah or Lewis, and Other Shawnee Chiefs to the President, December 1, 1808, Record Group 107, Records of the Secretary of War Relating to Indian Affairs, Letters Received by the Secretary of War, Main Series M221, Roll 25, 8148–50, National Archives and Records Collection, Washington, D.C. (hereafter all documents cited from the National Archives, after an initial full citation, will be cited by their microfilm number).

13. William Wells to William Kirk, June 18, 1807, M221, Roll 9, 2878–79; Chiefs and Headmen of the Shawnees to the President, April 10, 1809, M221, Roll 25, 8053–54. See also Edmunds, "'Evil Men,'" 8–12.

14. The best discussion of the emergence of the Tenskwatawa can be found in R. David Edmunds, *The Shawnee Prophet* (Lincoln: University of Nebraska Press, 1983), 28–66.

15. R. David Edmunds, *Tecumseh and the Quest for Indian Leadership* (Boston: Little, Brown, 1984), 93–95. See also Kirk to Dearborn, July 20, 1807, M221, Roll 9, 2874–78; Joseph Vance to Benjamin Drake, n.d., Tecumseh Papers, Draper Manuscripts, 2YY108–117, State Historical Society of Wisconsin, Madison; see also Simon Kenton Papers, 9BB1, ibid. (hereafter documents from this collection will be cited by title and collection number, i.e., Tecumseh Papers, 2YY108–117, Draper MSS).

16. Edmunds, *The Shawnee Prophet*, 67–70. See also "Articles of a Treaty Made and Concluded at Brownstown, November 25, 1808," in Kappler, *Indian Treaties*, 99–100. Some historians have argued that Captain Lewis supported Tecumseh and the Prophet at this early period, but there is little evidence to support such a position. By 1807 Lewis had emerged as a proponent of acculturation and was much more closely associated with Black Hoof and the Shawnees at Wapakoneta. Indeed, his adoption of many American cultural patterns made him vulnerable to the Prophet's threats and denunciations. For a perspective associating Lewis with Tecumseh, see John Sugden, *Blue Jacket: Warrior of the Shawnees* (Lincoln: University of Nebraska Press, 2000), 229, 238–42.

17. "A Treaty between the United States and the . . . Delawares, Putawatamies, Miamies, and Eel River Miamies," September 30, 1809, in Kappler, *Indian Treaties*, 101–102; Wyandots of Sandusky to William Hull, June 27, 1810, Wyandot File, GLOVEC.

18. John Johnston to William Henry Harrison, June 24, 1810, in Esarey, *Harrison Papers*, 1:430–32; Wyandots of Sandusky to William Hull, June 27, 1810, Wyandot File, GLOVEC; Brownstown Wyandots to Hull, 1810, Lewis Cass Papers, William Clements Library, University of Michigan, Ann Arbor, Michigan; Joseph A. Badger, *A Memoir of Joseph Badger* (Hudson, Ohio: Ingersoll, 1851), 125.

19. Hull to the Different Nations, September 30, 1810, Cass Papers, William Clements Library; Chiefs at the Council at Brownstown to the President, September, 1810, Shawnee File, GLOVEC; John Johnston to William Eustis, October 20, 1810, Shawnee File, GLOVEC.

20. For the best account of these events, see R. David Edmunds, "Main Poc: Potawatomi Wabeno," *American Indian Quarterly* 9 (Summer 1985): 259–72. See also Harrison to John Johnston, September 1811, in Esarey, *Harrison Papers*, 1:583–84; William Hull to the Ottawas and other northern Indians, September 22, 1811, Shawnee File, GLOVEC.

21. Speeches by Captain Lewis and Black Hoof, August 24, 1811, enclosed in Johnston to the Editors of *Liberty Hall* (Cincinnati), August 27, 1811, Shawnee File, GLOVEC.

22. Speech from the Shawnee Chiefs at a Council at Ft. Wayne, November 18, 1811, Shawnee File, GLOVEC; Speech by Shawnee Delaware, Potawatomi, and Miami Indians at Ft. Wayne, November 22, 1811, in ibid.; deposition by James McElvain, December 4, 1811, Tecumseh Papers, 5YY8, Draper MSS.

23. Thomas Fish and Enos Terry to Return J. Meigs, January 14, 1812, Shawnee File, GLOVEC; John Johnston to William Eustis, May 1, 1812, ibid.; Eustis to Johnston, March 5, 1812, Records of the Secretary of War Relating to Indian Affairs, Letters Sent, M15, Roll 3, 118; William Perry to Return J. Meigs, April 30, 1812, Return J. Meigs Papers, Ohio State Historical Society, Columbus.

24. William Perry to Meigs, May 7, 1812, Meigs Papers; "From Our Western Frontier, May 14, 1812" an excerpt from the *National Intelligencer*, May 30, 1812, in ibid.; Johnston to Eustis, May 21, 1812, M221, Roll 46, 1064–66; Perry to Worthington, June 24, 1812, Thomas Worthington Papers, Ohio State Historical Society, Columbus.

25. Proceedings of a Council at Urbana Ohio, June 6, 1812, in Milo Milton Quaife, ed., *War on the Detroit: The Chronicles of Thomas Verchers de Boucherville and the Capitulation by an Ohio Volunteer* (Chicago: Lakeside Press, 1940), 197–207; Agreement with the Wyandot, Shawnee, and Mingo Chiefs, June 8, 1812, Shawnee File, GLOVEC; Hull to Eustis, June 18, 1812, Shawnee File, GLOVEC; Circular by Eustis to Meigs et al., June 19, 1812, Shawnee File, GLOVEC.

26. The best brief account of these events can be found in Alec Gilpin, *The War of 1812 in the Old Northwest* (East Lansing: Michigan State University Press, 1958), 63–83.

27. Hull to Eustis, June 9, 1812, Shawnee File, GLOVEC; Hull to Eustis, July 14, 1812, ibid.; Hull to Eustis, July 21, 1812, ibid.; Hull to Eustis, July 19, 1812; *Collections of the Michigan Pioneer and Historical Society* (Lansing: Michigan Historical Commission, 1929), 40:419–21.

28. Report by R. J. Meigs, T. Worthington, and J. Morrow to Eustis, September 10, 1812, M221, Roll 49, 4163–66; Worthington to Eustis, September 11, 1812, ibid., 4105. See also R. David Edmunds, "A Watchful Safeguard to Our Habitations: Black Hoof and the Loyal Shawnees," in *Native Americans in The New Republic*, ed. Frederick E. Hoxie, Ronald Hoffman, and Peter J. Albert (Charlottesville: United States Capitol Historical Society and the University of Virginia Press, 1999), 181–83.

29. A good account of the Potawatomi attacks upon Ft. Dearborn and Ft. Wayne can be found in R. David Edmunds, *The Potawatomis, Keepers of the Fire* (Norman: University of Oklahoma Press, 1978), 184–93.

30. S. W. Culbertson to Mr. Chambers, 1812, in Esarey, *Harrison Papers*, 2:139–40;

31. Edward DeWar to Colonel McDonnell, October 19, 1812, British Military and Naval Records, Record Group 8, C Series, vol. 676, 136–39, Library and Archives of Canada, Ottawa. See also Tarhe to Meigs, October 28, 1812, Meigs Papers; Edward Tupper to Meigs, November 28, 1812, Meigs Papers; Edmunds, "A Watchful Safeguard," 185–86.

32. Tarhe to Meigs, October 28, 1812, Meigs Papers; Tupper to Meigs, January 26, 1812, ibid.; Benjamin Stickney to John Armstrong, July 8, 1813, M221, Roll 49, 4105.

33. Tupper to Meigs, January 26, 1813, Meigs Papers; Benson J. Lossing, *Pictorial Fieldbook of the War of 1812* (New York: Harper and Brothers, 1868), 345–46n2.

34. Edmunds, *Tecumseh and the Quest*, 189–91.

35. Edmunds, "A Watchful Safeguard," 187–89.

36. Johnston to John Armstrong, June 4, 1813, Shawnee File, GLOVEC; Stickney to Armstrong, June 1813, M221, Roll 57, 1201–206; Edmunds, "A Watchful Safeguard," 189–90.

37. Report of an Indian Council, July 21, 1813, Harrison Papers, Draper MSS, 26S114–16; William Barbee to Tomas Worthington, July 21, 1813, Worthington Papers; Harrison to the Secretary of War, July 23, 1813, Esarey, *Harrison Papers*, 2:494–95.

38. Johnston to the Secretary of War, August 3, 1813, Esarey, *Harrison Papers*, 2:509; Harrison to the Secretary of War, August 11, 1813, ibid., 522–24; Harrison to Meigs, September 4, 1813, ibid., 533–35; "From the *Ohio Eagle*, August 11," quoted in the *National Intelligencer*, August 3, 1813; "Extract of a Letter from a Correspondent, August 22, 1813," in ibid., September 8, 1813.

39. Harrison to the Secretary of War, September 27, 1813, Esarey, *Harrison Papers*, 2:550–51; Lossing, *Pictorial Field Book*, 545–46; Robert Breckinridge McAfee, *History of the Late War in the Western Country* (Lexington: Worsley and Smite, 1816), 363; Edmunds, *Tecumseh and the Quest*, 207–10.

40. Harrison to the Secretary of War, October 9, 1813, Letters Received by the Secretary of War, Unregistered Series, M222, Roll 8, 3007–13; Lossing, *Pictorial Field Book of the War of 1812*, 545–46.

41. Harrison to the Secretary of War, October 9, 2013, M222, Roll 8, 3007–13; McAfee, *History of the Late War*, 389–99.

42. Johnston to Meigs, August 22, 1813, Meigs Papers; Benjamin Whiteman to Meigs, August 22, 1813, ibid.; H. M. Perry to Meigs, November 29, 1813; ibid.; Harrison to Johnston, October 15, 1813, M221, Roll 54, 8339; Johnston to John Armstrong, March 25, 1814, M221, Roll 54, 8399.

43. Tecumseh Papers, Draper MSS, 3YY143; Harrison to Armstrong, February 11, 1814, Shawnee File, GLOVEC; Journal of the Treaty Commissioners, July, 1814, *American State Papers*, 1:827–36; "A Treaty of Peace and Friendship between the United States and the Tribes of Indians . . . ," July 22, 1818, in Kappler, *Indian Treaties*, 105–107.

44. Edmunds, "A Watchful Safeguard," 194–95.

45. McArthur to George Izard, November 18, 1814, Duncan McArthur Papers, vol. 19, Library of Congress, Washington, D.C.; McArthur to Stickney, January 30, 1815, ibid., vol. 22; John Brant to

William Claus, November 16, 1814, Indian Affairs, Record Group 10, Records of the Superintendent's Office, Correspondence, 29:1367–68, Library and Archives of Canada; General Order issued by C. S. Todd, November 18, 1814, in Stuart A Rammage, *The Militia Stood Alone: Malcolm's Mills, 6 November 1814* (Summerland, B.C: Valley Publishing, 2000), 129–30. Rammage's volume has the best account of McArthur's raid into Ontario. The author would like to thank Don Hickey for his suggestions regarding access to Rammage's volume.

46. McArthur to Captain Lewis, Captain Wolf, Captain Johnny, and Anthony Shane, February 13, 1815, Duncan McArthur Papers, vol. 23; McArthur to James Monroe, March 15, 1815, ibid., vol. 24; McArthur to the Acting Secretary of War, March 15, 1815, in Clarence E. Carter, ed. *Territorial Papers of the United States* (Washington, D.C.: Government Printing Office, 1934–), 10:519–20 (hereafter cited as Carter, *Territorial Papers*). See also Leonard U. Hill, *John Johnston and the Indians in the Land of the Three Miamis* (Piqua, Ohio: Leonard U. Hill, 1957), 83.

47. McArthur to the Acting Secretary of War, March 15, 1815, Carter, *Territorial Papers*, 10:519–20; Shawnee Chiefs to Johnston, April 27, 1815, M221, Roll 63, 6471; Johnston to the Secretary of War, May 4, 1815, M221, Roll 63, 6469.

48. Journal of the Proceedings of the Commissioners, August, 1812, *American State Papers*, 2:17–25; George Ironsides to William Claus, October 23, 1815, Records of the Superintendent's Office, Correspondence, vol. 13, 1838, Indian Affairs, Record Group 10, Library and Archives of Canada; Harrison and John Graham to William Crawford, September 9, 1815, William Harrison Papers, Indiana Historical Society; "A Treaty between the United States and the . . . Indians," September 8, 1815, in Kappler, *Indian Treaties*, 117–19.

49. Harrison to Armstrong, March 20, 1814, Shawnee File, GLOVEC; Harrison to Crawford, September 9, 1815, Harrison Papers, Indiana Historical Society. See also Andrew R. L. Cayton, *Ohio: The History of a People* (Columbus: Ohio State University Press, 2002), 13–16.

50. John Johnston to the Secretary of War, November 23, 1815, Shawnee File, GLOVEC; Shawnee Chiefs to the Secretary of War, December 29, 1815, ibid.; Report of James Ellicott and Philip E. Thomas, August 1, 1816, ibid.

51. The Ohio Shawnees' desire for a clear legal title to their lands was longstanding. In 1802 Captain Lewis and Black Hoof had asked Jefferson and Dearborn for such a delineation of Shawnee lands in Ohio, but the latter had refused. See note 8 above. For good brief discussions of the Shawnees' desire to combine traditional Native American and white economic practices to defend their Ohio homelands, see Stephen Warren, *The Shawnees and Their Neighbors*, 49–55; and Lakomäki, *Gathering Together*, 151–52.

52. John Johnston to Lewis Cass, June 13, 1817, Shawnee File, GLOVEC; Cass to McArthur, June 13, 1817, ibid. See also Warren, *The Shawnees and Their Neighbors*, 56.

53. "Articles of a Treaty Made and Conducted at the Foot of the Rapids of Lake Erie," September 29, 1817, in Kappler, *Indian Treaties*, 145–55. See also Henry Harvey, *History of the Shawnee Indians, from the Year 1681 to 1854* (Cincinnati: E. Morgan and Sons, 1855), 165–68.

54. "Articles of a Treaty Made and Concluded at St. Mary's . . . ," September 18, 1818, in Kappler, *Indian Treaties*, 162–63. See also Francis Paul Prucha, *American Indian Treaties: The History of a Political Anomaly* (Berkeley: University of California Press, 1994), 136–38; William J. McMurray, *History of Auglaize County, Ohio* (Indianapolis: Historical Publications, 1923), 1:126–30.

55. McMurray, *History of Auglaize County*, 1:91–96; John Johnston, "A Table Showing the State of the Indians in Ohio," October 1819, Shawnee File, GLOVEC; John Johnston to Unknown, June 17, 1819, in Hill, *John Johnston*, 187–92. See also Warren, *The Shawnees and Their Neighbors*, 60–61; Lakomäki, *Gathering Together*, 155–56.

56. Johnston to Cass, April 11, 1821, Shawnee File, GLOVEC; Warren, *The Shawnees and Their Neighbors*, 64–65.

57. See Hill, *John Johnston*, 106; Warren, *The Shawnees and Their Neighbors*, 62–63; Philip E. Thomas to John C. Calhoun, April 26, 1820, in W. Edwin Hemphill, ed., *The Papers of John C. Calhoun* (Columbia: University of South Carolina Press, 1959–2003), 5:77 (hereafter cited as Hemphill, *Calhoun Papers*).

58. Thomas to Calhoun, April 11, 1820, Shawnee File, GLOVEC; Warren, *The Shawnees and Their Neighbors*, 62–63.

59. Thomas Forsyth to William Clark, September 30, 1818, Thomas Forsyth Papers, Missouri Historical Society, St. Louis; Johnston to Cass, July 17, 1819, Shawnee File, GLOVEC; Hill, *John Johnston*, 106.

60. Excellent brief overviews of this emigration can be found in Lakomäki, *Gathering Together*, 165–80; and Warren, *The Shawnees and Their Neighbors*, 71–84.

61. Lakomäki, *Gathering Together*, 176–80; Warren, *The Shawnees and Their Neighbors*, 81–87.

62. Warren, *The Shawnees and Their Neighbors*, 85, 90–91; Calhoun to Kiscallawa, Mayesweskaka, and Petecaussa (Western Shawnee chiefs), March 2, 1825, Record Group 75, Records of the Michigan Superintendency, M1, Roll 28, 165. In the letter Calhoun mentions that Clark set aside the lands for the Shawnees in southwestern Missouri in 1821. See also James F. Keefe and Lynn Morrow, eds., *The White River Chronicles of S. C. Turnbo* (Fayetteville: University of Arkansas Press, 1994), 5, 50, 264–65, 264n6.

63. Grant Foreman, *Indians and Pioneers: The Story of the American Southwest before 1830* (Norman: University of Oklahoma Press, 1930), 185–88. See also George Lankford, "Shawnee Convergence: Immigrant Indians in the Ozarks," *The Arkansas Historical Quarterly* 59 (Winter 1999): 408–11. Lankford's article, which provides several anecdotal "reminiscences" by early Shawnee settlers in northern Arkansas, contains several references to Captain Lewis, but it also contains inaccurate and very questionable materials describing his emigration to Arkansas prior to 1820.

64. Clark to Calhoun, September 5, 1823, Shawnee File, GLOVEC.

65. Ibid.; Foreman, *Indians and Pioneers*, 191. See also Willard H. Rollins, *The Osage: An Ethnohistorical Study of Hegemony on the Prairie-Plains* (Columbia: University of Missouri Press, 1984), 249–54; John Joseph Matthews, *The Osages: Children of the Middle Waters* (Norman: University of Oklahoma Press, 1961), 517–20.

66. Grant Foreman, *Last Trek of the Indians* (Chicago: University of Chicago Press, 1946), 49–50.

67. Foreman, *Indians and Pioneers*, 192–93.

68. Foreman, *Last Trek of the Indians*, 50.

69. Acting Governor Robert Crittenden to the Secretary of War, September 28, 1823, in Carter, *Territorial Papers*, 19:546–50; Francis Paul Prucha, *The Great Father: The United States Government and the American Indians* (Lincoln: University of Nebraska Press, 1984), 1:187–88. See also Foreman, *Last Trek of the Indians*, 50–51; and Calhoun to the Western Shawnee Chiefs, March 2, 1825, M1, Roll 28, 165.

70. Cherokee Delegation to the Secretary of War, March 12, 1825, in Carter, *Territorial Papers*, 20:4–5; Speech by John Lewis, March 2, 1825, M1, Roll 28, 163; Calhoun to Lewis, March 2, 1825, M21, Roll 1, 186; Lewis to Calhoun, February 28, 1825, Record Group 75, Letters Received by the Office of Indian Affairs, Ohio Agency, M234, Roll 300, 11–12. See also *Niles Register*, March 26, 1825; Foreman, *Last Trek of the Indians*, 51.

71. Report of the Council at Wapakoneta, May, 1825, M1, Roll 28, 148–63; Thomas McKenney to Cass, June 11, 1825, M1, Roll 16, 143; Council with Shawnee Chiefs, April 10, 1830, M234, Roll 300, 143–46.

72. Johnston to Cass, April 4, 1825, M1, Roll 16, 87; Speech by Waysaosheka, the Cherokee Chief, November 10, 1825, M234, Roll 747, 325–31; Council with the Cherokee Chiefs, April 10, 1830, M234, Roll 300, 143–46; Edmunds, *The Shawnee Prophet*, 170–71.

73. Edmunds, *The Shawnee Prophet*, 166–70.

74. Minutes of a Council at Wapakoneta, May 1825, M1, Roll 28, 148–61.

75. Speech by Captain Lewis, May 23, 1825, ibid.

76. Edmunds, *The Shawnee Prophet*, 171–73.

77. Speech by Waysaosheka, November 10, 1825, M234, Roll 747, 325–31; Menard to Graham, January 17, 1827, in Foreman, *Indians and Pioneers*, 196n27; Treaty with the Shawnees, November 7, 1825, in Kappler, *Indian Treaties*, 262–64.

78. Speech by Lewis, November 10, 1825, M234, Roll 747, 335–31.

79. Entries for July 13, 1826, and August 7, 1826, in Louise Barry, ed. "William Clark's Diary: May 1826–February, 1831," *Kansas Historical Quarterly* 16 (February 1948): 11, 12n29; Lakomäki, *Gathering Together*, 162; Warren, *The Shawnees and their Neighbors*, 91–92; McKenney and Hall, *History of the Indian Tribes*, 1:168–71.

80. Published in the first volume of the portfolio in 1837, Lewis's portrait is probably based on an earlier watercolor painted by James Otto Lewis, who accompanied Cass during his meetings with Great Lakes tribes. Charles Bird King later used some of the earlier watercolors or sketches by Lewis as the basis for many of the portraits that were included in the McKenney-Hall portfolio. There seems to be no evidence that King painted Lewis in 1820 or 1825, when the latter visited Washington. Tragically, the original sketch or watercolor and King's later painting of the Shawnee chief were destroyed in a fire at the Smithsonian Institution in January 1865.

McKenney and Hall, *History of the Indian Tribes*, 1:168–71; Herman J. Viola, *The Indian Legacy of Charles Bird King* (Washington, D.C.: Smithsonian Institution Press, 1976), 55, 58, 118; R. David Edmunds to Herman Viola, February 11, 2016, personal correspondence in the possession of the author; Viola to Edmunds, February 13, 2016, personal correspondence; Edmunds to Viola, February 13, 2016, personal correspondence; Edmunds to Brian Dippie, February 10, 2016, personal correspondence; Dippie to Edmunds, February 16, 2016, personal correspondence; Edmunds to Dippie, February 17, 2016, personal correspondence.

81. Johnston to Cass, April 4, 1825, M1, Roll 16, 87; Speech by Waysaosheka, November 10, 1825, M234, Roll 747, 325–31; McKenney to Cass, June 11, 1825, M1, Roll 16, 143.

82. Clark to Calhoun, September 5, 1823, in Hemphill, *Calhoun Papers*, 8:255–58; Calhoun to Lewis, March 2, 1825, ibid., 9:612.

83. Speech by Waysaoshka to Clark, November 10, 1825, M234, Roll 747, 325–31.

84. The nature and evolution of Shawnee political structure has been admirably analyzed and discussed in Warren, *The Shawnees and Their Neighbors*; Warren, *The World the Shawnees Made*; and Lakomäki, *Gathering Together*. The in-depth delineation and analyses of Shawnee politics by both of these historians is far too detailed for inclusion in an essay of this length, but readers interested in pursuing this subject are encouraged to read these excellent histories of the Shawnee people.

2

From Ohio to Oklahoma and Beyond

The Long Removal of the Lewistown Shawnees

SAMI LAKOMÄKI

In mid-July 1831 the people of Lewistown, the multinational and multilingual community of some three hundred Shawnees and Senecas on the headwaters of the Great Miami River in northern Ohio, gathered to attend a council with a delegation sent by the U.S. government. Many of the locals must have come to the meeting deeply concerned. For years federal officials had been pressing them and their Shawnee, Seneca, Wyandotte, and Ottawa neighbors to sell the small reservations the Indians still owned in the region amid a growing American population. So far the Lewistown chiefs and elders had refused all such offers, but they worried that eventually the Americans would run out of patience and simply force them to sell. Their worst fears were soon confirmed. As the negotiations got under way, the federal representatives bluntly announced that the United States intended to buy the Lewistown reservation and relocate the people west of the Mississippi River.

The American plans for the Lewistown people formed a small part in a much larger federal project known as Indian removal. Briefly, the aim of the removal policy was to transplant all Native peoples from the organized U.S. states and territories in the eastern part of the continent to "Indian country" west of the Mississippi River. This was a massive program of forced relocation. During the 1830s and 1840s the federal government pushed approximately 80,000 Indians from their homes in the eastern United States to new reservations in what are now Oklahoma, Kansas, and Nebraska. In theory, removal was voluntary; in practice, the government was prepared to use arms to force the Indians to the West. For the Indian nations, the consequences of the removal program were horrendous. Thousands of Native Americans perished on the exhausting journeys, typically badly planned and inadequately funded by U.S. officials, while millions of acres of Indian land were incorporated into the United States to benefit the federal and state governments as well as American farmers and businessmen. Indeed, "removal" is a euphemism for the immense physical pain, emotional suffering, violence, and territorial theft these events entailed. Today, any similar state-organized displacement of national or cultural minorities would unquestionably be termed ethnic cleansing—a crime that, according to one recent historian, should "haunt America."[1]

An ethnic cleansing had not always been on the U.S. government's agenda. In the 1790s some federal authorities hoped that teaching Christianity and other Euroamerican cultural practices to the Indians would gradually assimilate them into the Republic. However, even during the heyday of this so-called civilization program, many U.S. officials asserted that those Natives who were unwilling or unable to adopt American culture would have to move west to make room for white settlers. Such arguments grew louder after the War of 1812. As the population of the United States grew rapidly, increasing numbers of citizens coveted Indian homelands across the East. Many Americans now began to question the feasibility of the civilization program. Some suggested that the Trans-Mississippi West would offer a safer setting for the Natives to learn the "civilized" lifestyle than the East, where they were allegedly "depraved" by "the wasting influence" of alcohol and other vices taught by the Americans. Others insisted that the Indians were an inferior race, incapable of ever attaining the cultural level of the whites; therefore, they had to be segregated beyond the Mississippi. In the 1820s the advocates of states' rights joined their voices in the proremoval chorus. For them, Indian nations living on their own lands, within state boundaries but outside of state jurisdiction, defied the states' constitutional rights to sovereignty. Motivated by such complex agendas, American officials began pressuring and persuading the eastern Indian nations to move beyond the Mississippi in the late 1810s. Their efforts received a major boost in 1828, when the strongly proremoval Andrew Jackson was elected president. Less than two years later, in May 1830, Congress passed the Indian Removal Act, which made the relocation of the eastern Native nations a priority of the federal government and provided funding for it.[2]

Today the Indian removal is often remembered as a tragic but relatively simple story in which the Indian nations were forced off their lands in the East, travelled harrowing "trails of tears" over the Mississippi, and settled on new tribal reservations in the West, where they gradually recovered from the horrors of displacement. The reality, however, was far messier. For one thing, many Indian nations were divided over removal: some communities and families migrated to the West decades before the Indian Removal Act to escape the pressures of colonialism, while their tribespeople remained on their old homelands until they were forced at gunpoint to leave. Second, arrival to the West did not put an end to Native mobility and coerced migrations. Indians often found harsh conditions on their new trans-Mississippi reservations, and many decided to seek better futures on the lands of their relatives, neighbors, and allies. This promoted continuous movement of individuals, families, and larger bands among the various reservations stretching from modern Nebraska to Oklahoma. Indeed, instead of being a single one-time event, removal was a long process of displaced peoples adjusting to the loss of homelands, learning to make a living in unfamiliar environments, fighting impoverishment, and moving in search of better opportunities. It is important to recognize that Native peoples were not simply hapless victims in these complex processes. No one can deny the trauma they endured. But through it all, they found ways to defend their rights, make their own decisions, and shape their futures. The history of the Indian removal is therefore not only about loss and suffering but also about survival, creative adaptation, and resilience.

The removal of the Lewistown Shawnees and Senecas was long and complex. It began well before that day in mid-July 1831 when the federal negotiators announced to the townspeople that they would have to migrate west of the Mississippi. Likewise, it lasted long after Lewistown's people had traveled from Ohio to a new reservation in what is now Oklahoma. The Lewistown Shawnees and Senecas first encountered the specter of removal during the War of 1812, when U.S. officials threatened to drive all Ohio Indians beyond the Mississippi if any Natives joined the British in the conflict. After the war, pressure for removal became more insistent as politicians such as Michigan's territorial governor Lewis Cass insisted that the security and economic progress of the Great Lakes region depended on pushing the Indians away. In both 1817 and 1818 the federal government proposed that the Lewistown people and their Shawnee, Seneca, Wyandotte, Lenape, and Ottawa neighbors sell their lands in Ohio to the United States and move west. Despite the Indians' firm refusal, Governor Cass renewed the offer in 1825, claiming that the Shawnees and Senecas would soon be completely "hemmed in by white people" and that eventually they would "be compelled to remove." Once more, Skilloway (Robin), Methomea (Civil John), and other Lewistown headmen refused to give up their homes. "We all feel anxious to remain" in Ohio, they insisted.[3]

However, not all Lewistown Shawnees and Senecas shared this view. After the War of 1812, life in Ohio became increasingly difficult for Indians. The state's non-Indian population boomed

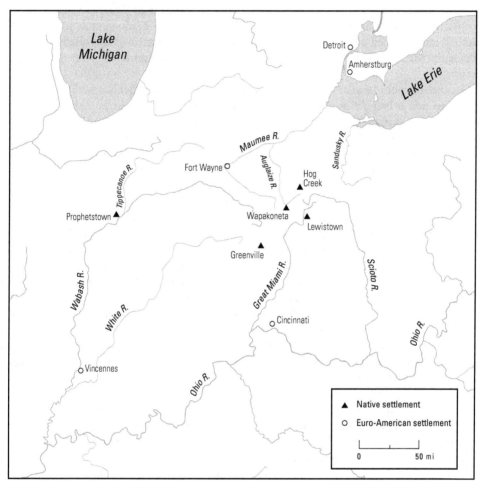

2.1. Lewistown and other Ohio Shawnee communities, c. 1800–1832. Map by Erin Greb.

from 230,000 in 1810 to 940,000 in 1830.[4] Even though the Lewistown people and the neighboring Shawnees, Senecas, Ottawas, and Wyandottes managed to secure small reservations for their communities in tense negotiations with the federal government in 1817 and 1818, many Indians felt that these asylums did not afford enough game and farmland for their people. Others complained about the alcohol trade, which brought liquor to the Native communities and caused violence, poverty, and other social problems. Worst of all, the Indians' American neighbors were a constant threat. White settlers regularly trespassed on the reservations, stole horses, robbed hunting camps, killed cattle and hogs, and most seriously, sometimes assaulted the Natives. During the winter of 1825–26, for example, four Shawnees were murdered in the space of a few months.[5]

Frustrated, some Lewistown people turned their eyes toward the Trans-Mississippi West, hoping to find a better future there, far from the pressures of American colonialism. Most famously, Quatawapea (Captain Lewis) explored southwestern Missouri and northern Arkansas in 1823, and about thirty of his followers settled in the area among other Shawnee, Cherokee, Lenape, and Kickapoo refugees from the East. Encouraged by U.S. officials who were eager to push the Indians west, Quatawapea led another group from Lewistown across the Mississippi two years later, though this time most of the migrants apparently settled on a new reservation that the federal government had just established for the Shawnees in what is now eastern Kansas. In 1826 more Lewistown Shawnees and Senecas migrated there with more than two hundred Shawnees from the neighboring community of Wapakoneta. By 1830 at least sixty, and probably many more, migrants from Lewistown lived west of the Mississippi, most of them on the Kansas reservation. In contrast, 332 Shawnees and Senecas remained in Lewistown.[6]

The future looked increasingly dark for the Lewistown people still in the East. During the 1820s Indian removal gained more and more support among the American citizens of Ohio. State officials, including Governor Ethan Allen Brown, forcefully advocated for the removal of the local Natives, arguing that the economic development of Ohio was hindered by the Indians who owned some of the best lands in the state. Other Ohio citizens portrayed the Natives as "morally depraved" drunkards and thieves, whose mere presence formed a constant nuisance, even a danger, to the growing white population. By the late 1820s some Ohio Indians, including the Senecas and Lenapes living on the Sandusky River, had determined to leave their homes and move west to escape the constant American encroachments and maltreatment. Federal, state, and territorial officials in the Great Lakes region added pressure on them and their neighbors. In 1830 Michigan's governor Cass, the longtime champion of Indian removal, sent a detailed plan to Washington, outlining how the Ohio Indians could be relocated west of the Mississippi quickly and cheaply. Impressed by his arguments, federal officials lost little time in putting his plans into effect.[7]

The Americans' first target was the Seneca community on the Sandusky River in northern Ohio. In negotiations with the federal government in February 1831, the Sandusky Senecas agreed to relocate to a new reservation in what is now northeastern Oklahoma. News of the treaty must have worried the people of Lewistown. They had long had a close relationship with the Sandusky Senecas, as intermarriage, ties of kinship, and political cooperation had weaved the two communities together. The removal of the Sandusky Senecas threatened these intimate bonds. Moreover, the people of Lewistown feared that the Americans would soon demand their relocation, too. Indeed, Lewistown and the two neighboring Shawnee reservations, Wapakoneta and Hog Creek, were next on the federal government's list. In early June, Indian agent John McElvain toured the three communities to convince the locals that removal was necessary. He was followed by James Gardiner, an Ohio politician appointed by the federal government to negotiate removal treaties with the Native nations in the state. During July and August, Gardiner treated with the leaders of the Shawnee communities in a series of councils. Fiercely proremoval, he bullied the Natives relentlessly to pressure them to accept relocation. In a council in Wapakoneta, for example, Gardiner threatened the local Shawnees, claiming that if they refused to leave Ohio, they would face racial discrimination and violence, and the state would impose its jurisdiction, laws, and taxation on them, essentially turning them from a sovereign nation into second-class citizens.[8] It was a grim prospect indeed.

Such threats convinced many of the leaders of Lewistown, Wapakoneta, and Hog Creek that the Americans intended to remove them at any cost. The chiefs and elders were left with one remaining option: to strike the best possible deal for their people. Therefore on July 20 Skilloway, Methomea, Pewyache, John Jackson, and other Lewistown leaders signed a treaty in which they ceded their reservation to the United States in exchange for a new one in Indian Territory in what is now northeastern Oklahoma.[9] It must have been a hard decision for the chiefs, who had successfully resisted removal for more than fifteen years before succumbing to American pressure.

The decision of the Lewistown Shawnees to remove to Oklahoma may seem perplexing given that there was a Shawnee reservation in Kansas, where several hundred Shawnees, including at least thirty from Lewistown, had already settled. American documents do not explain the decision unambiguously, but they offer some hints about the complex reasons behind it and demonstrate that Lewistown's people were not unanimous about the issue. Federal agents may have first suggested relocating the Lewistown Shawnees and Senecas to a separate reservation in northeastern Oklahoma. They had already decided to transplant the Sandusky Senecas there and possibly regarded removing the Lewistown Senecas to the same area as logical. On the other hand, many Lewistown people—both Senecas and Shawnees—quite likely wished to reunite with their Sandusky Seneca allies and relatives in the West. Indeed, Lewistown Senecas had already been discussing removal plans with the Sandusky chiefs in the spring, more than two months before the Lewistown treaty was signed. However, some Lewistown Shawnees were not happy with the decision to move to Oklahoma because it threatened to separate them from their tribespeople. For decades they had shared their lives with the Shawnees of Wapakoneta and Hog Creek. The leaders of the three communities had regularly met in joint councils to discuss common concerns, while the townspeople had participated in one another's rituals, married each other, and gathered together for work and fun. When the Wapakoneta and Hog Creek Shawnees signed their removal treaty in early August and agreed to relocate to the tribal reservation in Kansas, many Lewistown Shawnees grew concerned about losing their relatives, allies, and friends. Several families now decided that they too would "join [their] own Nation" in Kansas rather than migrate to Oklahoma with the Senecas.[10] The removal, then, began to tear apart the Lewistown community.

Federal officials scheduled the removal of the Lewistown Shawnees and Senecas to take place in 1832. They designed a removal route that would take the Lewistown people, along with the Wapakoneta and Hog Creek Shawnees and a small group of Ottawas, to the Mississippi River. At this juncture, the Lewistown Shawnees and Senecas would turn southwest toward Oklahoma, while their kinsmen and allies would continue west to what is now Kansas. The Indians began to get ready for the journey early, for they wanted to arrive at their new homes well before winter. By March 1832 the people of Lewistown were anxiously asking their Indian agent when the removal would begin in order to know whether they should plant their fields in Ohio or not. When Gardiner, who had been appointed to organize and lead the relocation, instructed the Shawnees to start preparing for the trip in May, many Indians decided not to waste time and resources in sowing. Unfortunately, U.S. officials were far slower in their preparations. Indeed, the planning and organization of the Ohio removal was haphazard and confused. Congress did not even allocate money for the removal until June, and almost two months later Gardiner and his assistants were still waiting to receive the funds. It took until late August for President

Jackson to allow the Indians to travel by land, like they wanted, instead of by steamboats, which the American officials had initially deemed a cheaper option. Such delays wasted away the summer. By mid-August the Indians, still waiting for the journey to begin, had depleted their food stores and were forced to live on meager government rations. Recognizing the difficulties of traveling in winter with little, if any, of their own supplies, the Lewistown people were increasingly worried.[11]

The abusive policies of the federal government also began to impoverish the Lewistown Shawnees and Senecas even before the removal started. The government had promised to reimburse the Indians for the farms they would have to leave behind in Ohio, but the compensation fell considerably short of the actual value of the Lewistown farms.[12] To make matters even worse, federal instructions decreed that the Indians could only take "necessary clothing, bedding, &c, light cooking utensils, and a few tools for agricultural and mechanic purposes" with them on the removal journey. While all Natives probably did not follow these orders to the letter, many had to sell much of their property, including such vital possessions as plows and other farming implements, furniture, and cattle and hogs. They must have wondered how they would ever be able to get new farms going in the West. Others worried if they would even reach their new reservation, for they had heard news of a deadly smallpox epidemic in the Trans-Mississippi West. Concerned, the Lewistown leaders pressed the removal agents to have their people inoculated, threatening that they would not leave their homes until this was done. During their last weeks in Ohio, the Shawnees and Senecas also performed a long and complex "round of religious ceremonies" that included leveling old graves to protect them from the intruding curiosity of American settlers.[13]

After months of preparations and delays, the removal finally got under way on September 19, disconcertingly close to autumn rains and colder weather. It was a massive operation. Some eight hundred people—258 Shawnees and Senecas from Lewistown, more than 400 Shawnees from Wapakoneta and Hog Creek, and almost 100 Ottawas—set out in several parties that together formed a long, slow column stretching over several miles on the road.[14] Federal officials had prepared strict regulations for the removal that were supposed to keep the traveling costs low, but which threatened to make the human toll of the migration intolerable. For example, officials had originally tried to persuade the Indians to give up most of their horses before the journey, worrying that buying fodder for the animals would mean a considerable expenditure to the government. Likewise, official instructions allowed the Indians merely one wagon per fifty people and decreed that only "those who [were] too young or too infirm" to walk would have the right to travel in them or on horseback. The Natives ignored such restrictions, however. Most of them rode their own horses, which they had kept despite government orders. Some had also furnished wagons of their own to travel more comfortably.[15] They knew it would be a long way to their new homes.

Once on the road, Gardiner organized the journey according to his own notions of order and economy. Instead of traveling in one group, he divided the Indians into three detachments. First came the Lewistown Shawnees and Senecas, followed by the Ottawas, while the Shawnees from Wapakoneta and Hog Creek took the rear. Gaps up to forty miles long—more than two days' travel—often separated the groups, and sometimes there were as many as eighty miles between the first and the last migrants. This made it challenging for Gardiner's assistants to purchase and distribute food for the Indians and fodder for their horses. Sometimes the meat bought from the farms the migrants passed went bad before everyone had received their share. Even then, Gardiner protested when Native men stopped to hunt in order to supplement their insufficient provisions.[16]

Gardiner and the Indians continually clashed over their divergent interests and differing cultural understandings of travel and discipline. Gardiner had envisioned the removal as an orderly

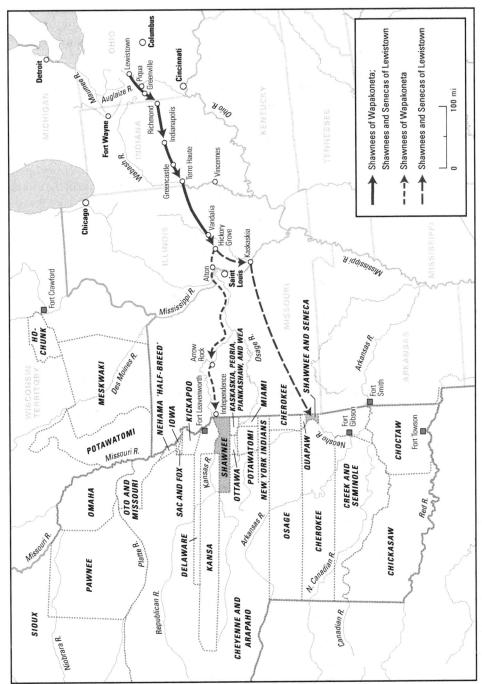

2.2. Indian Territory, c. 1840, with Shawnee routes westward in response to the Indian Removal Act of 1830. Map by Erin Greb.

march under his sole command. When the eight hundred Native men, women, and children, including newborn babies and infirm elders, did not proceed as quickly and economically as a military unit, he appeared surprised. He complained that the Indians were "obstinate and refractory" and grumbled that their leaders were unconcerned about wasting government money. The Shawnees, Senecas, and Ottawas, in turn, often found Gardiner's orders unreasonable and simply ignored them. Instead of remaining in tightly separated detachments, they constantly visited relatives and friends in the other groups for mutual help and socializing. Likewise, many Shawnees had traveled back and forth between Missouri and Ohio for decades. They knew the country better than their federal conductors and frequently left the road chosen by Gardiner to take shortcuts through the woods or to trade at the American settlements near their route. For Gardiner, all this amounted to insubordination, and he feared that the Shawnees, in particular, were plotting against him.[17] The Indians were at least equally annoyed.

Despite these collisions, over the last two weeks of September the removal party crossed western Ohio. Covering between six and nineteen miles a day, the migrants traveled from Lewistown to Piqua, and thence to Greenville, reaching Richmond, Indiana, by the end of the month. Yet traveling was not easy. The weather soon turned bad. Sometimes it rained so hard that the Indians had to stop for a whole day afterwards to dry their tents and other equipment. Fall storms often made traveling impossible. Recurrent downpours also ruined roads that, especially in Indiana, were described as "extremely bad." This slowed down the migrants and compelled them to change from light two-horse teams to four-horse ones, which were better able to pull the wagons on the muddy roads. Crossing rivers became a serious challenge, too. The Wabash River, for example, was so high that women and children could not ford it safely, but had to be taken over in boats. Far worse, sickness began to spread among the Indians. The Wapakoneta Shawnees were hit particularly badly, with several people, mostly children, dying in early October.[18]

The removal was not made any easier by the fact that the federal government had grossly underestimated its expenses. The migrants had traveled less than three weeks and had barely reached Indianapolis when Gardiner and his assistants realized that they had run out of government money. Incredibly, the removal agents borrowed cash from the Indians to keep the migration going while waiting for more funds from Washington. These problems exacerbated tensions between Gardiner and his chief financial officer to the point that the two refused to talk to one another. The conflict further complicated what was already a difficult journey. Finally, federal officials stepped in and replaced Gardiner with a new officer, Colonel John Abert.[19]

In late October, as the removal party crossed into Illinois, both the weather and the roads improved. Unfortunately, news of a cholera epidemic in Saint Louis reached the migrants, who were intending to cross the Mississippi River there. Concerned, they left the main road to avoid people escaping from the infected city and halted in central Illinois to decide how to proceed. The entire party collected at a place called Hickory Grove to rest and negotiate for three days. While there, they resolved that the Lewistown Shawnees and Senecas would now turn southwest toward Oklahoma and the others would skirt Saint Louis and continue west to Kansas.[20]

The separation of two parties must have been difficult for the Lewistown Shawnees. They now had to choose whether to follow their Seneca friends and relatives to Oklahoma or their Shawnee tribespeople to Kansas. Many ignored the dictates of the removal treaties and made their own decisions on the basis of their personal interests and networks. In the end, about forty Lewistown people joined the Wapakoneta and Hog Creek Shawnees and headed for Kansas. Many of them probably did so for family reasons. For example, Lewis and John Dougherty may have wanted to reunite with five Shawnees known as "Doughartys," who had already moved from Lewistown to the Kansas reservation in 1826. In other cases, however, families broke at Hickory Grove. Skilloway, one of Lewistown's most prominent headmen, decided to continue toward Oklahoma, while his son, Wayawpapea, or Joe White, joined the party going to Kansas.

Similarly, two men separated from the family of the Seneca leader Methomea to go to Kansas instead of Oklahoma. Although we can only guess at their motives, Methomea's wife apparently had Shawnee ancestry, making it possible that these men, too, had relatives living among the Shawnees in Kansas.[21] As these examples demonstrate, the Lewistown people had wide-ranging social networks and complex personal motives that shaped the choices they made to navigate their harrowing circumstances.

Leaving behind many relatives and friends, the main body of the Lewistown party set out from Hickory Grove toward Oklahoma on October 29. They still faced a long journey, and winter was approaching fast. The next challenge was crossing the Mississippi. In little more than a week, the Lewistown migrants arrived at Kaskaskia, where they had been instructed to take the ferry across the great river. That proved a difficult task. For a whole day the wind blew so hard over the "Father of Waters" that the local ferrymen did not dare to try a crossing. Even when the wind settled down, it took two days to ferry all of the migrants to the west side of the wide river.[22]

The journey became increasingly challenging west of the Mississippi. One federal agent described how "sickness, bad weather, high waters, [and] the poor condition of their horses" plagued the travelers. As the removal party pushed southwest across Missouri, American settlements along the way grew more and more sparse, making it difficult to buy new provisions. Once again, Shawnee and Seneca men had to hunt to procure food both for their families and for the federal agents overseeing the journey. Horses, too, had trouble finding enough to eat. Several mornings the migrants spent hours collecting horses that had strayed far from the camp in search of grass. The animals grew weaker and many died, further slowing down the travelers. The terrain presented its own obstacles: the roads grew worse again, and one day the migrants had to cross a meandering, deep river six times. After mid-November the weather turned severe, with rain and snow alternating. Some days were so stormy and cold that the Indians refused to travel at all, preferring to remain in camp, where they could at least try to stay relatively dry and warm in their tents. Given these conditions, it is surprising that the federal agents reported that only one person, a young child, died on the road.[23]

The long and grueling journey finally came to an end on December 13, when the Lewistown people reached the new reservation of their old allies, the Sandusky Senecas, immediately east of the Neosho River in what is today the northeastern corner of Oklahoma. They had traveled for almost three months and covered nearly eight hundred miles. Exhausted, the migrants stopped to rest among their Seneca friends before settling on their own reservation, located on the other side of the Neosho. Unfortunately, their trials were far from over. As the Lewistown people reconnected and swapped news with the Sandusky Senecas, they learned that the lands reserved for them were of poor quality. The Sandusky Senecas explained that the Lewistown reservation "cannot be cultivated: that there is scarcely any timber upon it, and but little good soil." All in all, they concluded, the reservation was "entirely unadapted" to the needs of the Lewistown people.[24]

Concerned, the Lewistown leaders inspected the land and confirmed the Senecas' assessment. They flatly refused to accept the reservation, arguing that it did not fulfill the promises made to them in their removal treaty. Even the federal removal agents who had conducted the Lewistown people to Oklahoma agreed and invited U.S. Indian commissioners from Fort Gibson, an American post located ninety miles from the reservation, to settle what was threatening to become a serious conflict. Arriving the day after Christmas, the commissioners assented that the Lewistown reservation "was not fit for agricultural purposes" and called the Indians to a council to discuss the situation. The Lewistown and Sandusky leaders decided to meet the Americans as a united front to give more force to their grievances. They had some success. In the negotiations, the U.S. commissioners granted a new reservation to the Lewistown people, this time located on the east side of the Neosho, immediately north of the Sandusky Seneca reservation. They also agreed to pay $400 to the Lewistown migrants and $600 to the Sandusky people to compensate for the money, horses, and other property the Indians had lost during their long, hard journeys to Oklahoma. Finally, the vocal complaints of the Shawnees and Senecas led to the dismissal of the local Indian agent, who was deemed to have "a total disregard for the welfare of the Indians."[25] The cooperation of the Lewistown and Sandusky leaders had scored important victories for their people.

Yet other problems remained. The Lewistown people settled on their new reservation during the winter, and in the spring they began preparing fields for planting. However, a lack of farming implements impeded their work. In the 1831 removal treaty, the federal government had promised to provide the Shawnees and Senecas with new plows and other farming utensils to replace those that the Indians had had to sell before their removal. Yet when planting time arrived in the spring of 1833, no tools had materialized. Without plows and gear for horse teams, the Shawnees and Senecas were able to open and sow only small fields. Many of these were destroyed in June, when the Neosho River flooded after heavy rains. As the Indians' food stores ran low, American officials provided little help. In the removal treaty, the federal government had agreed to supply the Lewistown people with provisions for one year after their arrival to their new reservation. However, the private contractor hired to do the job was either remarkably dishonest or astonishingly inept. For the first six months he used an undersized measure for issuing corn to the Shawnees and Senecas, delivering five hundred bushels fewer than had been agreed on. Moreover, his shipments seemed to always arrive late. By late May 1833 the scarcity of food had left the Lewistown people "in a truly destitute situation."[26]

Faced with systematic neglect and abuse, Shawnee and Seneca leaders repeatedly demanded that the federal government fulfill its treaty obligations more punctually. Throughout the summer they insisted on getting a new Indian agent who would "befriend them" and "see that their treaty-stipulations are carried into effect." In August the chiefs asked federal authorities to finally deliver the promised plows and other farming implements well before the next planting season. During the ensuing winter American officials distributed some tools to the Shawnees and Senecas, but only half of the promised number. By March 1834 the Indians were again "in a starving condition." The chiefs Skilloway, Methomea, Pewyache, John Jackson, and Totella twice made the ninety-mile trek to Fort Gibson to ask for extra money from the U.S. Indian commissioners. They explained that they needed cash for food "or they must starve."[27]

Clearly, the first years that the Lewistown Shawnees and Senecas lived on their new reservation were extremely hard. In Ohio many of them had owned prosperous farms; in Oklahoma they had to start from scratch with minimal resources while struggling with hunger and poverty. Their impoverishment was largely produced by federal disregard of treaty obligations. In addition to the tardy delivery of the farming equipment, it took U.S. officials years to build a sawmill, a gristmill, and a smith's shop at the reservation—all crucial infrastructure for starting and operating farms—in accordance with the Lewistown removal treaty and subsequent agreements. Federal agents were also late in paying annuities to the Indians, and at least once they accidentally sent half of the Lewistown annuity—$500—to the Shawnee reservation in Kansas. Although one of the stated goals of the federal removal policy was to relocate Indians to a safe distance from unscrupulous frontier whites, the new Shawnee and Seneca reservation bordered the state of Missouri, whose population was growing fast. Many of the Americans settling near the reservation were far from ideal neighbors. Some sold alcohol to the Indians despite tribal and federal prohibitions. Others stole horses from the Shawnees and Senecas, seriously disrupting the Indians' farmwork, hunting, and everyday lives. Even with the help of the federal Indian agents, Senecas and Shawnees found it next to impossible to get any compensation for such thefts. Frustrated, their headmen complained that they were constantly "harassed and ill treated by their white neighbors" and demanded better protection from federal officials.[28]

Yet, in the vortex of removal, land loss, and violence, the Lewistown reservation looked like a safe haven to some Indians. In the 1780s and 1790s hundreds of Shawnees had fled from U.S.

expansion in the Ohio Valley to what is now eastern Missouri. In the 1820s they had again been driven from their homes by American settlers, and many of them had scattered along the White River in southwestern Missouri and northern Arkansas. When the Lewistown Shawnees and Senecas arrived on the nearby Neosho River in December 1832, the refugees from Missouri began reestablishing old social and political ties with them. Impoverished and without allies, the Missouri Shawnees needed help and support from their eastern tribespeople. By 1835 more than three hundred refugees had gathered next to the Lewistown reservation. The cooperation between the Lewistown and Missouri Shawnees suggests that old bonds of kinship and alliance continued to connect the two groups despite decades of separation. Unfortunately, the federal government remained blind to such Native ties. American officials griped that the Missouri Shawnees had no right to government assistance at the reservation of the Lewistown people. They likewise refused to grant any land to the refugees and instead pushed them to move to the Shawnee reservation in Kansas. Under constant pressure, most of the Missouri Shawnees reluctantly left during the late 1830s. Some migrated to Kansas, others fled American interference, moving to Texas and elsewhere.[29]

The Lewistown Shawnees, too, were invited to move to the Kansas reservation, but not by the federal government. In 1834 Kansas Shawnee leaders summoned their Lewistown relatives to come and join them.[30] The invitation formed a part of an ambitious plan of the Kansas Shawnees to gather the entire Shawnee nation together after more than a century of dispersal and migration. Although American records are silent about Lewistown Shawnees moving north, there are hints in the documents suggesting that some migration may have taken place. The split at Hickory Grove had not destroyed the intimate bonds of kinship, friendship, and alliance that connected the various Shawnee groups, and some Lewistown individuals and families seem to have traveled from Oklahoma to Kansas after 1832 to escape the hardships in the South and to reunite with, or simply visit, relatives and tribespeople. In 1838, for example, some Lewistown Shawnees who had settled on the Kansas reservation six years earlier demanded that U.S. officials pay a part of the Lewistown annuity there, claiming that most of the Lewistown Shawnees now lived in Kansas rather than in Oklahoma.[31] This was an exaggeration, however. Federal annuities were a crucial resource to the removed and impoverished Indian communities trying to start a new life in the West, and struggles over their control were common among the various Shawnee bands. But even if the Lewistown Shawnees in Kansas overstated their number—and understated that of the Lewistown Shawnees remaining in Oklahoma—their demand suggests that some Lewistown people had indeed left Oklahoma and joined their tribespeople in Kansas after the removal.

Life on the Oklahoma reservation improved gradually in the 1840s. Little by little, the local Shawnees and Senecas, now often known as the "Mixed Band" or the "Senecas Shawnees," became more familiar with their new land and learned to use it more efficiently. In 1845 the local Indian agent opined that they were "the best farmers of any of the tribes" in the region. By then the Shawnees and Senecas had 1,200 acres under cultivation, producing corn, wheat, oats, potatoes, beans, and cabbage. They had also acquired respectable stocks of cattle and hogs. Most supplemented their farming and husbandry with hunting. Many old cultural practices and beliefs continued to shape daily life in Oklahoma. In 1846 the U.S. Indian agent reported that all Shawnees and Senecas "adhere[d] to their national or ancient religion" and that there were no missionaries, Christian churches, or schools on the reservation. Contrary to the claims of the Lewistown Shawnees living in Kansas, the Shawnee and Seneca population had remained stable. According to federal officials, 241 Shawnees and Senecas lived on the reservation in 1845. This was actually slightly *more* than the number of Lewistown people who had originally settled there at the conclusion of their long removal journey thirteen years earlier.[32]

The Lewistown Shawnees and Senecas enjoyed political stability as well. Prominent preremoval chiefs and their descendants continued to lead the community through the 1830s and

1840s. These leaders included men like Skilloway and Methomea, whose careers extended back to at least the 1810s. Quatawapea's relatives, especially his nephew Pewyache and a more "distant relation" called John Jackson, also played important roles on the reservation. The leaders of the Mixed Band worked hard to protect and promote the interests of their people, negotiating with American agents about day-to-day reservation business, protesting against mistreatment and treaty violations, and fighting for the federal funding they were owed. In 1845 John Jackson and Methomea, together with a Sandusky Seneca chief, even visited Washington, D.C., to meet with U.S. authorities.[33]

Life in Oklahoma was far from easy. The climate was erratic; droughts in one year could be followed by floods during the next one. In the summer of 1844, for instance, severe rains destroyed the Shawnee and Seneca crops, forcing people to buy provisions on credit well into the next year. In addition, the federal government remained incapable of promptly fulfilling its treaty obligations and developing the reservation's infrastructure. As late as 1844 the Shawnees and Senecas were still waiting for the gristmill and sawmill promised years earlier. There were also disturbing rumors that a part of the reservation actually fell within the borders of Missouri and might be claimed by that state.[34]

Not surprisingly, some Shawnees apparently continued to move north to the tribal reservation in Kansas in search of a better future and the aid of their kinspeople. In 1850 the leaders of the Kansas Shawnees again demanded that the Lewistown annuity be delivered to the Kansas reservation, claiming that the majority of the Lewistown Shawnees had settled there. Once again, however, their figures were exaggerated to impress federal officials. In fact, while some Shawnees almost certainly had migrated from Oklahoma to Kansas, this was not one-way traffic. For example, between 1845 and 1846 the Shawnee and Seneca population on the Oklahoma reservation jumped from 241 to 282, suggesting that people were moving in as well as out.[35]

Most likely, many Shawnees trying to cope with the economic, social, and political challenges created by the removal moved back and forth between the Oklahoma and Kansas reservations and may also have lived temporarily on the reservations of other nations as well as on non-reservation lands. Such mobility was facilitated by the extensive webs of kinship, alliance, and friendship borne out of decades, even centuries, of cooperation, diplomacy, and intermarriage that had weaved lasting bonds between the Lewistown people and other Native communities across eastern and central North America. Through the hard years of removal, the Lewistown Shawnees remained connected to the Shawnees in Kansas as well as to other old allies, including the Sandusky Senecas, Cherokees, Creeks, Quapaws, and Absentee Shawnees. Even as the Lewistown people gradually transformed the Oklahoma reservation from a strange place to a home, they maintained their networks and were ready to utilize their wide social ties to survive the harsh realities of the Trans-Mississippi West.[36]

The removal of the Lewistown Shawnees was not a single traumatic trail of tears from Ohio to Oklahoma, but rather a long cycle of migrations, political struggles, impoverishment, and reinvention. From the 1820s to the 1850s and beyond, mobility and land loss became ubiquitous and recurrent experiences. Some families and individuals escaped the pressures of American colonialism to the Trans-Mississippi West early, others were later forced there by the federal removal program, and still later economic hardships pushed many from their new reservation in Oklahoma to look for brighter futures among relatives and friends across Indian Territory. Through these difficult decades the Lewistown community was in constant flux: some people left, some returned, and newcomers joined in. Yet a strong sense of community remained, as kinship, rituals, and traditional leadership bound people together. As late as 1850 the Kansas Shawnees identified the Lewistown Shawnees in Oklahoma as the relatives of Quatawapea, the headman who had first explored the area almost thirty years before.[37] In a world unsettled by U.S. expansion, forced dislocation, and impoverishment, enduring webs of kinship and emerging ties to the new western homeland anchored the Lewistown Shawnees' lives and provided paths to the future.

NOTES

1. Gary Clayton Anderson, *Ethnic Cleansing and the Indian: The Crime That Should Haunt America* (Norman: University of Oklahoma Press, 2014), 7, 170–71; Theda Perdue and Mike Green, *The Cherokee Nation and the Trail of Tears* (New York: Penguin, 2007), 42.

2. Anderson, *Ethnic Cleaning and the Indian*, 128–72; John P. Bowes, *Exiles and Pioneers: Eastern Indians in the Trans-Mississippi West* (New York: Cambridge University Press, 2007), 38; John P. Bowes, *Land Too Good for Indians: Northern Indian Removal* (Norman: University of Oklahoma Press, 2016), 37–38, 52–58; Theda Perdue, *Cherokee Women* (Lincoln: University of Nebraska Press, 1998), 109–13; Perdue and Green, *Cherokee Nation*; Francis Paul Prucha, *The Great Father: The United States Government and the American Indians* (Lincoln: University of Nebraska Press, 1984), 1:179–213; Anthony F. C. Wallace, *Jefferson and the Indians: The Tragic Fate of the First Americans* (Cambridge, Mass.: Belknap Press of Harvard University Press, 1999), 17–20; "depraved" from Exchange of Public Lands with the Indians, January 9, 1817, *American State Papers: Documents, Legislative and Executive, of the Congress of the United States*, Class II, *Indian Affairs*, ed. Walter Lowrie, Matthew St. Clair Clarke, and Walter S. Franklin (Washington, D.C.: Gales and Seaton, 1832–34), 2:124 (hereafter cited as *American State Papers*); "deprived" and "wasting influence" from Isaac McCoy, *History of Baptist Indian Missions* (Washington, D.C.: William M. Morrison, 1840), 124.

3. Leonard U. Hill, *John Johnston and the Indians in the Land of the Three Miamis* (Columbus: Stoneman, 1957), 66; Graham to Cass, March 23, 1817, *American State Papers*, 2:136; Cass and McArthur to Calhoun, September 18, 1818, *American State Papers*, 2:177; quote from Minutes of a Council Held at Wapaghkonnatta, May 1825, Record Group 75, Records of the Bureau of Indian Affairs, M234, Roll 28, 363, 371–72, National Archives and Records Administration, Washington, D.C. (hereafter any document cited from the National Archives, after the document's full title, will be cited by its microfilm number).

4. Bowes, *Exiles and Pioneers*, 39.

5. Sami Lakomäki, "'Our Line': The Shawnees, the United States, and Competing Borders on the Great Lakes 'Borderlands,' 1795–1832," *Journal of the Early Republic* 34 (2014): 597–624; Clark to Calhoun, September 5, 1823, Shawnee File, Great Lakes and Ohio Valley Ethnohistory Collection, Glenn A. Black Laboratory of Archaeology, Indiana University, Bloomington (hereafter cited as GLOVEC); Minutes of a Council held at Wapaghkonnetta, May 1825, Record Group 75, M234, Roll 28, 366–67; Proceedings in Council with Genl. Clark, November 10, 1825, Record Group 75, M234, Roll 747; Johnston to Cass, January 25, 1826, Record Group 75, M1, Roll 18; Stephen Warren, *The Shawnees and Their Neighbors, 1795–1870* (Urbana: University of Illinois Press, 2005), 60.

6. Speech of Col. Lewis, January 7, 1825, Record Group 75, M234, Roll 747; Proceedings in Council with Genl. Clark, November 10, 1825, ibid.; Menard to Clark, September 30, 1825, ibid.; An Enumeration of the Shawnees and Senecas of Lewistown Who Have Emigrated to the West of the Mississippi, April 15, 1830, Record Group 75, M234, Roll 300, frame 0142; Graham to Clark, April 4, 1827, Record Group 75, M234, Roll 300, frames 0070, 0072; Copy of a Speech from Emigrating Shawnees from Wapaghconnetta & Lewis Town, April 3, 1827, Record Group 75, M234, Roll 300, frames 0082–83; No Title, Record Group 75, M234, Roll 300, frame 0149; Thomas L. McKenney and James Hall, *The Indian Tribes of North America with Biographical Sketches and Anecdotes of the Principal Chiefs*, ed. Frederick Webb Hodge (Edinburgh: John Grant, 1933), 1:170; R. David Edmunds, *The Shawnee Prophet* (Lincoln: University of Nebraska Press, 1983), 173–83.

7. Stephen Warren, "The Ohio Shawnees' Struggle against Removal, 1814–30," in *Enduring Nations: Native Americans in the Midwest*, ed. R. David Edmunds (Urbana: University of Illinois Press, 2008), 84–87, "morally depraved" from 85; Bowes, *Land Too Good for Indians*, 123–27; Mary Stockwell, *The Other Trail of Tears: The Removal of the Ohio Indians* (Yardley, Penn.: Westholme, 2014), 192–93.

8. Bowes, *Land Too Good for Indians*, 127; Convention with the Senecas, February 28, 1831, *Public Statutes at Large of the United States*, ed. Richard Peters (Boston: Charles C. Little and James Brown, 1846), 7:348–50; Disbursements by John M'Elvain, *Document 512: Correspondence on the Subject of the Emigration of Indians, between the 30th November, 1831, and the 27th December, 1833* (Washington, D.C.: Duff Green, 1834–35), 5:85 (hereafter cited as *Document 512*); Henry Harvey, *History of the Shawnee Indians, from the Year 1681 to 1854, Inclusive* (reprint; Millwood, N.Y.: Kraus, 1977), 190–96.

9. Convention with the Senecas and Shawnees, July 20, 1831, *Public Statutes*, 7:351–54.

10. An Enumeration of the Shawnees and Senecas of Lewistown Who Have Emigrated to the West of the Mississippi, April 15, 1830, Record Group 75, M234, Roll 300, frame 0142; Brish to Eaton, May 4, 1831, *Document 512*, 2:443; McLean et al. to Clark, January 16, 1838, Record Group 75, M234, Roll 301, frame 0155.

11. McElvain to Cass, March 15, 1832, *Document 512*, 3:260–61; Gardiner to Cass, June 2, 1832, ibid., 1:686; Gardiner to Gibson, June 20, 1832, ibid., 1:689; Lane to Gibson, July 20, 1832, ibid., 1:724; Lane to Gibson, July 25, 1832, ibid., 1:725; Hook to Gardiner, September 1, 1832, ibid., 1:153; Journal of Occurrences kept by the conductors of the "Lewistown detachment," ibid. 4:78–79; Harvey, *History of the Shawnee Indians*, 216; Carl G. Klopfenstein, "Westward Ho! The Removal of the Ohio Shawnees, 1832–1833," *Bulletin of the Historical and Philosophical Society of Ohio* 15 (1957): 3–31.

12. Journal of Occurrences, *Document 512*, 4:80. The Quaker missionary Henry Harvey took part in evaluating the Shawnee farms in Wapakoneta and delivering the government compensations to the locals. According to him, the reimbursements were, in many cases, far lower than the actual value of the farms. Though Harvey does not discuss Lewistown, the situation was likely similar there. Harvey, *History of the Shawnee Indians*, 224–27.

13. "Necessary" from Regulations Concerning the Removal of the Indians, May 15, 1832, *Document 512*, 1:345; Gardiner to Gibson, June 3, 1832, ibid., 1:692; Journal of Occurrences, ibid., 4:79–80; "round" from Henry Howe, *Historical Collections of Ohio* (Cincinnati: C. J. Krehbiel, 1904), 1:299.

14. Muster Roll of a Company of Senecas and Shawnee Indians, September 1832, Record Group 75, M234, Roll 603, frame 267; Stockwell, *Other Trail of Tears*, 247; Lane to Commissary General, March 15, 1833, *Document 512*, 1:742.

15. Quote from Regulations Concerning the Removal of the Indians, May 15, 1832, *Document 512*, 1:344; Gardiner to Cass, June 2, 1832, ibid., 1:688; Gardiner to Cass, February 25, 1833, ibid., 4:114; Harvey, *History of the Shawnee Indians*, 221.

16. Gardiner to Gibson, October 8, 1832, *Document 512*, 1:704–705; Lane to Gibson, October 3, 1832, ibid., 1:732–33; Gardiner to Cass, February 25, 1833, ibid., 4:114.

17. "Obstinate" from Gardiner to Gibson, October 3, 1832, ibid., 1:704; Gardiner to Gibson, October 8, 1832, ibid., 1:705; Gardiner to Cass, February 25, 1832, ibid., 4:114; Journal of Occurrences, ibid., 4:80.

18. Journal of Occurrences, ibid., 4:80–81; "extremely bad" from Gardiner to Gibson, October 8, 1832, ibid., 1:705; Stockwell, *Other Trail of Tears*, 239.

19. Gardiner to Gibson, October 8, 1832, *Document 512*, 1:706; D. Dunihue to A. Dunihue, October 23, 1832, in "Dunihue Correspondence of 1832," *Indiana Magazine of History* 35 (1939): 423; Klopfenstein, "Westward Ho," 23–24.

20. Journal of Occurrences, *Document 512*, 4:81–82; Abert to Cass, January 5, 1833, ibid., 4:4–5.

21. Van Horne to Gibson, December 7, 1833, ibid., 1:929; Copy of the Remarks to the Muster Roll of the Senecas and Shawnees, December 18, 1832, ibid., 4:77; "Doughartys" from An Enumeration of the Shawnees & Senecas of Lewistown Who Have Emigrated to the West of the Mississippi, April 15, 1830, Record Group 75, M234, Roll 300, frame 0142; Methomea's wife from An Enumeration of all the Mixed Blood Shawnees and Senecas of Lewistown, April 15, 1830, Record Group 75, M234, Roll 300, frame 0141; Wayawpapea/Joe White from Parks et al. to Brown, January 8, 1850, Record Group 75, M234, Roll 303, frame 0873. Note that Wayawpapea/Joe White was sometimes also known as Red Skillaway, making it easy to confuse him with his father in the documents (*Document 512*, 4:92).

22. Journal of Occurrences, *Document 512*, 4:82.

23. Quote from Lane to Gibson, December 2, 1832, ibid., 1:738; Journal of Occurrences, ibid., 4:82–83; Stambaugh to Secretary of War, January 6, 1833, ibid., 4:11.

24. Journal of Occurrences, ibid., 4:84.

25. Lane to Gibson, December 31, 1832, ibid., 4:739; "was not" from Stambaugh to Secretary of War, January 6, 1833, ibid., 4:10; Articles of Agreement with the Senecas and Shawnees, December 29, 1832, Peters, *Public Statutes*, 7:411–13; "total disregard" Letter from Ellsworth at al., January 10, 1833, Record Group 75, M234, Roll 921, frames 0055–56; Stambaugh to Arbuckle, January 2, 1833, Record Group 75, M234, Roll 78, frame 0262; Ross to Herring, December 11, 1833, Record Group 75, M234, Roll 78, frame 0366.

26. Stokes to Cass, November 20, 1834, Record Group 75, M234, Roll 79, frames 0181–82; Convention with the Senecas and Shawnees, July 20, 1831, *Public Statutes*, 7:352; Van Horne to Gibson, June 10, 1833, *Document 512*, 1:923–25; quote from Ross to Cass, May 28, 1833, Record Group 75, M234, Roll 78, frame 0359.

27. Van Horne to Cass, June 27, 1833, Record Group 75, M234, Roll 78, frame 0455; "befriend" and "see" from Van Horne to Cass, August 1, 1833, ibid., frame 0462; Stokes to Cass, November 20, 1834, Record Group 75, M234, Roll 79, frame 0182; "in a" and "or they" from At a Meeting of the Board, March 4, 1834, Record Group 75, M234, Roll 79, frames 182–83; Commissioners' Report, June 7, 1834, Record Group 75, M234, Roll 79, frame 0185.

28. Luce to Armstrong, January 18, 1842, Record Group 75, M234, Roll 530, frame 0369; Barker to Crawford, February 20, 1844, ibid., frames 0536–37; Proceedings of a Council, January 19, 1835, ibid., frames 0155, 0162; Harris to Butler, January 18, 1837, ibid., frames 0158–59; Van Horne to Crawford, December 1, 1838, Record Group 75, M234, Roll 922, frames 0185–86; "harassed" from Van Horne to Harris, March 23, 1837, Record Group 75, Roll 922, frame 204; Van Horne to Cass, August 1, 1833, Record Group 75, M234, Roll 78, frames 0461–62.

29. Warren, *Shawnees and Their Neighbors*, 81–91; Sami Lakomäki, *Gathering Together: The Shawnee People through Diaspora and Nationhood, 1600–1870* (New Haven, Conn.: Yale University Press, 2014), 183–84; Van Horne to Gibson, December 7, 1833, *Document 512*, 1:930.

30. Perry et al. to Cass, February 7, 1835, Record Group 75, M234, Roll 300, frame 0666.

31. McLean et al. to Clark, January 8, 1838, Record Group 75, M234, Roll 301, frame 0155.

32. "Best farmers" from Raims to Armstrong, August 30, 1845, Record Group 75, M234, Roll 530, frame 0650; "adhere" from Census and Statistics of the Mixed Band of the Senecas and Shawnee for the Year 1846, ibid., frame 0716; Van Horne to Gibson, December 7, 1833, *Document 512*, 1:929–30.

33. Skilloway and Methomea had been prominent headmen already in 1817; see Treaty with the Wyandottes, Senecas, Delawares, Shawanees, Pattawatamies, Ottawas, and Chippewas, *American State Papers*, 2:132. For Pewyache's and John Jackson's relationship to Quatawapea, see Parks et al. to Brown, January 8, 1850, Record Group 75, M234, Roll 303, frame 0872. For the trip to Washington, see [No title], February 1, 1845, Record Group 75, M234, Roll 530, frame 0670.

34. The Mixed Band of Senecas and Shawnees to Crawford, June 18, 1845, Record Group 75, M234, Roll 530, frames 0663–64; Barker to Crawford, February 20, 1844, ibid., frame 0537; Barker to Crawford, June 12, 1844, ibid., frame 0568.

35. Parks et al. to Brown, January 8, 1850, Record Group 75, M234, Roll 303, frames 0871–73; Raims to Armstrong, August 30, 1845, Record Group 75, M234, Roll 530, frame 0650; Census and Statistics of the Mixed Band of the Senecas and Shawnee for the year 1846,Record Group 75, M234, Roll 530, frame 0716.

36. For the importance of Native mobility within Native networks in the West during the removal era, see Bowes, *Exiles and Pioneers*, 18.

37. Parks et al. to Brown, January 8, 1850, Record Group 75, M234, Roll 303, frame 0872.

3

Divided Lands and Dispersed People

Allotment and the Eastern Shawnees
from the 1870s to the 1920s

JOHN P. BOWES

"I am a member of the Eastern Shawnee Tribe, and I live on the same section that I was born on in 1884," Thomas Andrew Captain Jr. stated in May 1969, "and I lived on starvation wages all my life." Sitting next to his wife, Florence, Tom reminisced about a variety of topics, including the implementation of allotment and the early years of Oklahoma statehood. He helped farm the allotment of his father, Thomas Captain Sr., and portions of his younger sister Cordelia's allotment. He married in 1907, and he and Florence "kinda existed through life together sixty-two years." At the time of the interview, Tom had been the owner and operator of a store in Miami, Oklahoma, for almost twenty years.[1] Elsie May "Sis" Captain Hoevet was one of Tom Captain Jr.'s nieces, the daughter of his younger brother William. In the spring of 1969, while her uncle discussed his long history in Oklahoma, Sis was living in Salem, Oregon, and working for the state. Born in Miami, Oklahoma, in 1919, she moved away in 1941 and did not return. She remembered her grandparents' allotment, what she called "the Home Place." From what she recalled, her aunts and uncles constantly debated whether or not to sell it. "Then as time went by," she noted, "the heirs were more scattered and that was a mess trying to locate them."[2]

Tom's and Elsie's accounts provide more than a tantalizing glimpse into a particular family history—they shine a bright light on a transformational period for the Eastern Shawnee Tribe as a community. At first glance, the Eastern Shawnee experience in the late nineteenth and early twentieth centuries fits the common understanding of how federal allotment policy altered the landscape of Indian reservations and lives. Indeed, the history of allotment most often makes people think of the Dawes Act and of the division of reserved lands that led to traumatic dispossession throughout the American West from the late 1880s to the 1920s. The Eastern Shawnees are a part of that story, but their experience does not necessarily fit the more familiar arc. It is true that the acreage held by the Eastern Shawnees at the end of the allotment era was vastly diminished compared to their holdings at the beginning. Yet a closer examination of the process that led to such land loss reveals three particular trends shaping those events. First, permissive leasing policies within the Quapaw Agency, along with Eastern Shawnee economic needs, created an environment in which allotment was not always the main story. Second, the desire to finance new homes or business ventures also played a role in the land sales that accompanied allotment, and that connection suggests that the diminishment of the Eastern Shawnee land base may not always be best described as dispossession. In the early 1910s in particular, more than just poverty, debt, or inexperience explained why many Eastern Shawnees sold the parcels assigned to them through allotment. The third point is that leasing and land sales fragmented the Eastern Shawnees' sense of themselves as a community and furthered an ever-growing Eastern Shawnee diaspora. The reserve lands set aside by treaty in 1832 had been the central focus of the Eastern Shawnee community in Indian Territory. By the 1930s, however, the Eastern Shawnee

Tribe spanned a much larger geographic space, a change that had been initiated in large part by turn-of-the-century policies and economies. Put in simpler terms, the extended period of leasing and allotment not only divided up Eastern Shawnee lands but also ended up dispersing the Eastern Shawnee people.

LEASING BEFORE ALLOTMENT

Three separate treaties provide the foundation for Eastern Shawnees' historic land base in present-day northeastern Oklahoma. The first agreement, signed in 1831, arranged for the removal of the Mixed Band of Shawnees and Senecas then living at Lewistown, Ohio. In exchange for the cession of forty-eight square miles of land (about thirty thousand acres) in Ohio, the Shawnees and Senecas would receive "a tract of land to contain sixty thousand acres, to be located under the direction of the President of the United States." A second treaty, signed in 1832, provided the boundaries of that western territory, where the Shawnees and Senecas from Lewistown joined with the Senecas removed from Sandusky, on a reserve that was bounded on the west by the Neosho River. The citizens of this new United Nation of Shawnees and Senecas resided together on this reserve until 1867, when they signed a third and final treaty with the federal government. The 1867 agreement described the provisions by which the Shawnees separated from the Senecas. They now had claim to a separate reserve of approximately 16,000 acres and officially became known as the Eastern Shawnees. The location of their lands in relation to the other Indian participants in the 1867 treaty can be seen in the map drawn for the Indian Bureau in the spring of 1871.[3]

The creation of reservations in general, and the designation of Indian Territory in particular, demonstrated the long-held public position of American officials that the best chance for the survival of tribes like the Eastern Shawnees rested in separating them from the vices of American society. Or as acting commissioner of Indian affairs Charles E. Mix wrote in his annual report for 1867, "The greatest obstacle to the consummation of ends so much desired," namely the civilization of Indians, "is to be found mainly in his almost constant contact with the vicious, unscrupulous whites."[4] Similar sentiments appeared in the 1870 annual report of Enoch Hoag, the superintendent of the central superintendency, the regional bureaucracy that presided over affairs in Indian Territory. The Eastern Shawnee reservation, located on Missouri's southwestern border, compelled Hoag to request federal protection for the Indians under his jurisdiction from white squatters. He described how "this last and only home of our red brother" had been beset by a series of "impending evils." Yet he also had a very firm idea about what kind of protection would work best. "The first step towards effectual improvement of the tribes must be based upon permanent locality," Hoag opined. "The Indian must be secure in his home, one that he can call his own. He must feel that he is 'sitting under his own vine and fig tree, with no one to make him afraid.'" For Hoag, however, it was more than just a feeling of security. Similar to those who within the next twenty years would advocate for a national allotment policy, the superintendent believed the answer rested in private property: "His cottage, however humble, must be his, in fee simple, and he must realize this ownership. Then, and then only, can he successfully commence to travel the upward road to a better and higher life, drawing around him his family, with the comfort and happiness of real ownership. This reality once fixed in the Indian mind, we may hope for his advancement in all the avenues to civilization." As more non-Indians began to descend on Indian Territory, the Indians could protect themselves best and make real progress toward civilization by finally adopting land-ownership practices that mirrored those of American society.[5]

Interestingly enough, Hoag composed his letter six months after the Eastern Shawnees had negotiated a lease agreement with Richard M. Jones and Henry H. Gregg, two non-Indians

3.1. The Quapaw reserve, 1871 (Record Group 77, Central Map File, No. I.R. 60-1, National Archives). This map displays more than just the Quapaw reserve, as it shows the Eastern Shawnee reserve created by the 1867 treaty. Courtesy of National Archives II, College Park, Maryland.

who lived across the border from the Eastern Shawnees in Seneca, Missouri. In that agreement, signed on April 7, 1870, by William Jackson as first chief and William McDaniel as second chief, the Eastern Shawnees leased out approximately two hundred acres for a period of five years, or "until the Indian title to said land shall be extinguished if such event first occurs." The terms of the lease required the two men to "fence, cultivate, and improve" forty of the two hundred acres by the end of the first year and the remaining 160 acres by the end of the second year of the lease. As payment, Jones and Gregg would hand over one-third of the "profit arising in any way from the use or occupation of said premises." The lease would be subject to the approval of the proper authorities, and the U.S. agent would "at all times have free access to the books containing the accounts between" the Eastern Shawnees and the lessees. Jones and Gregg were also required, as part of the contract, to peaceably relinquish the lands and leave them once the terms of the lease had expired. Enoch Hoag approved this agreement, with the provision that the Eastern Shawnees had the right to terminate the lease after three years if they so desired. In January 1871 Richard Jones sold his portion of the lease to Gregg, leaving the latter as the sole lessee moving forward.[6]

This lease, which began as an agreement with several individuals, created a bounded area on the reservation that became known as the Eastern Shawnee National Farm. Gregg was the first to break the land, but he was not the last to cultivate it as a tenant. In July 1881 D. D. Dyer, then the agent for the Quapaw Agency, wrote of the National Farm that "it has always been worked by town people living in Seneca and has no other improvements than a rail fence which encloses it." Those rails bounded a total of 126 acres, and the typical lease agreements provided a payment of two dollars per acre or one-third of the crop, though Dyer did not mention how those rental payments were distributed within the Eastern Shawnee community.[7] Yet while the farm remained under cultivation by non-Indian tenants into the 1880s, it was not the only piece of property used in such a manner. It did not take long for the practice of leasing land to white men to extend well beyond the boundaries of the National Farm. By the end of 1879, Agent J. M. Haworth of the Quapaw Agency reported that of the 794 acres cultivated on the Eastern Shawnee reserve, white renters worked 671 of them. The population numbers tell an even bigger story. Haworth reported that eighty Eastern Shawnees lived on the reserve at the end of 1879. That same year the number of white renters came to sixty-six. In fact, according to Haworth, because of the number of renters, "the country presents very much the appearance of a white man's country." The agent also acknowledged that the leasing seemed to be in direct contravention of the very idea of the Indian Territory. Had the leasing "been confined to such lands as the Indians could not farm themselves and been sanctioned by law," he asserted, "the result might have been beneficial." Haworth firmly believed that, rather than adding any value to the lives of the Eastern Shawnees, this practice "has encouraged idleness and dependence among the Indians." He had hope that the situation was about to change, however, because only four months earlier President Rutherford B. Hayes had issued a proclamation to remove from Indian Territory white men who did not have permission to be there.[8]

The proclamation issued by President Hayes underscored some critical differences between the federal government's perspective of leasing and the attitude of the Indians negotiating the rental agreements on their reserves. The proclamation referred to "certain evil disposed persons" who had "begun and set on foot preparations for an organized and forcible possession of, and settlement upon the lands of what is known as Indian Territory." Yet while it appeared that Agent Haworth was hoping to see the white renters removed from the Eastern Shawnee lands, the Eastern Shawnees did not share that sentiment. Shawnee leaders called a council for all the tribes of the Quapaw Agency in July 1879 to discuss their response to the new policy. Only the Senecas supported the proclamation, while the others wanted the agent to communicate their concerns to Washington. "The renter leases were making farms for minors and orphans who

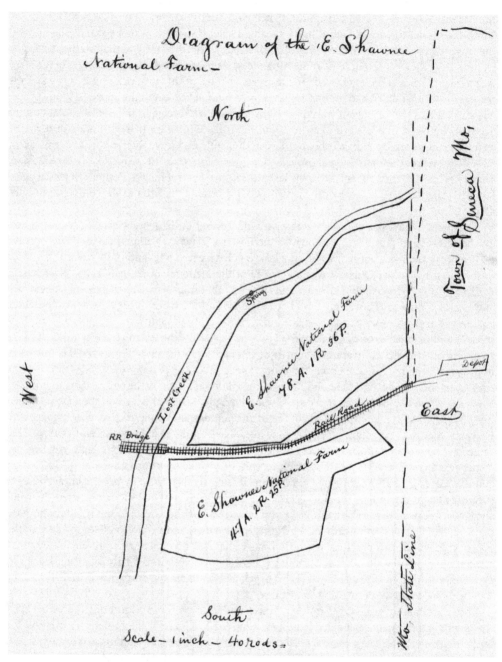

3.2. Eastern Shawnee National Farm (Record Group 75, Central Map File, No. 822, National Archives). This map shows, in part, the official recognition of the acreage designated as the Eastern Shawnee National Farm. Courtesy of National Archives II, College Park, Maryland.

without it was done for them would have nothing when they grew up," the Indian delegates noted. Other renters cultivated "the farms of widows," who, without such labor, would have no means of supporting themselves.[9] John Jackson, first chief of the Eastern Shawnees, wrote his own letter one month later, explaining his specific reasons for wanting to keep white men on the reserve. "Labor and its fruits are inseparable," he wrote, "and I cannot cultivate all my improved lands myself, and no one has as yet been able to carry on any extensive business requiring constant manual labor by Indian aid." Jackson requested that the commissioner of Indian affairs allow his white neighbor George Wallace to stay, for, "to enforce his removal would be a great hardship and manifest injustice to him, as well as a serious loss to me."[10]

Therefore, despite the proclamation issued by Hayes, the leasing of lands on the Eastern Shawnee reserve did not stop. Instead, the federal government in 1886 still permitted "widows, minor orphans, and aged or disabled Indians at this [Quapaw] agency . . . to lease their lands to reliable white renters for a period of not to exceed one year."[11] However, Eastern Shawnee leases granted by the Indian agent demonstrate that more than widows, orphans, or minors contracted leases. The agent for the Quapaw Agency kept a record of the contracts made, and in the early 1880s at least thirteen different Eastern Shawnees leased land to whites. Susan Jackson leased fifty acres to William Harper for the term of one year starting in March 1880, while Thomas Stand leased thirty acres to Samuel Neil for one year beginning in August of that same year. George Wallace, the white neighbor that John Jackson had been so concerned about, leased forty acres from John starting in March 1881 and then leased ninety acres from Anna Jackson starting in April 1882.[12]

Despite the apparent economic benefit of leasing, however, federal agents saw the need for a different approach to Indian lands in the region. Leasing may have brought money into the Eastern Shawnee reserve, but the practice did not promote civilization or the work ethic that American officials thought was lacking within the Indian population. The agents stationed at Quapaw would not or could not surrender their belief that allotment remained the best solution to many of the problems they saw in Indian Territory. At the very end of his annual report of 1878, Agent Hiram Jones advocated the enactment of allotment, a policy he believed would "promote a better and more permanent class of improvements, by giving the people a feeling of security in the ownership of their homes."[13] Year after year, the agents who succeeded Jones echoed this sentiment through familiar phrases, for instance, that allotment "would encourage and advance [the Indians] in civilization."[14] Then, in his report of 1887, following the passage of the Dawes Act, Agent J. V. Summer reported, "The Indians are gradually coming to see that it will benefit both themselves and their children."[15]

If leasing did anything, then, it would seem that it served as a bridge to understanding the benefits of private land ownership. Federal agents were pleased to know that, under the auspices of allotment, the Eastern Shawnees and their neighbors would now find the security and civilization that others deemed so necessary.

ALLOTMENT AND THE EASTERN SHAWNEES

The federal action that the agents at Quapaw called for finally arrived in 1887 in the form of the General Allotment Act. More commonly known as the Dawes Act, this is the legislation that aimed to take reservation lands held in common by Indian nations, divide them into smaller plots of 40 to 160 acres, and distribute them to individual Indians. The distribution would occur according to specific guidelines. Each head of family would receive 160 acres, the equivalent of one-quarter of a surveyed section of land. A single man or woman over the age of eighteen and any orphan under the age of eighteen received eighty acres. The smallest allotments of forty acres went to any child under the age of eighteen at the time allotment occurred on that tribe's reservation.[16] This act had numerous origins and was not passed by unanimous acclaim.

Instead, the legislation took what one scholar has termed a "crooked path" to its passage as a number of groups and individuals presented alternate ways to protect tribal lands and sovereignty.[17] Ultimately, however, the supporters of allotment won out, as did the most powerful and longstanding ideologies underlying the legislation—the desire to force Indians into becoming private landowners and the hunger of Americans to acquire more land. But perhaps the most succinct statements regarding the hopes American officials had for this legislation came out of the mouth of President Theodore Roosevelt. In his first State of the Union address in December 1901, he declared the need "to recognize the Indian as an individual and not as a member of a tribe." More to the point, he then described the Dawes Act as "a mighty pulverizing engine to break up the tribal mass."[18] For the better part of five decades the federal government used this legislation to transform the landscape of the western half of the nation.

The Dawes Act was not implemented equally throughout the United States, and no tribe had the same experience with its measures. The 1887 legislation also served as an umbrella for additional bills that targeted particular tribes and eased restrictions on land sales. Because of specific treaty provisions, for example, the Cherokees, Choctaws, Chickasaws, Seminoles, and Creeks had been exempted from allotment when it first passed through Congress. However, the 1898 Curtis Act altered that situation and brought allotment to the so-called Five Civilized Tribes despite their strong resistance to the policy.[19] Yet the Curtis Act did not establish a singular experience for any one of those five nations. Allotment among the Creeks, as was the case for any of the other four nations, intertwined with their specific history and demography. As David Chang asserts, "Land has been central to the ways people in the Creek Nation and the United States have defined their races, nations, and classes," which means that Creek allotment could not be separated from the racial issues arising from the presence of former slaves who, by treaty, had become Creek citizens after the Civil War.[20]

The Eastern Shawnee Tribe did not face the same kind of racial politics that influenced Creek allotment, but their experience is still unique and is a product of their particular history. Most notably, Eastern Shawnee allotment did not proceed according to the vision of federal agents, because leasing did not end. Between 1888 and 1902 federal commissioners implemented four different allotments of the Eastern Shawnee reserve. The first distribution made under the terms of the Dawes Act proceeded along a straightforward timeline. In early 1888 allotment agents recorded a total of 14 allotments encompassing 1,071.15 acres. The very next year commissioners allotted 5,201.72 acres to another 58 individuals. Additional allotments totaling 4,278.35 acres were confirmed in 1892. The final distribution occurred in 1902, when 33 allotments totaling 2,173.27 acres were recorded for those Eastern Shawnees who, having been born in the previous 10 years, had missed out on the previous implementations.[21] All told, the 4 different rounds of allotment encompassed 12,724.49 acres of land divided among 117 different members of the Eastern Shawnee Tribe.[22]

Those numbers provide a surface-level perspective on the status of Eastern Shawnee lands, but do not accurately capture the more complex developments shaping the lives of the newly crowned individual landholders. In February 1891, even as the distribution of allotments was at its peak among the Eastern Shawnees, the federal government passed further legislation to regulate leasing. In an amendment to the Dawes Act, Congress authorized the Department of the Interior to permit leasing of allotted lands for a period of three years for agricultural or grazing purposes, or ten years for mining.[23] It did not take long for problems to arise. In 1896 Indian agent George Doane fielded a large number of complaints about leases. The white lessees "were working under a labor contract running from three to seven to twelve years, and the Indian getting very little, if anything, for his share, possibly a dollar or two now and then." Doane took actions to combat this problem, issuing an order in December 1895 that voided all labor contracts made by non-Indians with allottees and required any individuals wishing to maintain a lease to register at his office. By early spring 1896 Doane had forcibly removed twenty-four men from the Quapaw Agency who refused to comply with his new regulation.[24]

Despite Doane's efforts, the situation did not improve, but instead became even more problematic. In 1897 Congress went to work again, this time authorizing leasing within the Quapaw Agency specifically if, "by reason of age or disability, any such allottee can not improve or manage his allotment properly and with benefit to himself." This language was not all that different from the 1891 amendment to the Dawes Act, and it specified that the secretary of the interior would make such judgments about the allottee. Agent Doane believed it compromised his efforts of the previous year and viewed the 1897 legislation as permitting leasing without any departmental oversight. "The majority of the Indians will now be at the mercy of the lessee," Doane protested to his superiors. "The white man comes into the Indian Territory, not for his health, but purely for gain, and too many of them care very little how they get it. The Indian gets but very little for his allotment land, which should bring the Indian something more than a living under the aforesaid act, and, left entirely with the lessees to say what they will give, will have a very poor show to get anywhere near the value." All indications were that the lack of strong regulation in leasing practices would not simply undermine the benefits allotment was intended to provide; it would also be dangerous because it would "be an incentive for the shrewd mixed-blood and the mercenary white man to speculate."[25]

When the new century dawned three years later, the situation had worsened, at least as far as the agents stationed at the Quapaw Agency were concerned. Alcohol sales on the Missouri border exacerbated the disorder caused by the presence of so many white men trying to get their hands on Indian lands. "Contracts are made between the Indians and their lessees without the advice of the agent," Edward Goldberg reported. "It is impossible to give figures as to the number of leases made during the year, as very few are filed for record with the clerk of the United States court in this district." This permissive leasing environment also meant that very few Indians were even working their allotments. "Unless laws can be enacted which will prevent the Indian from leasing all of his land," Goldberg noted, "the time will be very short when at least 95 per cent of the agricultural lands in this agency are controlled by white men."[26]

Goldberg wrote that report in the summer of 1900. Within two months he was dead because he mistakenly ate a poisonous toadstool he thought was a safe mushroom. He may have had poor judgment about fungi, but his statements about the control of the allotments in the Quapaw Agency seemed more like a prophecy as the environment of the territory shifted with the anticipation of upcoming statehood. In the summer of 1901 the official records reveal that the Eastern Shawnees had eighty-four total allotments covering 10,484 acres. This meant that the tribe had a surplus of 2,543 acres, indicating that not all of the land bounded by their reserve in 1887 had been allotted. The tribe's population had risen to one hundred with the birth of six children in 1900, and those six infants were not the only additions to the tribe since the last round of allotments made in 1892. In response to these developments, the federal government passed legislation in May 1902 that enabled one more distribution of the reserve land. The surplus acreage was allotted in 120-acre plots to thirty-three minors who had not been alive when the first allotments were made in the nineteenth century. This ended up being the final allotment, as the Eastern Shawnees then sold the remaining 405 acres of land from their original reserve.[27]

COMPETENCY COMMISSIONS AT THE QUAPAW AGENCY

In 1906 Congress found it necessary to once again amend the Dawes Act, this time taking action that allowed for the sale of a deceased allottee's land by his or her heirs.[28] Policies that loosened restrictions on the sale or leasing of land appeared repeatedly from that point forward. Indeed, over the next three decades allotment legislation resembled a pendulum that swung back and forth between loosening and tightening protections. In 1909 Congress passed a law that removed the restrictions on the sales of allotted lands in the Quapaw Agency. The only condition given was that at least forty acres had to be retained for the allottee as a homestead.[29] Then, in 1916, President Woodrow Wilson issued an executive order that extended the trust period for forty-four Eastern Shawnee allotments by ten years, granting a reprieve for those who had no interest in losing their trust status until 1926.[30]

In the midst of these policy swings, which first allowed for the sale of allotted lands and then extended the trust period on allotments, came another instrument that facilitated land exchange in Indian country. What became known as competency commissions were born out of the Burke Act. Passed by Congress in 1906, the Burke Act gave the secretary of the interior authority to determine the competency of individual Indians to manage their private lands. In brief, the Dawes Act stated that, once allotted, an individual Indian's land could not be sold for a period of twenty-five years. The Burke Act declared that the federal government could cut that trust period short if it determined that an Indian was competent to make decisions about his or her land independently. And when an individual was deemed competent, that individual received "a patent in fee simple, and thereafter all restrictions as to sale, incumbrance, or taxation of said land shall be removed."[31] Instead of waiting for Indians to apply for an assessment of their competency, the federal government decided to send agents to the reservations to force such an evaluation. Competent Indians were those with some knowledge of white society and the ability to survive within that context. Determining competency, not surprisingly, involved a series of standard questions provided on a government form. Questions included "Do you use intoxicating liquors?" and "Do you work?" which highlighted the effort to assess moral fiber and work ethic. Other questions posed by appointed members of the competency commission about educational backgrounds and the manner of business experience targeted the individual's ability to survive in the "real world" of twentieth-century America. The questions were both intrusive and telling, and the process had an impact. At least 200,000 acres of land throughout the western United States transferred from trust to fee simple patents in the two years these competency commissions did their work.[32]

The Quapaw Competency Commission had its genesis in the Burke Act, but its interviews also charted the impact of the 1909 legislation that had removed land sale restrictions for allottees within the Quapaw Agency. From 1910 to 1911 the members of the Quapaw Competency Commission spoke to Eastern Shawnee landholders about their circumstances and desires. In the process they assessed and passed judgment on each man or woman's capacity to act independently and responsibly in early-twentieth-century Oklahoma. Or, as the acting commissioner of Indian affairs stated in his letter to one of the commissioners, it was their responsibility to examine whether the allottee "has made advancement equal to his opportunities and has progressed in a degree that will enable him to assume all the responsibilities that come with the full control of his property."[33] Although each form also noted the interviewee's blood quantum and appearance, the commission never explicitly commented on any connection between racial appearance and potential for worldly success. The resulting records provide a wealth of insight into a number of issues, including how much land had been sold by this time, how much land was being retained, and how much land was still being leased. The same documents also indicate the manner in which the Eastern Shawnee community had become more geographically fractured.

Although the commission records cover only forty-three individuals, the information supplied in those interviews illustrates distinct trends among those with allotments. First, it is clear that many individuals took advantage of the 1906 law that allowed for the heirs of deceased allottees to sell the land before the end of the official trust period for the original allotment. Many also moved quickly to sell sections of their own allotment under the 1909 law that removed restrictions on allotted lands within the Quapaw Agency. All in all, the records indicate that

Eastern Shawnees sold at least 1,522 acres of allotted lands prior to 1910. The reasons for such actions varied, though often an individual sold enough land to obtain money that was then used to fund improvements on the remaining land. That was the case for William Hampton, who sold eighty acres of his allotment for a total of $460, which he then put to use "improving other land, paying debts, & buying stock." Both Lewis Beaver and William Prophet had more entrepreneurial visions. Beaver used the $1,600 he made by selling half of his father's allotment and all of his mother's allotment to buy "an interest in [a] grocery store at White Oak." Unfortunately the store went broke after one year, and as of December 1910 he was working as a carpenter. William Prophet had worse luck. He used the $950 he received for the forty acres of his mother's allotment and "went into the bakery business." That business did not end well when his unnamed partner "got the money & skipped."[34]

The sale of more than 1,500 acres by 1911 means that at least 12 percent of Eastern Shawnee allotted lands had already changed hands two decades into the allotment era. However, it was leasing that remained just as, if not more, significant. The records show that non-Indians rented 2,030 acres, or an additional 16 percent of the Eastern Shawnee allotted lands. Perhaps even more important than the total acreage is the fact that, of the forty-three Eastern Shawnees interviewed by the Quapaw Competency Commission, twenty-nine of them leased out part or all of their allotments. Such rentals provided supplemental income or additional produce, depending on the contract. The lease agreement William Stand had with C. C. Masterson brought the former $175 per year for the use of forty acres, and that did not count the additional seventy-five dollars per year he earned for hay gathered on another forty acres of his allotment. David Dushane Jr. rented out thirty acres to Henry Hamilton and received one-third of the grain produced in return. Ora Hampton rented out forty acres to a man named Fred Roche, who had lease agreements with at least two other Eastern Shawnees. Roche also paid in grain. Yet not all lease agreements worked in favor of the landowner. Ella Thomas rented out her allotment, but she was not aware of the exact terms of the contract or the total acres under cultivation, a situation that led the commission to assert that, she "needs some one to look after her interests all the time."[35]

However, the Quapaw Competency Commission, led by J. F. Murphy, had not traveled to northeastern Oklahoma simply to document lands already sold or ongoing lease arrangements. Instead, they wanted to know which Eastern Shawnee allottees wanted restrictions removed from their allotments so that they could sell them. According to their conversations, thirteen men and women wanted restrictions removed from a total of 927 acres. Six, or nearly half of that number, wanted to sell land so that they could fund improvements on the remainders of their allotments. Minnie Turkeyfoot House, for example, wanted restrictions removed from 120 acres so that she could build a house. Her current house was "old and nearly fallen down." Thomas Captain Sr. needed money to pay off debts at the store and the bank, while Ida Prophet hoped to make a real estate investment where she was living in Muskogee. Lillian Prophet was the only one recorded as saying that she wanted "to be on equal footing with the white man," a phrase that undoubtedly pleased Mr. Murphy and his colleagues.[36]

More Eastern Shawnees expressed their opposition to living like white men during the course of the commission's inquiries. Indeed, the notes from Mary Turkeyfoot Punch's interview indicate that, when asked why she did not want the restrictions removed from her 160-acre allotment, she stated, "Don't want to be no white—don't want to pay tax." Her distaste for taxes was shared by most of those who declined the offer to make their lands unrestricted and open to sale. Ida BlueJacket Holden did not think twice about the idea, noting that she did not want to pay taxes because "[I] have enough to pay now." Carrie BlueJacket, Ida's mother, shared that sentiment but gave another important reason why she wanted to keep the restrictions intact. "[I] want to keep it to leave to my children," she informed the commission.[37] Carrie BlueJacket's statement makes sense and is the type of response we might expect under the circumstances.

Yet, as the numbers of acres sold and leased demonstrate, it was not easy to hold on to the land and support a family.

Of course, allotted land did not automatically equate to good farmland, which meant that selling and leasing might not even prove to be much of an option when it came to developing a source of income to sustain a family. Mary Punch Tucker leased out twenty acres of her allotment for twenty-five dollars per year, another twenty acres was where she lived with her parents but was not cultivated, and she described the remaining forty acres as "rough." That same term came up with Anna Belle Deweese, who said her allotment was "too rough to sell." John Prophet declared that the forty remaining acres of his original allotment was both "not tillable" and "no good for anything." He had leased it out for seven years for mining purposes, but an extended investigation did not reveal any minerals worth digging up, and Prophet did not receive any royalties from the deal. Not even the land that the Eastern Shawnees held on to, therefore, guaranteed a sustainable future.[38]

In fact, just over twenty years into the allotment era Eastern Shawnee tribal members had already begun to disperse in search of other opportunities, not only throughout the region but also throughout the country. The very first question posed on the competency commission interview form shows that trend clearly. After filling in the name of the interviewee, his or her marital status, and the names of spouses and children, the commission asked, "Do you reside on your allotment?" Only thirteen of the forty-three Eastern Shawnees answered yes. That number is a bit shocking until a closer examination reveals that, among those Eastern Shawnees who answered no, eleven of them lived on the allotments of their Eastern Shawnee relatives. Nevertheless, that still means nineteen of the forty-three did not live within the boundaries of what had been the Eastern Shawnee reserve prior to the institution of allotment. Some did not live far, such as John Mohawk, who resided on his wife's allotment on the Quapaw reserve. Six of the interviewees made their homes on the allotments of relatives or spouses within the boundaries of the Cherokee Nation. Yet others had moved farther afield, perhaps drawn by the careers they had pursued. William Stand, who was twenty-nine years old in 1910, lived in Kansas City, Missouri, and earned more than $1,000 per year as a bookkeeper. Twenty-three-year-old Ida Prophet was earning sixty-five dollars per month as a stenographer in Muskogee, and Levi Nichols's job with a railroad company had taken him to Las Cruces, New Mexico. Levi was twenty-four years old and had a wife, four children under the age of four, a ranch in New Mexico, three city lots in Tobin, Texas, and four hundred Angora goats. In short, he was doing well. But his success occurred away from northeastern Oklahoma.[39]

Allotment had not simply led to the loss of land but to the gradual dispersal of the community. It is not necessarily surprising that William Stand, Ida Prophet, and Levi Nichols would have to leave Ottawa County to find work. It also makes sense that these three individuals were younger and perhaps more willing to move farther away from the region to make a living. Nevertheless, their migrations from what had been the Eastern Shawnee reserve also had an impact. Even from a numbers standpoint, those three individuals and their respective families comprised ten of the 127 names on the census of Eastern Shawnee tribal members for 1911. Just those three examples contain almost 8 percent of the tribal roll.[40]

THE END OF THE ALLOTMENT ERA

The trends that had defined the allotment experience for the Eastern Shawnees did not disappear even as the implementation of allotment on the national level slowed down in the early 1920s. In 1926, when federal officials revisited the forty-four Eastern Shawnee allotments that had received a trust extension by executive order ten years earlier, their reports contained familiar tales.[41] Of the forty-four allottees who received those first extensions in 1916, only twenty-four were still alive in 1926. J. L. Suffecool, the superintendent of the Quapaw Agency at the time, was required to submit information about the twenty individuals who had died and whether or not designated heirs were alive and identifiable. The first allotment reported on by Suffecool was that of Cora Hampton. Cora had retained all 160 acres of her original allotment until her death. As decided by probate in 1920, however, those 160 acres were divided up amongst ten different individuals, with the largest portions going to her twin daughters, Opal Fay Hollandsworth and Ida May Hollandsworth, who had only just come of age. They received forty acres each, and they, along with eight other siblings, received a joint patent in fee simple for the remaining eighty acres. The next allotment on Suffecool's list was that of Mary Punch. His report in this instance was much more succinct: "This entire allotment has been sold and disposed of; and the Indian title extinguished."[42]

Overall, Suffecool's reports revealed not only that land sales and leasing continued but also that the dispersal of the Eastern Shawnees had not abated. Including Mary Punch, eight of the twenty allotments of those who had died had been sold off completely. For the heirs of Jane Williams, Suffecool recommended that the trust period be extended because "the heir who holds the major share is getting old, and the rentals furnish her some means of support." In three different instances the heirs in question were non-residents. Suffecool recommended that a patent in fee simple be issued to Mamie Chisholm Starr for the 120 acres she inherited from Jennie Chisholm, for Mamie, "has never resided within this jurisdiction, but lives with her husband near Shawnee, Oklahoma." Meanwhile, the two designated heirs for Eliza Ball's intact allotment lived in Canada and Kansas City, respectively.[43]

For the allottees who were still alive, some of the trends were even more dramatic. Eleven requested to have the extensions on their lands removed so they could sell whatever acreage remained from their original allotment. Nine out of those eleven made the request because they no longer lived in the area or had not lived in the area for a significant period of time. Ida Holden informed Suffecool that "she never expected to live or make a home on her allotted lands." Rosa BlueJacket had always lived among the Cherokees and never in the jurisdiction of her allotment, and Mary Quick Gibson had not lived in northeastern Oklahoma since she was a small child. Those who sought to sell their lands did not speak for all, as the other fourteen requested to have their trust period extended. Yet the fact remained, by the late 1920s fewer and fewer Eastern Shawnees were living on smaller and smaller parcels of land in northeastern Oklahoma.[44]

The official end of allotment as a national policy did not come until 1934, with the passage of the Indian Reorganization Act. The IRA is a complex piece of legislation that shaped the lives of American Indians for decades, but for the purposes of this discussion, its most relevant element appears in the very first sentence, where it reads, "That hereafter no land of any Indian reservation, created or set apart by treaty or agreement with the Indians, Act of Congress, Executive order, purchase, or otherwise, shall be allotted in severalty to any Indian."[45] Under the auspices of the IRA, the policy of allotment officially ended, forty-seven years after its official enactment. The landscape had been transformed during that five-decade period, and any assessment of the Dawes Act's impact starts with the startling numbers relating to Indian lands. Of the approximately 138 million acres in Indian hands in 1887, only an estimated 48 million acres remained so in 1934. Allotment equaled dispossession.[46]

The history of the Eastern Shawnee tribal lands fits well within that allotment narrative when it comes to land loss, but the diminishment of the land base is only one part of the larger story. In 1930 the federal government reported that only fifty-two Eastern Shawnees still retained allotment lands totaling 3,469.93 acres. This roughly parallels the allotment profile on the national level, in that the Eastern Shawnees retained only 27 percent of their allotted lands at the end of the allotment period.[47] However, the voluminous paperwork produced by federal agents and others as they documented Indian affairs from the 1870s to the 1930s reveals that, while federal allotment policy played a role in the transformation of the Eastern Shawnee reservation, ongoing leasing practices may have been just as influential. Well before allotment became the national policy, the leasing of Eastern Shawnee tribal members' land by white men had become an entrenched practice and a substantial piece of the local economy. Allotment did not dramatically change that economic framework. The distribution of individual lands did, however, affect the ways in which decisions about landholdings could be made. In short, individual Eastern Shawnees now had the ability to decide what they wanted to do with their assigned piece of property. The changing nature of Eastern Shawnee lands, then, became a matter of individual decisions and not communal ones. Thus individual circumstances, attitudes, and desires mattered.

It cannot be denied that the Eastern Shawnee land base diminished from the time of allotment's inception to its official end as a government policy in 1930. And the fact that only 3,469.93 acres of land were still retained under the auspices of fifty-two different allotments speaks to the devastating consequences of the national effort to break up Indian tribes. Yet just as important to note is the manner in which the loss of land sparked a significant dispersal of the community as a whole. It was a dispersal that would only increase once the Great Depression provided another impetus for migration in the 1930s. In other words, the impact of allotment should not simply be viewed in terms of acres lost or in connection with permissive leasing. The division of the Eastern Shawnee reserve may have had a much greater impact on the people than it did on the land.

NOTES

1. Tom Captain Interview, Doris Duke Collection, Western History Collections, University of Oklahoma, Norman; Allottee Examination Reports, 1910–11, Records of the Quapaw Competency Commission, Records of the Quapaw Agency, Record Group 75, National Archives and Records Administration Federal Records Center, Fort Worth, Tex. (hereafter Allottee Examination Reports).

2. Elsie May Hoevet, "As I Remember," chapter 11, this text.

3. Treaty of 1831, *Indian Affairs: Laws and Treaties*, comp. and ed. Charles J. Kappler (Washington, D.C.: Government Printing Office, 1904), 2:327–31 (hereafter *Indian Affairs*); Treaty of 1832, ibid., 2:383–85; Treaty of 1867, ibid., 2:960–69; "Statistical return of farming, etc., 1871," Office of Indian Affairs, Annual Reports of the Commissioner of Indian Affairs (hereafter ARCIA), Documents Relating to Indian Affairs, History Collection, University of Wisconsin Digital Collections, 624.

4. Charles E. Mix to Orville Browning, November 15, 1867, ARCIA, 1.

5. Enoch Hoag to Ely S. Parker, October 8, 1870, ARCIA, 260.

6. Lease Agreement of April 7, 1870, Record Group 75, Records of the Quapaw Agency, M234, Roll 704, Letters Received by the Office of Indian Affairs, 1824–81, National Archives and Records Administration, Washington, D.C. (hereafter any document cited from the National Archives, after the document's full title, will be cited by its microfilm number).

7. D. D. Dyer to Hon. H. Price, July 29, 1881, Item 1881, Record Group 75, LR13351, Box 32, Eastern Shawnee Tribe of Oklahoma Digital Collection.

8. J. M. Haworth to Commissioner of Indian Affairs, August 27, 1879, ARCIA, 75–78; Statistics of Stock Owned, Acreage Cultivated, Crops, and Other Results of Indian Labor, ibid., 250–51; Proclamation by President Rutherford B. Hayes, ibid., 188–89.

9. Proclamation by President Rutherford B. Hayes, ibid., 188–89; J. M. Haworth to Ezra A. Hayt, July 11, 1879, Record Group 75, M234, Roll 708.

10. John Jackson to E. A. Hayt, Commissioner of Indian Affairs, August 26, 1879, Record Group 75, M234, Roll 708.

11. J. V. Summers to the Commissioner of Indian Affairs, August 30, 1886, ARCIA, 139–42.

12. Records of Leases and Contracts, 1875–94, Record Group 75, E45, Box 1.

13. Hiram Jones to the Commissioner of Indian Affairs, 1878, ARCIA, 68.

14. D. B. Dyer to the Commissioner of Indian Affairs, August 25, 1880, ARCIA, 86–90.

15. J. V. Summer to the Commissioner of Indian Affairs, August 23, 1887, ARCIA, 90–93.

16. General Allotment Act of 1887, 24 Stat. 388, chap. 119.

17. C. Joseph Genetin-Pilawa, *Crooked Paths to Allotment: The Fight over Federal Indian Policy after the Civil War* (Chapel Hill: University of North Carolina Press, 2012), 2–3.

18. Theodore Roosevelt, "First Annual Message," December 3, 1901, *The American Presidency Project*, ed. Gerhard Peters and John T. Woolley, www.presidency.ucsb.edu/ws/?pid=29542.

19. Andrew Denson, *Demanding the Cherokee Nation: Indian Autonomy and American Culture, 1830–1900* (Lincoln: University of Nebraska Press, 2004), 232–40.

20. David A. Chang, *The Color of the Land: Race, Nation, and the Politics of Landownership in Oklahoma, 1832–1929* (Chapel Hill: University of North Carolina Press, 2010), 6; Treaty of 1866, *Indian Affairs*, 2:931–37.

21. Totals for 1888 and 1892 from Land Allotment Records Entries 97A and 97B, Record Group 75.

22. Ibid.

23. 26 Stat. 794 (1891), ARCIA, 631–32.

24. George S. Doane to the Commissioner of Indian Affairs, 1896, ARCIA, 143–49.

25. 30 Stat. 62, *Indian Affairs*, 1:619–20; George S. Doane to the Commissioner of Indian Affairs, August 27, 1897, ARCIA, 133.

26. Edward Goldberg to the Commissioner of Indian Affairs, August 26, 1899, ARCIA, 190; Edward Goldberg to the Commissioner of Indian Affairs, August 13, 1900, ARCIA, 224–25.

27. Edgar A. Allen to the Commissioner of Indian Affairs, August 29, 1901, ARCIA, 217–19; 1902 legislation noted in *Indian Affairs*, 1:752.

28. 34 Stat. 182, *Indian Affairs*, 3:182.

29. 35 Stat. 751, ibid., 3:387–88.

30. Executive Order of President Woodrow Wilson, February 15, 1916, ibid., 4:1035–36

31. 34 Stat. 182, ibid., 3:181–82.

32. Frederick E. Hoxie, *A Final Promise: The Campaign to Assimilate the Indians, 1880–1920* (Lincoln: University of Nebraska Press, 2001), 176–80.

33. C. F. Hauke to Charles L. Ellis, August 9, 1910, Report of Quapaw Competency Commission on Removal of Restrictions from Allotted Land, 1910–11, Record Group 75, Box 3, Records of the Superintendent's Office, E.1 Correspondence.

34. Allottee Examination Reports, 1910–11.

35. Ibid.

36. Ibid.

37. Ibid.

38. Ibid.

39. Ibid.

40. 1911 Census of the Eastern Shawnee Tribe, Seneca, 1910–11, Indian Census Rolls, 1885–1940, Record Group 75, M595, Roll 489.

41. Executive Order of President Woodrow Wilson, February 15, 1916, *Indian Affairs*, 4:1035–36.

42. E. B. Merritt to J. L. Suffecool, February 6, 1926, Record Group 75, Allotments—Extended Restrictions Folder, Box 3, Records of the Superintendent's Office, E.1 Correspondence; accompanying reports on individual allotments also in Allotments—Extended Restrictions Folder, ibid.

43. Allotments—Extended Restrictions Folder, ibid.

44. Ibid.

45. An Act, to Conserve and Develop Indian Lands and Resources, 48 Stat. 984.

46. Mark R. Scherer, "Dawes Act," in *Encyclopedia of the Great Plains*, ed. David J. Wishart (Lincoln: University of Nebraska Press, 2004), 450–51.

47. Statistics for Annual Report of 1930, IMG_0833, Eastern Shawnee Tribe of Oklahoma Digital Collection.

4

"Each Band Knew Their Own Country"

Land, Cooperation, and Community in
Nineteenth-Century Eastern Shawnee
Intertribal Interactions

AMY DIANNE BERGSETH

The common bond between American Indians in Northeastern Oklahoma grows out of the complex and difficult legacy of forced removal. Despite this dark past, the Eastern Shawnees have had a relatively peaceful history of intertribal relations with their Native neighbors in the nineteenth and twentieth centuries. Like other Indians who were forcibly evicted from their homelands in the early 1830s, the Eastern Shawnees lived near other removed Indians from the East. The Shawnees and Senecas who lived together in Lewistown, Ohio, chose to reside next to familiar neighbors when the United States government removed them to Indian Territory. During the American Civil War a new round of migrations occurred when the Eastern Shawnees fled their reservation and lived among the Ottawas in Kansas. After the Civil War, Reconstruction-era treaties transformed intertribal relations yet again, as the United States demanded that the Eastern Shawnees, Senecas, Quapaws, and Cherokees each sell a portion of their lands to other Native nations moving into the territory. The Eastern Shawnees cooperated with other tribes, ceding land to make way for newcomers who had also been forced to leave their homes. By 1880 the Eastern Shawnee reservation was cut down to 13,000 acres—a loss of 47,000 acres—to make way for tribes forced from Kansas. As northeastern Oklahoma became even more diverse, the Eastern Shawnees joined with their neighbors and participated in intertribal dances and Seneca ceremonies. Yet they managed to retain their distinctive identity and autonomy while fostering friendly relationships with their neighbors and participating in intertribal political assemblies. The Eastern Shawnees met the challenge of maintaining their independence and strength, but while sustaining their autonomy and individuality, they established alliances with their Indian neighbors that continue to this day. Thus, paradoxically, the Eastern Shawnee Tribe, a politically sovereign nation, survived in large part because of their postremoval intertribal cooperation.[1]

One might naturally expect the Eastern Shawnees to become insular and reserved after the extensive disruption of forced removal. But instead of merely defending their own personal interests, the Eastern Shawnees actively sought to make friends and allies. This helped them survive the upheaval. Historical studies have often not explored these sorts of connections. Many scholars, such as Wendy St. Jean and David LaVere, focus on the intertribal conflicts as a result of removal.[2] Other historians have recounted other tribal stories of survival, assertions of sovereignty, and identity formation.[3] The term sovereignty has also been used to describe a state of fundamental independence, authority, and self-governance, as well as the right to maintain one's own values and traditions. Anishinaabe scholar Heidi Kiiwetinepinesiik Stark has aptly described the use of sovereignty as a word that has lost its meaning and value in the present day. Tribal sovereignty is more than just political and legal power; it can also include Native concepts of interdependence and accountability and the formation of relationships.[4] The story of postremoval nation building and the maintenance of sovereignty, then, requires an examination of intertribal interactions. For the Eastern Shawnees, cultural and political sovereignty and intertribal cooperation intersected in the postremoval years. Cooperation and the renewal of relationships facilitated Eastern Shawnee survival and resilience after the devastating disruptions of removal.

The Eastern Shawnees were one of the first removed tribes to settle in what is now northeastern Oklahoma. Because they were among the first, the Eastern Shawnees witnessed the wholesale transformation of the land and its people. In 1969 the Eastern Shawnee chief Tom Captain explained how the federal government "moved us in here. And at the time they gave us twenty miles up and down the Missouri and Kansas lines, square. And now the Quapaws, Peorias, Miamis, Pi[a]nkashaws, we got everything but the Choctaws. [We have] the Wyandots and the Senecas and the Modocs."[5] Many different Indian nations ended up in the northeastern corner of Oklahoma. While some were completely new and foreign to them, most of the Eastern Shawnees' Indian neighbors were familiar relations from their homelands in the Ohio valley. In the winter of 1832 the Eastern Shawnees and Senecas from Ohio settled next to other Senecas in Indian Territory.[6]

Earlier in 1832 the United States had created the Stokes Commission to verify the physical locations of the removed nations and to resolve existing land disputes between them. Former North Carolina governor Montfort Stokes chaired the commission, which had two years to visit, comment on, and make recommendations regarding the conditions of removed tribes in Indian Territory. The Stokes Commission settled substantial discrepancies such as those between the Muscogees (Creeks) and the Cherokees, conferred with Osages to try to induce removal and resettlement, and planned for further removals of Native peoples who remained east of the Mississippi River on vestiges of their original homelands. In December 1832 the Stokes Commission concluded a treaty with the Senecas and the Shawnees regarding the boundaries between their lands.[7] For the Eastern Shawnees, the Stokes Commission's treaty and council arbitration resulted in the establishment of new reservation locations and boundaries. Whereas the Eastern Shawnee lands had previously been located on the western side of the Neosho (or Grand) River, in the new treaty the Eastern Shawnees traded their reserved land for land on the waterway's eastern bank. Thus, instead of having the Grand River separate the Sandusky Senecas from the Lewistown Senecas and Shawnees, their reserves would both be on the eastern side of the river.[8]

This 1832 treaty was not only a clarification and confirmation of the Eastern Shawnees' new homelands, but also a solidification of a newly formed, symbolic political alliance between the Lewistown Senecas and Shawnees, who are often identified as the Mixed Band in federal correspondence, and the Sandusky Senecas, which secured their respective interests. They joined together as the United Nation of Senecas and Shawnees. The Senecas and Shawnees, well-acquainted friends and neighbors, safeguarded their own lands and communities with their solidarity. The treaty explained that "the said Senecas from Sandusky, and the mixed Band of Senecas and Shawnees[,] have lately formed a confederacy, and have expressed their anxiety to unite as one Tribe or Nation."[9] Despite the unification, the Senecas and Shawnees retained their individuality and autonomy as separate bands and nations. The Iroquoian-speaking Senecas with Longhouse traditions differed greatly from the Algonquian-speaking Shawnees with their own dances. For all political purposes, however, they would act as a singular intertribal alliance, a united nations of sorts.[10]

Because they had joined symbolically, the Senecas and Shawnees worked together, but they did so as distinctive kin and individual tribal groups. Notwithstanding federal attempts at governmental consolidation, the Sandusky Senecas and the Mixed Band of Senecas and Shawnees maintained their distinctions. The confederation did not dissolve tribalism and individual sovereignties. Rather, as anthropologist Brian Joseph Gilley explains, "The Sandusky people and Lewistown people had their own distinct and autonomous councils."[11] Despite the treaty's language of confederation, the Senecas and Shawnees still maintained their own separate leadership, territories, and customs. In 1837 William Armstrong, the Western Territory superintendent, reported to the commissioner of Indian affairs, "Each band knew their own country, and they were making arrangements for their permanent settlement."[12] The Shawnees and Senecas were seizing the initiative and managing their own affairs rather than letting the federal government take control. In the 1842 report the commissioner clarified that, of the Indian nations in the Neosho subagency—the Senecas, the Mixed Band of Senecas and Shawnees, and the Quapaws—"each of the three mentioned have separate annuities and mechanics, under treaty stipulations. Their lands, although adjoining, are laid off separately for each tribe."[13] The Eastern Shawnees served as a small nation within a much larger figurative political network that included the Sandusky and Lewistown Senecas, but they also retained their separate acreage and independent communities.

This 1830s administrative unification may have strengthened social and cultural ties between the Senecas and the Eastern Shawnees. In 1969 an interviewer asked Eastern Shawnee chief Julian BlueJacket, "Do you think the Senecas and Shawnees had any ceremonies together? Or were they just put together for the government to deal with?" It is unclear whether the question referred to the Lewistown or Sandusky Senecas, or both as implied by the 1832 treaty. "Did they ever really consider themselves combined as far as being in the same tribe?" the interviewer continued. Julian BlueJacket answered, "No, I don't think they were ever, they of course undoubtedly had some ceremonies together. We know they had elections together. . . . But ah, I'm sure both sides were loyal to their own blood sides. But they did have this agreement."[14] BlueJacket believed that the Senecas and Shawnees continued their own traditions and community gatherings separately but had a political arrangement to work as one diplomatic unit when it came to their reservation lands, which were all held east of the Grand River, south of Kansas, and west of Missouri.

This political unit tied together the three smaller groups—the Sandusky Senecas and the Lewistown Senecas and Shawnees—into a larger confederation and also concentrated and centralized all of their lands. In the new 1832 treaty the Senecas and Shawnees sought to "occupy their land as tenants in common—and have the whole of the country provided for them by the United States located on the east side of Ne-o-sho or Grand river." Instead of dividing the groups into separate reservations and splitting them apart, the treaty documented that the Senecas and Eastern Shawnees wanted "a more convenient and satisfactory location" together. The Senecas and Shawnees relinquished any lands formerly treated to them west of the Grand River in exchange for more acreage on the eastern side of the waterway. The Sandusky Senecas would occupy the lower half of the lands while the Mixed Band of Senecas and Shawnees would occupy the upper half. As a whole, however, the land was "occupied in common."[15] Julian BlueJacket explained the Senecas and Shawnees, saying, "At one time they were a unit"; the U.S. federal government was "dealing with Seneca and Shawnee as a unit."[16] Eastern Shawnees and Senecas confederated, and they did so in the eyes of the federal government, which served to strengthen their land base and the custody of their acreage northeast of the Grand River, although they continued as distinctive nations and communities.

At the same time, the federal government and the Stokes Commission made negotiations to remove other tribes to the same area. The Quapaws, originating in Arkansas Territory, were one of the first groups to settle near the Shawnees and Senecas in what would become northeastern Oklahoma. In an 1833 treaty the Quapaws exchanged their lands on the Red River near the Caddos, where some of the tribe had originally chosen to reside, for 96,000 acres of land in northeastern Indian Territory. According to the treaty, the Quapaws' new home was to be on lands "not heretofore assigned to any other tribe of Indians," possibly "between the lands of the Senecas and Shawnees." The Quapaw location itself was nonspecific in the treaty, except that it was on lands to be determined in the future and on acreage that the federal government had not already allocated to other Indian groups.[17]

The way it turned out in practice, nonetheless, was that the Quapaws settled on land that already belonged to the Shawnees and Senecas because the Seneca and Shawnee treaty had consolidated their lands so that they had "become contiguous to each other," not leaving any land in between for the Quapaws.[18] A couple of years after the Quapaw treaty, the U.S. federal government surveyed the Quapaw lands and discovered that they had settled on Seneca treaty lands. Many Quapaws left to live among other communities: back with the Caddos at the Red River, with the Cherokees in Texas, or with the Choctaws in southeastern Indian Territory. Only decades later would the Quapaws finally resolve the northeastern Indian Territory land disputes with the Senecas and Eastern Shawnees.[19]

When the Civil War broke out, many Indian nations from Indian Territory, including the Eastern Shawnees, sought refuge with tribes in Kansas. At that time an Ottawa named Joseph B. King (Kotohwan) co-owned a general store with John Tecumseh Jones in Ottawa, Kansas. In 1913, although he was more than ninety years old at the time, King detailed his life story (including the forced removal of the Ottawas to Kansas) to a University of Oklahoma history professor. In his interview he noted, "Several tribes from the Indian Territory were temporarily quartered on the Ottawa reservation during the Civil War." This included the Eastern Shawnees, Senecas, Quapaws, and Osages.[20]

With the United States Army's abandonment of Indian Territory during the Civil War, many Indian nations witnessed the cutoff of protection and security that had been promised in treaties. When approached by the Confederate States of America, then, many tribal nations, including the Eastern Shawnees, entered into agreements with the United States' enemies. On October 4, 1861, Lewis Davis, Joseph Mohawk, John Tomahawk, White Deer, and Silas Dougherty signed the Shawnee and Seneca treaty with the Confederacy on behalf of the Shawnees. The treaty insisted that they "place themselves under the laws and protection of the Confederate States of America" and that they must likewise remain loyal to the Confederacy. In return, the Confederacy was to protect the Indian communities and their properties. The Confederate States of America promised to not allow the cession of any of these lands without the consent of both the tribal communities and the Confederacy. Article 4 of the treaty stated that the tribes could incorporate, with a majority vote, any Indians (including the Shawnees in Kansas) into their tribal memberships. The Confederate states were required to resume some of the annuities that had been promised, but dropped, by the United States federal government. The treaty also upheld the legality of slavery and prohibited any further negotiations with the Confederacy's enemy, the United States of America.[21]

While the bulk of the treaty between the Eastern Shawnees and Senecas and the Confederacy focused on loyalty and defense between the parties, some provisions focused on intertribal relations. Article 10 called for "perpetual peace and brotherhood" between the Shawnees and Senecas and the other Indian Territory nations—the Osages, Cherokees, Muscogees (Creeks), Seminoles, Choctaws, Chickasaws, Wichitas, Caddos, Comanches, and others. Article 11 reinforced that those listed would "henceforth be good neighbors to each other" and that "the horses, cattle and other stock and property of each nation, tribe or band, and every person of each, is his or its own."[22] The treaty ultimately focused on peaceful relations with other Indian nations, Confederate protection of the Indians, and tribal loyalty to the Confederates.

After the violence and upheaval of the American Civil War, many of the tribes of northeastern Oklahoma returned south from Kansas to their reservations. With their homecoming came a slew of treaty renegotiations with the United States.[23] In 1865 the U.S. federal government called to council the tribal nations of Indian Territory in order to reestablish a trust relationship and to discuss making new postwar treaties. At Fort Smith, Arkansas, thirteen different Indian nations, including the Eastern Shawnees, came to hear what the federal government had to offer. The U.S. commissioner of Indian affairs, Dennis N. Cooley, came with specific stipulations for the nations. He demanded that the Indian nations give a "portion of the lands hitherto owned and occupied" to "be set apart for the friendly tribes in Kansas and elsewhere, on such terms as may be agreed upon." Tribal representatives balked at these demands and at the request for immediate treaty making without community consultation.[24]

The Indian nations' dissatisfaction and disdain for the federal government's slippery negotiations at the Fort Smith council exemplified the difficulties that the Eastern Shawnees and other Indian nations confronted after the Civil War. As Daniel Littlefield Jr. has noted, it was not the violence and refugee crises but rather the postwar diplomacy that ultimately hurt American Indian communities the most. Littlefield maintains, "The most destructive consequences of the war were the treaties that concluded it."[25] These Reconstruction-era treaties would have pronounced repercussions for the Eastern Shawnees and their neighbors.

The Seneca, Shawnee, and Quapaw leaders reiterated that they had a long tradition of treaty making with the United States and had kept up their end of the agreements. Seneca leader Isaac Warrior spoke on behalf of the tribes, stating, "We feel happy because we have made this treaty and shaken hands anew with you. We three nations would say that the old treaties made between you and us many years back have been lived up to. And now that we find that our Great Father intends to protect us from this on we are glad, and will henceforth expect his protection forever a long time."[26]

In the omnibus Reconstruction treaty of 1867, the Shawnees, Senecas, Quapaws, Peorias, Miamis, Ottawas, and Wyandottes signed more land cessions and removals. It was not until 1868 and 1869 that the Quapaws ultimately moved next to the Peorias and bought land from the Eastern Shawnees. This came about as a result of the negotiations between Quapaw leader John Wilson (Pastee) and Eastern Shawnee leader Thehconagah (Lewis Davis).[27] Issues such as confusion over the Quapaw lands, displacement during the American Civil War, and retribution through land cessions during Reconstruction contributed to the continued removal of other Indian tribes to northeastern Oklahoma. The Eastern Shawnees sold much of their land, more than 40,000 acres, to new and old arrivals.[28]

The Eastern Shawnees sold more of their new homelands for other removed Indians—the Ottawas and Wyandots—to resettle on after the Civil War. The Ottawas purchased 14,000 acres of the western part of the Eastern Shawnee reservation.[29] Ottawa tribal leader Joseph B. King described the Ottawas' move from Kansas to Oklahoma, explaining that "John Wilson, our chief, realizing that they could not care for the money received from the sale of their lands and believing that most of the Ottawas would soon be penniless if not protected, entered into a contract with Theh-con-a-gah (Davis), who was chief of the Shawnees, for the purchase of a part of the Shawnee reservation, in the Indian Territory." The tribal nations themselves initiated negotiations with each other, perhaps in spite of the United States' pressure to do so. The southern superintendency summary in the 1866 annual report of the commissioner of Indian affairs echoed the sentiment of self-initiative on the part of the Eastern Shawnees and other Indian nations, noting the creation of "treaty arrangements between themselves." John Whitetree, John Young, and Thehconagah (Lewis Davis) were some of the Shawnee leaders who initiated such treaty discussions.[30]

Not only did the Shawnees and Senecas begin the treaty discussions, their old alliances and friendships also influenced the agreements. The Office of Indian Affairs recommended postponing any endorsement of the treaty because it saw an opportunity to include in the negotiations some land sales for other Indian communities that currently resided in the state of Kansas. The report explained that the present idea was that the "Senecas confederated with the Shawnees propose to sell to their allies, the Shawnees, their interest in the reservation, and to become confederated with the other band of Senecas; and then to sell or give to the Wyandotts of Kansas a home with them." The rationale was that "under an old understanding . . . the Senecas acknowledge their obligations to the Wyandotts for giving them a home in Ohio, and desire to reciprocate the favor."[31] Decades-old obligations that the Senecas had to the Wyandottes resurfaced in the post–Civil War treaty negotiations. Similarly, the Eastern Shawnees and Senecas would sell their lands to the Ottawas, their old allies from Ohio who had welcomed them as refugees onto their Kansas reservation during the Civil War. A reunion of sorts in northeastern Oklahoma made sense, given these shared histories. Eastern Shawnee resilience and political sovereignty well into the twentieth century depended—ironically—on the help of other tribes from the era of removal.

Although the Eastern Shawnees were confederated with the Senecas, one of their closest allies since preremoval times, the tribes decided in their post–Civil War treaty to politically split from each other and divide their reservation. In 1867 the Eastern Shawnees not only officially ended their recognition as a confederation united with the Seneca reservation to the south, they also separated from the Lewistown Senecas. The 1867 treaty detailed that the two groups would separate and divide up any of their monies held in common as a mixed band. It specified, "The said Shawnees thereto consenting," the Senecas "agree to dissolve their connection with the said Shawnees, and to unite with the [Sandusky] Senecas."[32] At the same time, the Shawnees agreed to the Senecas' sale of some of the joint Shawnee-Seneca reservation to the Peorias and other confederated tribes. According to the 1867 annual report of the commissioner of Indian affairs, "The [Lewistown] Senecas, joined with the Shawnees, have agreed to sell their half of the present reserve of the two tribes to the Miamies and Peorias of Kansas, and to unite with the other [Sandusky or Cowskin River] Senecas."[33] By September of 1868 the Indian agent stated, "The mixed Senecas have nearly all moved down with the Cowskin Senecas." The physical and geographical separation between the Eastern Shawnees and Senecas was thus complete.[34]

In theory the Senecas and Shawnees decided and began the process of fiscal and territorial detachment just after the Civil War. In practice, however, their political and geographic separation continued into the next century. Julian BlueJacket explained that some Eastern Shawnee finances were still jointly owned with the Lewistown Senecas even into the latter half of the twentieth century. In 1969 BlueJacket clarified, "In fact, [until] only about three years ago, we had some money jointly with the Senecas. They call it the Seneca-Shawnee fund." He continued: "It was a joint account, and they divided it out about two years ago." BlueJacket and the Eastern Shawnees conferred with the Seneca-Cayugas and their chief, Vernon Crow. Detailing the discussions, BlueJacket clarified that he remembered the discussion on the joint account, "'Cause Vernon and I flipped, well we almost were going to flipped [*sic*] a coin to see who got the odd penny."[35]

The resettlement of other Indian nations alongside the Eastern Shawnees in northeastern Oklahoma did not end with the implementation of the nineteenth-century reconstruction treaties. The U.S.-Modoc War of 1872–73 also brought Modoc prisoners of war to Eastern Shawnee lands. The army brought the exiled Modoc families, shackled and transported in cattle cars, to Baxter Springs, Kansas, and then finally to northeastern Oklahoma in the middle of November 1873. Tom Captain, chief of the Eastern Shawnees in 1969, said that the federal government just "brought them down here. They settled them on our reservation just east of us."[36] Originally, people believed that the Quapaws, the largest tribal nation in terms of population in northeastern Oklahoma at that time, would be the ones to sell land to the Modocs.[37] Instead, the Eastern Shawnees sold a small amount of land to them. It was not until June 23, 1874, that the federal government finally bought the land from the Eastern Shawnees as a permanent location for the Modoc exiles.[38]

The U.S. Army took the Modocs to "Seneca Station (on Shawnee land) . . . at the Quapaw Agency." The federal government also selected the location for the Modocs to build their temporary home. The army and the federal authorities forced them to build their own shelters out of $524.40 worth of "scrap lumber" only two hundred feet away from the Quapaw Agency headquarters. Eventually the Modoc settlement was no longer temporary. In 1874 the Eastern Shawnees sold four thousand acres to the federal government to be the permanent home of the Modocs in exchange for $6,000.[39] Eastern Shawnee Tom Captain said, "We sold Modocs some land and we never did get a dime out of it, off of our reservation, that I know of."[40] It is unclear whether this is true or not. The Eastern Shawnees did, however, agree to the Modocs' purchase of a small portion of their reservation lands—creating a square-shaped anomaly on the northeastern Oklahoma Indian reservation maps.[41]

With these geographic reorganizations, and with additional Native communities settling in northeastern Indian Territory, the Eastern Shawnees and other Indian nations began to meet in intertribal councils in an effort to protect their political integrity and strengthen their sovereignty. Despite the physical reservation divisions and political separations, intertribal councils dealt with shared concerns in Indian Territory. They first met in the winter of 1870 at Okmulgee, in the Muscogee (Creek) Nation, as the General Council of the Indian Territory. Representatives included leaders from the Eastern Shawnee Nation as well as the Cherokee, Muscogee (Creek), Ottawa, Quapaw, Seneca, Wyandotte, Confederated Peoria, Sac and Fox, and Absentee Shawnee nations. Legal scholar David Wilkins describes the Okmulgee Constitution—the intertribal constitution created and drafted at the first General Council of the Indian Territory meeting—as setting an "intertribal diplomatic precedent." Scholar Curtis Nolen explains that, alternatively to the federal government's aspirations for territorial organization, the American Indian delegates for the Okmulgee Constitution organized "to preserve their basic organization and culture—a movement that today would be referred to as self-determination."[42] Although it was not completely ratified by all tribal parties, the Okmulgee Constitution still served as a way to unify the disparate Native nations in the Indian Territory for the collective security of their sovereign rights.[43]

The 1870 Okmulgee Constitution stated its purpose as being "in order to draw themselves together in a closer bond of union, for the better protection of their rights, the improvement of themselves and the preservation of their race."[44] It created a tripartite government for Indian Territory with a bicameral legislature—a general assembly. Because the senate was based on population, it consolidated the smaller nations, including the Eastern Shawnees, into one agent. One senator represented the Senecas, Wyandottes, and Shawnees, while another one stood for the Ottawas, Peorias, and Quapaws. The house of representatives was centered around a single representative for each tribe, plus additional delegates for greater tribal population sizes.[45]

In the Okmulgee Constitution the tribes retained their separate, distinct jurisdictions, and the judicial branch of the Indian Territory government would abide by the individual laws of the tribal nations as noted in their treaties.[46] Lazarus Flint was the Eastern Shawnee delegate on the general council. He also served on the committee on relations with the United States, which reported on their relationship to the U.S. federal government, "as defined by treaty stipulations." This committee also served as the general council's main assembly for "protesting against any legislation by Congress impairing the obligation of any treaty" and against sale of lands and the creation of any other government of Indian Territory without Indian consent.[47]

In the post–Civil War era the Eastern Shawnees and other Indian nations worked together to create an Indian state in Indian Territory in order to avoid the threat of Oklahoma's statehood. Similar to the interest in Shawnee-Seneca unity in the 1830s, the Eastern Shawnees once again found avenues to protect their own interests by collaborating with other Indian nations in Indian Territory. Possibly the biggest threat to the Indian nations' political sovereignty was the creation of an external territorial government without tribal consent. The general council emphatically pressed that the Indian nations would not accept the United States Congress's imposition of an outside territorial government. The general council's Report of the Special Committee on Permanent Organization maintained that the numerous Indian nations did and would "cling to their homes, to their laws, to their customs, to their national and personal independence, with the tenacity of life itself," and it was "of the opinion that the organization of the people here represented, and such as may hereafter unite with them, should be a government of their *own choice.*"[48] Lazarus Flint, representing the Eastern Shawnees, approved this communal proclamation and also voted to send the Okmulgee Constitution to the various tribes for ratification.[49] Although funded, mediated, and promoted by the United States, the general councils served as Native voices for discussion regarding reorganization and reconstruction after the Civil War.

The Indian Territory nations, however, failed to authorize the Okmulgee Constitution. The Chickasaws' Indian agent explained that they disapproved because the proportional representation hindered smaller nations' interests.[50] In 1871 only the Muscogees (Creeks) had ratified the Okmulgee Constitution. Seminole representative E. J. Brown offered an amendment to provide for equal representation among the Five Tribes—the Cherokee, Muscogee (Creek), Choctaw, Chickasaw, and Seminole nations. The amendment was supported by the majority of the Chickasaws and all of the Seminoles, yet it was shot down by a majority of the Cherokees, Choctaws, Muscogees (Creeks), Absentee Shawnees, Absentee Delawares, and Caddos. In 1873 Choctaw and Cherokee delegates debated the "phraseology" in the amendments. A general quarrel ensued, and a Cherokee delegate accused the amendment writer of using "bad English." A Choctaw rebutted that the amendment committee "was competent to write and transact its business much better in Indian, but that he feared the gentleman objecting could not well manage business coming up in that shape."[51] At the June 1872 general council, representatives still included the Eastern Shawnees, but the Chickasaws did not send any delegates. By the end of the month the Muscogees (Creeks), Choctaws, Sac and Foxes, Senecas, Eastern Shawnees, Wyandottes, Peorias, Ottawas, and Quapaws had all indicated to the general assembly their acceptance of the Okmulgee Constitution.[52] Although the constitution never came to fruition, the council continued until 1875. At its last meeting the General Council of the Indian Territory included not only the Eastern Shawnees, other small tribal nations, and the Five Tribes, but also western Plains nations—the Pawnees, Kickapoos, Wichitas, Comanches, Caddos, Kaws, Cheyennes, and Arapahoes.[53]

When given the opportunity to provide a report of the Eastern Shawnee Nation, Lazarus Flint emphasized the amiable relations between the Eastern Shawnees and their neighbors. He admitted, "The fact that we get along so peaceably among ourselves, as well as with others, has always seemed strange." Flint believed that the Shawnees' respect for their leaders' call for peace explained this. "Now the Shawnees, while they are but few, entertain great respect and veneration for their chiefs, so much so that his word is to the Shawnees very much as written laws are to other nations," Flint reasoned. "Besides this, it is made his principal duty to call the people together from time to time, and advise and encourage them to be industrious, honest, kind, and loving toward all men."[54] With the support of their tribal leadership such as himself, Lazarus Flint saw the Eastern Shawnees as promoting general cordiality with their nearby tribes.

The Modocs also sent representatives to the 1875 general council and shared their positive feelings of being amid such welcoming neighborly tribes as the Eastern Shawnees. Modoc leader Bogus Charley addressed his northeastern Oklahoma neighbors at the assembly, explaining, "The Government brought us here in irons about two years ago." Charley then detailed how the Modocs settled on the new lands, adjusted to the new life in Indian Territory, and purchased a parcel of land for themselves. Charley continued, "We number about one hundred and fifty, and have now about four or five sections [equivalent to 2,500 to 3,200 acres] of land in this Territory, in the north-east part, purchased for us by the Government of the United States from the Eastern Shawnees." The Modocs, he explained, then established themselves by constructing new residences and starting work in industry and farming. Charley underlined the importance of their neighbors' goodwill and welcome. He said, "The Shawnees, Wyandotts, Ottawas, Peorias, Quapaws, Senecas, are all like brothers toward us." Charley went on, "We feel like we are amongst good friends. We feel at home." He assured the assembly, "we intend to be good to our neighbors and the people generally."[55] As Bogus Charley detailed in his speech, the Modocs adjusted to becoming friendly neighbors in their new homes on reservation lands bought from the Shawnees.

Although the Eastern Shawnees sold their lands to other Indian nations, they sometimes did not necessarily interact closely with their neighbors. In the 1960s Eastern Shawnee chief Tom Captain explained that, riding his horse one day, he came across four or five Modoc women who were sitting on a log with their cane fishing poles. When he was passing by them, they suddenly "all raised up at once. . . . I put that pony down the road," he exclaimed.[56] Captain's tale illustrates the occasional awkwardness and the difficulties for woodland Indians such as the Eastern Shawnees to socialize with Pacific Northwest and plateau Indians. One of Captain's favorite pastimes when he was young was to "borrow" the Quapaws' ponies. "I would run across a bunch of them Quapaw ponies[.] I'd drive them up and put them in pasture and then on Sunday morning I'd go to Sunday School and tell boys." The children would have fun riding them all day. Captain explained, "We'd ride on Sundays and then I'd run 'em back on the range."[57] He did not necessarily interact with the culturally unfamiliar Quapaws, but instead borrowed their ponies for some horseback riding on the weekends in the rural northeastern Oklahoma backcountry. It was not permanent theft for economic benefit and social standing, as was omnipresent in the nineteenth-century West and the Great Plains, but rather a unique Eastern Shawnee temporary appropriation of Quapaw horses. Captain's reminiscences show that despite their proximity to other Indian nations, the Eastern Shawnees did retain some tribal insularity.

Despite the isolating atmosphere of the disparate reservation lands, the Eastern Shawnees did have opportunities to interact with other tribal members periodically in the late nineteenth century. Often it was trips to the border towns that provided them the opportunity not only to pick up necessary goods and foodstuffs but also to socialize with others. A Wyandotte named Donna Elliot Vowel detailed how initially there were not many people on the Wyandotte reservation and her family would often take opportunities to see others. She explained, "To most of the Indians the trip to Seneca, Missouri, for buying and trading also afforded an opportunity to visit with friends of their own and other tribes of this part of Indian Territory."[58] The circumstance must have been similar for the Eastern Shawnees who lived near the border, across from Seneca, Missouri.

The Eastern Shawnees and White Oak Shawnees collaborated, participated, and shared their dances and songs with each other. In the late 1960s Eastern Shawnee Rosa Kissee said that she remembered always having a dance among the Eastern Shawnees, but that the White Oak Shawnees would come up to assist. Kissee said that at this Eastern Shawnee dance, "they didn't do the singing now they ah, the Cherokee Shawnee came up and sang. . . . [There] aren't too many of 'em that can sing."[59] Ceremonial customs and dances provided one very sure way in which Eastern Shawnees interacted with other tribes—especially with other Shawnee peoples in the northeastern Oklahoma region.

Eastern Shawnees also traveled to White Oak, near what is now Vinita, Oklahoma, in Craig County, to participate in their dances. Clyde BlueJacket explained that because many of the elders of the Eastern Shawnees had passed away, the Eastern Shawnees no longer hosted their own dances. They did, however, go down to participate in dances with other Shawnee kin. "We do have Cherokee Shawnee Indians located around from BlueJacket on west, White Oak, where they make and carry on tribal dances in which we do have several of our Eastern Shawnee members that participate," he detailed. Julian BlueJacket echoed Clyde BlueJacket's sentiments and affirmed, "When I was a kid, everyone went down there a lot."[60] Similarly, a Wyandotte named Robert Long stated that "the Eastern Shawnees they go over here to a place they call White Oak" and that many Wyandottes would also go to participate.[61] White Oak was—and still is today—a place for Eastern Shawnees to congregate and meet other relatives and their extended Shawnee kin and to interact with other northeastern Oklahoma Indian people.

By the end of the nineteenth century many Eastern Shawnees participated in both ceremonial and secular social dances such as powwows hosted by other tribes. In the 1960s Clyde BlueJacket said that the "Eastern Shawnee, . . . scattered in different parts in the state of Oklahoma, . . . come and participate with the Quapaws."[62] Julian BlueJacket noted that he would meet with a Widow BlueJacket and travel around to all the dances in the area. "She'd come and get me. She had a set of horses and a buggy. We'd throw the saddle in the back of the buggy and take off," he explained. "Then we'd go to White Oak. We'd go to Quapaw. We'd go to every Indian pow-wow there was."[63] The Eastern Shawnees participated in this broader pan-Indian powwow culture, especially during the large annual Quapaw Powwow on the Fourth of July weekend, one of the oldest powwows in the country.

The Eastern Shawnees also engaged in Seneca dances, songs, and ceremonies in northeastern Oklahoma. Bill Connor, a Quapaw, recalled hearing about the Senecas' Shuck Face ceremonies in which the Eastern Shawnees participated when he was younger. He recollected, "Here in Oklahoma, the Seneca had a Shuck Face and the Shawnees partake a lot with the Senecas in this particular dance." He continued, "They would send runners out. Sometimes it would be a Shawnee man, but you didn't know who he was until you were told who he was and he'd come running through." The runners would travel up to twenty-five miles to let people all across the area know about the happenings. Connor explained that he would often see that when a runner came to tell another person about the event, "the man that was plowing or doing the chores or whatever they were doing—the men that belonged to this organization, would drop the things that they were doing immediately, and go get their shuck faces and they would be off to this—to this meeting."[64]

Close proximity to other small Indian nations enabled the Eastern Shawnees to speak many different Indian languages. Many Eastern Shawnees also married other Indians and became intertribal families. Janie Blalock Logan, whose mother married a Peoria, reflected on her upbringing, saying that her mother, Marry Blackgut, "spoke Shawnee to us all the time."[65] When considering the many different languages spoken in the area, Ottawa leader Clarence King noted that the Quapaws and the Iroquoian peoples—the Senecas and Cayugas—all spoke their own separate languages. Most of northeastern Oklahoma's tribes, including the Eastern Shawnees, Ottawas, Miamis, Peorias, Piankashaws, and Weas, spoke closely related Algonquian languages. They could often recognize meaning and similarities in words and phrases.[66] Cayuga elder Kenneth Oyler noted that in many of the northeastern Oklahoma stomp dances, multiple communities who spoke different languages would come together. "There's a lot of different tribes. Some of 'em talk Indian. You can see and hear where the different tribes can understand one another," he said.[67] Many Eastern Shawnees knew multiple languages. Sarah Longbone, in an interview in the 1930s, said that she grew up around many different languages. She recollected, "I was taught to speak the Seneca, Wyandotte and Shawnee languages, and was interpreter for the Shawnees between the Senecas and Wyandottes."[68]

Being in the diverse northeastern corner of the state of Oklahoma, the nineteenth-century Eastern Shawnees interacted with other Indian nations in the area and utilized intertribal cooperation to support their tribal sovereignty. The Neosho subagent reported that the Indians in "each band knew their own country." Although the agent meant the landscapes and settlement of their new postremoval homelands, this idea of "knowing" also expands to other aspects of life. The Eastern Shawnees knew the country that was surrounded and filled by other Indian communities. Over several decades they had been the ones to sell portions of their reservation lands for the settlement of other Indian neighbors. Some, like the Senecas and Ottawas, the Eastern Shawnees knew well from their preremoval and Civil War pasts. Others, such as the Quapaws and Modocs, the Eastern Shawnees had just become newly acquainted with. By the end of the nineteenth century the Eastern Shawnees had come to intimately know the land and people in northeastern Oklahoma.

NOTES

1. Treaty with the Seneca, etc., 1831, in July 20, 1831, 7 Stat. 351, Proclamation, April 6, 1832, *Indian Affairs: Laws and Treaties*, comp. and ed. Charles J. Kappler (Washington, D.C.: Government Printing Office, 1904), 2:328 (hereafter cited as *Indian Affairs*); Annual Report of Commissioner of Indian Affairs (hereafter ARCIA), November 1, 1880, 83, H. R. Doc. No. 1 (1880), 209.

2. David LaVere, *Contrary Neighbors: Southern Plains and Removed Indians in Indian Territory* (Norman: University of Oklahoma Press, 2000); Wendy St. Jean, *Remaining Chickasaw in Indian Territory, 1830s–1907* (Tuscaloosa: University of Alabama Press, 2011).

3. William McLoughlin, *After the Trail of Tears: The Cherokees' Struggle for Sovereignty, 1839–1880* (Chapel Hill: University of North Carolina Press, 1994); Clara Sue Kidwell, *The Choctaws in Oklahoma: From Tribe to Nation, 1855–1970* (Norman: University of Oklahoma Press, 2008); Andrew H. Fisher, *Shadow Tribe: The Making of Columbia River Indian Identity* (Seattle: Center for the Study of the Pacific Northwest/University of Washington Press, 2010); David A. Chang, *The Color of the Land: Race, Nation, and the Politics of Landownership in Oklahoma, 1832–1929* (Chapel Hill: University of North Carolina Press, 2010); William J. Bauer Jr., *We Were All Like Migrant Workers Here: Work, Community, and Memory on California's Round Valley Reservation, 1850–1941* (Chapel Hill: University of North Carolina Press, 2009). John P. Bowes covers earlier postremoval intertribal councils such as the one at Tahlequah in John P. Bowes, *Exiles and Pioneers: Eastern Indians in the Trans-Mississippi West* (New York: Cambridge University Press, 2007), chap. 4.

4. Heidi Kiiwetinepinesiik Stark, "Nenabozho's Smart Berries: Rethinking Tribal Sovereignty and Accountability," *Michigan State Law Review* 2013, no. 2 (2013): 341–43, 346, 352–53.

5. Tom Captain (Eastern Shawnee), interview by Peggy Dycus, May 16, 1969, Vol. 52, Tape No. T-428-1, 4, Doris Duke Collection of American Indian Oral History, Western History Collections, University of Oklahoma, Norman (hereafter cited as Duke Collection).

6. Frank H. Harris, "The Seneca Sub-Agency, 1832–1838," *Chronicles of Oklahoma* 42, no. 2 (Summer 1964): 82–83.

7. William Omer Foster, "The Career of Montfort Stokes in Oklahoma," *Chronicles of Oklahoma* 18, no. 1 (March 1940): 36–39; John Bartlett Meserve, "Governor Montfort Stokes," *Chronicles of Oklahoma* 13, no. 3 (September 1935): 339; Grant Foreman, "The Life of Montfort Stokes in the Indian Territory," *North Carolina Historical Review* 16, no. 4 (October 1939): 373; Curtis L. Nolen, "The Okmulgee Constitution: A Step towards Indian Self-Determination," *Chronicles of Oklahoma* 58, no. 3 (Fall 1980): 26; Linda Parker, "Indian Colonization in Northeastern and Central Indian Territory," *Chronicles of Oklahoma* 54, no. 1 (Spring 1976): 106–108; Harris, "Seneca Sub-Agency," 82–83.

8. Treaty with the Seneca and Shawnee, 1832, December 29, 1832, 7 Stat., 411, Proclamation, March 22, 1833, *Indian Affairs*, 2:383–85.

9. Ibid., 2:383–84. See also T. Hartley Crawford to William Wilkins, December 10, 1844, Record Group 75, M234, Roll 642, National Archives and Records Administration, Washington, D.C. (hereafter any document cited from the National Archives, after the document's full title, will be cited by

its microfilm number); Julian B. BlueJacket (Eastern Shawnee), interview by Peggy Dycus, May 14, 1969, Vol. 52, Tape No. T-428-2, 3, Duke Collection.

10. Treaty with the Seneca and Shawnee, December 29, 1832, 7 Stat. 411, Proclamation, March 22, 1833, *Indian Affairs*, 2:383–84; ARCIA, November 30, 1849, 937, S. Doc. No. 1 (1849), 1115. See also T. Hartley Crawford to William Wilkins, December 10, 1844, Record Group 75, M234, Roll 642.

11. Brian Joseph Gilley, *A Longhouse Fragmented: Ohio Iroquois Autonomy in the Nineteenth Century* (Albany: State University of New York Press, 2014), 92. See also ARCIA, November 28, 1833, 168, H. R. Doc. No. 1 (1833), 170.

12. ARCIA, December 1, 1837, 525, S. Doc. No. 1 (1837), 543; Carolyn Thomas Foreman, "The Armstrongs of Indian Territory: Part II William Armstrong," *Chronicles of Oklahoma* 30, no. 4 (1952): 422; Harris, "Seneca Sub-Agency," 88.

13. ARCIA, November 16, 1842, 370, H. R. Doc. No. 2 (1842), 445.

14. Julian BlueJacket interview, T-428-2, 6, Duke Collection.

15. Treaty with the Seneca and Shawnee, 1832, December 29, 1832, 7 Stat. 411, Proclamation, March 22, 1833, *Indian Affairs: Laws and Treaties*, 2:383–84; ARCIA, November 28, 1833, 168, H. Doc. No. 1 (1833), 170; ARCIA, December 1, 1836, 367, H. R. Doc. No. 2 (1836), 378, 388; Minnie Thompson (Seneca), interview by J. W. Tyner, June 24, 1970, Vol. 52, Tape No. T-618-1, 1, Duke Collection; Robert Long (Wyandotte), interview by J. W. Tyner, May 26, 1970, Vol. 54, Tape No. T-589-1, 2, Duke Collection. See also Julian BlueJacket's commentary on "United Nations," Julian BlueJacket interview, T-428-2, 4–5, Duke Collection.

16. Julian BlueJacket interview, T-428-2, 3, Duke Collection.

17. Treaty with the Quapaw, May 13, 1833, 7 Stat. 424, Proclamation, April 12, 1834, *Indian Affairs*, 2:396; ARCIA, November 24, 1835, 260, H. R. Doc. No. 2 (1835), 291, 296; ARCIA, November 25, 1834, 240, H. R. Doc. No. 2 (1834), 271; ARCIA, November 25, 1844, 305, S. Doc. No. 1 (1844), 459; Jerome O. Steffen, "Stokes Commission," *Encyclopedia of Oklahoma History and Culture*, Oklahoma Historical Society, 2009, www.OKHistory.org/publications/enc/entry.php?entry=ST040; W. David Baird, *The Quapaw Indians: A History of the Downstream People*, (Norman: University of Oklahoma Press, 1980), 76–79; Parker, "Indian Colonization," 109; Frank H. Harris, "Neosho Agency, 1838–1871," *Chronicles of Oklahoma*, 43, no. 1 (Spring 1965): 42; Harris, "Seneca Sub-Agency," 89–90.

18. Baird, *Quapaw Indians*, 78–79. See also ARCIA, November 25, 1839, 327, S. Doc. No. 1 (1839), 474.

19. Baird, *Quapaw Indians*, 79.

20. Joseph B. King, "The Ottawa Indians in Kansas and Oklahoma," in *Collections of the Kansas State Historical Society, 1913–1914, Together with Addresses at Annual Meetings, Memorials, and Miscellaneous Papers*, ed. William E. Connelley, (Topeka: Kansas State Printing Plant, W. R. Smith, 1915), 13:377; Gilley, *A Longhouse Fragmented*, 103–105; Arrell Morgan Gibson, "America's Exiles," *Chronicles of Oklahoma*, 54, no. 1 (Spring 1976): 15; Parker, "Indian Colonization," 113; Harris, "Seneca Sub-Agency," 94; ARCIA, November 26, 1862, 169, H. R. Doc. No. 1 (1862), 287; ARCIA, October 31, 1863, 129, H. R. Doc. No. 1 (1863), 143; ARCIA, November 15, 1864, 147, H. R. Doc. No. 1 (1864), 176, 448; ARCIA, October 31, 1865, 169, H. R. Doc. No. 1 (1865), 476, 478. Historical sources spell the Native names with hyphens, but I have chosen to use spellings without hyphens here. Hereafter in this chapter, all Native names use spellings without hyphens.

21. Treaty with the Senecas and Senecas and Shawnees, October 4, 1861, Articles of a Convention, in Charles D. Bernholz et al., eds., *As Long as Grass Shall Grow and Water Run: The Treaties Formed by the Confederate States of America and the Tribes in Indian Territory, 1861*, Center for Digital Research in the Humanities, University of Nebraska, Lincoln, http://CSAIndianTreaties.unl.edu/, accessed February 24, 2016.; Joyce Ann Kievit, "Trail of Tears to Veil of Tears: The Impact of Removal on Reconstruction" (Ph.D. diss., University of Houston, 2002), 102; Kinneth McNeil, "Confederate Treaties with the Tribes of Indian Territory," *Chronicles of Oklahoma*, 42, no. 4 (Winter 1964–65): 415;

Harris, "Neosho Agency," 53; Dean Trickett, "The Civil War in Indian Territory, 1861," *Chronicles of Oklahoma*, 17, no. 4 (December 1939): 402, 410; Harris, "Seneca Sub-Agency," 94; ARCIA, October 31, 1865, 169, H. R. Doc. No. 1 (1865), 482.

22. Treaty with the Senecas and Senecas and Shawnees, October 4, 1861, Articles of a Convention, in Bernholz, *As Long as Grass Shall Grow*, quoting Confederate States of America, *The Statutes at Large of the Provisional Government of the Confederate States of America*, 375–76. The website has a transcription misprint in the order of articles of the treaty. The scanned original has the correct article numbers.

23. Gilley, *A Longhouse Fragmented*, 105–107. See also Dean Banks, "Civil War Refugees from Indian Territory, in the North, 1861–1864," *Chronicles of Oklahoma*, 41, no. 3 (Fall 1963): 297; Harris, "Neosho Agency," 54–55.

24. "The Fort Smith Council of 1865," *Proceedings: War and Reconstruction in Indian Territory: A History Conference in Observance of the 130th Anniversary of the Fort Smith Council, September 14–17, 1995, Fort Smith, Arkansas*, 3–4; Edwin C. Bearss, "The Civil War in Indian Territory and the Fort Smith Council: Transcript of Keynote Address," ibid., 9; Kievit, *Trail of Tears to Veil of Tears*, 130, 136; ARCIA, October 31, 1865, 169, H. R. Doc. No. 1 (1865), 480–86.

25. Daniel F. Littlefield, "The Treaties of 1866: Reconstruction or Re-Destruction?" *Proceedings: War and Reconstruction in Indian Territory: A History Conference in Observance of the 130th Anniversary of the Fort Smith Council, September 14–17, 1995, Fort Smith, Arkansas*, 97, 107.

26. ARCIA, October 31, 1865, 169, H. R. Doc. No. 1 (1865), 487, 497, 518.

27. Baird, *Quapaw Indians*, 79; Blue Clark, "Quapaw," *Indian Tribes of Oklahoma: A Guide* (Norman: University of Oklahoma Press, 2009), 301–12; Muriel H. Wright, "Quapaw," *A Guide to the Indian Tribes of Oklahoma*, (Norman: University of Oklahoma Press, 1986), 218–22; Oklahoma Tourism and Recreation Department, "Quapaw Tribe of Oklahoma," *Oklahoma Indian Country Guide* (Oklahoma City: Oklahoma Tourism and Recreation Department, 2010), 53–54; Rennard Strickland, *The Indians in Oklahoma* (Norman: University of Oklahoma Press, 1980), 4–5; Treaty with the Seneca, Mixed Seneca and Shawnee, Quapaw, etc., 1867, February 23, 1867, 15 Stat. 513, *Indian Affairs*, 2:961–62.

28. In 1880 the Eastern Shawnee reservation consisted of 13,088 acres. ARCIA, November 1, 1880, 83, H. R. Doc. No. 1 (1880), 209.

29. Treaty with the Seneca, Mixed Seneca and Shawnee, Quapaw, etc., 1867, 15 Stat. 513, *Indian Affairs*, 2:963–64; Clarence King (Ottawa), interview by Peggy Dycus, May 16, 1969, Vol. 49, Tape No. T-443-1, 2, Duke Collection; Ottawa Tribe of Oklahoma, *History Archives Library*, www.OttawaTribe .org/history-archives-library/, accessed February 11, 2016.

30. King, "Ottawa Indians in Kansas and Oklahoma," 13:377; Clark, "Ottawa," *Indian Tribes of Oklahoma*, 258–60; Oklahoma Tourism and Recreation Department, "Ottawa Tribe," *Oklahoma Indian Country Guide*, 48–49.

31. ARCIA, October 22, 1866, H. R. Doc. No. 1 (1866), 55–56.

32. Treaty with the Seneca, Mixed Seneca and Shawnee, Quapaw, etc., 1867, February 23, 1867, 15 Stat. 513, *Indian Affairs*, 2:961. See also Gilley, *A Longhouse Fragmented*, 92–93, 107; ARCIA, December 23, 1869, 443, H. R. Doc. No. 1 (1869), 476.

33. ARCIA, November 15, 1867, 541, H. R. Doc. No. 1 (1867), 22.

34. ARCIA, November 23, 1868, 461, H. R. Doc. No. 1 (1868), 733; ARCIA, November 1, 1872, 389, H. R. Doc. No. 1 (1872), 425.

35. Julian BlueJacket interview, T-428-2, 1–3, Duke Collection; Roberta White Smith and Ruby White Sequichie, *A Brief History of the Seneca-Cayuga Tribe* (Wyandotte, Oklahoma: Gregath Publishing for the Seneca-Cayuga Tribe, 2000), 122–23.

36. Tom Captain (Eastern Shawnee), interview by J. W. Tyner, September 16, 1969, Vol. 52, Tape No. T-535-2, 1, Duke Collection; See also J. W. Tyner's summary of the Modoc exile.

37. Lela Barnes, ed., "An Editor Looks at Early-Day Kansas: The Letters of Charles Monroe Chase, the Letters of 1873," in *Kansas Quarterly* 26, no. 3 (Autumn 1960): 288–91.

38. Odie B. Faulk, *The Modoc People* (Phoenix: Indian Tribal Series, 1976), 83; Clark, "Modoc," *Indian Tribes of Oklahoma*, 203–208; Wright, "Modoc," *A Guide to the Indian Tribes of Oklahoma*, 184–86; Oklahoma Tourism and Recreation Department, "Modoc," *Oklahoma Indian Country Guide*, 44; Strickland, *Indians of Oklahoma*, 5; Modoc Tribe of Oklahoma, "Tribal History and Photos," *The Modoc Tribe of Oklahoma*, 2014, www.ModocTribe.net/history.html; Parker, "Indian Colonization," 113–16.

39. Faulk, *Modoc People*, 83, 86, "Settlement, etc., of Modoc Indians," 18 Stat. 447, *Indian Affairs*, 1:157–58; Julian BlueJacket interview, T-428-2, 4, Duke Collection; Julian BlueJacket interview, T-545-1, 4–5, Duke Collection; ARCIA, November 1, 1873, 369, H. R. Doc. No. 1 (1873), 450; ARCIA, November 1, 1874, 311, H. R. Doc. No. 1 (1974), 330, 391; ARCIA, November 1, 1878, 439, H. R. Doc. No. 1 (1878), 466.

40. Tom Captain interview, T-428-1, 3–4, Duke Collection. See also Lucille J. Martin, "A History of the Modoc Indians: An Acculturation Study," *Chronicles of Oklahoma*, 47, no. 4 (Winter 1969–70): 422–28.

41. Interviewer commentary explains that "Indian Territory maps as late as the 1900 showed those separate Indian reservations" in northeastern Oklahoma. Robert Whitebird (Quapaw), interview by J. W. Tyner, December 23, 1969, Vol. 51, Tape No. T-546-3, 1, Duke Collection.

42. Nolen, "Okmulgee Constitution," 264.

43. "Okmulgee Constitution (Several Indian Nations in Indian Territory, 1870)," in *Documents of Native American Political Development: 1500s to 1933*, ed. David E. Wilkins (New York: Oxford University Press, 2009), 134; La Vere, *Contrary Neighbors*, 187; *Journal of the General Council of the Indian Territory [1870] . . .* (1871; Reprint, Wilmington, Del.: Scholarly Resources, 1975), 3–4; Nolen, "Okmulgee Constitution," 267–71.

44. "Okmulgee Constitution," in *Documents of Native American Political Development*, 135.

45. Ibid., 135–36.

46. Ibid., 139; Nolen, "Okmulgee Constitution," 271–73.

47. *Journal of the General Council of the Indian Territory [1870] . . .* , 3, 8, 11. Lazarus Flint, the Eastern Shawnee delegate, was not present at the December 6, 1870, assembly but attended December 12 (ibid., 15–16, 24–25). There was no Eastern Shawnee representative at the third session of the general council, but Flint was present the next year. *Journal of the Third Annual Session of the General Council of the Indian Territory [1872] . . .* , in *Journal of the General Council of the Indian Territory, 1871–75* (Topeka, Kansas State Historical Society, 1959), 3, University of Oklahoma Microfilm Serial 160; *Journal of the Fourth Annual Session of the General Council of the Indian Territory [1873] . . .* , in *Journal of the General Council of the Indian Territory, 1871–75*, 3, 6; *Journal of the Fifth Annual Session of the General Council of the Indian Territory [1874] . . .* , in *Journal of the General Council of the Indian Territory, 1871–75*, 3, 7.

48. *Journal of the General Council of the Indian Territory [1870] . . .* , 23–24.

49. Ibid., 25, 37.

50. Nolen, "The Okmulgee Constitution," 274; Ohland Morton, "Reconstruction in the Creek Nation," *Chronicles of Oklahoma* 9, no. 2 (June 1931): 175. The Eastern Shawnee representatives in 1871 included David Dushane as interpreter and William McDaniel as delegate. *Journal of the Second Annual Session of the General Council of the Indian Territory [1871] . . .* , in *Journal of the General Council of the Indian Territory, 1871–75*, 3–4, 6–7. In the general council minutes, the Eastern Shawnee interpreter's last name is spelled Duchine but should be adjusted to the modern spelling, Dushane.

51. *Journal of the Second Annual Session of the General Council of the Indian Territory [1871]*, 7, 10–14; *Journal of the Fourth Annual Session of the General Council of the Indian Territory [1873] . . .* , 7, 10–11, 15–17.

52. La Vere, *Contrary Neighbors*, 189–91; Nolen, "The Okmulgee Constitution," 275. See also Muriel H. Wright, "A Report to the General Council of the Indian Territory Meeting at Okmulgee in 1873," *Chronicles of Oklahoma* 34, no. 1 (Spring 1956): 7–8, 13.

53. *Journal of the Sixth Annual Session of the General Council of the Indian Territory [1875] . . .* , in *Journal of the General Council of the Indian Territory, 1871–75*, 3–4, 10, 81.

54. *Journal of the Fifth Annual Session of the General Council of the Indian Territory [1874] . . .* , 14–15.

55. *Journal of the Sixth Annual Session of the General Council of the Indian Territory [1875] . . .* , 21. See also La Vere, *Contrary Neighbors*, 201.

56. Tom Captain interview, T-428-1, 6.

57. Ibid., 7–8.

58. Donna Elliot Vowel (Wyandotte), interview by J. W. Tyner, July 20, 1970, Vol. 54, Tape No. T-618-4, 3, Duke Collection. For another commentary on nearby border towns, see May Snell Butler (Cherokee), interview by J. T. Tyner, July 6, 1970, Vol. 11, Tape No. T-618-2, 1, ibid.

59. Rona Kissee (Eastern Shawnee), interview by Peggy Dycus, May 15, 1969, Vol. 52, Tape No. T-428-3, 2, ibid.

60. Clyde L. BlueJacket (Eastern Shawnee), interview by Velma Nieberding, May 15, 1970, Vol. 52, Tape No. T-654-1, 5–6, Duke Collection; Julian BlueJacket interview, T-545-1, 6, Duke Collection.

61. Robert Long interview, T-589-1, 13, Duke Collection. See also Janie Blalock Logan (Shawnee), interview by Velma Nieberding, January 5, 1970, Vol. 52, Tape No. T-619-4, 1, Duke Collection; Tom Captain interview, T-535-2, 2, Duke Collection.

62. Clyde L. BlueJacket, interview, T-654-1, 5–6, Duke Collection.

63. Julian BlueJacket interview, T-545-1, 9–10, Duke Collection.

64. Bill Connor (Quapaw), interview by Velma Nieberding, December 15, 1969, Vol. 51, Tape No. T-621-2, 3–4, Duke Collection.

65. Janie Blalock Logan interview, T-619-4, 2, 5, Duke Collection.

66. Clarence King interview, T-443-1, 8, Duke Collection.

67. Kenneth Oyler (Cayuga), interview by J. W. Tyner, April 13, 1970, Vol. 10, Tape No. T-572-3, 4, Duke Collection.

68. Sarah Longbone (Eastern Shawnee), interview by Nannie Lee Burns, July 27, 1937, Indian-Pioneer Interview No. 6962, 4 [197], Indian-Pioneer Papers Oral History Collection, Western History Collections, University of Oklahoma, Norman.

5

Shawnee Resilience

Eastern Shawnees and the Boarding School Experience

ROBIN DUSHANE WITH SARAH MOHAWK DUSHANE
LONGBONE AND ROBERT "BOBBY" BLUEJACKET

Learning about different kinds of schools, especially schools my husband's family attended, is a particular interest of mine. My husband's father, Howard Spear Dushane, attended boarding schools and went on to become superintendent of various schools and reservations in the West for the Department of Interior's Office of Indian Affairs, which was known as the Indian service. His grandfather, Charles Dushane Sr., was also a boarding school graduate, who went on to become an educator employed by the Indian service. Consequently, both men acquired collections of photographs and family stories, particularly in regard to education. Their family records and keepsakes inspired me to learn more and to share the rich history of the Eastern Shawnee people. I have learned that mobility and resilience are enduring characteristics of the Shawnee people. My husband's family, from their commitment to education to their working lives, epitomize these traits.

My husband's great-great-grandmother Kenefease Jackson lived to be well over one hundred years old. The Methodist missionary Joab Spencer interviewed her in 1896, when she recalled "crossing the Mississippi, the life at Cape Girardeau, the abandonment of that country, the migration to the Delawares on the James Fork of White River, and the journey to the Kansas River."[1] Like the stories of many Eastern Shawnees, hers is one of constant movement, even before she first migrated to the Shawnee reservation in northern Indian Territory, which would soon become Kansas Territory (in 1854). In 1861 Kansas became a state, and in 1862 the Homestead Act was passed, opening millions of acres to white settlement.[2] After the Civil War, Kenefease Jackson moved yet again when the Shawnees were removed to Oklahoma. Some, such as Jackson, settled among the group that was in what would become Ottawa County. She then became an Eastern Shawnee. Others were removed to Cherokee lands in Indian Territory, and they became known as the Loyal Shawnees (presently the Shawnee Tribe of Oklahoma). Kenefease and her husband, John Jackson, were the progenitors of several families in the Eastern Shawnee community.

Kenefease Jackson lived in Missouri at a time when various churches were just beginning to establish missions among her people. North of the land grant, in the region known as the Ozark highlands of Missouri, was a Shawnee village at the mouth of the Bourbeuse River. The village was named Rogerstown after Chief Louis Rogers.[3] Years earlier in Ohio, Rogers had been adopted by Chief Blackfish. After migrating to Missouri, Rogers established a school in this village in 1817. John Peck, a Baptist preacher, assisted in the development of this school, which enrolled both Indian and non-Indian children. Rogers and other Shawnees financed the school and provided a house for the teacher as well. Sadly, Indian education at this school was short-lived. Between 1818 and 1821, as Missourians prepared for statehood, residents of Rogerstown were displaced by land-hungry settlers. As a result, Shawnees who occupied lands in and near the Spanish Land Grant, people such as Kenefease Jackson, moved to lands in northern Indian Territory along the Kansas or Kaw River.[4]

A decade later, in the fall of 1832, another contingent of Shawnees, the Mixed Band of Shawnees and Senecas, also known as the Lewistown Band, arrived in Indian Territory. As a result of the Indian Removal Act, 258 Shawnees and Senecas departed from the Lewistown reserve in Logan County, Ohio, in September 1832. After three months of travel, 220 members of the Mixed Band arrived during the final days of December in the area known today as Ottawa County, Oklahoma.[5]

In the same year, Shawnees from the Wapakoneta reserve of Ohio arrived in northern Indian Territory near the Kaw River (or Kansas River), about two hundred miles to the north of the Ottawa County site. Surnames listed on the muster roll from the Wapakoneta reserve removal are some of the same names on the rolls of the Eastern Shawnee tribe. These current family names include Bluejacket, Daugherty, and Dushane, as well as family names from the Eastern Shawnee rolls of the 1870s, such as Blackhoof, Cornstalk, and Wolf.[6] Movement of the Shawnees, intermarriage, and shared religious practices between the various Shawnee bands were all commonplace both before and after removal.

In the 1830s, while the ink was still wet on President Jackson's signature on the Indian Removal Act, missionaries, particularly in northern Indian Territory, began to establish schools among the Shawnees.[7] Missionaries had far-reaching objectives, beyond simply educating American Indians. In 1836 Baptist missionary Isaac McCoy believed, "The whole country inhabited by the Indians is, or has been, ours. It has or can become theirs only as we have made, or may make it so. We control both their person and their property." McCoy believed that the Shawnees could not govern their own affairs. He wrote, "We decide what they may sell, and what they may not, and who shall be the purchasers." Like all Jacksonians, McCoy denied that American Indians were citizens of sovereign nations. He believed, "We have always enacted laws for the regulation of Indian affairs, and have repealed them at pleasure. We have created agencies among them to attend to the execution of our laws and we have abolished them when we deemed it expedient to do so."[8] The United States, then, had absolute power over the Shawnee people.

Another Baptist missionary, Jonathan Meeker, engaged two Shawnee men as assistants to translate his writings for a small newspaper called the *Siwanwi Kesibwi/Shawnee Sun*. Initially published in 1836, it was the first Indian newspaper printed entirely in the Shawnee language. Shawnee-speaker George Blanchard, grandson of Eastern Shawnee allottee Mary Quick, has translated the only existing issue of this newspaper, dated 1841.[9] His translation reveals that Biblical teachings, drawn particularly from Proverbs and Genesis, were the exclusive content of this newspaper.[10] Perhaps this resource hastened literacy for Shawnees during that era, especially if it was used as a resource at mission schools, but it does point to a close relationship between education and Christian missionary efforts in the colonization process.

In 1836 McCoy wrote, "Between one and two hundred of the Shawnanoes, Delawares and Potawatomies have become capable of reading, and some of them can write." Interestingly, McCoy described how literate Shawnees had begun teaching their kinsmen. Armed with literacy, "many of the Shawnees, have thus learned to read from their associates, without the knowledge of the missionaries." McCoy seemed surprised by the fact that many preferred to learn without the pressure to convert to Christianity.[11] But the Biblical teachings presented in the *Shawnee Sun* conflicted with religious observances of the Shawnee people. For example, the Shawnees believed in multiple powerful deities rather than one "Great Spirit."[12] Thus it is not surprising that Shawnees were more receptive to literacy when Christian teachings were not involved.

Even so, many Eastern Shawnee surnames appear in the records of the Methodist Mission in Kansas. These names include Black Hoof, BlueJacket, Daugherty, Kyser, Prophet, Tooley, and Tucker. Quaker and Methodist Mission Schools in northern Indian Territory existed alongside the Baptist Mission School. Several buildings of the Methodist Mission School, which was the largest of the three mission schools, still exist today within a historic district of Kansas City, Kansas. Each of these schools received government assistance through the Civilization Fund. Set aside by Congress, this fund provided missionaries money to educate Indian people. The main objective of this education was to break children's ties to Indian culture.[13]

In contrast to northern Indian Territory, where mission schools proliferated, to the south, in what is now Ottawa County, Oklahoma, federal officials struggled to establish schools among the Mixed Band of Shawnees and Senecas. In the 1842 annual report of the commissioner of Indian affairs, the Indian agent states, "The Mixed Band of Senecas and Shawnees have an absence of schools among them." In the 1848 report he explained, "The Mixed Band refused to let teachers come among them." In 1851 the stalemate continued; the Indian agent again reported that the Mixed Band had an absence of missionaries and schools among them and that many opposed education for their children.[14] For nearly a decade the Shawnees in southern Indian Territory resisted missionaries. By keeping the reservation of the Mixed Band free from missionaries, the community was able to safeguard their culture, and in this way they maintained Shawnee language and lifeways. Nina Dushane (b. 1897), the daughter of Charles Dushane Sr. and Ethel Helena Chandler (non-Indian), shared with her family, "I didn't speak Shawnee, but as a young child sometimes my mother would take me to meet with my grandmother [Nancy Dushane, b. 1845] out in the woods where we would play. Even though we were unable to talk with one another, we still enjoyed being together."[15]

These are remarkable efforts of resistance and resilience. In an 1852 report the agent observed, "They adhere to many of the ancient customs and partake of as few of the habits and manners of the white people as possible." In 1880 the Indian agent reported, "The Eastern Shawnees, that while orderly and generally temperate, punctual and honest, many nevertheless cling fast to the old ways. They have their dance to drive away sickness and the Buffalo Dance, at both of which the men and women dance in a circle around the fire and sing." Additionally, the agent's 1890 report states, "Their favorite custom is the Stomp Dance."[16]

In spite of their resistance to education, many among the southern Indian Territory Shawnees were proficient bilingual speakers. This is evidenced in the series of ethnographic interviews conducted by Albert Gatschet in 1884. Among those who provided Shawnee translations or served as professional translators for Gatschet were Thomas Stand, Tom Captain, Lazarus Flint, Lot Whiteday, David C. Dushane, William Prophet, and William Tooley, two of whom (Stand and Captain) were Eastern Shawnee chiefs.[17]

It is significant that Shawnees living in northern Indian Territory had schools available to them nearly forty years before schools were established for Shawnees living in Ottawa County, Indian Territory. However, when the United States' federal program of Indian education, commonly referred to as the boarding school era, began after the Civil War, all Shawnees were affected. Children were often sent great distances for long periods of time to attend boarding schools across the United States. Shawnee children were sent to all of the more famous schools, such as Carlisle, Chilocco, and Haskell, as well as to local boarding schools, including the Seneca, Wyandotte, and Eastern Shawnee Mission Boarding School (referred to as the Seneca Indian School or SIS). In the agent's report of 1872 it was noted that the Quakers had established this school, although few Shawnees or Senecas were enrolled initially.[18]

Carlisle Indian Industrial School

Carlisle Indian Industrial School was founded in 1879 by a retired Civil War captain named Richard Pratt, who coined the phrase, "Kill the Indian and save the man." This school was established in the remnants of an old Pennsylvania Cavalry barracks from the Civil War era, and it became the model for Indian boarding schools throughout the country. Pratt's intention was to separate children from their families and communities during the critical developmental years of childhood in order to transform the Indian into the white man's image. His mode of operation included the use of bells, whistles, bugles, military-style punishment, and a daily regimen. It remained an institution of learning for forty years, and approximately ten thousand Indian children were sent there. It closed in 1918 with the onset of an influenza epidemic.[19]

Rosa Skakah and Anna Skakah (Eastern Shawnees, daughters of Susan Tomahawk) attended Carlisle. Rosa was nineteen years old and her sister was one year younger when they both left Ottawa County, Oklahoma, in 1916 to study there. Rosa's descendants, including Dorma Hollis, Robert Kissee, Chris Samples, and Wanda Stovall, have all served as members of the Business Committee, the governing body of the Eastern Shawnee Tribe.[20] Nancy "Nan" Prophet, sister of John Prophet, also attended Carlisle. Nan was born in 1897 to Mariah Dushane and William Prophet. She introduced classmate Ellen Thomas to her brother John, and the two married and have many descendants in the Eastern Shawnee Tribe.[21]

Chilocco Indian Agricultural School

Still more Eastern Shawnee children attended Chilocco Indian Agricultural School. In 1882 the United States Congress passed the Indian Appropriation Act, which entailed a sum of money for the building of a school for Indian youth, adequate to care for 150 children. Located in northeastern Indian Territory, this school was built near the present-day Oklahoma-Kansas state line. It began with one building located on a desolate prairie. In 1894 six boys and six girls graduated. In 1925 the school began offering a high school curriculum. Then, in 1932, Chilocco began a vocational program. By this time school enrollment totaled nine hundred Indian students who lived in six dormitories—tremendous growth in five decades. It is likely the growth was due, in part, to the addition of secondary education to the curriculum.

With the addition of a high school curriculum, many Shawnees who attended Chilocco did so after having spent time at other boarding schools. For example, Dennis James, of the Tooley family, began his education at the age of four at the Seneca Indian School. He graduated high school at Chilocco in 1956 and went directly into the United States Marine Corps. During his professional career as a health care specialist, he served in Indian Health Services for twenty years.[22] John Peacock, of the BlueJacket family, graduated high school at Chilocco in 1969. After serving as a United States Marine, he began his career in the Indian service and retired after thirty years.[23]

Another tribal member who served in the armed forces was Jim Greenfeather Jr., who conveyed the following information:

> I knew what it was like at Seneca Indian School because I went there during sixth and seventh grades. When my mom passed away in 1954, I quit school. Then they tried to put me in white-man schools and I rebelled. During the 1950s I went to Chilocco, but I ran away from there twice before I finally stayed and graduated in 1961. While I was there I was in the National Guard and played football and baseball. I took academic classes and studied carpentry. When I left Chilocco, I went directly into the army, where I was a paratrooper.
>
> I went back and worked at Seneca Indian School during the late 1970s. First I worked in the dormitory, and then in the kitchen. This was right before all the students transferred out and the school closed.[24]

Haskell Institute

Students from the Eastern Shawnee Tribe also attended the Haskell Institute, located in Lawrence, Kansas. John Prophet, who was raised by his grandmother Kenefease Jackson, was the

5.1. John Peacock (b. 1951) graduated from Chilocco High School and entered the marine corps in 1970. John also served in the army and national guard for a total of twenty-one years in the armed services. His professional career included thirty years in the Indian service. Photo courtesy of John Peacock.

first Eastern Shawnee to attend Haskell during the 1880s.[25] It opened in 1884 with just three buildings. Admitted students were compelled to stay for a minimum of four years, which is a long time for children to be away from their homes. Some students appealed to the Indian agent back home for permission to return and visit their families. Their cases had to be strong, because boarding school officials at Haskell required the preapproval of an Indian agent or local reservation superintendent before children were given permission to go home.[26] Homesickness was endemic at this school, and for the very young it most likely was the hardest part of attending. In 1927 Lucinda, Ira, and Earl Peacock learned this the hard way. They were not allowed to return home for the summer after they had made a written request to go home.[27]

During a discussion I had with Glenn Stoner, he shared that his mother, Lucy Bluejacket, never liked Haskell. She told her children that she "walked in the front door at Haskell and walked straight out the back door to catch a ride back home."[28] In a letter to the agent of the Eastern Shawnees, she wrote, "Dear Agent Suffercoal, Just to inform you that I want to come home on June 5, 1927. That is, if I don't have to stay here for summer school. I have written my parents telling them to send my transportation monies for both ways. Please let me know. I remain, Lucy Bluejacket."[29]

Other children ran away from the boarding school. Shirley Alexander (granddaughter of Annie Jackson Daugherty) shared this story with me: "My father, Buck Deweese, went to school at Haskell. He always told us he didn't have enough to eat there, but the student athletes always ate well. He also said that he often had to work long hours in the gardens, and one rainy day he woke up [and] ran away from school. He managed to make it all the way home by walking and catching rides. He told us that he started feeling so good once he got to the area around Joplin. After leaving Haskell, he never returned to school."[30]

Some children died during their stays at the boarding schools, and a small cemetery housing the graves of 122 students is located on the southeastern side of Haskell's main campus. The name of each student and his or her tribal affiliation has been compiled. George Evans and Jonah Moharty, both from other Shawnee communities, are buried there.[31] While some children died in boarding schools, other children experienced the deaths of family members who passed away while they were away at school. Nina Dushane attended Haskell, and her daughter Lora Ethel shared her mother's memories with me. Nina remembered, "My sister Jessie and I were both at Haskell when our three year old sister, Lula Mae, died. I had been at Haskell and never got to see my little sister. Jessie had only been up there about a year when Lula Mae died."[32]

In spite of these losses and hardships, a number of Shawnee students drew upon their education and contributed to Native communities as educators and in the government, demonstrating the resiliency of the people. Howard Spear Dushane (father of Laurence "Larry" Dushane, my husband) graduated from Haskell in the 1940s. During World War II he served in the Asian-Pacific theatre. Following his service in the U.S. military he began a long career in Indian service (the Bureau of Indian Affairs).[33] Dorma Hollis (daughter of Rosa Skakah and granddaughter of Susan Tomahawk) graduated from Haskell in the spring of 1943. She served on the Eastern Shawnee Business Committee as one of the first women on the committee. Her professional career included serving as the head clerk to the superintendent of the Seneca Indian School.[34]

In the agency files of the Eastern Shawnee Tribe there were many letters that revealed interesting information about tribal members' school experiences, demonstrating a wide range of Shawnee responses to boarding schools. There was a letter from the Haskell superintendent regarding a railroad ticket being arranged for Thomas Hampton to arrive at Haskell. Another letter concerned Edna Holden, who reenrolled at the age of eighteen to complete the commercial course at the school. Then there was a letter from the Haskell authorities, asking the agent in Wyandotte if a certain student could attend a different school because this student was a constant source of trouble. A letter from Haskell Institute dated 1927 explained that Leo Captain, age twelve, was accepted for a term of four years. Additionally, it stated that since he was under fourteen years of age, he would be expected to come to Haskell at the expense of his family.[35]

Haskell continues to be an important school for Indian people. It is currently known as Haskell Indian Nations University and is located in Lawrence, Kansas, just west of the Wakarusa River in Douglas County, Kansas.

Seneca Indian School

In 1872 Quakers established the Seneca Indian School (SIS), but the school got off to a shaky start. By 1874 the Wyandotte Tribe formed a committee to inspect the school. They reported the following deficiencies:

The teacher, through negligence or want of discipline is not advancing his scholars in their studies and that he suffers them to idleness in and about the school rooms and premises during school hours. It is for this reason that some of our neighbors among the Shawnees and Senecas refuse to send their children to school any longer. The matron pays no regard to teaching the children habits of cleanliness or decency. The beds and the clothing and bodies of the children are infested with vermin the greater part of the time and the appearances in and about the premises are deplorable. Boys wear red duck pants put together with rivets, hickory shirts of blue and white, brogan shoes, common black hats and no

5.2. Charles Dushane Sr. with daughter Nina Dushane (1897–1988). Nina attended Haskell Industrial School in Lawrence, Kansas. Her Eastern Shawnee land allotment is the current location of the Eastern Shawnee Tribal Headquarters, located in Oklahoma, just west of downtown Seneca, Missouri. Photo courtesy of the Dushane family.

socks nor underwear. The girls wear matching blue denim dresses with coarse canton flannel underwear and heavy shoes and the little girls have copper toes on their shoes.[36]

The 1882 annual report of the agent states that spring classes were not conducted that year due to an outbreak of measles, which claimed the lives of three children.

The SIS did eventually become more established, and graduates began to seek secondary education. In the 1886 annual report, the agent notes that fourteen graduates in the class of 1885 went on to study further at Indian schools in other states. Eight were selected to attend Carlisle, five were enrolled at Haskell Institute, and one was enrolled elsewhere.[37]

Charles Dushane Sr. (grandson of Kenefease and John Jackson) attended Seneca Indian School as a child and later graduated from Seneca High School in 1896. Family stories include that he made box traps to catch quail and rabbits to feed his family before he went to Stillwater, Oklahoma, to attend teacher-training school. His first teaching certificate, dated 1908 and signed by the superintendent of schools in Indian Territory, was issued from Cherokee Nation, Oklahoma. He began teaching school just down the road from his own allotment, at Brushy Hollow School, where his students were Eastern Shawnee children as well as non-Indians. In 1911 he began working for the Department of the Interior's Office of Indian Affairs, which sent him to teach at the Kickapoo Agency in Kansas for a year, at the Sac and Fox Day School, where he earned sixty dollars per month. He had several teaching posts throughout the years, and most were at day schools, with the exception of Riverside Indian School in Anadarko, Oklahoma. Though not a veteran himself, Charles was the son of Civil War veteran David C. Dushane, and he fathered three generations of U.S. veterans as well.[38]

By 1910 the agent's report stated that there were 132 students enrolled at the Seneca Indian School. Seventy of these students had lost their father or mother and were essentially homeless. In spite of the school's close proximity to the community, students were unable to return home very often. The removal of Native children from their families and communities was critical to the boarding-school philosophy—to erase the influence of Native culture during the

5.3. Charles Dushane Sr. (1873–1945) attended Seneca Indian School and graduated from Seneca High School in 1896. He studied education in Stillwater, Oklahoma, and received his first teaching certificate in 1908. Charles worked as an educator in the Indian service from 1911 through 1928. He was the father of Nina, Jessie, Everett, Nadine, Lula May, Howard, and Charles Jr. Dushane. Photo courtesy of the Dushane family.

assimilation process. The children and grandchildren of Carrie BlueJacket (daughter of Lucinda Dick) attended the SIS, which was less than three miles away from her home; her allotment was across Spring River from the school. She put her children, and later her grandchildren, on the bus in September, and they didn't return home until May.[39]

As was common among boarding schools across the country, the daily routine was a mix of academics and physical labor. Children participated in academic studies for five hours each day. Thereafter, boys labored in the gardens and fields while the girls worked at laundering, cooking, and sewing for an additional four hours per day.[40] Betty Drake James McIntosh submitted her memories of the routine:

At Wyandotte [Seneca Indian School] the fall brought autumn changes. Sadly, some of the children were unable to go home for Thanksgiving Day. We would stay at the school dormitory and continue with our daily regimen. Our matron, Mrs. Garrison, woke us up before sunrise to prepare for the day. We would dress in our uniform, which was a blue dress, "bloomers," and big black shoes. Before going down we would have to clean our rooms, sweep and mop the hallways and bathrooms.

Although we had several jobs, my job was to work in the kitchen; being seven years old, sometimes it was very hard. One Thanksgiving we had to prepare a lot of food for the remaining staff and the children who were not able to leave for the holidays. As we were preparing and cleaning, men brought in big silver vats filled to the brim with fresh turkeys, turkeys that had to be cleaned and plucked before time to start cooking them. Tedious work that never seemed to end, turkey after turkey, over and over until they were all finished!

After that, big vats of fresh milk came in that had to be hauled to the freezer by myself and the other children, which was quite a feat for seven-year-olds. The work was grueling at times; just do the work and go to class afterwards. Since this was a holiday, class was not in session, but there was still work. When we had to haul those big vats of milk into the freezer, we would carry out a small retaliation for working so hard by scooping all the cream off and drinking as much as we wanted. It sure was good, as most of our daily meals consisted of beans and gravy, so this was quite a treat![41]

In a personal interview, tribal elder Robert "Bobby" BlueJacket shared, "I went to the Mission School in 1935 through 1936, and then for another year in 1944. On the first day, when they opened the school bus doors, they motioned for us to go the washtub where you bent over while they poured kerosene on your head. This was our welcome to Indian school."[42]

Norma Kraus (Jessie Millhollin's daughter) shared, "I know my mother missed her family very much while she was at boarding school. She wasn't allowed to come home during the holidays, and she constantly yearned to be with them, although the school provided a warm, dry place to live with regular meals."[43]

Janet Hansen shared this writing by her mother, Doris James McIntosh (who was granddaughter of William Tooley and Mattie Williams):

Mornings were hectic at Seneca Indian School. Many chores had to be completed before we were allowed to go to school. Cleaning, sweeping, and mopping before school—then to class, then after class—more work in the kitchen. One of the matrons did not treat us very good. We all had different jobs to do in addition to group assignments. Being nine years old, working in the kitchen was my last job. Lots to do there, washing all the dishes, in addition to the huge cooking pots. I would take my thumbnail and scrape off the burned on food from the sides of the pots as I was washing them. After all the dishes were washed, we began to prepare food for the next day. Cleaning and sorting beans was often done by the younger girls in the kitchen. Food had to be cleaned, chickens needed [to be] plucked and seared to have the remaining feathers removed before cooking them. If you did not do your job right or talked too much, being slapped on the hands with a big wooden spoon was not uncommon. The older kids were mean to the younger kids, pushing and shoving them, trying to get them to do their chores. They would also steal their money if they had any. Sometimes if you did not give in to them, you would have to fight back or run away to get them to leave you alone, as they would pull your hair or scratch you.

My sister and I saw each other from time to time, but we had a little brother who we rarely saw, and we worried about him, knowing how the older kids treated us. When we did get to go home for a rare visit, he was always sick or hurt before we got there. He would get better and have to go back. We stayed there for about three years.

Sometimes if we were given any money, we might get to go to town. Candy was a special treat. If I could, I would buy a cherry mash or necca candy wafers [sic]. You would have to hide them or the other kids would try to get them from you. You had to be extra good to get to go to the movie and have popcorn and soda.

One day, when the old school was still standing, my daughters and I returned and walked through the old dorm. Memories both good and bad flooded my mind as I looked in the mirror. I told my daughters, whatever you have to do in life—do the best you can do.[44]

During the later years of SIS's operation, the school became more open to cultural influences from tribal members. Ozina Dixon, an Eastern Shawnee tribal citizen, participated in an important program at the SIS to encourage community engagement. In what was referred to as the Grandmother and Grandfather Program, students visited with members of the community to build a personal connection with an elder. These elders came to the school dorms to stay overnight with the children.[45]

Once, during the 1960s, Senator Robert Kennedy toured the SIS. Eastern Shawnee tribal member Dorma Kissee Hollis was the boarding school superintendent's assistant at that time. She told me once that she was so busy that day with managing the various details surrounding the event that she didn't even get to shake his hand.[46]

During the long history of Western education for Native peoples, students had a variety of complex responses to the harsh situation. In spite of the difficulties, many went on to contribute to their communities. Some, such as my husband's family, entered the Indian service as educators. Others worked on the tribe's Business Committee, such as Dorma Hollis, Robert Kissee, Chris Samples, and Wanda Stovall. In spite of the hardships they endured, their story is one of resilience, holding on to their unique Shawnee identity in spite of extreme efforts to erase their sense of themselves as Native people. It is my hope that this chapter provides historical context for discussions that families will have concerning their relatives who attended mission and boarding schools and how their experiences affected families and the Eastern Shawnee Tribe as a whole. There are many more stories to be told, and the experiences that children had at boarding schools continue to impact Indian families. We have limited ways of knowing how those who attended boarding schools felt and reacted to the mission and boarding school experience. None of the first generation of students who attended are alive to share their stories—only paper trails left by the schools and Indian agents remain. The following two sections provide insight into the lives of Eastern Shawnees who attended boarding schools through oral histories they've left for future generations.

SARAH MOHAWK DUSHANE LONGBONE (1887–1968)

Early Life

My mother died when I was eight months old and my grandparents reared me. I always lived there at their home. I was the youngest of three children. One incident of my early life in Kansas stands out clearly. One day grandfather came home dragging an animal and asked us children what it was. We looked at it. It had hoofs and ears like a mule, we thought he had killed a young mule, but it was a deer, the first one I ever remember seeing.

I went to school there before we came to the Indian Territory.

Removal to the Indian Territory

I was about twelve years old when we came to the Indian Territory. We came in wagons driven by horses. We never owned any oxen. We settled about ten miles south of Wyandotte on the now–Jim Logan place, and our first home was a crude log building with plaster between the logs. The first years were hard. My grandfather cut and sold wood for sixty cents per rick. I do not mean he received that much. The money was divided three ways, between the man who cut the trees, the man who sawed them, and the man who hauled it to Wyandotte and Seneca, Missouri.

The poor horses got nothing and had to live on sticks and leaves through the winter and grass in the summer.

The Eastern Shawnees are very particular about their clothes. They never wore each other's clothes and were also careful to take baths. They would buy yards of cloth. It was not cut up and sewed into a dress in those days. They wrapped and draped it around themselves. When wash day came, they would go the creek, and seat themselves in the water, and take off and wash the suit they had on. Wash it clean on the hands, and if they had only the one suit, would wear it until it was dry. They usually had an extra suit and both suits would be washed. Grandmother used to say to me, "You won't do that way, you'll learn to do the white man's way."

Grandmother often used to tell me, "Someday the Indian language will fade away, be no more Indians. We have full bloods and half bloods now, some day they be one-eight, one-thirty-second, one-sixty-fourth, black eyes and hair be gone, all be white. There will be no more horses, some day you fly in the air like birds. Old Indian be gone." I was taught to speak the Seneca, Wyandotte, and Shawnee languages, and was interpreter for the Shawnees between the Senecas and Wyandottes.

School Days

After we came here, grandmother took me to the Wyandotte Mission and placed me there. We learned to scrub, had to get on our hands and knees and scrub with a brush. They didn't give us much to eat either. Sundays we had breakfast, no dinner, and for supper two pieces of light bread with or without molasses. We wore blue hickory, I should call them shirting dresses. Danny Cochran was the superintendent.

Grandmother came to see me and she saw a louse in my hair. She got a bottle and went through my hair and nearly filled it with them. Then she took the bottle and went to the superintendent and told him, handing him the bottle, that he could have them, she didn't want them, but that she was taking her granddaughter home. She was mad.

Then I was sent to Lawrence, Kansas, to school. This was in 1900, and I stayed there for nine years, or until 1909. Here we had good schools and, with my other studies, I had domestic art, domestic science and the laundry course. I applied for the position of matron in this Indian School (SIS) and had several letters, but my daughter who has since died, became sick so I could not go.

Marriage

I try to tell my daughters how we were raised, and how we were taught. Those were horse and buggy days, and when I had company and went in a buggy, grandmother usually went with me; or if she could not go, someone else went. She reared us right.

I was twenty-one when I returned home from school, and shortly afterwards Mrs. Dushane, my husband's mother, came to my grandmother and asked for me for her son. Dan and I had gone to school together in Kansas and had always played together, and I had always known him, but I had never thought of marrying him. They arranged the marriage, and his grandmother talked to me and told me that I was now a woman and should have a home of my own, that Dan was a good man and they wanted me for a daughter.

We were married the old Indian way. They dressed me up in red dress with blue ribbons, big bow in my hair on top of my head. My hair was plaited into two braids and one brought over each shoulder, had beaded moccasins. I painted my face, not like they do now. I had two red marks up and down on each cheek. The paint was made by taking a piece of dead wood that is like a sponge and burning it, saving the ashes, then there is a flower that looks like a sunflower, only the petals are red, I do not remember the name of it. You grind the red petals and you mix them with the ashes of the dead wood.

Then his people gave a big feast; they furnished everything. They killed a hog, a beef, had pies, etc. a big feast. All were seated at the big table, my folks below me on my side, his people all on his side. Then the chief talked and told them why they were there. He talked and they answered him. They did not eat till the sun went down. After the feast all shook hands and talked to us. Some gave us presents, anything they wanted to give, shawls, hogs, blankets, etc. His people gave money to build a house. It was a two-room log house with a fireplace. I had to cook on the fire in a Dutch oven. They all danced after the feast. After this I could go with him, or I could go back to my people.

Dan and I made our home on this land one and a fourth miles west of Seneca, Missouri, after we were married, May 26, 1909. We lived together for twenty years and had nine children, five of whom are living. We lived on the old place till about two years before his death, when we went to live east of Quapaw, where he worked for Alex Beaver. Dan was killed in a car wreck in South Dakota while he was still working for Alex Beaver. My husband, like myself, an Eastern Shawnee, was born in Kansas.

I joined the Baptist Church when in school at Lawrence, but I have always been glad to take part in the dances of my people, as all of them have a religious significance.

January 31, 1930, I married Jack Longbone, a Delaware Indian. This time we were married like other people.[47]

A TRAGIC EDUCATION, BY ROBERT "BOBBY" BLUEJACKET (B. 1930)

The chill that ran through the three-year-old boy standing, tightly holding on to his five-year-old sister's hand, steadying her as she stood with her legs in iron-twisted braces from illness, was like a winter's breath down the back of your neck. But it was only yet August. The chill came from watching their brothers, Tommy, Junior, and Dennis, board the government bus returning them to the Seneca Indian School at Wyandotte, Oklahoma. The younger boy could not comprehend what happened to his brothers. It was as if they did not exist after boarding that bus. He turned and walked the old worn path back to his native home. He did not understand it then; no, not even now, and not knowing that in three short years, the bus would come for him.

That was eighty-three years ago, but I remember the day that the bus came for me. I knew then that the chill was the loss within my soul, the crying of my people, the voice of the old ones shattered by that tortured ride. I knew, but I did not understand. How many seasons must pass until I could be Shawnee again? This I am only now beginning to know.

In the winter of my days, now, I see barren limbs that stretch to the sky. Yet the life that flows through these branches is connected with the earth and feels the wind of the sky sift softly through my fingers. That which flows in me is Shawnee and has always been. It is in the circle, the Great Circle, that we honor our old ones and speak our ancient words. We hear the drums and they beat within our heart as we stretch our limbs to the stars. The trimming of these branches in the spring of my life did not stop their growth.

The "Indian" School

I remember sticking my head in a bucket of kerosene as I stepped off the bus. No greeting here. Only derisive remarks and "names" directed to some of the kids who had lice in their hair. Names they would carry for years—"Bugs," "L.," and "L. L."—meaning live and little lice. There were many bald heads of children, their hair shaved off. And like the length of hair that hit the ground, we learned that our language would also be gone, forbidden to speak it as we learned the white man's words.

Eight decades could not erase these memories and even those of a more sordid nature. There were whippings and even more despicable things that I thought would leave my mind, but the strength of it was not equal even to the years. No longer would we hear the ancient words. No more would we feel the warmth of the lit fires. No more would our songs and dances spring from us. No more would we sit in the tribal circle. All of that which we were was stripped from us. All of that which was Shawnee at this Indian school—stripped from us. We missed Christmas and Thanksgiving and never went home until the end of the year in May.

Grandmother Carrie BlueJacket

It seemed forever to walk the one-and-a-half-mile dusty road that led from the Indian school to Grandmother Carrie BlueJacket's house, and the torrid summer days of 1936 only made the distance more unbearable. But that didn't matter. Because each step I took even then took me farther away from that stifling atmosphere of the Indian school. It took me away from the deceit, the empty promises, the regimentation, the assimilation, the loneliness, the yearning for home, the hunger for affection that to this day pervades the lives of too many former Indian school students. Grandmother, with dimming eyes, would sit in her rocker facing the door. She could not see us at a distance. But her clouded eyes only lent to her perception of sound. "Is that you? Dennis? Tommy? Bobby?" She would hold each of us, cupping our faces in her hands, pulling us to eye level to better see each of our features. She held us like precious gifts, like finest china. She would say again and again, "I love you," as if the words would protect our hearts and cleanse our spirits. I always found myself standing close to grandmother. Her arm around my waist, I would touch her hand and her skin. My fingers rubbing furrowed wrinkles—wrinkles that hid her sadness, wrinkles that hid her tears.

The Ancient Lessons

There was never a display of anguish at Grandmother's. Only the stories and the fun of finding images in the wondering sky, and at night finding the star that grandmother said belonged to each of us. Grandmother's rainbow stretched across the sky with colors from the mahogany skin of my beautiful sister, Marjorie, to the sunny brown of Brother Junior, the ruby red of Dennis and Tommy, to my own sun-drenched red. Together, Grandmother said, we were her rainbow.

There were more than games at Grandmother's, too. There were sobering lessons, especially when she spoke of nature. There was seriousness in her words. There was ancient wisdom. There was the heart of Shawnee.

Though imperfectly spoken in English, she had an unyielding spirit in the conveying of our responsibility to nature—living not on the land or off the land, but rather being a part of the land. Her heart sang the ancient words. To know the forest, the wind, the rain, the Shawnees—all together they were one. Each nurtured the other. The old Indians knew from the beginning of creation, they had the responsibility to the other to be respectful. The creation is to be one with the Creator—an unbroken circle like the swirling wind. Thus, anguish always lay idle at Grandmother's house. Her joy, like all of the old ones, was rooted in the land and the seasons.

Grandmother's Words

We were all born in Grandmother's little house, high on what we, as children, thought was a mountain. It is only a hill, east of the Spring River on the Eastern Shawnee reservation. Grandmother's allotment ran west and fronted on the river. In terms that were spoken at the Indian school, we still own the land. In Grandmother's words, we are still one with the land. Like the sap that moves through the greatest tree, it is our roots and our branches, an ever-flowing legacy to that which was as the Creator intended.

The old house lies in ruins, but the family it spawned, seven uncles and aunts, have left a legacy of honor, dedication, and caring—a living creation. (Fifty-nine acres are left in Carrie BlueJacket's allotment.)

It was Grandmother who changed the message, even in her days of quiet torment. She said that we were to prepare ourselves to live in the white world, to be like the white people. "But don't believe their words. You are Shawnee. Your heart will always be Shawnee," she said. "Don't ever forget these words." My mind began to understand. My heart understood even greater.

An Indian Is . . .

The language within me, although it has been erased from my mouth, beats in me like the ceremonial drums. I try to recapture it with the words of my adopted language. Isn't it unique the Shawnee was replaced by English at the Indian school? I begin to understand, but not all of it.

These are the words written by me in the journey along a path as worn as to my Grandmother's house: "An Indian is . . . the golden light of morning, the river flowing, the wind blowing, the whisper of the trees. At dusk, as battle between day and night builds; an Indian is . . . the blood red of mountains, the myriad colors of life, the heart and soul of this iridescent land. An Indian is . . . eternal.

Indian culture is not of contradictions—we have dreams, aspirations, and inspirations. But what confuses many are our moments of retreat—"seeking the silence of nature"—striving to keep the traditions alive. It is the dances and the drums—the heartbeat of a people—each of us—together and alone at the Sacred Circle.

—Eastern Shawnee Pow Wow Committee Program, 2007, Bobby BlueJacket

I saw the rainbow and remembered that we were the rainbow for Grandmother, we ruddy children walking from the Indian school to the house of our birth. I see the colors in the sky and I know that the rainbow never ends. It is eternal in the heavens, put there by the Creator as a promise to us—the old ones shall be forever honored in the colors of the young ones, and the brighter colors even still yet to come. We only see part of the circle that fills the sky and touches the earth. My heart begins to see the sounds of the drum and feel the ancient song. I can understand.

Sweat Lodge

The ceremonies of my people had been driven from me. I knew that I was Shawnee, Grandmother Carrie BlueJacket made sure I knew. But as a man in the fall of my seasons, at well over eighty, I needed the connection to the old ones, to our ways and to our spirit—the Sacred Circle.

I could hear the drums—the sound of voices—the language I didn't know, yet understood. It was the echo of their voices—bewailing the anguish of their seasons—a call from the past and now.

This night, for the first time, I could begin to know . . . to be what I was born to be—to touch, to feel, to sense a part of their past.

I feel a foreboding, not knowing the ceremonial steps, as I stripped to my trunks—stillness. Quiet—no songs, no coyote call—only the sound of the wood smoke spiraling skyward. We entered on our knees, forming a circle—the Sacred Circle. We faced the four doors, in Shawnee tradition, reverent on our knees. The first direction is facing east for the sunrise—thanksgiving for a new day and the elements, wind, rain, moon, and sun. The second direction is to the south, in praise for all creatures, plants, food, animals, trees, and growth. The third is to the west—prayer for all people and all needs. The fourth door is a prayer for ourselves and faces north. I say the words that are now forever part of me, my children, and my children's children's children. Words uttered by Wah-wey-ah-pier-sen-wah (Blue Jacket), the words of Grandmother Carrie—thankfulness for being Shawnee—for being a part of a great people.

The words of my prayer erased the two hundred years between then and now. I remember wondering as a six year old what it would be like to be like all of the old Indians. I feel their spirit. I hear their words. I understand.

I felt a touch to my knee as I sat. It was the passing of the pipe. I took the pipe and held it as grandmother taught, gently with the left hand forward under the bowl and the right moving it steadily to my lips.

Exhilaration . . . euphoria . . . not from the tobacco, but from the connection I shared with the past. For the first time, my heart felt complete—to be what I was born to be—to be Shawnee.

As I left, I saw the stars and remembered Grandmother's heart and words. The countless stars, who each were an old Indian that had passed on, were always watching over us. I had shared in the lives of the old Shawnees.

The Sacred Ground

Much as the old Indian school tried to take away our identity, our language, and our culture, today there is a more "cleansing" threat not only to our ways, but to the ways of all peoples. We no longer see each other, but through a picture on Facebook or a cell phone camera.

Technology has brought us a great communication, but it has dangerously moved us from the things that make us Shawnee. Can we touch the blade of grass with our feet? Can we see the hawks circle the sky? Can we smoke the pipe in the Sacred Circle if we do not know the presence of one another? The tool is good as long as it does not become our culture, assimilating us.

We are unique as a tribe in that we have set aside a ceremonial ground. We have a ceremonial chief in Shawn King. His appointment leads us to the old ones. His spiritual guidance and leading to our ceremonial grounds, where we can feel the water of the brook and let the grass tickle our feet in the very view of our children's playground.

The hawks blessed our people in the first ceremony held at the grounds. Two red-tailed hawks circled over the wedded couple, gracefully soaring closer and tighter as the ceremony went on. As the couple shared their song, the hawks circled over their heads and dipped their wings in blessing.

We must see this as a people with our own eyes, feel it with our own hearts, and hear the ancient words and songs in the silence of the drifting breeze under the hawk's wings.

As Eastern Shawnees, we are fortunate. We have this sacred land.

We Hear the Drum

Our children have spent many happy times on these ceremonial grounds . . . this small piece of earth dedicated to our beginning. Only this parcel remains of the millions of acres once held so dear. This place holds time still . . . and sorrow is lifted with no thought of the morrow. Here, Indian hearts are troubled less. Here, where we hear the beat of the drum, is a sacred place.

The sound of the drum—the beat—comes with the ease and certainty of the small stream that moves past our ceremonial grounds, it lingers in our mind like a melody . . . telling us to take our dream and vision into the future with pride in who you are, where you live, and what you accomplish. In its sound—in each beat is that call—about faith, not simply religious faith, but faith in people, in the land, in the need to comfort and ease the burden of others—the comfort that is found in simply doing what is right—in being Indian.

An Acorn

We teach the children our dances. We teach them our songs. They can sing in the language of the old ones. We teach them some words of the Shawnees, but are we growing them? They are more precious to us than anything. I tell them of the acorn that drops from the tree. It touches the earth—a small nugget of life. The days come, and it is watered by the rains until it grows to be the mightiest tree. The circle is complete with roots in the ground and branches in the sky. The hawk takes comfort and finds a home in its branches.

Another acorn falls from the mighty tree. . . .

The children are more than the rainbow in our life. They are the new color that glows so magically in the iridescent marvel that colors the sky. Imbue their hearts with the altruistic spirit the old ones gave us.

Their dreams—ask them to bring and share their dreams with us—that we may embrace their yearning, binding them to our hearts as they were formulated and born in their hearts.

Our children need to learn the warm joy and the sense of belonging—of being Indian. They need to learn to walk away from scorn . . . to be generous and forgiving. Our children need to know compassion is not a limited resource, but replicates itself, imbuing the compassionate with the gentle fragrance of truth . . . of what it means to be Indian.

Nothing can move our memories more than the time spent watching our children at the ceremonial grounds. The importance of this place of repose and contemplation is a place where spirit and nature come together to guide us to the Indian way.

We teach them of the past and to use that which is harmonious with today. We remind them of the almost-forgotten pathway the old ones walked. Oh, how those memories stir our hearts. We do this as a mark, a mark upon this day, a mark upon our conscience to commemorate and confirm our thoughts and what is most important to us—a committal for all time to come—that the old ones never be forgotten, remembering that in everything they told us, they told no lies, only the fragrance of truth.

A Winter of Understanding

The chill that I felt in the youth of my life, even on those August days that led to the missing of my family and my heritage, is gone. Now in the winter of my life, I am warmed by the sunshine and the rainbow. There can be no greater joy for an old tree than to feel the acorns at his feet and to know the ancient songs will go on. This is a circle stronger than any one moment of life. It is our way. It is Shawnee.[48]

NOTES

Robin Dushane would like to thank Professor Sandra Garner (American Studies, Miami University, Oxford, Ohio) for her invaluable assistance writing this chapter.

1. Joab Spencer, "Interview with Robert Sidney Douglas," *History of Southeast Missouri: A Narrative of Its Historical Progress, Its People, and Its Principle Interest* (Chicago: Lewis Publishing, 1912), 386.

2. "Homestead Act," *Kansapedia*, www.kshs.org/kansapedia/, Kansas Historical Society, created 2010, modified 2013; "Shawnee Indians," ibid., created July 2015, modified December 2015.

3. Stephen Warren, *The Shawnees and Their Neighbors, 1795–1870* (Urbana: University of Illinois Press, 2005), 78.

4. Spencer, "Interview with Robert Sidney Douglas," 386.

5. Carl G. Klopfenstein, "Westward Ho: Removal of Ohio Shawnee, 1832–1833," *Bulletin of the Historical and Philosophical Society of Ohio* 15, no. 1 (January 1957): 16, 26.

6. Richard W. Cummins, "Muster Roll of Company of Shawnee Indian Emigrants from the Hog Creek and Wahpahkonnetta, Ohio and Turned Over to My Agency on the 3rd Day of December 1832, by Col. J. J. Aberts—Agent and Superintendent of Ohio, Indians," Record Group 75, M234, Roll 603, National Archives and Records Administration, Washington, D.C. (hereafter any National Archives document, after the full document title, will be cited by its microfilm number).

7. "An act to provide for an exchange of lands with the Indians residing in any of the states or territories, and for their removal west of the river Mississippi," 4 Stat. 411, 148 (1830).

8. Isaac McCoy, *The Annual Register of Indian Affairs: In the Western (or Indian) Territory* (1835; Springfield, Mo.: Particular Baptist Press, 2000), 50–51.

9. James K. Beatty, "Interpreting the Shawnee Sun: Literacy and Cultural Persistence in Indian Country, 1833–1841," *Kansas History: A Journal of the Central Plains* 31, no. 4 (Winter 2008): 244.

10. Ibid., 254.

11. McCoy, *Annual Register*, 21.

12. Beatty, "Interpreting the Shawnee Sun," 256.

13. Martha B Caldwell, *Annals of Shawnee Methodist Mission and Indian Manual Labor School* (Topeka: Kansas State Historical Society, 1977), 72, 105, 110.

14. Annual Report of the Commissioner of Indian Affairs (hereafter ARCIA), November 16, 1842, S. Doc. No. 1, 413 (1842); ARCIA, November 30, 1848, H. R. Doc. No. 1, 537 (1848); ARCIA, November 27, 1851.

15. Lora Ethel, interview with Robin Dushane, November 3, 2001, transcript in author's possession.

16. ARCIA, November 30, 1852, S. Doc. No. 1, 658 (1852); ARCIA, November 1, 1880, H. R. Doc. No. 1, 1959 (1880); ARCIA, November 30, 1852, S. Doc. No. 1, 613 (1852); ARCIA, November 1, 1890, H. R. Doc. No. 1, 2841 (1890).

17. "1879–80 [Loyal Band Shawnee field notes]," Albert Gatschet MSS, National Anthropological Archives, Smithsonian Institution, Washington, D.C.

18. ARCIA, November 1, 1872, H. R. Doc. No. 1, 1560 (1872).

19. Robert N. Utley, ed., *Battlefield and Classroom; An Autobiography by Richard Henry Pratt* (Norman: University of Oklahoma Press, 2003).

20. Robert Kissee, interview with Robin Dushane, February 23, 2016, transcript in author's possession.

21. Lola Prophet Perkins Callahan, interview with Robin Dushane, January 27, 2016, transcript in author's possession.

22. Dennis James, interview with Robin Dushane, November 10, 2015, transcript in author's possession.

23. John Peacock, interview with Robin Dushane, February 17, 2016, transcript in author's possession.

24. Jim Greenfeather Jr., interview with Robin Dushane, January 31, 2016, transcript in author's possession.

25. Ibid.

26. Records of the Superintendent's Office, 1910, Record Group 75, E.1 Box 17, National Archives And Records Administration Federal Records Center, Fort Worth, Tex.

27. Ibid.

28. Glen Stoner, interview with Robin Dushane, February 28, 2016, transcript in author's possession.

29. Records of Superintendents Office, 1910, Record Group 75, E.1 Box 17.

30. Shirley Alexander, interview with Robin Dushane, February 27, 2016, transcript in author's possession.

31. Theresa Milk, *Haskell Institute: 19th Century Stories of Sacrifice and Survival* (Lawrence, Kans.: Mammoth Publications, 2007), 140, 152.

32. Laurence H. Dushane, personal records, accessed December 13, 2012.

33. Ibid., accessed March 20, 2003.

34. Records of Superintendents Office, 1910, Record Group 75, E.1 Box 17.

35. Ibid.

36. A. M. Gibson, "Wyandotte Mission: The Early Years, 1871–1900," *Chronicles of Oklahoma* 36 (Summer 1958): 151.

37. ARCIA, November 1, 1882, H. R. Doc. No. 1, 2100 (1882).

38. Laurence H. Dushane, personal records, accessed November 14, 2000.

39. Robert BlueJacket, interview with Robin Dushane, February 27, 2016, transcript in author's possession.

40. Records of Superintendents Office, 1910, Record Group 75, E.1, Box 5.

41. Betty Drake James McIntosh, personal writing, accessed December 8, 2015, in author's possession.

42. Robert BlueJacket, interview with Robin Dushane, February 27, 2016, transcript in author's possession.

43. Norma Kraus, interview with Robin Dushane, February 29, 2016, transcript in author's possession.

44. Memoir of Doris James McIntosh, submitted to author by Dora's daughter, Janet Hansen, in author's possession.

45. Lola Purvis, interview with Robin Dushane, February 27, 2015, transcript in author's possession.

46. Dorma Hollis, interview with Robin Dushane, November 23, 2001, transcript in author's possession.

47. Sarah Mohawk Dushane Longbone, interview with Nannie Lee Burns, July 27, 1937. Permission to reproduce courtesy of the Oklahoma Historical Society. Family note: Sarah's father, John Mohawk, was born in Canada and was known by his grandchildren as a healer.

48. Robert "Bobby" BlueJacket, "A Tragic Education," permission to print given by Robert "Bobby" BlueJacket.

PART II
RECOVERING EASTERN SHAWNEE SOVEREIGNTY AND HISTORY

The Eastern Shawnee Tribe of Oklahoma is a jealous guardian of its sovereignty. But, as Chief Glenna Wallace admits, "We have not been the best at recording or preserving our history." The following three chapters seek to correct this trend. Robert Miller offers a careful analysis of the political sovereignty of the Eastern Shawnee Tribe. Miller is both a tribal citizen and a professor of Native American law at Arizona State University. As such, he is supremely qualified to explain how "Indian nations are expressly recognized as governments in the U.S. Constitution." The federal policy of assimilation, a protracted campaign to destroy tribal cultures, has certainly left its mark. However, throughout it all, the Eastern Shawnee Tribe has not relinquished its "reserved rights": rights possessed by Native nations before colonizers stepped foot on the sovereign lands of the Native nations who now live as "domestic dependent nations" within the United States. Moreover, Miller writes that because of "political and contract-like negotiations" with the United States, tribes have a well-documented history as sovereign nations. From there we move to Glenna Wallace, who offers the first comprehensive study of Eastern Shawnee chiefs, showing how each, in his or her own way, has contributed to the present strength of the tribe. In the chapters that follow, Miller and Wallace describe the people, as well as the treaties and laws they signed, that convey an unbroken history of sovereignty and self-determination from before contact to the present day.

6

Treaties between the Eastern Shawnee Tribe and the United States

Contracts between Sovereign Governments

ROBERT J. MILLER (EASTERN SHAWNEE)

The Eastern Shawnee Tribe of Oklahoma (ESTO) and its political ancestors have long engaged in political and diplomatic relations with other Indian nations, European powers that attempted to colonize North America, and the United States. This chapter starts its analysis with the ESTO's role in the Treaty of Greenville of 1795. Including that treaty, the ESTO and its predecessors signed eleven treaties with the United States that were ratified by the U.S. Senate and thus became constitutionally binding. The tribe also signed three agreements with the United States, one of which was approved by Congress. The tribe entered into one treaty with the Confederate States of America in 1861. In addition, throughout its history, the ESTO has been involved in nearly constant political dealings, relationships, and agreements with other tribal governments. These negotiations and arrangements demonstrate the tribe's political existence and show how the Eastern Shawnee Tribe has always engaged in government-to-government diplomatic relationships with other governments and with the United States.[1]

In colonial times the English, French, Spanish, Dutch, and American colonies entered into hundreds of treaties with indigenous peoples and nations across North America. In turn, the United States adopted its procedures for dealing with Indian nations through treaty making from England, the thirteen original colonies, and other European nations. The United States ultimately ratified 375 treaties with Indian nations from 1778 to 1871. But even after Congress ended official treaty making with Indian nations in 1871, the U.S. executive and legislative branches continued to interact with tribes as governments through political and diplomatic negotiations and agreements in which tribal consent was a requirement.[2]

The significance of Indian treaty making cannot be overstated. The U.S. Supreme Court has stated, "A treaty, including one between the United States and an Indian tribe, is essentially a contract between two sovereign nations." And a federal judge has written in his book on American Indian law that "Indian treaties stand on essentially the same footing as treaties with foreign nations." These statements are not surprising, because President George Washington showed great respect for Indian treaties. In fact, he established many of the U.S.-Indian treaty procedures, and he handled Indian treaties from the beginning of his presidency in the same fashion as he did international treaties. The U.S. Constitution recognizes Indian treaties and recognizes Indian tribes as governments. Furthermore, the United States has continued to deal politically with tribal nations to this very day. This history of Indian treaty making and the continued existence of binding treaties continue to be important components of federal Indian law today.[3]

THE HISTORY AND LAW OF TREATY MAKING BETWEEN
INDIAN NATIONS AND THE UNITED STATES

The issue of Indian treaty rights is often hotly contested because some people perceive them as giving Indians special rights. These property rights have often been vigorously opposed by state officials, and issues about tribal treaties are regularly in the news. Many people misunderstand the nature of Indian treaties, the promises that were given in them, and the reservations that were formed by them. For the most part, Native governments and peoples were not *given* rights or land by the United States in treaties. Instead, through political and contract-like negotiations, tribes reserved rights they already owned and traded other rights with the United States. In 1905 the U.S. Supreme Court clearly showed its understanding of the true nature of Indian treaties: "The treaty was not a grant of rights to the Indians, but a grant of rights from them—a reservation of those not granted." Thus, in treaty making tribes were giving up certain rights they already owned—in lands, resources, and assets—in exchange for payments, promises, and protection from the United States. The Indian nations agreed to sell some of their property rights, while they preserved other assets that they already possessed and wanted to retain. It is obvious, then, why American Indian homelands are called "reservations" and why the lands of the First Nations in Canada, for example, are called "reserves."[4]

Moreover, it is well recognized that Indian treaties are contracts between the United States and Indian nations. The Supreme Court has recognized this fact, as has already been shown above. And, in fact, several of the ESTO treaties expressly name the tribe and the United States as "the contracting parties."[5] Consequently, treaties are correctly analyzed under the principles of both contract law and international law.

The History of Indian Treaties

Long before Europeans arrived in North America, Indian nations dealt politically and diplomatically with other Native governments through negotiations and consensual arrangements. The Shawnee nations and peoples entered many voluntary relationships, in particular with the Iroquois Confederacy and the Delaware Nation. As mentioned above, once European countries began attempting to colonize North America, they uniformly followed the recognized pattern of dealing with Indian nations through governmental and political means by treaty making. France, the Netherlands, Spain, and England, and those countries' colonial governments, signed scores, even hundreds, of treaties with American Indian nations. Once the United States was created, it naturally adopted the accepted practice of dealing with tribal nations as governments and through treaties.[6]

In 1778, under the Continental Congress, the United States negotiated its first Indian treaty with the Delaware Nation. The Congress respectfully requested permission to cross Delaware territory to attack the British at Fort Detroit during the Revolutionary War. In this treaty the United States even asked the Delawares to consider joining the Union of the thirteen states as a separate, fourteenth state.[7]

After winning the war, the new United States government, now known as the Articles of Confederation Congress, was at first far less solicitous of tribes. Although this Congress signed eight treaties with Indian nations between 1784 and 1789, the Confederation Congress approached the tribes with a very bellicose attitude at first because many tribes had supported the British in the Revolutionary War. In fact, the United States claimed that it had "conquered" the tribes by defeating England and that, under international law, tribal lands were now forfeited to the United States. That argument was vigorously disputed by Indian nations, and it did not help the United States' relationship with the tribes. Thus, in 1795, Secretary of War Timothy Pickering specifically instructed U.S. treaty commissioners to drop any claims of conquest and to strive to reach fair diplomatic agreements with tribal governments.[8]

Once the current United States government commenced operations under the new Constitution in the spring of 1789, President George Washington and his administration dealt with tribal governments and treated Indian treaties in the same manner and with the same respect as they did international treaties with foreign powers. The United States ultimately entered into 375 treaties with Indian tribes. In these treaties the United States negotiated cessions of land, recognized other areas of land—usually known as reservations—that the tribal governments reserved to themselves, and respected the self-governing powers of Indian nations. Even though Congress ended treaty making with tribes in 1871, the preexisting treaties contain promises that still bind the United States today. In fact, under the Constitution, treaties are "the supreme Law of the Land." In addition, the United States continues to deal with the tribal nations on a political basis to this day.[9]

The United States developed fairly standard procedures for proposing, negotiating, and ratifying Indian treaties. Many of these procedures, as they were used in specific Eastern Shawnee treaties and agreements, are discussed below. But it is also helpful to note here the standardized and generalized procedures that the United States developed for Indian treaty making.

Tribal treaties were most often negotiated by U.S. commissioners who were officially appointed by the executive branch and funded by appropriations from Congress. Commissioners were instructed to travel to specific tribes to attempt to reach agreements on certain objectives. The United States was almost always seeking land sales (cessions) from tribes and was often trying to control tribal trade, keep the peace, and settle grievances that Indians had with American settlers who were invading tribal lands. Occasionally, Indian leaders traveled to Washington, D.C., for negotiating sessions, and sometimes Indian nations requested that the United States treat with them. But in the vast majority of situations, the United States sought out the tribes.

Federal treaty commissioners were usually given fairly specific instructions on what to seek from the tribes.[10] Many of them kept detailed notes or journals of the treaty negotiations to record what was discussed at the sessions. These journals and signed treaties were then submitted to the secretary of war (and later to the secretary of interior after the Department of the Interior was created in 1849). The secretary would then submit the proposed treaty to the president, who, if he approved, would send it to the Senate for consideration. The Constitution provides for the president to negotiate and draft treaties, but they must be ratified by a two-thirds vote in the Senate before they become binding on the United States.[11]

Several practices that were regularly used by U.S. treaty commissioners raise serious questions about the meaning and fairness of American Indian treaties. First, questions arise in almost all Indian treaties whether the "chief" or tribe that signed a particular treaty even had the authority or right to sell the lands and surrender the various rights addressed in the treaty. Numerous allegations have been made by historians and tribal citizens that federal commissioners, including ones that signed treaties with the ESTO, purposely selected the tribal leaders they wanted to negotiate with or picked a specific tribe to speak for others. William Henry Harrison, for example, who negotiated three treaties with the ancestors of the Eastern Shawnee Tribe in 1803, 1814, and 1815, and other U.S. treaty negotiators, were well known to select the tribal chiefs they would negotiate with and then would only give gifts to the chiefs who signed treaties.[12]

Second, all Indian treaties, including the ones with the Eastern Shawnees, were negotiated and written in English. Hence, Indians had to trust that the U.S. commissioners and the interpreters were telling them the truth. In addition, tribal leaders were expected to understand exactly the legal meaning and significance of the English words used in the treaties. Third, the federal commissioners had the assistance of trained personnel. For example, in regard to Indian treaties in the Pacific Northwest, the U.S. commissioner even had a Harvard-trained attorney on

his staff. Fourth, federal negotiators were known to badger and coerce tribal leaders to sign treaties, and alcohol often flowed freely at treaty sessions. The federal commissioner at the Shawnee
treaty negotiation in August 1831 at Wapakoneta, Ohio, apparently even refused to take the time
to read the full treaty to the tribal leaders, but still tried to force them to sign it. Suspiciously,
treaty interpreters and other Americans often received grants of tribal lands in these treaties.
And fifth, in many of the treaty negotiations—including, again, the treaty with the Shawnees at
Wapakoneta in August 1831—Indians and Indian leaders were heavily influenced by businessmen who claimed that the tribal government or individual Indians owed them enormous debts
for past purchases. One eyewitness at the 1831 Wapakoneta Shawnee negotiation claimed that
traders paid bribes to some Shawnees and provided alcohol to federal officials and Shawnees to
get them to agree to a treaty that ensured the traders were paid for blatantly false claims.[13]

Notwithstanding these problematic issues, Indian nations negotiated many of the early treaties with the United States from a position of some strength. In the late 1700s and early 1800s
the newly formed United States had almost no army, no funding, little ability to fight wars with
tribal governments, and it faced internal problems and external conflicts with European countries. Consequently, early treaty making between the United States and tribes was somewhat
favorable to the tribes. After the Louisiana Purchase in 1803 and the War of 1812, however, tribal
nations could no longer rely on European support against the United States, and their weaken-
ing position led to more one-sided treaty negotiations in favor of the United States.[14]

The Law of Indian Treaties

As constitutionally authorized and ratified treaties, and, by analogy, as legally binding contracts,
Indian treaties are applied and interpreted under well-settled principles of law.

INDIAN NATIONS AND INDIANS IN THE U.S. CONSTITUTION   Indian nations are expressly recognized in the U.S. Constitution as governments, and individual Indians are expressly recognized as citizens of their tribal governments. Indian tribes are explicitly named only once in the
Constitution, but they are also referred to one other time. In what is known as the Interstate (or
Indian) Commerce Clause, the Constitution states, "Congress shall have Power . . . to regulate
Commerce with foreign Nations, and among the several States, and with the Indian Tribes." This
provision clearly acknowledges Indian nations as governmental entities somewhat on a par with
the states and with foreign nations. This clause was expressly designed to grant the United States
Congress the exclusive authority to deal with tribal governments and to exclude the states from
meddling in Indian affairs.[15]

In addition, Indian treaties, and thus tribal governments, are included in the Treaty Clause
of the Constitution. This clause states, "All Treaties made, or which shall be made, under the
Authority of the United States, shall be the supreme Law of the Land." By the time the United
States began operating under its Constitution, the country had already entered into nine treaties
with tribal governments and twenty-three treaties with other foreign countries. Thus, the Treaty
Clause was a ratification of those previous thirty-two "treaties made," including the ones with
the Indian nations, and a recognition that tribal treaties "which shall be made" in the future
would also be constitutionally recognized treaties and "the supreme Law of the Land."[16]

Individual Indians are mentioned twice in the constitutional provisions that require a census
every ten years to count state populations in order to determine how many U.S. House representatives each state receives. In 1789 the Constitution stated that Indians were not to be counted
as part of a state's population—in essence, they were not to be considered state or federal citizens—unless they paid taxes. In 1868, when African Americans were granted citizenship rights

through the Fourteenth Amendment, Indians were once again expressly excluded from being counted in state populations, or as state or federal citizens, unless they paid taxes. These exclusions demonstrate that the founding fathers of the Constitution in 1787 and of the Fourteenth Amendment in 1868 recognized that Indians were citizens of their own separate nations. (The majority of Indians were not made U.S. citizens until 1924.)[17]

The U.S. Supreme Court has also recognized the constitutional significance of treaty making with tribal nations and that these actions by the United States are themselves a recognition that tribes are sovereign governments. For example, in 1831, in *Cherokee Nation v. Georgia*, the court stated that Indian tribes are governments (that is, they are distinct political entities capable of managing their own affairs) and that, by repeatedly entering into treaties with tribes over many decades, the United States had acknowledged that tribal nations are governments.[18] In the very next year the Supreme Court made an even stronger statement about the significance of the U.S.-Indian treaty relationship: "The words 'treaty' and 'nation' are words of our own language, selected in our diplomatic and legislative proceedings. . . . We have applied them to Indians, as we have applied them to the other nations of the earth. They are applied to all in the same sense."[19]

THE RULES OF INDIAN TREATY INTERPRETATION (CANONS OF CONSTRUCTION) In light of the facts set out above, and the often questionable tactics that the United States used during Indian treaty making, it is no surprise that the Supreme Court has developed fairly liberal rules for interpreting and enforcing these treaties that favor Indian nations. The suspect manner in which most tribal treaties were negotiated has led the court to develop special rules, called canons of construction, to interpret the treaties in favor of tribes. In fact, Indian treaties receive a broad construction, or reading, in favor of the signatory tribe by a mixture of principles borrowed from international treaty construction and contract law.

In 1832 the court stated this general standard for Indian treaty interpretation: "The language used in treaties with the Indians should never be construed to their prejudice. If words be made use of which are susceptible of a more extended meaning than their plain import, as connected with the tenor of their treaty, they should be considered as used only in the latter sense. . . . How the words of the treaty were understood by this unlettered people, rather than their critical meaning, should form the rule of construction."[20] The court reaffirmed this standard in an 1866 case regarding the Shawnees in Kansas and refused to read their treaty in a narrow manner that would have injured tribal interests.[21]

The court has also set out more specific interpretive rules. First, courts resolve any ambiguous expressions in a treaty in favor of the tribe. This seems fair, since the United States drafted the treaties, and since they were written in English, which very few Indians spoke and almost none could read. Second, courts interpret treaties as the tribes themselves would have understood them at the time, so that we can understand today what the tribe agreed to in the document. The Supreme Court repeated as recently as 1999 that courts must "give effect to the terms [of a treaty] as the Indians themselves would have understood them." Third, courts factor in the history and circumstances behind a treaty and its negotiations to interpret its provisions. Obviously, then, the Supreme Court has ruled that treaties should never be interpreted to a tribe's prejudice, but that they should be liberally construed in favor of the tribes to accomplish the treaties' protective purposes.[22]

Since treaties are also contracts, it is not surprising that contractual principles and ideas are also used to interpret them. In fact, many of the very liberal-sounding canons of construction listed above are really only general rules for interpreting contracts and are not as friendly to tribes as they may sound. First, in interpreting contracts, courts look to enforce the actual agreement the parties reached. This is known as the "meeting of the minds." What exactly did the parties to the contract agree to sell or to do? If a court can figure that out from the language of a contract, then it will enforce that bargain. Just as in contract law, courts try to interpret treaties to achieve the intent of the parties and to ensure that the United States and the tribes had a meeting of the minds and were discussing and agreeing to the same things. One unique aspect of interpreting Indian treaties, however, arises from the recognition of the disadvantaged bargaining position that Indians often held during treaty negotiations. Hence, courts narrowly interpret treaty provisions that might injure tribal interests.

Second, in a contract, ambiguous expressions are interpreted against the party that wrote the contract. That is fair because if one party caused the problem by writing a confusing, ambiguous contract, it should be interpreted against that party. Third, the idea behind the Indian canons of treaty construction listed above is similar to the judicial treatment of what are called adhesion contracts. An adhesion contract is one that was not fairly bargained for because one party was operating from a much weaker position than the other. In such instances, courts will not interpret a contract against the interests of the weaker party. Under contract theory, contracts negotiated in this manner should not be enforceable due to undue influence, unequal bargaining position, and the lack of arms-length bargaining. The situations under which the vast majority of Indian treaties were negotiated are analogous to adhesion contracts and thus justify the liberal rules of Indian treaty interpretation.

As with any contract, both parties to a treaty must fulfill the terms or suffer legal consequences. In cases where the United States has violated its treaty duties to Indian nations, or where its action would take or adversely affect the property rights that tribes possess under treaties, the Supreme Court has presumed that the United States would then be subject to a lawsuit for compensation for taking or destroying the property rights recognized by the treaty.[23]

The End of Indian Treaty Making

Congress ended constitutional treaty making with Indian nations in 1871. But the act that ended the practice also expressly provided that all preexisting treaties remained in effect, and thus many of those old treaty promises are still binding in the United States today.[24]

The decision to stop making treaties with Indian nations was undertaken because of political infighting between the U.S. Senate and the House of Representatives, not because of some change in the status, existence, or powers of Indian governments. The House was upset because it was expected to agree to the treaty commissioners selected by the executive branch and to provide funding for any and all potential treaties, and then to allow the executive alone to negotiate and draft treaties, while the Senate considered the draft treaties and ratified them. The House wanted to increase its role in this process and consequently inserted a provision into an appropriations bill in 1871 that ended tribal treaty making.[25]

But this was by no means the end of federal relations, negotiations, or the making of agreements with Indian governments. It just meant that these negotiations now had to be conducted by the executive branch and then approved as agreements or contracts by acts of both houses of Congress instead of being ratified as constitutional treaties by just the Senate. In fact, Indian treaty making continued unabated after 1871 because there was a constant stream of negotiations and agreements entered into by the United States and Indian nations. The agreements produced by these negotiations were even called treaties by many people and courts long after 1871, although they were then more correctly termed agreements and contracts. Commentators and historians call these agreements "treaty substitutes." The Eastern Shawnee Tribe entered just such an agreement with the United States in 1874. And in the modern day the ESTO and other tribes continue to enter into agreements with the United States and with state governments on many issues, such as gaming, taxes, jurisdiction, water, and fishing and hunting matters.[26]

Finally, it is important to note when discussing the law of Indian treaties that, as is the case with all United States treaties, Congress has the legal authority to unilaterally abrogate or destroy them. In 1986 the Supreme Court even developed a test to determine whether Congress has abrogated an Indian treaty. But as mentioned above, the court has stated that in such a situation Congress should have to compensate a tribal nation for the taking of any treaty property rights.[27]

THE TREATIES AND AGREEMENTS OF THE EASTERN SHAWNEE TRIBE AND THE UNITED STATES

From 1795 through 1874 the Eastern Shawnee Tribe and its direct political predecessors entered into eleven treaties with the United States that were ratified by the Senate and thus became valid and binding under the Constitution. The tribe also signed a treaty with the Confederate States of America that was ratified by the Confederate Congress. In addition, the tribe executed three agreements with the United States, only one of which appears to have been accepted by Congress. We examine each of these documents to review the significant aspects of the ESTO's political and diplomatic dealings with the United States as part of our examination of the history of the Eastern Shawnee Tribe.[28]

United States' Objectives

The European countries that attempted to colonize North America were interested in acquiring land, resources, and empires. As part of worldwide colonization, Europeans developed the international law of colonialism, known today as the Doctrine of Discovery, in which they almost totally ignored the rights of indigenous peoples.[29] In 1823 the U.S. Supreme Court affirmed the application of the doctrine in the United States:

> On the discovery of this immense continent, the great nations of Europe were eager to appropriate to themselves so much of it as they could respectively acquire. Its vast extent offered an ample field to the ambition and enterprise of all; and the character and religion of its inhabitants afforded an apology for considering them as a people over whom the superior genius of Europe might claim an ascendency. The potentates of the old world found no difficulty in convincing themselves that they made ample compensation to the inhabitants of the new, by bestowing on them civilization and Christianity, in exchange for unlimited independence.[30]

The new United States—the thirteen American states and their citizens—almost unanimously pursued these same objectives. In fact, on September 7, 1783, General George Washington clearly expressed these goals in an influential letter of advice he wrote to Congress and in which he foretold the probable extermination of Indians. In his letter General Washington laid out many of the principles that became federal Indian policy for nearly two hundred years.[31]

A congressional committee asked Washington how the United States should deal with the Indian nations after winning the Revolutionary War and gaining its freedom from England. Washington provided advice on the Indians and "Settlement of the Western Country." He argued that the United States should inform the Indians that they had been conquered along with England and had consequently lost their lands to the United States. He also advised drawing a boundary line between the American states and Indian country, but noted that "care should be taken neither to yield nor to grasp at too much." He also encouraged the United States to engage in trade with Indian tribes to "fix them strongly in our Interest." He clearly realized how important Indian relations were to the United States, because he stated that "the Settlemt.

of the Western Country and making a Peace with the Indians are so analogous that there can be no definition of the one without involving considerations of the other." He then explained to Congress his suggestion to pursue peace and to purchase Indian lands instead of engaging in warfare with tribal nations:

> Policy and oeconomy [*sic*] point very strongly to the expediency of being upon good terms with the Indians, and the propriety of purchasing their Lands in preference to attempting to drive them by force of arms out of their country; which as we have already experienced is like driving the Wild Beasts of the Forest . . . ; when the gradual extension of our Settlements will as certainly cause the Savage as the Wolf to retire; both being beasts of prey tho' they differ in shape. In a word there is nothing to be obtained by an Indian War but the Soil they live on and this can be had by purchase at less expence [*sic*], and without that bloodshed.[32]

The cynicism and lethal nature of this advice is obvious. Washington was clearly comparing Indians to animals ("the Savage as the Wolf . . . both being beasts of prey tho' they differ in shape"), and he also clearly envisioned a future in which the United States would spread across the continent and Indian nations and peoples would retreat and even disappear. Thereafter the United States pursued this exact policy under the rubric of Manifest Destiny until at least the early 1960s. For example, presidents Thomas Jefferson, James Madison, John Quincy Adams, Andrew Jackson, and many other presidents, politicians, and American citizens expressly foresaw extermination as the future of Indian nations, peoples, and cultures. Federal Indian policies and treaty making with American Indians were expressly designed to accomplish these goals. These national objectives are also reflected in the United States' relationship with the Eastern Shawnee Tribe.[33]

Eastern Shawnee Tribe's Objectives

Indian nations were forced to deal with the expansive and aggressive United States. Tribal nations, cultures, and leaders faced the difficult and perhaps impossible task of holding on to their lands and retaining their lifeways, economies, cultures, and lives under the onslaught of American expansion. Some tribal leaders advocated warfare, and some were successful for brief times in slowing American Manifest Destiny. Some tribal nations attempted partnerships with England and Spain, for example, to attempt to hold back or to avoid the United States. But perhaps a majority of tribal leaders and Indian governments attempted to accommodate American expansion while at the same time preserving their lives and homelands.

In the early 1800s Shawnee chief Black Hoof and other Shawnee leaders in Ohio appear to have decided to accommodate the United States and also attempt to keep their lands. Black Hoof is considered to have been one of the primary Shawnee leaders in the late 1790s and early 1800s in the Ohio area. While Tecumseh and his brother, the Prophet, are far more famous for fighting the United States and supporting the English in the War of 1812, Black Hoof, Captain Lewis (chief of the Lewistown reservation in Ohio, where the Eastern Shawnee Tribe removed from), and other Shawnees in Ohio actively fought for the Americans. Yet Black Hoof adamantly refused the United States' attempts to remove his people, and he attempted to keep his tribe on its reservation in Ohio. Black Hoof believed that if tribes started removing westward, the United States would never stop seeking more removals. He told a U.S. Indian agent, "Go where we may your people will follow us, and we will be forced to remove again and again and finally driven to the sea on the other side of this great island." Black Hoof died in 1830 or 1831, still resisting removal.[34]

As we examine the Eastern Shawnee treaties and agreements with the United States, we will see the continual tension between these countervailing themes: the George Washington federal policies of the inevitable expansion of the United States and the retreat, and even extermination, of Indian nations and peoples versus the attempt by Indian nations and peoples to preserve their lives, governments, cultures, and lands.

Eastern Shawnee Treaties and Agreements with the United States 1795–1874

Treaties and agreements from 1795 forward are part of the political lineage and history of the modern-day Eastern Shawnees. In 1795 Chief Black Hoof signed the first of many treaties between the Shawnees and the United States that directly involved the ancestors of the Eastern Shawnee Tribe and people.

AUGUST 3, 1795, TREATY WITH THE WYANDOTTES, ETC., AT GREENVILLE, NORTHWEST TERRITORY The tribal nations located north and west of the Ohio River had long insisted on that river being the boundary line between the United States and Indian country. A pan-Indian confederacy, led primarily by Shawnee chief Blue Jacket and Miami chief Little Turtle, had defeated American military invasions north of the river in 1790 and 1791. These defeats led the United States to attempt to sign treaties with the tribes in order to establish peace and a boundary line.[35]

The American treaty negotiators were instructed to discover which Indians were the "proprietors of the country lying to the northward of the Ohio" and to guarantee them their rights to "the remaining Indian lands," but they were also to get them to agree to allow some American forts north of the Ohio River. The tribes would be paid $50,000 in trade goods. The secretary of war instructed the negotiators to "form separate contracts, or treaties . . . with the several tribes to whom the lands actually belong, avoiding as much as possible, to confirm the idea of an union, or general confederacy of all the tribes." The negotiators were to insist, however, on the United States' Doctrine of Discovery, their "rights of pre-emption . . . to the Indian country, against all other nations and individuals. . . . When they choose to sell any portion of the country, it must be sold only to the United States." The secretary was also very crafty and ordered the negotiators to try to get permission for American agents, traders, and missionaries to live among the Indians, so as to further induce them to peace with the United States. The secretary also directed the negotiators to forbid anyone from talking to the Indians about selling or ceding land. As George Washington had advised in 1783, that subject could be left for another day.[36]

At this treaty conference the tribes countered the United States' points: "We have only been defending our just rights against your invasions. We want peace. Restore to us our country, and we shall be enemies no longer." The tribes also argued vigorously against the Doctrine of Discovery, the idea that the United States had any right to tribal lands: "You have talked, also, a great deal about pre-emption, and your exclusive right to purchase Indian lands, as ceded to you by the King, at the treaty of peace. Brothers: We never made any agreement with the King, nor with any other nation, that we would give to either the exclusive right of purchasing our lands." These treaty negotiations ultimately failed because the tribes continued to insist on the Ohio River as the boundary.[37]

Thereafter the United States sent a new army north of the river under General Anthony Wayne. Wayne defeated the tribes at the Battle of Fallen Timbers in August 1794, and now the United States negotiated a treaty from a much stronger position.[38]

The sachems, chiefs, and warriors of twelve named tribes signed the Treaty of Greenville on August 3, 1795. The treaty restored peace with the United States, required the release of prisoners by both sides, and drew a borderline between the tribes and the United States that ceded up to 17 million acres of Indian land. In fact, the tribes ceded up to two-thirds of the present-day state of Ohio and various other tracts of land in modern-day Illinois, Indiana, and Michigan for American forts and posts. One of the specific tracts ceded was 150,000 acres at the rapids of the Ohio (around modern-day Clarksville, Indiana), which the United States had given to General George Rogers Clark and his soldiers as payment for their services in the Revolutionary War. The United States paid the tribal nations $20,000 in goods and promised annual payments of $9,500 in goods (including $1,000 annually for the Shawnees) for all these concessions.[39]

The United States allegedly relinquished its claim to the lands that the tribes retained, but it still claimed the Doctrine of Discovery preemption right over those lands: the lands could only be sold to the United States. Also, any white persons or citizens of the United States that tried to settle on the retained Indian lands would lose American protection and would be subject to the tribes' punishments or to being driven away. The United States could also break up such settlements or punish the settlers as it saw fit so as to "effect the protection of the Indian lands herein before stipulated."[40]

The Indians retained the right to hunt on the lands they had ceded to the United States if they did so peaceably and without creating injury to Americans. The tribes also agreed to limit their trade and to only admit into their territory U.S.-licensed traders, and they "acknowledge[d] themselves to be under the protection of the said United States and no other power whatever." They also agreed to allow U.S. citizens free passage across Indian country to various American posts and forts by land and water.[41]

The Shawnee signers of this treaty were Black Hoof, Red Pole, Captain Reed, Blue Jacket, and five others.

After the Greenville Treaty, historians state that the Shawnees generally moved back as closely as possible to their former homes. They established their principal village at Wapakoneta on the Auglaize River, and Lewistown (Stony Creek, the Ohio home of the ESTO) was established nearby, as well as another village at Hog Creek. These three locations became recognized by the United States as Shawnee reservations within the state of Ohio in the treaties of 1817 and 1818.[42]

JUNE 7, 1803, TREATY WITH THE DELAWARES, ETC., AT FORT WAYNE, INDIANA TERRITORY In 1803 William Henry Harrison, then the governor of Indiana Territory, summoned various chiefs to Fort Wayne to discuss a new treaty. He explicitly threatened tribal leaders and "announced that only those chiefs who signed the treaty could receive their annuities." He continued to use that strategy in future negotiations with tribal governments, and he is also noted for purposely choosing to negotiate with relatively weaker tribes. In fact, he would treat with tribes who were new to a particular area because they would be more likely to sell land. Moreover, he tried to buy land from tribes with the weakest claims to avoid the need "to Negotiate with the other tribes who are more tenacious of their land." Governor Harrison also knew full well the true value of the Indian lands that the United States was buying. In 1805 he wrote that the United States was paying tribes one penny an acre but would sell the same lands for two dollars an acre.[43]

The introduction to this 1803 treaty states that the signatory chiefs were properly authorized by their tribes to enter the treaty. An 1826 book states that the tribes ceded another 1.2 million acres of land in this treaty. The Shawnees and the other tribes also reaffirmed that the United States were "their only friends and protectors," and they ceded to the United States a salt spring on Saline Creek, which flowed into the Ohio below the mouth of the Wabash River. The United States agreed to share the benefits of this spring and agreed to give the signatory tribes 150 bushels of salt each year. The United States was also authorized to build "houses of entertainment for the accommodation of travelers" on the roads between several American towns. The Indian citizens of the signatory tribes would receive free passage on any ferries built by Americans near these inns. For some unknown reason, the Shawnee signers of this treaty are listed in two separate sections on the signature page: Neahmemsieeh signed his X mark, as did Black Hoof and Methawnasice, although the latter two signed in a separate Shawnee listing.[44]

JULY 4, 1805, TREATY WITH THE WYANDOTTES, ETC., AT FORT INDUSTRY, OHIO, MIAMI OF THE LAKE   In spring 1805 Charles Jouett was appointed a U.S. treaty commissioner to negotiate a new treaty with the Wyandottes, Shawnees, and other tribes. Jouett was instructed by the secretary of war to attempt to purchase from the tribes 1 to 1.25 million acres of land south of Lake Erie and not pay more than one cent per acre. But he was also to buy any other lands the chiefs would sell, and he could pay up to two cents per acre. On July 4, after concluding the treaty with the tribes, he submitted to the secretary of war the treaty and a letter in which he stated that he had not been required to give the tribes any money in advance and that the United States simply had to pay annuities equaling one cent per acre: "You will see by those treaties, that an annuity is to be paid, of one thousand dollars, to the Wyandot, Delaware, and such of the Seneca and Shawanese nations that reside with the Wyandots."[45]

In this treaty the tribes once again acknowledged that they were under the protection of, and in friendship with, the United States. They reaffirmed that they had sold forever the lands south and east of the 1795 Greenville Treaty Line. For these new land sales, the nations were to be paid, annually and forever, a $1,000 annuity that would be distributed at Detroit. The "Indian nations, parties to this treaty," also retained for themselves the right to "fish and hunt within the territory and lands which they have now ceded to the United States, so long as they shall demean themselves peaceably." This treaty was signed by Shawnee chiefs Blue Jacket, "Black Hoff" [*sic*], Civil Man, and Isaac Peters.[46]

NOVEMBER 25, 1808, TREATY WITH THE CHIPPEWAS, ETC., BROWNSTOWN, MICHIGAN TERRITORY   In this treaty the United States requested to build a road across Indian lands to connect its settlements in the state of Ohio with its settlements in the Michigan Territory. The treaty states that lands still owned by the "Indian nations" blocked the United States from building a "convenient road." Consequently, the treaty claimed that, since the road would be "beneficial to the Indian nations," and because of the United States' "liberal and benevolent policy" towards Indians, the tribes should "give" the United States, "for free," a 120-foot-wide right-of-way to build the road as well as the right to establish settlements on the lands within one mile on each side of the road. The United States also asked for the right to build another road, but only asked for a 120-foot-wide right-of-way and not the additional lands. But the United States was to have the right to take materials and timber as needed from the adjacent lands to keep the roads and any necessary bridges in repair. It is worth noting that the United States was requesting an enormous amount of land—one commentator says it was two hundred square miles—yet the treaty asserts that the tribes "gave" this land to the United States.[47]

The "Indian nations" would once again "retain the privilege of hunting and fishing on the lands given and ceded as above, so long as the same shall remain the property of the United States." And, once again, the tribes acknowledged that they were "under the protection of the United States, and of no other sovereign." This treaty was signed for the Shawnees by chiefs Black Hoof and "Col. Lewis (Koitawaypie)." Lewis, who was most often called Captain Lewis, was the chief of Lewistown, the Ohio home of the ESTO.[48]

We must note that building American roads through Indian lands created very dangerous situations for the tribes. Roads, and the right of the United States to establish settlements along those roads, just invited more American settlers to invade Indian country. In fact, in 1826 Governor Lewis Cass of Michigan Territory wrote to the secretary of war after he concluded a treaty with the Potawatomis in which they agreed to allow the building of a road. In that letter he expressly stated the devious intent behind building roads through tribal territories: "What is much more important to us, it will sever their possessions, and lead them at no distant day to place their dependence upon agricultural pursuits, or to abandon the country."[49]

JULY 22, 1814, TREATY WITH THE WYANDOTTES, ETC., AT GREENVILLE, OHIO   During the War of 1812 the United States was very interested in ensuring the neutrality and even the assistance of the Indian nations in Ohio. As perhaps few people are aware, up to two hundred Shawnees from Wapakoneta (Black Hoof's village) and from Lewistown (Captain Lewis's village and the Ohio home of the ESTO), as well as more than two hundred Indians from other tribes located in Ohio, scouted and fought for the American army in 1813. Yet even while these tribes were supporting the United States, it had its eye on further Indian land cessions in Ohio.[50]

In March 1814 General William Henry Harrison and the secretary of war exchanged letters discussing the removal of tribes from Ohio. The secretary reported that Governor Lewis Cass of Michigan Territory and Ohio members of Congress were suggesting that a treaty should be arranged to remove the tribes to lands west of the Mississippi River. The secretary stated that a policy of separating Indians and Americans was useful because, as long as Indian settlements touch "ours, . . . collisions are to be feared." The secretary directed Harrison to query the tribes and report on their interest in removing so that the secretary could draft treaty instructions. Harrison reported on the Shawnees at Stony Creek (Lewistown) and at Wapakoneta: "The chiefs of this band of Shawanoese, Black Hoof, Wolf, and Lewis, are attached to us from principle as well as interest—they are honest men."[51]

In a June 11, 1814, letter, the secretary of war informed Governor Lewis Cass and General William Henry Harrison that they had been appointed as treaty commissioners. He first instructed them to meet with the Indian nations in Ohio to conclude a treaty of peace and alliance. He also set out the objectives to be attained: "1st A peace sincere & lasting, between the contracting parties, 2nd An alliance between the said parties in prosecuting the present War against Great Britain, and, 3d An arrangement for the extinction of the Indian title to the tract of land." The secretary also directed that any Indians who would fight for the United States would be taken into the army and would receive the same pay and subsistence of other soldiers.[52]

For some reason, however, the secretary changed his mind about the objectives for this treaty. One week later, on June 18, he made two changes to his instructions (one of which was more harsh on the Indians and one more lenient): "1st That instead of an article stipulating alliance and subsidy, by pay &c, one shall be substituted, simply obligatory on the Indians to assist in prosecuting the War against Great Britain, if so required to do, by the United States, and, 2nd That nothing be said or stipulated with regard to an exchange of lands, or opening of roads."[53] Perhaps the secretary did not want to antagonize tribes that were actively fighting for the United States at that very moment in the ongoing war.

Remember, this short treaty of "peace and friendship" seems to primarily have been designed to ensure the tribes' support or neutrality during the War of 1812. The United States was rightfully concerned that tribes would ally with the British, as Shawnee leaders Tecumseh and the Prophet and many others had already done. In this treaty the United States and some of the tribes, including the Shawnees and Senecas from Lewistown, granted peace to other tribes who had perhaps been fighting for England. The Indian nations agreed to aid the United States in its war with Great Britain and agreed to "make no peace with either [England or hostile tribes] without the consent of the United States." The tribes also agreed to provide warriors to support the United States. Shawnee Captain Lewis and many others from the Mixed Band of Senecas and Shawnees had already been fighting, scouting, and interpreting for the United States. The United States and its treaty commissioners expressly stated that the Sandusky Seneca, the Stony Creek (Lewistown), and the Delaware and Shawnee tribes had remained faithful to the United States throughout the war.

All the signatory tribes "again acknowledge[d] themselves under the protection of the said states, and of no other power whatever." The United States then granted the tribes, in essence, an illusory promise for signing the treaty: if the tribes performed the treaty, the United States would confirm and establish all the boundaries of the tribal lands as they had existed before the war. This was not a new promise and thus was not legal consideration (payment) for these tribes' support in the war and for signing a new treaty. Rather, the boundaries of their lands had already been established by prior treaties.[54]

The treaty conference was attended by nearly three thousand Indians. Five tribes and up to sixty-five chiefs and warriors, including Black Hoof, Blue Jacket, Captain Lewis, and eleven other Shawnees signed the treaty. Several Senecas who later signed other ESTO treaties also signed this treaty: Civil John, Wiping Stick, Big Turtle, and John Harris.[55]

SEPTEMBER 8, 1815, TREATY WITH THE WYANDOTTES, ETC., AT SPRING WELLS, MICHIGAN TER-RITORY In December 1814 the Treaty of Ghent ended the War of 1812 between England and the United States. England attempted to provide some protection for the Indian nations, many of whom had been English allies. That treaty required the United States to end hostilities with the Indians and to restore to the tribes "all the possessions, rights, and privileges which they may have enjoyed . . . previous to such hostilities." In the September 8, 1815, treaty with the tribes, which included the Lewistown Shawnees, the United States restored peace and relations with the tribal nations, but it did not bring up the subject of restoring tribal lands.[56]

In contrast, General Duncan McArthur, who later became one of the federal treaty negotiators for this 1815 treaty, had previously proposed to the secretary of war that now was the time for a new treaty because the United States could make "valueable [*sic*] purchases" of Indian lands "on better terms at this time." The federal government apparently took his advice because a new treaty conference was scheduled with the tribes in the state of Ohio and the territories of Michigan and Indiana.[57]

In a June 1815 letter the acting secretary of war instructed the U.S. treaty commissioners, William Henry Harrison, Duncan McArthur, and John Graham, regarding this newly proposed treaty. The secretary wrote that the federal objectives were to remind the tribes of their existing relations with the United States, to explain the peace treaty just concluded with England, and to end all hostilities with tribal nations. And, using a little subterfuge, the commissioners were to tell the Indians that the United States did not now want any new cessions of land. However, the tribes were to be told that they must allow the surveys for roads to proceed on the lands the United States had purchased in past treaties. The commissioners were also to tell the Indians that the United States would build trading posts so that they could buy goods. A later letter of instructions requested the commissioners to ascertain whether federal troops had taken livestock and grain from Indians during the war, and if so, the commissioners were to promise fair payments.[58]

In the subsequent treaty the United States granted peace to the tribes, and to bands of certain tribes who had allied with Great Britain in the war, including some Shawnees and Senecas. These specific tribes were restored to the possessions, rights, and privileges they enjoyed before the war, and they now again placed "themselves under the protection of the United States, and of no other power whatsoever."[59]

In addition, because of the fidelity to the United States manifested by, among others, the Seneca and Shawnee tribes, the United States pardoned certain chiefs and warriors of those tribes that may have fought for England, and they also were restored to their stations and property from before the war. The parties then renewed and confirmed all prior treaties, from the 1795 Treaty of Greenville forward. Similar to the 1814 treaty, this treaty was signed by many tribes, sachems, headmen, and warriors, including Black Hoof, Captain Lewis, and six other Shawnees, as well as Senecas who also signed several ESTO treaties, such as Civil John, Wiping Stick, and John Harris.[60]

SEPTEMBER 29, 1817, TREATY WITH THE WYANDOTTES, ETC., AT RAPIDS OF THE MIAMI OF LAKE ERIE The U.S. Senate refused to ratify this 1817 treaty with the Shawnee tribes and others in the form that it was first negotiated and signed. As will be seen in the next section, the Senate insisted that some changes, which were included in an 1818 supplemental treaty, be negotiated and signed by the tribes before the Senate would ratify both the 1817 and 1818 treaties.

Soon after the Shawnee tribes in Ohio had assisted the United States in the War of 1812, the United States repaid them by seeking even more land cessions and attempting to move them west of the Mississippi. In March 1817 the acting secretary of war wrote to Michigan Territory governor Lewis Cass indicating that the president wanted "to make an effort to extinguish the Indian title to all the lands now claimed by them within the limits of the State of Ohio." So he directed Cass to negotiate with the chiefs and see if they would relinquish their lands and on what terms. The president also proposed that individual Indians who demanded to remain in Ohio, even if the tribes sold all of their lands, "should have a life estate in a reservation of a certain number of acres, which should descend to his children in fee . . . and that those who do not wish to remain on those terms should have a body of land allotted to them on the west of the Mississippi." As a backup position, the president directed that if the tribes refused to sell, the treaty commissioners were to try to get them to relinquish certain portions of land so that the United States could build a road from Ohio to the Michigan Territory.[61]

Governor Cass and General Duncan McArthur were then appointed commissioners and given additional instructions in a May 1817 letter from the secretary of war. The secretary reported that Ohio's congressional delegates were telling the president that now was the time to buy Indian lands and to extinguish their claims in Ohio. The secretary repeated to the commissioners that it was politically important to remove tribes from the vicinity of Lake Erie, to connect the American populations in the state of Ohio and Michigan Territory, and thus they were authorized to pay "a more liberal compensation for its relinquishment than has hitherto been given for the relinquishment of Indian claims." Cass wrote back in July regarding the importance of giving gifts to the chiefs: "To attain with more certainty the proposed cession of land from the Wyandots, a timely distribution of presents to the influential chiefs is all-important."[62]

The commissioners met with at least seven different tribes at the Rapids of the Miami of Lake Erie in September 1817. After signing the treaty on September 29, the commissioners submitted it and a report on the negotiations to the secretary. They were worried that they had paid too much for the lands that the tribes ceded, but they knew how important this treaty and these lands were to the United States. They also reported, "The Wyandots, who owned it, and the Shawanees and Senecas, who live upon it, are fully aware of its importance to us and to them." In fact, the tribes were well aware of the extravagant prices the United States was receiving for selling former Indian lands to American settlers, hence the tribes demanded higher prices themselves. The commissioners also reported difficulties in negotiating the treaty and the terms for establishing Indian reservations because everyone was aware of the great changes to tribal life that these sales caused and of the increasing American population and the pressure on the Indians and tribes. Interestingly, the tribes insisted on being given copies of the treaty, and the commissioners promised them six copies printed on parchment and enclosed in tin cases.[63]

The secretary was delighted. He replied to the commissioners that this was the most important treaty the United States had ever negotiated. He was pleased with the vast amount of tribal lands purchased and the price paid. In fact, he stated that the only objection anyone could make to the price was that it was "not an adequate one."[64]

The 1817 treaty was equally important to the tribes. They now ceded to the United States millions of acres, almost all their remaining lands in the state of Ohio, and reserved for themselves only small islands of reservations as well as perpetual annuity payments. Black Hoof and the Shawnees at Wapakoneta retained ten square miles of land, while the Hog Creek Shawnees reserved twenty-five square miles, and the Mixed Band of Senecas and Shawnees at Lewistown reserved forty-eight square miles.[65]

The 1817 treaty is a long document compared to other Indian treaties, and it addresses many different issues and tribal nations. It appears from the text that the United States did not think the Senecas, Delawares, or Shawnees really owned the lands they lived on in Ohio. In articles 1 and 2 of the treaty the Wyandottes, Potawatomis, Ottawas, and Chippewas ceded various lands in Ohio to the United States. But in article 3 the Shawnees, Senecas, and Delawares (and four other tribes) were only asked to agree to the land cessions described in articles 1 and 2. In exchange, the United States agreed to pay all the tribes, annually and forever, annuities including, "[t]o the Shawnese tribe, annually, forever, the sum of two thousand dollars, in specie, at Wapaghkonetta."[66]

The United States treaty commissioners, however, made two mistakes. First, they stated in the treaty that the United States was "granting" land to the tribes. That was not legally or factually correct. In reality, the tribal nations were *reserving* to themselves some of the lands they already owned in Ohio, and thus they did not sell all their lands to the United States. Consequently, it is correct to use the term *reservations* for these reserved, or retained, lands. Second, the commissioners made a far more important mistake when they stated that the United States granted the reservation lands to the tribes "in fee simple" ownership. Under American property law, this is the highest and most protected form of land ownership. But this is not how international law and Anglo-American law assumed that indigenous peoples "owned" their lands. This is the exact reason the Senate refused to ratify the 1817 treaty until the "fee simple" language was amended in the supplemental 1818 treaty discussed below.[67]

Moreover, in what looks like an early attempt to create what is known as Indian allotments, this treaty purported to grant ownership, and specific amounts of land within the described reservations, to named individuals of each of these tribes. Consequently, lands were to be granted within the Wapakoneta, Hog Creek, and Lewistown reservations to Indian individuals that were specifically named in the treaty. The forty-eight square miles at Lewistown were to be "equally divided among" eighty-two named Shawnees and fifty Senecas. However, the actual decision to divide, or allot, these reservations and to grant titles to the named individuals was left up to the chiefs. Once the parcels of land had been conveyed to individuals, the treaty appeared to allow the individual Indians to sell the lands to anyone. In addition, the tribes apparently asked the United States to grant land to certain individuals connected to the tribes by blood, by adoption, or as prisoners. For example, Nancy Stewart, the daughter of Shawnee chief Blue Jacket, received 640 acres immediately south of the Lewistown reservation. Three of the interpreters who worked on this treaty also received land.[68]

The United States also agreed to provide Indian agents to reside with the tribes, ostensibly to help protect the Indians and their property, and to manage their interactions with the United States. One agent was appointed for the three Shawnee reservations at Lewistown, Hog Creek, and Wapakoneta. Pursuant to the treaty, the United States also appointed a blacksmith to serve the three Shawnee reservations.[69]

This treaty repeated a similar provision from earlier Shawnee treaties, that the Indians could hunt on the lands they had ceded to the United States as long as the United States continued to own them. The 1817 treaty also contained a new provision that Indians could make sugar from the trees on lands they had ceded to the United States as long as the United States owned the lands and as long as they caused "no unnecessary waste upon the trees."[70]

The United States also agreed to pay for the damages that loyal tribes and Indians suffered during the War of 1812, as determined by the secretary of war. Furthermore, the treaty expressly stated the amounts that the Shawnee Indians at Lewistown and Wapakoneta were to receive.[71]

This treaty was signed by dozens of chiefs, sachems, and warriors of the seven tribes, including Black Hoof, Captain Lewis, and ten other Shawnees and eight Senecas.

SEPTEMBER 17, 1818, TREATY WITH THE WYANDOTTES, ETC., AT SAINT MARY'S, OHIO The 1818 ESTO treaty is a supplement to the 1817 treaty. As already mentioned, the U.S. Senate would not ratify the 1817 treaty without some amendments. The Senate objected to the tribes retaining their Ohio reservations in fee simple ownership, which meant that chiefs could transfer land to individual Indians who could then sell their lands to whomever they wished. Thus, that treaty was returned to the tribal nations to reconsider in light of the Senate's proposed changes as stated in the 1818 supplemental treaty. The U.S. Senate then ratified both treaties after the tribes agreed to the changes, and they both became effective in 1819.

When the Senate considered the 1817 treaty in December of that year, one senator from the committee charged with reviewing it stated,

> The committee view as exceptionable that clause of the seventh article, which, without any control on the part of Government, authorizes the individuals of those tribes, after separate allotments have been made by the chiefs, to dispose of their lands, and grant them in complete title to any person whatever. This provision, it is believed, is unprecedented by any former treaty, and at variance with the general principles on which intercourse with the Indian tribes has been conducted. The laws . . . have also prohibited any sale of their lands, except made in public council, and to authorized agents of the Government.

Consequently, the Senate proposed that the 1817 treaty be amended by a new treaty, which stated that the tribes would hold their lands "in the same manner as Indian reservations have been heretofore held" and which required that no sale of the Ohio reservation lands could be made by an Indian "without the permission of the President."[72]

The 1817 treaty commissioners were now instructed to carry out the Senate's order. A Senate resolution of February 5, 1818, stated that it would not ratify the 1817 treaty and called for the negotiation of a new treaty "under which the Indians will not be granted the right to own their new lands individually in fee simple." Hence John Calhoun, the secretary of war, informed commissioners Lewis Cass and Duncan McArthur to renew negotiations with the Shawnees and other tribes.[73]

The commissioners were also instructed to once again try to force the tribes to move west. They were told to offer the tribes very generous terms if they would remove beyond the Mississippi. But once again the tribes refused. The commissioners wrote the secretary that they had pushed the issue "as far as we believe it politick [*sic*] to enforce it." The commissioners also stated that the time had not yet come for the tribes to voluntarily leave Ohio, but as Americans surrounded them with settlements, the Indians would become anxious to move, and echoing George Washington, the commissioners said that it would cost the United States far less to remove them then than to try to force removal now.[74]

However, as the government had feared, the commissioners had to offer the tribes more compensation before they would accept the proposed changes to the 1817 treaty. In regard to the Lewistown Shawnees and Senecas, their reservation was enlarged by 8,960 acres, and the United States agreed to pay annuities "to the Shawnese, and to the Senecas of Lewistown, an additional annuity of one thousand dollars, forever."[75]

The relatively short 1818 supplementary treaty only contains five articles. Article 1 amended the status of the lands in the 1817 treaty that had been granted in fee simple title. The 1818 treaty said they "shall not be thus granted" but shall be "reserved for the use of the said Indians, and held by them in the same manner as Indian reservations have been heretofore held." However, these reservations "shall be reserved for the use of the Indians named in the schedule to the said treaty, and held by them and their heirs forever, unless ceded to the United States." This treaty reinforces the political nature of Indian treaty making when it states, "This treaty shall take effect, and be obligatory on the contracting parties, as soon as the same shall be ratified by the President of the United States, by and with the advice and consent of the Senate thereof." For some reason, the sachems, chiefs, and warriors of only four of the seven tribes from the 1817 treaty signed this 1818 treaty, including Black Hoof, Colonel (Captain) Lewis, and ten others for the Shawnees, and eight for the Senecas.[76]

For an unknown reason, the Lewistown reservation was then divided in half. The northern part was set aside "for the use of the Senecas who reside there, and the south half for the use of the Shawnese who reside there."[77]

JULY 20, 1831, TREATY WITH THE SENECAS, ETC., AT LEWISTOWN, OHIO The 1831 treaty is very significant in the history of the Eastern Shawnee Tribe. In July 1831 the citizens of the tribe finally agreed to sell all their lands and homes in Ohio and most of their personal property and remove to Indian Territory. The United States had long been working to get the tribes in Ohio to remove. In 1830 Congress passed the Removal Act, under which tribes that consented would be moved to the West. So now removal was an official federal Indian policy, and even more pressure was put on the eastern tribes to remove westward.

In February 1831 the Sandusky Seneca Tribe of Ohio signed a treaty in Washington, D.C., and agreed to remove. The commissioner, James B. Gardiner, who had successfully concluded the treaty of removal with the Seneca Tribe, was then appointed as a treaty commissioner to go to Ohio. He was instructed to treat with the tribes there and convince them to remove also. John McElvain, the U.S. Indian agent for the Wyandottes, Senecas, and Shawnees, was also appointed a commissioner.[78]

In July 1831 Gardiner and McElvain conducted a treaty negotiation with the principal chiefs and warriors of what this treaty calls the "mixed band or tribes of Seneca and Shawnee Indians residing at and around Lewistown." According to several commentators and historians, Gardiner put intense pressure on the tribe to remove. Echoing President Andrew Jackson's comments to other tribes, Gardiner threatened the Mixed Band that if it stayed in Lewistown, its lands would come under state jurisdiction and they would become subject to state laws and taxes, all without the benefits and protections of being U.S. or state citizens.[79]

Gardiner's negotiations with the Mixed Band of Senecas and Shawnees in July 1831 were no doubt very similar to the nearly contemporaneous negotiations he held with the Wapakoneta Shawnees for their August 8, 1831, removal treaty. Regarding that negotiation, an eyewitness and unofficial transcriber of the proceedings accused Gardiner of using underhanded tactics against the Wapakoneta Shawnees. This witness, a Quaker missionary, wrote that Gardiner made many promises that the tribal leaders did not trust. Gardiner also read aloud from his instructions from the president and the secretary of war that he was instructed to tell the Indians that they were in a deplorable condition, surrounded by bad white people, that conditions would get worse, that they were overrun with whiskey, that the game was nearly gone, and that Ohio would soon extend its laws over them and tax the Indians for the benefit of white Americans. Not all of these statements were true, of course.[80]

Gardiner also gave glowing reports regarding the area in Kansas Territory to which the Wapakoneta Shawnees were to be removed. He stated that there was plenty of buffalo and game, and that they would live well without even working. In fact, he said, the government would make them rich. He also stated that the United States would grant them their lands "forever" and build them a gristmill and sawmill. Interestingly, the eyewitness claims that Gardiner coerced the Wapakoneta Shawnees to sign their August treaty without even reading it to them in full.[81]

This same eyewitness recorded that traders used false claims to pressure the Wapakoneta Shawnee Tribe and individual Indian debtors to sell their reservation so that the traders could be paid. This reporter stated that the traders also offered large bribes to chiefs, and that, in reality, the traders would get most of the money paid to the tribe. All the parties, including government officers, were allegedly intoxicated.[82]

On July 20, 1831, the Mixed Band of Senecas and Shawnees signed its treaty and agreed to sell its remaining land in Ohio. According to the treaty, the tribe agreed to sell its land "in order to obtain a more permanent and advantageous home" in the West. In exchange, the United States agreed to help the tribe of about three hundred people to remove west. The United States also agreed to "grant by patent, in fee simple to them and their heirs forever, as long as they shall exist as a nation and remain on the same," 60,000 acres of land "contiguous to the lands granted to the Senecas of Sandusky." The land would be granted to the Mixed Band in fee simple ownership, but it was a restricted title because the land could only be sold to the United States. And, similar to treaty promises made to the Five Civilized Tribes, which courts have held to be legally significant, the United States "guarantee[d]" that the land granted to the Senecas and Shawnees "shall never be within the bounds of any State or Territory, nor subject to the laws thereof."[83]

The United States agreed to pay all costs of the removal, to provide the Senecas and Shawnees with a one-year supply of provisions upon arriving in Indian Territory, and due to their former good conduct and friendly disposition, the United States would give "presents" to the tribe (blankets, guns, tools, and more) after they arrived in the territory. In addition, the United States sold the Mixed Band's Ohio lands and used that money to build a sawmill and blacksmith shop for the tribe in Indian Territory, and the United States paid the expenses and salary for a blacksmith, as long as the president deemed necessary. The United States also sold the tribe's improvements in Ohio, such as houses, farm buildings, and other property, and the chiefs were to distribute those sums to the individuals who owned the improvements. Moreover, the United States promised to remove the tribe with care, under the protection "of some competent and proper person" friendly to the tribe.[84]

Any monies left over from the sale of the Ohio lands, after the United States deducted its expenses, were to be invested in a fund for the tribe's needs and paid out 5 percent annually to the chiefs for the use and benefit of the tribe. This fund would last as long as Congress desired, or it could be terminated sooner if the chiefs, with the consent of the general council of the people, requested the fund to be paid out. Furthermore, all annuity monies due to the Senecas and Shawnees under past treaties were to be paid at their new location.[85]

The treaty was signed for the "contracting parties" by the commissioners and by thirteen Seneca and Shawnee principal chiefs and warriors: Civil John (Methomea), Robbin (Skilleway), John Young (Totala Chief), Pewyache, Mingo Carpenter, John Jackson, Little Lewis (Quashacaugh), James McDonnell, Civil John's son (Honede), Run Fast, Yankee Bill, Cold Water, and John Sky.

DECEMBER 29, 1832, TREATY WITH THE SENECAS AND SHAWNEES, AT SENECA AGENCY, INDIAN TERRITORY The Mixed Band of Seneca and Shawnee Indians left Lewistown, Ohio, on September 19, 1832, and arrived at the Seneca Agency in Indian Territory on December 13. They were displeased with the 60,000 acres of land that were selected for them west of the Neosho/Grand River, and they began negotiating for 60,000 acres east of the river.[86]

Federally appointed commissioners Henry L. Ellsworth, John F. Schermerhorn, and Montfort Stokes were already in the territory and were charged with dealing with multiple issues regarding the resident tribes and the removal of the eastern Indians. These commissioners had no specific instructions regarding the Mixed Band, but they were in the territory at the general orders of the secretary of war to inspect it, to receive the emigrating tribes from the East, to locate them on appropriate lands, and to make them happy as far as was possible. They were also instructed that their negotiations with these tribes were actually part of constitutionally based treaty making with the Indian nations, because the Senate would have to approve any agreements the commissioners made. The commissioners then conducted negotiations with the Mixed Band at the Seneca Agency at the headwaters of the Cowskin River and quickly agreed with the request to locate their reservation on the east side of the Neosho River.[87]

The commissioners' secretary reported on the negotiations with the Senecas and Shawnees to the secretary of war and submitted the draft treaty signed by the parties. He reported that the Senecas and Shawnees from Lewistown would not settle west of the river because the lands were not fit for agriculture. Their new lands were east of the river and immediately north of the lands assigned to the Sandusky Senecas. Interestingly, the Sandusky Senecas and the Mixed Band of Senecas and Shawnees now formed a confederacy and merged into one nation to be called the United Nation of Senecas and Shawnees.[88]

Furthermore, the treaty provided for the Mixed Band to receive title to its land "in fee simple; but the lands shall not be sold or ceded without the consent of the United States." The United States also agreed to immediately build a gristmill, a sawmill, and a blacksmith shop and to provide all needed tools and machinery. The United States also agreed to pay the "United Nations" $1,000 ($400 of which was to go to the Mixed Band from Lewistown) for money they had advanced to the United States to pay for their own removal and for property lost during the removal. And nothing in this 1832 treaty was to affect the rights that the tribes enjoyed under any previous treaty, which presumably means they were to continue receiving all annuities due under previous treaties. This treaty would become binding and obligatory "upon the contracting parties" after it was ratified by the president and the Senate. The treaty was signed by fourteen Sandusky Seneca chiefs and, for the Mixed Band, by first chief Civil John (and two of his sons), Robbin, John Jackson, Little Lewis, John Young, Mingo Carpenter, Jemmy McDaniel, Yankee Bill, Big Ash, and Pe-wy-a-che.[89]

AUGUST 23, 1854, AGREEMENT (UNRATIFIED TREATY) WITH THE SENECAS AND SHAWNEES, AT NEOSHO AGENCY, INDIAN TERRITORY   In August 1854 the United Nation of Seneca and Shawnee Indians (the Sandusky Senecas and the Senecas and Shawnees of Lewistown) signed a proposed treaty with U.S. commissioner Andrew Dorn. These parties clearly understood this document to be a treaty. The Senate, however, never ratified it as a treaty, and Congress never approved it as an agreement either, so it never became effective. Thus little time will be spent here discussing it.[90]

Pursuant to this document, the Senecas of Sandusky and the Senecas and Shawnees agreed to sell to the United States some of their land in Indian Territory. However, the tribes would keep a total of 160 acres per individual for the Cowskin/Sandusky Seneca Tribe, to be held as common property of the tribe, and the Mixed Band of Senecas and Shawnees of Lewistown would retain eighty acres of land per person, plus sixteen additional sections of land, all of which would be held as common property of the Mixed Band. The lands not selected to be reserved by the tribes would have been sold at public auction by the United States, and all net funds would have been paid to the Indians.[91]

Apparently, the United States also wanted to end its obligation to pay the annuities due under earlier treaties. This document would have relinquished those rights, and any other claims the tribes had against the United States, and for any injuries caused by U.S. citizens, for a one-time payment of $16,000 to each tribe. The Indians also promised to renew their efforts to prevent alcohol use and to encourage industry, thrift, and morality, all "to promote their advancement in civilization." The document also would have provided for the building of roads, highways, and railroads on the lands the tribes ceded to the United States and on the lands they reserved.[92]

This proposed treaty was signed by six chiefs and warriors for the Sandusky Senecas and by eight chiefs and warriors for the Mixed Band of Senecas and Shawnees: Pe-ny-a-che, George McDaniel, John Lamb, David Civil John, Peter Knox, John Melton, Yankee Bill, and John Lewis. The interpreter for the Senecas and Shawnees was Lewis Davis, who is no doubt the same Lewis Davis who later signed the 1861, 1865, and 1867 agreements and treaties as a chief of the Shawnees of the Mixed Band and of the ESTO.

OCTOBER 4, 1861, TREATY WITH THE SENECAS AND SHAWNEES WITH THE CONFEDERATE STATES OF AMERICA, AT PARK HILL, CHEROKEE NATION During the Civil War many Indian nations in Indian Territory signed treaties with the Confederate States of America (CSA). It was without question a political and human necessity, as the tribes were desperately trying to survive the war and had to accommodate the South. This was especially the case after Union troops and officials, and even the Neosho Indian agent, abandoned the territory and the United States ceased paying treaty annuities. In fact, historians write that the Senecas of Sandusky and the Mixed Band of Senecas and Shawnees "were forced by their location to sign a treaty with the CSA" and that the United States violated its treaty promises by not protecting these tribes. By 1862 most of the Senecas and Shawnees had to flee to Kansas to avoid depredations caused by both Northern and Southern troops. All of their horses and "hogs and cattle [were] taken by Union and rebel soldiers." Notwithstanding this egregious situation, more than six hundred Quapaw, Seneca, and Shawnee Indians in Kansas served in the Union Army, and the commissioner of Indian affairs praised them as "good and efficient soldiers." Nevertheless, these CSA treaties ultimately cost all the tribes dearly because the United States used them as excuses to extract new concessions from the tribes after the Civil War.[93]

In late September 1861 the CSA negotiated treaties with the Senecas and Shawnees and other tribes at the home of Cherokee chief John Ross. The CSA representative, Lieutenant Albert Pike, and the Sandusky Senecas and the Mixed Band signed a treaty on October 4, 1861. It was ratified December 21, 1861, by the CSA Congress. One historian claims that Lieutenant Pike threatened the tribes to force them to sign. But it seems clear from the text of the treaty that the Senecas of the Lewistown Mixed Band did not sign. The CSA and Lieutenant Pike were assisted at this treaty session by Andrew Dorn, the U.S. commissioner who had negotiated the Mixed Band's 1854 unratified treaty.[94]

The Confederate States made significant promises to the Sandusky Senecas and to the Mixed Band of Senecas and Shawnees in this very long treaty. The CSA even paid the tribes one annuity payment that was due under their treaties with the United States. Other than that, the provisions of the Mixed Band–CSA treaty were never fulfilled. Not surprisingly, this treaty was very similar to Indians' treaties with the United States. For example, the tribes placed themselves "under the laws and protection of the Confederate States of America, in peace and war forever," and the Confederacy guaranteed the tribes their land "title in fee simple, as long as each, respectively, shall exist as a nation and remain thereon, and the exclusive possession and undisturbed use, occupancy and enjoyment, as long as grass shall grow and water run." There were also several provisions in the treaty regarding slavery. For example, the tribes agreed to return any "negroes, horses or other property stolen from white men," and "all negroes and mulattoes" would be subject to the criminal laws of the tribes; they also agreed that "the institution of slavery in the said Seneca and Seneca and Shawnee Tribes is legal, and has existed from time immemorial."[95]

The treaty was signed by twelve Seneca chiefs and by Lewis Davis (entitled the principal chief of the Senecas and Shawnees), Joseph Mohawk (second chief of the Shawnees), two Shawnee councilors (White Deer and Silas Doughtery), and John Tomahawk.

SEPTEMBER 13, 1865, AGREEMENT WITH THE CHEROKEES AND OTHER TRIBES IN INDIAN TERRITORY, AT FORT SMITH, ARKANSAS After the Civil War, Washington, D.C., policy makers clearly intended to use the fact that many tribes in Indian Territory had signed treaties with the South as an excuse to extort land cessions, to remove Indians in Kansas to Indian Territory, and to wrest other rights from the Indian nations. Thus the United States called at least eleven tribes from the territory, including the Mixed Band of Senecas and Shawnees, to a conference at Fort Smith, Arkansas, in September 1865. Ostensibly, the meeting was to begin reconciling the tribal nations once again to the North.[96]

President Andrew Johnson appointed five commissioners for this conference, which convened on September 8. The commissioner of Indian affairs, Dennis Cooley, was the president of the conference. Colonel Ely Parker, a Seneca Indian from New York and a member of General U. S. Grant's staff, was also one of the commissioners.[97]

The meeting began on a harsh note when commissioner Cooley told the tribes that they had erred badly by allying with the Confederacy. Cooley told them that they were all now supplicants for whatever favors the United States might deem to grant. He also stated that the tribes had committed a "great crime" and had forfeited their former treaty annuities, nullified their existing treaties, and lost all rights to their lands. He specifically named the Mixed Band of Senecas and Shawnees as one of the tribes that had signed treaties with the Confederacy and forfeited their treaties and rights. He laid out seven conditions for making new treaties to reconcile the Indian nations to the United States, which included agreeing to make room on their reservations to accept removed tribes from Kansas.[98]

The tribal representatives correctly responded that the United States had abandoned them in Indian Territory, had not protected them from the CSA, and had stopped paying treaty annuities. The representatives—including Cowskin/Sandusky Seneca chief Isaac Warrior, speaking for the Senecas, Mixed Band of Senecas and Shawnees, and Quapaws—stated that they were innocent victims, had been forced to accept treaties with the CSA to save their lives, and had sent warriors to the Union army. The commissioners recognized that many of these tribes, specifically the Senecas and Shawnees, had sent warriors to fight for the United States. Yet commissioner Cooley still responded that the tribes had committed treason.[99]

The hypocrisy and evil intent on the part of the United States was obvious. The United States had previously used a similar bellicose and demanding strategy toward Indian nations in 1784–86 after the Revolutionary War. That position had been mistaken and was quickly abandoned. The 1865 position was even more blatantly false and seemed politically and economically motivated as a mere bargaining chip, because the rebellious Southern states and their soldiers and politicians were accepted back into the Union after the war with few, if any, permanent repercussions. But the innocent tribes would not be so lucky.[100]

As historians have noted, the primary purpose of the Fort Smith conference, and of the Americans' demand for new treaties, was to get more Indian land. Consequently, this conference was conducted as a punitive measure and in an atmosphere of coercion, oppression, and bitterness. More or less tentative agreements were reached and new treaties outlined to restore peace and friendship between tribes and the United States, and tribal delegates were ordered to select treaty commissioners to go to Washington, D.C., in 1866.[101]

The Mixed Band of Senecas and Shawnees was not the main target of this conference, probably due to its miniscule land base and population. The Mixed Band did not send representatives to D.C. until 1867, and it does not appear that the United States imposed a punitive treaty on the tribe at that time. Instead, the Senecas and Shawnees appear to have visited D.C. to request that the United States ratify agreements they had made among themselves and with other tribes. But it must be noted that the 1867 arrangement included the Mixed Band selling some of its land to tribes removing from Kansas, which did serve the express objectives of the United States and was one of the conditions the U.S. commissioners at Fort Smith insisted on for future treaties.[102]

The 1865 Fort Smith agreement states that the named tribes (Cherokees, Creeks, Choctaws, Chickasaws, Osages, Seminoles, Senecas, Senecas and Shawnees, and Quapaws) "were induced . . . to throw off their allegiance to the government of the United States . . . [and] made themselves liable to a forfeiture of all rights." But the United States pledged to act with magnanimity and reestablish order and its authority among these tribes. The representatives of the Indian nations did "acknowledge themselves to be under the protection of the United States of America, and covenant and agree, that hereafter they will in all things recognize the government of the United States as exercising exclusive jurisdiction over them, and will not enter into any allegiance or conventional arrangements with any state, nation, power or sovereign whatsoever." Pursuant to these stipulations, the United States was willing to reestablish peace and friendship with these nations and to protect the persons and property of these tribes. The United States was also willing to enter new treaties to settle questions growing out of former treaties. Chief Isaac Warrior signed the agreement for the Cowskin/Sandusky Senecas, and it was signed for the Senecas and Shawnees by Chief Lewis Davis, A. McDonald, Goodhunt, Jas. Tallchief, and Lewis Denny. Lewis Davis also served as the Seneca and Shawnee interpreter, as he had done for the unratified 1854 treaty.[103]

FEBRUARY 23, 1867, TREATY WITH THE SENECAS, MIXED BAND OF SENECAS AND SHAWNEES, QUAPAWS, ETC., AT WASHINGTON, D.C. Representatives of the Mixed Band and other tribes traveled to Washington, D.C., in February 1867 to conclude treaties with the United States. As is briefly mentioned in the previous section, these tribes appear to have already reached several agreements and were asking the United States to approve and ratify these decisions in a treaty. However, the United States welcomed this treaty because it instituted one of the most important U.S. conditions as stated at the 1865 Fort Smith conference—removing tribes from Kansas to Indian Territory.[104]

United States special commissioner W. H. Watson conducted two long interviews with these tribal representatives in Washington, D.C., on February 5 and 9, 1867. Watson was apparently trying to ascertain exactly what agreements the tribes had reached. Then he took these proposals to the commissioner of Indian affairs to see if the commissioner would agree to the terms and draft a treaty for the executive branch and the Senate to consider. Regrettably, Shawnee chief Lewis Davis of the Mixed Band was too sick to attend on February 9, and he must have also been absent for the interview on February 5, because the minutes do not record his presence or that he said anything. Moreover, two U.S. Indian agents served as witnesses to his signature on the February 23, 1867, treaty. So it is probable that he did not attend the treaty-signing event.[105]

These interviews primarily addressed moving tribes from Kansas to the lands of the Senecas, the Mixed Band of Senecas and Shawnees, and the Quapaws in Indian Territory. The tribes in Kansas who were discussing removing to Indian Territory were the Wyandottes, Ottawas, Miamis, Peorias, Absentee Shawnees, the Black Bob Band of Shawnees, and the Shawnees connected with Chief Charles BlueJacket.[106]

In the interviews John Whitetree, primarily, and John Young, to a much lesser degree, spoke for the Mixed Band. Both of these representatives signed the resulting February 23 treaty for the Senecas and Shawnees, as did Lewis Davis. Significantly, the Senecas and the Shawnees of the Mixed Band now desired to separate. The tribes had apparently decided to split so as to join other tribes who spoke their same languages. Thus, the Senecas wanted to join the Cowskin/

Sandusky Senecas, and the Shawnees—who were now to be called the Eastern Shawnee Tribe— discussed having Shawnees from Kansas move to their reservation. There were also discussions and agreements about how to handle the Mixed Band's joint treaty annuities and government-provided blacksmith, how to divide their reservation, and about placing the tribes from Kansas on the Sandusky Senecas' or on the Mixed Band of Senecas and Shawnees' lands. In addition, the U.S. representative proposed that the Senecas and the Mixed Band of Senecas and Shawnees move further south, but they declined.[107]

The tribes signed the treaty in Washington, D.C., on February 23, 1867. But in June 1868 the Senate insisted on several amendments before it would ratify the treaty. Two changes affected the Senecas and Shawnees. The Senate insisted on deleting language in the treaty stating that the United States had failed to protect the tribes during the Civil War ("the government being under obligations to protect them, but for the time unable to do so"), and the Senate removed a monetary cap on the amount of possible damages the tribes could be paid by the United States for losses suffered in the Civil War. The amended treaty was then re-signed by many tribal nations and representatives at the Neosho Agency in the Shawnee Nation during the first two weeks of September 1868. John Whitetree, John Young, Alfred McDaniel, and William Jackson signed for the Mixed Band of Senecas and Shawnees. President Andrew Johnson proclaimed the treaty in October 1868, and it became constitutionally effective.[108]

The treaty reflected the agreements discussed above. Most relevant to the ESTO was the agreement that the Mixed Band of Senecas and Shawnees would separate. The Senecas would join the Cowskin/Sandusky Senecas and live on their reservation, and the Shawnees would now become known as the Eastern Shawnee Tribe. The Eastern Shawnees and Senecas split the funds they were due under their past treaties. And the United States was required to investigate and pay the claims of the Mixed Band and other tribes for the loss of homes and property in the Civil War.[109]

Ironically, because the United States had not protected the tribes during the Civil War, and because the tribes had suffered grievous losses, the treaty stated that the tribes wanted to sell land to rebuild their houses and reopen their farms. Conveniently, the United States just happened to know of tribes from Kansas that were ready to buy these lands and to move to Indian Territory. The Senecas of the Mixed Band sold 30,000 acres to the United States for $24,000, which was the north half of the 60,000-acre reservation it owned with the Eastern Shawnees. The United States sold this land to the Peorias, who were joined by the Weas, Kaskaskias, Piankashaws, and Miamis. The Senecas then moved onto the reservation of the Cowskin/Sandusky Senecas.[110]

The Eastern Shawnee Tribe sold 12,000 acres on the west side of its remaining 30,000-acre reservation to the United States for $12,000. The United States then sold that land to the Ottawa Tribe for the same price. Two thousand dollars of the $12,000 payment were to be paid immediately to the Shawnees to build homes, and the balance was invested for the tribe "under the name of Eastern Shawnees." This fund was to pay 5 percent to the tribe semiannually, and these monies were to be used under the direction of the chiefs and with the consent of the U.S. Indian agent to buy farm tools and general articles.[111]

June 23, 1874, Agreement with the Eastern Shawnees, at Quapaw Agency, Indian Territory In 1872–73 the Modoc Tribe fought a war with the United States on the California-Oregon border. Approximately 155 Modocs were then removed in 1873 as prisoners of war and temporarily located on the ESTO reservation in Indian Territory. In 1874 the Eastern Shawnee Tribe agreed to sell four thousand acres in the northeast corner of its reservation to the United States for $6,000 to provide a permanent home for the Modoc Tribe. The United States agreed to pay the $6,000—one-half upon ratification of the agreement by the secretary of interior and then the balance one year later "per capita" to the Eastern Shawnee Indians to enable them to "enlarge their farms and otherwise improve their condition in civilization." The agreement was signed for the ESTO by chiefs James Choctaw and Thomas Captain, councilors John Logan and John Williams, and "Young Men" Good Hunt, Billy Dick, John Mohawk, Corn Stalk, George Beaver, Samson Kyzer, and John Jackson. In March 1875 Congress confirmed the agreement.[112]

CONCLUSION

The political interactions between the governments of the United States and the Eastern Shawnee Tribe are amply demonstrated in the history and in the treaties and agreements detailed above. Under the U.S. Constitution, federal Indian law, and these treaties, the Eastern Shawnee Tribe has an ongoing government-to-government relationship with the United States. The tribe is a sovereign government that exercised in the past, and still exercises today, jurisdiction and political authority over its territory, its citizens, and the people and events within ESTO territory. It is crucial for Eastern Shawnee citizens and for all Americans to be aware of this history and law.

In stark contrast, however, the ESTO history of treaty making also demonstrates a very disturbing aspect of American history. It is hard to deny, in fact, that the actions of the United States toward the Eastern Shawnee Tribe and other Indian nations would be defined today as ethnic cleansing and even perhaps as genocide. While the United Nations has apparently not adopted an official definition of ethnic cleansing, the working definition accepted by UN experts and bodies defines it as "a purposeful policy designed by one ethnic or religious group to remove by violent and terror-inspiring means the civilian population of another ethnic or religious group from certain geographic areas." And the official UN definition of genocide, adopted in a UN international treaty in 1948, states, "Genocide means any of the following acts committed with intent to destroy, in whole or in part, a national, ethnical [*sic*], racial or religious group, as such: (a) Killing members of the group; (b) Causing serious bodily or mental harm to members of the group; (c) Deliberately inflicting on the group conditions of life calculated to bring about its physical destruction in whole or in part." Moreover, in 2007 the United Nations General Assembly adopted a resolution that states, "Indigenous peoples shall not be forcibly removed from their lands or territories" or be forcibly assimilated or have their cultures destroyed. In sum, the policies and history detailed above seem to meet the definition of ethnic cleansing, and they certainly followed the pattern that General George Washington predicted in 1783.[113]

But it would be a mistake to focus on treaty making only as a matter of historical interest. These treaties have modern-day effects. Even though the majority of their provisions are no longer applicable, the very existence of these treaties continues to reinforce that the ESTO is a government as recognized under the Interstate Commerce Clause and the Treaty Clause of the U.S. Constitution. In addition, Indian "treaty making" is really not even over, notwithstanding the congressional act of 1871. In the modern day, the Eastern Shawnee Tribe continues to have a consensual and diplomatic relationship with the United States and consults on and consents to various activities with the United States and also with the state of Oklahoma. For example, the ESTO is what is known as a self-governance tribe due to the signing of a continuing self-governance agreement with the United States in 1996. The tribe has also signed gaming and tobacco tax compacts with Oklahoma and has entered into numerous agreements, contracts, and memoranda of understanding with other tribal governments and several Oklahoma towns. All of these political and diplomatic activities demonstrate, as one law professor has written, that Indian nations have created a "modern form of treaty," and thus "treaty making therefore has undergone a resurgence, and the process continues."[114]

In conclusion, the eighty-year history of treaties and agreements concluded by the Eastern Shawnee Tribe with the United States demonstrates the kinds of issues that these two governments dealt with through official political and diplomatic means. The ESTO was a partner of the United States in war, but was also treated as an adversary and a conquered people as the tribe struggled to accommodate the expansion of the United States and still maintain its tribal relations, existence, and homelands. The ESTO was nearly overrun by American Manifest Destiny, but it has endured as a government and as a people to the modern day. The Eastern Shawnee Tribe continues to fight today for interests that are remarkably similar to what its ancestors have fought for throughout history—to preserve its people, its culture, its history, its homeland, and its existence.

Table 6.1 Treaties between the Eastern Shawnee Tribe and the United States

Treaties Date Location	Statute at Large	Significant Terms	Shawnee and Seneca Signers
Treaty with the Wyandottes, etc. (Treaty of Greenville) Aug. 3, 1795 Greenville, Northwest Terr.	7 Stat. 49; *Indian Affairs*, 2:39	• Ceded 17 million acres in and around Ohio • Drew boundary line • Tribal nations were placed under U.S. protection • United States to pay $9,500 in goods for tribes annually ($1,000 for Shawnees) • Indians retained right to hunt on ceded lands, if peaceable and causing no injury to United States • White settlers that entered Indian lands would be subject to tribal punishment • Exclusive trade agreements	*Shawnees:* Black Hoof (Cutthewekasaw) Red Pole (Misquacoonacaw) Captain Reed (Hahgooseekaw) Blue Jacket (Weyapiersenwaw), Long Shanks (Waytheah) (Kaysewaesekah, Weythapamattha, Nianymseka, Nequetaughaw) Seneca Tribe not mentioned; no Seneca signers
Treaty with the Delawares, etc. June 7, 1803 Ft. Wayne, Indiana Terr.	7 Stat. 74; *Indian Affairs*, 2:64	• Ceded land, including a salt spring in exchange for salt • Acknowledged United States as protector • Allowed United States to build inns and ferries on roads between U.S. towns • Indians allowed free passage on ferries	*Shawnees:* Neahmemsieeh Black Hoof (Cuthewekasaw) Methawnasice Seneca Tribe not mentioned; no Seneca signers
Treaty with the Wyandottes, etc. July 4, 1805 Ft. Industry, Ohio	7 Stat. 87; *Indian Affairs*, 2:77	• Indian nations remained under U.S. protection • Moving of boundary line and cession of land • U.S. would pay $1,000 annuity forever to the tribal nations (including Shawnee and Seneca nations that lived with the Wyandottes) • Indian nations would have the right to hunt and fish on ceded lands, so long as peaceable	*Shawnees:* Blue Jacket (Weyapurseawaw) Black Hoof (Cutheaweasaw) Civil Man (Auonaschla) Isaac Peters No Seneca signers

Treaty	Citation	Terms	Signatories
Treaty with the Chippewas, etc. Nov. 25, 1808 Brownstown, Mich. Terr.	7 Stat. 112; *Indian Affairs*, 2:99	• Nations ceded land for roads to join U.S. settlements in Ohio and Michigan Terr. • One road 120 feet wide, another two miles wide • United States could build settlements on one of the roads and take timber and materials off adjacent lands • Indian nations retained right to hunt and fish on ceded lands as long as they were U.S.-owned • Indian nations remained under U.S. protection	*Shawnees:* Black Hoof (Makatewesha) Col. Lewis (Koitawaypie) (ESTO Capt. Lewis) Seneca Tribe not mentioned
Treaty with the Wyandottes, etc. July 22, 1814 Greenville, Ohio	7 Stat. 118; *Indian Affairs*, 2:105	• Restatement of peace with tribes loyal to United States in War of 1812 • Tribes would give aid and warriors to fight for the United States • Tribes would not make peace with England or hostile tribes without U.S. consent • Sandusky and Stony Creek Senecas and Shawnee Tribe preserved fidelity to United States • Tribes acknowledged themselves to be under U.S. protection	*Shawnees:* Black Hoof (Cutewecusa) Captain Lewis (Quitawepeh) Blue Jacket Snake (Shammonetho) Wolf (Piaseka) Walker (Pomtha) Capt. Tom (Chiachska) Butter (Tamenetha) 6 others *Senecas:* Civil John (Corachcoonke) Big Turtle (Cuntahtentuhwa) Wiping Stick (Renonnesa) John Harris (Endosquierunt) 9 others
Treaty with the Wyandottes, etc. Sept. 8, 1815 Spring Wells, Mich. Terr.	7 Stat. 131; *Indian Affairs*, 2:117	• To restore peaceful relations with these tribes, and certain bands of the Shawnees and Senecas that joined England in War of 1812 • United States and tribal nations renewed and confirmed all treaties signed 1795–1815	*Shawnees:* Black Hoof (Cutaweskeshah) Capt. Lewis (Quatawwepay) Capt. Reid (Mishquathree) Big Snake (Shemenetoo) Butter (Tamenatha) 3 others *Senecas:* Civil John (Masomea) Wiping Stick (Saccorawahtah) John Harris (Yonundankykueurent) 1 other

Table 6.1 Treaties between the Eastern Shawnee Tribe and the United States (*continued*)

Treaties Date Location	Statute at Large	Significant Terms	Shawnee and Seneca Signers
Treaty with the Wyandottes, etc. Sept. 29, 1817 Rapids of the Miami of Lake Erie	7 Stat. 160; *Indian Affairs*, 2:145	• Tribes ceded more land and set aside reservations • Shawnees and Senecas at Lewistown reserved a 48-square-mile reservation in fee simple ownership (this 1817 treaty was not ratified because the Senate demanded a supplemental treaty changing the fee simple title to the land to "the same manner as Indian reservations have been heretofore held") • Reaffirmed payment of all annuities due under past treaties • Reservation lands would be for use and ownership of named individuals (including land for Shawnee and Seneca chiefs at Lewistown) • Many other individuals (i.e. adopted and and non-Indians) granted lands in fee simple on these reservations • Indian agent and blacksmith appointed for Shawnee reservations at Lewistown, Hog Creek, and Wapakoneta • Indians could hunt and make sugar on the ceded lands as long as U.S.-owned • United States agreed to pay damages loyal Indians incurred in War of 1812, including at Lewistown and Wapakoneta • United States could build roads, taverns, and ferries • Land rights at Lewistown granted by name to eighty-two Shawnees and fifty Senecas	*Shawnees:* Black Hoof (Cateweekesa) Wolf (Biaseka) Walker (Pomthe) Big Snake (Shemenetu) Tail's End (Chacalowa) Perry (Pemthata) Yellow Feather (Othawakeska) Capt. Reed (Wawathethaka) Tecumtequa, War Chief (Quitewe) Captain Tom (Cheacksca) Captain Lewis (Quitawepea) *Senecas:* Civil John (Methomea) Wiping Stick (Sacourewceghta) Big Turtle (Shekoghkell) Joe (Aquasheno) White Man (Wakenuceno) Captain Sigore (Samendue) Robbin (Skilleway) Dasquoerunt

Treaty	Citation	Provisions	Signatories
Treaty with the Wyandottes, etc. Sept. 17, 1818 St. Mary's, Ohio	7 Stat. 178; *Indian Affairs*, 2:162.	• Supplement to the 1817 treaty, changing the fee simple title of lands granted to tribes and chiefs to "the same manner as Indian reservations have been heretofore held" • Both treaties ratified by Senate and proclaimed by president on Jan. 4, 1819 • United States granted tribes more land in exchange for agreement to change 1817 treaty • Shawnees and Senecas at Lewistown received 8,960 more acres and an additional annuity payment of $1,000 "forever" • Lewistown reservation divided in half by an east-west line with northern half for Senecas and southern half for Shawnees	*Shawnees:* Black Hoof (Cuttewekasa) Wolf (Biaseka) Walker (Pomthe) Big Snake (Shemenetu) Long Tail (Chacalawa) Perry (Pemthata) Capt. Reed (Red Man) Elk in the Water (Tecuntequa) Captain Tom (Chiakeska) Colonel Lewis (Quitawepa) Captain Pipe James Armstrong *Senecas:* Civil John (Methomea) Wiping Stick Big Turtle (Skekoghkell) White Bone (Waghkonoxie) Yellow Bone (Tochequia) Captain Togone Harris (Cunneshohant) Blanket Down (Tousonecta)
Treaty with the Senecas, etc. July 20, 1831 Lewistown, Ohio	7 Stat. 351; *Indian Affairs*, 2:327.	• Ceded lands in Ohio and agreed to remove to Indian Territory • Granted 60,000 acres in fee simple with restricted title to hold "forever, as long as they shall exist as a nation and remain on the same" lands • "Said lands shall never be within the bounds of any State or Territory, nor subject to the laws thereof" • United States would pay costs of removal and provide one-year supply of goods upon arrival • United States would sell Ohio lands to build a sawmill and blacksmith shop, pay operational expenses, and employ a blacksmith • Balance on sale of Ohio lands would be invested for the tribe, held by the United States and paid out 5 percent annually • Annuities due under past treaties would be paid in Indian Territory • United States gave presents for loyal and good conduct of the Seneca and Shawnee Tribes	Civil John (Methomea) Robbin (Skilleway) John Young (Totala Chief) Pewyache Mingo Carpenter John Jackson Little Lewis (Quashacaugh) James McDonnell Civil John's Son (Honede) Run Fast Yankee Bill Cold Water John Sky

Table 6.1 Treaties between the Eastern Shawnee Tribe and the United States (*continued*)

Treaties Date Location	Statute at Large	Significant Terms	Shawnee and Seneca Signers
Treaty with the Senecas and Shawnees Dec. 29, 1832 Seneca Agency, Indian Terr.	7 Stat. 411; *Indian Affairs*, 2:383.	• Mixed Band of Senecas and Shawnees, who were unhappy with the 60,000 acres assigned to them west of Neosho/Grand River, traded for 60,000 acres east of Neosho, to be held in fee simple titles but requiring U.S. consent to sell • Mixed Band formed a confederacy with Senecas of Sandusky, which would be called "United Nation of Senecas and Shawnees" • United States to build gristmill, sawmill, and blacksmith shop and furnish tools and machinery • United States to pay claims for horses and property lost during removal • Treaty would not change the terms of any preceding treaty	*Mixed Band (Shawnee and Seneca):* Civil John (Me-tho-mea) (first chief Senecas and Shawnees) Pe-wy-a-che Robbin (Skilleway) John Jackson Little Lewis (Quash-acaugh) John Young (To-ta-la) Mingo Carpenter Jemmy McDaniel Civil John's son Yankee Bill Big Ash Civil John's young son *Seneca Chiefs:* Comstick (first chief Seneca nation) Seneca Steel Small Cloud Spicer George Curly Hair Tall Chief Captain Good Hunter Hard Hickory Wiping Stick Seneca John John Johnson John Sky Isaac White Joseph Smith Captain Smith

Agreement with the Senecas and Shawnees Aug. 23, 1854 Neosho Agency, Indian Terr.	(Agreement rejected by Congress; see Deloria and DeMallie, *Documents*, 1:850–53)	• "United Nation of Seneca and Shawnee Indians" attempted to cede their 60,000 acres of land in Indian Territory to United States • Reserved 160 acres for each Seneca of the Sandusky band and 80 acres for each person in the Mixed Band of Senecas and Shawnees, as well as sixteen sections to be held as common property of the Mixed Band • Disputes about selecting lands would be decided by chiefs, subject to appeal to the Indian agent • Lands not selected would be sold by United States and funds paid to Indians • For $16,000 each, the Senecas of Sandusky and the Mixed Band attempted to relinquish their permanent annuities amounting to $1,000 per year due under former treaties, to discharge the United States from all claims or damages due to the nonfulfillment of former treaties, and to discharge the United States from injuries caused by U.S. citizens • Indians promised to renew efforts to prevent alcohol use and to encourage industry, thrift, morality, and "to promote their advancement in civilization" • Roads, highways, and railroads could be built on lands ceded and on lands reserved	*Senecas and Shawnees:* Pe-ny-a-che George McDaniel John Lamb David Civil John Peter Knox John Melton Yankee Bill John Lewis Lewis Davis, interpreter *Sandusky Senecas:* Little Town Spicer Young Henry William King Moses Crow George Douglass Cayuga John Smith

Table 6.1 Treaties between the Eastern Shawnee Tribe and the United States (*continued*)

Treaties Date Location	Statute at Large	Significant Terms	Shawnee and Seneca Signers
Treaty with the Senecas and Shawnees with the Confederate States of America Oct. 4, 1861 Park Hill, Cherokee Nation Introduction says the treaty is with the Senecas of Sandusky and the Shawnees, formerly known as the Seneca and Shawnee of Lewistown or the Mixed Band.	Ratified by CSA Congress Dec. 21, 1861; Deloria and DeMallie, *Documents*, 1:650–59.	• Andrew J. Dorn, CSA agent to Osages and Senecas, had been the U.S. commissioner who negotiated the ESTO's unratified 1854 agreement • A long treaty assuring friendship, included many provisions common to U.S.-Indian treaties • Confederacy required to provide attorneys for Seneca or Shawnee Indians charged in Confederate or state court • At least nine statements that the Senecas of the Mixed Band either did not attend this treaty session or did not agree to sign • Slavery in the Seneca and Shawnee Tribes "is legal, and has existed from time immemorial" • Senecas and Shawnees would aid Confederacy in fighting the United States • Confederacy would pay many of the annuities that the United States owed the tribes • CSA would build schoolhouse, sawmill, and gristmill and would hire teachers, a physician, a blacksmith, a wagon maker, a wheelwright, and a miller	*Senecas:* Little Town Spicer (principal chief) Small Cloud Spicer (second chief) Moses Crow (councilor) John Mush (councilor) George Spicer (councilor) *Seneca warriors:* John Smith James King Isaac Warrior Jim Big-Bone Buck Armstrong Jo Crow David Smith George Keron (CSA interpreter) *Shawnees:* Lewis Davis (principal chief of the Senecas and Shawnees) Joseph Mowawk (second chief of the Shawnees) John Tomahawk White Deer (councilor of the Shawnees) Silas Dougherty (councilor of the Shawnees) William Barbee (CSA interpreter)

Treaty	Citation	Provisions	Signatories
Agreement with the Cherokees and Other Tribes in Indian Territory Sept. 13, 1865 Ft. Smith, Ark.	Not ratified as a treaty; see *Indian Affairs*, 2:1050 (appendix); Deloria and DeMallie, *Documents*, 2:1355	• United States willing to treat again and reestablish peace and friendship with tribes that signed treaties with Confederate states • Tribes acknowledge themselves to be under U.S. protection and will not enter allegiance or arrangements with any other state, nation, or sovereign	*Senecas and Shawnees:* Lewis Davis (chief) A. McDonald Goodhunt, Jas. Tallchief Lewis Denny (interpreter Lewis Davis) Isaac Warrior (chief of the Cowskin Senecas) Charles Bluejacket (first chief) Graham Rogers (second chief) Moses Silverheels Solomon Madden Eli Blackhoof
Treaty with the Senecas, Mixed Band of Senecas and Shawnees, Quapaws, etc. Feb. 23, 1867 Washington, D.C.	15 Stat. 513; *Indian Affairs*, 2:960	• Mixed Band of Senecas and Shawnees split: Senecas joined the Cowskin/Sandusky Senecas; Shawnees now to be known as Eastern Shawnee Tribe • Senecas, formerly confederated with Shawnees, ceded 30,000 acres (north part of the Seneca and Shawnee reserve) to United States for $24,000 • Shawnees, "heretofore confederated with the Senecas," ceded "that portion of their remaining lands," about 12,000 acres, to the United States for $1 an acre • West part of Shawnee reservation ceded to United States, sold to Ottawas for $1 an acre • $2,000 of the Shawnees' $12,000 to be advanced to establish homes, the balance to be invested for the tribe "under the name of Eastern Shawnees" with 5 percent to be paid semiannually • Shawnees to split with the Senecas the fund for a blacksmith, and United States would pay $500 more annually for five years • Mixed Band's claims for loss of homes and property in the Civil War would be investigated and reported to Congress	*Senecas and Shawnees:* John Whitetree John Young Lewis Davis (for some reason there were witnesses listed for Lewis Davis's signature—G. L. Young, and G. C. Snow, the Indian agent at Neosho Agency) *Other Senecas (probably Cowskin/Sandusky Senecas):* George Spicer John Mush

Table 6.1 Treaties between the Eastern Shawnee Tribe and the United States (*continued*)

Treaties Date Location	Statute at Large	Significant Terms	Shawnee and Seneca Signers
Agreement with the Eastern Shawnees June 23, 1874 Quapaw Agency, Indian Terr.	Deloria and DeMallie, *Documents*, 1:260–61; Congress approved March 3, 1875, 18 Stat. 447; *Indian Affairs*, 1:158	• ESTO ceded about 4,000 acres of land in the northeast corner of its reservation to United States for Modoc Indians, who were "temporarily located on the Eastern Shawnee Reservation" • United States paid $6,000, to be paid per capita to enable Shawnees "to enlarge their farms and otherwise improve their condition in civilization"	*Chiefs:* James Choctaw Thomas Captain *Councilors:* John Logan John Williams *Young Men:* Good Hunt Billy Dick John Mohawk Corn Stalk George Beaver Samson Kyzer John Jackson

NOTES

The author is extremely grateful to Arizona State University law librarian David Gay for his extensive and very helpful assistance.

1. Colin G. Calloway, *Pen and Ink Witchcraft: Treaties and Treaty Making in American Indian History* (New York: Oxford University Press, 2013), 245; Benjamin Franklin, *Pennsylvania, and the First Nations: The Treaties of 1736–62*, ed. Susan Kalter (Chicago: University of Illinois Press, 2006), 35, 63, 69, 149, 160, 166, 282, 358, 369; Francis Jennings, *The Ambiguous Iroquois Empire: The Covenant Chain Confederation of Indian Tribes with English Colonies from its beginnings to the Lancaster Treaty of 1744* (New York: W. W. Norton, 1984), 236, 241, 259; Dorothy V. Jones, *License for Empire: Colonialism by Treaty in Early America* (Chicago: University of Chicago Press, 1982), 75. The treaties are available in *Indian Affairs: Laws and Treaties*, ed. and comp. Charles J. Kappler, vol. 2, *Treaties* (Washington: Government Printing Office, 1904), which has been digitized at http://digital.library.okstate.edu/kappler /vol2/tocyr.htm. In this chapter and in table 6.1 the spelling of the treaties' titles has been made consistent with the spelling of tribal names throughout the rest of this book, but the spelling of such names in the notes remains consistent with the source texts.

There are three federally recognized Shawnee tribes today: the Eastern Shawnee Tribe of Oklahoma (www.ESToO-nsn.gov/), the Absentee Shawnee Tribe (www.ASTribe.com), and the Shawnee Tribe (www.Shawnee-Tribe.com). This chapter addresses only the ESTO and the tribal governments and communities that are the direct ancestors of the ESTO. Consequently, we will not examine the treaties that were signed by the other two tribes, nor will we examine treaties that Shawnee tribes signed with Europeans, the United States, or American colonies before 1795.

2. Francis Paul Prucha, *American Indian Treaties: The History of a Political Anomaly* (Berkeley: University of California Press, 1994), 446–502; Jeffrey Glover, *Paper Sovereigns: Anglo-Native Treaties and the Law of Nations, 1604–1664* (Philadelphia: University of Pennsylvania Press, 2014), 3, 9, 12, 19, 119; Vine Deloria Jr. and Raymond Demallie, *Documents of American Indian Diplomacy: Treaties, Agreements, and Conventions 1775–1979* (Norman: University of Oklahoma Press, 1999), 1:3–5; Henry F. De Puy, *A Bibliography of the English Colonial Treaties with the American Indians: Including a Synopsis of Each Treaty* (Union, N.J.: Lawbook Exchange/Martino Fine Books, 2001). See also ESTO 1874 Agreement in Vine Deloria Jr. and David E. Wilkins, *Tribes, Treaties, and Constitutional Tribulations* (Austin: University of Texas Press, 1999), 60–61; Act of March 3, 1871, 16 Stat. 544, chap. 120, 566, codified as amended at 25 U.S.C. § 71.

3. Washington v. Washington Commercial Passenger Fishing Vessel Association, 443 U.S. 658, 675 (1979); William C. Canby Jr., *American Indian Law in a Nutshell*, 5th ed. (St. Paul: West Academic Publishing, 2009), 119; Prucha, *American Indian Treaties*, 21, 67, 72–73.

4. United States v. Winans, 198 U.S. 371, 381 (1905). See Judith V. Royster et al., *Native American Natural Resources Law*, 3rd ed. (Durham, N.C.: Carolina Academic Press, 2013), 475–76; Fay G. Cohen, *Treaties on Trial: The Continuing Controversy over Northwest Indian Fishing Rights* (Seattle: University of Washington Press, 1986).

5. See Treaty with the Wyandot, etc., 1817, art. 21 *Indian Affairs*, 2:151; Treaty with the Wyandot, etc., 1818, art. 5, ibid., 2:163.

6. See note 2 above.

7. Delaware Nation Treaty, 1778, *Indian Affairs*, 2:3.

8. Francis Jennings, *The History and Culture of Iroquois Diplomacy: An Interdisciplinary Guide to the Treaties of the Six Nations and Their League* (Syracuse, N.Y.: Syracuse University Press, 1985), 59.

9. Prucha, *American Indian Treaties*, 21, 23, 59, 67, 72–73; U.S. Constitution, art. VI; Act of March 3, 1871.

10. But, see Deloria and Demallie, *Documents of American Indian Diplomacy*, 1:177. Treaty instructions could also be quite vague, for example, quoting a May 2, 1818, letter to U.S. commissioners: "The

terms to be offered depend so much on the whims and tempers of the tribes interested in the land, that no particular instructions can be given you."

11. U.S. Constitution, art. II, § 2, cl. 2.

12. Adam Jortner, *The Gods of Prophetstown: The Battle of Tippecanoe and the Holy War for the American Frontier* (New York: Oxford University Press, 2012), 90–92, William Henry Harrison to Thomas Jefferson, May 12, 1804, ibid., 160n60; Robert J. Miller, "Speaking with Forked Tongues: Indian Treaties, Salmon, and the Endangered Species Act," *Oregon Law Review* 70, no. 3 (1991): 543, 552–55; Prucha *American Indian Treaties*, 212. There was no clear criterion "except, perhaps, expediency" for determining what Indian political unit would be used for negotiations.

13. Robert J. Miller, "Exercising Cultural Self-Determination: The Makah Indian Tribe Goes Whaling," *American Indian Law Review* 25, no. 2 (2001): 165; Miller, "Speaking with Forked Tongues," 552–55; Henry Harvey, *History of the Shawnee Indians, from the year 1681 to 1854, Inclusive* (1855; New York: Kraus, 1971), 196, 199–200; Robert J. Miller and Maril Hazlett, "The 'Drunken Indian'—Myth Distilled into Reality through Federal Indian Alcohol Policy," *Arizona State Law Journal* 28, no. 1 (1996): 223, 232, 249. There are instances in which federal treaty negotiators paid bribes to Indian negotiators who signed treaties and refused them to Indians who did not sign, and alcohol was sometimes provided.

14. Prucha, *American Indian Treaties*, 129; Deloria and Wilkins, *Tribes, Treaties, and Constitutional Tribulations*, 33; Robert J. Miller, "American Indian Influence on the United States Constitution and Its Framers," *American Indian Law Review* 18, no. 1 (1993): 133, 138.

15. U.S. Constitution, art. I, § 8, cl. 3; James Madison, No. *42, The Federalist Papers*, ed. Clinton L. Rossiter (New York: New American Library, 1961), 268–69; John Jay, No. 3, *Federalist Papers*, 44–45; County of Oneida v. Oneida Indian Nation, 470 U.S. 226, 234n4 (1985) ("Madison cited the National Government's inability to control trade with the Indians as one of the key deficiencies of the Articles of Confederation, and urged adoption of the Indian Commerce Clause"); Miller, *American Indian Influence*, 151–54, 151–54nn145–62.

16. U.S. Constitution, art. VI, cl. 2. See also Worcester v. Georgia, 31 U.S. 515, 559 (1832).

17. U.S. Constitution, Art. I, § 2, cl. 3; Amendment XIV, § 2; Act of June 2, 1924, 43 Stat. 253, chap. 233, codified at 8 U.S.C. § 1401(b).

18. Cherokee Nation v. Georgia, 30 U.S. 1, 16–17 (1831).

19. *Worcester v. Georgia*, 559.

20. Ibid., 582.

21. In re Kansas Indians, 72 U.S. 737, 760 (1866).

22. Minnesota v. Mille Lacs Band of Chippewa Indians, 526 U.S. 172, 204 (1999); Oliphant v. Suquamish Indian Tribe, 435 U.S. 191, 208n17 (1978); Choctaw Nation v. Oklahoma, 397 U.S. 620, 630–31 (1970); Tulee v. Washington, 312 U.S. 681, 684–85 (1942); Carpenter v. Shaw, 280 U.S. 363 (1930); Jones v. Meehan, 175 U.S. 1, 11 (1899). See, by way of comparison, State v. Tinno, 497 P.2d 1386 (Idaho 1972). A treaty that did not use the word "fish," but did expressly protect the tribe's "right to hunt," was interpreted to include fishing since the Indian words used in the negotiation meant "to obtain wild food" and would mean both hunting and fishing, and the treaty minutes indicated that both hunting and fishing were discussed.

23. See, for example, United States v. Sioux Nation, 448 U.S. 371 (1980); Menominee Tribe of Indians v. United States, 391 U. S. 404 (1968). See also David H. Getches et al., *Federal Indian Law*, 6th edition (St. Paul, Minn.: West Publishing, 2011), 267–68. In 1946, Congress created a process for tribes to bring claims against the United States for violations of their treaties and for other causes of action.

24. Act of March 3, 1871.

25. Antoine v. Washington, 420 U.S. 194, 202 (1975).

26. See, for example, Oklahoma Tax Commission v. Sac and Fox Nation, 508 U.S. 114, 117 (1993), which calls an 1891 agreement between the United States and Sac and Fox a "treaty" and states that

"Congress ratified the treaty"; Deloria and Wilkins, *Tribes, Treaties, and Constitutional Tribulations*, 61. The basic treaty format was followed long after 1871.

27. United States v. Dion, 476 U.S. 734, 738–40 (1986); Menominee Tribe of Indians v. United States, 391 U.S. 404 (1968); Lone Wolf v. Hitchcock, 187 U.S. 553, 566 (1903). See also Charles F. Wilkinson and John M. Volkman, "Judicial Review of Indian Treaty Abrogation: 'As Long as Water Flows, or Grass Grows Upon the Earth'—How Long a Time is That?" *California Law Review* 63, no. 3 (1975): 601, 609.

28. See table 6.1 for general information on all the treaties and agreements. The full treaties are available in *Indian Affairs*, vol. 2, and online at http://digital.library.okstate.edu/kappler/Vol2/tocyr .htm.

29. Robert J. Miller, "The International Law of Colonialism: A Comparative Analysis," *Lewis and Clark Law Review* 15, no. 4 (2012): 847; Robert J. Miller, *Native America, Discovered and Conquered: Thomas Jefferson, Lewis & Clark, and Manifest Destiny* (Westport, Conn.: Praeger Publishers, 2006).

30. Johnson v. M'Intosh, 21 U.S. 543, 572–73 (1823).

31. George Washington to James Duane, September 7, 1783, in *Documents of United States Indian Policy*, 3rd ed., ed. Francis Paul Prucha (Lincoln: University of Nebraska Press, 2000), 1–2.

32. Ibid.

33. See, for example, Miller, *Native America*, 78, 92–94, 115–61, 200n98; *Memoirs of John Quincy Adams: Comprising Portions of His Diary from 1795 to 1848*, ed. Charles Francis Adams (Philadelphia: J.B. Lippincott, 1875), 7: 90, 410–11 (in the latter, see Henry Clay and President John Quincy Adams's conversation).

34. Sami Lakomäki, *Gathering Together: The Shawnee People through Diaspora and Nationhood, 1600–1870* (New Haven, Conn.: Yale University Press, 2014), 161–62; Jortner, *The Gods of Prophetstown*, 103; Stephen Warren, *The Shawnees and Their Neighbors, 1795–1870* (Urbana: University of Illinois Press, 2005), 7, 11, 13–14, 29, 49, 57–58; R. David Edmunds, "A Watchful Safeguard to Our Habitations: Black Hoof and the Loyal Shawnees," in *Native America and the Early Republic*, ed. Fred Hoxie (Richmond: University of Virginia Press, 1999), 162–63, 184–86; Leonard U. Hill, *John Johnston and the Indians: In the Land of the Three Miamis* (Columbus, Ohio: Stoneman Press, 1957), 19.

Captain Lewis, however, became an advocate for removal by the early 1820s, and he led a small group from Lewistown to the West long before the ESTO removed. John P. Bowes, *Exiles and Pioneers: Eastern Indians in the Trans-Mississippi West* (New York: Cambridge University Press, 2007), 43–44; Lakomäki, *Gathering Together*, 162.

35. Calloway, *Pen and Ink*, 108, 113; Bowes, *Exiles and Pioneers*, 28.

36. *American State Papers: Documents, Legislative and Executive of the Congress of the United States*, ed. Walter Lowrie, Matthew St. Clair Clarke, and Walter S. Franklin (Washington, D.C.: Gales and Seaton, 1832–34), 1: 340, 342. Preemption is one of the elements of the international law doctrine Europeans and Americans used to claim power over Indian nations and their lands. Miller, *Native America*, 3–5, 50–56.

37. *American State Papers*, 1:356.

38. Ibid., 1:488–91. Wayne's troops destroyed the Indians' houses and cornfields; he described their cornfields as being more extensive than what he had seen anywhere in the United States.

39. Treaty with the Wyandot, etc., 1795, arts. I–IV, *Indian Affairs*, 2:39–42.

40. Ibid., arts. V, VI, *Indian Affairs*, 2:42.

41. Ibid., arts. V, VII, VIII, X, *Indian Affairs*, 2:42–44.

42. See *Messages and Letters of William Henry Harrison*, ed. Logan Esarey (New York: Arno Press, 1975), 2:637; Hill, *John Johnston and the Indians*, 19; Lakomäki, *Gathering Together*, 137, 141; Jerry E. Clark, *The Shawnee* (Lexington: University Press of Kentucky, 1993), 24–25.

43. Jortner, *Gods of Prophetstown*, 90–92, 160n60 (the latter quoting William Henry Harrison to Thomas Jefferson, May 12, 1804).

44. *Indian Treaties, and Laws and Regulation Relating to Indian Affairs* (Washington City: Way and Gideon, 1826), 591; Treaty with the Delawares, etc., 1803, arts. I–IV, *Indian Affairs*, 2:64–65.

45. *American State Papers*, 1:702–704; Prucha, *American Indian Treaties*, 124.

46. Treaty with the Wyandot, etc., 1805, *Indian Affairs*, 2:77–78.

47. Treaty with the Chippewa, etc., 1808, arts. I, II, *Indian Affairs*, 2:99–100; Prucha *American Indian Treaties* 126; Harvey, *History of the Shawnee Indians*, 135.

48. Treaty 1808, arts. IV, V, *Indian Affairs*, 2:100.

49. Lewis Cass to Secretary of War James Barbour, October 23, 1826, *American State Papers*, 2:684.

50. John Johnson to Secretary of War, Aug. 3, 1813, *Messages and Letters of William Henry Harrison*, 2:509; Edmunds, "A Watchful Safeguard," 179, 181.

51. *Messages and Letters of William Henry Harrison*, 2: 631, 636–37.

52. Secretary of War to Governor Cass, June 11, 1814, Clarence Edwin Carter, ed., *The Territorial Papers of the United States* (Washington, D.C.: Government Printing Office, 1934–), 10:462–63.

53. Carter, *Territorial Papers*, 10:463.

54. Treaty 1814, arts. I–IV, *Indian Affairs*, 2:105–106. See also Edmunds, "A Watchful Safeguard," 194, 196–98.

55. Prucha, *American Indian Treaties*, 130; *Indian Affairs*, 2:106.

56. Prucha, *American Indian Treaties*, 132–33.

57. Duncan McArthur to Acting Secretary of War, March 15, 1815, Carter, *Territorial Papers*, 10:519.

58. *American State Papers*, 2:13–14; Carter, *Territorial Papers*, 10: 548, 548n69; Hill, *John Johnston and the Indians*, 86, 89 (the latter indicates that the United States apparently did pay some Indians for wartime pillaging of their property, including Shawnees at Lewistown).

59. Treaty with the Wyandot, etc., 1815, preamble, arts. 1–2, *Indian Affairs*, 2:117–18.

60. Ibid., arts. 3–4, *Indian Affairs*, 2:118.

61. George Graham, Acting Secretary of War, to Gov. Lewis Cass, March 23, 1817, *American State Papers*, 2:136.

62. George Graham, Acting Secretary of War, to Commissioners Gov. Lewis Cass and Gen. Duncan McArthur, May 19, 1817, *American State Papers*, 2:137; Gov. Lewis Cass to George Graham, July 3, 1817, ibid.

63. Governor Lewis Cass and General Duncan McArthur to Acting Secretary of War George Graham, September 30, 1817, *American State Papers*, 2:138–39.

64. *American State Papers*, 2:140.

65. Ibid., 2:148–50; Warren, *The Shawnees and Their Neighbors*, 56.

66. Treaty with the Wyandot, etc., 1817, arts. 1–3, *Indian Affairs*, 2:145.

67. Ibid., art. 5, *Indian Affairs*, 2:146. See also Treaty with the Wyandot, etc., 1818, art. 1, *Indian Affairs*, 2:162; Miller, *Native America*, 3–5, 26–27, 47, 51–53.

68. Treaty with the Wyandot, etc., 1817, arts. 7–8, *Indian Affairs*, 2: 147–49, 152–55. Although the lands were claimed to be granted to the tribes by the United States, the U.S. government still claimed the right to build roads, taverns, and ferries on them, and the lands granted to the various chiefs "shall not be liable to taxes of any kind so long as such land continues the property of the said Indians." Ibid., arts. 14–15, *Indian Affairs*, 2:150.

69. Ibid., art. 9, *Indian Affairs*, 2:149.

70. Ibid., art. 11, *Indian Affairs*, 2:149. Compare to Treaty with the Wyandot, etc., 1795 (Treaty of Greenville), art. VII, *Indian Affairs*, 2:42. The United States still owns wildlife refuges, national forests, military bases, and a national park in Ohio. See U.S. Geological Survey, "Printable Maps List: Federal Lands and Indian Reservations," http://NationalMap.gov/small_scale/printable/fedlands.html#list, accessed December 30, 2015. An interesting question arises as to whether the Eastern Shawnees can still hunt and gather tree sap on these lands. It must be noted, however, that two other tribes have already litigated and lost somewhat similar treaty claims to own filled land on Lake Erie and for

fishing rights on Lake Erie. Williams v. City of Chicago, 242 U.S. 434 (1917); Ottawa Tribe of Oklahoma v. Logan, 577 F.3d 634 (6th Cir. 2009).

71. Treaty with the Wyandot, etc., 1817, art. 12, *Indian Affairs*, 2:149.

72. Senate Committee on Public Lands, to the Senate, December 28, 1817, *American State Papers*, 2:148–49 (quoting Mr. Morrow); Treaty with the Wyandot, etc., 1818, arts. 1, 3, *Indian Affairs*, 2:162; Prucha, *American Indian Treaties*, 136–37.

73. *American State Papers*, 2: 166, 175; *The Papers of John C. Calhoun*, ed. W. Edwin Hemphill (Columbia: University of South Carolina Press, 1959), 2: 121, 288.

74. Chief Clerk of the War Department C. Vandeventer to Lewis Cass, June 29, 1818, *American State Papers*, 2:175; Lewis Cass and Duncan McArthur, Commissioners, to John Calhoun, Secretary of War, September 18, 1818, ibid., 2:177. See also Ratified Treaty No. 181, Documents Relating to the Negotiation of the Treaty of December 29, 1832, with the Seneca and Shawnee Indians, Documents Relating to the Negotiation of Ratified and Unratified Treaties With Various Indian Tribes, 1801–1869 (hereafter DRNRUT), Documents Relating to Indian Affairs, History Collection, University of Wisconsin Digital Collections, 1–2 ("The time has not yet arrived for them voluntarily to abandon the land of their fathers and seek a new residence in a country with which they are unacquainted and among powerful and hostile Indians. As our settlements gradually surround them, their minds will be better prepared to receive this proposition, and we do not doubt, but that a few years will accomplish, what could not now be accomplished, except at an expense greatly disproportional to the object."); Lewis Cass and Duncan McArthur Letter, September 18, 1818, *Papers of John C. Calhoun*, 3:138.

75. John C. Calhoun, Secretary of War, to Gov. Lewis Cass and Gen. McArthur, *American State Papers*, 2:175; Prucha, *American Indian Treaties*, 138–42; Treaty with the Wyandot, etc., 1818, arts. 2, 5, *Indian Affairs*, 2:162–63.

76. Treaty with the Wyandot, etc., 1818, arts. 1, 2, *Indian Affairs*, 2:162–63.

77. Ibid., art. 2, *Indian Affairs*, 2:162. Stephen Warren states that it was part of the United States' strategy to create separate tribal governments. Warren, *Shawnees and Their Neighbors*, 59; he also states that William Henry Harrison worked to consolidate tribal power and authority around a handful of leaders who were willing to negotiate (18).

78. Prucha, *American Indian Treaties*, 186; Hill, *John Johnston and the Indians*, 114; *The New American State Papers: 1789–1860: Indian Affairs*, ed. Thomas C. Cochran (Wilmington, Del.: Scholarly Resources, 1972), 1: 202, 282–84.

79. Lakomäki, *Gathering Together*, 163; Warren, *Shawnees and Their Neighbors*, 67; Harvey, *History of the Shawnee Indians*, 194; President Jackson, Message to Congress, December 8, 1829, *Indian Treaties, and Laws and Regulation*, 591–93.

80. Harvey, *History of the Shawnee Indians*, 190–93.

81. The August 8, 1831, treaty signed by the Wapakoneta and Hog Creek Shawnees provided for them to be removed to Kansas. Hill, *John Johnston and the Indians*, 113; Harvey, *History of the Shawnee Indians*, 196, 199.

82. Harvey, *History of the Shawnee Indians*, 196, 199–200. Those "backed by the traders with bribes, outnumbered the others, and word was conveyed, by a few of the chiefs to the commissioner, to come on and close the contract"; the traders "paid some of the chiefs" and all parties were intoxicated.

83. Treaty with the Seneca, etc., 1831, preamble, arts. I, II, XI, *Indian Affairs*, 2: 327–28, 330; Choctaw Nation v. Oklahoma, 397 U.S. 620 (1970).

84. Treaty with the Seneca, etc., 1831, arts. III–VIII, X, *Indian Affairs*, 2:332–33.

85. Ibid., arts. VIII–IX, *Indian Affairs*, 2:333.

86. Laurence M. Hauptman, *The Iroquois in the Civil War: From Battlefield to Reservation* (Syracuse, N.Y.: Syracuse University Press, 1993), 88; Hill, *John Johnston and the Indians*, 116–17.

87. Secretary of War Lewis Cass to Indian Territory Commissioners, July 14, 1832, Ratified Treaty No. 181, 107–14, DRNRUT.

88. S. C. Stambaugh to the Secretary of War, January 6, 1833, Ratified Treaty No. 181, 1–4, DRNRUT; 7 Stat. 411, *Indian Affairs*, 2:383.

89. Treaty with the Seneca and Shawnee, 1832, arts. II–VI, *Indian Affairs*, 2:384–85.

90. Agreement/Treaty (unratified) with the Seneca and Shawnee, 1854, art. XIII, Deloria and Demallie, *Documents of American Indian Diplomacy*, 2:853 ("This instrument shall be obligatory on the contracting parties whenever the same shall be ratified by the President and Senate of the United States").

91. Ibid., 2:850–51.

92. Ibid., 2:851–52.

93. Hauptman, *Iroquois in the Civil War*, 85, 89, 94, 96; Grant Foreman, *A History of Oklahoma* (Norman: University of Oklahoma Press, 1942), 101–102. According to federal reports in 1853 and 1854, the Senecas and Shawnees were doing quite well in farming and were in comfortable circumstances before the Civil War. *New American State Papers*, 2:415.

94. Foreman, *History of Oklahoma*, 104–105. The signature page shows Shawnee signers from the Lewistown Mixed Band of Senecas and Shawnees and from the Sandusky Senecas, but apparently there were no Seneca signers from the Mixed Band. There are also multiple references in the treaty that appear to indicate that the Senecas of the Mixed Band did not attend the treaty negotiation or else did not agree to sign it. See, for example, Treaty with the Seneca and Shawnee with the Confederate States of America, 1861, art. XXX, Deloria and Demallie, *Documents of American Indian Diplomacy*, 1:656, in which the CSA agree to pay funds due under the treaty solely to the Shawnees of the Mixed Band until "the Senecas shall have united in this treaty."

95. Treaty with the Seneca and Shawnee with the Confederate States of America, 1861, Arts. I, III, XII, XX, XXVIII, Deloria and Demallie, *Documents of American Indian Diplomacy*, 1:651–55. See also Hauptman, *Iroquois in the Civil War*, 94.

96. Official Report of the Proceedings of the Council with the Indians of the West and Southwest, Held at Fort Smith, Arkansas, September 1865, Annual Report of the Commissioner of Indian Affairs, 312–14; Hauptman, *Iroquois in the Civil War*, 85; LeRoy H. Fischer, ed., *The Civil War Era in Indian Territory* (Los Angeles: Lorrin L. Morrison, 1974), 25 ("The Indian treaties with the Confederacy provided a convenient excuse for taking land from the Five Civilized Tribes as a penalty for secession, and then relocating the Kansas tribes on it").

97. Official Report [Ft. Smith Council], 313–15; Foreman, *History of Oklahoma*, 133.

98. Official Report [Ft. Smith Council], 318–19; C. Joseph Genetin-Pilawa, *Crooked Paths to Allotment: The Fight over Federal Indian Policy after the Civil War* (Chapel Hill: University of North Carolina Press, 2012), 60; Fischer, *Civil War Era*, 26; Hauptman, *Iroquois in the Civil War*, 97–98. See also Documents Relating to the Negotiation of an Unratified Treaty of September 13, 1865, with the Cherokee, Creek, Choctaw, Chickasaw, Osage, Seminole, Seneca, Shawnee, and Quapaw Indians, DRNRUT, 14, 19–20, which consists of 230 pages of handwritten notes of the 1865 conference; one of the conditions of the treaty was to accept emigrant Indians from Kansas. Foreman, *History of Oklahoma*, 133–34.

99. Official Report [Ft. Smith Council], 320–22, 327–29, 332; Fischer, *Civil War Era*, 25; Hauptman, *Iroquois in the Civil War*, 98; Documents Related to the Negotiation of an Unratified Treaty of September 13, 1865, 52, 56 (quoting commissioner Ely Parker).

100. Calloway, *Pen and Ink*, 102; Anthony F. C. Wallace, *The Death and Rebirth of the Seneca* (New York: Random House, 1969), 154; Southern acceptance into the Union discussed in "Reconstruction Era," *Wikipedia*, https://en.wikipedia.org/wiki/Reconstruction_Era#Loyalty, accessed January 30, 2016; "Reconstruction," *U.S. History: Pre-Columbian to the New Millennium*, www.USHistory.org /us/35.asp, accessed January 30, 2016.

101. Foreman, *History of Oklahoma*, 134, 137. U.S. politicians, the railroads, and Kansas also wanted to remove all Indians from that state. Indian Territory was a convenient location, so the U.S.

government wanted land from the tribes in the territory, and the CSA treaties were the excuse. See ibid. 137, 140. Commissioner Cooley expressly stated that in any new treaties the tribes must agree to accept emigrant Indians from Kansas. Documents Related to the Negotiation of an Unratified Treaty of September 13, 1865, 20.

102. Official Report [Ft. Smith Council], 318–19, 322, 327. At the Ft. Smith 1865 conference Chief Isaac Warrior, a Cowskin/Sandusky Seneca, agreed to accept Indians from Kansas if the tribes could reach agreements and if "our Grand Father" approved; Commissioner Ely Parker thanked the Neosho agency Indians for accepting the president's stipulations. At least one historian expressly ties the ESTO's 1867 treaty to the punitive actions of the United States at the Ft. Smith conference and the treaties that followed. Hauptman, *Iroquois in the Civil War*, 99, 99n33 ("Under the guise of aiding the Indians who had suffered during the Civil War, federal officials, on February 23, signed a treaty with the Seneca, Mixed Seneca and Shawnee, Quapaw, Etc. in D.C.").

103. Agreement with the Cherokee and Other Tribes in the Indian Territory, 1865, *Indian Affairs*, 2:1050–52. While the agreement is dated September 13, 1865, it was actually signed by the commissioners and the representatives of eleven tribes on September 14. Official Report [Ft. Smith Council], 333–34, Cowskin/Sandusky Seneca chief Isaac Warrior stated, for the Senecas, the Mixed Band of Senecas and Shawnees, and the Quapaws, that the tribes were "happy because we have made this treaty and shaken hands anew with you." This agreement was repeatedly called a treaty by the commissioners and the tribal representatives, but it was never ratified by the Senate, and several authorities state that it was never intended to be a treaty but instead was just designed to make arrangements for future treaties.

104. Cowskin/Sandusky Seneca chief George Spicer expressly recognized that at Ft. Smith in 1865, the government demanded that the tribes let Indians from Kansas move onto their lands. February 5, 1867, Ratified Treaty No. 361, Documents Relating to the Negotiation of the Treaty of February 23, 1867, with the Seneca, Mixed Seneca and Shawnee, and Quapaw Indians, DRNRUT, 45. *See also* Hauptman, *Iroquois in the Civil War*, 100. The U.S. motive was to serve the interests of Americans in Kansas and get the tribes removed to Indian Territory.

105. The apparently verbatim notes for these two interviews cover nearly one hundred handwritten pages. See February 5, 1867, Ratified Treaty No. 361, 50; February 9, 1867, ibid., 38.

106. For example, February 5, 1867, interview, ibid., 3–4, 20–21, 23–25, 31–34 51; February 9, 1867, interview, ibid., 1, 5, 27, 29–30, 32, 35–37.

107. February 5, 1867, ibid., 17, 19–21, 29, 37–38.

108. Treaty with the Seneca, Mixed Seneca and Shawnee, Quapaw, etc., 1867, *Indian Affairs*, 2:960–69; Ratified Treaty No. 361, 118–21. Lewis Davis, who signed the original February 23, 1867, treaty, died on March 5, 1868, and obviously could not sign the amended treaty. Christopher B. Chaney, "Lewis Davis—Protector of the Seneca and Shawnee People," *The Shooting Star* (February 2015), 2, 28.

109. Treaty with the Seneca, Mixed Seneca and Shawnee, Quapaw, etc., 1867, arts. 5, 8, 12, 16, *Indian Affairs*, 2:961–64.

110. Ibid., preamble, arts. 2, 21–22, 26, *Indian Affairs*, 2: 960, 965.

111. Ibid., art. 3, 8, 16, *Indian Affairs*, 2:961–64.

112. National Park Service, *A Brief History of the Modoc War*, www.NPS.gov/labe/planyourvisit/upload/MODOC%20WAR.pdf, accessed, December 17, 2015; Oregon Historical Society, *Modoc War*, *The Oregon Encyclopedia*, www.OregonEncyclopedia.org/articles/modoc_war/#.VnNfx5VIiUk; Deloria and Demallie, *Documents of American Indian Diplomacy*, 1:260–61, 18 Stat. 447 (1875).

113. Report of the Commission of Experts Established Pursuant to United Nations Security Council Resolution 780 (1992), May 27, 1994, 33, para. 130, available at www.icty.org/x/file/About/OTP/un_commission_of_experts_report1994_en.pdf. See also Robert M. Hayden, "Schindler's Fate: Genocide, Ethnic Cleansing, and Population Transfers," *Slavic Review* 55, no. 4 (1996): 727–48. The United Nations has defined ethnic cleansing as "rendering an area ethnically homogeneous by using force

or intimidation to remove from a given area persons of another ethnic or religious group." "Ethnic Cleansing," *Wikipedia*, https://en.wikipedia.org/wiki/Ethnic_cleansing, accessed January 18, 2016); Convention on the Prevention and Punishment of the Crime of Genocide, Adopted by Resolution 260 (III) A of the U.N. General Assembly on December 9, 1948, Entry into force, January 12, 1951, art. II; United Nations Declaration on the Rights of Indigenous Peoples, arts. 8, 10, September 13, 2007, G. A. Res. 61/295, reprinted in, S. James Anaya, *International Human Rights and Indigenous Peoples* (New York: Wolters Kluwer, 2009), 321–32.

114. The following information and documents were provided by the ESTO attorney Audrey Dixon. Email, January 4, 2016, Tobacco Tax Compact Between the State of Oklahoma and the Eastern Shawnee Tribe (2012) (hard copy on file with author); EPA-Tribal Environmental Plan, Eastern Shawnee Tribe of Oklahoma and U.S. Environmental Protection Agency Region 6, Fiscal Years 2016–2020 (hard copy on file with author); Gaming Compact with Oklahoma, www.estoo-nsn.gov/wp-content /uploads/2011/08/Eastern-Shawnee-State-Compactnew.pdf; Self-Governance Agreement (FY2016), August 6, 2015 (hard copy on file with author); Bearskin Clinic Memorandum of Understanding (MOU) with the Wyandotte Nation (2013); MOUs with Modoc Tribe, Cherokee Nation, Miami Tribe, Ottawa Tribe, Peoria Tribe, Quapaw Tribe, and Seneca-Cayuga Tribe; Oklahoma towns including Fairland, Commerce, and Quapaw (all concerning interagency cross deputation); Robert N. Clinton, "Treaties with Native Nations: Iconic Historical Relic or Modern Necessity?" in *Nation to Nation: Treaties Between the United States & American Indian Nations,* ed. Suzan Shown Harjo (Washington, D.C.: National Museum of the American Indian, 2014), 32–33.

7
Tribal, Federal, and State Laws Impacting the Eastern Shawnee Tribe, 1812 to 1945

ROBERT J. MILLER (EASTERN SHAWNEE)

The Indian nations in North America developed traditions and laws to manage and control their societies and peoples and their interactions with other tribal governments. No society or community can exist without developing control mechanisms. Likewise, indigenous peoples governed themselves pursuant to well-established codes and rules. The vast diversity of the myriad cultures of Indian peoples across what is now the United States is well represented through the diverse governing schemes and laws they developed. All Indian nations had well-understood laws and even highly organized societies.[1]

The Euro-American societies that established themselves on the North American continent, and especially in the United States, developed policies, courts, and hundreds of laws that had enormous impacts on tribal governments and Indian peoples. Many of these court cases, policies, and laws played an important role in the history, operation, and existence of the Eastern Shawnee Tribe of Oklahoma (ESTO) and its citizens during the time period this book addresses. In addition, the state of Oklahoma and its courts and laws impacted the ESTO. This chapter examines some of the constitutional and legal provisions that the governments of the Eastern Shawnee Tribe, the United States, and Oklahoma adopted from roughly 1812 to 1945 that impacted the Eastern Shawnee people.

EASTERN SHAWNEE LAWS AND CONSTITUTION

All societies develop laws, traditions, dispute-resolution systems, and property rights to govern themselves and their territories. Societies that did not develop writing, like American Indian peoples, utilized oral traditions and unwritten laws to manage their internal actions and interactions with other groups. Similarly, the Shawnee peoples and their separate nations governed themselves pursuant to well-defined systems, laws, and procedures. The Shawnees appear to have exercised their political power and governance via division, clan, and village structures.

Historians state that Shawnees were originally organized into five divisions. Each of these divisions exercised relatively specific and separate governmental and cultural functions for the nation as a whole. For example, national leaders primarily came from two of these divisions, the Chillicothe and Thawegila. In contrast, the Piqua division maintained tribal rituals and religious affairs, the Kispokothas most often supplied the war chiefs and advised on matters concerning war, and the Maykujays specialized in medicine and health. Yet each division was also politically autonomous and often occupied a separate village that was named after the specific division. Historians seem to agree that sometime in the distant past the nation as a whole split into separate tribes, primarily along the lines of their division affiliations. Each tribe thereafter carried out all the functions of government, religion, and culture for each distinct tribal entity. There was, naturally enough, some mixing of division members into towns or tribes primarily composed of members of other divisions. The nation further divided and organized itself into twelve patrilineal clans by 1795, according to at least one historian. Consequently, the Shawnee people came to be divided into perhaps five or more separate nations or tribes and governed themselves more as village entities rather than as one unified Shawnee nation.[2]

Akin to most American Indian cultures, the Shawnees distributed power among the various branches of their governments and among different individuals. The well-known governance principle of separation of powers is nothing new to Shawnee peoples. The Shawnees had war chiefs and peace chiefs and male chiefs and female chiefs. The peace chief position was generally a hereditary position, while war chiefs were selected based on proven military prowess. Peace chiefs exercised their political powers during peacetime, and war chiefs assumed authority once decisions were made to engage in warfare. In addition, every Shawnee village was built around a large council house in which tribal governance meetings occurred and in which decisions, by a vote of the chiefs, were made. The village councils were comprised of men, and sometimes women, with experience and common sense. Women were an important part of the town councils and played a significant and pervasive role in tribal affairs. They controlled certain tribal activities, such as planting and some rituals, and they even exercised some prerogatives over warfare.[3]

The Shawnees exercised criminal and civil jurisdiction within their territories and enforced established laws regarding conduct. For instance, Shawnee customary law controlled adjudications and punishments for murder, theft, and consistent infringement of community standards. Corporal punishment and even revenge killings (capital punishment, in essence) were mandated by Shawnee law. Public beating, ostracism, and expulsion (a penalty tantamount to a death sentence) could be imposed by town councils. Civil disputes were most often handled by families or by kinship groups.[4]

In addition to the criminal laws mentioned above, the Shawnees had other well-recognized laws and traditions that regulated their societies, communities, cultures, economies, and property rights. For example, individual households owned their own fields, and women harvested and owned their crops. Other laws defined modes of conducting rituals and proper sexual conduct.[5]

Mixed Band of Senecas and Shawnees, Lewistown, Ohio, 1812–1832

The Mixed Band of Senecas and Shawnees located at Lewistown, Ohio, and the Shawnee tribes at the Wapakoneta and Hog Creek reservations in Ohio operated under established governmental leaders, laws, governing mechanisms, and traditional practices. The chief at Wapakoneta, Black Hoof, appears to have been the leading Shawnee chief in Ohio, and Captain Lewis was the recognized leader of the Mixed Band of Shawnees and Senecas at Lewistown. These leaders represented the nation in diplomatic relations, and along with others, they helped formulate and carry out political, diplomatic, and commercial decisions for their tribes. Chiefs Black Hoof and Lewis also led nearly two hundred Shawnees who fought for the United States in the War of 1812, in direct opposition to England, Tecumseh, and the Prophet. In addition, they signed numerous treaties for the Shawnee people. Most Shawnee peoples in Ohio appear to have agreed with, complied with, and supported these leadership decisions. The United States also recognized these individuals as political leaders who could act for their peoples.[6]

Political, diplomatic, and military decisions would only seem to have been made after consulting the Lewistown and Wapakoneta Shawnee communities and with the concurrence of a vast majority of these populations. Black Hoof and Captain Lewis also led their people to the decisions to attempt to accommodate American expansion, to remain in Ohio, and even to attempt to adopt American farming lifestyles and to accept Christian missionaries, practices which one historian says carried over to Oklahoma.[7]

We can also glean evidence of tribal governance and laws from the treaties Captain Lewis and others signed with the United States for the Lewistown Seneca and Shawnee people. In the treaty of 1817, for example, the decision of whether to allot the communally owned reservation into specific parcels of land for named individuals, and then to grant titles to those individuals, was left up to the discretion of the chiefs. Moreover, in the treaty of 1831, the Mixed Band tribal chiefs made an agreement with the United States for the tribe to sell its land and homes in Ohio and remove to Indian Territory. The Lewistown chiefs were to decide how to distribute the money that the United States paid the Mixed Band for the sale of the improvements they were leaving in Ohio. The chiefs also had the authority, after obtaining the consent of the general council, to request that the United States pay the Mixed Band the balance of the funds the United States would withhold from the sale of the Ohio lands. It is clear that the United States and these tribal leaders thought that the chiefs had the authority to sign treaties binding the tribal government and the Shawnees to sell their lands and to make decisions settling disputes and dividing tribal assets. Subsequently, these treaties demonstrate Shawnee governance, politics, and political decision making.[8]

But it is also important to note that Shawnee peoples voted with their feet and would leave communities or tribes when they no longer agreed with the direction the tribal leadership was taking. For example, Captain Lewis himself decided by the early 1820s that the Ohio Shawnees should remove to better lands and a better situation west of the Mississippi. He tried to convince other Shawnees to move with him. In 1825, however, he led only a small group of Senecas and Shawnees westward.[9]

Eastern Shawnee Laws and Governance, 1832–1945, Indian Territory and Oklahoma

There is minimal written evidence of how the Mixed Band (and, after its division, the Eastern Shawnee Tribe) governed itself and the laws it enacted and enforced in this time period in Indian Territory and, after statehood in 1907, in Oklahoma. We must once again mostly infer tribal laws and the exercise of sovereignty and governance from various actions of the tribal government and the Eastern Shawnee people during this time. But it is important to note that in 1951 one historian stated that the Eastern Shawnee Tribe had preserved its tribal organization and governed itself via chiefs and tribal council members throughout its entire time in Indian Territory and Oklahoma.[10]

In 1832, immediately upon arriving in Indian Territory, the tribal government negotiated a change in the land it had been assigned and signed a treaty in December 1832, exchanging the 60,000 acres of land on the west side of the Neosho River for the same amount of land east of the river. The tribal government also engaged in other treaty making with the United States in 1854, in 1867 (when the Shawnees of the Mixed Band split from the Senecas and became the Eastern Shawnee Tribe), and in 1874 (when the Eastern Shawnees decided to sell four thousand acres of land to the United States for the Modoc Tribe). In the 1854 agreement the Seneca and Shawnee chiefs were to select which lands the Mixed Band would retain if it sold the majority of its reservation to the United States. If individual Indians disagreed on their private land selections within the retained lands, the chiefs were to investigate and decide the disputes. Thus the chiefs would in essence be acting as a judicial body.[11]

Tribal leaders would not have undertaken these political actions without consulting with tribal citizens or without authorization from a wide array of community leaders and citizens. In fact, in 1867, when the Mixed Band representatives were in Washington, D.C., to negotiate a treaty with the United States, they referred several times to their credentials, which proved that they had been authorized by the community to speak officially for the tribe. In addition, these treaty negotiators referred to and then produced the written instructions they had been given by their tribe, which authorized them to negotiate a treaty only on specific issues. These facts demonstrate the political process of the tribe and the exercise of sovereign powers by both the Seneca and Shawnee people and their chosen leaders.[12]

Moreover, during this time period, as is also discussed below, the Mixed Band was heavily involved in attempting to create an Indian Territory tribal confederacy to protect the tribal land base and rights. Representatives of the Senecas and Shawnees attended informational and organizational meetings in the 1830s, '40s, and '50s, as well as in 1870 and 1888. These actions also constitute the exercise of governmental and sovereign powers by the Mixed Band.

Furthermore, in 1870–71, the tribe decided to consent to sell land to the Atlantic & Pacific railroad. In 1866 Congress authorized the A&P to build a transcontinental railroad, which included building track through Indian Territory. The A&P finished its line from Saint Louis to Seneca, Missouri, in 1871. The line was then built from Seneca, Missouri, through Eastern Shawnee land, to Vinita, Indian Territory. The tribal government must have consented to this action, because the 1866 Act of Congress required tribal consent.[13]

Significantly, in 1901 the Eastern Shawnee Tribal Council enacted a law that was expressly confirmed and ratified by the U.S. Congress. On December 2, 1901, the tribe passed a law to allot its remaining land to Eastern Shawnee children who had been born since the tribal land allotments of 1888–92. The tribe also decreed that it would sell any remaining surplus land, that is, any reservation land that was left over after all of the allotments. In an act dated May 27, 1902, Congress "ratified and approved" the law enacted by "the council of the Eastern Shawnee . . . nation . . . providing for the allotment of lands to certain minor children and for other purposes."[14]

The tribal council also negotiated with the United States to settle its right to annuity payments under multiple treaties, and for the payment of all Eastern Shawnee trust funds that were then on deposit with the U.S. Treasury. The tribe agreed to take all of these funds in one lump-sum payment. This money was distributed in 1902 in payments of $286.45 to each tribal citizen.[15]

In contrast to the exercise of tribal sovereignty, however, the governments of all the tribes in the Quapaw Agency were heavily influenced by the U.S. Indian agents, the agency police force, and the Courts of Indian Offenses. The Bureau of Indian Affairs (BIA) started using reservation and agency police forces in 1878 and started creating reservation and agency courts in 1883. The Quapaw Agency police force was first mentioned in an agent report in 1879, and the annual reports thereafter state that the police force comprised one captain and six privates and was of great service to the agents. The police primarily worked to evict white trespassers; to stop timber, wildlife, and horse theft; and to control alcohol issues. In addition, the Courts of Indian Offenses began operating informally in 1883. Apparently, the original instructions for these courts were also issued in 1883, and an amended version issued in 1892 specified a range of penalties the courts could impose. The court system at the Quapaw Agency was composed of three Indian judges. Their tribal identities, at least in 1896, were Wyandotte, Seneca, and Ottawa. They mostly handled minor cases and were praised in multiple agents' reports for doing an excellent job and contributing to the security and control of the agency. Today the Eastern Shawnee Tribe continues to use one of the few remaining descendants of the old Courts of Indian Offenses, the BIA Court of Federal Regulations, as its judicial branch.[16]

These facts demonstrate that the Eastern Shawnee Tribe and its people governed themselves and exercised sovereign prerogatives through law in the Indian Territory and Oklahoma from 1832 to 1945.[17]

Indian Territory Tribal Confederacy

The governments of the removed tribes were obviously interested in continuing to operate and govern their peoples and lands in Indian Territory. An intriguing effort along these lines was the multidecade attempt to create a confederacy of tribal governments in order to protect and represent the interests of the Indian nations. A wide array of tribal nations and delegates held numerous meetings on this subject over many decades. The Eastern Shawnee Tribe was heavily involved in many of these meetings and discussions.[18]

Tribal delegates met at various times and locations in northeastern Indian Territory to discuss forming a confederacy. Apparently, the first meeting was held on October 14, 1837, at the Tahlontuskee council grounds near the mouth of the Illinois River in Indian Territory. The Mixed Band of Senecas and Shawnees attended and also signed invitations asking other tribes to attend. An even larger council meeting was held the next year, September 15 to 25, 1838, east of Tahlequah. Delegates from eleven tribes attended, and officers were elected.[19]

Another council was held in May 1842, and the Senecas and Shawnees attended again. This council adopted rules of conduct intended for the common good. In 1843 the largest of all these conferences met at Tahlequah, and at least eighteen tribes and more than four thousand Indians met for four weeks. They discussed mutual concerns and worked to provide improvements and protection for Indians. In a throwback to issues raised by Tecumseh and other leaders in Ohio, these tribes wanted to restrict any individual tribe from selling its land without the consent of all other tribes. This council drafted a treaty, but it was only signed by the Cherokee, Creek, and Osage nations. Other meetings occurred in 1845 and 1853, and in 1859 the Creeks held an "international council of nations" at North Fork Town to adopt a code of international laws for Indian Territory.[20]

Furthermore, in June, September, and December 1870, other council meetings occurred. The tribal delegates discussed creating a constitution and organizing themselves to maintain the territory as an Indian home. These councils adopted resolutions opposing U.S. plans to set up a government over the territory and demanded compliance with their treaties. Up to forty tribes sent delegates to these meetings, including the Eastern Shawnees. At the December 6 to 20, 1870, meeting, the council apparently adopted a constitution and bill of rights and set up a form of government. The last of this chain of meetings appears to have occurred in 1888, when a score of tribes attended another of the so-called international councils at Fort Gibson.[21]

The Eastern Shawnee Tribal Constitution, Bylaws, and Charter of 1939–1940

In 1934 Congress enacted the Indian Reorganization Act (IRA), but this law had little application to the tribes in Oklahoma. Thus, in 1936 Congress enacted the similar Oklahoma Indian Welfare Act (OIWA) and applied it to the tribes in that state. In conjunction, these laws encouraged Indian nations to draft constitutions and corporate charters so as to operate business entities and assist tribal economic development. The United States provided model constitutions to tribes under the IRA and the OIWA, and many tribal governments adopted them with very little change. Consequently, many of the IRA and OIWA tribal constitutions are very similar to one another and to the U.S. Constitution.[22]

The Oklahoma Indian Welfare Act offered to tribal nations in that state the opportunity to draft and adopt written constitutions and to organize and operate their governments pursuant to these constitutions and through bylaws and corporate charters. The Eastern Shawnee government thereafter worked with federal authorities to draft, vote on, and adopt a constitution and bylaws in December 1939. The tribal community then adopted a corporate charter in December

1940. These actions and these documents help to demonstrate the continued operations of the Eastern Shawnee Tribe in this time period.[23]

Once the Eastern Shawnees made the decision to draft a constitution, various meetings, drafting sessions, and consultations with the federal government ensued. A tribal election was held on December 22, 1939, deciding whether to ratify the constitution that had been drafted, and the constitution was approved by a vote of 54–2. The Eastern Shawnee Business Committee was, of course, heavily involved in these political activities and decisions. The committee comprised Walter L. BlueJacket, Thomas A. Captain, Ora S. Hampton, Edward H. BlueJacket, and David Dushane Jr. The tribe then drafted a corporate charter, which was ratified by a 60–1 vote of the citizens of the tribe on December 12, 1940. This election was certified by the chief of the ESTO, Walter L. BlueJacket, and by Thomas A. Captain, the tribe's secretary-treasurer.[24]

The IRA and the OIWA conferred extensive powers on the secretary of the interior to influence the tribal constitutions that were enacted and the tribal governments that operated under them. In fact, many of the tribal constitutions that were adopted granted the secretary a veto power over future tribal constitutional amendments and required the secretary to approve certain actions of a tribe's governing body before they could become effective. The ESTO amended its 1939 constitution in 1999 and removed that secretarial power.

In conclusion, this brief discussion demonstrates that the Eastern Shawnee Tribe and its people have consistently exercised their inherent sovereign powers over many centuries to govern themselves and to control their external relations with other governments. The ESTO is a sovereign government and possesses political and governing authority over its citizens, its territory, and anyone who comes within its jurisdiction.

FEDERAL INDIAN POLICIES, LAWS, AND CASES IMPACTING THE EASTERN SHAWNEE TRIBE

The United States has pursued various policies and enacted innumerable laws and regulations regarding Indian nations since 1789. In addition, the U.S. Supreme Court has decided literally hundreds of cases on federal Indian law issues. We concentrate here only on the most significant of these policies, laws, and cases, mostly from 1812 to 1945, and briefly point out the impact on the Eastern Shawnee Tribe and its citizens.[25]

United States Constitution

The U.S. Constitution addresses Indian nations and Indian peoples. In Article I the Interstate Commerce Clause of the Constitution recognizes tribal governments as political entities. This clause enforced the objective of the founding fathers to ensure that only Congress would manage diplomatic and commercial affairs with Indian nations. This provision was expressly designed to exclude state governments from Indian affairs. "The Congress shall have Power . . . to regulate Commerce with foreign Nations, and among the several States, and with the Indian tribes."[26]

In Article VI the Supremacy Clause and the Treaty Clause refer to the Indian nations: "This Constitution, and the Laws of the United States . . . and all Treaties made, or which shall be made, . . . shall be the supreme Law of the Land; and the Judges in every State shall be bound thereby, any Thing in the Constitution or Laws of any State to the Contrary notwithstanding."[27] Although tribal governments are not expressly named in the provision, they are definitely covered by the clause, because in 1789, when the Constitution became operative, the United States had already entered into twenty-three treaties with foreign nations and nine treaties with Indian nations.[28]

Indians as individuals are mentioned in the Constitution in the provisions that require a national census of state populations to determine how many members of Congress each state can have in the House of Representatives. Article I states: "Representatives . . . shall be apportioned among the several States . . . according to their respective Numbers . . . excluding Indians not taxed." The Fourteenth Amendment, adopted in 1868, stated in nearly identical language that populations were still to exclude Indians: "Representatives shall be apportioned among the several States according to their respective numbers, counting the whole number of persons in each State, excluding Indians not taxed."[29]

The meaning of these provisions, and the clear intent of the founding fathers who wrote them, is that tribal nations are recognized as governments and that Indian peoples are citizens of their own political entities, not citizens of the federal or state governments.

U.S. Indian Policies

General George Washington penned the first, most enduring, and most infamous federal Indian policy. In 1783 he compared Indians to animals and foretold that American Manifest Destiny—the United States' expansion across the continent—would lead to the probable extermination of Indians. He wrote to Congress: "Policy and oeconomy [*sic*] point very strongly to the expediency of being upon good terms with the Indians, and the propriety of purchasing their Lands in preference to attempting to drive them by force of arms out of their country; which as we have already experienced is like driving the Wild Beasts of the Forest . . . when the gradual extension of our Settlements will as certainly cause the *Savage as the Wolf* to retire; *both being beasts of prey tho' they differ in shape*."[30] As Washington assumed, Indian nations owned lands and resources that American settlers and the United States wanted. Thereafter, the U.S. government adopted the European and English tradition of dealing politically with tribal governments. The United States also developed official policies to deal with tribal nations. These policies often changed slowly over time, but occasionally they changed drastically and within very short periods. This has left American history and law with a schizophrenic mix of federal actions taken toward Indians and Indian nations that reflect the contrary goals of either assimilating Indians into American society or exterminating them.

The first national government of Colonial America organized itself as the Continental Congress in September 1774. This Congress, which existed from 1774–81, pursued tribal policies that attempted to either keep Indian nations neutral in the American Revolutionary War or gain their support for the colonies. During this time the Continental Congress dealt with tribes on a diplomatic basis and sent negotiators and gifts to tribal governments. The fledgling government even entered into one treaty with the Delaware Tribe in 1778.[31]

After winning its independence, the new United States government, operating as the Articles of Confederation Congress from 1781–89, was heavily involved in dealings with Indian tribes. This new government was very weak and had neither funds nor an army to fight tribes. Consequently, the Confederation Congress strongly desired to avoid wars with the Indian nations.[32]

The Confederation Congress was organized under the Articles of Confederation, which were adopted in 1781 by the thirteen states. A very important function of this new Congress was to handle Indian affairs and to exclude the states from this business. Thus Article IX provided that Congress "shall also have the sole and exclusive right and power of . . . regulating the trade and managing all affairs with the Indians."[33] As mentioned above, the United States Constitution, under which the United States began operating in the spring of 1789, adopted this same principle, reserving Indian affairs for Congress alone and not for the states.

TRADE AND INTERCOURSE ERA (1789–1830) One of the important duties of the new United States government was to keep the peace with the Indian nations while conducting all affairs with the tribes. The first Congress under the new Constitution immediately assumed the exclusive power it had been granted to manage Indian affairs. In the first five weeks of its existence, Congress passed four laws regarding tribes. It established the Department of War, which was granted responsibility over Indian affairs; it appropriated funds to negotiate Indian treaties; and it appointed federal treaty commissioners to negotiate with tribal governments. On July 22, 1790, Congress enacted the first of a series of laws called the Indian Trade and Intercourse Acts. Most of the provisions of this 1790 law are still in effect today.[34]

These acts forbade—and federal law today still forbids—states or individuals from buying Indian lands. Consequently, the federal policy of dealing with tribes as political sovereign governments, excluding states and individuals from any role in the process, was instituted from the very beginning of the United States government.

REMOVAL ERA (1830–1850) In the mid-1820s the federal government began to openly discuss moving all tribes west of the Mississippi River. President Thomas Jefferson had written privately as early as 1803 that the tribes would have to be moved west of the Mississippi, and as mentioned above, George Washington assumed all along that Indian nations would disappear before the advance of the American frontier.

Andrew Jackson, who became president in 1829, was the first president from the western part of the United States, and he advocated a land-hungry, hostile attitude toward the Indians. Jackson supported, and Congress enacted, the Removal Act of 1830, making official the policy to remove tribal nations and peoples west of the Mississippi River.

Ultimately, the vast majority of tribes and Indians who lived east of the river were removed to the West. Tribes from the Pacific Northwest and other areas were also removed to Indian Territory. Many tribes were removed via treaty agreements, such as the Eastern Shawnees. The Modoc Tribe was removed there, essentially, as prisoners of war. Many tribal communities suffered grievously from these removals, which are known as the "trails of tears."

RESERVATION ERA (1850–1887) Most historians state that the reservation era of federal Indian policy began in 1849–50, when Indian reservations were first created in Texas and California. But the Eastern Shawnee Tribe's lands in Ohio, and the lands of other tribes in Ohio, were called reservations as early as 1817.

Notwithstanding that fact, the federal policy to remove all tribes to Indian Territory was expedited by a rush of events. The discovery of gold in California and the opening of the Oregon Trail caused a leapfrog effect, as U.S. citizens swarmed across the continent and began invading areas owned and used by Indians. This massive migration, and the problems and violence that it caused, resulted in federal attempts to set aside separate, specifically designated tracts of land as reservations for Indian nations. Tribes were asked or forced to give up rights to most of their lands and to "reserve" for themselves clearly defined areas. Reservations were designed to create a measured separatism to keep Indian peoples and governments separate from Americans and state governments. More than three hundred Indian reservations still exist today in the contiguous forty-eight states.

ALLOTMENT AND ASSIMILATION ERA (1887–1934) Federal Indian policy changed dramatically in 1887, when Congress enacted the General Allotment Act. The idea behind allotment was to impose on Indians the American form of individual, private landownership and to further diminish the tribal land base. The General Allotment Act, and the many tribally specific allotment acts and presidential orders that followed, usually divided (allotted) tribally owned reservations into 160-, 80-, and 40-acre plots, which were then given to tribal citizens to be owned individually. Any excess lands that exceeded the amount needed for allotment to individual Indians were called surplus lands and were often sold to non-Indians. Consequently, most of the reservation lands on allotted reservations were no longer owned by the tribal governments and held in common for tribal citizens.

This era is more fully known as the "allotment and assimilation era," because the goal of the United States was to "civilize" Indians and bring them into the American melting pot by assimilating them into mainstream society. Indians would not be allowed to live separate lives and maintain their governments, religions, and cultures, even on their own reservations. Hence, the well-recognized and longstanding goal of either exterminating or assimilating Indians became official federal policy. The government expressly tried to force assimilation on the Indians and to end their identity as Indian peoples. The Eastern Shawnees felt the effects of this era. In fact, the Bureau of Indian Affairs was used to take absolute control of life on reservations in order to squeeze out Indian governments, religions, and cultures. Missionaries and church- and government-run schools were major tools used to assimilate Indians.[35]

This policy also had the specific goal of opening reservations for settlement by Americans. It mostly succeeded because a significant amount of the reservation lands that were allotted to individual tribal citizens were ultimately lost from Indian ownership due to voluntary sales or forced state-tax foreclosures. Furthermore, reservation lands that were not allotted to individual Indians, surplus lands, were often sold to non-Indians. The loss of Indian land allotments and the sale of surplus lands to non-Indians resulted in a major loss of tribal reservation lands and created a checkerboard effect of non-Indian landownership mixed in with Indian and tribal lands on many reservations today. In total, the Allotment Act resulted in a loss of about two-thirds of all tribally owned lands between 1887 and 1934. In addition, of the remaining 48 million acres of tribally owned lands in 1934, 20 million acres were nearly worthless because they were desert or semidesert lands.[36]

INDIAN REORGANIZATION ERA (1934–1953) The absolute failure of allotment to assimilate Indians into American society or to improve their economic situations and the resulting poverty, ill health, and undereducation on reservations led to a major change in federal Indian policy. In 1934, under the new administration of President Franklin D. Roosevelt, Congress passed the Indian Reorganization Act (IRA) and commenced an entirely new federal Indian policy called, appropriately enough, the Indian reorganization era, running from the early 1930s to the mid-1950s. Although the era is considered to have ended in the 1950s, the IRA is still binding law today; it substantially impacts most tribal governments today and is very significant to the ESTO because the tribe organized its government under a constitution it drafted pursuant to the 1936 version of the IRA.[37]

Under the IRA, the United States completely reversed its allotment policy and its efforts to destroy tribal governments and cultures. Congress and the executive branch decided instead to support Indian governments and sovereignty. The IRA ended further allotments of reservations and stopped further sales or losses of remaining Indian allotments by freezing in place the individual Indian allotments. Consequently, on reservations today individual Indians still own more than 11 million acres of allotted lands in trust with the United States.

The IRA also took a first step toward assisting Indian peoples to regain control of their lives and to wrest power over their lives and governments from the United States and the BIA. The policy also tried to strengthen tribal governments and help them to function more effectively as governments. Tribes were encouraged to form governing entities under constitutions that were similar to the U.S. Constitution. In fact, these IRA tribal constitutions had to be approved by the secretary of the interior, a requirement which provided the secretary with great power over tribal governments. As discussed above, the ESTO used the 1936 Oklahoma Indian Welfare Act when it adopted its constitution in 1939. Indian nations were even encouraged to form tribal corporations under federal law to provide economic development on reservations.

TERMINATION ERA (1953–1961) The final two eras of U.S. Indian policy occurred after 1945, after the time period this book covers. Thus they will barely be mentioned.

In a nutshell, in 1953 Congress passed a resolution to terminate the federal political relationship with tribal governments as quickly as possible. Thereafter, Congress and the executive branch terminated the federal relationship with 109 tribes and bands. Most of these tribal governments, however, were restored to federal recognition in the 1970s and 1980s.

SELF-DETERMINATION ERA (1961–2016) Most historians state that the termination era ended in 1961 with the inauguration of President John F. Kennedy. While his administration completed some tribal terminations that were already in progress when he took office, it began no new tribal terminations.

This era of federal Indian policy is named after a statement President Richard Nixon made in 1970, and also the title of a very significant 1975 federal law called the Indian Self-Determination and Education Assistance Act. The ESTO has benefitted from that law, and especially from the subsequent 1994 Tribal Self-Governance Act, under which the ESTO is a self-governance tribe.

Federal Laws

Stated briefly below are the more significant federal Indian laws that specifically impacted or benefitted the Eastern Shawnee Tribe and its people.

THE NORTHWEST ORDINANCE OF 1787 The Northwest Ordinance, enacted by the Articles of Confederation Congress in 1787, established the Northwest Territory, which comprised what are now the states of Ohio, Indiana, Illinois, Michigan, and Wisconsin. This was the area where Shawnee tribes and peoples were living at the time. The ordinance set out how the territory would be governed by the United States, how new states could be formed, and how the United States would deal with the tribal nations. The act stated, "The utmost good faith shall always be observed towards the Indians, their lands and property shall never be taken from them *without their consent*; and in their property, rights and liberty, they never shall be invaded or disturbed, unless in just and lawful wars."[38]

The United States nominally complied with this ordinance, although it continually pressured and coerced Indian nations to consent to removal. The Lewistown Mixed Band of Seneca and Shawnee Indians finally did consent to remove from Ohio to Indian Territory in its treaty of 1831.

THE TRADE AND INTERCOURSE ACT The Trade and Intercourse Acts have already been mentioned in connection with the federal Indian policy of the same name. The original temporary act of 1790 was renewed in 1793, 1796, and 1799, and it was made permanent in 1802. The 1802 act was amended in 1834 and remains part of federal law today.[39]

In addition to restraining states from interfering in Indian affairs, these acts exercised Congress's constitutional authority to regulate American trade with Indians and Indian tribes. These laws tried to implement Indian treaties and force frontier Americans to obey reservation boundaries and Indian rights. Under the acts, persons who desired to trade with Indians had to obtain a federal license, had to provide a bond guaranteeing their compliance with the acts, and could not trade alcohol in Indian country. Interestingly, in 1796, 1799, and 1802 Congress even required non-Indians to obtain federal passports to enter tribal lands.

THE FEDERAL FACTORY SYSTEM In 1795 Congress enacted President George Washington's proposal to establish U.S. trading posts (also called factories) along the Indian frontiers. Washington believed it was good policy to promote trade with the Indian nations. His goals were to foster peaceful relations with tribes, to bind the tribes economically to the United States, to keep the trade fair, to prevent the alcohol trade, and to avoid the friction, fraud, and other problems that private traders often caused. From 1795 to 1822 the federal government operated up to twenty-eight federal trading posts across the frontier. Congress repeatedly renewed this bill at the urging of President Washington, and later President Jefferson. Jefferson was especially interested in using the posts to control the Indian nations through trade and commerce. He was also very crafty; he purposefully used this trade to get Indians into debt so that they would be inclined to sell their land to pay debts.[40]

These federal trading posts impacted the Shawnees in Ohio. One of the closest U.S. factories to the Lewistown Senecas and Shawnees, Fort Wayne in Indiana Territory, operated from 1803 to 1812. It was, in fact, the second most important trading post in the region after Detroit, and Shawnee people were regular customers. Shawnees also often used the post at Sandusky, Ohio. One scholar states that the Fort Wayne post, in particular, created an American-influenced economy that radiated throughout the region. He writes that Shawnee men traded deer, raccoon, and muskrat skins at the fort, and that Shawnee women made goods, including maple sugar, beeswax, moccasins, and feathers to trade at the fort.[41]

CIVILIZATION FUND The United States government long claimed to be interested in assimilating Indians into American society. In pursuit of this goal, the United States attempted to educate Indians according to American standards in order to convince Natives to emulate American-style farming societies and economic endeavors (ignoring the excellent Indian farming practices that had sustained Indian nations for centuries) and to convert Indians to Christianity. In pursuit of these objectives, Congress created the Civilization Fund in 1819 with regular appropriations to support Indian education efforts and missionary societies.[42]

Missionary activities among the Indian nations were not entirely the private church functions they might at first have appeared. At least one historian notes that missionaries worked in partnership with the U.S. Indian agents and reservation superintendents and were oftentimes even funded with federal dollars. President Grant, for example, appointed churches to be in charge of education and religious operations on many reservations. Congress and the Bureau of Indian Affairs even gave churches Indian-owned land on which to build churches and schools. The Seneca, Shawnee, and Wyandotte Indian School, located on the Wyandotte reservation, was apparently built in 1872 by a Quaker missionary and supported by federal funds. Although the government soon assumed operation of this school, it was repeatedly called a mission in the annual reports of the Quapaw Agency, and it was obviously working to convert Indian children to Christianity in addition to providing basic education. The United States actively encouraged churches to provide schools to Indians in order to teach them American-style farming and to convert them.[43]

The Mixed Band, and later the Eastern Shawnees, experienced the effects of missionary activities and federal programs under the civilization fund in both Ohio and Indian Territory. In 1802 Chief Black Hoof at Wapakoneta convinced fellow Shawnees in Ohio to adopt some elements of European farming. At his request, the United States sent a Quaker missionary to assist them. At the Seneca Indian School many Eastern Shawnee children were immersed in American history, culture, and religion. U.S. Indian agents at the Quapaw Agency and superintendents at the Seneca Indian School regularly reported on the number of students and the conditions at the school. Included in the reports were the number of churches on the lands of the eight tribes in the Quapaw Agency, the number of converted Indians, the number of services and Indian attendees, and the number of those that could speak and write English. The United States, Indian agents, and missionaries continually encouraged and worked with tribes to develop Euro-American farming, religion, and lifeways.[44]

INDIAN REMOVAL ACT The removal era has already been mentioned, and the Eastern Shawnee Tribe felt the heavy hand of removal policies. Most politicians and American citizens long agitated for the removal of Indian tribes west of the Mississippi, so that their lands could be owned by American citizens. Congress enacted the Indian Removal Act in 1830 and authorized the president to exchange lands in the West for lands the Indian nations owned east of the Mississippi if they consented to be removed westward.

This act and U.S. initiatives led to the removal of almost all Indian nations west of the Mississippi. The act itself required that tribal consent be obtained before a tribe was removed: "It shall and may be lawful for the President . . . to cause so much of any territory belonging to United States, west of the river Mississippi . . . To be . . . for the reception of such tribes or nations of Indians *as may choose* to exchange the lands where they now reside, and remove there."[45]

The removal era is considered to have officially commenced in 1830, but the United States had long been trying to remove eastern tribes. The federal government and various Indian agents had continually badgered and encouraged the Mixed Band of Senecas and Shawnees to remove long before the tribe finally signed its treaty of removal in 1831. Obviously, the removal era of federal policy and the Removal Act played an important role in Eastern Shawnee history.

ATLANTIC & PACIFIC RAILROAD American politicians and citizens were not inclined to allow Indian Territory, tribal lands, and treaty promises to stand in the way of economic development, one example of which is the transcontinental railroad. Consequently, on July 27, 1866, Congress chartered the Atlantic & Pacific Railroad (later called the Saint Louis–San Francisco Railroad), and authorized it to lay track through Indian Territory. To reimburse the railroad for building the line, Congress granted it every other section of land, comprising 3.1 million acres across the territory, "subject only to Indian occupancy which will soon be extinguished." Congress did require, though, that these land cessions only be by "voluntary cession, [of] the Indian title to all lands falling under the operation of this act."[46]

The A&P railroad line was completed as far as the boundary of Indian Territory at Seneca, Missouri, by April 1, 1871. Thereafter, track was built through Eastern Shawnee land, and by November 1871, A&P trains were crossing Indian Territory as far as Vinita. It is unclear when and how the tribe decided to sell these lands for the railroad or what was done with the proceeds. But obviously the Eastern Shawnee government had the authority and procedures in place to make this decision. One commentator states that the Eastern Shawnee Tribe received $25 per acre for its land, while the Wyandotte Tribe received only $15 per acre.[47]

BIA POLICE AND COURTS OF INDIAN OFFENSES United States Indian agents had long desired more control over reservation populations, so in the late 1870s the already nearly dictatorial control of the BIA over reservations was greatly strengthened by the creation of reservation police forces. Although this action was not specifically authorized by Congress, agency police forces, and appropriated funds to pay them, were apparently first referenced in an act dated May 27, 1878.[48]

The U.S. agent at the Quapaw Agency, which encompassed the Eastern Shawnee reservation, apparently first reported the existence of an agency police force in 1879. Thereafter, the agents regularly reported to the commissioner of Indian affairs that the police force consisted of one captain and six privates. The police helped to keep trespassers and timber thieves at bay and to restrict the alcohol trade.[49]

Moreover, the Courts of Indian Offenses were developed by the commissioner of Indian affairs in 1883 to help control and punish reservation Indians. Many scholars have stated that these courts, which were created by an executive branch administrative agency, were unconstitutional.

But reservation agents got tribal governments to accept the courts and persuaded reservation Indians to submit to their rulings. Congress appears to have enacted its first appropriation to pay the Indian judges on these courts in 1888.[50]

FEDERAL CRIMINAL AND CIVIL JURISDICTION IN INDIAN TERRITORY The United States rarely, if ever, tried to interfere with Shawnee internal affairs while the tribe was located in Ohio. However, once the tribe moved to Indian Territory in 1832, the United States became more active in creating courts and laws that applied to the Eastern Shawnees and other tribes in the territory. This chapter will not attempt to trace this complex history, but will simply note some major features.

In 1834 Congress annexed all judicial matters and the punishment of crimes in Indian Territory to Arkansas Territory. Litigants had to travel to Fort Smith in Arkansas Territory. After Arkansas became a state in 1836, its courts continued to have jurisdiction in Indian Territory. Congress apparently first transferred jurisdiction over cases arising from the Quapaw Agency—and thus those concerning Eastern Shawnees—to the judicial district of Kansas in Fort Scott in 1880. In 1896 all criminal cases in Indian Territory, except for those in tribal courts, were to be tried in Muskogee, which was now the headquarters of the U.S. Northern District Court of Indian Territory. Vinita, Miami, and Tahlequah were the other court towns. In 1902 Vinita became the headquarters for the Northern District Court.[51]

In addition to creating United States courts, jurisdiction, and power over Indian Territory, Congress enacted numerous laws regulating the activities of Indians in the territory. These laws included bans on bigamy in 1862 and on other "immoral" actions in 1887. In fact, adultery and fornication were felonies if they were committed by U.S. citizens in Indian Territory. Congress also imposed taxes on alcohol and tobacco and allowed any Indian nation or individual to sue or be sued by railroads. In 1887 Congress created federal jurisdiction over any Indian who committed an act upon an Indian policeman.[52]

GENERAL ALLOTMENT ACT The allotment era of federal Indian policy has been briefly addressed above. This policy and the 1887 General Allotment Act (GAA) had enormous impacts on the Eastern Shawnee Tribe.[53]

Pursuant to allotment policy, Congress now desired to break up the communal, tribal governmental ownership of reservation lands and to grant parcels of land to individual Indians. Ostensibly, the goal was to teach individual Indians private property ownership, to help them support themselves, and to further acculturate them to American society. Many people, however, including President Theodore Roosevelt, recognized that the act was a further attempt by American society to acquire Indian lands and assets. The GAA was another application of George Washington's "Savage as Wolf" policy and the United States' efforts to ultimately acquire all Indian lands. In fact, the General Allotment Act is viewed today as an absolute disaster for tribal governments and for the ownership and use of reservation lands. Additionally, the vast majority of Indians who received allotments of tribally owned lands—and received fee simple titles to those lands—lost their lands through voluntary sales or by state and county tax foreclosures. Furthermore, many minors in Indian Territory were literally robbed of their lands and their assets by unscrupulous lawyers and judges.[54]

The first allotments at the Eastern Shawnee reservation began in 1888 under the authority of the GAA and instructions from the commissioner of Indian affairs dated March 5, 1888. Further allotments were then undertaken in 1889–92, mostly under the direction of Special Agent Spencer Hartwig. By 1892, 10,484 acres of the reservation had been allotted to eighty-four Eastern Shawnee citizens.[55]

The tribe still owned 2,543 acres of surplus land on its reservation after these allotments. Agents from the Quapaw Agency reported that the eight tribal councils in the agency engaged in much discussion about how to handle their surplus lands. The Eastern Shawnee Tribal Council ultimately decided to keep those lands in the ownership of tribal citizens and passed an act on December 2, 1901, authorizing "the allotment of lands to certain minor children." Congress ratified and approved this Eastern Shawnee Tribal Council law on May 27, 1902. Most of the tribe's surplus lands were then allotted to thirty-three Eastern Shawnee minors, and the tribe sold the remaining 405 acres of surplus land on its reservation.[56]

This action by the tribe was probably designed to ensure that the reservation surplus land was allotted to Shawnee children rather than sold to non-Indians. The tribal council that made this decision, which was also called the "allotment committee of the Eastern Shawnee Tribe," is identified in BIA records: Chief Andrew Dushane, councilmen Charles Dushane, Elkin B. Grindstone, and Stonewall Jackson. The BIA records also state that the council certified that the allotments were completed properly.[57]

CURTIS ACT, JUNE 28, 1898 This law was no doubt primarily directed at the Five Civilized Tribes in Indian Territory, but the statute expressly addresses all tribes in the territory, which includes the Eastern Shawnees.

At this time Congress decided to destroy these tribal governments, courts, and tribal laws, to establish town sites on reservations, to manage mineral leases, and to address other technical matters. Congress also authorized the Dawes Commission to draw up tribal rolls so as to allot the communally owned lands of the Five Civilized Tribes. (The Eastern Shawnee reservation had already been mostly allotted.)[58]

UNITED STATES CITIZENSHIP Until Congress amended the General Allotment Act in 1906, the act provided that Indians who took allotments became United States citizens immediately upon receiving their allotment. Consequently, the eighty-four adult Shawnee citizens who received allotments between 1888 and 1892 and the thirty-three Shawnee minors who received allotments between 1902 and 1904 should have been considered U.S. citizens at the time of their allotment. In addition, in 1901 Congress made all Indians in Indian Territory United States citizens, which included the Eastern Shawnees, of course. If there were any remaining doubts about the citizenship status of the Eastern Shawnee people, Congress made all Indians U.S. citizens in 1924.[59]

JOHNSON O'MALLEY ACT In 1934 Congress authorized the secretary of the interior to enter into contracts with states, and later with public and private institutions and corporations, wherein the federal government would pay those entities to provide educational, medical, and other services to Indians. The secretary was authorized to pay for those services from funds appropriated by Congress for Indians. States were allowed to use the existing schools, hospitals, and other facilities already owned by the federal government to provide those services.[60]

OKLAHOMA INDIAN WELFARE ACT In 1934 Congress enacted the Indian Reorganization Act. This act and others during the era of federal Indian policy have already been addressed above. However, Congress excluded, for the most part, the tribes in Oklahoma from the application of the IRA.

But in 1936 Congress extended most of the powers and opportunities of the IRA, and more, to the tribes in Oklahoma by enacting the Oklahoma Indian Welfare Act. Tribes in Oklahoma were now encouraged to draft constitutions and organize themselves under those documents and to adopt corporate charters to engage in economic activities. The Eastern Shawnee Tribe took this opportunity and adopted its constitution and charter in 1939 and 1940.[61]

INDIAN CLAIMS COMMISSION By 1946 Congress had become weary of tribal allegations that the United States had violated treaties and engaged in fraud and abuse. Congress was approached nearly every year to enact multiple laws allowing specific tribes to sue the United States for such claims. Instead, in 1946, Congress created an administrative body called the Indian Claims Commission to address these claims once and for all. Tribes would have a five-year deadline to file claims against the United States with the commission, which was intended to exist for ten years. The claims would be decided by that administrative body, and appeals from its decisions would go to the U.S. Court of Claims and to the United States Supreme Court. The number of claims that were ultimately filed and the complexity of the cases led Congress to repeatedly extend the life of the commission until it ultimately terminated on September 30, 1978.[62]

The Eastern Shawnee Tribe was involved in several Claims Commission cases. In 1964 Congress authorized the payment of one Shawnee claim, and it was paid per capita to Eastern Shawnee citizens as well as the citizens of the Absentee Shawnee Tribe and the Cherokee Band of Shawnee Indians.[63]

U.S. Supreme Court Cases

The United States Supreme Court has decided hundreds of cases regarding Indian affairs in the past 227 years. Rather than attempt to discuss this enormous body of law here, it is sufficient to mention that the court cases have essentially taken two contradictory lines of analysis. In any lawsuit, both parties can point to Supreme Court cases that are favorable in regard to tribal sovereignty and authority, and also to cases that are very limiting and even derogatory of tribal sovereignty. But even cases that might seem antitribal recognize and start with the premise that Indian nations are sovereign governments and possess inherent political and governmental powers.

Supreme Court case law regarding Indian nations really commences with what is called the Marshall trilogy, three decisions written by Chief Justice John Marshall in the mid-1800s. In 1823, in *Johnson v. McIntosh*, the court affirmed the international law principle known as the Doctrine of Discovery and held that the property and sovereign rights of Indian nations were automatically diminished upon their "discovery" by Euro-Americans.[64]

In *Cherokee Nation v. Georgia* in 1831 the court had to decide whether the Cherokee Nation was a foreign state or a foreign government for constitutional purposes. In a fractured decision Chief Justice Marshall and one other justice decided that the Cherokee Nation was a state (that is, a government), but that it was not a state foreign from the United States. Marshall's opinion made this significant statement: "In any attempt at intercourse between Indians and foreign nations, they are considered as within the jurisdictional limits of the United States. . . . They occupy a territory to which we assert a title independent of their will, which must take effect in point of possession when their right of possession ceases. Meanwhile they are in a state of pupilage. Their relation to the United States resembles that of a ward to his guardian."[65] The court then held that Indian nations have been incorporated into the United States and are "domestic dependent nations," not foreign governments.[66]

The very next year, in *Worcester v. Georgia*, the court had to decide whether Georgia could apply its laws in Indian country, inside the Cherokee Nation's territory. The court held that "the laws of Georgia can have no force" in Indian country and were void because they conflicted with the U.S. Constitution, Indian treaties, and federal laws, which established that all relations between Americans and Indian tribes were the exclusive business of the federal government.[67]

Throughout the years, the court recognized some very important facts about Indian nations. In 1896, in *Talton v. Mayes*, the court stated, regarding the Cherokee Nation and all tribes in general, that Indian nations exist as governments separate from the United States and the U.S. Constitution and that their sovereignty predates the United States and does not spring from the

U.S. Constitution. Instead, tribal sovereignty and governmental existence arise from the will and the consent of their own peoples.[68]

In addition, in *United States v. Wheeler* in 1978, the court recognized, "Before the coming of the Europeans, the tribes were self-governing sovereign political communities . . . [and] had the inherent power to prescribe laws for their members and to punish infractions of those laws. . . . Indian tribes have not given up their full sovereignty. . . . 'Indian tribes are unique aggregations possessing attributes of sovereignty over both their members and their territory.' . . . Indian tribes still possess those aspects of sovereignty not withdrawn by treaty or statute, or by implication as a necessary result of their dependent status."[69]

Finally, it is very relevant to the ESTO to note the 1993 case *Oklahoma Tax Commission v. Sac and Fox Nation*. Here the court stated that an Indian living and working in Indian country was exempt from state income taxes. "Indian country" includes not just "a formal reservation" but also any "land set aside for a tribe or its members."[70] Consequently, under this decision, the lands owned by the ESTO, in trust with the United States, should be deemed Indian country.

OKLAHOMA AND THE ESTO

A statement by Governor Johnston Murray (Chickasaw) well sums up the state's view of its power over Indians and Indian nations. In 1953 the governor wrote to the assistant secretary of the interior about the "Indians citizens" of Oklahoma: "When Oklahoma became a state, all tribal governments within its boundaries became merged in the State and the tribal codes under which the tribes were governed prior to Statehood were abandoned and all Indian tribes, with respect to criminal offenses and civil causes, came under State jurisdiction."[71]

This statement was, and is, false. In fact, Congress had specifically required Oklahoma to disclaim any and all jurisdiction over Indian nations as a condition to becoming a state. Many western states were admitted to the Union pursuant to similar disclaimers of jurisdiction over Indian nations and tribal lands and assets. The Oklahoma Enabling Act of 1906 allowed Oklahoma Territory and Indian Territory to become a state so long as

> nothing contained in the said [state] Constitution shall be construed to limit or impair the rights of the person or property pertaining to the Indians of said territories (so long as such rights shall remain unextinguished) or to limit or affect the authority of the government of the United States to make any law or regulation respecting such Indians, their lands, property, or other rights by treaties, agreement, law, or otherwise which it would have been competent to make if this [statehood] act had never been passed. . . . The people inhabiting said proposed state do agree and declare that they forever disclaim all right and title in or to any unappropriated public lands lying within the boundaries thereof, and to all lands lying within said limits owned or held by any Indian, tribe or nation.[72]

Oklahoma complied with this requirement and adopted the following provision in its constitution: "The people inhabiting the State do agree and declare that they forever disclaim all right and title in or to any unappropriated public lands lying within the boundaries thereof, and to all lands lying within said limits owned or held by any Indian, tribe, or nation; and that until the title to any such public land shall have been extinguished by the United States, the same shall be and remain subject to the jurisdiction, disposal, and control of the United States."[73]

Despite the disclaimers in the Enabling Act and the Oklahoma Constitution, the government and courts of Oklahoma endorsed the 1953 position of Governor Murray, and for many decades after statehood Oklahoma assumed it had jurisdiction over tribal nations, Indians, and their lands and assets. For example, in 1936, in *Ex Parte Nowabbi*,[74] the Criminal Court of Appeals of

Oklahoma "held that the state court had jurisdiction to prosecute a Choctaw Indian for murdering a Choctaw Indian on the victim's restricted allotment. The Court reached this result by concluding that a 1906 amendment to the General Allotment Act precluded Indian Country jurisdiction in the so-called Indian Territory which is now eastern Oklahoma."[75] And as late as 1979, the attorney general of Oklahoma issued a legal opinion that, due to the dissolution of the Indian tribes in the former Indian Territory, there is no "Indian country" in the former Indian Territory (now eastern Oklahoma), over which tribal and federal jurisdiction could exist.[76]

The 1936 case and the 1979 attorney general opinion have since been overruled by Oklahoma courts. In 1985, in *State v. Seneca-Cayuga Tribe of Oklahoma*, the Oklahoma Supreme Court stated that *Nowabbi* and the attorney general's opinion were inconsistent with current law and were "disapproved and withdrawn."[77] And in 1989 the Oklahoma Court of Criminal Appeals expressly overruled the *Nowabbi* case.[78]

But the 1953 statement of Governor Murray—that the tribal governments had come under state jurisdiction and that tribal laws were abandoned—was, sadly, mostly a fact for many decades. After finding their governments, jurisdictions, lands, and cultures under attack from the United States, the Bureau of Indian Affairs, "boomers," churches, American settlers, and corporations—and all too often by fraudulent means—the tribal nations in Oklahoma were decimated and nearly inactive for many decades after statehood.[79] Three highly esteemed Indian lawyers from Oklahoma wrote in 1978 and 1980 that the tribes had been adversely affected by the state's attitudes and actions and that statehood had changed forever the nature and authority of tribal governments. These commentators also noted that the Indian nations in Oklahoma were not even asserting and exercising the governmental powers that they did possess.[80]

That is no longer the case today.

CONCLUSION

The Eastern Shawnee Tribe has governed itself and its people since time immemorial. The evidence and facts addressed above demonstrate the truth of that statement. Through well-recognized laws, established governmental entities, and traditional control mechanisms, the tribe has exercised its inherent sovereign powers and operated as a government and a political body in its interactions with its people, with the United States, with European nations, and with other tribal nations.[81]

The Eastern Shawnee people are citizens of three political entities: the United States, the states in which they are domiciled, and the Eastern Shawnee Tribe. The Eastern Shawnee nation continues today to exercise its inherent sovereign powers and to govern its territory, its citizens, and all who enter its jurisdiction.

NOTES

The author thanks Arizona State University law student Christine Reyes for her valuable research assistance, and Arizona State University law librarian David Gay for his very helpful assistance for more than two years.

1. See Robert J. Miller, "American Indian Influence on the United States Constitution and its Framers," *American Indian Law Review* 18, no. 1 (1993): 141–46; Rennard Strickland, *Fire and the Spirits: Cherokee Law from Clan to Court* (Norman: University of Oklahoma Press, 1976); Karl N. Llewellyn and E. Adamson Hoebel, *The Cheyenne Way: Conflict and Case Law in Primitive Jurisprudence* (1941; reprint, Getzville, N.Y.: W. S. Hein, 1967).

2. Jerry E. Clark, *The Shawnee* (Lexington: University Press of Kentucky, 1993), 32–33; R. David Edmunds, *Tecumseh and the Quest for Indian Leadership* (Boston: Little, Brown, 1984), 46, 51; Charles

Callender, "Shawnee," *Handbook of North American Indians*, ed. William C. Sturtevant and Bruce G. Trigger (Washington, D.C.: Smithsonian Institution, 1978): 15, 623–24, 627.

3. Clark, *The Shawnee*, 31, 33–36; Edmunds, *Tecumseh*, 48–49, 59; James H. Howard, *Shawnee!: The Ceremonialism of a Native Indian Tribe and Its Cultural Background* (Athens: Ohio University Press, 1981), 106–107; Callender, *Shawnee*, 622, 624–25, 627–28.

4. Clark, *The Shawnee*, 36; Edmunds, *Tecumseh*, 50–51; Callender, *Shawnee*, 628.

5. Robert J. Miller, *Reservation "Capitalism": Economic Development in Indian Country* (Westport, Conn.: Praeger, 2012), 62–63; Edmunds, *Tecumseh*, 56; Callender, *Shawnee*, 628.

6. William H. Bergmann, *The American National State and the Early West* (New York: Cambridge University Press, 2012), 195; Clark, *The Shawnee*, 16, 24–25, 31–33.

7. Clark, *The Shawnee*, 24–25, 41, 46; Edmunds, *Tecumseh*, 67–69; R. David Edmunds, *The Shawnee Prophet* (Lincoln: University of Nebraska Press, 1983), 16–18, 171. Following Black Hoof's lead, most Ohio Shawnees wanted to stay in Ohio.

8. Treaty with the Wyandot, etc., 1817, arts. 7–8, *Laws and Treaties*, ed. Charles J. Kappler (Washington D.C.: Government Printing Office, 1904): 2:147–49 (hereafter Kappler); Treaty with the Seneca, etc., 1831, preamble, arts. I, II, V, VIII, XI, Kappler, 2: 327–28, 330, 332–33.

9. Edmunds, *The Shawnee Prophet*, 169.

10. Muriel H. Wright, *A Guide to the Indian Tribes of Oklahoma* (Norman: University of Oklahoma Press, 1951), 244.

11. Treaty with the Seneca and Shawnee, 1832, Kappler, 2:383; Agreement/Treaty (unratified) with the Seneca and Shawnee, 1854, art. II, ibid.; Treaty with the Seneca, Mixed Seneca and Shawnee, and Quapaw Indians, 1867, Kappler 2:960; Agreement with the Eastern Shawnees, 1874, Vine Deloria Jr. and Raymond Demallie, *Documents of American Indian Diplomacy: Treaties, Agreements, and Conventions 1775–1979* (Norman: University of Oklahoma Press, 1999), 1:260, 2:850.

12. February 5, 1867, Ratified Treaty No. 361, Documents Relating to the Negotiation of the Treaty of February 23, 1867, with the Seneca, Mixed Seneca and Shawnee, and Quapaw Indians, Documents Relating to the Negotiation of Ratified and Unratified Treaties With Various Indian Tribes, 1801–1869, Documents Relating to Indian Affairs, History Collection, University of Wisconsin Digital Collections, 29, 30; February 9, 1867, ibid., 38, 39, 40.

13. Grant Foreman, *A History of Oklahoma* (Norman: University of Oklahoma Press, 1942), 173, 177–78, 180.

14. Act of May 27, 1902, 32 Stat. 245, 262.

15. Ibid.; Report of School Superintendent in Charge of Quapaw Agency, September 1, 1903, Annual Report of the Commissioner of Indian Affairs (hereafter ARCIA), Documents Relating to Indian Affairs, History Collection, University of Wisconsin Digital Collections, 1:161.

16. Report of the Quapaw Agency, Indian Territory, August 27, 1879, ARCIA, 78; Report of the Quapaw Agency, Indian Territory, August 20, 1888, ibid., 109; Report of the Quapaw Agency, Indian Territory, August 21, 1893, ibid., 141; Report of the Quapaw Agency, Indian Territory, August 24, 1895, ibid., 148; Report of the Quapaw Agency, Indian Territory, August 26, 1896, ibid., 144–45. See William T. Hagan, *Indian Police and Judges: Experiments in Acculturation and Control* (New Haven, Conn.: Yale University Press, 1966), 49, 51–52, 120, 122–23, 156, 171.

17. Report of the School Superintendent in Charge of Quapaw Agency, Seneca Indian Training School, Indian Territory, August 12, 1902, ARCIA, 188 (each tribe has its own chief and council).

18. John P. Bowes, *Exiles and Pioneers: Eastern Indians in the Trans-Mississippi West* (New York: Cambridge University Press, 2007), 122; Grant Foreman, *The Five Civilized Tribes* (Norman: University of Oklahoma Press, 1934), 289.

19. Foreman, *History of Oklahoma*, 44, 47–48; Bowes, *Exiles and Pioneers*, 137–38, 145. See also "Tahlonteeskee (Cherokee Chief)," *Wikipedia*, https://en.wikipedia.org/wiki/Tahlonteeskee_(Cherokee_chief), accessed February 12, 2016.

20. Foreman, *History of Oklahoma*, 48, 52; Bowes, *Exiles and Pioneers*, 122, 145, 147; Jeffrey Burton, *Indian Territory and the United States, 1866–1906* (Norman: University of Oklahoma Press; 1995), 14.

21. Foreman, *History of Oklahoma*, 171–72, 230; Annie H. Abel, *The American Indians and the End of the Confederacy, 1863–1866* (1925; Lincoln: University of Nebraska Press, 1993), 89.

22. Indian Reorganization Act, June 18, 1934, 48 Stat. 984, codified at 25 U.S.C. § 461ff.; Oklahoma Indian Welfare Act, June 26, 1936, 49 Stat. 1967 codified at 25 U.S.C. §§ 501–509.

23. Robert J. Miller, "American Indian Constitutions and Their Influence on the United States Constitution," *Proceedings of the American Philosophical Society* 159, no. 1 (2015): 32–56

24. Wright, *Guide to the Indian Tribes*, 245. The 1939 constitution and bylaws of the ESTO are available through the Native American Constitution and Law Digitization Project at http://thorpe .ou.edu/IRA/okeshawcons.html, and the 1940 corporate charter is at http://thorpe.ou.edu/IRA /okeshawchrtr.html, both of which were last modified April 21, 2005.

25. Title 25 of the United States Code is composed entirely of laws about Indian nations and Indians. And that title contains only a miniscule portion of all the federal laws enacted since 1789 concerning Indian nations and Indians. By comparison, see Kappler, vols. 1, 3–7. Also, Title 25 of the Code of Federal Regulations addresses only tribal governments, Indians, and federal programs regarding Indians.

26. U.S. Constitution, art. I, § 8, cl. 3.

27. Ibid., art. VI.

28. Chapter 6 of this book demonstrates that the United States has always treated and dealt with tribal nations as governments.

29. U.S. Constitution, art. I, § 2; ibid., 14th amend., § 2.

30. George Washington to James Duane, September 7, 1783, *Documents of United States Indian Policy*, ed. Francis Paul Prucha, 3rd ed. (Lincoln: University of Nebraska Press, 2000), 1–2 (emphasis added).

31. Francis Paul Prucha, *The Great Father: The United States Government and the American Indians* (Lincoln: University of Nebraska Press, 1995), 35–39.

32. Prucha, *Great Father*, 39–50.

33. Articles of Confederation, art. IX (1781); Prucha, *Great Father*, 38.

34. Charles F. Wilkinson, *American Indians, Time, and the Law* (New Haven, Conn.: Yale University Press, 1987), 13; Act of August 7, 1789, 1 Stat. 49; Act of August 20, 1789, 1 Stat. 54; Act of July 22, 1790, 1 Stat. 137. The Indian Trade and Intercourse Act was made permanent in 1802 and amended in 1834, but it is still the law today. See, for example, 25 U.S.C. § 177 (2012).

35. Report, Quapaw Agency, Indian Territory, August 24, 1877, ARCIA, 102–104, 140. The Seneca, Shawnee, and Wyandotte mission school taught boys farming and gardening, and girls household and kitchen work; religious meetings and Sabbath schools were held in the schoolhouse and a Sabbath school, and an occasional religious meeting was held at the agency office.

36. Delos Sackett Otis, *History of the Allotment Policy*, Hearings on H. R. 7902, Before the House Committee on Indian Affairs, pt. 9, 434 (1934); Montana v. United States, 450 U.S. 544, 560n9 (1981) ("the avowed purpose of [Congress's] allotment policy was the ultimate destruction of tribal government"); General Allotment (Dawes) Act, 24 Stat. 388 (1887), codified as amended at 25 U.S.C. §§ 331–34, 339, 341–42, 348–49, 354, 381; John Collier, Memorandum, *The Purposes and Operation of the Wheeler-Howard Indian Rights Bill*, Hearings on H. R. 7902, Before the Senate and House Committees on Indian Affairs, 15–18 (1934). *Felix S. Cohen's Handbook of Federal Indian Law* (San Francisco: Lexis Law Publisher, 1982), 130–38.

37. 25 U.S.C. § 461. In 1936 Congress extended the IRA to the tribal nations in Oklahoma. Oklahoma Indian Welfare Act, June 26, 1936, 49 Stat. 1967.

38. Journals of the Continental Congress 32:340–41 (1787), reprinted in Prucha, *Documents of United States Indian Policy*, 9 (emphasis added).

39. Act of July 22, 1790, 1 Stat. 137, reprinted in Prucha, *Documents of United States Indian Policy*, 14; Act of March 1, 1793, 1 Stat. 329, ibid., 17; Act of May 19, 1796, 1 Stat. 469, ibid., 19; Act of March 3, 1799, 1 Stat. 743, ibid., 34; Act of March 30, 1802, 2 Stat. 139, ibid., 63.

40. Act of April 18, 1796, 1 Stat. 452. See also Robert J. Miller, "Economic Development in Indian Country: Will Capitalism or Socialism Succeed?" *Oregon Law Review* 80 (2002): 757, 808–809; Prucha, *Great Father*, 116, 120; Ora B. Peake, *A History of the United States Factory System, 1795–1822* (Denver: Sage Books, 1954); *A Compilation of Messages and Papers of the Presidents 1777–78*, ed. James D. Richardson (Washington, D.C.: Government Printing Office, 1910), 1: 191, 322; Robert J. Miller, *Native America, Discovered and Conquered: Thomas Jefferson, Lewis & Clark, and Manifest Destiny* (Westport, Conn.: Praeger, 2006), 86–90; Jefferson to William Henry Harrison, February 27, 1803, in Prucha, *Documents of United States Indian Policy*, 22; *The Writings of Thomas Jefferson*, ed. Andrew A. Lipscomb and Albert Ellery Bergh (Washington D.C.: Government Printing Office, 1903), 17:374; Colin G. Calloway, *The American Revolution in Indian Country: Crisis and Diversity in Native American Communities* (New York: Cambridge University Press, 1995), 242.

41. Bergmann, *American National State*, 185–87 (among others, the text cites Secretary of War Henry Dearborn to William Henry Harrison, July 29, 1802).

42. Act of March 3, 1819, 3 Stat. 516. See also Prucha, *Great Father*, 151–58, 517–19.

43. Report of the Quapaw Agency, Indian Territory, September 1, 1872, ARCIA, 244 (the school and boardinghouse for the Shawnees, Senecas, and Wyandottes opened June 1, 1872); Report, Quapaw Agency, Indian Territory, August 25, 1880, ibid., 90 (this report states that missionary work was being conducted nearly every Sunday and that a Sabbath school was conducted at the mission schools); Report of the Commissioner of Indian Affairs, Washington, D.C., September 14, 1894, ibid., 38 (this report states that Indian lands were granted to missionary and religious societies for religious and educational purposes); Report of the Commissioner of Indian Affairs, September 16, 1893, Washington, D.C., ibid., 12 (this report states that a Seneca, Shawnee, and Wyandotte school was begun by the Society of Friends as an orphan asylum in 1867 under contract with the tribe); Report of the Quapaw Agency, Indian Territory, August 16, 1883, ibid., 81 (this report states that the Shawnees were the only Agency tribe that, with regularity, kept up the dances, but the agent stated that its influences, aside from the wasted time, were harmless); Bergmann, *American National State*, 174, 183–84, 196 (this text states that reservation superintendents were to manage the Indians and get them to adopt Euro-American agriculture and animal husbandry; missionary projects were not just private endeavors but were "in fact, partnerships with the federal government"); *Indian Treaties, and Laws and Regulation Relating to Indian Affairs* (Washington City: Way and Gideon, 1826), 414 (in this text Congress authorized the annuity payment to Christian Indians on May 26, 1824).

44. Report of the Quapaw Agency, Indian Territory, August 25, 1891, ARCIA, 235 (this report states that the morals of the reservation had been raised by the missionary work and that the Indians seemed to be taking a deeper interest; six Sunday schools within the Agency had an attendance of 325 children); Report of the Quapaw Agency, Indian Territory, August 30, 1890, ibid., 85; Report of the Quapaw Agency, Indian Territory, August 20, 1888, ibid., 110; Wright, *Guide to the Indian Tribes*, 240.

45. 4 Stat. 411 (emphasis added).

46. One section equals 640 acres. Act of July 27, 1866, 14 Stat. 292, 294.

47. Foreman, *History of Oklahoma*, 173, 177–78, 180; H. Craig Miner, *The Corporation and the Indian: Tribal Sovereignty and Industrial Civilization in Indian Territory, 1865–1907* (Columbia: University of Missouri Press, 1976), 43; H. Craig Miner, *The St. Louis–San Francisco Transcontinental Railroad: The Thirty-Fifth Parallel Project, 1853–1890* (Lawrence: University Press of Kansas, 1972), 47, 51, 79, 103; Burton, *Indian Territory and the United States*, 54–55.

48. Foreman, *History of Oklahoma*, 199; Burton, *Indian Territory and the United States*, 66.

49. See note 16 above.

50. Foreman, *History of Oklahoma*, 199.

51. 4 Stat. 731–38; 27 Stat. 24–25; 32 Stat. 275–76; Burton, *Indian Territory and the United States*, 10–11, 71, 121, 151–54, 170, 196, 216, 241; Foreman, *History of Oklahoma*, 42–43, 278–79, 283–84.

52. 12 Stat. 301; 15 Stat. 125–68; 19 Stat. 240; 19 Stat. 244; 23 Stat. 69–76; 24 Stat. 449; 24 Stat. 635–42; Burton, *Indian Territory and the United States*, 26, 46–47, 50, 66, 109, 136, 196.

53. General Allotment (Dawes) Act, 24 Stat. 388 (1887), codified as amended at 25 U.S.C. §§ 331–334, 339, 341–42, 348–49, 354, 381. See also chapter 3 by John Bowes in this book.

54. Prucha, *Great Father*, 903; Kenneth R. Philp, *John Collier's Crusade for Indian Reform: 1920–1954* (Tucson: University of Arizona Press, 1977), 180 (probate abuses were found in Oklahoma state courts); U.S. House Committee on Indian Affairs, Hearings H. R. 6234, *General Welfare of the Indians of Oklahoma*, 1935, 75, 197; *Meriam Report: The Problem of Indian Administration* (Baltimore: Johns Hopkins Press, 1928), 798–804.

55. Land Allotment Records Entries 97A and 97B, Miami Agency, Records of the Bureau of Indian Affairs, Record Group 75, National Archives and Records Administration Federal Records Center, Fort Worth, Texas; Report, Quapaw Agency, Indian Territory, August 20, 1888, ARCIA, 109; Wright, *A Guide to the Indian Tribes of Oklahoma*, 241 (this text describes allotments made to 84 Eastern Shawnees by 1893).

56. Act of May 27, 1902, 32 Stat. 245, 262; Report, of the School Superintendent in Charge of the Quapaw Agency, Seneca Indian Training School, Indian Territory, September 1, 1903, ARCIA, 161.

57. Land Allotment Records Entries 97A and 97B, Record Group 75.

58. An Act for the Protection of the People of the Indian Territory, 30 Stat. 495, 497–98, 502–505 (1898). See also F. Browning Pipestem and G. William Rice, "The Mythology of the Oklahoma Indians: A Survey of the Legal Status of Indian Tribes in Oklahoma," *American Indian Law Review* 6, no. 2 (1978): 277, 292, 302.

59. Act of February 8, 1887, 24 Stat. 388; Prucha, *Great Father*, 668; Act of March 3, 1901, 31 Stat. 1447; Act of June 2, 1924, 43 Stat. 253, codified at 8 U.S.C. § 1401(b); Foreman, *History of Oklahoma*, 285 (the Act of March 3, 1901, made all Indians of the Indian Territory U.S. citizens without consulting them); S. T. Bledsoe, *Indian Land Laws*, 2nd ed. (Kansas City: Vernon Law Book, 1913), 37, 73, 669.

60. Act of April 16, 1934, 48 Stat. 596, codified as amended at 25 U.S.C. §§ 452–54; *Cohen's Handbook of Federal Indian Law*, 146–47, 695.

61. Act of June 26, 1936, 49 Stat. 1967, codified as amended at 25 U.S.C. §§ 501–509; Pipestem and Rice, *Mythology of the Oklahoma Indians*, 304–306.

62. 60 Stat. 1049–56; Prucha, *Great Father*, 1017–23; H. D. Rosenthal, *Their Day in Court: A History of the Indian Claims Commission* (New York: Garland Publishing, 1990); *Cohen's Handbook of Federal Indian Law*, 160–62.

63. Indian Claims Commission 31:89 (1973); Indian Claims Commission 12:161 (1963); Act of August 20, 1964, 78 Stat. 555.

64. 21 U.S. (8 Wheat.) 543 (1823). See also Miller, *Native America, Discovered and Conquered*, 50–53; Robert J. Miller, "The International Law of Colonialism: A Comparative Analysis," *Lewis and Clark Law Review* 15, no. 4 (2012): 851–54.

65. 30 U.S. (5 Pet.) 1, 17, 20 (1831).

66. Ibid., 17.

67. 31 U.S. (6 Pet.) 515, 561–62 (1832).

68. 163 U.S. 376, 379–80, 382–84 (1896).

69. 435 U.S. 313, 322–23 (1978). The court also quoted with approval a statement from the leading Indian law treatise (ibid., 322): The powers of Indian tribes are, in general, "*inherent powers of a limited sovereignty which has never been extinguished.*" *Cohen's Handbook of Federal Indian Law*, 122 (emphasis in original).

70. 508 U.S. 114, 124–25 (1993). See also Oklahoma Tax Commission v. Citizen Band Potawatomi Indian Tribe of Oklahoma, 498 U.S. 505, 511 (1991) (land "held by the Federal Government in trust for

the benefit of the [tribe] . . . is 'validly set apart' and thus qualifies as a reservation for tribal immunity purposes."); *Cohen's Handbook of Federal Indian Law*, 291–93. This states that Indian country includes trust lands retained for a tribe within its original reservation, that is, original treaty land subsequently acquired or reacquired within original tribal boundaries and taken into trust, citing United States v. Roberts, 185 F.3d 1125, 1130, 1137 (10th Cir. 1996); Cheyenne-Arapaho Tribes v. Oklahoma, 618 F.2d 665, 667–68 (10th Cir. 1980).

71. Quoted in Rennard Strickland, *The Indians in Oklahoma* (Norman: University of Oklahoma Press, 1980), 76; Pipestem and Rice, *Mythology of the Oklahoma Indians*, 278.

72. 34 Stat. 267.

73. Oklahoma Constitution, art. 1, § 3.

74. 60 Okl. Cr. 111, 61 P.2d 1139, 1156 (Okla. Crim. App. 1936).

75. The quoted language is from a 1989 Oklahoma case explaining what the *Nowabbi* court had done. State v. Klindt, 782 P.2d 401, 403 (Okla. Crim. App. 1989).

76. Op. Atty. Gen. No. 79–216 (Dec. 31, 1979).

77. 711 P.2d 77, 81, 81n17 (Okla. 1985).

78. State v. Klindt, 782 P.2d 401, 403–404 (Okla. Crim. App. 1989). "The holding in *Nowabbi* is inconsistent with the Oklahoma Supreme Court's holding in *Seneca-Cayuga*. In *Seneca-Cayuga*, the Court held that a tribal allotment to the Quapaw and Seneca-Cayuga Tribes is Indian Country even though the land is located in eastern Oklahoma. See *Seneca-Cayuga*, 711 P.2d at 82. . . . We resolve this inconsistency in favor of the holding in *Seneca-Cayuga*. There is ample evidence to indicate that the *Nowabbi* Court misinterpreted the statutes and cases upon which it based its opinion. . . . *Nowabbi* is hereby overruled."

79. Strickland, *Indians in Oklahoma*, 32–38, 40–42, 46, 52–53, 72–73, 82, 113; Pipestem and Rice, *Mythology of the Oklahoma Indians*, 302; Angie Debo, *And Still the Waters Run: The Betrayal of the Five Civilized Tribes* (Princeton, N.J.: Princeton University Press, 1940), viii, 313; Gertrude Bonnin, *Oklahoma's Poor Rich Indians: An Orgy of Graft and Exploitation of the Five Civilized Tribes—Legalized Robbery* (Philadelphia: Indian Rights Association, 1924).

80. Pipestem and Rice, *Mythology of the Oklahoma Indians*, 306–07; Strickland, *Indians in Oklahoma*, 113.

81. See, for example, chapter 6 in this book; Clark, *Shawnee*, 18, 59, 63, 67–68, 70, 73.

8

Chiefs of the Eastern Shawnee Tribe

CHIEF GLENNA J. WALLACE

They stand there, an adult woman and a young child, perhaps an elder teaching a child. Their heads held erect, their eyes gazing upward, they appear to be looking into the future. They stand by a large boulder. Unlike other immense, formidable boulders that seem impervious to pressure, this one has cracked from the force of a struggling but persistent tree, which embodies the spirit of the Eastern Shawnee Tribe that refuses to be denied its birthright. The sculpture symbolizes the struggles and ultimate victory of our people. We placed this sculpture on the southeast edge of our casino, Indigo Sky, to remind us of our resilience through adversity.

Led by chiefs throughout the ages, the Eastern Shawnee Tribe wishes to pay tribute to our former chiefs from the time we came to Indian Territory, now Oklahoma. Each has walked the red road, and each has contributed to our present strength. Unfortunately, we have not been the best at recording or preserving our history. Perhaps we did not because of our oral traditions. Perhaps the red-road life was so difficult when our ancestors arrived here that all their energies had to be focused on survival. Whatever the reason for not recording our history in the past, now is the time to begin the discovery and preservation process. I dedicate this chapter to those chiefs who have served the Eastern Shawnee Tribe since 1830. Each faced challenges and forged new trails. Sometimes the footprints along those trails have become indistinct, some are barely visible, and in some cases, at least for the moment, some have been erased. Gaps remain. Every chief has not been identified. Not every contribution has been noted. Lengths of leadership often remain unclear, unknown. But it is a beginning. This is a work in progress. It is my hope that others will pick up this important challenge and discover those missing footprints that helped to build the unique red road of the Eastern Shawnee Tribe of Oklahoma.

CIVIL JOHN OR METHOMEA (C. 1800–1845)

The Shawnees' world had been torn asunder. At one time a mighty force, their influence continued to decline following losses at the Battle of Fallen Timbers in 1794, the Battle of Tippecanoe in 1811, the War of 1812 (where many sided with the British), and the death of Tecumseh (the greatest of the resistance element) in 1813. One chief who lived through much of this chaotic, ever-changing world was Civil John, or Methomea.

Civil John, first chief of the Mixed Band in Indian Territory, was politically active as early as 1815, when he signed for the Senecas at Spring Wells "to restore peaceful relations with tribes and certain bands of the Shawnee and Seneca, that joined England in War of 1812—USA and the tribal nations renewed and confirmed all treaties they signed 1795–1815." His name, and his mark of X, is the first listed under the Seneca signers of the 1817 Fort Meigs Treaty, which involved several tribes and resulted in the Shawnees ceding their remaining lands in exchange for three reservations in Ohio: Wapakoneta, Hog Creek, and Lewistown. This 1817 treaty was not ratified by Congress. As a result, on September 17, 1818, in the Treaty with the Wyandottes, etc., the Lewistown reservation was established as the home of the Mixed Band of Senecas and Shawnees.

Quatawapea, or Captain Lewis, the person for whom the town was named, also signed the 1818 treaty, along with Chiakeska, or Captain Tom. Later treaties, signed in 1831 and 1832, relinquished land in western Ohio in exchange for land west of the Mississippi River, land that would be known first as Indian Territory, and later Oklahoma.[1] Many wanted the Indians to leave, but not all. Referring to themselves as "the feeblest of the feeble," several ladies in Steubenville, Ohio, originated and signed a petition in protest of Indian removal. These ladies addressed the Senate and House of Representatives of the United States, writing, "As the constitutional protectors of the Indians within our territory, and as the peculiar guardians of our national character, and our country's welfare, we solemnly and honestly appeal, to save this remnant of a much injured people from annihilation, to shield our country from the curses denounced on the cruel and ungrateful, and to shelter the American character from lasting dishonor. . . . And your petitioners will ever pray."[2] Their petition was ignored.

It is a rare feat for a person to be the last and the first, but that is exactly the position Civil John holds in the history of the Eastern Shawnee Tribe of Oklahoma. He was the last chief of the Mixed Band of Shawnees and Senecas to serve in Ohio, signing his mark of X to the July 20, 1831, treaty, where he is listed as first chief of the Senecas and Shawnees. His Indian name was Methomea, also at times spelled Mesomea. Our last chief in Ohio was Seneca, not Shawnee. He was also the first chief of the Mixed Band to serve in Indian Territory, which is verified by his signing of the December 29, 1832, Mixed Band document entitled "Seneca Agency, Head Waters of the Cowskin River." In this document the Mixed Band of Senecas and Shawnees voiced their dissatisfaction with the 60,000 acres west of the Neosho (or Grand) River, which was in Cherokee jurisdiction. They agreed to trade these lands for 60,000 acres on the east side of the river. The first name listed under the Mixed Band reads, "Civil John (Me-tho-mea) (first chief Senecas and Shawnees)."[3]

Little is known about his personal life. The April 15, 1830, "Enumeration of Shawnees Senecas Remaining East of Mississippi River" lists Civil John, his wife, and three children. Several years later he signed, as chief of the Mixed Band, a document dated March 1845 regarding "the sum of $250, being in part payment the sum of the annuities for $400 due the Seneca and Shawnee under the treaty of 1818 for the years 1837."[4] At least two of his children signed Mixed Band treaties. His oldest son is identified only as "Civil John's son" in some places, with the name Honede added in others. His younger son was referred to as exactly that: "young son of Civil John." Years later, on August 23, 1854, in an agreement in which the Senecas and Shawnees attempted to cede 60,000 acres of land in Indian Territory to the United States, David Civil John was a signatory.[5] His relationship to Civil John remains unclear.

Civil John also witnessed the Treaty of Greenville (1814), which was called a treaty of peace and friendship between the United States of America and the tribes of Native Americans, specifically the Wyandottes, Delawares, Shawnees, Senecas and Miamis. This treaty, concluded in Greenville, Ohio, on July 22, 1814, established peace between the tribes and the United States and sealed their alliance against Great Britain. It followed the earlier 1795 Treaty of Greenville, which had ended the Northwest Indian Wars and allowed peaceful American expansion and trade into the Northwest Territory.[6] Some Eastern Shawnees protested against Civil John and John Jackson (another Shawnee signer) because both leaders had tried to remove their Indian agent from his position. Eastern Shawnees, including Battusha, W. R. Johnson, Pea-wy-a-chee, Mohawk Jo, and Peter Knox, protested by traveling to Washington, D.C., to show support for their Indian agent. The signers of this document state that Civil John and John Jackson "have no authority to act for us in any capacity except as agents in looking after four hundred dollars . . . for a saw mill due us by the U.S. Government and to look after money due us for lost property. . . . We are not only pleased with our agent but that we do not want his removal. We are satisfied that a change would be of disadvantage to our people."[7]

After 1845 Civil John fades from the archival record. For at least thirty years he was active on behalf of the Senecas and Shawnees. It would appear that he was chief of the Mixed Band from 1831 through 1845.[8] As a young man he and his people could live where they wanted to in Ohio. But as an adult, he and his people were confined to the Lewistown reservation, and soon thereafter they were forced to relocate from Ohio to Indian Territory. He saw people die and endure hunger on the march there. Surely he hoped for a better future. On their arrival in Indian Territory, he learned that he was chief of a homeless band of people because they had been placed on Cherokee lands. He had to both accept and challenge the promises of a government that often took years to uphold its promises, if it ever did. He held a position no other chief of the Eastern Shawnee Tribe of Oklahoma will ever hold—our last chief in Ohio and our first chief in Indian Territory—and the irony of it all is that he wasn't even Shawnee.

LEWIS DAVIS OR QUASHACAUGH (C. 1810–1868)

Check the documents signed by the Mixed Band of Senecas and Shawnees from 1831—when they signed the treaty to leave Ohio—to 1867—when they signed the omnibus treaty that formally separated the Shawnees and the Senecas into two distinct tribes, the Eastern Shawnee Tribe of Oklahoma and the Seneca-Cayuga Tribe. It is quite likely that within this nearly-four-decades' worth of documents you will find an X mark representing the signature of a man who was known, at least at first, by his Indian name, Quashacaugh. He then became known as Little Lewis, and later, as an adult, as Lewis Davis. At times he made that X mark as an interpreter, at times as a general laborer, at times as a blacksmith, at times as a councilman, and in later life as chief of the Mixed Band.

Unlike Civil John, Lewis Davis was both Seneca and Shawnee. Family census records indicate that he was born sometime between 1800 and 1810 on a Seneca reservation located in New York.[9] Exactly when or why the family moved to Ohio can only be speculated on. Perhaps the hostilities leading up to the War of 1812 were a factor. The reservation was near the U.S.–British border, and fighting was quite common there. Perhaps they wanted to distance themselves from the turmoil. Perhaps it was an opportunity to be with both tribes in Ohio. Whatever the reason, it wasn't the last move Davis would make.

In 1817 a Seneca and Shawnee reservation was established near Lewiston, Ohio, with the Senecas living on one half of the reservation and the Shawnees on the other. In 1831 papers were signed between the United States and Seneca and Shawnee representatives, forcing the Mixed Band to leave Ohio and relocate to Indian Territory. Little Lewis signed his mark of X on that treaty, indicating another move for him and other Senecas and Shawnees.[10]

On September 19, 1832, 258 people left their lands, their homes, and most of their possessions for an unknown existence. They refused to go by waterway as the government desired. Instead they went by foot, horse, and wagon. Four months and seven hundred miles later, on December 13, 1832, they reached their intended destination.[11] Or so they thought, for the U.S. government had placed them on Cherokee lands. Thirty-eight people had died, the remainder had survived on little more than pumpkins for days on end, and they often had to finance the trip themselves because of the government's woeful lack of planning. They had arrived in a land of strangers. On December 29, 1832, a new treaty was signed, relocating them east of the Neosho River. Quashacaugh (or Little Lewis) signed the treaty and was listed as one of the chiefs of the Mixed Band.[12]

Several decades later, in 1861, the winds of war swirled around Quashacaugh's people. In February of that year the Confederate States of America had organized, and April brought the first battle of the Civil War. May saw Arkansas secede from the United States and join the Confederacy. On October 4, 1861, the Senecas, Quapaws, and the Mixed Band met with the Confederate general and envoy to Native Americans, Albert Pike, at Park Hill near what is now Tahlequah,

Oklahoma. Many tribes, including the Mixed Band, signed a treaty of alliance with the Confederate States of America. The Mixed Band was now part of the Confederacy. Signing that treaty as principal chief of the Senecas and Shawnees was none other than Lewis Davis.[13]

Less than one year later the Civil War had a direct and far-reaching effect upon the Mixed Band. On July 3, 1862, in the Battle of Cowskin Prairie, Union soldiers attacked a Confederate encampment in the Mixed Band's jurisdiction, near present-day Grove, Oklahoma. As a result of that battle, and in acknowledgement that Indian lives were in jeopardy, the Mixed Band fled to the Ottawa reservation. Appreciative of their hospitality and protection, Chief Lewis Davis promised Ottawa chief John Wilson and his people that he would return the favor that had been extended to him, and the Ottawas would have a place to live if they ever wished to relocate to Indian Territory. Later, the Ottawas took Davis up on his promise.[14]

When the Civil War ended with the defeat of the Confederacy, the Mixed Band wondered if there would be consequences for tribes who supported the Confederacy. September 1865 found a number of tribes signing a treaty in Fort Smith, Arkansas, with the intent of reestablishing a formal relationship with the United States. Lewis Davis signed this treaty as a chief of the Mixed Band, but the treaty was never ratified. Eighteen months later—this time in Washington, D.C., on February 23, 1867—Lewis Davis signed a new treaty on behalf of the Mixed Band, reestablishing tribal relationships with the United States. This treaty had far-reaching effects, as one of the provisions formally separated the Senecas and Shawnees into two distinct tribes. It was the end of an era; the Mixed Band would be no more.[15] Lewis Davis would never sign a treaty again. He had lived most of his life in support of the Mixed Band. Interestingly enough, when Lewis Davis died on March 5, 1868, he was still a member of the Mixed Band, as the treaty separating the tribes was not ratified until June 18, 1868. Three years later, in 1871, the United States ceased making treaties with tribes, thus marking the end of another era.[16]

Throughout his life, the roads Lewis Davis travelled were difficult ones. First was the bitter removal road, where people died, some literally starved. Next was the endless road of delayed or broken promises. Then there was the road of punishment. Because the Senecas, Quapaws, and Seneca-Shawnees entered into a treaty with the Confederate States of America in January 1862 and drew an annuity payment in gold and silver from the Confederate States, the United States government accused them of treason. Davis was imprisoned at Fort Leavenworth "for a short time for this action," according to Barney Armstrong, a great-nephew of Davis.[17] Throughout it all, Lewis Davis fought to protect the Seneca-Shawnees. His death was reported as a "serious loss," especially for the Shawnees. The X mark that Lewis Davis so frequently made is part of his legacy. As his great-great-grandson Chris Chaney writes, it "unites him with all Seneca-Cayuga and Eastern Shawnee tribal members today. Lewis Davis protected his people and paved the way for the survival of the Seneca-Cayuga Nation and the Eastern Shawnee Tribe. As members of these tribes, we owe a great debt of gratitude to our ancestors. May we learn from their lives as we forge our own paths in history."[18]

WILLIAM JACKSON

Between 1860 and 1870 the United States endured one of the most tumultuous decades in its history. Events leading up to the Civil War, the Civil War itself, the assassination of President Lincoln, and the dramatic changes following the war affecting African Americans, slave owners, and others were far reaching. The same was true for the Eastern Shawnee Tribe during this ten-year span of time.

In 1860 Eastern Shawnees lived in fear. Lawlessness in Indian Territory was rampant. Located on the edge of Missouri, a state that had proven it had no sympathy for Indian people, the Eastern Shawnee reservation was in a difficult position. The United States was gearing up for war. Federal agents failed to protect Indians from unscrupulous whites in a land that wasn't even a state. Consequently, no Eastern Shawnee was safe. Stealing, violence, destruction of property, and threats to life were everyday occurrences. The Eastern Shawnees had no choice but to vacate their lands, their animals, and most of their personal belongings and relocate to Kansas as guests of the Ottawa Tribe. Led by the Mixed Band chief Lewis Davis, they remained on the Ottawa reservation in Kansas until the war ended.[19]

They returned to what would one day become Ottawa County to find that whatever improvements they had made to their lands were for naught. Fences were destroyed, buildings were burned, their animals were nowhere to be found, and their gardens had reverted to a wild state. But their challenges didn't end there. In 1867 an omnibus bill was passed, requiring the Mixed Band to relinquish large parcels of their land to other tribes. Included in that bill were the separation of the Mixed Band and the creation of two distinct tribes: the Seneca-Cayuga Tribe and the Eastern Shawnee Tribe. Other challenges beset them. Lewis Davis, chief of the Mixed Band, died in March 1868.[20] The Eastern Shawnees, who were particularly decimated, keenly felt the loss of Lewis Davis.

What happened immediately after the separation of the Mixed Band and the death of Lewis Davis is unclear. It would seem reasonable to assume that the Eastern Shawnee Tribe would have chosen a chief. If that happened, when it happened, how that happened, and who that person was—all are questions begging for answers at this point. Whoever that person was would have faced immense challenges.

What is known is that in April of 1870 William Jackson and William McDaniel signed a lease agreement between the Eastern Shawnees and two non-Natives from Missouri, Richard M. Jones and Henry H. Gregg. This land lease required Jones and Gregg to "fence, cultivate and improve" approximately two hundred acres of Eastern Shawnee land. This land was part of what would become known as the Eastern Shawnee National Farm, which would ultimately encompass 13,088 acres. William Jackson signed as first chief, and William McDaniel was listed as second chief. This document proves that the Eastern Shawnees had a chief in 1870, and that chief was William Jackson.[21]

In the years 1871 and 1872 Jackson and McDaniel signed a document acknowledging annuity receipts from Enoch Hoag, the superintendent of Indian affairs who had designated them as first and second chief, respectively. Jackson's name appears first, followed by McDaniel's, which was the customary means of acknowledging chieftainship at the time. The document reads, "We the Chiefs, Head men, Head of families and individual with our families of the Eastern Shawnee Tribe of Indians acknowledge the receipts . . . being our proportion of the annuity of said Tribe of Indians." Jackson's family consisted of two men, two women, and two children, for a total of six. William McDaniel was second signer, listing one man, one woman, and two children, for a total of four. Also signing this document was Tom Captain, listing one man, no women, and no children, for a household total of one.[22]

Tom Captain's name is included in this discussion of William Jackson because, in the year 1874, James Choctaw and Tom Captain were listed as chiefs on a document entitled "Articles of Agreement," authorizing the sale of four thousand Eastern Shawnee acres to the Modocs. Two years later, in 1876, John Jackson was elected principal chief. This two-year cycle seems to suggest that a chief was elected for a term of two years.

In short, we know that Lewis Davis was chief when he died in 1868, we can assume someone was elected for the years of 1868 to 1870, we know that William Jackson was chief 1870 to 1872, we're unsure about the years of 1872 to 1874, we know that James Choctaw served as chief from 1874 to 1876, and we know that John Jackson was elected chief in 1876. Whether William Jackson served as chief following the death of Lewis Davis and whether he was chief during the years 1872 to 1874 are blank spots in the historical record that remain to be filled.

Whatever the length of his service, William Jackson held the Eastern Shawnee Tribe together during a most tumultuous time. The Eastern Shawnees had experienced yet another removal, this time from Indian Territory to Kansas and back; had been traumatized by the Civil War; had separated from a kindred tribe; had mourned the death of its longtime leader Lewis Davis; and had declined in number to its all-time low of sixty-nine citizens in 1872. Yet he continued leading the people forward, embodying an attribute that has become a character trait of the Eastern Shawnees: resiliency.

JOHN JACKSON (1799–1852)

The facts regarding John Jackson are few, hard to come by, and in need of sorting out. To begin with, John Jackson lived in Ohio and participated in the removal march from Ohio to Indian Territory. Records from that time period are scarce. Complicating the research even further, he fathered a son, also named John Jackson. Names, dates, and events are a constant challenge. His father was William Jackson, a white man who was adopted by Blackfish. Little is known of Blackfish, a Chillicothe war chief who lived circa 1725–79, other than his experiences with Daniel Boone and Simon Kenton during the last three years of his life. William Jackson was married three times, and his third wife was Blackfish's granddaughter Polly Rogers, who is listed as half-Shawnee Métis. William and Polly were the parents of Elizabeth (born c. 1798), John (c. 1799–1852), and William (born c. 1800) Jackson.[23]

John Jackson's early involvement with the Mixed Band is readily discernible. He signed the treaty with the Senecas on July 20, 1831, in Ohio, along with Civil John and Lewis Davis. Historian Randall Buchman discusses Jackson's participation in the removal march from Ohio to Indian Territory. Jackson's name is also listed on the 1832 muster roll (the U.S. military's list of members leaving the Lewistown reserve in Ohio). The first name on the list is Civil John, as head chief (Seneca); the second name is Totala, also listed as chief; and the third name is John Jackson, who is listed as headman.[24] Later he signed the treaty with the Senecas and Shawnees on December 29, 1832, in Indian Territory. Jackson's leadership role with the Mixed Band continued throughout his lifetime, as he, along with Chief Civil John, signed a document dated March 1845 regarding "the sum of $250, being in part payment the sum of the annuities for $400 due the Seneca and Shawnee under the treaty of 1818 for the year 1837." John Jackson married Ke-ne-fe-ase, a Shawnee woman who later became legendary in the tribe for taking in and rearing two children, John Prophet, a Shawnee, and Stonewall Jackson, a Mexican. John and Ke-ne-fe-ase's biological children were James, John, and Nancy. Nancy married David Dushane Sr., a member of another prominent family in the tribe. John Sr. died around the age of fifty-three in 1852, and Ke-ne-fe-ase's death is recorded as August 1, 1897. Etched into her tombstone at Calamus Pond (a Shawnee cemetery established in 1832 and located in Oklahoma about one mile west of the Eastern Shawnee BlueJacket Complex) are the words "about the age of 95."[25]

John Jackson's death in 1852 is verified by two different sources. A document entitled "Emigrant Tribes" records that John Jackson, chief councilor of the Mixed Band of Senecas and Shawnees, died of cholera in May 1852. A second document, the 1852 Indian agent's official records submitted to the commission of Indian affairs at the Department of the Interior, reads, "The death of John Jackson, the chief counselor of the mixed Band is noted."[26]

In the same report, the Indian agent makes mention of the Mixed Band's "opposition to sending their children to school" and further states, "They adhere to many of the ancient customs and partake of as few of the habits and manners of the white people as possible." It was the agent's responsibility to report annually upon what he considered progress, or lack of progress, in the tribal community. Assimilation of tribal populations into the mainstream way of life, and away from their tribal lifestyles, was always the goal of the government. What better and faster way could there be to accomplish this acculturation than to have children spend time outside of their communities, outside of their homes, away from their "ancient customs" and parents' influence? The government's desire, and the agent's responsibility, was to get those children inside the schoolhouse walls, with all instruction geared toward abandoning the Native way of life and replacing it with the "habits and manners of the white people."

What is known is that various sources use the term chief councilor interchangeably with chief or lesser chief, making John Jackson one of our earliest chiefs after the Ohio removal.[27]

JAMES CHOCTAW

It was a significant document. It was significant because it established a permanent home for the Modoc Indians, where they could "settle down and become self-supporting," and because it listed the names of two Eastern Shawnee chiefs, James Choctaw and Thomas Captain. The year was 1874, the place was the Quapaw Agency, and the document was an agreement between the United States (represented by Indian agent H. W. Jones) and the Eastern Shawnee Indians. Six thousand dollars was to be paid per capita for four thousand acres. Jones justified the sale of Eastern Shawnee lands, arguing that it would enable them to "enlarge their farms and otherwise improve their condition in civilization." Ultimately, the Eastern Shawnee Tribe of Oklahoma did cede four thousand acres to the Modocs.[28]

The name James Choctaw first surfaces in 1870 and again in 1872, when he is listed on Eastern Shawnee tribal rolls. Then, in 1874, his name and mark appear as one of two chiefs on the Articles of Agreement referenced above. In a later report, the federal subagent, H. W. Jones, stated that the Eastern Shawnees had a "paucity" of adult men. In 1874 James Choctaw and Tom Captain responded to the death of their "old men" by requesting a trip to Washington. They explained that "they know little about their business and wish to see the commissioner so as to find out all about it."[29]

James Choctaw's name appears again in 1875, when he is listed as the representative of the Eastern Shawnees at the sixth session of the Indian Territory General Council. Following the Civil War, leaders of several tribes realized that they needed to meet in order to discuss matters of common interest. Called the Indian Territory General Council, this organization convened at Okmulgee in the Creek Nation on September 27, 1870, and met annually through 1878. Tribes represented included the Cherokees, Muscogees (Creeks), Ottawas, Eastern Shawnees, Quapaws, Senecas, Wyandottes, Confederate Peorias, Sac and Foxes, and Absentee Shawnees.[30]

In 1876 James Choctaw was elected vice chief, or second chief, when it was noted, "The Shawnees commenced the year by making a change in the office of Principal Chief by selecting John Jackson for that position, vice James Choctaw." The wording, "making a change in the office of Principal Chief," could be interpreted as saying that James Choctaw was chief in 1874 and 1875, then elected second chief in 1876. How long he was in that position is yet to be determined. In 1877 Choctaw is listed as receiving rent or payment from the Shawnee National Farm. In the 1870s the Eastern Shawnee Tribe owned 13,088 acres, half tillable and half timber, known as the Eastern Shawnee National Farm, and in 1878 the tribe leased out 671 acres, the proceeds from which were paid out to tribal members.[31]

We may never know when James Choctaw was born, who his parents were, or if he married or had children. Like the wilderness trails he must have traveled, those facts aren't visible at this point. However, one thing is certain: the Modocs are surely thankful that he enabled them to have a home.

TOM CAPTAIN (C. 1850–1920)

Tom Captain was chief of the Eastern Shawnee Tribe in 1874 and second chief in 1893. He lived in Ottawa County much of his life, died there in 1920, and is buried in Captain Cemetery on

8.1. Young Tom Captain in Kansas. Later, he and his people were forcibly removed to Indian Territory. He fathered eleven children with Martha Gullett and one with Oreillia Keno. Photo courtesy of Larry Kropp.

land that he was allotted.[32] His descendants are numerous. Those are undisputed facts. Other less certain facts of his life are much greater in number. What is known about Tom Captain comes from two types of sources: the written word and oral history. At times they parallel; sometimes they converge; and other times they disconnect. Such is the case with Tom Captain.

His Quapaw Indian Competency Commission papers indicate that he was born about 1850 on what was then known as the Quapaw reservation.[33] His tombstone bears the inscribed birthdate of 1853. A much later document states he was born "at the place of his current residence," which is in all probability the same as the one listed as the Quapaw reservation, where he died. Family member Lamont Laird writes, "All family sources that I know consider that he was born in Kansas. All dates regarding his birth were wild guesses as no documents were ever kept about births or deaths amongst Shawnees of his time. Even he had no clue." Several descendants agree with Laird, and they cite the Kaw (or Kansas) River as his birthplace. Census papers for the Shawnee Tribe of Indians within the Fort Leavenworth agency for the year 1842 show two Tom Captains residing there, one being in the category of "[over] 10 and under 40," and the second listed as "over 40."[34]

Those same competency papers inform us that he was one-quarter French and three-quarters Eastern Shawnee. Later testimony from his son Thomas A. Captain and daughter Mary Captain affirm that he was a full-blooded Eastern Shawnee and that his wife (their mother), Martha Ellen Gullett, erred when she maintained that he was three-quarters Eastern Shawnee blood. His records were consequently corrected. The competency papers list his Indian name as Na-na-he-pu-ma-ka, his father's as Wau-a-ha-gu-ma, and his mother's as Ma-ta-haw-e-seec. Tribal historian Lamont Laird points out that there is a problem in writing the Shawnee language, that he has heard the names spoken, and that Tom Captain's was Nuh-naw-he-buh-nuck, his father's was Non-ho-gom-wee, and his mother's Maw-tah-wah-see.[35]

He seems to have come from the Shawnee reservation in what is now Kansas. So where did he live, and when did he unite with the Eastern Shawnee Tribe? Oral history holds that Tom Captain was from the band of Black Bob Shawnees, who left Ohio in 1779, went west to Missouri,

8.2. Tom Captain (c. 1853–1920) in later years in Oklahoma. Photo courtesy of Glenna Wallace.

and then were the first to relocate to the Kansas reservation, which explains how Tom Captain was born on the Kansas River. Once the Black Bobs left Kansas, they went to White Oak, where the Cherokee Shawnees lived, and there they basically broke up, with the main Black Bob body moving on to the Little Axe or Absentee Shawnee area. As for Tom Captain specifically, his family first went to the White Oak area. Then he, his mother, and his aunt joined the Eastern Shawnees in the late 1860s or early 1870s.[36]

Agency files from 1910 indicate that Tom was married at least four times—the first three times in the Indian custom—to Skaw-wan-ah-dee Davis (Seneca); Tee-dee-day, or Bluebird (Shawnee); and Orillia Keno Mohawk (Peoria and Wea), whom he divorced in 1878 according to her Competency Commission papers; and lastly to Martha Gullett on January 4, 1884. These files list a daughter, Mary, by his first wife. His great-grandson Lamont Laird states that this daughter's name was Mary Gibson, which she later changed to Mary Quick Mohawk, and that her mother was Shawnee, not Seneca. Orillia Keno Mohawk bore Tom a daughter named Minnie Captain around 1870. She later married Solomon Quapaw and gave birth to four children: Bertha Quapaw, Annie Quapaw, Katie Quapaw, and Jessie Quapaw. Tom and Martha were blessed with eleven children, namely Thomas Andrew (born 1884), Cordelia Jane Hampton (born 1886), Mary Ellen Ross (born 1888), Charles Selby (born 1890, died at the age of ten), William Henry (born 1894), Sarah May Crain (born 1892), Michael Francis (born 1895), Grace Dixon (born 1897), George Philemon (born 1899), Martha Eveline (born 1901), and Sophronia "Babe" Rickner (born 1903).[37]

At least two documents bear witness to Tom Captain being a chief of the Eastern Shawnee Tribe, in one as principal chief, in the other as second chief. The first is dated 1874, the year the Eastern Shawnee Tribe sold four thousand acres to the Modocs so that they could "settle down and become self-supporting." James Choctaw and Thomas Captain are listed as chiefs in articles of agreement between the United States (represented by Indian agent H. W. Jones) and the Eastern Shawnee Indians, selling the four thousand acres in exchange for $6,000 to be paid per capita, which would enable Eastern Shawnee Indians to "enlarge their farms and

8.3. *Left*, Tom Captain; *right*, Martha Gullett Captain; *center*, Babe (Tom's youngest child) and Thurman Captain (Tom's first grandchild) on their allotment in Ottawa County, Oklahoma, c. 1907. Photo courtesy of Glenna Wallace.

otherwise improve their condition in civilization." Oral history expands upon the situation, highlighting the personal relationship Tom Captain had with this tribe: it is said that Tom took in the Modocs because they were prisoners of war and had nothing, and no other tribe would help them.

In a similar story, Tom helped Chief Joseph and the Nez Perces, who were removed from their lands and loaded into railroad cars to relocate to Baxter Springs, Kansas. Many of Chief Joseph's people died en route, and the rest were briefly moved to the area near the Indian agency west of Seneca, Missouri, not far from Tom Captain's farm. Tom invited Chief Joseph and his band to live on his land for a while, as they, too, were prisoners of war. He was saddened by their condition and took pity on them, feeding them and such.[38]

A third example of Tom's character is illustrated by a time when he inherited land from a family member. Tom and each of his children inherited an allotment, with the exception of his youngest daughter, Sophronia (Babe), who was born in 1903, after the cutoff date for allotment eligibility. When Tom inherited land from Sa-pa-ta-wa-se Flint, a relative who lived at White Oak, he and his children gave that allotment to Babe, confirming the fairness that Tom lived by and taught his family.[39]

Tom Captain later served his tribe as second chief. A document recorded the 1893 election of Andrew Dushane as first chief and Tom Captain as second chief. Andrew Dushane ran against Tom Stand for the position of first chief, whereas Tom Captain was unopposed. Dushane, at twenty-five years old, was much younger than Tom Captain, who would have been about forty-five. Voting members included Tom Captain, Stonewall Jackson, Charlie Dushane, and Andrew Dushane. The term of office was two years.[40]

Tom Captain's daughter Grace Captain Dixon provides insight into the family's day-to-day life. She writes that, although her mother was non-Native, she was a fluent Shawnee speaker. However, the parents chose not to teach the language to their children, believing they were doing

8.4. The Captain children. Photo courtesy of Glenna Wallace.

what was best for them. Grace "learned to cook on a wood cookstove, to sew, quilt, crochet, etc. by hand and wash clothes, using a tub and washboard." Their washing was done outdoors, with the water heated on an open fire. Her father was very particular about the appearance of the yard around the house, so he made them a wash-area outside the yard. The boys had to carry the wood and water for the washtubs and keep the fires going while the girls did the washing. They always had a farm and raised their own animals and vegetables. Butchering day was always a busy day, as they usually killed several animals at a time. They had their own smokehouse, so they preserved everything themselves, by either canning or smoking. She and her brothers and sisters always had their own special chores to perform.

Her father always had hired hands to help on the farm, and part of their job was teaching her brothers how to farm. Several times, when the boys were supposed to be working, Tom would walk out to see how they were doing and would catch them napping under the trees, but they did eventually learn how to farm.[41]

According to Grace, Tom's wife Martha was very particular with her chickens. Because they were raised to produce eggs to sell or trade for something else they might need, very few were killed for eating; however, her husband dearly loved fried chicken. At one time they had a pig that also had a taste for chickens. It seems that one day, when Tom got chicken-hungry, somehow or other a chicken "accidently" got into the pigpen. Of course, Tom was there in time to rescue the chicken, just not soon enough to save its life. Since you didn't waste good meat, he got fried chicken. Another time, while the parents were away from home, the kids decided that fried eggs would be awfully good and were well into cooking some when their parents came home and caught them in the act. Grace says she can't remember getting into too much trouble over it, but is sure they were well scolded.[42]

The first school Grace and her siblings attended was the Seneca Indian School. She, her brother Frank, and sister Evie ran away and went home. They convinced their father that they were being "badly mistreated," and when school officials arrived to take them back, Tom said, "Children not go back." They then attended schools around the Peoria area.[43]

Grace recalled that her mother served as a midwife many times, but didn't recall much sickness in the family, giving credit to her father, who "knew many roots, plants and herbs that could be used for medicinal remedies."[44] Lamont Laird elaborated further, stating, "The one primary role that great-grandpa held in his life . . . was a traditional healer or medicine man. This was his main occupation. Traditionally, he would have received a kind of compensation for treating people." Laird goes on to say that Tom had a certain power that was hereditary, a power he had received from his father and all the male relatives before him, and that Tom had tried to pass this power on to one of his sons, but the son refused, and the power no longer exists in the family. Continuing, Laird stated,

> Because there were no other healers in this entire region, great-grandpa doctored many other Indians and learned to speak fluently five other Indian languages so that he could help them. He traveled to White Oak extensively and conducted many public healing ceremonies down there with a sort of men's society that he was in charge of. He had a counterpart down at Little Axe, [who was] also the last healer down there, and he traveled there a couple times that I know of. That man, [who was] also a relative, died in the 1930s sometime. Neither man was successful in passing on this power, knowledge, and ability, which is why the Shawnees no longer have traditional healers. When great-grandpa died, his wife—great-grandma Martha—took all his medicine and healing items that same day and drove them down to White Oak and gave everything to his sisters. Grandma always said she was pretty scared of these items, as we have always been taught that these items were alive.[45]

Tom was a role model for Eastern Shawnees in life and death. Velma Nieberding, in her book *History of Ottawa County*, writes that "the Eastern Shawnee were still observing the ancient burial rites for the dead," citing an article from the *Miami News-Record* of September 17, 1920, with the headline Aged Shawnee's Spirit Goes to Happy Hunting Ground after Feast and Tribal Ceremony. The article notes that Thomas Captain had died at his home near Wyandotte. The rites were held on Sunday afternoon, with some seventy-five persons attending the night ceremony. Briefly, the story includes mention of such rituals as the Supper for the Dead, the notching of the coffin, the feast served to those who attended the funeral, the ritual burning of cedar, and the watch kept for three nights with a fire built at the head of the grave. The reporter stated, "Every favorite dish of the aged Indian were [*sic*] prepared by 9 o'clock of the night of the ceremony. A table was prepared for one, a dish of everything he liked in life placed on it, even a cup of steaming coffee placed beside the plate. The chair was vacant. At the stroke of nine the lights were put out and remained so until midnight. A feast was then served to the visitors in the home." The writer describes the washing of hands with water and the smoking of the house with cedar and reports, "The oldest son washed first; the others followed until the youngest son was washed. The youngest daughter came next, graduating up to the oldest." The article continues: "After burning cedar wood in every part of the house, the guests departed. . . . The old Indian had supposed his coffin would be wood and had kept a saw in his smokehouse with which to make a hole for the spirit to pass out." The writer concluded, saying that the deceased was one of the oldest Indians in the county and had scores of warm friends.[46]

He was a chief, a full-blood Eastern Shawnee, and a father of many. His descendants are abundant. Most of all, he was a good man who cared about people. His walk was long and his footprints deep. Hopefully one day someone will be able to locate more of those footprints to fill in more of the puzzle pieces. That will be a significant contribution.[47]

JOHN JACKSON JR. (1842–1882)

Drive across the field and enter the cemetery through the gate of the chain-link fence, which protects the graves of those buried within from the herd of cattle feeding nearby. Pause to take in the tranquility of the isolated area, the stream pooling nearby, the age of the stones, and the old trees guarding those who sleep in the dust. You have traveled back in time to Calamus Pond, a Shawnee cemetery established in 1832. Step a few feet to the right and you will find the grave of one of our earliest chiefs, John Jackson Jr. He was not our first chief, but his burial site, complete with headstone, was one of the first to be maintained.[48]

According to oral history, he died in a tragic accident; he was killed when a team of horses ran away with him. He was still a young man when he died, not yet forty, but he had accomplished much in those few years. The son of former chief John Jackson Sr. and Kenefease Jackson, John Jackson Jr. was born December 28, 1842, and crossed over April 16, 1882, according to his headstone. He became a man early in life, as he was only ten years old when his father died. He had two biological siblings, James and Nancy, and two young men, raised by his mother, who were like brothers to him, John Prophet and Stonewall Jackson.[49]

John Prophet was a Shawnee, but Stonewall Jackson, buried at Calamus Pond in 1920, was not. Stonewall's story is an interesting one. It seems that when a raiding party came through a Shawnee encampment, they encountered a group of people who had little to eat. This war party had been off south fighting with other Indians, and possibly Mexicans, as they had with them a tiny Mexican baby. Kenefease Jackson traded a horse and a sack of flour for him. The story also claims that this transaction took place by a stone wall, which accounts for the name of Stonewall Jackson.[50]

As for John Jackson Jr. himself, he married Annie Elizabeth Daugherty (Mah Chilquah). They had children, but only one child, Cora Jackson Hampton Hollingsworth Van Sant, lived to adulthood. Cora married Alfred Corn Hampton (1855–97), and their first child, William Howell Hampton, was born in 1884, when she was sixteen. Bill married Cordelia Captain, thus connecting the Hampton and Captain families.[51]

John lived during a tumultuous time period. He was born in 1842, ten years after the Mixed Band of Senecas and Shawnees was removed from Ohio to Indian Territory. Times were difficult and changes were many. He was a teenager when the Civil War began. At the age of thirty-one, John Jackson Jr. is listed as one of the "Young Men" who, on June 23, 1874, signed a document ceding approximately four thousand acres of land to the United States government for Modoc Indians who had been "temporarily located on the Eastern Shawnee Reservation."[52]

The year 1876 was important for John Jackson Jr., as that was when he was elected principal chief of the Eastern Shawnee Tribe of Oklahoma, with James Choctaw chosen as vice chief. Jackson was approximately thirty-three years old. The Quapaw agent viewed the outcome of that election favorably, describing Jackson as energetic and industrious. The agent also noted that Jackson owned perhaps the best farm in the tribe. Believing that the new chief's work ethic and lifestyle would serve as a catalyst for forward momentum, the agent commented, "I find that the habits of the head men greatly influence the remainder of a tribe and that much more can be accomplished in elevating and improving the rank and file of a tribe when the leaders are sober, industrious and energetic men, than when they are the reverse."[53]

Rent receipts from the Shawnee National Farm in 1877 show payments from Jackson, further indicating that he was active in farming. In a letter dated January 4, 1882, First Chief John Jackson and Second Chief George Beaver wrote to "Honorable H. Price," requesting financial relief for tribal members. Referencing $2,000 from sale of twelve thousand acres of the Eastern Shawnee reservation to the Ottawa Tribe, Jackson and Beaver asked if it could be paid early because of drought and the ravages of "chinch-bugs." John Jackson died approximately three and a half months after he signed that letter as first chief, which suggests that he was chief of the Eastern Shawnee Tribe from the time he was elected in early 1876 until his death on April 16, 1882.[54]

Possibly the greatest legacy of John Jackson Jr. is the number of family footprints that came after him. A vast number of Eastern Shawnee families are related to the Jackson family, many of them through marriage, including the Daugherty family, the Deweese family, the Hampton family, the Prophet family, the Hauser family, the Amos family, the Tayrien family, the Dushane family, and others.[55]

GEORGE BEAVER (1853–?)

It was a time when the Eastern Shawnee Tribe experienced a dearth of adult males. The old men had died off, and consequently the young ones had to step into leadership roles at a young age. Such was the case with George Beaver.

He was born in 1853 with the Indian name of Na-tah-wa-ka-kah. His brother, To-Ta-Se, was two years younger. Additional facts, like the old men, are scarce. In 1874 or 1875 he married Amanda Splitlog, a Wyandotte, and that same year they had a son named Lewis (or Louis). The three names—George, Amanda, and Lewis—appear on tribal rolls from 1882 through 1889, with the exception of 1884. In 1878 his brother, To-Ta-Se, had a son named Charles. Only two other individuals with the Beaver surname can be found: Enoch, born in 1872, and John, born in 1874 to William and Lucinda Duck, who were born in 1832 and 1836, respectively. Why Enoch and John were named Beaver when their parents' name was Duck and what, if any, relationship they had to George and To-Ta-Se are still mysteries.[56]

In the 1874 agreement whereby the Modocs received four thousand acres from the Eastern Shawnee reservation, George Beaver was a signer listed as one of the "young men." He was twenty-one at the time. In 1876 and 1877 he was listed as receiving payment for rent from the Shawnee National Farm. He is listed as the second chief behind John Jackson on the 1882 treaty through which $2,000 was appropriated in relief aid from the sale of 12,000 acres to the Ottawas. He is listed as chief of the Eastern Shawnees in government correspondence with Cherokee principal chief Joel B. Mayes regarding the status of Eastern Shawnees on citizenship rolls of both nations. In 1890, at the age of thirty-seven, he is still referred to as principal chief in correspondence with the Cherokee chief regarding the subject of allotment. He is also referred to as principal chief in correspondence related to U.S. government attorneys Geyer and North and a contract they entered into with the Eastern Shawnee tribe at the Quapaw Agency. This correspondence indicates that the government was to pay just over $9,000 to the tribe, with interest, and was to erect a blacksmith shop. A document from September 24, 1891, lists T. J. Moore as a U.S. Indian agent and gives George's age as thirty-eight and his son Louis Beaver's as seventeen. The three names—George, Amanda, and Louis—continue to appear on tribal rolls through 1889 with no other notation. In 1890 the Quapaw Indian agent wrote that, under Beaver's watch, "this tribe continues to make progress, and has promised me to forever discontinue their favorite custom, 'the stamp [*sic*] dance.'" Perhaps it was the Eastern Shawnees' small number of men at the time, or perhaps it grew out of the federal government's campaign against Native American religions at the time. Likely, the decision to end the stomp dance grew out of both trends. Regardless, with this final mention, George Beaver's footprints disappear at the age of thirty-eight.[57]

ANDREW DUSHANE, "A YOUNG CHIEF" (1868–1924)

In the year of 1893, running against Tom Stand, Andrew Dushane was elected first chief and Tom Captain was elected second chief of the Eastern Shawnee Tribe. Andrew was twenty-five years old, which was extremely young to be a chief. Voting members included Tom Captain, Stonewall

Jackson, Charlie Dushane, and Andrew Dushane. The term of office was two years. An interesting side note to this is that in the September 6, 1893, letter reporting this election, the author remarks that only six votes were cast: "This comprised all of the male members of the tribe who resided on the reservation, except Tom Stand who, though present, did not vote. The band comprises about 83 persons in all, and number only 7 or 8 men who are over 21 years of age."[58]

The son of David C. Dushane and Nancy Jackson Dushane, Andrew was born March 19, 1868, on the eve of the Shawnee removal from Kansas. (His father was born in Kansas, his mother in Ottawa County, Ohio.) According to his relative Jack Dushane, Andrew was probably born in Johnson County, near Olathe, where his father was born.[59] Andrew was the eldest of four boys, each of whom received an allotment: Andrew (Eastern Shawnee allottee No. 9), Charles (Eastern Shawnee allottee No. 22), David Jr. (Eastern Shawnee allottee No. 3), and Daniel (Eastern Shawnee allottee No. 4). Allotments of land were made to tribal individuals rather than the tribe as a whole, which is why the Eastern Shawnee Tribe of Oklahoma does not have a reservation. The Eastern Shawnee allotments were made at four different times: in 1888, 1889, 1892, and 1902. Allotment numbers simply coincide with the order of allotment; Andrew Dushane was No. 9 because he was the ninth person to receive an allotment. The one difficulty with this is that the numbers one through eighty-four were assigned to those allotted in 1888, 1889, and 1892, but for the additional allotments in 1902, they started back at one, which sometimes makes the government's system confusing. All told, 12,724 acres were distributed to 117 different tribal members.[60]

In a 2014 letter tribal citizen and descendant Jack Dushane explained that he believes David and Nancy "came down to Oklahoma after the Civil War, when the Federal Government forced the Cherokees to take them on their tribal rolls and give the allotments. They brought Mariah Louisa Dushane with them on the trip. Mariah was the child of David's first marriage to Hanna Evans, who must have died in childbirth." According to a 1937 interview with Andrew's younger brother David Jr., David and Nancy married in Kansas (c. 1865) and lived there six years before coming to Indian Territory in 1871. Andrew must have been about three years old at that time. Jack went on to say that David and Nancy "must have resided over by Vinita and White Oak for a while, but then moved over to live with the Eastern Shawnees and Nancy's family, John and Kenefease Jackson."[61]

Andrew, who was one-quarter French, one-quarter Cherokee, and one-half Eastern Shawnee, was allotted 180 acres, according to the Department of Interior's records. Much of this information about Andrew actually came from an interview of Andrew's wife, Rebecca (Wyandotte), by noted Canadian ethnographer, folklorist, and anthropologist Charles Marius Barbeau, who did extensive research with the Huron-Wyandottes of Oklahoma during the first decades of the twentieth century. In testimony regarding the estate of Andrew after his death, Rebecca stated that she was allotted land as Rebecca McDaniel, under the name of her first husband, George McDaniel, who died before allotment. Later Andrew and Rebecca "were married by the Indian Agent where the old agency used to be," north of the Seneca Indian School at Wyandotte. This would have been approximately 1888, when Andrew was about twenty years old, and Rebecca was about eighteen. Following their marriage, Rebecca Hicks McDaniel Dushane always signed her name as Becky Dushane. Andrew and Becky first lived on Andrew's allotment, but then moved to Becky's allotment, some three miles east of Wyandotte, where they lived until Andrew died on March 24, 1924, at the age of fifty-six.[62]

Not many details are known about Andrew. He was a deputy sheriff and once owned a restaurant named Andrew's Restaurant. His granddaughter Colleen Carpenter (Clifford's daughter) said she never knew her grandfather, as he had already passed away when she was born. She was, however, able to provide a photograph of Andrew's Restaurant. Andrew's name surfaces again in Stonewall Jackson's last will and testament. In 1920 Stonewall Jackson bequeathed his property and other belongings to Andrew and his brothers, stating that they should "share and share alike."[63]

In Barbeau's interview, Becky Dushane indicated that she was born in 1870 and was the daughter of Mary Splitlog Logan and Henry Hicks. "Becky was a descendant of Chief Thomas Splitlog, the younger brother of Roundhead. The two were allies of Tecumseh and the Shawnee Prophet," according to Barbeau. "Becky was a leader in her own way." Because she was such an excellent craftsman, Barbeau bought many of her beadwork items and took them back to Canada, where they now remain in the Canadian Museum of History. Andrew and Becky were married for thirty-six years, until his death in 1924. Andrew's younger brother David (or Dave) became chief of the Eastern Shawnee Tribe of Oklahoma in 1940.[64] The red road was not easy for Eastern Shawnees in the early 1900s. Andrew Dushane was a man who travelled it well and helped keep the Eastern Shawnee Tribe alive by serving as a young Eastern Shawnee Tribal chief.

WALTER L. BLUEJACKET: THE FIRST EASTERN SHAWNEE CHIEF IN MODERN TIMES (1885–1941)

His picture is the first of several. It is only fitting that the first person on the Eastern Shawnee Tribe of Oklahoma's Wall of the Chiefs is a BlueJacket. It is also appropriate that the building where the picture hangs bears the name BlueJacket Center. Walter BlueJacket was first elected chief in October 1928 in a meeting presided over by Lloyd LaMotte, chief clerk of the Quapaw Agency. Elected at that same meeting were T. A. Captain as secretary and Dave Dushane, Ed BlueJacket, and Ora Hampton as councilmen.[65] It would seem that these men remained in office for at least twelve consecutive years, as their names appear on the tribe's first charter, ratified in December 1940. The constitution and bylaws were ratified December 22, 1939, by a vote of 54–2. Shortly thereafter, on October 17, 1940, the acting assistant secretary of the interior issued a charter, which was voted upon and ratified on December 12, 1940, by a vote of 60–1. Signatures on this document are historic, as three of the five signatories became the first three chiefs of the Eastern Shawnee Tribe in modern history: Walter L. BlueJacket, David Dushane Jr., and Thomas A. Captain. Walter's tenure as chief of a tribe with a constitution was brief, however, as he died at the age of fifty-five from type 2 diabetes on July 29, 1941, some nineteen months after the constitution was adopted and eight months after the charter was ratified.[66]

On October 22, 1941, the Eastern Shawnee Business Committee declared that, "Believing ourselves to be entitled to annuities and rights under signed treaties by the United States Government," they elected a chief—W. L. BlueJacket—and a Business Committee—T. A. Captain as secretary and Dave Dushane, Ed BlueJacket, and Ora Hampton as councilmen. Two documents record this transaction, the first the handwritten and the second the typewritten minutes of that meeting. The latter lists W. BlueJacket as chairman, which suggests that chairman and chief were considered interchangeable titles.[67]

This chief's impact is everlasting. Born August 16, 1885, in Indian Territory, Walter L. Blue-Jacket's grandparents were George BlueJacket (Na Wah Tah Thu) and Mary Blackhoof. Walter's father, Charles Jr. (1831–1907), was apparently married four times, which was seemingly not uncommon in Shawnee culture, particularly in the 1800s, when many died young. His wives included Mary E. Barnett, Susan Mohawk (Na Ta Wah Sa), Julia Tiblow (whom he married and divorced in Indian custom), and Carrie Elizabeth Foreman. With Susan he had one child, Rosa BlueJacket. Julia gave birth to Ida (c. 1867), who died at sixteen months. Carrie gave birth to at least seven children: Ida May Holden (1883–1959), Walter Lane (1885–1941), Edward "Tobe" Harrison (November 27, 1887–October 20, 1959), William T. (September 24, 1893–February 12, 1943), Blanche Bear Greenfeather Hawk (1895–1972), Amy Lunette Peacock (November 25, 1898–May 23, 1969), and Clyde BlueJacket (1903–1985). Various genealogical sites list three other children: Teressa BlueJacket, Annie (March 12, 1881–September 1882), and Grover.[68]

8.5. Chief Walter Lane BlueJacket, the first chief after the tribe's first constitution was adopted in 1939, plowing corn with a cultivator, c. 1939. Photo courtesy of Glenna Wallace.

Several documents dated from October 1909 through March 14, 1917, indicate that Walter attended the Quapaw Boarding School and the Seneca Boarding School for a period of about ten years. These documents involve Walter's applications for the removal of restrictions from land he owned, which at that time required action from the secretary of the interior. In his initial application, Walter, referred to as Allottee No. 14, was described as twenty-four years old, three-quarters Indian blood, single but contemplating marriage, and seeking removal of restrictions on a forty-acre tract under the act of Congress approved on March 3, 1909.[69]

Apparently a standard set of approximately thirty questions had to be answered by the superintendent of the local agency or clerk in charge. It seems that the superintendent recommended to the secretary of the interior that BlueJacket's restriction be removed. In a document dated October 1, 1909, Walter stated that his desire was "to sell this forty acre tract and to use the proceeds in improving and building himself a home on the balance of his allotment." Federal officials deemed that Walter Lane BlueJacket was up to the challenge of civilization. They believed, "He has the necessary business qualifications to enable him to manage his own affairs fairly successfully." As evidence they testified to his "good character and reputation" as well as his industriousness, the fact that he supported himself and his family, that he was a farmer, and that he did not drink and was in good physical health.[70]

American officials offered a very complimentary picture of his homestead. They described how he cultivated fifteen acres of his own allotment and possessed a wagon and team and various farming implements. He and others farmed a total of seventy-five acres of his allotment, a mix of grain and pasture, likely for the large number of domesticated animals raised on his farm. Superintendent Ira C. Deaver wrote, "About 75 acres of his entire allotment is under cultivation. He has built a good house on the balance of his allotment with proceeds derived from a sale in

8.6. Ed BlueJacket and Walter BlueJacket performed as part of the Seneca Indian School band during President Theodore Roosevelt's inauguration in 1901. Photo courtesy of Glenna Wallace.

the past year, and made other improvements on his homestead." Deaver added, "He rents his lands from year to year for grain rent; receiving 1/3 of all grain produced thereon." Deaver's only reservation regarding Walter was that his experiences were limited to working at home and on his own land, though he lauded Walter's credit-worthiness, noting that he had debts of $200 to Jim McGannon of Seneca, Missouri, for farm implements, but had a history of promptly settling his debts.[71]

Removal of restriction freed Walter to make his own decisions in life, and he wasted little time. On December 6, 1909, just two months after the superintendent's decision, he married Doris Longan. Telling the story of their grandparents' meeting, Judy Brown, Janice Brossett, and Jeff BlueJacket said they were told that Walter and other Indian friends, including Thomas A. Captain, frequently traveled together on government business, catching the train at Wyandotte, Oklahoma. One extremely cold evening, the train didn't arrive. Doris Longan's parents invited the men into their home to get out of the frigid temperatures. The men spent the night sleeping on the floor, with Doris and her sister Florence giggling, slyly peeking around the corner at the Indians.[72]

Other grandchildren, Walter Jr. and Brenda, shared a similar story, but this one involved Walter, T. A. Captain, and John Longan (Doris's father) each owning a team of horses that they would rent or hire out for the day at the Wyandotte train depot. In this story, Walter and T. A. were at one end of the depot, with John Longan and his daughters Doris and Florence at the other. The girls and men peeked at each other, but it took a week of peeking before they spoke and formally met each other. After all, in those days it wasn't proper for two Irish girls to be talking or keeping company with two Indians.[73] Either way, Walter and Doris met and married, as did T. A. and Florence.

Walter loved horses and was known for always having one of the best teams around. Walter treated his horses well. After all, successful farming was largely dependent upon a successful team. The picture of Chief BlueJacket hanging in the BlueJacket Center shows Walt sitting on a corn planter, which would have been drawn by a team of horses, possibly a pair named Duke and Prince, as his grandson Walter Jr. recalls. In that picture Walt has the left side of his face toward the camera, a detail consistent with information provided by Bobby BlueJacket, who said that Walter had a huge goiter on the right side of his neck that was as big as a softball, and thus he always turned his head to the right when taking pictures.[74]

Another application dated July 6, 1910, asked for the removal of restrictions from one acre of land in the southeast corner of a forty-acre tract. Walter was paid twenty-five dollars for the acre. A school, called BlueJacket School, or District No. 6, was then built on the site. Walter was highly respected in the community, and especially so in the Indian community. In his earlier days he played tuba in the Wyandotte Band and was an excellent baseball player. In fact, he built a ballfield on his front acreage, where all the Indians would gather on Saturday and Sunday to play. Walter was also an advocate of education and believed his children should be fluent in English because that was the language they would need to know to survive in this world. Glen Stoner indicated that when he once asked his mother, Lucy, why she and her brothers and sisters didn't teach their children Shawnee, she replied that she couldn't teach them Shawnee because she didn't know the language. Even though Walt and Doris conversed in Shawnee, they didn't permit their children to do so because they believed it would be a hindrance to them.[75]

Life continued. Following his marriage to Doris Longan, daughter of John and Elisha Cook Longan, Doris gave birth to their first son, Julian, followed by two daughters, Lucy Stoner and Ercel "Ert" Sample Palmer, and then another son named Walter BlueJacket Jr.[76] On an application for the removal of restrictions filed March 14, 1917, the age of Walt's fourth child is listed as one month. It also indicates that Walter obtained his support from the rentals derived from his lands and from his trade as a carpenter.

Studying the archival record of Walter BlueJacket's life reveals a man whose every decision was cross-examined by government officials. The United States government was totally involved in the lives of Eastern Shawnees, and more often than not, it placed profound limits on their choices. Superintendent Ira C. Deaver of the Quapaw Agency at Wyandotte, Oklahoma, observed, "[Walter is] industrious and has always supported his family as well as the average white men." He describes Walter's wife, Doris, as "a white woman of good character and reputation." He goes on to relate that Walter lived on the portion which he desired released, where he farmed a small portion and worked at the Century Mining Camp as a carpenter. He had a frame house of three rooms and outbuildings, and the property, worth about $2,800, was best adapted to the growing of corn, wheat, oats, etc., and he rented land at $2.50 per acre per annum.[77]

In a third request, Walter asked for the land restrictions to be removed because he wanted to get a loan on his land in order to erect two small houses in a mining camp, so that he could live in one while renting out the other. Superintendent Deaver questioned Walter's managerial abilities. He denied Walter's request, writing, "I am of the opinion that it would not be for his best interest to remove the restrictions from this land." Deaver's harsh tone is readily apparent. He compared Indians to non-Indians and implied that Indians are inferior and need the government to watch over them.

Adversity was definitely a hallmark of Walter's life. His application for unconditional removal of restrictions from forty acres of his surplus allotment had been denied; the government had spoken. And then, in 1918, Walter BlueJacket Jr. died at the age of eighteen months. It has been said that adversity introduces a man to himself. Never a quitter, Walter continued farming, continued his carpentry work, continued working in his Indian community and continued with life, fathering a fifth child, Leonard. In 1921 the BlueJacket School, or District No. 6, consolidated with the Wyandotte Public School District. For several years the old school building continued as a community building. Ironically, one document stated, "The Indians recently desired to use the building for community purposes and objections were raised by some of the white members." Land that had been an Indian allotment, land that had been for years the gathering place of the Eastern Shawnee people to play baseball, land that had helped keep a tribe together, land

8.7. Jake Robbins and Henry Turkeyfoot, dressed in a manner that was typical of the time in northeastern Oklahoma. Photo courtesy of the Wallace family.

that was used to educate all people was now land whose use was being denied to the very people who provided it. Obviously not everyone who went to school there became educated.

Nevertheless, the building became the hub of the community as a meeting center. It also served as the polling place on election days. Supposedly, lots of campaigning, whiskey drinking, and story swapping occurred with great gusto on Election Day. Walter was an avid Republican, while Doris preferred the Democrats. Heated discussions took place between the two, as each was known to be quite opinionated. Ultimately they agreed it would be better if they didn't participate in politics because there were too many heated arguments and they were just canceling out each other's vote. A story is told that one election day Doris noticed Walter was gone from the house. Thinking he was out farming, she seized the opportunity to finally have her vote count. She told her son Leonard to drive her down to the polls inside the schoolhouse. She got in line only to discover Walter three people ahead of her.[78]

Walter was also known for his honorable interactions with people. Walt BlueJacket Jr. (Walter Sr.'s grandson) told of the time that his grandfather had a new knife, which Henry Turkeyfoot wanted. Henry followed Walter around all day, admiring the knife, telling Walter how much he liked the knife, asking Walter if he would give it to him. Unfortunately Henry was known to sometimes drink more than he should and become violent. Walter feared that Henry would drink too much and slash someone with the knife. Turkeyfoot assured him that this would not happen. But that's exactly what did occur. Always a soft-spoken man, not prone to violence, Walter learned of the misdeed, went to Turkeyfoot, and fought with him. Successfully reclaiming the knife, Walter dropped it in Turkeyfoot's bottle of whiskey and smashed the bottle on Turkeyfoot's head.[79]

From his concern for each individual tribal member, even if it meant disagreeing with that person, to his overarching desire to advance the Eastern Shawnee Tribe as a whole, Walter Blue-Jacket was a man who lived life and tried to learn from each experience, be it success or failure. William Hazlitt once wrote, "Prosperity is a great teacher, adversity is a greater." Lucretius observed, "Watch a man in times of . . . adversity to discover what kind of man he is." Just as the tribe's original constitution stated that it was adopted "to take advantage of the opportunities of economic independence and social advancement offered by the Thomas-Rogers Oklahoma Indian Welfare Act of June 26, 1936," Walter BlueJacket was a man who recognized opportunity for his people.[80] So it was that a man who had known prosperity, a man who had experience interacting with the government, a man who had known adversity, a man who had known love, a man who had known disappointment, and a man who had earned the respect of others came to the forefront and was elected the first chief of the Eastern Shawnee Tribe of Oklahoma in modern times. His leadership enabled the good road to continue so that future Eastern Shawnee citizens could travel it.

DAVID DUSHANE JR.: SECOND CHIEF OF EASTERN SHAWNEE TRIBE OF OKLAHOMA (1878–1954)

The tombstone located on the Missouri side of the Seneca Cemetery erroneously reads that David Dushane Jr. died in 1955. Obituaries state that he died on May 3, 1954.[81] Such is the difficulty in researching tribal citizens born more than a hundred years ago. So many research errors can occur. Not researching and not writing about those Eastern Shawnee historical subjects would be a greater error. Chief David Dushane's life and impact upon the Eastern Shawnee Tribe of Oklahoma should not go unnoticed.

David Dushane Jr. left us an invaluable family history on October 26, 1937, when he sat down for an interview with Nannie Lee Burns. In this interview David indicated he was born July 10, 1878, to David Dushane and Nancy Jackson Dushane. Dave, as he was later known, stated that his father was a full-blood Shawnee Indian born in Johnson County, Kansas, near Olathe. Dave's mother, Nancy Jackson Dushane, came with her parents from Sandusky, Ohio, during the Indian removal era. However, Jack Dushane, a grandson of Dave's brother Charles, and one who has done considerable genealogical research, points out that according to Nancy's allotment paper, Nancy was born in Ottawa County around 1845. Obviously, there is a discrepancy between the two accounts.[82]

According to Dave's interview, his parents married in Kansas and lived there six years before coming to Indian Territory in 1871. David Sr. and Nancy had four sons: Andrew, Charles, Daniel, and David. Two of those sons later became chiefs of the Eastern Shawnee Tribe. Dave's father was previously married to Hannah Evans, and later to Mary Chick. From his father's first wife,

Hannah Evans, Dave had a half-sister, Mariah Louisa Dushane, who married Bill Prophet, a Cherokee-Shawnee. Dave stated that his parents lived on land "located on the state line just west of Seneca, Missouri," a place that became known as the Dushane farm, a place where Dave was born, raised his family, and lived until the time of his death. Today the place is still known as the old Dushane place and makes up part of the site where Indigo Sky Casino is located.

In that 1937 interview with Nannie Lee Burns, Dave explained,

> My father's family were among those who were moved for protection to Kansas. Many things have not been understood by the Indians, and under the treaty between the Shawnees, in 1854, they agreed among themselves that those who chose to do so might take their lands in severalty, and those who did not like that plan might retain a part of the land we had acquired from the Senecas, in common. Later, this led to a dispute and a division of the tribe as part of them contended that those who had accepted their lands in severalty had severed their tribal relations. This condition existed when the Civil War began.

Dave went on to state,

> The Shawnees were driven out of here in the fall of 1862 when they went to Kansas, taking with them only what was easy to carry, leaving most of their stock on the range and many things in their houses, thinking, no doubt, that they would not be gone very long. Homesick, in the fall of 1863, under the leadership of Black Bob, about a third of them returned to their home in the Indian country where many of them, including their leader, Black Bob, sickened and died. In 1864, there were more than eight hundred Shawnees in Kansas and there were more than a hundred of these Shawnees in the Union Army. . . . In the spring of 1865 we started with an agent back to the Indian country in the Indian Territory . . . traveled about eighty miles, stopped on Big Creek and here we remained through the summer months . . . where we farmed some.

Dave concludes this history by stating, "Our band of Shawnees completed their trip home in the fall of 1865; however my father did not come till later," 1871, as he indicated earlier in the interview. In 1884, at the age of six, Dave started at the Wyandotte Mission School, which he attended nine years, until he had to quit to work on the farm and care for his parents. In 1892 lands were allotted, with heads of families receiving 160 acres and each child receiving forty. Dave would have been about fourteen years old at that time, and according to his grandson Bud Nelson, Dave had to wait until he turned twenty-one to take over his allotment. Later the "Too-Lates," people born after the date of the last allotment, were given forty acres each.[83]

On Christmas Day, 1907, at the age of twenty-nine, Dave married Allie Frazier, whom he described as "a white woman who was born in Kansas, January 10, 1888, but who had been raised in the Indian Territory." Dave and Allie had four daughters (Vance Nelson, Genevieve Golden, Jewell Crain, and Madelyn Rosenow Dowd) and three sons (David M., June Warren, and Jimmy Curtis). Jimmy died when he was a teenager as the result of a fall from the bluffs while running traps. At the time of Dave's death in 1954, Dave and Allie also had eighteen grandchildren and four great-grandchildren.[84]

Dave was proud to be an American Indian. He was proud of his ancestry and his heritage, so much so that he named his youngest son Jimmy Curtis after Charles Curtis, the thirty-first vice president of the United States (1929–1933) who was "the first person with significant acknowledged Native American ancestry and the first person with significant acknowledged non-European ancestry to reach either of the two highest offices in the United States Government's executive branch. His maternal ancestry was three-quarters Native American, of ethnic

Kaw, Osage and Pottawatomie ancestry. Curtis spent years of childhood living with his maternal grandparents on their Kaw reservation." A later grandson of Dave's, Buddy Charles Nelson, was named in honor of Charles Curtis as well.[85]

Dave often referenced the difficulties of living on the state line. Living on the border between Oklahoma and Missouri "made it very easy for us to be attacked and robbed by bushwhackers who preyed on the settlers along the Oklahoma border. We were too far from fort to get any protection." After the Civil War, when Shawnees returned from Kansas, those houses still standing "were occupied by a band of thieves and robbers who, by living on this side of the state line, escaped from the law of the Border States. This condition caused the agent, Major Snow, to request that a Company of United States Soldiers be stationed at Baxter Springs, Kansas, for the protection of the Shawnees, the Senecas, the Peorias and the Quapaws."[86]

Ironically, years later the Dushane place had another experience involving thieves, robbers, and killers. According to Dee Griffith (daughter of Vance Nelson and the first grandchild of Dave and Allie), two of Dave and Allie's daughters had walked to Seneca, Missouri (about two miles away), made some grocery purchases, and were walking back home carrying the merchandise when a car stopped and offered them a ride home. The girls accepted and rode home with the strangers, whereupon Allie offered iced tea and food to them for being so kind and gracious to her daughters. The individuals declined and drove away. Only after their departures were the girls able to tell Dave and Allie that the car was full of guns. Later they learned the identity of the strangers—Bonnie and Clyde, who had just come from their infamous shootings in Joplin, Missouri.[87]

Both Dee and Buddy Charles spoke of what a calm, quiet man their grandfather Dave Dushane was. He believed in talking as opposed to spanking or whipping. Never a violent person, Dave always demonstrated a calm, cool demeanor. That did not mean he could not be forceful, because he always had the markings of a thoughtful decision maker. Dee recalled a time when she spent the night with her grandparents and one of her uncles came home after having far too much to drink. Allie, typically the disciplinarian, could do nothing with her son. Dave went outside with the son and returned alone. All was quiet and peaceful. Only the next morning did Dee look outside and realize how Dave had handled the situation: there was the son chained and locked to a tree. (For years Dave had been employed as a jailer in Miami, Oklahoma.)

Dee also recalled one of the few times she heard her grandfather raise his voice. It was shortly after the tragic death of the youngest child, Jimmy Curtis. Allie was extremely distraught long after his death, and Dave finally spoke in a stern, loud voice, telling her, "That's enough. We have lost a son but we have two other ones. Life goes on." From that point on, Allie collected herself, dealt with the grief, and moved forward. Dee also spoke of the deep, rich love her grandparents shared. She recalled seeing them every Sunday afternoon leaving the house, hand in hand, to stroll down to the creek.[88]

Dave Dushane played an important role in Eastern Shawnee history. When the first constitution and bylaws were ratified on December 22, 1939, Walter L. BlueJacket, Thomas A. Captain, Ora S. Hampton, Edw. H. BlueJacket, and David Dushane Jr. signed the document. Walter L. BlueJacket was the first elected chief of the tribe after the constitution was adopted in 1939, followed by David Dushane, who was the second chief elected in 1940, and Thomas A. Captain was the third chief of the tribe. Bud Nelson recalled listening to many of the conversations between his grandfather Dave Dushane and Thomas A. Captain. Both men focused on how tribal citizens needed to get along and thrive. Each recognized the need to blend in with the United States government and the rest of the population without giving up our traditions.[89]

David Dushane Jr. died May 3, 1954, at the age of seventy-six from peritonitis caused by a ruptured appendix. Howard Moore, in an article entitled "Rural Ramblings," stated, "Old Dave

Dushane died yesterday 8:25 A.M. He died in the Baptist hospital in Miami, Okla. 'Ruptured appendix' the doctors called it. Dave would have said, 'I've got a belly ache.'" A plethora of words could be used to describe David Dushane Jr.—honest, fair, calm, rational, loving. Two words that he refused to acknowledge were "can't" and "quit."[90] The Eastern Shawnee Tribe of Oklahoma has progressed so much because of the leadership provided by our founding fathers. May we all learn from them and heed the advice of David Dushane Jr., who admonished us to get along and thrive. In other words, we are all traveling this same road. Let's respect each other. Good advice then; good advice now.

THOMAS A. CAPTAIN (1884–1980)

One word comes to mind when you think of Thomas A Captain: chief. He was chief of the Eastern Shawnee Tribe of Oklahoma for twenty-five years. He was also the son of a chief (Tom), the father of a chief (George, usually referred to as Buck) and the grandfather of a chief (Nelis). Born December 21, 1884, Thomas A. Captain (Ske-te-pu-ska-ka) died February 11, 1980, at the age of ninety-five. He married Florence Longan, and they became parents of nine children: six sons—Thurman, Leo, John, Charlie, George, and Dennis—and three daughters—Thelma, Marjorie "Sue," and Virginia. Thomas gave nicknames to his children; Thurman was Windy, Thelma was Irish, and Charlie was Chud. Leo became known as Peanut, George was Buck, Virginia was Ginger, and Dennis was Sandy. He referred to the nicknames as their Indian names. Everyone always laughed at Thomas's sense of humor. At the time of his death in 1980, he was survived by seven children, twenty-three grandchildren, thirty-nine great-grandchildren, and seven great-great-grandchildren.

Having a large family was nothing new to Thomas, as his parents, Tom Captain Sr. and Martha Ellen Gullett, had had eleven children, of whom Thomas, born in 1884, was the oldest. His siblings included Cordelia Jane (born 1886), Mary Ellen (1888), Charles Selby (1890), Sarah May (1892), William Henry "Bill" (1894), Michael Francis "Frank" (1895), Gracie "Grace" (1897), George Philemon (1899), Martha Eveline "Evy" (1901), and Sophronia "Babe" (1903). All the children grew to adulthood with the exception of Charles Selby, who died from a gunshot accident at the age of ten and was buried on the family farm, thus establishing the Captain Cemetery.

Thomas's life begins and ends in Eastside, a community located nine miles east of Miami, Oklahoma. Many of the allotments made to Eastern Shawnee individuals were located in this area. Thomas lived his entire life within ten miles of Eastside, with the exception of one year when he attended school at Haskell. From the Quapaw Indian Competency Commission papers, we learn that Thomas married Florence Longan, a white woman who was born November 7, 1888, in Taney County, Missouri. Thomas was allotted 120 acres and sold forty of them for $220 to Kelsie B. Ross and another forty acres to M. B. Sparlin for $1,200. When asked what he did with the money, Thomas stated, "Paid off what I owed, bought 2 mares and lost both of them, bought hogs, one horse, wagon and buggy, farm machinery." He described the forty remaining acres as being "all in timber. About 15 acres can be cleared and farmed—not even fenced and the land is worth $10 an acre."

In the same interview, which is titled "Noncompetent Indian Land Form," Thomas' business experience is listed as "lineman, firing stationary engine." In response to the question "Do you use intoxicating liquor?" Thomas responded, "Yes." The most humorous response occurred when Thomas was then asked to what extent he used intoxicating liquor and he replied, "Once in a while when I can get it." Anyone who knew Thomas A. Captain knows he loved his beer and in his later life made a daily beer run in his old pickup from his home in Eastside across the Missouri line. Those who lived in the community during this time could be heard fondly saying, "Thar goes Thomas," and about an hour later observing, "Well, Tom's back." Thomas and his wife, Florence, were living on Walter BlueJacket's allotment at the time of the Indian Competency interview, and the agent concluded, "Seems to be on an equal with the average white man as to intelligence, but has nothing left from the sale of his best land," concluding that "he is a progressive and industrious man."

The agent was correct. Possibly no other person influenced the Eastside community more than Thomas A. Captain. In 1908, like Walter BlueJacket, he sold one acre of land for the construction of a new school. For this act, Thomas received twenty dollars. The District No. 5 School was built and named Moccasin Bend. Some say the origin of this name is the fact that Spring River is located in the vicinity, and water moccasins could always be found in the bend of the river. According to Tom, it began as a one-room school with seventy-five kids. Later, in the 1940s, it became a two-room rural school, with grades one through four on the north end of the building, separated from grades five through eight by a white wall that could be moved, much like a garage door. A potbellied coal-burning stove heated the structure. Like the Blue-Jacket School, Moccasin Bend No. 5 became a community gathering place, where many political gatherings and family reunions were held as well as school functions, including Christmas parties and pie suppers. It was a progressive rural school, consistently winning first place when all of the rural schools competed against each other academically and athletically. Graduates went on to Wyandotte to attend high school.

Another one-acre plot owned by Thomas also contributed to the Eastside community. This was an acre of land he and his wife, Florence, sold to the Christian church in 1917, which later became Eastside Assembly, and then Eastside Baptist. From baptisms, weddings, and baby showers to funerals and elections, the community repeatedly gathered. And then there was the acre of land that became the business district of Eastside, which included Captain's Grocery, fondly called Captain Store. Originally started by their son Charlie, Thomas and Florence purchased the store and operated it for many years. It was a rural grocery, measuring about twenty by forty feet, including a gas station, with living quarters in the rear. Later the gas pumps were removed, and the small structure became the community's town hall.[91] Everyone traded at Captain Grocery, most charging their groceries and running a monthly bill. They also gathered there for community news and to visit with rural neighbors. People remembered that Thomas "near always had a chaw of 'baccy in his mouth," and that Florence, clad in her calico dress topped with a white bibbed apron, could frequently be seen cooking a pot of beans. Many Indian meetings were held at Captain Store as Chief Captain kept interest in the tribe going.

Next to the store, Tom and his neighbors constructed a roping arena in the late 1940s. The place was packed on weekends. Across the road, on the land of his brother-in-law, Arthur Crain, they developed one of the best baseball fields in Ottawa County. Youngsters, especially boys, either rode horses or walked up to five miles every weekend to be part of the action. Families came and spent the day. One day they roped, and the next day they played baseball. It was the place to be.

In an interview conducted in 1969, when he was eighty years old, Chief Captain talked about the tribe, specifically referring to the tribal land near Seneca, Missouri. He described the land as being fifty-seven acres of creek-bottom land, which made the tribe $250 a year. At the time, the tribe had no meeting place. But in the mid-1950s the government wanted to build the tribe a council house. Captain told them the tribe didn't need it. He advised them, "If you got money . . . to build . . . take it down the Seneca nation." He went on to say, "Some of them give me the devil because I give it away but heck what did we want with it."[92] Captain's last year as chief was 1966. In that context, it is understandable why he didn't see a need for a building. The building would have to be placed on trust land, and the only property the tribe possessed at that time was the 58.19 acres from Nina Dushane's allotment located west of Seneca, Missouri. This location is at least ten miles from the Eastside community, fifteen from the BlueJacket community

8.8. Interior of Captain's Grocery Store, the hub of the Eastside Community. Thomas A. Captain and Florence Captain, c. 1947. Photo courtesy of Larry Kropp.

near Wyandotte, and nearly fifteen from Peoria, all areas inhabited by many Eastern Shawnees. Seneca, Missouri, was simply not thought of as a tribal community. Even if the 58.19 acres were in Oklahoma, that land was seen as being in Missouri. A building for meetings would not be constructed on the 58.19 acres until more than ten years later, and even then many would have preferred Miami, Oklahoma. However, Miami is out of the Eastern Shawnee jurisdictional area. Today many tribal citizens realize the value of developing a tribal community, a sense of place. Thomas A. Captain simply wanted the right place. He was a candid individual, saying what he thought, and you have to give him credit for that.

Possibly one of Thomas's greatest contributions to the tribe was holding on to that land. The City of Seneca offered $15,000 to purchase it, but in a tribal meeting held on January 9, 1965, the tribe turned it down. The city raised its bid to $18,000, but once again the tribe voted no. In the 1950s and 1960s the U.S. government promoted the termination of federal recognition, and many feared that the Eastern Shawnee Tribe would be terminated if it sold its remaining land.

The topic of land surfaced in other conversations as well. In the 1969 interview Tom was asked if the Eastside community had its own cemetery. Tom responded that the old Indians are buried in Flint Graveyard, two miles east and a quarter mile south of Eastside, but that most burials now go to Miami or Seneca, with a few going to Wyandotte and other family cemeteries. He then told how Captain Cemetery came to be. His father was hunting with Charles Selby, one of his younger brothers, when a dog treed a squirrel up a dead tree.

> My dad cut this tree down. And my brother, he was only about ten or eleven years old. But he had my gun and a hunting dog. And the tree started to fall and he was trying to drag the gun and the dog too and the gun went off and shot him right in under there. I

don't know what my dad ever done to that gun. He got rid of it before I got back from school.[93]

Tom Captain was a good man. He gave generously to the community. He could also be a stern man; ask his children. He believed in the adage, "Spare the rod and spoil the child." Tom didn't have any spoiled children. Captain descendants, sometimes humorously and sometimes not so humorously, refer to the legendary "Captain temper," and Thomas was one of many who created this legacy.

Thomas A. Captain proved that his father, Tom Sr., was a full-blood Shawnee. It took from 1939 to 1954 to accomplish this. In an affidavit dated June 14, 1954, Thomas wrote,

> I am the son of Thomas A. Captain, Sr., deceased Eastern Shawnee Allottee #58 and do know that from my earliest childhood until his death in 1920 that always he said he was a full-blood Shawnee Indian. My dad could speak only limited English and his sister Nancy could not speak English at all. My grandparents on my father's side were full-blood Shawnee Indians and their names were Nan-ho-gom-we and Me-tah-way-see. My father's Indian name was Nan-na-ha-ya-be-nuck. As shown above, the names of my grandparents and my father's name show no influence of any nationality other than Shawnee Indian. My mother, Martha E. Captain, tried in many ways to influence my father's life so that she could gain control of his property and in many ways she was successful. It is my earnest belief that she, rather than my father had him enrolled as a 3/4 Shawnee and 1/4 French in order to set aside the restrictions on the land my father was allotted and the land he inherited. In some instances she did succeed and sold the land, of which my father received little or none of the proceeds.
>
> Tom Captain June 14, 1954

Thomas A. Captain's sister Mary Captain Ross wrote a similar affidavit maintaining that her "mother, a white woman, gave erroneous statement" about her husband, Tom, when she stated that he was three-quarters Eastern Shawnee and one-quarter French in order to pursue her own personal gain. Mary found out in 1938, when her children were refused readmission to Indian service schools because they were said to have less than the required one-quarter Indian blood. Three other affidavits from "old people who knew my father" were also presented. Upon receipt of these affidavits, the Department of Interior declared Tom Captain Sr. to be a full-blood Shawnee Indian, thereby affecting the blood quantum of every Captain from that point on. It has been said that Martha Gullett was fearful that, because she was non-Native, she would be ineligible for any inheritance if her husband was a full-blood Native.

Today, Captain's Store is gone, as is Moccasin Bend No. 5. The rock from that school now covers Eastside Assembly of God Church, located near the original site of the school. Still standing, on a corner not far away, is a church identified as Eastside Baptist Church. South of that church, in a cemetery near Wyandotte, lie Thomas and Florence Captain. Still very much alive is a grateful and thriving Eastern Shawnee Tribe whose chief for twenty-five years was Thomas A. Captain.

JULIAN BOLES BLUEJACKET (1910–1970)

His father was the first elected chief of the Eastern Shawnee Tribe following its formal reorganization in 1939. He became the second BlueJacket to serve in this prestigious office, both of whom died while serving as chief. Julian Boles BlueJacket was the fourth chief of the Eastern Shawnee Tribe of Oklahoma in this modern era, serving from 1966 to 1970.[94]

Born March 6, 1910, in Vinita, Oklahoma, to Walter Lane BlueJacket and Doris Longan, he was the grandson of Charles BlueJacket (1846–1907), whose Indian name was Ma Ta Me A, and Carrie Elizabeth Foreman (1859–1943). The oldest of five children, Julian's siblings were Lucy Stoner, Ercel Palmer, Walter BlueJacket Jr. (who died as a child), and Leonard. Following graduation from Wyandotte High School, Julian attended what was then known as the Haskell Institute, a tribal university located in Lawrence, Kansas. During World War II, when our country was in dire need of troops, he entered the military and served in both World War II and the Korean War. In 1935 he married Louella Florence Gunnels, who gave birth to their son, Darrell Lee, September 7, 1937. Florence tragically died September 29, 1940, during childbirth. She and her daughter, Caroline, are buried in the Seneca, Missouri, cemetery. Young Darrell went to live with Julian's parents, Walter and Doris BlueJacket. Later Julian married Juanita Fay Yocum, and shortly thereafter his father died. Doris didn't feel she could cope with losing a husband and having her grandson Darrell, whom she had been raising, leave her, too, so Julian made the difficult decision that Darrell's home would continue to be with his beloved Grandma Blue.[95]

Following his military service, Julian joined the Bureau of Indian Affairs, serving in Arizona and New Mexico on the Navajo reservation, where he lived for a number of years. Over a period of time the J-family came to be: Julian, Juanita and five little J's, Judy, Janice, Joetta "Jodi," Jeanette, and Jeff. Northeast Oklahoma was always home to Julian and Juanita, so several years later he transferred as a realty officer to the Muskogee office, where he later retired prematurely due to ill health.[96]

After retirement he truly returned to his roots, moving back to Ottawa County. Sacrifice had always been in his blood—sacrifice to serve in the military, sacrifice to let his oldest son be reared by Julian's mother, sacrifice to move away from the area and his parents to work and live on a Navajo reservation—so it was only natural for him to sacrifice his free time and be willing to follow in his family's heritage by serving the Shawnee people. Julian became chief of the Eastern Shawnee Tribe in 1966.[97] At that time there were no tribal buildings, and some area tribes had been terminated.[98] The tribe had only a 58.19-acre plot, which was almost sold the previous year, and we had little hope, little vision.[99] The same was true of our neighboring tribes. Julian set out to change that.

Julian understood that strength lies in numbers. He joined with other chiefs in the county and sought to unify with them around their shared interests. Historian Velma Nieberding describes this: "In April, 1967, a group of Indian leaders representing the tribes living within the boundaries of the Miami Agency met to organize an Inter-Tribal Council." Julian BlueJacket was one of those leaders. The Inter-Tribal Council (ITC) was formed by seven tribes, but only five tribes could vote on BIA programs, because the Modocs and Peorias had been terminated. These five tribes—Quapaw, Seneca-Cayuga, Eastern Shawnee, Miami, and Wyandotte—were known as the Five Tribes Council. At this time, according to Nieberding, "Oklahoma ha[d] a larger Indian population than any other state, it ha[d] no reservations. Some thirty million acres, about 67 percent of the state, were initially allotted to Indians. Slightly more than 1.5 million acres (about 3.6 percent of the state) are in Indian hands today [1983]." It was the ITC that united the small tribes in Ottawa County. Nieberding explains that the "ITC worked to secure BIA grants, title programs and direct assistance from state and federal agencies. It was this unity that would enable the tribes to develop into self-sustaining entities." Julian BlueJacket was a vital force in changing a termination policy into a self-determination policy.[100]

Afflicted with a heart condition the entire time he was chief, Julian BlueJacket had heart surgery in Houston, Texas, in April 1970 and died one week later, April 9, 1970. The Eastern Shawnee Tribe lost another warrior. His obituary says it best:

Julian B. BlueJacket, chief of the Eastern Shawnee, was buried yesterday as a warrior—a modern warrior. His tribe long ago gave up warfare after its defeat by Anthony Wayne in 1794. Although the Shawnees were known as fierce warriors, this defeat was so crushing, they never afterwards, as a nation, made war on the white man. Julian . . . used his excellent training in fighting for his people in another way—by ballot, tribal resolutions, conferences with Indian Service officials, and for the past few years as an active member of the Inter-Tribal Council of this area.

Appropriately, Miami Inter-Tribal Council chiefs served as honorary pallbearers.[101]

Julian came from a family steeped in Shawnee history. The first Blue Jacket fought during the Revolutionary War and reportedly acquired his name because of a blue hunting shirt he frequently wore. "Julian's father was the late Walter BlueJacket who was chosen as chief when the tribe was reorganized under the Oklahoma Indian Welfare Act of 1936. His grandfather, Charles BlueJacket, also served the tribe as chief for many years."[102]

The town of BlueJacket, in Craig County, is named for yet another BlueJacket, Reverend Charles BlueJacket, the uncle of Julian's grandfather, who was the first postmaster there.[103] The BlueJacket legacy of sacrifice and service did not die with Julian BlueJacket. His sons, Darrell and Jeff, served on the Business Committee when the Eastern Shawnees first established a bingo hall in 1984. His daughter Jodi, who lived in Texas, was interested in bringing business opportunities to the Eastern Shawnee Tribe. His daughter Jeanette developed the first Eastern Shawnee Facebook page. Judy Brown has served as secretary of the Eastern Shawnee Business Committee for several years, and Janice Brossett served on the election board.[104] He was the fourth chief of the modern Eastern Shawnee Tribe, he was a fighter for his people, he refused to let the red road deteriorate, and his name was Julian B. BlueJacket.

CLYDE LEROY BLUEJACKET (1903–1985)

Second row, second picture, the portrait of the fifth modern chief and third BlueJacket chief is probably the first one people notice of the eleven chiefs' portraits hanging in the BlueJacket Center. Why? Clyde Leroy BlueJacket, often known as Blue, is the only chief wearing a prominent full headdress. Bobby BlueJacket, the last surviving son of Chief Clyde BlueJacket, recalls a time when a tour group was looking at the pictures of chiefs on the wall and someone asked why Clyde was in full headdress. The man giving the tour said that wearing a full headdress was not within the Eastern Shawnee tradition, but Bobby corrected him and said that it was indeed his father's place to wear it, since it honored the fact that it was given by the chief of the Kiowa Tribe.[105]

Born July 22, 1903, to Charles BlueJacket (1831–1907) and Carrie Elizabeth Foreman Blue-Jacket (1859–1943), Clyde was one of ten children. (Charles BlueJacket's large family is detailed in the section discussing Walter L. BlueJacket, above.) Clyde stated in an interview with Velma Nieberding on May 15, 1970, that he attended Public School No. 6, also known as BlueJacket School; the Seneca, Missouri, public school; and Seneca Indian School from the time when he was nine or ten years old through the eleventh grade.[106] He and Ethel L. Welch (1904–99) married when he was only seventeen, and later divorced. Together they had five children: Junior William BlueJacket (1920–82); Dennis Wayne BlueJacket (1922–44), who died overseas in World War II; Thomas Lee BlueJacket; Marjorie BlueJacket; and Robert Denton BlueJacket.[107]

Clyde served honorably in the United States Navy Seabees for three years during World War II, a time when the United States desperately needed servicemen. In 1942, shortly before his induction into the service, his son Bobby was asked if he had heard the story of their great-great-great-grandfather Blue Jacket, that he was a white boy captured by the Shawnee tribe. In what is now Ohio, tourists used to be able to see a play that perpetuates this legend of the white Blue Jacket. The play tells a story of two brothers from the Swearingin family who were captured by the tribe. The boy who became known as Blue Jacket asked his capturers to release his brother in exchange for his staying with them and learning Shawnee ways. Later on, as adults, the brothers met on the field of battle, where the freed Swearingin brother (now an American soldier) was killed by his brother (now named Blue Jacket) just as he learned of his identity. Bobby recalled that Clyde told every member of the family, "When you hear this story, know that it is a lie." Sixty years later, the scientific discovery of DNA led to the discovery of the truth and conclusively proved that Blue Jacket had no English matches in his DNA; rather, all of his genetic markers were of North American tribal descent. "Dad was right," says Bobby. "It was a lie. Our family had always followed a more altruistic life and could not be involved in such a thing."[108] The popular play later had to stop performances, as the truth became known.

Bobby BlueJacket explains, "I did not know my father in my early childhood. . . . I was told that the younger man was a carouser and a boozer. It led to separation and divorce shortly after my birth, in 1930. We became better known to one another when Clyde became a Christian in 1953, affiliated with the Indian Baptist Church. He traveled and worked extensively with the convention throughout the United States, where he spoke of its influence on the Native people." At the age of sixty-seven, Clyde became chief of the Eastern Shawnee Tribe upon the death of Julian BlueJacket on April 9, 1970. He finished out Julian's term, then went on to win a two-year term himself, serving from 1970–74. He lived in Quapaw, Oklahoma, for a number of years.[109]

Clyde thought it an honor and a great responsibility to be chief. His son Bobby wrote, "He tried with every breath to walk in the steps of the old ones and share the heritage that was rightly proven to be his. He wore the full headdress because it was a gigantic honor, bordering on a spirituality of the connection between the tribes. It was hardly ever done, but it honored my father with their [the Kiowas'] song and their gifts. For Clyde, it was not about the symbol of position or power, but in honoring the old ones, the giver of gifts, and in service of his fellow tribal members." Bobby went on to say,

> When visiting my family in Minneapolis years ago he spoke at several schools about being chief and aspects of his life in white society. He spoke of Shawnee being his first language and about being forbidden to speak it while attending the Seneca Indian Boarding School in Wyandotte. He stayed a year there before going to his home with his mother, Carrie BlueJacket. He was reared in a small four-room house by his mother, Carrie, and older brother Edward "Tobe," the house where my sister and brothers and I was born. His dad died when Clyde was four years old from the aftereffects of saving a man from drowning. Given the tribe's financial stability today, [there is] a most interesting story. . . . He said that when it was necessary to inform tribal members of issues by regular mail that they would all donate and pay for the mailings themselves. Though they had not financial resources to work with, they were some of the ones that laid the foundation for the tribe's success today.[110]

Now that I am chief of the Eastern Shawnee Tribe, I can remember when my mother, Vergie Enyart, served as secretary and treasurer of the tribe during Clyde's tenure as chief. I can remember many occasions when Mom and Clyde reviewed the minutes, laboring over basically non-existent tribal funds, discussing options, hoping for better things, serving the tribe out of love and convictions. There were no monetary rewards, few praises. "Someday," Blue would say, "someday we will win these land claims. Somehow we must hold on."[111]

And hold on we did. In 1939 we owned just 58.19 acres. In 1974 we still owned just 58.19 acres. But we were resilient. Blue died in February 1985, two months after the tribe opened its first bingo hall.[112] That hall would not have happened if Chief Clyde Leroy BlueJacket had given up. Instead he chose to put one foot in front of the other, believing that our red road would be a thriving place one day.

JAMES GREENFEATHER: BEFORE AND AFTER (1920–1983)

He served four short years, from 1974–78, but the Eastern Shawnee Tribe of Oklahoma was forever changed after James Greenfeather was elected as the sixth chief following reorganization in 1939. Before James Greenfeather became chief, the tribe had 58.19 acres, no buildings, no enterprises, and no developments. Business was conducted in offices located in Miami, Oklahoma, over Dawson's Jewelry Store. Business Committee meetings and general council were held in the Ottawa County Courthouse annex or elsewhere.[113] Perhaps it was the 1976 bicentennial preparations and celebrations held in honor of the nation's birth that helped energize all tribes in the area, including the Eastern Shawnees, perhaps it was the personality and leadership style of Greenfeather, perhaps it was a combination of both—but dramatic changes did occur while he was chief.

James Isaac "Big Boy" Greenfeather was born July 18, 1920, to Luther Oce Greenfeather and Blanche BlueJacket Hawk. His maternal grandparents were Charles Jr. and Carrie Elizabeth Foreman BlueJacket. James, or Big Boy, was the oldest of three children born to Luther and Blanche. His siblings were Lois "Cissy" Greenfeather Nowlin and Alonzo Greenfeather. James also had several older half brothers and sisters from his mother's previous marriage to Frank Bear. These included Wynona Evelyn Bear Hollandsworth, Edgar Lee Bear, Richard Vance Bear, Thurman Walker Bear, Herman Wilfred Bear, and Lucy Nadine Bear Captain. Additionally he had A. J., Carl, and Roy Greenfeather as half brothers from another marriage of his father's.

Big Boy attended Seneca Indian School, completing the tenth grade. A natural athlete, Big Boy tried out for the Brooklyn Dodgers professional baseball team, but a broken ankle cut that career short. He was also a professional boxer.[114]

At the age of eighteen Big Boy enlisted in the army, where he served four years. His military duties took him to North Africa and Sicily. Wounded more than once, he was awarded the Purple Heart for his bravery in World War II. James married Esteline Kist, and they became the parents of Thurman James Greenfeather, who is often called Little Jim. James and Esteline divorced, and Little Jim went to live with his grandmother Mary Francis Beaver Kist when he was three or four. Married several times, James also had one other son, Herman Jay Greenfeather, who currently lives in Florida. Although Little Jim lived with his maternal grandmother, he states that he had lots of contact with his father and has good memories of him.[115]

James Greenfeather had a way with words and actions. Little Jim remembers his father as being headstrong, while at the same time having a gentle side. Jim states that his father never talked mean to him, never laid a hand on him. Big Boy realized that more could be gained by scolding his son than spanking him. Jim recalls his father saying, "If you've got something to say, well say it and get it off your chest. If you see a person you don't like, stay away from him. Speak to people you don't necessarily care for but let it end there." And if it didn't end there, James took care of that, too. He didn't let anyone sway him or intimidate him. He could be up for a good fight. He was chief at a time when men still invited other men outside to settle their political differences. James let it be known that he wasn't afraid, that he was prepared to defend himself and his ideas if he had to, and that he was going to run the meetings. Some of those meetings were notorious for less-than-mild behavior, from women as well as men.[116]

"Before and after" could also refer to James's drinking. It has been a pattern in so many Native American lives. Before James stopped drinking he had a temper. Before he stopped drinking he went through several marriages. Before he stopped drinking he would argue. Before he stopped drinking, if he lost his temper, look out! His son Jim pointed out that after his father stopped drinking, he straightened up, mellowed out. No longer would he argue. Instead he would just laugh at you. It was at this time in his life, even though he was still an over-the-road truck driver, that he became easygoing. He spent lots of time with his son Jim; they even made a saddle together, which is on display in our museum today. Proud of his Shawnee heritage, he was a stomp dance leader at White Oak, dressed in regalia, participated in sweats, and did whatever he wanted to accomplish. Little Jim's face lit up as he proclaimed, "What a great guy he was to me in later years. He treated me like I was special."[117]

James Isaac Greenfeather became chief of the Eastern Shawnee Tribe of Oklahoma in 1974. Shortly thereafter the tribal newsletter, *The Shooting Star*—named after Tecumseh, which means "shooting star"—made its debut. In 1975 the Inter-Tribal Council (ITC) obtained an Indian Grant to design and construct tribal flags in order to participate in the bicentennial celebrations. All of the ITC tribes began the process of developing tribal flags. Jim Greenfeather involved himself in extensive research and enlisted the aid of Robert Alexander, who is credited with designing the flag's logo, along with Clark Frayser and George Phelps, who wrote a play about Tecumseh entitled "The Panther and the Swan." This production was staged in August 1976 at the Quapaw Powwow Grounds, and Greenfeather appeared in the play. A tribal flag and a tribal play can be attributed to the efforts of James Greenfeather as well as the initiation of Miami Heritage Day.[118]

In 1977 Greenfeather led the tribe in securing its first grant—obtained through the Department of Commerce at no cost to the tribe. A contractor was hired to construct an industrial building, which Greenfeather hoped to name the Tecumseh building, the groundbreaking for which was held December 2, 1977. Jim said it was his father's idea to get a contract with someone in the East to build stainless steel sinks in hospitals. This was news to me, as I had always heard that the building was built to house a truck-driving school. In any case, the contractor hired to construct the industrial building disappeared, leaving an unfinished building along with $31,000 in unpaid bills. Ultimately the bonding company took care of the unpaid bills, but the building project was never completed for its original purpose.[119] The red metal barn sat unfinished and vacant until 1984, when entrepreneur David Allen entered into a contract with the Eastern Shawnee Tribe of Oklahoma. He remodeled the building and turned it into a bingo hall, the Eastern Shawnees' initial venture into gaming.[120] Greenfeather died in May 1983, prior to the December 7, 1984, opening, without seeing the building utilized. Nevertheless, had he not taken the bold leadership steps he took, the tribe might not be where it is today.

In 1978 the tribal park and recreation area was developed and named Tecumseh Park. Playground equipment from the Seneca Indian School was moved to this location, which is now part of the ceremonial grounds.[121] Also in 1978 plans were initiated to construct a second building on the 58.19 acres, the tribe's administration building. Following the construction of the BlueJacket Center in 1992, that original building came to be known as the education building, and it has housed the gaming commission since 2013.[122]

Before James Greenfeather, the Eastern Shawnee people dreamed of a time when they would have their own meeting spaces, their own enterprises. Each chief helped advance the tribe to make the dream become reality. Each held on, paving the way for the next chief. Before James Greenfeather, we were a tribe with 58.19 acres and a dream of development. After James Greenfeather, our tribe had a newsletter, a seal, a flag, a play, and buildings that would one day be used for the good of the Eastern Shawnee Tribe of Oklahoma. The dream continues.

GEORGE JACOB "BUCK" CAPTAIN (1922–1997)

"I see changes," George Jacob "Buck" Captain said regarding the Eastern Shawnee Tribe of Oklahoma in a 1994 interview.[123] The seventh Eastern Shawnee chief to be elected following the tribe's adoption of a constitution in 1939, Buck reflected on his life, stating, "I didn't know it, but I guess I've had an uncanny ability to figure things out that a lot of people couldn't see. And they turned out to be right, so I kind of established a reputation." Buck Captain used this uncanny ability throughout his life.[124]

Born August 14, 1922, in Ottawa County to Thomas A. Captain and Florence Longdan, he was one of nine children: brothers Thurman, John, Charles, Leo, and Dennis "Sandy" and sisters Thelma Captain Sullivan, Marjorie "Sue" Captain Kropp, and Virginia Captain Welch Hart. Recalling his early years, Buck relayed, "We lived in an oak house my dad built. I went to a country school, Moccasin Bend, District Number 5, and I went through the eighth grade there. My whole childhood was fairly rugged. I was raised during the Depression. We did have plenty to eat. We lived on a farm. We raised everything we had. But we didn't have any money. But we had a lot of company. It wasn't just us. It was everybody."[125]

Following high school graduation, Buck enlisted in the Air Force. On November 17, 1945, at the age of twenty-three, he married Betty Cole in Baxter Springs, Kansas. Becoming a career military man, Buck was in the Air Force for thirty years, serving the Security Service in the intelligence department. He flew more than twenty missions during World War II. During this time Buck and Betty became the parents of two sons, George Jacob IV and Sandy Nelis Captain.[126]

Buck retired from the military in the 1970s and returned to the Miami, Oklahoma, area. In 1978 he was elected chief, a position he held for eighteen years until he resigned in 1996. His son Nelis, who had been second chief, then became chief. Buck explained, "When my people moved to Oklahoma . . . our group most of them came from the Chillicothe Division in Ohio. That was the group that most always produced the Chiefs of the Shawnee Nation back in Indiana and Ohio. We always had a chief, my dad, Thomas Andrew Captain was a Chief for over twenty five years and my grandfather before him and so forth."[127]

Buck was an active chief. In 1984 a third building was constructed on the 58.19 acres. The first two, an administrative building and a still-unfinished industrial building, had been constructed during Chief James Greenfeather's term. The third was the nutrition building (now the Sandy Captain Cultural Building). Shortly thereafter, the previously empty and unfinished building opened on December 7, 1984 as the Eastern Shawnee Tribe of Oklahoma's bingo operation, catapulting the tribe into the gaming world. As a result of bingo profits, the tribe made its first land purchase in 1987, 112 acres on State Highway 10C.

In 1990 Buck made an unprecedented move. Knowing that the three federally recognized Shawnee tribes in Oklahoma had not been together as a single nation for almost two hundred years, Buck contacted the Absentee Shawnee Tribe, based near Little Axe, and the Loyal Shawnee Tribe and invited them to a dinner in the nutrition building. The rest is history. Governor Kenneth Blanchard, Chairman Ron Sparkman, and Chief Buck Captain met, and the three tribes have been trying to work together ever since.[128]

The year 1992 saw the construction of the BlueJacket Center, the adoption of a new constitution that made the position of chief a full-time position, and the purchase of the Rickner property—a sixty-acre parcel—for $40,000. In 1995 the tribe made its first purchase of 1,750 shares in People's Bank of Seneca at $200 per share. As of 2016 the value exceeds $1,000 per share.

In his final year as chief, Buck oversaw the establishment of the George F. Captain Library. That same year the Eastern Shawnees became a self-governance tribe and the tribe jointly established the Bearskin Clinic, a health venture, with the Wyandotte Nation of Oklahoma. Buck recalled that when the Eastern Shawnees were removed from Ohio, all they had were fifteen hoes, two chopping axes, and a blacksmith's shop. He thought that was appropriate because it signified that it was up to the individual to make a living. Buck wanted to see the tribe provide benefits, but even more important than that, he observed that in his lifetime, "the biggest change within the tribe has been going from poverty to being capable of holding good jobs. . . . I see changes." Buck Captain facilitated these changes.

NELIS CAPTAIN (1948–2000)

"I am not my father. I am not my father." It was a phrase Nelis Captain often repeated. And he was not, nor should he have been expected to be. On May 18, 1996, when his father George J. "Buck" Captain resigned in a special general council meeting, Nelis Captain, who had previously been second chief, became the eighth chief to serve the Eastern Shawnee Tribe of Oklahoma following its reorganization as a modern tribe in 1939.[129] Buck died one year and one day later, on May 19, 1997.

Nelis (more commonly referred to as Neil) and his father, Buck, were a study in contrasts. Neil worked at a fast pace. He could whip out a grant seemingly effortlessly. Ask for a letter, and you didn't leave to come back later because his response was "I'll have it for you within five minutes." And he did. He wrote fast, worked fast, made decisions fast. Buck, on the other hand, was methodical; he pondered over the words he chose, labored over his decisions, and mulled over his thoughts. They each demonstrated these traits in the minutest of tasks. Take, for instance, mowing the yard. Buck would take all afternoon to mow a lawn; placing the gear in slow mode, he would take his time to mow it to perfection. Neil, however, would get on that mower, put it in high gear, and he was off. Neil was high energy. It was as if he had unlimited tasks to accomplish, but limited time in which to complete them.

Born July 5, 1948, in Roswell, New Mexico, to Buck and Betty Cole Captain, he was the second of two sons. His father was a career military man, so Nelis Sandy Captain was an army brat. Later he joined the U.S. Army himself during the Vietnam War and built a distinguished record. During his service Neil received a National Defense Service Medal, a Vietnam Campaign Medal with a 1960 device, a Vietnam Service Medal with one bronze service star, a Combat Infantry-man Badge, a Bronze Star Medal, an Army Commendation Medal with an oak-leaf cluster and a V device, and a Purple Heart.

After leaving the military, Neil settled in Colorado. There he married Lillian "Lee" Carlson on April 26, 1974. He was employed as a firefighter and fire inspector for the Aurora, Colorado, fire department and was a member of the American Legion in Denver. In 1987 Neil and Lee relocated to Miami to be near his parents and his son, Scott, from a previous marriage.

Prior to serving as chief of the Eastern Shawnee Tribe of Oklahoma, Neil was employed at the Miami Nation as director of the Title VI program (the equivalent to the Shawnees' Administration on Aging nutrition program) and then as grant writer. Later he became a full-time employee as grant writer for the Eastern Shawnee Tribe of Oklahoma. Ron Kaiser, the Wyandotte planning director and longtime best friend of Nelis Captain, describes their first meeting:

> I met Nelis in 1987, when I wrote a successful Housing Rehab Grant for the Eastern Shawnee Tribe. At that time I worked at the Intertribal Council. Nelis asked me what the secret was for getting grants. I answered, "Just follow directions and listen to what the federal line staff has to say." I was being smart but Nelis thought it was funny. That conversation began our friendship. Nelis was the kind of person that could solve problems and would help anyone. Early one Saturday morning, when a renovation project went so wrong at my

house, it was Nelis who came to the rescue. Over the years that followed, my wife Mary and I became part of Nelis and Lee's family, spending holidays and meeting a broad range of local characters.[130]

Elected second chief when the tribe adopted its new constitution in 1994, Neil served as the day-to-day tribal administrator, as his father, Buck, chose not to make his position full time. Buck enjoyed his retirement as well as his travels and did not want to work full time. Thus when Neil became chief, he was the first chief of the Eastern Shawnee Tribe of Oklahoma to serve in a full-time paid position. It was one of many firsts for Neil. His first day as chief he made changes in the staff, a practice that is oftentimes unpopular but also not uncommon with the changing of the guard. It just hadn't been done before at the Eastern Shawnee Tribe. Being chief was a learning process for Neil, as he and the Business Committee struggled with the balance of power between the executive branch and the legislative branch as outlined in the new constitution. He was the first chief to sue the Business Committee. It was a complicated and trying time for everyone, but particularly for the Captain family. Having a Captain as the chief (Neil) and two Captain family members on the Business Committee (Sandy and Danny) made it even more difficult on them and on the extended family as well.

Although Neil Captain was chief for only seventeen months, he used his high energy to achieve two extremely important milestones that affect every Eastern Shawnee tribal citizen today. First, he gained for the Eastern Shawnees the designation as a self-governance tribe. This is important because tribes can avoid following a cookie-cutter model of governance predetermined by the Bureau of Indian Affairs. Self-governance enables tribes to determine their own needs rather than having people in Washington, D.C., determining what our needs are. Second, he entered into a joint venture with the Wyandotte Nation in the Bearskin Clinic. An additional contribution is that Neil Captain named the administration building the BlueJacket Center, and he also did the landscaping for the building.[131]

Nelis resigned in October 1997, the first chief in modern times to do so. Sadly, just as his tenure as chief was brief, so was his life. Nelis Sandy Captain died on April 18, 2000 at the age of fifty-one. His only child, Scott Captain, died in 2015. Chief Nelis Sandy Captain was the son of Chief George F. "Buck" Captain, who was the son of Chief Thomas A. Captain, who was the son of Chief Tom Captain (Nan-na-ha-ya-be-nuck), who was the son of Wau-a-ha-gu-ma (or Nan-ho-gom-we).[132] What a lineage! What a history! The Eastern Shawnee Tribe of Oklahoma would not be the tribe it is today without each of these chiefs.

GLEN BROCK: A SHAWNEE THINKER (B. 1956)

Born on leap day, the 29th of February, the ninth child in a family of nine children, and the ninth elected chief of the Eastern Shawnee Tribe of Oklahoma in modern times, Glen Brock followed John F. Kennedy's famous admonition from his 1961 inaugural address: "Ask not what your country can do for you; ask what you can do for your country." After attending Business Committee meetings for several years, Brock became interested in the tribal government and decided to run for the position of second chief, to which he was elected, unopposed, in 1996. When Chief Nelis Captain resigned, Glen Brock advanced to the position of chief in October 1997 to fill the vacancy as the constitution dictates. It was a position he neither asked for nor particularly wanted, but he served his tribe willingly and ably until the term ended in September, 1998, just shy of one year in office. He chose not to run for reelection.[133]

The son of Lawrence D. Brock and Ruthie May Tucker Brock, Glen was born February 29, 1956. His mother was the daughter of Silas Tucker and Mary Punch Tucker. Mary Punch was a full-blood Shawnee, and Silas Tucker was four-fourths Shawnee/Peoria. Thus Glen's mother was classified four-fourths Native American, meaning 100 percent Native American, just not 100 percent of one tribe, the technical definition of full blood. When Ruthie died at the age of ninety-five in 2013, she was the last person in the Eastern Shawnee Tribe of Oklahoma to be four-fourths Native American. An era had ended. Silas and Mary Punch Tucker were from White Oak, Oklahoma. Glen's mother, Ruthie May, was Shawnee/Peoria, but Glen proudly states that she always considered herself Eastern Shawnee, and all nine of the children are Eastern Shawnee: four daughters (Virginia Clark, Florence Routh, Geraldine Loftin, and Linda Shores) and five sons (Lawrence Duke, Johnny, Darrell, Gary, and Glen Brock).[134]

Glen was raised in the Oak Grove school district, near Peoria, Oklahoma. He went to grade school at Oak Grove, and then graduated from Quapaw High School. After receiving his high school diploma, he attended Northeastern Oklahoma A&M College (NEO A&M) in Miami, Oklahoma, receiving a certificate in marketing and management. He then changed majors and graduated with an associate of arts degree in nursing. He passed state boards, becoming a registered nurse. He didn't stop there, but continued his education at Southwest Missouri State University in Springfield, Missouri, graduating with a bachelor of science degree in nursing in 1986.[135] He continues to work in his chosen field of nursing today.

Even though his education and his career kept him busy, Chief Glen Brock always found time—or more appropriately, made time—to serve his tribe. He first began attending Business Committee meetings when he was a teenager. At that time the tribe did not have any buildings, so the meetings took place in the Ottawa Tribal Building across from NEO A&M. He has attended every Eastern Shawnee annual powwow since its inception, serving on the original powwow committee, and then as chairman of the powwow committee for several years.

Those cultural traditions led him to become interested in tribal government. During his tenure as chief, he and the Business Committee were involved in several endeavors. The first was the acquisition of additional shares in People's Bank of Seneca. Chief Brock indicated that he was also in negotiations with the city of Fort Scott, Kansas, and with the state of Kansas to place a gaming facility on property near the Eastern Shawnees' motel in Fort Scott. Other projects included planning for a convenience store and truck plaza on the property on State Highway 10C and discussion of expanding the sewer treatment plant at Seneca to accommodate continued growth at the tribal complex. The tribe obtained a grant of more than one million dollars for the housing authority and began planning for the current housing development. Chief Brock indicated that during his time as chief he enjoyed interacting with tribal members and other Indian people. He stated that he learned the meaning of being a sovereign nation.[136]

In a statement for this book, Chief Brock wrote,

> Our tribe has come a long way from a time when the Business Committee met in the Ottawa Tribal Building across from NEO A&M College when I was a teenager and first attended these meetings. I believe our success has been due to very strong, intelligent, forward-thinking individuals. Our tribal heritage comes from a historically independent and wise people. I think for all Shawnees to continue to exist as a sovereign people, we will have to work together to maintain tradition and culture, maximize our effort to learn our Shawnee language, which is an integral part of our being, as Shawnee people.[137]

Glen Brock lived up to the challenge of doing what he could for his tribe, our tribe. He continues to work in the nursing field, continues to be one of the "seven in seven,"—a term his mother, Ruthie May, laughingly referred to as seven of her nine children living within seven miles of each other—and continues to "think Shawnee," a phrase he used to end every article he wrote for the tribal newsletter, *The Shooting Star.*

CHARLES ENYART (B. 1936)

At six feet two inches, when Charles Enyart enters a room, people notice. His height comes from the Captain line, where it is not uncommon for the men and women to be tall. It certainly did not come from the Enyart side, where the men tend to be—well, to be blunt—short. But he has always stood tall, even as a young man. And that is his distinguishing characteristic.

Born to Champ and Vergie Crain Enyart on November 24, 1936, at Pawnee Indian Hospital, Charles Dewayne Enyart was the second of what would ultimately be five children. He always questioned why his mother had to spell his middle name the way she did, and he had to wonder why the third child, a sister named Glenna, had to be born on his birthday two years later. He grew up in the Eastside Community, nine miles east of Miami, where most of the land had been allotted to Eastern Shawnee tribal members. His youth was spent on the allotted land of his grandmother, Sarah Captain Crain, a woman he never met as she died at age twenty-nine, when his mother was only seven years old. Living in a rural area, it was only natural for him to be introduced to hunting, fishing, swimming in creeks, milking cows, slopping pigs, butchering hogs, smoking grapevines, and playing sports. Graduating from the eighth grade at Moccasin Bend No. 5, he then went to Wyandotte High School and graduated in 1954.

In high school he emerged as a leader. Beginning in his freshman year, he played football and basketball, the two dominant sports at Wyandotte High School. In his senior year he was the captain of both winning teams. His fellow classmates elected him most likely to succeed as well as class president, a role he still feels responsible for more than sixty years later. He has kept his classmates connected; his 1954 graduating class raised more money throughout the years for Wyandotte High School than any other class in the school's history. Today that money is set aside for scholarship purposes. Also, years after graduating, he was honored with the Outstanding Alumni of Wyandotte High School award. He never had a car in high school, never had possessions, and had to hitchhike each weekend to and from Miami if he wanted to attend a movie.[138] But he always had friends and he always stood tall.

Following high school graduation, Enyart enlisted in the United States Army, where he served four years, some of it overseas. He then went to college on the G.I. Bill, enrolling at NEO A&M at Miami while working at the Eastern State Hospital mental facility at Vinita. He ultimately transferred to Pittsburg State University at Pittsburg, Kansas, where he earned a bachelor's degree with an emphasis in psychology. While he worked at Eastern State Hospital, he met and married Betty, a single mother with three children—Gary, Cathy, and Ronnie—whom he later adopted. Making the Vinita area their home, Charles went on to the University of Oklahoma, where he received his master's degree and was honored as the outstanding social worker of his graduating class. He remembers those lean times, when he was working his way through college, as a time when he and his family ate lots of neck bones and chicken wings. He continued to work at Eastern State Hospital until he retired in 1995.[139]

It was after retirement from Eastern State Hospital that Enyart became involved in tribal matters. He was first elected as third councilperson in 1996, then ran for and was elected chief in 1998. He was then reelected to another four-year term in 2002 and retired in December 2006. Ordinarily, his term would have ended in September, but he remained chief an additional three months while a run-off election was conducted to determine his successor.[140]

His eight-year tenure was an active time for the Eastern Shawnee Tribe of Oklahoma. The land at BlueJacket Complex is in a floodplain, and the Department of Housing and Urban Development ruled that federal money could not fund projects in floodplains. In response, Enyart turned his vision to the 112 acres on State Highway 10C that had been purchased in 1988 and the contiguous 221 acres purchased in 1997 (two lots, or forty-eight acres, of that land were designated for the housing authority). First came the housing authority buildings—twelve existed at that time. Next, he contracted the services of Sherry Rackliff, a dedicated and gifted grant writer employed by the Delaware Tribe. She wrote a grant for the Eastern Shawnees' water system and for the social service building, which is now occupied by the tribal administrator, accounting, and the Environmental Protection Agency. The building was built in 2001 with dedication services scheduled for September of that year. A week before the dedication, the 9/11 attacks occurred. At a time when the rest of the world was cancelling events, Enyart said that the dedication would go forward, as would our tribe and our nation.[141]

Other construction projects during his tenure included the travel center, an addition to the old bingo hall that culminated with the 2003 completion of Bordertown Casino and Bingo, a structure of more than 56,000 square feet and costing more than $7 million, which was paid in cash. During this time the tribe also purchased a motel in Fort Scott, Kansas, with intentions of pursuing gaming there. Those plans never came to fruition, and ultimately the hotel was sold.[142]

Policies, procedures, and programs received major attention during Enyart's time as chief. The Twenty-Year Plan was formulated, the tribal tag program was implemented, tribal photo CDIB cards were initiated, the revenue sharing formula was developed and implemented, and the first annual tribal golf tournament was hosted.[143]

Enyart expended a great deal of energy attempting to open Ohio to gaming for the Eastern Shawnee Tribe. He was one of two Oklahoma Indian leaders selected to testify before Congress, telling them that federal rules regulating tribal acquisition of "off-reservation land for casinos are strict enough and that an outright prohibition isn't necessary." In addition to being active nationally, he served as chairman of the Claremore Indian Hospital Board and vice chairman of the local Inter-Tribal Council, and he was appointed by Governor Keating to the Oklahoma Indian Affairs Commission.[144]

Gaming flourished during Enyart's tenure. Revenues from gaming increased, and tribal citizens enjoyed increased benefits. But there were difficulties and challenges in these years as well. The adoption of a new tribal constitution in 1994 brought with it legal challenges of interpretation. Several lawsuits involving individual tribal members or members of the Business Committee were filed against Enyart. Some threatened to recall him. He was victorious in each incident.

In 2006 Enyart chose not to run for reelection. As of 2016 he lives in Vinita near his three children and his grandchildren. He and his wife, Betty, also raised one granddaughter and one great-grandson, who recently graduated from high school. Betty passed away in 2014. Enyart remains active in his church, where he is a deacon, and continues to be interested in the tribe.

Six feet two inches—that's tall. Serving your country—that's tall. Being willing to sacrifice for your family by routinely eating boiled neck bones or chicken wings—that's tall. Charles Enyart, tenth chief of the Eastern Shawnee Tribe of Oklahoma in modern elected times, is a tall man. His footprints are firmly implanted.[145]

NOTES

1. *Indian Affairs: Law and Treaties*, comp. and ed. Charles J. Kappler (1904; Washington, D.C.: Government Printing Office, 1904), 2: 117, 147, 162, 327–31, 381–85 (hereafter *Indian Affairs*).

2. Memorial of the Ladies of Steubenville, Ohio, to the United States Senate and the House of Representatives, 1830, in Walter Hixson, *American Foreign Relations: A New Diplomatic History* (New York: Routledge, 2015), 53–54.

3. *Indian Affairs*, 2: 330, 383.

4. United States, *Laws of the United States of America: From the 4th of March, 1789, to the [3rd of March, 1845]: Including the Constitution of the United States, the Old Act of Confederation, Treaties, and Many Other Valuable Ordinances and Documents; with Copious Notes and References*, (Philadelphia: J. Bioren and W. J. Duane; 1815–1845), 8:145.

5. Vine Deloria Jr. and Raymond J. DeMallie, eds., *Documents of American Indian Diplomacy: Treaties, Agreements, and Conventions, 1775–1979* (Norman: University of Oklahoma Press, 1999), 3:850–53.

6. *Indian Affairs,* 2:105–106.

7. Numerous Eastern Shawnee citizens can trace their lineage to John and Ke-ne-fe-ase Jackson, including the Deweese family, the Amos family, and the Daugherty family as well as the Hamptons, Hausers, and Dushanes.

8. Muriel H. Wright, *A Guide to the Indian Tribes of Oklahoma* (Norman: University of Oklahoma Press, 1951). An excerpt of Wright's book is available on the Seneca-Cayuga Nation website, http://SCTribe.com/history/a-guide-to-the-Indian-tribes-of-ok-excerpts, accessed March 5, 2015.

9. "Taylor Davis," U.S. Census Bureau, Fourteenth Census of the United States, 1920—Population, Ottawa County, Oklahoma, image of records available at FamilySearch.org.

10. "Treaty of the Maumee Rapids (1817)," OhioHistoryCentral.org; Treaty With the Seneca, Etc. (July 20, 1831), 7 Stat. 351.

11. Charles Banks Wilson, *Indians of Eastern Oklahoma including Quapaw Agency Indians* (Afton, Okla.: Buffalo Publishing, 1956), 25–26; Randall Buchman, *A Sorrowful Journey* (Defiance, Ohio: Defiance College Press, 2007), 15, 59.

12. Treaty with the Seneca and Shawnee (December 29, 1832), 7 Stat. 411.

13. Treaty with the Senecas and Senecas and Shawnees (October 4, 1861), Statutes at Large of the Provisional Government of the Confederate States of America, *Documenting the American South*, University of North Carolina at Chapel Hill, http://DocSouth.unc.edu/imls/19conf/19conf.html#p374.

14. Jeff Konrei Minde, "July 3, 1862—The Battle of Cowskin Prairie," *Once a Civil War*, http://Konrei CivilWar.blogspot.com/2013/06/july-3-1862-battle-of-cowskin-prairie.html; Velma Nieberding, *The History of Ottawa County,* (Marceline, Mo.: Walsworth Publishing 1983).

15. Treaty with the Cherokee and Other Tribes in the Indian Territory September 13, 1865, *Indian Affairs,* 2:1050; Deloria and DeMallie, *Documents,* 2:1355; Treaty with the Seneca, Mixed Seneca and Shawnee, Quapaw, Etc. (February 23, 1867), 15 Stat. 513.

16. 1868, Annual Report of the Commissioner of Indian Affairs (hereafter ARCIA), Documents Relating to Indian Affairs, History Collection, University of Wisconsin Digital Collections; for a brief definition of the Indian Appropriation Act, see Peter Nabokov and Lawrence Loendorf, *Restoring a Presence: American Indians and Yellowstone Park* (Norman: University of Oklahoma Press, 2004), 34.

17. Frank H. Harris, ed., "Neosho Agency 1838–1871," in *Chronicles of Oklahoma,* 43, (1965): 45.

18. Chris Chaney, "From This Corner" *Shooting Star* (Eastern Shawnee Tribe newsletter), February 2015.

19. Nieberding, *History of Ottawa County,* 306.

20. Treaty with the Seneca, Mixed Seneca and Shawnee, Quapaw, etc., 1867, arts. 5, 8, 12, 16, *Indian Affairs,* 2:961–64.

21. D. D. Dyer to Hon. H. Price, July 29, 1881, Item 1881 RG75LR13351B32, Eastern Shawnee Tribe of Oklahoma Digital Collection.

22. Eastern Shawnee Annuity Roll, 1871, Enoch Hoag, Annual Report of the Central Superintendency, ARCIA, October 5, 1871, 461.

23. Troy O. Bickham, "Blackfish (1729?–1779)," *Oxford Dictionary of National Biography*, Oxford University Press, 2004, www.OxfordDNB.com/view/article/74802; Don Greene, *Shawnee Heritage I: Shawnee Genealogy and Family History* (Oregon: Vision ePublications, 2008).

24. *Indian Affairs,* 2:330; Buchman, *Sorrowful Journey,* 29; Lewistown Reservation Muster Roll, 1832, in the author's possession.

25. *Indian Affairs,* 2:385; Heirship Cards for Ke-ne-fe-ase and John Jackson, Eastern Shawnee Tribe of Oklahoma Digital Collection, www.OhioMemory.org/cdm/landingpage/collection/p16007coll27 /id/8600/rec/1; Tombstone of Ke-ne-fe-ase, Calamus Pond Cemetery, Oklahoma.

26. Larry K. Hancks, *The Emigrant Tribes: Wyandot, Delaware & Shawnee, a Chronology* (Kansas City, Kan.: Larry K. Hancks, 2003), www.Wyandot.org/emigrant.htm; Records of the Secretary of the Interior, Record Group 48.5.4 (Records of the Indian Division), National Archives and Records Administration.

27. 1852, ARCIA, 104.

28. Articles of Agreement Made and Concluded at Quapaw Agency, Indian Territory, June 23, 1874, between the United States, by United States Indian Agent, and the Eastern Shawnee Indians, 1882, ARCIA, 271.

29. Eastern Shawnee Tribal Rolls for 1870; Eastern Shawnee Tribal Rolls for 1872.

30. *Journal of the Sixth Annual Session of the General Council of the Indian Territory*, (Lawrence, Kans.: Republican Journal Steam Printing Establishment, 1875); "Journal of the Indian Territory," *Chronicles of Oklahoma* 3, no. 1 (March, 1925): 34.

31. Quapaw Agency Monthly Report January/February 1876; Buchman, *Sorrowful Journey*, 29.

32. Articles of Agreement, 19; "Aged Shawnee's Spirit Goes to Happy Hunting Ground after Feast and Tribal Ceremonial," *Miami Record-Herald*, September 17, 1920.

33. Quapaw Agency Competency Commission reports (Eastern Shawnee), Record Group 75, 7RA36, roll 1, 973.

34. D. C. Gideon, *Indian Territory: Descriptive Biographical and Genealogical Including the Landed Estates, County Seats Etc., Etc. with a General History of the Territory,* (New York: Lewis Publishing, 1901); Lamont Laird, e-mail correspondence with Glenna J. Wallace, February 28, 2016; Census papers for the Shawnee Tribe of Indians within the Fort Leavenworth Agency for the Year 1842.

35. Quapaw Agency Competency Commission Reports, 973; Laird e-mail.

36. Ibid.

37. Quapaw Agency Competency Commission reports, 973; Laird to Wallace, February 28, 2016.

38. Articles of Agreement, 19; Laird to Wallace, February 28, 2016.

39. Estate of Sa-pa-ta-wa-se Flint February 10, 1921, Department of the Interior, Office of Indian Affairs.

40. Laird e-mail.

41. Grace Dixon interview, "A Stroll down Memory Lane," *The Shooting Star*, May 1985.

42. Ibid.

43. Ibid.

44. Ibid.

45. Laird e-mail.

46. *Miami News Record Herald*, September 19, 1920, quoted in Nieberding, *History*.

47. Numbered among his descendants are other Captains, the Ross family, the Dixon family, the Hampton family, the Crain family, the Rickner family, the Kropp family, the Sullivan family, the Huggins family, the Mitchell family, the Enyart family, the Sherwood family, the Devine family, the Miller family, the Hoevet family, the Wallace family, and the Purvis family et al.

48. In his May 15, 1970, interview with Velma Nieberding, shortly after he had become chief, Clyde BlueJacket referenced a Shawnee cemetery "located some three miles, or maybe three and half west of Seneca." The written transcript calls the road "Lawstreet Road," but in all probability BlueJacket said "Lost Creek Road," because the transcriptionist also states the cemetery was on the west side of "Modoc Bryant," which is more likely Modoc Branch. The cemetery is called Cress Pond Cemetery. When asked why it was called Cress Pond (two words in the transcript) Cemetery, BlueJacket explained by stating, "Well, they have that water cress growing, around the spring there right at it. And they call it the Cresspond [one word] Cemetery." Today we know it as Calamus Pond Cemetery.

49. Lola Purvis, Shawnee genealogist, interview with Glenna Wallace; Quapaw Agency Report, 1910, Record Group 75, 1021.

50. Nina Dushane letter, 1960, relating a story told to her by her father, Charles Dushane Sr., in the possession of the Dushane family.

51. Ibid.

52. United States President, "Modoc Reservation," *Executive Orders Relating to Indian Reservations, May 14, 1855–July 1, 1912* (Washington, D.C.: Government Printing Office, 1912), 1:144.

53. Correspondence with the Central Superintendency, 1871–18711875–78, Quapaw Agency Monthly Report, January/February 1876, Records of the Miami (Quapaw) Indian Agency, Record Group 75.

54. Some Eastern Shawnees believe that John Jackson Jr. died in 1877. That belief possibly stems from a letter written by Chief David Dushane in which he states that John Jackson Jr. died about the year of 1877. However, the 1882 letter cited proves that the 1877 date is inaccurate. "Commemoration Ceremony, Honoring Our Ancestors," December 13, 2012, www.ESToO-nsn.gov/wp-content/uploads/2012/12/commemoration-handout.pdf.

55. James Jackson (John's brother) married Laura Jaco or Lah le quah. James died prior to allotment and Laura died November 17, 1901. They were the parents of one child, Jane Jackson Daugherty Pender. Nancy married David Dushane Sr., and they were the parents of four sons—Andrew, Charles, David, and Daniel. Two of them became chiefs: Andrew and David Jr. David Dushane Sr. died November 20, 1910, and Nancy the following year, December 1911.

56. For more on the family of George Beaver and Amanda Splitlog, see Carrie Ann Cook and Fredrea Cook, *Ottawa County Families, Volume 1* (Wyandotte, Okla.: Gregath, 2002), with an index available online at www.GregathCompany.com/ottco/v1Index.html.

57. For particular details related to George Beaver, see "Eastern Shawnee Census, 1890, Quapaw Agency" and "George Beaver Heirship Card" on the Eastern Shawnee Tribe of Oklahoma Digital Collection, www.OhioMemory.org/cdm/search/collection/p16007coll27/searchterm/George%20Beaver/order/nosort; Agreement with the Eastern Shawnee, June 23, 1874, Deloria and DeMallie, *Documents of American Indian Diplomacy*, 1:260. For T. J. Price, see 1890, ARCIA, 83–84.

58. United States Indian Service, Cheyenne and Arapahoe Indian Agency.

59. Quapaw Agency Report, 1910, Record Group 75, 986; Jack Dushane interview, March 2016.

60. John P. Bowes, e-mail, March 2, 2016. See chapter 3 of this book for more information regarding allotments.

61. Jack Dushane to Glenna Wallace, May 6, 2014, in author's possession; Nannie Lee Burns, interview with David Dushane Jr., October 26, 1937, Indian-Pioneer Papers Oral History Collection, Western History Collections, University of Oklahoma, Norman.

62. See C. M. Barbeau, *Huron and Wyandot Mythology* (Ottawa: Government Printing Bureau, 1915), available online at https://babel.HathiTrust.org/cgi/pt?id=uc1.32106000740347;view=1up;seq=15; Quapaw Agency Report, 1910, Record Group 75, 1002.

63. Colleen Carpenter interview with Glenna Wallace, April 2014; Jeff Bowen, *Indian Wills 1911–1921: Records of the Bureau of Indian Affairs* (Baltimore: Clearfield, 2007).

64. Earlene Angel Roskob and Sallie Cotter Andrews, "Rebecca Hicks Dushane," *Wyandotte Nation*, www.Wyandotte-Nation.org/traditions/biographical-panels/rebecca-hicks-dushane/; when Walter BlueJacket died in office, second chief David Dushane succeeded him.

65. T. A. Captain, "Minutes," October 22, 1928, Quapaw Indian Agency, Miami, Oklahoma, Record Group 75.

66. Judy Brown, Janice Brossett, and Jeff BlueJacket, interview with Glenna Wallace, July 25, 2011. Research compiled in 2015 at the Fort Worth Archives reveals that Walter L. BlueJacket was chief longer than originally known. In a document dated April 26, 1928, at the request of Mr. Lloyd LaMotte, chief clerk of the Quapaw Indian Agency at Miami, Oklahoma, J. E. DeVore provided the names of various tribal business committees to Mr. J. L. Suffecool, agency superintendent. A statement is provided for the Shawnees: "No active committee, two of the old members are Chas. Dushane, Councilman, John Prophet, Secy." A note at the end states, "The Seneca and Wyandotte committees are elected for life or until a vacancy occurs through the member moving away." Records of the Quapaw Indian Agency, Record Group 75. United States Department of the Interior, Indian Field Service, Wyandotte, Oklahoma, April 26, 1928, 5–1142.

67. October 22, 1928, Records of the Quapaw Indian Agency, Record Group 75.

68. Ibid.

69. Ibid.

70. Ibid.

71. Ibid.

72. Brown, Brossett, and BlueJacket interview.

73. Walter BlueJacket and Brenda Himes, interview with Glenna Wallace, August 1, 2011.

74. Bobby BlueJacket interview with Glenna Wallace, August 3, 2011.

75. Glen Stoner interview with Glenna Wallace, August 3, 2011.

76. Brown, Brossett, and BlueJacket interview.

77. The Deaver correspondence is located in Records of the Miami Agency, Record Group 75, E.1, box 4.

78. Brown, Brossett, and BlueJacket interview.

79. Walter BlueJacket and Brenda Himes interview.

80. Constitution and By-Laws of the Eastern Shawnee Tribe of Oklahoma, December 22, 1939, available at http://thorpe.ou.edu/IRA/okeshawcons.html.

81. *Seneca News Dispatch*, May 6, 1954.

82. David Dushane, interview with Nannie Lee Burns October 26, 1937, Indian-Pioneer Papers Oral History Collection.

83. Bud Nelson, interview with Glenna Wallace, January 2011. According to Dave, "the balance of our land was sold to Judge Harvey of Wyandotte."

84. Ibid.

85. Ibid.

86. Glenna Wallace, "From This Corner: David Dushane, Jr., Second Chief of Eastern Shawnee Tribe of Oklahoma," Chiefs of the Eastern Shawnee Tribe of Oklahoma, http://history.estoo-nsn.gov/wp-content/uploads/2015/01/FROM-THIS-CORNER-Eastern-Shawnee-Chief-David-Dushane.pdf.

87. Marcella Dee Griffith interview with Glenna Wallace, January 2011.

88. Ibid.

89. Bud Nelson interview.

90. Howard Moore, "Rural Ramblings," *The Neosho Daily News*, December 14, 1954; Bud Nelson interview.

91. Larry Kropp interview with Glenna Wallace, February 2011.

92. Tom Captain, interview with J. W. Tyner, September 16, 1969, Doris Duke Oral History Collection, Western History Collections, University of Oklahoma, Norman.

93. Ibid.

94. Brown, Brossett, and BlueJacket interview.

95. Ibid.

96. Ibid.

97. Ibid.

98. Acts of August 1–3, 1956, which terminated the federal relationship with Wyandotte, Ottawa, Modoc, and Peoria Tribes of Oklahoma.

99. *Seneca News Dispatch*, May 6, 1954.

100. Nieberding, *History*, 238.

101. Obituaries, *Miami News-Record*, 1970.

102. Ibid.

103. Brown, Brossett, and BlueJacket interview.

104. Personal knowledge of Glenna Wallace.

105. Bobby BlueJacket interview with Glenna Wallace, November 2012.

106. Nieberding, *History*.

107. "Clyde BlueJacket," Find A Grave Memorial, http://FindaGrave.com/cgi-bin/fg.cgi?page=gr& GRid=9425151.

108. Bobby BlueJacket interview, November 2012.

109. Nieberding, *History*.

110. Bobby BlueJacket interview, November 2012.

111. Glenna Wallace, "From This Corner," *The Shooting Star* (December 2012).

112. The Eastern Shawnee bingo hall opened December 7, 1984.

113. Glen Brock interview with Glenna Wallace, 2013.

114. Little Jim Greenfeather (son of Chief Greenfeather) interview with Glenna Wallace, January 2013.

115. Ibid.

116. Ibid.

117. Ibid.

118. Nieberding, *History*.

119. Greenfeather interview.

120. Melanie Chase interview with Glenna Wallace, March 2010.

121. Perry Hauser interview with Glenna Wallace, April 2014.

122. Ibid.

123. George J. "Buck" Captain, interview with in Rita Kohn and William Lynwood Montell, eds., *Always a People: Oral Histories of Contemporary Woodland Indians* (Indianapolis: Indiana Historical Society, 1996), 56–62.

124. Ibid.

125. Nieberding, *History*.

126. Ibid.

127. Ibid.

128. Personal archive of Glenna Wallace.

129. Eastern Shawnee General Council Minutes, May 18, 1996.

130. Ron Kaiser interview with Glenna Wallace, April 2012.

131. Personal knowledge of Glenna Wallace

132. Larry Kropp interview.

133. Glen Brock interview.

134. Ibid.

135. Ibid.

136. Ibid.

137. Ibid.

138. Sonny Jones (high school classmate of Charles Enyart) interview with Glenna Wallace, August 2013.

139. Ibid.

140. Ibid.

141. Ibid.

142. Ibid.

143. Ibid.

144. Ibid.

145. Charles Enyart's family is as follows: great-grandfather Tom Captain, 1853–1920; grandmother Sarah Captain Crain, 1892–1921; father Champ Clark Enyart, 1911–1985; mother Vergie Ellen Crain Enyart, 1913–2005; sister Jean Buxton, 1934–2011; sister Glenna J. Wallace, b. 1938; sister Dixie Martin, b. 1941; brother Bud Enyart, b. 1943; three adopted children Gary, Ronnie, and Kathy.

PART III
BECOMING OUR OWN STORYTELLERS

In a recent essay, the novelist, literary critic, and Leech Lake Ojibwe tribal citizen David Treuer describes how "language and cultural revitalization are the new activism" in both urban and rural indigenous communities.[1] In the chapters that follow, Benjamin J. Barnes and Catherine Osborne-Gowey are prime examples of the new activism. As second chief of the Shawnee Tribe, Ben has become an avocational linguist, archaeologist, and historian. Together with Chief Wallace, Ben has done a great deal to restore the long-dormant connection between his people and their homeland in the middle Ohio valley. In contrast, Eastern Shawnee tribal citizen Catherine Osborne-Gowey devotes much of her time and energy to domestic violence prevention programs in her community. Finally, Elsie Mae Hoevet left behind an extraordinarily intimate life history for her grandchildren. She survived many hardships, from boarding schools and the Dust Bowl to migration to Oregon. Nevertheless, she embodied resilience through adversity. More than anything else, she wanted her grandchildren to know that "life is not a bed of roses, it's a book of experiences; and if you really weigh them against each other, the good seems to overbalance the bad." Thankfully, with her family's permission, we can all regard her sage advice.

Each in their own way, Barnes, Osborne-Gowey, and Hoevet showcase how tribal communities are now telling their own stories. Like so many tribal citizens and authors in this volume, they demonstrate that Native peoples are no longer dependent on non-Native scholars for basic knowledge about their people. Indeed, it is our hope that the Administration for Native Americans grant, "A Search for Eastern Shawnee History," becomes the foundation for grassroots activism and scholarship for years to come.

NOTE

1. David Treuer, "The Cultural Twilight," *American Indian Culture and Research Journal* 35, no. 1 (Winter 2011): 53, 49.

9

Becoming Our Own Storytellers

Tribal Nations Engaging with Academia

BENJAMIN J. BARNES, SECOND CHIEF, SHAWNEE TRIBE

For more than eighty years, the three federally recognized Shawnee tribes have initiated conversations with scholars, dignitaries, and institutions in our ancestral homelands. The persistent goal has been to create opportunities to form collaborative relationships with stakeholders in our ancestral lands. By examining the histories of these shared dialogues and projects, along with our successes and failures, I hope to encourage academics and tribal citizen-scholars to reach out and create networks in the old homelands that our peoples vacated during the removal era. Tribal citizens awakened to past missteps as well as the rewards of engagement can use these networks to rediscover and further understand our past and present. The digital age has given us unprecedented access to our ancestral records. By working with academia, we can unlock the treasure trove of ethnographic materials and rehabilitate it with cultural sensitivities and understandings. Beyond the benefits of scholarship, these relationships become valuable to all participants, and from these partnerships the nations have developed strong allies on indigenous issues in our ancestral homelands. Through the active engagement of Shawnee citizens and leaders with our institutional partners, we have created valued, lasting partnerships with a variety of institutions, including the Ohio History Connection, the University of Iowa, the Ohio State University at Newark, Indiana University at Bloomington's Glenn A. Black Laboratory of Archaeology, and many of the historic sites across our homeland. These renewed and fragile relationships created by the three federally recognized Shawnee tribes and our academic allies help us to reinterpret the past with an eye on the future, and we now act as our own advocates, interpreters, and storytellers in the homelands of our ancestors.

When I travel in the old homelands of the Ohio valley, I often find myself among professors, historic societies, and institutions. I feel compelled to remind those educators, archaeologists, and anthropologists that when we Shawnee people speak about our ancestors, they are not abstractions for us. The people of our past still live in recent memory with us through our stories, traditions, and ceremonies. We continue to honor their perseverance and tenacity and can see how they enabled the modern Shawnee tribes to survive.[1] This living memory of our ancestors may seem foreign to non-Native students of history, but for Shawnee people, we remember them at our Bread Dance, our War Dance, our death feasts, and in the stories we tell our children. Even when we recall them in the most agnostic of ways, such as researching family histories and genealogies, our ancestors live on through collective memory. In contrast, academics have a deeply ingrained habit of describing our ancestors in impersonal, abstract ways. For us, as Shawnee people, we see how this leads to error-plagued assumptions about the history and culture of the Shawnee people. We know that these errors sometimes result in paternalistic decisions regarding our federal right to protect the graves of our ancestors and the ancient, sacred places in the East that my people once called home.

Non-Native readers should imagine their own homes, lands, and precious belongings. While we consider all of the comforts of our homes, imagine that some dire family emergency arises and we must leave our homes and all our belongings behind. This place where we were born, where our people have lived for generations, and where our beloved departed ancestors rest in the soil beneath must be left behind for an unspecified period of time. Our urgency to leave does not allow us the time to arrange for our household, precious belongings, and departed family members.

Perhaps after we have left, there might be the well-intentioned neighbor who has decided to watch our house for us. As time wears on, those intentions fade, and soon the house is overrun with people rifling through the silver drawer, vandalizing the walls, breaking windows, defacing old family photos, defiling our most important religious symbols, and creating caricatures of our beliefs. Even more time passes, and we still have yet to return home. People begin to talk among themselves and create false stories about us and our homes. Soon, people impose their own imagined idea of us on what remains of our presence. Some even claim to be our long-lost cousins, and they often act in our name. Self-proclaimed gurus have moved into our master bedroom and founded a club for new-age spiritualists. Someone even has taken down the old family Bible and begun inserting their own family's names into our family tree in an attempt to establish some sort of kinship and claim to our cherished home and land.

For Native people such as myself, the forced removal of my ancestors is part of my inheritance. The first time Shawnees returned to our homelands to reclaim our ancestors' legacy, if not their belongings, was both exhilarating and degrading. It seemed as if Shawnees were brought in to fill the public's appetite to celebrate the conquest of the Indian. In the fall of 1931, Thomas Wildcat Alford, an Absentee Shawnee, returned to Xenia, Ohio. Alford had been educated at boarding schools and later advocated for the allotment of reservation lands in Oklahoma. He traveled to Ohio as the guest of William Albert Galloway, a man who had something of an obsession with Tecumseh, our most famous Shawnee warrior. Thomas Wildcat Alford was a direct descendant of Tecumseh, and so he served Galloway's needs. One of the accounts of Alford's month-long visit to the homeland occurs in the Xenia newspaper, *The Evening Gazette.* The paper describes how dignitaries, local clergy, and "Chief Alford" traveled to a local cemetery to dedicate the new entryway to the graveyard of the hallowed dead early-Ohio settlers and war veterans.[2] On the very same page of the paper, there is another article, which gleefully regales the reader with a more macabre story. Headlined SKELETON, RELIC OF PAST, TAKES RIDE IN AUTO, the story describes how a complete Native American skeleton had been excavated from a local mound and driven through town in a shiny, brand-new automobile. The dissonance of the newspaper editor could not have been any more painful for the modern Shawnee reader. But it gets worse. The newspaper reported that Alford's visit and our ancestor's ride in the automobile were dated October 5, 1931—the centennial of the Shawnees' removal from Ohio and the anniversary of Tecumseh's death at the Battle of Thames.[3]

William Galloway had more than just an interest in Alford, Tecumseh, and the Shawnees. He was in pursuit of a family legend involving his ancestor Rebecca Galloway. Locals believed that she had a romantic relationship with Tecumseh. William Galloway subsequently created a vision of courtship between Rebecca and "Tecumtha" that included star-crossed lovers, a doomed suitor plagued by conflicts between his people, the Christian Rebecca Galloway, and an imminent war that would separate them forever.[4]

Galloway's romance resonated well with his audiences in the Ohio valley. The story of a fair maiden equipped with beauty, virtue, and Christian faith, who sought to convert the noble savage and save him from his inevitable doom, played well in our former homeland. On the Newberry Library's *Indians of the Midwest* website historian R. David Edmunds states, "We know that their paths may have crossed, but there's no evidence at all, no historic evidence at all, that there was any kind of relationship there."[5]

Despite the complete lack of evidence for Galloway's family fable, the legend persists to the present day. The public, hungry to feed romantic notions of the vanishing noble savage, can enjoy a performance of Galloway's myth written for the theatre by the novelist Allen Eckert. Since May 1970, the outdoor drama *Tecumseh!* has been an annual event in Chillicothe, Ohio. This fictional portrayal of Tecumseh and Native Americans dressed in garish outfits does not represent Shawnee material cultural traditions, or any of the peoples of the Ohio valley. Shawnee people have visited the outdoor drama as recently as June 2014, when a group of Absentee Shawnees visited the spectacle as audience members. It is my hope that someday Shawnees will be able to visit with the cast and crew of *Tecumseh!* as advisors rather than as ticket holders.

Books, dramas, and daily news presses were not the only ones to feed into the public notion of the "vanishing Indian." Universities began to document our people in a misguided attempt to salvage what they could of the Shawnees before we became extinct. Near the end of the nineteenth century, academics began to flood into Shawnee communities in Kansas and Oklahoma, seeking to fill notebooks with data about our culture, language, and religion. Salvage anthropologists, ethnographers, and linguists were not interested in preserving the material for our latter generations; rather they published their research with very little context or input from the communities from which they reaped their information. In spite of what professors and researchers thought were noble intentions, they, too, reinforced the idea that the Indian has simply vanished from the Ohio valley. With the wave of a newspaper and sheets of research, the sons and daughters of the colonizers were able to wipe away the sins of their forebears.

In the 1980s Shawnees once again returned to the homelands of our people. They had received letters and information from people back east, telling of Shawnees who had defied the odds during removal and remained behind. I remember the contingent of eager, yet skeptical, White Oak Shawnees who went back to Ohio to meet our supposed long-lost kin. What they found were culture clubs—people dressed in garish outfits, engaging in pantomimes of Shawnee ceremonies. The Shawnees came home having borne witness to a new form of minstrel show performed by the very descendants of the people who had dispossessed them of their towns and sacred sites. Long before this visit Shawnees had become wary of outsiders who asked too many questions. But now in Ohio our elders saw the extent to which these new inhabitants of the homelands would go to pretend to be Shawnee. In response, we became even more cloistered and protective of our language, culture, songs, and ceremonies. The righteous indignation against the cultural predations of the colonizers' children created a long-term apathy for us, the original children of the Ohio region. With no one to speak on behalf of our sacred sites and ancestral remains, the new occupiers of our homelands sullied the sacred. Absent our voice, the poor treatment of our sacred sites is everywhere in evidence. For example, the Newark Earthworks' Great Octagon is now part of Moundbuilders Country Club. To us, golfing on the mounds of our Hopewell ancestors represents the ultimate defilement. The Moundbuilders Country Club website features a history of the course and quotes a 1911 *Newark Advocate* article, which, in what I can only describe as either arrogance or ignorance, cautions the golfer, "The fourth hole is named 'The Veldt.' . . . One must maintain a straight course or the mound on one side and the gully on the other will play havoc with his score."[6]

Visitors to the Newark Earthworks and the Great Octagon may observe the site during daylight hours, but are limited to an interpretive trail skirting the golf course; or one can view the sacred majesty of the mounds from a viewing platform near the parking lot. Only recently have tribal citizens been afforded a mere four days per year for the opportunity to walk the entirety of the site without paying for a nonresident membership and green fees. Open access to the

9.1. The Moundbuilders Country Club golf course cuts across the Newark Earthworks in Newark, Ohio. The Hopewell people constructed this earthen mound complex more than 1,500 years ago. Visitors to the sacred site are warned off by this sign. Photo courtesy of Marti Chaatsmith, Newark Earthworks Center, Ohio State University.

Newark Earthworks and the Great Octagon is subject to a yearly negotiation process between the Moundbuilders Country Club and the Ohio History Connection. The days are typically Memorial Day and the following Tuesday, with additional days in April and October. Without the advocacy of individuals from Ohio State University's Newark Earthworks Center, the Ohio History Connection, and Chief Glenna Wallace, tribal descendants of the Mound Builders would have even less access to a wonder of ancient America.

The debasement of our homeland is not limited to the land itself. Even the bones of our ancestors are subjected to abuse by those who do not view Native Americans as people. The hallowed remains of the ancestors are no more regarded than a mastodon tusk found in a cornfield. Ohio burial laws do not protect the remains of our old ones that happen to be located on private property. The state of Ohio only protects the bones of people who died less than 125 years ago. Recent efforts to change the law to protect all people interred in Ohio's soil, as voiced by the Ohio Historical Society and Chief Glenna Wallace of the Eastern Shawnee Tribe to the Ohio legislature, were stymied by state politics.

Removal left nothing sacred or secure for Indian people. In our absence from the East, our very identity is jeopardized. The fraudulent voices filling the vacuum of our absence have performed minstrel shows of our sacred ceremonies and begun to speak and act on our behalf.[7] More than thirty fake Shawnee tribes have organized as 501(c)(3) nonprofits, entities that syphon away resources and grant monies from federal, state, and private sources.

These problems are not unique to just the Shawnees. The three Cherokee tribes, whose removal is perhaps the most well known by the American public, have more than two hundred fake nonprofit tribes, while the Delaware tribes have a number similar to the Shawnees. The level of the fraud has become so pervasive that it should be cause for concern to all state and federal legislatures. Between the years of 2007 and 2010, more than $100 million of federal aid was given to just twenty-six fake tribes.[8] These $100 million were monies that would have gone to real Indian people, nations, and the many services we provide for our people. Instead, it was diverted to newly created culture clubs using our identities for economic gain. In Alabama a fake Shawnee tribe ran a gambling parlor, and because they are only state recognized instead of federal, they did not have to abide by the Indian Gaming Regulatory Act, as the real nations must.[9] The uninformed general public falls prey to their fables and yarns, and well-meaning people who feel empathy for the plight of the removed nations bestow a largess of money and donated land unto these so-called culture clubs.

During the summer of 2012 the Cumberland Gap National Park, under the aegis of the Department of the Interior's National Park Service, allowed a group of "pretendians" calling themselves Shawnees to perform a Green Corn ceremony within the park as a public spectacle, all the while representing this as a sacred ceremony.[10] But there is only one place on the earth that can hold the Shawnee Green Corn ceremony. As a member of the White Oak Shawnees' ceremonial ground, I took extreme offense to the minstrel show performed in the Cumberland Gap. In spite of my formal protests, in spite of letters of condemnation from Absentee Shawnee governor George Blanchard and Eastern Shawnee chief Glenna Wallace, we were unable to stop the sacrilege in the Cumberland Gap National Park. It is worth noting that our efforts were not completely in vain. The Cumberland Gap has not repeated this mistake.

It would be easy to blame the Shawnee Tribe, the Eastern Shawnee Tribe, the Absentee Shawnee Tribe, the Seneca-Cayuga Tribe, the Wyandottes, Delawares, Potawatomis, Peorias, and Miamis for not taking care of their collective business back in the old homelands. For the thirty-nine federally recognized tribes in Oklahoma today, the immediate needs of our tribal nations—economic development, healthcare for our children and elderly, and grant-funded governmental services for our citizens—often eclipse our desire to return to our aboriginal homelands. As our tribal nations' economies have developed, so too have our governmental authorities and responsibilities. With the inclusion of tribal nations in the 1992 amendment to the National Historic Preservation Act (originally passed in 1966) and with the legislative victory of Native American Graves Protection and Repatriation Act (NAGPRA) in 1990, tribes received some limited funding and legal authority to examine our nations' roles in the ancestral homelands. The Shawnee tribal nations now had a tool, and incentive, to reengage with the eastern states. NAGPRA mandated that the ancestral remains and funerary objects of our ancient people be inventoried. These acts forced discussions with universities, laboratories, and museums. Although negotiations between tribes and institutions had a slow, difficult start, productive conversations have occurred, and some common ground has been found between tribal and academic parties. Tribal nations and historic sites were both interested in site preservation and in telling the story of the ancient past. Museums became interested in the material cultural conversations about objects of art and ceremony, and the tribes' own specialists were acquired and trained to aid them in the process of repatriating ancient remains and funerary objects.

For the first time, our modern nations had the opportunity to walk on the soil of our ancestors' ancient places. We learned new things about our ancient homeland. More importantly, we found that, in spite of removal, no matter how much loss we had experienced, not only did we still remain, so did the story of the land. Seeing the earthen walls and ramparts of the Fort Ancient village, Shawnees were able to behold the marvel of the artisanship of previous centuries and to know that our ancestors dwelt in some of these places. For the first time, we saw the

Serpent Mound and recognized how the counter-clockwise loops of that ancient earthen snake are reflected in our ongoing ceremonies and beliefs.

While we cannot forget the horrible things done to our ancient places and the misinterpretations of our people, Chief Glenna Wallace, Councilman Roy D. Baldridge, and I know that renewing our relationship with the land and speaking on its behalf are not just dreams but also moral imperatives. A half-dozen or so years ago, Chief Glenna Wallace of the Eastern Shawnees began the first thawing of relations between the Shawnees and the Ohio Historical Society (which is now the Ohio History Connection). Discussions have not always been easy, and neither have the solutions. The Newark Earthworks is perhaps a fine example of a difficult problem with no immediate solution. The long-term lease held by Moundbuilders Country Club poses a problem not only for Shawnee people, but also for the Ohio History Connection. Burt Logan, CEO of the Ohio History Connection, and his staff and interested parties in Ohio would like to see the Newark Earthworks become a UNESCO World Heritage Site. However, we have learned that the mistakes of the past haunt both the removed tribes and the descendants of the removers. A World Heritage designation for the Newark site and its Great Octagon will remain elusive until a solution is found.

Shawnee delegations to the Ohio valley and its institutions soon began to realize that they had more in common with academics and cultural institutions than we previously believed. The modern-day enemies of Indian people, archaeologists, discovered that they needed the tribes to preserve and interpret archaeological sites. As the Ohio History Connection and the Hopewell Culture National Historical Park began to propose nominating the Hopewell Ceremonial Earthworks and Serpent Mound as UNESCO World Heritage Sites, the Shawnees and our Ohio valley allies often provided the necessary consultations and support for these designations.

The more we rediscovered the mounds and walls of our ancient places, the hungrier we became to learn more from the scientists who had been trying to tease out the stories of our people that had been trapped in the soil. While we may never completely agree on NAGPRA, we are discovering exciting things about our old ones. During a consultation with the University of Indianapolis, I had a conversation with Christopher Schmidt about a NAGPRA site known as the Meyer Cemetery site in Spencer County, Indiana.[11] The Meyer site was approximately 5,300 years old, and the graves had numerous distinct burial features that led archaeologists to associate them with the Shawnees.[12] Numerous graves of young children had inadvertently been discovered, and in one particular grave they found a woman who was approximately twenty-five years old. The University of Indianapolis performed osteological testing on the bones of this young woman without consulting the tribes. However, something interesting was discovered. It was easily discovered with a casual observation of the remains by the archaeologists and osteologists that this woman had suffered a terrible wasting, syphilitic disease that had twisted and contorted her arms, legs, and jaw bone to such a degree that she was unable to walk or feed herself. But the testing that was done without our knowledge had a story to tell. This young woman had enjoyed a high level of nutrition throughout her life, and it was only her terrible disease that had killed her.

I confess to being extremely conflicted. Things had been done to this ancestor without our knowledge. But here was evidence of a Shawnee ancestor, buried with Shawnee mortuary features, who had been completely crippled, but her village and family had loved her so much that she was not a burden to them. They had kept her nourished and safe. She was 5,300 years old, and her burial spoke to our religious and mortuary beliefs, calling to us from the ancient past through the evidence of the ritualistic burial practices that still exist within contemporary traditional Shawnee communities. This ritual expression of faith was a singular affirmation of the continuity of our Shawnee beliefs, religion, and burial practices that continue into the present, beliefs practiced by Shawnee ancestors long before the religions of the colonizers and older than religions of the ancient Far East. When I think of this memory of discovery, I feel the gravity of the past and know that it is our moral obligation to protect these people while attempting to balance the pursuit for our truth.

NAGPRA activities require extensive consultations between tribal governments and universities, laboratories, and museums. The relationships created from these long conversations allow for bridges to be built between parties and for expanded understanding between the consulting parties. Inevitably, people come to know each other, and trust begins to build between us when we speak truthfully about our concerns and listen to each other. During these consultations, tribes are afforded the time to understand the scientists' perspectives, the methods used to unlock the past, and their need to unlock ancient stories. Likewise, the anthropologists, archaeologists, and osteologists are able to listen to our concerns, customs, and beliefs and find mutual satisfaction as we pursue the true histories of our people together. Through the hard work of NAGPRA and by overcoming hurdles from the missteps of the past, the Shawnees have new allies at the Ohio History Connection and Indiana University Bloomington.

Indiana University Bloomington has become one of the Shawnees' valued partners, particularly the Glenn A. Black Laboratory of Archaeology. The Glenn A. Black Laboratory awarded a summer research fellowship to a Shawnee tribal citizen and donated resource books and journals to our fledgling Shawnee archive. Perhaps more importantly, the laboratory houses the records of the Great Lakes and Ohio Valley Ethnohistory Collection, a vast record of land-usage documents spanning 108 feet in length. These documents are excerpts of the material that was used by the Indian Claims Commission to settle land-related claims for the Great Lakes and Ohio valley tribes. The Shawnee material takes up fifteen feet of space, each excerpt consisting of a few pages from a primary-source document or book. If each excerpt were recontextualized back to its primary source, the fifteen feet of Shawnee material would result in a massive collection of information, measuring hundreds of feet, documenting the lives of our people and homelands. The Glenn A. Black Laboratory of Archaeology is working with the Shawnee Tribe to digitize the entire Shawnee collection so that our people can benefit directly from the materials held in that treasure trove. The digital age has brought our history to our door, and we must step through and recontextualize the narratives of our Shawnee people.

We should not just rely on the stories already discovered by academics, however; rather *we* should be examining the archives of museums, historic societies, and universities to recontextualize the published material from the past. Shawnee people are collaborating with institutions, such as the Ohio History Connection, and making breathtaking new discoveries. Archaeologists, museum professionals, and archivists are now coming to Oklahoma to meet and discuss our interests. One such visit occurred at the Eastern Shawnee Complex, just outside of the language-learning area. In a glass case in the foyer was a collection of cultural objects including a brass water drum. Brad Lepper, curator of archaeology for the Ohio History Connection, asked us a series of questions about the objects. I began to explain to Lepper that the brass water drum in the display was an atypical example of a Shawnee water drum. As I described the water drum that is used at the White Oak Ceremonial Ground and how we use the small black stones to hold the tanned hide in place, Brad became very animated and inquisitive. Lepper then began to describe the stones from the Seip-Pricer Mound.

The excavation of the Seip-Pricer Mound from 1925 to 1928 was led by Ohio Historic Society archaeologists Henry Shetrone and Emerson Greenman. In an area that they termed a "burnt offering" pit, they discovered five round steatite stones with intricate carvings on their surface. Shetrone, with his European bias, described them as marbles, perhaps a child's toy, since a child's remains were not too distant from the stones.[13]

Continuing with my explanation of the water drum and how it is constructed, I told Brad that in tying the drum, we use an odd number of stones because the rope-work that we use to secure

9.2. These five steatite spheres were discovered at Seip-Pricer Mound by Ohio Historical Society archaeologists Henry Shetrone and Emerson Greenman during their 1925–28 excavation of the mound. Photo courtesy of the Ohio History Connection.

the tanned hide dictates such a number. The water drums of our ancient past would have been fabricated from wooden stumps or from cypress knees.[14] Since the Seip-Pricer Mound stones were found in the burnt offering pit, the plant-fiber cordage, drum hide, and wooden vessel would all have been destroyed, leaving only these five steatite spheres.

In preparing a paper about our idea of the Seip-Pricer Mound spheres for a presentation at the Ohio Archaeological Council's Third Hopewell Conference, we found a tantalizing bit in the records surrounding the excavation of the stones. Among the discovery at the site were "a total of 37 pieces of wood . . . some of which were in sufficient state of preservation to enable recognition of the original object," including "several fragments of a wooden bowl or plate from the Burnt Offering."[15] Could it possibly be that we have found the drum? Our efforts to build a case for the wooden drum continue as Brad Lepper searches the shelves of the Ohio History Connection for charred bits of wood from a past millennium.

The implications of this could be that conversations between the Ohio History Connection and the Shawnees regarding the Seip-Pricer Mound excavation have recontextualized the stone spheres. The original interpretation of the spheres was a conjecture based solely on a Euro-American preconception. Now, through engaged academic collaboration, we have been able to offer an opinion on the stones based upon an indigenous cultural context. While we may never be certain of the presence of a water drum in the "Burnt Offering," our collaboration has offered a superior explanation based on a cultural coherency that can only be obtained through engaging with tribal nation partners.

The Shawnee Tribe has initiated another archaeological project, whose goal is the rediscovery of our ancestors' pottery traditions. This particular project is very exciting for professional historians, archaeologists, ceramicists, and our own Shawnee cultural community. To explain this project fully, we must wind back the clock to the Shawnee habitations of 1540 C.E. At that time Shawnees and other tribes from the Ohio valley received trade goods from the Hernando de Soto expedition as they wandered through the homelands of our southern neighbors in search of gold and silver. Our Shawnee ancestors had long been connected to the tribes that suffered through his visits. Waterways and footpaths led from the towns and villages of Georgia, Alabama, and Virginia to the interior regions of Pennsylvania, Kentucky, Ohio, and elsewhere. By the 1720s Shawnee artisans had stopped creating vessels of clay, as metal pots and tools began to flow from their new European trading partners.[16]

Details regarding traditional Shawnee pottery can only be guessed at from inferences of other tribes and the late Fort Ancient inhabitants of the Ohio valley. However, we do know—from ethnographic material and our own lived experience—what a Shawnee burial looks like. These mortuary practices have been confirmed in late Fort Ancient archaeological contexts. So by defining an overlap between the temporal and geographic locations where we find these burials

9.3. Replica Fort Ancient pot cooking Native corn and venison. The ceramic vessel shown above was created by the Shawnee Tribe's pottery partner and ceramic expert, Richard Zane Smith (Wyandotte). Photo courtesy of Richard Zane Smith.

in areas of Fort Ancient and subsequent Shawnee habitations, we can then begin to analyze the pottery fragments from those archaeological sites.

To properly tell the story locked within these ancient sherds, we must use powerful tools and highly trained professionals. The Shawnee Tribe has begun conversations with the staff of Indiana University Bloomington's Glenn A. Black Laboratory of Archaeology. Specialists there have offered to be our partners, to unlock our ceramic mysteries with a field polarizing metallurgical microscope. We hope to establish a definition of sorts, a compositional signature of Shawnee pottery from the recovered pottery sherds. The fine analysis will tell us the story of how Shawnee pottery was made, and from the sherd samples we will know what our pots looked like. A day is quickly approaching when Shawnee people will be able to cook in Shawnee clay vessels and eat food that tastes the same as what our ancestors prepared so long ago.

When we create such opportunities for universities and institutions, which serve their interests as well as our own, we become valued collaborators for what our partnerships can bring. We raise the public profile of the institution, and they find themselves incentivized to seek out future opportunities to work with us. When indigenous people become actively engaged with the universities and institutions of our historic homelands, we have an opportunity to recontextualize the misinformation of the past, and we become our own storytellers. Occasionally these partnerships will bring needed funding to the institution in the form of grant opportunities or by direct investment from our tribal nations. The Shawnee relationship with the ancestral homeland is a fragile one, freshly birthed from the efforts of a small handful of Shawnee people. Notable engaged tribal leaders—such as Glenna Wallace, chief of the Eastern Shawnees; Roy D. Baldridge, treasurer of the Shawnee Tribe; and myself, Ben Barnes, second chief of the Shawnee

Tribe—continue to build these relationships, but we must have more citizen voices. The voices of just this handful cannot tell the full spectrum of the Shawnee experience. To become our own storytellers, to be the voice of our people and the stewards of our sacred sites and ancestors, we must have more Shawnees engaged in the homeland. If this small handful of citizens were to falter in their pursuit of the Shawnee truth in our ancient homelands, our ancestors might have to wait for another generation to return home and protect our birthright, much like Thomas Alford tried to do in the Ohio valley.

Only by participating with universities and other institutions from our historic lands can we express our needs and guide future research projects, which in turn will lead to better research outcomes for the students, universities, and more importantly, our tribal citizens. When we create relationships of mutual collaboration and both sides are willing to listen to each other, a more complete truth of our Shawnee people can be told. We hope that a day will come when our homes, our lands, and our ancestors' remains will no longer be subject to bigotry, discrimination, and ignorance. We strive for the day when our cultural identity, our ancestral remains, and our sacred sites will be appreciated for what they really are: the legacy of an undefeated and thriving Shawnee people.

NOTES

1. Bureau of Indian Affairs, Notice, "Indian Entities Recognized and Eligible to Receive Services From the United States Bureau of Indian Affairs," *Federal Register* 81, no. 19, (January 29, 2016): 5019, https://www.gpo.gov/fdsys/pkg/FR-2016-01-29/pdf/2016-01769.pdf. The modern-day Shawnee nations are the Absentee Shawnee Tribe of Oklahoma, the Eastern Shawnee Tribe of Oklahoma, and the Shawnee Tribe.

2. "Will Dedicate Cemetery Entrance Saturday," *The Evening Gazette* (Xenia, Ohio), October 5, 1931, 3.

3. "Skeleton, Relic of the Past, Takes Ride in Auto," ibid.

4. William Albert Galloway and Charles Burleigh Galbreath, *Old Chillicothe: Shawnee and Pioneer History, Conflicts and Romance in the Northwest Territories* (Xenia, Ohio: Buckeye Press, 1934), 123–25, 135–39, 166, 276–80.

5. R. David Edmunds, "Edmunds—Tecumseh," *Indians of the Midwest*, 2009, http://publications .Newberry.org/indiansofthemidwest/indian-imagery/how-we-know/video-transcript-tecumseh -imagery/, accessed February 28, 2016.

6. Moundbuilders Country Club, "The Golf Course," Moundbuilders Country Club History, accessed February 22, 2016, www.MoundbuildersCC.com/files/The%20Golf%20Course.pdf/.

7. Mike Fitzpatrick, "Skull Session, Medicine Hawk Blesses Skull," *Sandusky Register*, May 9, 2009, 1, A-11. Gary Hunt, self-proclaimed "Principal Chief of the Shawnee," conducted a reinterment ceremony for a cranial remain that was discovered during construction of a Walmart parking lot. The federally recognized tribes from Ohio were never consulted, and in this case, two nonrecognized "Indian" groups argued over the reinterment. This is an example of why the federal NAGPRA processes are important to Native nations to ensure that we handle the ancestors respectfully.

8. United States Government Accountability Office, *Indian Issues, Federal Funding for Non-Federally Recognized Tribes*, Anu K. Mittal et al., GAO 12–348 (Washington, D.C.: Government Accountability Office, 2012), www.GAO.gov/products/GAO-12-348.

9. For discussion regarding the Piqua Shawnee bingo parlor and its closing, refer to the forum at http://www.topix.com/forum/city/corbin-ky/T1QOHBK48GAFL141M. For information on the Piqua Shawnees and the Alabama Indian Affairs Commission, refer to http://www.AIAC.Alabama .gov/tribes.aspx. The Piqua Shawnees are a tribe recognized by the Alabama Indian Affairs Commission, of which they are also a member. The Piqua Shawnees have never been able to show that they are

descendant peoples of any Shawnee, living or dead. The Piqua Shawnee bingo parlor ran for several years before closing in approximately 2009.

10. "Green Corn Dance with Piqua Shawnee Tribe at Cumberland Gap National Historical Park," *Cumberland Gap National Historical Park*, (blog), July 30, 2012, https://CumberlandGapNHP.word press.com/2012/07/30/green-corn-dance-with-piqua-shawnee-tribe-at-cumberland-gap-national -historical-park/.

11. On December 10, 2013, the Shawnee Tribe, the Eastern Shawnee Tribe of Oklahoma, the Miami Tribe of Oklahoma, and the Pokagon Band of Potawatomis consulted with the University of Indianapolis regarding the "Meyer Cemetery site" (12Sp1082), Spencer County, Indiana.

12. Anne Tobbe Bader, "Evidence of Ritualized Mortuary Behavior at the Meyer Site: An Inadvertent Discovery in Spencer County, Indiana," *Indiana Archaeology* 5, no. 2 (2010/2011): 10–49, accessed February 20, 2016, http://www.IN.gov/dnr/historic/files/hp-2010-2010ArchJournal.pdf.

13. Henry C. Shetrone and Emerson F. Greenman, "Explorations of the Seip Group of Pre-Historic Earthwork," *Ohio History Journal*, Ohio History Connection website, p. 378 (no. 36), accessed February 28, 2016, http://publications.OhioHistory.org/ohj/browse/displaypages.php?display%5B0%5D= 0040&display%5B1%5D=343&display%5B2%5D=509/.

14. Erminie Wheeler-Voegelin, "Shawnee Musical Instruments," *American Anthropologist* 44 no. 3 (1942): 469–70.

15. Shetrone and Greenman, "Explorations of the Seip Group," p. 449 (no. 107).

16. Stephen Warren, *The Worlds the Shawnees Made: Migration and Violence in Early America*, (Chapel Hill: University of North Carolina Press, 2014), 63–64, 66–67.

10

Eastern Shawnee Migration

Cultural Changes and Disconnection following the Move to the Pacific Northwest

CATHLEEN OSBORNE-GOWEY

It is a cold spring day and the sun is peeking through the bare trees. I am standing in a place that has been considered sacred to the Eastern Shawnees for more than a hundred years. My mother is fidgeting next to me while talking with my informant, and for the first time she really looks interested in the conversation. I think she feels the significance of this moment and where we are. This is my mother's first time to Oklahoma, the place where her father was born and her grandmother was buried. My informant begins to tell my mother which families camped at this dance area. Before she can stop herself, my mother proudly and publicly tells the woman I'm interviewing that our family camped here too, that she is a BlueJacket. Shocked, I think to myself that this is the first time my mother has publicly and happily announced that she's Eastern Shawnee, a BlueJacket, and a member of the Turtle clan. My interviewee turns, looks into my mother's eyes, embraces her, and says, "Welcome home."

I always knew something was different about my mother and her family; they had dark skin, brown hair, and dark eyes, and they called themselves Eastern Shawnee. When I was seven I asked my grandfather why we looked different, why he was so dark, and what was Eastern Shawnee? He gave me a book on Indians in the Americas. I just remember that it had pictures of Aztec women with their hair coiled on the sides of their head. They didn't look anything like my mother or aunties, and our only similarities were that we all were called "Indians." I was raised in a small logging town in southern Oregon, a predominantly white community, where I saw few or no examples of what it meant to be an Indian. While I spent my entire life around my grandfather and his sisters, they never really talked about being Eastern Shawnee or about tribal culture and identity. I didn't begin to think of myself as Eastern Shawnee until I was in college, taking a course on Native American history, and the instructor taught about the Shawnees moving to Oklahoma. I realized I was reading about my own history. As I began to travel back to Oklahoma, reconnect with my family there, and work for the tribe, I challenged my family's idea that, in order to be Eastern Shawnee, you had to live in Oklahoma.

Being an Eastern Shawnee tribal citizen, I understand the importance of documenting the history of our tribe to ensure that our cultural history is passed on to future generations. Therefore the focus of this chapter is telling the story of Eastern Shawnee tribal citizens who left Oklahoma from the 1930s to the 1950s for the Pacific Northwest, where they sought employment and a new life at the expense of their tribal culture. In this chapter I will tell the story of my family, the Millhollins, of their experience with the disconnection from tribal culture and their work to reclaim it. This chapter does not represent the experience of all Eastern Shawnee families who moved to other areas during this time, or the experience of all within the Millhollin family. However, it does give a general background on why many Eastern Shawnee tribal citizens felt the necessity to move, the consequent disconnection many have faced from their culture, and the tribe's subsequent work to reconnect all tribal citizens—one-third of whom live outside of Oklahoma—with our culture and history.

Through this chapter I hope to give a three-dimensional glimpse into one piece of Eastern Shawnee history—the process of relocation and the cultural-identity changes that came with that. By using oral narratives about the lives of my family and community members mixed with research, I hope to create a bridge that reaches across the pages of the text and gives a face to this piece of Eastern Shawnee history. We can never fully understand the pain that these Eastern Shawnee families felt when faced with the decision to leave, nor can we know exactly why they felt this was their only key to survival; we can only hear their stories and their children's stories and examine the historical and economic context of the time. This chapter is a story of persistence, change, adaptation, and survival.

In the summer of 2002 I began working on a study, which I titled "The Eastern Shawnee Oral History Research Project," as an undergraduate research project that would later turn into research for my master of arts thesis through Oregon State University.[1] This project was a case study of my Eastern Shawnee family. The research documented whether traditional knowledge still exists in the family, how it was transmitted, and what effects relocation to the Pacific Northwest had on that knowledge. I interviewed all of my great-aunts on my mother's side (all citizens of the Eastern Shawnee Tribe), most of whom I had met only once when I was a child.[2] They began relaying stories of my great-great-grandmother Rosa BlueJacket, of my great-grandmother Louisa BlueJacket Daugherty, of their own lives, and of the lives of their children. Our family matriarchs, Rosa and Louisa, through their choices both bad and good, would set the course of our family's connection to our Eastern Shawnee culture for generations to come. I had come to these interviews looking for information on traditional Eastern Shawnee knowledge regarding plant usage, ceremonies, and rituals. What I received were stories of Eastern Shawnee experiences with federal Indian boarding schools, migration, relocation, forced marriage, basic survival, and dramatic cultural change and loss. This sparked my interest. By examining information gathered from my research, I found a correlation between the amount of cultural knowledge Eastern Shawnees possess, their migration, and how they identified themselves in the tribe. This then led to research for my thesis, "'No One Cared We Was Just Indian Women': Plants as a Catalyst to Eastern Shawnee Women's Identity Change," which I completed in 2006 at Oregon State University.[3] In this study I used plants as a nonthreatening catalyst for discussion of the changing status of Eastern Shawnee women in the Pacific Northwest. I began to see that after our family left Oklahoma, the knowledge that women in our family had regarding the usage of plants for medicinal purposes dwindled with each generation born in the Pacific Northwest; plants became a metaphor of the disconnection we experienced from our culture.

BEFORE THE MOVE TO THE PACIFIC NORTHWEST

The Eastern Shawnees are distinctive in their experience with assimilation and its push toward individualism, relocation, and migration. From the mid-eighteenth century through the end of the nineteenth century, and again in the early to mid-twentieth century, the group that would become the Eastern Shawnee Tribe was in a continual state of forced westward migration. Though the tribe continually tried to reunify and re-create their communal society, the constant migration unraveled, separated, and inevitably disconnected many from Shawnee culture.

Prior to migration, the Shawnees were known as an eastern woodlands tribe, living primarily in what are now Indiana, Ohio, Michigan, Kentucky, Pennsylvania, West Virginia, and Tennessee.[4] During the spring and summer the small bands joined together, allowing for easier planting, harvesting, gathering, and hunting. What information I know about the Shawnees prior to assimilation and forced migration comes only from history books. Unfortunately, my family has no stories of Shawnee life prior to the move from Ohio to Oklahoma: what roles men and women had, where they lived or how they lived, and why they chose to break down their society along clan lines. However, through oral histories I was given a glimpse into Eastern Shawnee life during the migration to Oklahoma from Ohio and the life of Rosa BlueJacket Daugherty, my great-great-grandmother.[5] Rosa would, through her strength and determination to keep her cultural identity, lay the foundation of our tribal culture in our family that would reach through the generations.

My great-auntie recounted a story that her grandmother Rosa BlueJacket told her about fleeing, or being pushed from, their reservation during the Civil War, one of the stories that Rosa remembered from her childhood. This story has been passed down through the generations in the Millhollin family. While there may be cause to speculate on the historical accuracy of the story, and perhaps Rosa mixed many of her memories together, this story illustrates for our family how our tribe began and where our family roots began: "As the bushwhackers approached the moving line of Lewistown Mixed Band, chaos rang out.[6] Tribal citizens scattered, running as fast as they could. Mothers wrapped their babies in their skirts, trying to hide or outrun the bushwhackers. Rosa remembered that when the commotion was over, and the tribe realized they were safe, many of the women unwrapped their skirts to find their babies dead, beaten to death by their mother's legs while they ran for safety."[7] The value in this description isn't the specific events, dates, or terminology, which are certainly open to contention and interpretation. Rather, this story gives an illustration to the larger story of Rosa's experience with decades (and certainly centuries) of the tribe's experience with structural violence carried out by the state and federal government on the Shawnees. This story gives a visual to the feeling of Rosa's experience with ceding lands and moving to Oklahoma. While written accounts of the Shawnees ceding their Ohio lands and eventually migrating to reservation lands in Oklahoma are rather peaceful, my oral-history interviews say otherwise. As the lands in Oklahoma that they were promised slowly dwindled, the reestablishment of traditional Shawnee life would continue to be challenging for Rosa and her family.

The Dawes General Allotment Act further disconnected the Eastern Shawnees from the greater tribal community.[8] Continual relocations away from tribal lands fostered the spread of assimilation. Being separated from each other, it became easier to convince tribal citizens that they no longer needed their cultural ties in order to survive. Rosa and her family came to believe that farming an individual plot of land, as an individual or as a nuclear family, was preferable to communal living. Individualism meant survival. It was this type of thinking that would make Rosa's daughter Louisa (my great-grandmother) and her children choose to move away from our tribal community to the Pacific Northwest for what they saw as survival.

After allotment had carved up the reservation, Rosa BlueJacket, aided by her father, acquired as many adjoining allotments as possible. This was her attempt to create some form of continuity. Though allotments were granted mainly to men, Rosa's father purchased the allotments and then gave them to her.[9] On her allotments she was able to re-create a somewhat stable piece of Shawnee life, similar to life prior to forced migration and assimilation. She, along with her husband, Edward, built a cabin on the allotments, where they hunted, fished, farmed, and raised four children. The life they built was peaceful and would give safety and warmth to her children and grandchildren.[10] This story, as told to me by my eldest great-auntie (Louisa's oldest child), illustrates the peaceful life Rosa built and the connection to Eastern Shawnee culture that she gave to her grandchildren.

Before I got old enough to go to school, we went to the fall Stomp Dance out at White Oak. That was a harvest ritual. . . . I loved the quiet time of evening. The grandparents

[Rosa BlueJacket and Edward Daugherty] would light up their pipes and sit and talk in the Shawnee language and chuckle now and then, such tranquility and peace. I guess I remember this time of my life because it was truly the happiest time of my childhood. Oh, . . . you wonder, Did I not live with my family? Oh yes, the time came all too soon. After I started school [the Seneca Indian School] I never got to go to the grandparents anymore.[11]

Rosa BlueJacket possessed the subsistence skills necessary to help ensure familial and cultural survival. After moving to Oklahoma, although the geographic location of the community had changed, she attempted to reestablish a traditional Shawnee life.

However, with the creation of the Society of Friends Mission School and the rise of churches, assimilation found its way into the lives of Rosa and her children. Rosa's daughter, Louisa Blue-Jacket, my great-grandmother, felt the pressure of assimilation.[12] Marrying an Irish immigrant, Louisa attempted to do what I assume the church and the school told her would ensure her survival: step away from her traditional Shawnee roots and begin to blend in to dominant society. By the 1920s and 1930s the Seneca Indian School had become a federally run Indian boarding school, and all of Louisa's children would attend. I believe Louisa once again made the choice of assimilation to ensure survival. Though she understood that her children would lose even more of their culture than she had, I believe she felt it would be the only way they could escape the abuse and poverty they found at home. One of my eldest great-aunties (Louisa's second-oldest child) describes the home she grew up in and the poverty she and her siblings experienced:

We all [two women, one man, and more than ten children] lived in a one-room shack. It probably wasn't more [than] 16 x 18 or 20 feet, a rough door with a Z brace, a window at each end, no more than 20 x 24 inches. It was a dirt floor. One table, maybe 36 x 8 feet [*sic*], no cupboards, only a shelf above the table, a grouping of powder boxes served as a place for clothes. 1 double bed and 3 iron cots, 4 kids per cot, a bigger kid and a little one at each end. Mattresses were tow sacks filled with what we called buffalo grass. Sheets were mad[e] of feed sacks, as was all our clothing, and dyed with walnut hulls, ugly brown, ugly. But it was home, we knew no other. I think back. . . . I can't remember funerals for the little ones that died [siblings]. Baby one burned to death, baby two fell on a sharp stob [stick] and poked a hole in his neck and finally died. Baby three and four died of summer comfort, whatever that was. Baby five only lived a few days; she was so tiny. Baby six died soon after birth, and the state took baby seven, and he was adopted. I do know that the stillborn babies were buried in shoeboxes around the place. Who was to know? The births and deaths were never recorded, and nobody cared anyway. It was just that bunch of . . . half-breeds.[13]

During their time at the Seneca Indian Boarding School, all of Louisa's children would learn their place in dominant society. The girls had their hair cut and were forced to wear wool dresses; they abandoned the subsistence skills their mother used and learned only how to cook, clean, and work as white women did. Louisa's sons forgot the stories of their culture, the songs their mother sang, and replaced these traditional practices with training as blacksmiths, carpenters, and farmers.[14]

Allotment carved up what reservation land was left and scattered Eastern Shawnee community citizens across several thousands of acres. Hunting, fishing, gathering, planting, and harvesting became more and more difficult, causing poverty and disease. Federal Indian boarding schools stifled cultural language and subsistence life skills. Unaccustomed to their own language, gender roles, and subsistence survival, many who went through the Seneca Indian Boarding School found it hard to survive once they were released back into their communities. Boys could not find work and easily became discouraged. Girls no longer had their valued place in their tribal society; they lacked the skills to contribute economically to their family and community.

Far from the life Rosa tried to reestablish for them, Louisa's hard choices for survival created an everlasting break from traditional Shawnee society for this portion of the BlueJacket family. Future members of the family did not know their place of respect and value; my mother's generation and my own have had to struggle to learn and find our way back to our tribal culture. As told by one of my great-aunties (one of Louisa's children), this story below illustrates how the journey back to our cultural identity is difficult and has created a divide in our family between those who left Oklahoma and those who stayed. "It's up to our generation. It isn't fair, we try to learn [Eastern Shawnee culture]. It was up to the generations back who have all died off. When we ask now and they say, 'Well you weren't raised in it [Eastern Shawnee culture], so you don't know.' . . . I don't know one person around here who was raised Indian. We have to carry on."[15]

The situation was the same for many Eastern Shawnee families; the individual choices for survival—to attend the federal Indian boarding schools and later to move to the Pacific Northwest to find jobs—disconnected them from their culture. By the 1930s life in Northeastern Oklahoma had become increasingly difficult; the local and federal economic crises were beginning to take their toll. Once again, Eastern Shawnees faced relocation and further disconnection from their tribal culture.

THE MOVE TO THE PACIFIC NORTHWEST AND CULTURAL CHANGES

With the 1930s came tuberculosis, the Great Depression, and the Dust Bowl.[16] Jobs were scarce, and were even scarcer for Indians, no matter how educated they were. A generation of Eastern Shawnees emerged lacking Shawnee survival skills. Instead, in their search for survival in a white man's world, the Eastern Shawnees assimilated, leaving behind many of the skills they had formerly used for thousands of years.

By the 1940s and 1950s many Eastern Shawnee community citizens had relocated out of Oklahoma and off tribal lands in search of work, creating a tribal generation disconnected from its community and history. Currently, of the more than 3,277 enrolled Eastern Shawnee tribal citizens, only 1,133 live in Oklahoma.[17]

The move to the Pacific Northwest was a large undertaking and leap of faith; it is important to remember why tribal citizens felt the need to move. Louisa BlueJacket died in 1939 at the age of forty-three, while giving birth to twins in Miami, Oklahoma, leaving behind several children, ranging in age from infancy to teens. Faced with local and federal financial depression, many of her children felt that the key for survival was once again change. Rumors of jobs in the Pacific Northwest convinced Louisa's older children and her husband to take the smaller children and move to Oregon in order to work in the shipyards and the timber industry. They packed up what could fit in the old Model T, and as many kids as could fit in the rumble seat, and headed west.

This story of survival, relocation, and disconnection happened to many families within the Eastern Shawnee Tribe. Many others, faced with the Dust Bowl, poverty, and a lack of choices, decided to move. Some of those families stayed only as long as necessary and moved back to Oklahoma and to the Eastern Shawnees' allotted lands, while others stayed and made a life in Oregon, Washington, or California. Two generations of Eastern Shawnee tribal citizens would be born in the Pacific Northwest, and many of those Eastern Shawnee families would stay within close proximity to one another.

AFTER THE MOVE, AND THE DISCONNECTION
TO EASTERN SHAWNEE CULTURE

Once in Oregon, many of the Millhollins lived close to each other, for familial connection, in and around the small town of Sandy, Oregon (although some traveled to Eastern Washington, on the other side of the Columbia Gorge), to work in the shipyards of Portland and in the timber industry. Though termination and relocation often caused Indian communities to spread to larger urban areas, I believe that, because the Millhollin family came from a rural area in Oklahoma, they felt more comfortable in Sandy, a small agricultural town not far from the base of Mount Hood.[18] Travel to and from Oklahoma for family or cultural events became more and more difficult.

I found in my research that many of the people I collected oral histories from who lived in Oklahoma (that is, lived their entire lives either on or near tribal allotted lands in Oklahoma) spoke mainly of traditional plant knowledge and gathering practices as well as their identities, ceremonies, loss of culture, and tribal politics. However, those I collected oral histories from who either relocated to the Pacific Northwest or were born after that relocation spoke little about tribal identity or the passing on of knowledge or culture. Because they were detached from their tribal community, their knowledge about tribal culture and identity was far less than those who lived on or near allotted lands and were exposed to these topics on a daily basis.

For younger generations who lived in the Pacific Northwest, being Eastern Shawnee meant having darker skin and a vague connection to family who lived far away. There was little talk of history, such as the boarding school experiences, the family still living in Oklahoma, or the traditions the older generation practiced when they were growing up in Oklahoma. Many of the first- and second-generation folks born in Oregon feel a strong cultural tie to that region and see Oklahoma, and being Eastern Shawnee, as our past. Though now, many first-generation and curious second-generation folks like myself are beginning to ask about the stories of Eastern Shawnee identity: What was it like relocating to Oklahoma and going to boarding schools? And who were Louisa and Rosa BlueJacket? We have begun to explore the disconnection in our tribal identity.[19]

As Peter Iverson states in *We Are Still Here*, "Being an Indian today, as it always had, included the incorporation of change."[20] The gap between the generations has become quite deep. There are few or no fluent speakers of Shawnee left in the Eastern Shawnee Tribe. Only one of the tribal elders I interviewed in my research remembered speaking the language, and only those currently living in Oklahoma have regularly attended Eastern Shawnee ceremonies other than powwow dances. Change is a large part of culture. Eastern Shawnee citizens must work to keep our culture alive and to rebuild a positive identity and connection for future generations. Revitalizing our connection to Shawnee culture is important to those of us born of the generation of Millhollins who relocated to the Pacific Northwest.

The story below, as told by an Eastern Shawnee citizen raised in the Pacific Northwest, illustrates how sharing and passing on our cultural knowledge—even knowledge of growing plants or of general gardening—is our common ground. It is how we can bridge the divide between those who left Oklahoma and those who stayed, and how we can work together as one tribe to rebuild our connection to our culture, regardless of where we live: "Now you'll see this . . . like when we went to my aunt's. She remembers gathering plants with her mother, but what she and I have in common are the roses, and we went to the grapes and plants because it's like it was common ground for us, see, and the knowledge that I learned from her I can share. It's . . . it draws you together, and so it doesn't matter if we're not gathering camas, cooking it; it leads her into stories, telling me about things I didn't know about."[21] Though I found in my research that a great deal of the cultural knowledge that Rosa BlueJacket passed down is now gone, we can work to preserve and pass down what cultural knowledge we do have.

THE INCORPORATION OF CHANGE

Many Eastern Shawnee families who relocated have started to travel back to Oklahoma, to pow-wow, and to rebuild and reclaim our connection to the land and our tribal identity. However, I did not want it to take another seventy years for our family (those Eastern Shawnees who relocated to the Pacific Northwest) to talk about our cultural identity, about all of the changes that had come to it, and find a way to connect ourselves to this new identity of being Eastern Shawnee in the Pacific Northwest.

As a storyteller, I'd like to conclude this chapter with a story. I began the chapter with the story of how I brought my mother "home." I had started to build what I hoped was a bridge to our cultural identity. But through my work, I have realized that a bigger bridge must be built.

In the fall of 2009 I realized how important it is to find a way to tell the Eastern Shawnee history, all of the history, including the migration to the Pacific Northwest, our loss of cultural identity, and our search to find it again. My family, including my grandfather, was elk hunting in the Rogue River Wilderness area. My daughter was just over three, and my son was an infant. On the third night there, my grandfather seemed anxious and wanted my family to come to his motor home to watch a movie. This required running a generator for two solid hours and cramming into a tiny space. I couldn't figure out what he wanted to achieve. When we got there, he had the movie *The Education of Little Tree* ready and wanted my daughter to go sit with him while we watched it.[22] Through the entire film he was telling her about his life in Oklahoma as a boy, about going to the Indian boarding school and the fear that he felt in being forced to go. The film doesn't tell the exact story of my grandfather's experience, but it does illustrate the historical trauma of the Indian boarding school experienced by my grandfather and many other Eastern Shawnees.[23] I realized at that moment that he was doing with her what he wasn't able to do with his daughter or granddaughter: he was teaching her what it meant to him to be Eastern Shawnee, and he was telling her about his cultural identity and her own cultural identity.

Our tribal community, as a whole, is moving forward in ensuring that all tribal citizens, those who relocated to the Pacific Northwest and those who stayed in Oklahoma, can rebuild a healthy culture that is connected to our tribe. Our tribal chief and cultural preservation staff went to the Pacific Northwest and honored the tribal elders living there, and in doing so they demonstrated their cultural importance to the larger Eastern Shawnee community. Our language is being published in our monthly tribal newsletter to allow those who live remotely to expand their understanding of the language and to use it. Our cultural preservation department has put countless historical artifacts, oral histories, and other materials on an interactive website so that tribal citizens can access and connect with their tribal culture regardless of where they live. Modern technology is doing what Rosa BlueJacket tried to do all those years ago; it is allowing our families to stay connected to our language, our past, and our culture. The following story, as told by an Eastern Shawnee tribal citizen who was born and raised in Oklahoma, expresses the desire that many Eastern Shawnees have to see our culture live beyond our generation: "I would say to children, learn as much as you can possibly learn about your heritage. And be who you are. Be who you are. It's important! Now that I have children of my own, the will that wasn't there [to learn cultural knowledge] is there, 'cause I want to pass it down to my children."[24]

Like an heirloom handed down, disconnection to our Eastern Shawnee identity was passed down through the generations, starting with my great-grandmother Louisa BlueJacket, to my grandfather, to my mother, and now to me. We were taught that assimilation equaled survival, that connecting to our Eastern Shawnee roots was not possible unless we lived in Oklahoma. But my generation has the ability to give back the heirloom of disconnection from our tribal culture, to not accept assimilation, and to embrace our Eastern Shawnee roots with more freedom and less fear than previous generations. My work toward this action has been to reconnect my family to our roots, to connect Rosa's family back to our culture, and to take my mother home again.

NOTES

1. In the summer of 2002 I began this research project with the McNair Scholars program at Oregon State University.

2. Since my research was completed in 2006, all but one of my great-aunties whom I interviewed have passed on (the surviving great-auntie is one of the oldest tribal members living in the Pacific Northwest). The oral histories collected during my research are some of the only oral histories gathered from these Eastern Shawnee elders.

3. This was my master's thesis, which was completed in 2006 through Oregon State University. A copy can be found at the Oregon State University library or at the Eastern Shawnee library in Wyandotte, Oklahoma.

4. Historical information regarding the Shawnee lifestyle was found in James H. Howard, *Shawnee! The Ceremonialism of a Native Indian Tribe and it's Cultural Background* (Athens: Ohio University Press, 1981), 14, 23. Since its publication in 1981, more contemporary research has found conflicting historical information regarding the Shawnee Tribe. For a more comprehensive history of the Shawnees, see Stephen Warren, *The Shawnees and Their Neighbors, 1795–1870* (Urbana: University of Illinois Press, 2005), chap. 1.

5. Rosa BlueJacket Daugherty (July 24, 1874–November 13, 1966) married Edward Daugherty. Rosa and Edward had four children: Louisa, Susie, Fydellia, and Joshua.

6. Though the term bushwhackers is used in this story by Rosa, it was meant primarily in reference to pro-Confederate militia during the Civil War. Rosa was either using this as a colloquialism from her time or mixing her memories in this story.

7. Cathleen M. Osborne-Gowey, "'No One Cared We Was Just Indian Women': Plants as a Catalyst to Eastern Shawnee Women's Identity Change" (master's thesis, Oregon State University, 2006). This story (an interview conducted in 2002 during the research for my master's thesis), gauging by its terminology, was most likely a mix of Rosa's memories of stories from the march from Ohio and from the Civil War. While its accuracy is open to interpretation, its value lies in the illustration it makes.

8. The General Allotment Act of 1887 (also called the Dawes Act) authorized the United States to survey Indian tribal land and divide it into allotments for individual Indians. The Eastern Shawnee Tribe of Oklahoma was one of many tribes whose reservation was divided into allotments. For further information on the Eastern Shawnee Tribe's experience with the General Allotment Act, see chapter 3 of this text by John Bowes.

9. "Examination of Allottee Record, 1910 Census No. 21," Records of the Quapaw Competency Commission, Record Group 75, National Archives and Records Administration Federal Records Center, Fort Worth, Texas.

10. Osborne-Gowey, "'No One Cared.'"

11. Ibid. Excerpts from this interviewee's journal were given to me during an interview for my master's thesis in 2002.

12. Louisa BlueJacket Daugherty Millhollin, my great-grandmother, was born in 1898 and died in 1939.

13. Osborne-Gowey, "'No One Cared.'"

14. Stories that Louisa's children (my grandfather and his siblings) would tell about their experience at the Seneca Indian Boarding School do not represent everyone's experience at the school. Information on the experiences of those attending the Seneca Indian Boarding School were taken

from interviews I conducted from 2002 to 2006 with members of the Millhollin family who attended the school.

15. Osborne-Gowey, "'No One Cared.'"

16. Tuberculosis was often found in employees who worked in the lead, copper, and zinc mines in Oklahoma. Information can be found in the *Handbook of Labor Statistics, No. 616*, (Washington, D.C.: Government Printing Office, 1936).

17. Information regarding tribal population was made available by the Eastern Shawnee Tribe Vital Statistics Department.

18. The Eastern Shawnee tribal lands are located in a rural part of the state of Oklahoma in Ottawa County. At the time the Millhollins moved to Sandy, Oregon, it was almost as rural as the area that they had moved from in Oklahoma.

19. First-generation refers to Eastern Shawnee tribal citizens born in Oregon shortly after the move to the Pacific Northwest. Second-generation refers to Eastern Shawnee tribal members born in the Pacific Northwest of parents who are considered the first generation.

20. Peter Iverson, *"We Are Still Here": American Indians in the Twentieth Century* (Wheeling, Mich.: Harlan Davidson, 1998).

21. Osborne-Gowey, "'No One Cared.'" Camas are an important and abundant variety of edible plant native to the Pacific Northwest.

22. The film *The Education of Little Tree*, released in 1997, is based on the book *The Education of Little Tree* by Forrest Carter, originally published in 1976.

23. The film *The Education of Little Tree* tells the story of a young boy who is half Indian and half white in the 1930s (around the same time my grandfather was growing up) and his experience with being sent to an Indian boarding school. While my grandfather's experience differs from the boy's, the film illustrates my grandfather's experience of growing up half Indian and the historical trauma that my grandfather and many others experienced at Indian boarding schools.

24. Osborne-Gowey, "'No One Cared.'"

11

As I Remember

An Oklahoma Memoir

ELSIE MAE "SIS" CAPTAIN HOEVET
TRANSCRIBED AND WITH AN INTRODUCTION BY
CHIEF GLENNA J. WALLACE

Back in the 1930s and 1940s, when the economy in Oklahoma was so terrible, many Eastern Shawnees left Oklahoma and moved to the West Coast, particularly to California, Oregon, and Washington. They were able to find jobs there, and they remained, ultimately encouraging other relatives to join them, marrying, having families, and raising them there. Now, three generations later, Oregon is home to numerous Eastern Shawnee citizens.

Elsie Mae "Sis" Captain Hoevet was one of the first to leave Oklahoma and make Oregon her home. She was the granddaughter of Tom Captain and Martha Ellen Gullett. Her father, Bill, was born January 13, 1894, the sixth of Tom and Martha's ten children: Thomas Andrew (born in 1884), Cordelia Jane "Corny" (1886), Mary Ellen (1888), Charles Selby (1890, died at age ten), Sarah May (1892), William Henry "Bill" (1894), Michael Francis "Frank" (1895), Gracie (1897), George Philemon (1899), Martha Eveline "Evie" (1901), and Sophronia "Babe" (1903).

Bill, known as Pops to his children and grandchildren, and his wife, Edith Reaser, had several children, all of whom went by nicknames more often than their given names: Lulu Marie "Tick," Esther, Elsie Mae "Sis," Hazel Leona "Jimmer" or "Jim," Clyde Eugene "Duge," and Frank Henry "Ike." The following is a multipage document that Sis wrote in her later life about her childhood in Oklahoma and subsequent events. Sis was born March 30, 1919, in Miami, Oklahoma. She graduated from Haskell Institute in 1939, moved to Washington, D.C., in 1941, to Portland, Oregon, in 1942, and to Salem, Oregon, in 1949. She worked in the Kaiser shipyard in Portland as a veritable Rosie the Riveter. After the war she worked for the state of Oregon for thirty-one years. Sis passed away in 2006 at the age of eighty-seven.

Her father, Bill, had severe rheumatoid arthritis, and Elsie's son Frank (who was always called Bo) pulled Bill everywhere in a little red wagon. Bill joined his children in Oregon, where he crossed over on February 21, 1963. We are indebted to Elsie's sons Bo and Doug for sharing this historical document with us.[1]

AS I REMEMBER

I'm writing this in hope that my grandchildren will read it and realize that things haven't always been the same as they are now. That it is possible to exist with very little, materially. And it might seem a struggle at times, but with the hopes and dreams of children, things seem to have a way of solving themselves and turning out for the best. Life is not a bed of roses; it's a book of experiences, and if you really weigh them against each other, the good seems to overbalance the bad.

The first recollection I have of my life started when I was four. At that time, we lived at Corney's place. It belonged to Pop's sister, who had gotten the land as an Indian donation.[2] The last

11.1. Edith Reaser Captain and her daughter Elsie Mae Captain Hoevet. Photo courtesy of Bo Hoevet.

time we saw the place, it had practically fallen down and had blackberry bushes higher than the house.

I am sure it was when we moved here that I remember some guy bringing us there in his new car, which had little pull-down curtains in the back with balled fringe on them, and I was quite taken with it, which made him quite nervous about me fooling with the curtains. Our big dog, Dick, got carsick in it, which didn't make us any more popular with him.

It was here that Jim was born, and my teddy bear disappeared about the same time. I was much more interested in what happened to my bear than I was in that squalling baby. They had sent me to the Farrs' down the road to stay all night, and the next morning, their oldest girl was going up to our place to get a bucket of water. Her mother told her not to go in the house 'cause "Mrs. Captain had a new B-A-B-Y." I told her I knew that spelled "baby." I would have been four years and seven months then.

Then we had a cyclone there that blew trees down all over the house and over the pump. I crawled under the bed and hollered that I wanted my daddy. He worked in the mines, which was thirty miles or so from home, and he would board up there sometimes. I don't know what determined when he would stay up there, but I remember him doing it for years. I can remember seeing the miners go by real early in the morning and getting home late in the evening, with their carbide lights on their caps, and just black and tired from the dirty mines. Pop was a shoveler, and one week he made eighty-four dollars that everyone was talking about, because he had beaten them all that week. There was a high incidence of "miner's con" among these workers, and it was not uncommon when riding through the mining towns to see victims lying on the porch with this disease, coughing, and just skin and bones. I had one uncle that had it, but he lived for quite a while, because he had a place that broke out on his chest, and actual pieces of rock from the accumulation of dust would drain out.[3]

We still lived here when Tick was going to grade school and fell off the Giant Strides onto ice and cut her lower lip. I saw her coming down the road with cotton packed over the cut, so I ran in the house and told Mom that Santa Claus was coming. I always gave Tick a bad time because I liked to tease, and she was always more serious. But she was seven years older than I, and we had lost a brother and sister in between, so that might have accounted for some of it. I remember throwing a rock and hitting her and hollering, "three shots at the nigger baby," which I had heard at a carnival; she started after me, but I hid in the wagon—lying flat on my stomach until Pop came and told me she was over her mad spell. There were two babies in between us, Roy and Esther. They died of whooping cough and diphtheria. I kinda remember that Roy was about two when he died, but don't know about Esther. Guess Roy had a temper, cause Pop said he would have been killed if he'd grown up.

The first time I went to a powwow at Devil's Promenade, I was scared of the Indians. They would come from all over the state of Oklahoma and set up their teepees. It would last for about a week, and they had a big cookhouse, where all the Indians ate. Pop took me in there one time, and we had buffalo meat. I can remember it was very tough, and Pop got tickled at me trying to eat it. We also went to the Green Corn Feast, which was a longer distance from home. I was told they had a peach-seed game they played, and that determined how long the feast lasted.[4]

11.2. *Quapaw Powwow*, 1942, Charles Banks Wilson (1918–2013), oil on panel, GM 0127.2512, Gilcrease Museum, Tulsa, Oklahoma.

The Fourth of July was one of the main celebrations for us. We would have soda pop put in a tub of ice, homemade ice cream, fried chicken, and if we were lucky, roasting ears. We would eat a big dinner, go to Seneca, Missouri, to a baseball game, and then stay for fireworks in the evening. Once in a while, we would get another bottle of pop at the ballgame. We saw our first Negroes at some of these games, which was a treat because they were a novelty to us, and we thought they were so funny. Pop was always crazy about baseball and had a team of his own for a while. They would go around to little towns or small communities around there and play. He took me with him once, up to the mines, and he bought me a little doll lying on a blanket in an artificial peanut shell. We stayed up all night at his sister's place, who we always considered to be wealthy because she always had a nice house and furniture. It was kinda a bad night because we could hear the machinery at the mines chugging all night.

I can still see Pop standing around at those baseball games. Always very calm with hands in back pockets. He always wore khaki pants and shirt, tan Stetson hat, and good shoes. He said he felt dressed up if he had good shoes and a good hat. He had only one suit that I knew of. It was a navy-blue pinstripe. But he always believed in buying good merchandise because he felt it paid off in the long run. He had a tendency to buy shoes to fit us kids and not allow for any growing room. Tick had terrible feet when she got older and will always believe that is the reason, because by the time the rest of us kids were older, he wasn't able to buy shoes for us.

Then we moved to the home-place. This place had belonged to Pop's folks. As long as I could remember, the brothers and sisters bickered back and forth about selling the place. When one was in the notion, one of the others would get stubborn and refuse to sign. Then, as time went by, the heirs were more scattered, and that was a mess trying to locate them. But I must have been twenty years old by the time they sold it. About thirty years later, a former neighbor told me it was too bad the Johnsons got that place, because they were so anti-Indian. It was a nice place, a big house with an upstairs and a big screened-in porch, with a good well fairly close to the house, up by the barn.

But that graveyard was up in back of it, so I can remember always having an eerie feeling about it. All of the funerals went right by the house. We went home late one night, and some-one had left a pine box in our front yard for an upcoming funeral. Then we walked through the cemetery on our way to school because it was the shortest way. That is where Mom is buried, as well as Grandpa and Grandma Captain along with other relatives, but no one has used it for a number of years that I know of. Used to, on Decoration Day, the relatives would gather up there and cut the grass and weeds and clean the place up.[5] In those days, the whole family went to funerals, and the friends dug the grave.

One day we had a double funeral for two uncles. Aunt Evie's husband committed suicide, and her brother died from natural causes. Everyone thought she was quite an exhibitionist and pretended a lot. When they were lowering her husband in the grave, she acted as if she was going to jump in after him. Uncle Thomas, her brother, said, "Hell, let her jump," and just stood and watched. She has been married about ten times to date, and two committed suicide. She was tried for murder when the last one shot himself, but was acquitted, and the lawyer took her farm for representing her. She was quite a character in her own right, always very stout for her size, and would just as soon fight a man as a woman. If she got mad, she'd throw a burning kerosene light or anything she could get her hands on. She had one husband that did all the housework, and she did all the outside work along with farming. She could lift a hundred-pound sack of feed as readily as anyone. She was always good to all of us, though, so we had no complaint.[6]

I remember nothing about my grandparents, except for Grandma Captain. She was a tall, stately woman that always drove her horse, Dean, and a buggy. I can still visualize her going past on her way to the store. She would hardly wave and never stopped to visit. Pop always said she was really a nagger and drove Grandpa Captain, a full-blooded Shawnee, to drink. My cousin

11.3. Evaline "Evy" Captain, daughter of Tom Captain. Photo courtesy of Glenna Wallace.

Charlie and I stayed all night with her once that I can remember. Grandpa Captain, according to Uncle Thomas, had an Indian name, but when he was in a war he did some heroic deed and they nicknamed him "Captain," which he thought was a pretty good name, so decided to keep it.

Then we moved up to the mines for a short period. I remember the two-room house, or shack, because it was cold, and there always seemed to be a wind there that just whistled through the cracks. Tick had a friend that would come by and walk to school with her. This girl would stand at the front gate and holler, "U-la!" Tick always hated her first name, Lula, so would never use it. There were chat piles [piles of rough gravel from the mines] every direction you looked. The first picture we saw of a mountain, we thought someone was trying to fool us and say it was thirty miles away, because we thought it was just a chat pile.

Grandma Captain was living with a daughter over at the mines when she passed away. I remember the funeral being in the house, and we started back to the Captain Cemetery, which was up in the woods, in a fenced corner reserved for this purpose, back of the home-place. We were on a dirt road, which was all we had at that time, and the hearse became stuck in the mud. They had a farmer come with a team of horses and pull the hearse out, and we were on our way. It was a long, slow trip, so it was after dark when we got to the cemetery. So, by carbide lights and lanterns, they buried her.

It wasn't too long after that, I remember being in town with Mom. She was carrying Jim as a tiny baby. We went in a store, for what I don't know, but Mom became angry and walked out. When we got outside, she handed me a ring with a blue set in it and told me to put it on. I was surprised and kinda set back, but as I got older and thought about it, she must have stolen it. I shouldn't say that, 'cause I don't know.

I also remember being at a carnival, with her carrying Jim, that we were eating ice cream bars. In those days, there was always gypsies telling fortunes. Anyhow, we passed a tent, and a gypsy woman was holding a baby without a diaper, and this evidently turned Mom's stomach, because she just gave the ice cream to me and told me to eat it. These carnivals were on the Fourth of July and at fair time, but I really looked forward to them. Pop would give us a quarter, and I would spend mine on spinning a wheel for butterfly pins, and Tick liked the rides, which I could never understand. I remember going to sideshows, too. One time they had a little guy that was supposed to be about thirty-five years old. He was in a little deal, about like our strollers now. He had his hair parted in the middle with a little black mustache. He was about the height of a two-year-old and very skinny. Another time, I ran up and looked over the edge down on a guy that looked to me like he was about six feet tall and very skinny. He was just laying on a bench. The guy told him, "Here's a little girl that came to play with you." But I didn't stay around that long because he really scared me. The first cotton candy I ever had was at a carnival, and I was running toward the car to go home when some boys threw it full of gravel.

I had my fifth birthday and my very first birthday cake here [at the home-place]. About this time, I learned to milk cows. We had one old cow that wasn't very ambitious, so I would sit flat on the ground with one leg [in] back of her feet and the other on the outside of the milk bucket. She could still switch her tail, though, around in your face when the flies were after her. Mom always did all the milking, and I was anxious to learn. Don't remember her making me help, but I just liked to. Tick never did learn to milk or much of anything else, 'cause Mom was just one to do all the housework and cooking and didn't teach us much. Our chores were bringing in wood, carrying water, doing dishes, and going after the cows. One time, Tick and I were doing dishes. I was standing on a box to be tall enough to reach the dishpan on the stove, and we were talking about something, and I said, "Jesus Christ"–something, and she told me to never let Pop hear me say that. And I told her that was where I heard it, but she said that was different, but I couldn't understand at that time. I was going after the cows one time, and I saw a pretty bumble-bee and decided that I would catch it in my handkerchief. I didn't hang on very long after he bit me through my protection. One night, I had forgotten to bring in my wood, so had to go after it after dark. It was scary anyhow with that graveyard so close, but an owl started swooping after me; and I had always heard that they would get mixed up in your hair and draw all the blood out of the top of your head, so it didn't take me long to get to the house. I learned more from that punishment than getting a whipping.

We were always told that August was "mad dog" month, so they wouldn't let us go swimming lest a mad dog had been in the water; or they said to watch for them on the road. We could tell them by sight because they would froth at the mouth. One of Pop's dogs went mad one time, and they had him tied up, but he frothed and was just wild. He would try to bite a pitchfork or any-thing he could get hold of. They finally shot him, though, because there was evidently no cure for it. This dog was named Duck because he caught one of my pet ducks and was pulling on the head while I was pulling on the feet.

I had blood poisoning while we lived here. I had a boil on my leg, and I had been told that rusty pins were poisonous, but I had to see for myself, so I picked a boil with it. Pop never knew that, or no telling what my nickname would have been. We had so many boils on our feet and legs when we were little. It must have been from going barefooted all the time that we could, and whether it was the dew from the grass or what, I don't know.

The only whipping that Pop ever gave me was one time he was building a fence and sent me to the store to get him some tobacco. I stopped at the cousins' and played awhile, got the tobacco, went a different way home, and stopped at some neighbors' and played, and was going on home when I saw Pop coming. Thinking real fast, I picked up a stick and told him I was scared of the cows. He could hardly keep from laughing, but he switched me a little anyhow.

11.4. Moccasin Bend No. 5 school in the Eastside Community. *Back row, left to right*: Eugene Wyrick, Travis Green, Denny Mercer, and Norman "Corky" Munson. *Front row, left to right*: Mrs. Adams (teacher), Barbara Hollis, Patsy Munson, Barbara Crawford King. March 1950. Photo courtesy of Glenna Wallace.

Duge was born at this place, and I would have been seven by then. When Tick and I came by Uncle Thomas's place after school, he told me, "Pusy, you have a little brother at your place," but I thought he was teasing me because he did that a lot. When Pop came home from work, Jim, aged two and a half, ran out and told him that Mom had a little nigger baby in bed with her. I remember seeing an old suitcase around the place that was stained with what I thought was blood, and I thought for a long time that that was what they brought Duge in.

I started school while we lived here. On my first day, walking up through the woods with Tick, I kept jabbering about how it felt like we were just going to Sunday school, but she just told me to keep quiet. One time it was my turn to fix our lunch, and she had run off from me, so I took a couple of biscuits and put butter on them and dropped them in a half-gallon syrup bucket (which we always used for lunch buckets) and ran and caught up with her, with those biscuits bouncing around in that bucket. She told me she had a notion to send me back to the house, but she didn't. Pop most always had a bill at the grocery store by the school, so we bought a box of raisins on his bill once, ate a few of them on the way home from school, then hid the rest in a hollow log.[7] The next morning, we went to get our raisins, and there had been a fire and burnt the log and our raisins.

The school we went to was one room for all eight grades and one teacher. Once in a while for our lunch, we would take dry beans and some salt pork, and the teacher would cook them on the wood stove for our lunch. We really thought that was living. I made the second and third grades in one year, because I knew all my multiplication tables. Some of the kids, especially one boy I remember, was real jealous and mad at me. I helped the teacher check some test papers, though, and I marked a lot of them wrong because they said a quarter of an hour was fifteen minutes, and I believed that a quarter was a quarter—twenty-five. We always exchanged valentines, and I got one from a boy that was a real pretty bought one that said, "I hope thistle show you I want you for my valentine," with a purple thistle on it. That boy was Bo's dad. One girl was jealous, and when she got hers from this same boy, hers said, "Come into my parlor said the spider to the fly," and it was homemade. She was the same one that said she wanted to be a typewriter when she grew up.

My first feller usually got my name for Christmas, and he would buy me a little set of tin dishes. He even promised me the colt when his pony had a little one, but it turned out to be a male. He was killed in the war in the '40s.

I had some cousins that were the meanest kids in school. The teacher would try to whip them with a rubber hose, but they would fight like little demons. They would fight and wrestle around in the aisles. One teacher's name was Jenny, and we thought that was just the name of a donkey. Her little sister came to visit school from town a time or two, and we would get her to say her sister's name and then everyone would giggle. One cousin, Peanuts, was a smarty and would tease the teacher until she could have slapped him, but he was bigger. Then he would say with a smirk on his face, "horse feathers," "frog hair," or something about as silly. One time we were to ask riddles, and Buck, his younger brother, asked, "What is it a rich man puts in his pocket and a poor man throws away?" The answer was "snot." Another cousin was sitting right behind me one time when we had a test with the question, "Where did the Indians come from?" He whispered and told me he came from a sugar bowl but didn't know where I came from. The one treat was to be able to help the teacher ring the bell. The big one for the start of the day was pulled by a rope. She had a smaller hand-bell that was used for recess and lunchtime.

The schoolhouse was the gathering place for the community. We had pie suppers, church, and Christmas programs there. Money was made from the pie suppers to get money to buy candy and nuts for all the kids in the community. The folks would sew red and green mesh sacks, and then they would all meet one night before Christmas and sack everything up. We would have a program, singing, and the distribution of name-drawn gifts and sacks by Santa. For the pie supper, all the women would take a pie in a pretty box decorated with crepe paper, then the men would bid on the pies. There was one man in the community that always wanted to buy his wife's pie, but Pop and some of the other men would get together and bid him up. They would eventually let him have it, but that was always the most expensive pie there. My folks were embarrassed one time when Pop bought a pie for Duge, and it turned out to be his favorite, chocolate. He practically ate the whole pie by himself. The candidates for county offices would come out to make speeches and electioneer, so they would have a pie supper at the same time. When I got older, someone dared me to make a hot-pepper pie, which was just like a cream pie with the hot peppers in it. One member of the school board, who never combed his hair—Pop said he used "bushum"—but he always tried to impress the teacher and would sit with her every chance he got. But anyhow, he bid on and got this pepper pie and was sitting on the stage with the teacher when he took his first bite. They said his face turned red, and he made a run for the pump. Then some of the candidates got onto it and were giving bites to their opponents, so there was quite a string to the pump. The pump handle used to freeze in the winter, so the new kids were always being dared to stick their tongue on it. It would pull the skin off and really be sore. So don't try it on cold iron.

We played a lot of tag, Run Sheep Run, shinny-hitting a can with a club kinda like hockey, Today-Had, Giant Strides, and teeter-totters. I almost tore my heel off one time playing tag because I was barefooted and had backed up to this corrugated steel or tin garage for the teacher's car and had slid my heel under the edge. When I started to run, it just practically sliced it off. Jim was mad because the teacher took us home at lunchtime, and she brought her doll and was just getting ready to play house. A few years later, we had a basketball court outside, and we would compete with some of the nearby schools. Jim later was janitor at this schoolhouse when she was going to public high school. She would walk about a half-mile in the morning to open up and build the fire. In the evening, the school bus would drop her off there, and she would sweep and dust and carry out the ashes. On Saturdays, she would go up and scrub the floor, and oil it, and carry the wood in for a week. For this, she was paid five dollars a month. Pop had a house down across from the school where he, Duge, Jim, and Ike lived. I was living with Tick and Jack, working in Miami, when Bo was born. We played with old tires by rolling them around and racing each other or by turning them wrong side out, and crouching up inside, and rolling each other down a hill. We would also take an old tobacco can, bend it in a half circle, nail it to a stick, and guide a little iron rim or wheel with it.

Back to the farm. This was on the old home-place. There was a lot of farmland on this place, but Pop had a hired hand. I remember one summer we had a threshing crew come in. There was just one threshing machine in the country, and they would hire out and bring most of the crew. Some of the women in the neighborhood would come and help cook dinner for them. That was a busy day because it took a lot of food to feed a bunch of men. One time, Pop put Tick and me out to transplant corn. We planted until we got tired and just threw the rest in a ditch, not being smart enough to know that it would come up. Pop found it later and told us what a good job we had done planting that corn. The hired hand would start plowing early in the morning, but would take a long lunch break to let the horses rest up as well as himself.

Pop bought his only new car while living here. I don't know whether Mom knew about it beforehand, but us kids didn't. We usually went to town on Saturday night to do what little shopping we did. But this night Pop was late getting home, and it was after dark when we saw the lights coming down the lane, so we ran to open the gate for him, and here was this new 1926 Ford with isinglass curtains. We went to town, but it was a mighty slow trip because he had to drive so slow. But I can remember we were so proud sitting away up there. Another time, we walked down the lane to meet Pop to go to town. Mom noticed I had dirty eyebrows—most kids had dirty ears, elbows, or something, but I always had dirty eyebrows—so she sent me back to the house to wash again. I couldn't tell whether the darn things were clean or not, so I just shaved them off. Mom was so mad. She said she should make me stay home, but she really wouldn't, because she always said she wouldn't go anyplace that she couldn't take her kids.

They would go to barn dances or to dances in someone's home, but all the kids went along. When we got sleepy, they would line us up on a bed—maybe six or seven across—and cover us up with coats. There was very little drinking at these dances; in fact, Pop drank very little that I ever knew about. One night, when we lived on Corney's place, after coming home from a dance, Pop was out walking up and down the road in front of the house just hollering and making noises. He woke the roosters up, and they started crowing. Pop would holler, "Crow, you SOB, crow!" He talked plainer than that. We were told that he'd been poisoned on whiskey, but after getting older, decided that he was just plain drunk. One time, I ran out to his car when he came home from work—first one there got his lunch bucket and any leftovers—but I ran back in the house and told Mom that he had been drinking whiskey. Come to find out, it was the antifreeze that smelled that way. Pop had a passion for playing pool. One time, Mom got tired waiting for him because the kids were hot and hungry and wanted to go home, so she sent me in a pool hall after him. He was so surprised and mad at me that he just about hit me with a pool cue. Kids nor women were allowed in those places.

He also liked to fox hunt or listen to the dogs run. We always had a bunch of dogs, up to twelve or thirteen around the place, and I've made many a pan of dog bread [cornmeal, cracklings, and water] for his dogs. A bunch of guys would get together with their dogs, go out in the woods in any kind of weather, turn the dogs loose, and they could tell by the bark which one was ahead. I never heard of them catching a fox, but the guys would sit or lie out all night with a lunch and coffee pot. And I heard in later years that there was a little liquor involved. Then the next day was usually spent looking for their dogs, because sometimes they would run until they were so tired or their feet were so sore that they couldn't make it home. One night, before Decoration Day, Pop stayed out all night on one of these hunts and wasn't home to go with us to the graveyards, so he and Mom got in a big fight. The worst one we had ever heard, so Tick and I were sure they were going to separate, so we were laying on the floor bawling.

Mom always seemed to have a bunch of geese around. Don't know what for or anything, because she never picked them or ate them. But I've run a thousand miles for those things. The old ganders would get hold of my dress-tail, and they would just hang on, flapping their wings when we ran. Then when it would happen to rain, I would have to get out and find all the goslings, because they would just stand under a drip with their mouths open and would drown.

We missed very few Wednesdays in the summer going to the Ladies' Aid.[8] The women would quilt, and the kids played. I was usually the biggest one, so I would take care of all the kids. Mom drove her horse and buggy. She drove old Dean, the one that had belonged to Grandma Captain and was now blind in one eye. One time, she was driving across the meadow, and Tick and a cousin were riding on the back on a board. Mom hit the horse just for meanness, and those two disconnected from the board and lit on their bottoms out in the middle of the meadow. We thought that was real funny.

I can remember the Canady cousins coming down for a Sunday. We had very little company and didn't visit much, so it was a real big occasion when someone came. Us kids would just about run our legs off, mostly running off and hiding from the younger ones. I had no girl cousins my age around those parts, so was always a tomboy. I was the happiest in my overalls and shirt. We always ate dinner after the older folks were through because the table wasn't big enough for all of us. One time Uncle Walter brought Mom a ring that he had pounded out of a penny.[9] She wore it for a wedding ring and was always polishing it with a cloth. She had it so shiny that it looked like gold to us. He could also make them out of nickels and dimes, but maybe those were too expensive.

Pop let me ride with him one time when he took a wagonload of tomatoes to Seneca.[10] We went in a nice drugstore that had nice tile floors and high ceilings, so it was always cool in there. I can remember having ice cream in there on little ice cream chairs and table. I was wearing a black satin dress that Aunt Brin had given me, and I really thought I was dressed up, sitting up in the wagon seat with Pop. Anyhow, I spilled some of my ice cream on the floor and embarrassed Pop.

One time, Tick, Aunt Brin, and I were playing whip; and they put me on the end. I was thrown and knocked out. When I woke up, Mom was pounding on me. If she got scared or excited, she would just start beating. Jim used to hold her breath until she would practically turn blue, Mom would start beating or stick her head in a bucket of cold water.

The one food I really enjoyed was wild rabbit. Mom used to clean them, and then throw them upon the smokehouse in the snow, and leave them overnight. We really thought that made them good. Once in a while we would have beefsteak for breakfast. I thought that was just like music, to wake up and hear Mom pounding it with a saucer to tenderize it before she cooked it. Our main foods were beans and potatoes, though. As soon as the breakfast dishes were done, we would put on a pot of beans. In the summer, we would just cook enough for one meal, because we had no way to keep them from spoiling, and they would in one day back there. Very seldom did we have bought bread. Always biscuits or cornbread. Sometimes, for supper, we would just have leftover cornbread and milk or mush and milk. We would hang the milk in a tin bucket down in the well or spring to cool it. We thought it was real icy cold. We had very little canned fruit or vegetables. If we got one little box of blue plums [prunes] and peaches to can, it was a rare occasion. We had a few wild blackberries, so if we got some to can, it was a treat. Our "sweetening," as Pop called it, was usually syrup; or if we were feeling flush, we could buy a gallon of homemade molasses for fifty cents. They used sugar cane for that, and there was only one guy in the county that made it that I knew of. We usually had a good supply of milk, eggs, and butter, if they thought we could afford to eat them instead of trading them for beans, flour, and potatoes. We hardly ever had a good garden, because it was too dry, and we never seemed to have an oversupply of water. I can remember having tomatoes, some green beans, and turnips.

It's true that Pop made pretty good money at times, but it always seemed to go for rent, car payments, dogs, and paying somebody else's bills. He was always signing notes for someone and then getting stuck and having to pay them. Once in a while he would butcher a pig, but never a beef. When they would butcher, some of the relatives or neighbors would come and help. They would have a barrel of hot water, and some boards laying in front of that. After the pig was killed, they would tie a rope around its neck and dip it back and forth in the hot water. Then put it on the boards, and everyone would start scraping. Very little of it was ever wasted, because they would cut every little piece of flesh off and make headcheese or sausage out of it. The skin would be rendered [the fat cooked out for lard] and used for cracklings. The brains were usually cooked with eggs, because they were too rich to eat alone. They would use a smoke-flavored salt to preserve the meat in the smokehouse, or you could can it after frying it all down. Pop usually raised his own chickens. I remember the incubator sitting in the bedroom. It had to be kept at a certain temperature by kerosene burner, and the eggs turned ever so often. It was always my job to kill all of the little deformed or sickly chicks. Then, they [the chicks] would go out to the brooder house. They had to be watched very carefully there, because if they got too hot they would die; and if they got too cold, they would bunch up and smother. Pop would often go out there in the evening and just sit and watch them because it was always nice and warm.

It was at this place that I found out there was no Santa Claus. I had my suspicions, so decided to play possum [pretending to be asleep] and find out for sure. Our bed for three kids was in the front room, so Mom and Pop brought in the one present each to put in our socks. Mom told Pop that she thought they should give the present that he had gotten for me to Tick, but he said no, he had gotten it for Sis. It turned out to be a comb and brush set. Before that, though, I had seen a doll in the stairway that I was sure was going to Jim. Our socks were filled with candy, a few nuts, and an orange. That was usually the only orange we had all year, so we would hang on to it as long as we could and smell it. Even the nuts would get an orange smell, which we enjoyed. I don't remember ever having a Christmas tree at home. We had the big one at the schoolhouse, so just never expected one at home. If we were very, very lucky, we would have turkey at Christmas, but it was usually roasted chicken. One time, later on, Tick was snooping around before Christmas to see if she could find her present and was convinced she was goin' to get some amber beads, but she didn't. Later, she went back to take a better look and found out they were dog pills. Aunt Brin would occasionally bring us a gift to the school Christmas play.

She moved in with the Canadys after Aunt Ethel died and left six kids, the youngest being six weeks old. She was paid for this, so always had her own money, since Uncle Walter worked in the mines. She sure was a nut on cleanliness; the house always reminded me of a mortuary because it was always so cool and clean, but quiet. You didn't dare drip a drop of water on her floor, or she would see you and make you wipe it up. The kids were never allowed to get dirty, or they would be punished. The older boys built a little log cabin down in back of the house and had a stove and cots in it, so that was where they spent most of their time. We used to chase a lot of lightning bugs in the meadow in front of their place, and it was also a good place for footraces. The boys were allowed to come in the kitchen door and walk directly to the table for meals. They washed at the back of the house the year around. Then there was another door at the end of this big, cement, unroofed back porch into the bedrooms. They would go in there at bedtime, then use the same door leaving the house in the morning. There was never any talking at the table; and if she caught the two younger ones looking from their plate, she would slap them. They would eat just what she put on their plate. Uncle Walter never seemed to argue with her or anything, but he told Pop one time that he was sorry she ever came. I stayed with them quite a bit during vacations, and especially after Mom died. She had the first phonograph I had ever seen and had two records that I remember—"Four-Leaf Clover" and "Ramona." Uncle Walter had a radio with a big horn on it, and there was a lot of squeaking and squawking, and you had to listen real closely to hear anything. Aunt Brin took very good care of Walter after he got miner's con and seemed to have a lot of patience with him. As the kids grew older, and up until she died, they all seemed to think the world of her.

Then it was time to move again. For some reason we couldn't move out when we should have, so Aunt Grace, Virg, and Gracie moved in with us. I can remember Aunt Grace standing behind the cupboard door and eating hard candy, evidently trying to hide from us kids, but we would stand and watch her anyhow. Then Gracie was always a big spoiled kid, so she never had to help do anything. She would always have to go to the toilet when it was time to do dishes.

But we finally moved up in the woods. Pop had been donated forty acres from the Indian agency when he was born.[11] It was worthless land and covered with small oak. It did have a good spring down the hill, though. He built a sturdy two-room house, with a loft where us kids slept at one end and Uncle Bob at the other. We just had a ladder from the kitchen to get up there on. He put sheetrock on the walls downstairs, without any paint or anything, but we sure thought it was nice. Duge came outside one day and announced that he had written all our names. Sure enough, there they were with crayon—just marks for each one of us. I can remember carrying water from the spring in the winter; and if we spilled any water or happened to fall down, it would freeze, and we'd have a heck of a time getting up the hill.

Jim was always one to play house and with dolls. She would lay rocks around for the rooms, with gaps for the windows and doors. I would play with her until I got tired and then jump out a window, and then she would bawl. I never did like that or making mud pies, but she and Duge would sit and eat those things like they were really dining out.

We had a creek nearby, where we could go swimming, too. It wasn't very deep, but we could sure do a lot of mud-crawling, but we didn't care as long as it was cool. We had to walk over a log to get to school. When the water was high, it was just [r]oiling under that log, so we had to be surefooted. If we had ever slipped, that would have been the end. The folks never seemed to worry about it, though, and just sent us on our merry way. One time, walking home from school, Jim had had a cold that settled in her ears, which made her deaf. Anyhow, the community drunk, Ed Graham, drove up behind her and bumped her with the bumper. It scared her so bad that, for a long time after that, if she even saw a car coming down the road, she would run and get on the other side of the fence. I can remember we would get so tired walking home from school; but if we got a stick horse, we could run and race each other all the way home.

Jim always had some little animal to play with, like a little yellow kitten that was her Baby Blue Eyes. She would carry it around like a baby in a blanket and could lay it on the window sill, and the silly thing would lay there all stretched out until she came back after it. She also had some baby mice in a matchbox one time, and Pop told her to lay them down by the cat so they could suck. She laid them all out, and the old cat turned around and took one look and swooped them up with one bite. Jim just sat there with her big brown eyes and was flabbergasted.

One summer, Mom took Tick, Jim, and me down in Missouri to pick strawberries. We lived in what had been a chicken house, but was clean, but wasn't sealed inside, had no windows, and boards with cracks in them for the floor. Aunt Evie and her husband at that time, John [Longlegs], stayed with us. We had only a small stove, homemade table and chairs. I remember there were two men picking, too, who teased me a lot. I finally thought up a nickname [for one], which I thought was hilarious—"Specs" because he wore glasses. The owner of the patch had an older boy at home who had TB. He always wore a white shirt and was so clean, but skinny and pale. He gave Tick the words to a popular song at that time, "Ramona." One night, Pop and Duge, who had to stay home to take care of the chickens, came to see us. I was so glad to hear Pop's voice, but I pretended I was asleep and just laid real quiet and cried. I remember he said, "Whatta boar's nest," when he came in. I made my first five dollars picking that year and practically wore the bill out carrying it around and letting the other kids have a peek. Finally, we went to town and the first thing I bought was a pair of wool knee socks in about 120-degree weather. They were brown and white plaid, and Mom just about had a fit when she saw them, but I just had to put them on in the store so I wouldn't have to bring them back.

Don't know why, but it was time to move again. Always hated those moving days because it was usually cold the first of the year. We'd always go to a cold house, and it would take time to get the stove set up and a fire built. Then we wouldn't be able to find the groceries, so we'd be hungry, too. It was usually late at night by the time they could get the beds set up. It was a slow, drawn-out process because we had to do it with horses and wagon.

But we moved to the Farr place. It had quite a bit of land with it, and we still had a hired hand. This time it was Everett Bowman, and he gave us all the itch. Tick and I seemed to have it the worse. Someone told us to use pokeroot to get rid of it.[12] We boiled it and put it in a tub of warm water and took a bath in it. About midnight, we started itching more and were both up trying to keep warm around the old wood stove. Anyhow, we both had big welts all over that itched clear to the bone. We evidently just outgrew it, because I don't recall using any kind of medicine on it.

This house was a little bigger than the last, but we always had beds in the front room. We had our first toilet that we had ever had, except for down at the strawberry field. We, of course, were still bathing in a tub, using the same water for all of us, usually on Saturday night. In the summer, we would set the water out in the sun to warm it. The well was right next to the house, so we thought we were really progressing. Mom always washed outside in the summer, with P&G soap and bluing and a washboard, and always boiled the clothes for so many minutes. She didn't know what bleach was, but she was known around for having the whitest washings. In the winter, she washed inside but still boiled the clothes; and it was such a nuisance trying to get the clothes dry, because they would freeze out on the clothesline, so we would just bring a few in at a time and dry them in the house.

Ike was born at this place. One Sunday, they sent us kids down to Uncle George's place, and when they came after us in the evening, we had a little brother. I was eleven at the time, but I had no idea that he was on the way. The women always made all the baby clothes by hand, or otherwise it would be bad luck, and kept them hidden so the other kids never saw them. Mom stayed in bed for thirteen days, and she believed on the tenth day all the organs went back in place, so she would lie very still on that day. I can remember her eating a lot of charcoal and dirt daubers' nests, but they told me later that she just did that when she was pregnant. She could stand a lot of pain and never complained. She had terrible teeth, with some practically rotted out, but she wouldn't go to a dentist. She used aspirin and oil of peppermint and doctored herself until the pain went away. Pop got her in a dentist's chair once, but as soon as the dentist started toward her, she jumped up and ran.

I always played with Ike and carried him everyplace, so much that my hip stuck out where he rode. We would walk about a quarter of a mile down the road to meet Pop in the evening, so we could open the gate for him and get a ride back to the house. On this place, we raised sweet potatoes, sugar cane, potatoes, had a better garden (we always put a tin can with holes in the bottom by the tomato plants and kept water in them), and there were more berries around. We had the sugar cane made into molasses on shares, kept the sweet potatoes in the house so they wouldn't freeze, made an igloo-effect mound lined with straw to keep the potatoes from freezing, so we were beginning to eat a little better. I don't remember exactly how they made molasses, but I

11.5. *Sorghum Mill at 10 A.M.*, 1960, Charles Banks Wilson (1918–2013), oil on canvas, GM 0127–2455, Gilcrease Museum, Tulsa, Oklahoma.

know they had a horse that would walk around and around hooked onto a log, and someway it was fixed up so that would squeeze the juice out of the cane.[13]

One day, some guys were hauling hay to the barn, and Duge would run down the hill, across the creek, and up the hill and jump on back of the wagon for the ride back to the house. These guys decided to put a dead bull snake on the back of the wagon, and they still tell the joke on him. He looked, backed off, and said, "My Dod, what a nake." We had a lot of snakes around, and it was not uncommon to find the black snakes in the hens' nests, so you learned pretty young to look in before sticking your hand in after the eggs. They would swallow the eggs whole, then wrap themselves around something to crush them. We watched out for the copperheads and water moccasins because they were both poisonous. The copperhead was a pretty snake, but it was slow and treacherous and would strike.

The only camping trip we took when I was home was about two miles from the house. We went with the Canadys and just threw quilts over the weeds and slept. The men were fishing for catfish and would put trot lines across the river with several hooks on them, and ever so often, they would run the trot lines with a boat to see how many fish they had. They would use dough balls for bait—boiled balls of water and flour.

I got a real hard whipping from Mom when we lived here. It was just the second whipping that I ever got, but it was a doozy. My folks never whipped much, but we knew enough to mind; and there was no backtalk or sassing. She had sent me to the store with some eggs to trade for something, and she knew there was exactly twenty-five-cents worth. I was playing around and broke some of the eggs, so I stopped at a neighbor's house, and they weren't home, so I stole some of their eggs, and Duge or Jim told on me. But she used a peach limb, which is very pliable and strong, so I carried welts for a while. She didn't tell Pop, because I bet he would have given me another one. But when one kid got a whipping, we would all cry. But what really brought it to a head was when she told us to come home from the neighbors' at a certain time and I over-stayed, so that was the climax. I knew I deserved it.

One time, Jim and I walked up to the mailbox, which was about a mile from the house. But it was a holiday, so there was no mail. Had to do something, you know, so I told Jim to tell the folks that we had seen a snake with teeth, but she didn't want to, but I told her she'd better or else. She did, but they just took it as a joke. I was always good at making up stories, but I wouldn't really lie to get out of trouble. The folks always told us that they would come nearer whipping us for lying than if we told the truth.

We had some characters around these parts, too. Henry Turkeyfoot was the best. He was full-blooded Indian and always wore a big black hat, red handkerchief around his neck, and rode a pretty horse. He always said he wouldn't take a "tousand dollas" for his horse. He later moved his horses in his house when the barn burnt down. One Fourth of July it was raining hard, and he came by drunk. We were sitting on the porch, and we would ask him questions just to hear him talk. I asked him if he was a "Missouri puke," and he said he was an Oklahoma roughneck and pulled his pistol out and shot up in the air. He was also going to show us how to make it rain—it was already pouring down. We had to find an old bird's nest, he put some navy beans in it, and walked down and put it in the creek. A lot of people were scared of him, but he liked to scare people, so he would sneak up on them if he could, he thought that was real funny. One time he came by and had cut his hand wide open on barbed wire, but he wanted some salt to put in it. He put it in there and walked on up through the woods. He made me a bow and arrow one time

11.6. Henry Turkeyfoot and his loyal horse, Billie. Photo taken by Charles Banks Wilson. Courtesy of Carrie Wilson.

and printed "Home Sweet Home" on it, and someone figured he had copied it off a calendar. He would always go to Grandma BlueJacket's to find out how old he was—he could never remember. It was told that he beat Grandpa Captain up years ago, so he and Uncle George were out drinking one time and George beat him up once and again "for Paw." They would take Henry over to jail to sober up if he got too wild, and he would tell us he'd been to school. They would let him sober up, and then he'd run around town a day or two and sleep at the jail.

We had some stray jennies that would come and hang around the place.[14] We could ride them, but you couldn't tell them where to go. If one went in the chicken house or barn, you'd just as well get off and find another one, because they wouldn't go any farther. But we would just get on them without a bridle or anything and ride as long as they would keep moving.

One time Mom cooked a possum, and we were going to try to eat it. Uncle Bob sat and looked at it for a while and said he could just see the damn thing smilin' at him. That was enough, none of us would taste it.

One time we were getting ready to go to the Christmas party, and pretty soon we heard all this noise out on the back porch. Mom came in carrying me the prettiest blue mohair tam, and she said Santa Claus had left it. I knew it wasn't true, but still I was kinda hesitant to disbelieve her, because I thought that noise might have been him.

By this time, Tick was in high school, and Jim and I were going to the grade school. It was quite a ways, so Pop found me some old-fashioned lace-up, sharp-toed shoes so I could walk in the snow ahead of her and kinda make a path. But I would take just as big steps as I could so she would fall down. Another cousin had a pair just like them, and we really had fun with them at school, 'cause the boys didn't dare tease us or we'd kick their shins or chase them to the toilet. I was getting to be quite a cipherer and speller in school, and we would go around to other schools and compete with them. I had one cousin my age who could beat me sometimes.

Mom was a joker, and she liked to play jokes on someone. She liked to keep busy doing something, especially piecing quilts by hand and sewing. We always pointed out in the catalog the way we wanted a dress made, and she could do it after cutting a pattern out of newspaper. She was always devoted to her children and they came first. She always kept a very clean house with what she had to work with, which wasn't much. I remember she had one new cook stove when I was six or seven, and a new rug a few years later. The furniture, what we had, was hand-me-downs and not very fancy. In the summer, many times, we would sit out under a shade tree and play cards, like Rummy or Five Hundred. She always did all the milking and garden work. We never had a decent yard, so there wasn't much work there, because it was just dirt, and it would get so hard that it could be swept. One thing that really irritated her was for Pop to bring someone home for a meal unexpected.

One Monday night, September 14, when I was twelve, I came home from school, and Mom was laying on the floor in front of the stove. I was going to change my clothes and go get my wood and play as usual. But she told me I would have to make the cornbread for supper. I was pretty disgusted, but I did it with a little cussin' under my breath. I stayed home from school the rest of the week to take care of Ike, [who was] eighteen months. She passed away on Friday afternoon, September 18, 1931. They called us kids in the house, and Tick ran up through the woods to get Grandma Triggs—everyone called her that—and I was rubbing her leg. I heard Pop say something about "Tommy," which he always called her, but I didn't realize that she was gone when I went outside and started praying for her and asking for her life. I guess that was when I lost my faith, when I couldn't have one little wish granted. Uncle Bob was out in the yard, but he didn't say anything. I had been reading some of Tick's books about where all those places such as Bethlehem was, etc., and I had always thought that was up in heaven. Anyhow, she was buried the next day, and things really happened fast after that. Pop never did work a day after that. He had been bothered with arthritis for years, but was still able to work until that happened, but then he really went down.[15] Pop said we all should have hated her for running out when we all needed her. We went ahead and went to school, leaving Ike with Pop. Tick left school and was married in November. Pop went to the Indian Hospital in Claremore, and we took Ike up for Aunt Corney to take care of. Another couple and their little girl moved in with us and took care of the three of us until the next summer.

Pop came home from the hospital the next spring after school was out. He could kinda get around on crutches, but not very well. So we moved back up in the woods on his place. Ike stayed at Corney's most of the time, but he would get his "budget" and come home once in a while for a visit. He would tell us about his two girlfriends—Mis Ammy and Blue Busses. That summer was really a nightmare because I didn't know how to do anything, and Pop was in so much pain that I had to get up all hours of the night to give him his aspirin and water. One time I remember getting down and running the treadle on the sewing machine, and the more he would holler trying to wake me up, the harder I would treadle. One night, I ran outside and was quite a ways from the house when I finally woke up and realized where I was.

Pop had no insurance or income of any kind, so we lived on what few eggs and cream we could get and welfare, and the Indian agent would give us a five-dollar grocery order once in a while and when we could get a way to go see him. The neighbors or uncle would take the cream and eggs to town and trade them for a few groceries. This was during the Depression, but I thought it was just that way because Pop wasn't working. So about once a month, I would get my sack and go down to Shawnee Lake, about five miles away, to wait for the food surplus truck to come in.[16] Usually, I would get a ride along the way, and we'd just sit and wait for the truck. We would get a can or two of meat, some canned grapefruit, which we didn't like, some tomatoes, powdered milk, flour, and cornmeal. It wasn't much, but we were glad to get it.

The lake was a different place for us to go to, and we always enjoyed going down there. It had so many water lilies on it, had a big swing that went out over the water, a ball field, a cement enclosure for some catfish, and a little concession stand. It always seemed to be cool down there and would get flooded in the summer or early spring when the river would back up in there. It would get in the log cabin, but the people would just move the furniture upstairs and leave until the water went down and then go back and clean the mud out.

I didn't know a thing about cooking, but Pop would come in the kitchen in his little red wagon and coach me. I knew several kinds of wild greens, so I would pick those and cook them. We also had watercress and wild onions which we mixed with eggs. The first pie I ever made was a lemon meringue, and I didn't put any sugar in the meringue, so had to cut it with scissors. I made some noodles one time, but Ike wouldn't eat them because they were too long. I would take the washtub and lard can down to the spring to do the washing. I used to get so mad at Jim and Duge because I didn't think they were helping me enough and wouldn't hunt up wood to heat the water in the lard can. Duge was six and Jim nine by this time [Sis would have been about fourteen]. We had a hard time getting wood, because if me and one of the kids could get it sawed off, then half the time it would be too tough for me to split. We would pull Pop over the rocks to another tree, and he would tell us how to do it. Besides this, we had five milk cows running on free range that we had to chase down every evening. Don't know how we ever got through without a snake biting us, because we all went barefooted and would be out tromping in the woods until after dark. I usually managed to get them all milked. I remember only once not being able to find them, so had to chase them down the next morning. But there were no fences, and they could go for miles. We went to public school for one year like this, and then someone decided that we should go to the Indian school. I can remember when I was six or seven, if something didn't go my way, I would tell Mom that I was going to run off and go to the mission, but she told me I would get lice if I went there.[17] So Jim, Duge, and I went to the mission. Had more trouble leaving Duge, 'cause he would get back to the car before Tick, Jack, Pop, and Ike.

But the mission was like heaven to me, at least, because we didn't have to work so hard, had good food, electricity, indoor plumbing, and clean clothes. Although, they used buggy flour to make the bread out of it; we'd just hold a slice up to the light and pick the bugs out, then eat it. The worse thing I remember about that school was poor Duge. He didn't want to go down there in the first place, but he started wetting the bed and Pap Kagey, the principal, would take him and others like him and turn the cold water hoses on him outside. I would be pretty nippy some of those mornings. The older kids had a detail that we did, whether it was in the kitchen, dining room, sewing room, cleaning around the dormitory, or helping wash dishes. I received my first electric shock when I worked in the kitchen. The cook sent me down to the storeroom to get something, and I was running my hand around on the wall looking for the switch, when something bit me. At first I thought it was a snake or something until I got the light turned on and looked around. We had a lot of kids that came there that couldn't speak English, like Sequoyah Hair. He took a liking for Jim, and she was scared to death of him. He would chase her all over the place. One day I was upstairs in the school building talking to his brother, who was older than the rest of the kids, but up came Jim, scared and out of breath and wasn't even supposed to be upstairs, but old Sequoyah was right behind her. I was embarrassed because I was trying to make points with the brother and act dignified. One time, one of the matrons in Sequoyah's dorm told me to quit giving him so much, but I was at a loss until I found out that he had been stealing stuff and telling them that "Oshie Copton" was giving it to him. He called Jim "Hawshell Copton" [Hazel Captain].

The next year, I was able to work in the laundry and employees' mess, where they paid us a little because we were helping the employees, too. That way, I was able to save for my graduation from the ninth grade. We had to make our own dresses, but we had to buy shoes, hose, and underwear. They furnished very shapeless cotton dresses with no trimming nor a belt, brown stockings, and black oxfords. They also furnished long underwear, in which we had to stand inspection ever once in a while to see that we had them on. But we ninth graders got smart and would cut a leg and arm off and put them on for inspection. They also furnished navy blue serge dresses to wear to Sunday school downtown [in Wyandotte].

We were able to go home on school holidays; but I was never sorry having to go back to school. We weren't able to get by with any funny stuff, and we had ballgames, shows, dances, and quite a bit of other entertainment such as plays and programs on special holidays. They saw that we made our grades and kept up on our homework. We had a certain time for study, along with a regular schedule for meals, work, school, and recreation.

After holidays, we were combed and checked for lice, because quite a few of the kids would come back with them. But they would use a fine comb and kerosene, and we all had our turn. We always had some fresh fruit with our dinner, and that was the way to tell who liked you—the boy would send his fruit over by a waitress. My best boyfriend was Harlan Bushyhead. He was a year behind me, but older, so I graduated before he did. I ran into him the summer after I graduated, when I went down to get a grocery order, but I was a big shot by then and was going to Haskell the next year, so I would hardly talk to him.

Most of the girls slept in one big dormitory. At night we all settled down, the matron would come to the door, turn the lights off, and then we all sang, "Praise God from whom all blessings flow, Praise him all ye creatures below, Praise Him above ye heavenly hosts, Praise Father, Son, and Holy Ghost. Amen." We all made our own beds, and they were made according to specifications.

I still don't know what possessed me to cross Pop, because he was always the boss. But I had made up my mind that I wanted to go to Haskell, but he wanted me to stay home and keep the kids and go to a public school. But I had a feeling that I wouldn't go to school much because there would be too many other things to do and a lack of money. Maybe I was lazy or something,

11.7. Shawnee children transported to Wyandotte Schools from the BlueJacket community, c. 1920. Photo courtesy of Glenna Wallace.

but I just decided there was something better out there someplace than what we had; and the thought became stronger after I got my letter of acceptance. That summer of '34 was pretty much the same, except Pop couldn't walk at all, and we had to pull him everyplace in his wagon. He would sit outside all day and got to be pretty good forecasting the weather by watching the grasshoppers. He was in pain all the time and believed in keeping us kids busy all the time. We would have to get out and cut weeds, cut brush, cut wood, make beehives, work on his car—changing tires or spark plugs—or just anything to keep busy. He would call the little kids up to his wagon and try to paddle them with his sore, stiff arms if they played around too much. He couldn't hurt them, but they bawled like they were being beaten.

Uncle Frank [Michael Francis Captain] lived nearby and would come to the house quite often. He had been injured in the First World War, so he didn't work outside. He liked to hunt squirrels and bee trees. He would watch the bees at water and see what direction they would go, and then he would go the same direction and see where they were making honey. If found, he would cut the trees and "rob" the bees of their honey.

So I went to Haskell, and Jim went to the mission and graduated, then went to public high and graduated. I don't remember how long Duge stayed at the mission, but they, including Jim, all lived in the house across from the school.

By this time, we didn't know where Uncle Bob was, because he had stayed in the house when we left to go to the mission, then just disappeared. We heard that he was making booze and the revenuers were after him, so he took off.[18] We looked for him for a number of years; and every time we'd hear that he had been seen in that part of the country, we'd go and try to trace him down. About six years later, some of the neighbors found him roaming around in town. He wasn't even going to come out to our part of the country because he just supposed Pop was dead by this time and didn't have any idea where us kids were. He had been working on a dam in Missouri. So he went back and got his clothes and stayed with us the rest of his life.

This summer, Aunt Evie was with us for a while. She had sent her seventh or eighth husband to the spring for a bucket of water, and the next time she heard from him he was in Chicago. She did a lot of praying and mooning around. We used to joke that as soon as Uncle Buzz came back, she quit praying and wasn't nearly as religious.

One day, I was going up the ladder to the loft and happened to look up before I put my hand on the next rung. There was a big black snake coming down to greet me. I left the house in a hurry and never did know where he went because we never saw him again.

One time, Pop was making some home brew and had it out in a tin cowshed. A Watkins man was out in the yard talking to Pop, and those quart jars started exploding and making a lot of noise; Pop said those damn cows are sure restless today.

I left for Haskell, about three hundred miles from home, on the train. Aunt Brin had given me a pair of anklets and shoes, and I took forty-nine cents from cream money and bought myself a red print dress. Had two other dresses that I had made at the mission—a formal and one that had a blue serge skirt and dark maroon-print rayon top. I had fifty cents for food, but a Negro porter insisted on carrying my suitcase at the Kansas City station then reminded me that he got twenty-five cents for that, leaving me twenty-five cents to eat on. Another girl that I had known at the mission was on the same train, but she had worked for some wealthy folks that summer. She was dressed in a nice sweater and skirt, and I thought she looked so pretty.

Haskell was just about like the mission, except on a bigger scale and older students. We had a few students that were in their thirties or late twenties who had come to learn a vocation. In both schools we took mostly subjects in homemaking, and vocations for the boys. We had sewing, child care, cooking, buying food, and serving it. At Haskell we had one cottage where about ten girls would live for a month; and we took turns in each. By serving it, I mean we acted like maids and served the others after they were seated. We still sent the laundry out to be done at the laundry, but we did the rest. At Haskell, too, we took chemistry, biology, plain math, woodworking, and a little bookkeeping. I got my only D in biology just from stubbornness; they had a bull snake in a cage in the classroom but would let him out for exercise when we were supposed to be studying, and I could do nothing but keep my eyes under the desk and on my feet. Everyone coddled that thing around and pet it except me. I walked up to the cage one day telling myself that I was going to touch it at least; but I opened the cage door and it looked around at me, so I told myself differently.

It seemed different at Haskell, too, because at the mission where we were upperclassmen, now we were just like little kids. We couldn't hold an office or be asked to assist the younger ones or new ones. We didn't get paid for any detail but could work out in peoples' homes on weekends or at the local Shack.[19] I worked there for a while, but I put too much stuff on the hamburgers so lost my job. I worked one day as a substitute in a restaurant downtown and spent most of the time breading oysters. I hardly knew what an oyster was, let alone how to bread it. But I did a lot of babysitting and doing housework downtown. One place I worked for quite a while was in a U[niversity] of Kansas professor's home, but I was definitely "help." I was not allowed to eat with the family, but ate at a little table in the kitchen. I remember one Saturday, with my usual pay of one dollar, I bought a sleeveless blue-striped vest to go with a blue skirt and a pair of shoes. I was really dressed up for the dance that night. Our dances were by invitation, and they would post the list each Saturday morning. Maybe the guy hadn't even asked you, but your name might show up with anyone. They would have to walk to our dormitory to pick us up and then walk us back afterwards. If your boyfriend was playing sports that night, and expected to be back before the dance was over, he would have one of his friends invite you and then he would take over when he got back. Peter Sitting was a good substitute because he loved to dance, but was kinda odd and wasn't the best dancer, so many of the girls wouldn't dance with him, but I always danced with him at least once. Woodrow Goose had a habit of embarrassing me, but he was a good dancer, so you were always glad when he asked, but he liked to break the ice [being the first one on the floor] and dance the whole length of the floor, then everyone would clap and holler.

Even at this age, I was still scared of Negroes. I remember once we were walking downtown and we met this Negro doctor that would walk home from the office but had to have directions where to turn into his house. I let the other girl do the directing. Then when I would be walking downtown to work on Saturday, we would meet them on the street. One morning I was alone and was walking across a park when there was a young Negro in front of me a ways. But he was so happy and was singing and whistling, which was very pretty, so I think that was when I began to realize that they were people just like us, and so many of them were always so happy and enjoying themselves.

We had students here from practically every state and some very poor and some quite well-to-do. Some of our roommates professed to being part-Negro, and they were treated no differently than the rest of us, so it made me realize all the more that they were just like the rest of us but perhaps a little darker.

The fad of having your ears pierced was in full swing then, too. So I decided to be part of the crowd. So I asked Rachel Heap of Birds to do mine. She made the ears numb by pinching them and running a needle and thread through with a cork in the back.

There were two buildings each for the boys and girls. The old building for the girls was for the younger ones, and the new one for girls in the senior class. The new building was brick, only two stories, and smaller rooms. I lived in this building for two years—being a senior twice—in high school and commercial.

The detail I disliked the most here was working in the vegetable room. We would have to get up about five and go to this damp, cold room, where we prepared the vegetables for the day. I recall doing a lot of onions, carrots, and potatoes. We had a machine that would scrape the potatoes, but we would have to cut the bad spots and eyes with a knife. We would finish just in time to go back and get ready for breakfast.

We were allowed to go home on holidays and for the summer, but I usually just had enough money to go home for the summer. Some of the girls would work in homes all summer, but I was always anxious to go home. One summer, I worked for a while for a family in Miami. She had just had her third baby, and the other two were just babies too. I did housework, took care of the kids, and the cooking; but I remember nothing but insults about the cooking from those two little ones. Then I had a job working in a sewing room for the Indian service. I did pretty good at that and enjoyed it but spent the money for a five-gallon can of lard, a hundred-pound sack of sugar, and an ice cream freezer for the family. I must have figured that it was more important for them to eat than for me to have new clothes.

I had accumulated a few things by this time. We did a lot of sewing at school for ourselves, and one winter someone donated me a black, furry jacket because I had no coat. Something made me believe it was from one of the faculty, but never knew for sure, but I was thankful. Tick had sent a few things that she got from welfare, but she would take labels from some of her wealthy sister-in-law's hand-me-downs and sew in them so I didn't know the difference.

By this time, Duge, Ike, and Pop were living with Tick and Jack. Jim finished the ninth grade at the mission. So in the summer, we were all together again. Tick sure had a time with all of us, 'cause Jack was as much a kid as the rest of us, and we were always horsing around. She had to boss him, too. But we had our share of water fights, footraces, swims in the river, and our Fourth of Julys were about the same.

One time they left Jim and me home to cook supper while they went to a ball game, and then we were going to the stomp dance in the evening.[20] We had to chase the chickens down that we were going to fry. We ran and ran after one rooster until we caught him, and Jim was going to hold his head while I chopped it off. She looked at him and said, "Look at those pitiful eyes, he knows what we're going to do," and let him go. I just about hit her with the axe, but we just started chasing again. The boys would hunt for rabbits and squirrels a lot, so we would have a little meat. We would do a little fishing, but the best and easiest way to catch catfish was in traps, but slightly illegal.

The boys usually had their pet lambs or goats or something, so we all managed to have enough to keep us occupied. On hot afternoons after dinner, we—meaning Jack and us kids—would lay on the rug because it was cooler in there. One day Jack was teasing one of the other kids, so I grabbed the south end of a northbound cat and put it right up next to his face and then hollered at him. He turned over real fast with his nose you-know-where. We were always trying to think of something to outdo the others.

One night, when Pop had gone visiting, we decided to get some watermelons. It was darker than blue blazes, but we walked up through the woods and fields to Tight Barlow's patch. Jack and another guy would carry them to the fence until we all had a load. We had to be quiet because we always heard he slept in the patch with a shotgun.

Times were still hard, so we were still getting a little surplus food and selling a little cream and a few eggs. Tick and Jack cut wood in the winter, trapped and skinned a few animals and sold the skins, and Jack worked on a WPA project as long as his health would last.

Our diet still consisted of beans and potatoes with biscuits or cornbread. Once in a while, when we were over [in] town, we would walk to the other end for a loaf of day-old bread if we had the nickel.

They had a radio by this time, but it was battery [operated], so we wouldn't listen to it all the time. Usually tried to save the battery until Saturday night so we could listen to the Grand Ole Opry, but most of the time the battery would give out before the program was over. We had the daily newspaper, which we read quite thoroughly.

The mail was delivered by a big fat guy, Ike Williams; that's where our Ike got his nickname. Pop was great for nicknames. Tick, because she was so little, Duge after a well driller, Jim after the Katzenjammer Kids—a comic—first it was Katzenjammer, then Jammer, then Jimmer, then Jim. I don't know where mine—Sis—came from, but later it was Pokum, then Poke, because I was so slow working.

After I graduated from the twelfth grade, the Indian agency would have assisted me in going to school any place, and they would lend me the money. I had always thought I wanted to be a nurse, and still do, but Pop killed that hope when he said I was so slow I would let the patient die. But we had several students that went to the University of Kansas and boarded at Haskell. I had been on that campus several times, to programs or art exhibits or ball games, but everything always seemed to be immense in comparison to what we had at school, and the idea of going to classes in all those different buildings just seemed to be too far-out for a kid from the country. Don't remember all the pros and cons, but I decided to borrow $270 from the Indian agency and stay at Haskell for two more years and take the commercial course. [But,] 'cause Aunt Mary or Grace had an argument with someone at the Indian office and the agency told them we weren't one-quarter degree [I was expelled].[21] [As a] consequence, [I spent] practically thirty-four years behind a typewriter. Don't get me wrong, I have enjoyed my work, but think I could have made a greater contribution to mankind had I gone into some other field.

I cut this off at this time, because it wasn't very long that I got pregnant with Bo, and at that time it was quite disgraceful, and I thought I could hide my head and not advertise it. But I've never been sorry I had him and kept him, 'cause Tick and Evie both asked to adopt him, but I had him and he was mine. Couldn't have had much of a better boy. Thanx.[22]

The more I reread this, the more little incidents I can remember, but too lazy to write down. Doubt if you could read it if I did.[23]

Afterthoughts

Pop was an interesting individual. He always had control over the kids, and he could tell you a lot with his eyes—whether he liked what you said or did, or whether he liked anyone. If he said no, we knew that was what he meant. But if he didn't say anything, or maybe, we knew there was still a chance. He would always get the last word, even if he had to get a little nasty about it. He was always free-hearted with his money and seemed to live more for today and let tomorrow take care of itself. I can remember him giving money to some of our cousins or buying pies for them at pie suppers, because their dad wouldn't. He would spend his last dime for a can of salmon, one of his favorite foods. He was always very honest—stealing and lying were very much against his morals. He joined the Pentecost Church for a while, but I can remember Uncle Bob teasing him once about hearing him cuss, so Pop got mad and didn't profess to be religious anymore. He had read the Bible quite a bit and was pretty well versed in it. He would never admit to loving anyone, but we had him figured out pretty well. He did say once that he would never give his kids a stepmother. He relented to his handicap very well, I thought, but he never gave us hope that he would walk again. At first, we thought he was too demanding and asked us to do things that we thought he could have done for himself, but how do we know what we would be like under the same circumstances? He was always looking for a cure and spent a lot on patent medicines. He eventually settled down and made a little life of his own with his crossword puzzles, read a little, listened to the radio, and was always open for a game of checkers. He was a Cleveland Indians fan and liked to have a radio close by so he could listen to the ball games.

He wasn't too happy about going to the nursing home, but it didn't take him long to accept it, and then it was a struggle to get him to leave it for a day. He had a buddy there—a young guy, twenty-four or so, confined to a wheelchair—that he played checkers with. They had wheeled him downstairs to play checkers with Gene just two or three days before he died. They treated him very well at the home. He could have anything he wanted to eat (he was always very finicky about his food and didn't like too many things), and he controlled the remote control to the TV for his big room. His worldly goods were few and were easily carried out in one small box.

I didn't mean to demean Mom any, but she had less patience than Pop and had rather do everything herself instead of teaching us how to cook. She did try to teach me to hem dishtowels, but I looked outside more than I watched my fingers. But she always said she wouldn't go anyplace her kids couldn't go. She and Pops did go away and leave me and Tick alone with a sitter, Uncle George's girlfriend and his baby.

NOTES

1. Edith Reaser Captain, wife of Bill "Pop" Captain (February 6, 1894–September 18, 1931); William Henry "Pop" Captain (January 13, 1894–February 21, 1963); Elsie Mae "Sis" Captain Hoevet (March 30, 1919–April 7, 2006).

2. The land was not donated; it was allotted under the Dawes General Allotment Act of 1887.

3. She is recalling the Picher Lead Company, formed on the site of an allotment owned by Harry Crawfish, a Quapaw Indian, in Ottawa County, Oklahoma. Until the mine closed in 1967, it was one of the richest and most productive lead and zinc mines in the country. Today the town of Picher, Oklahoma, has been abandoned and the former mine is known as the Tar Creek Superfund site.

4. "Devil's Promenade" refers to the bridge one must cross to enter the Quapaw Powwow, the second oldest powwow in the United States. "The Green Corn Feast" refers to the Seneca-Cayuga Ceremonial Ground, which is called the Cowskin by some, Bassett Grove by others. The Seneca-Cayugas are a coalescent community of Haudenosaunee peoples from Ohio. Today their community

is composed of Sandusky Senecas and the Senecas who shared the reservation with the Shawnees at Lewistown and later in Oklahoma. The era of self-determination has enabled this community to reassert its Seneca and Cayuga identities in ways that were not possible in the removal era.

5. Decoration Day was widely celebrated among the Eastern Shawnees. It began in 1866 as a way of remembering soldiers who had been killed in the Civil War. Such an event must have been especially poignant to the Eastern Shawnees, who signed a treaty with the Confederate States of America but served proudly in the Union Army. The Eastern Shawnee Tribe lost everything during and directly after the Civil War.

6. The cemetery in question is Captain's Cemetery, located nine miles east of Miami, Oklahoma, in the community of Eastside, just south of the Eastside Baptist Church, on the east side of road. Tom Captain (1850–1920) owned the original allotment before it passed into non-Native hands. More recently the Eastern Shawnee Tribe has purchased part of the old Captain home-place and has provided new access to the cemetery.

7. She is referring to Thomas A. Captain's grocery store, which stood beside the school attended by many Eastern Shawnee children, Moccasin Bend No. 5. William "Pops" Captain was Thomas A. Captain's brother.

8. Ladies' aid societies formed during the Civil War to supply soldiers with medicine and other basic supplies. After the war they continued on as local civic organizations for women.

9. Here she refers to Walter Lane BlueJacket, who is described by Glenna Wallace, in chapter 8 of this book, which describes chiefs of the Eastern Shawnee Tribe.

10. Seneca, Missouri, is an off-reservation town that borders the Eastern Shawnee tribal land. Many Native people from Ottawa County experienced discrimination there.

11. The land was not donated; it was allotted. Under the Dawes General Allotment Act of 1887, and later the Curtis Act of 1898, which applied to Oklahoma's reservations, Indian children received forty acres of land when their reservations were allotted.

12. Poke root produces a highly poisonous berry. However, the leaves were often boiled into a tea that was used to cure skin disorders, in this case poison ivy.

13. Sugar cane was the local name for sorghum, which was a wildly popular crop in Oklahoma in the 1930s and '40s.

14. Jenny was the term for a female donkey.

15. After his wife, Edith "Tommy" Reaser Captain, died, William Henry "Pop" Captain, became an invalid and got around by sitting in a little red wagon pulled by one of his children.

16. She is referring to Shawnee Twin Lakes.

17. "The mission" was the local name for the Seneca Indian School in Wyandotte, Oklahoma.

18. By federal mandate, alcohol was prohibited in Indian Territory. Then, in September 1907, when Oklahoma became a state, prohibition was written into the state constitution. In December 1933, when the 21st Amendment banned prohibition, Oklahomans accepted the legality of beer. But it wasn't until December 1957 that the sale of liquor became legal in the state. Here Elsie Mae Hoevet describes the robust black market in moonshine that became a hallmark of rural life in Oklahoma. Revenuers were agents of the U.S. Treasury Department tasked with enforcing liquor laws.

19. The Shack was a café on Barker Street, in Lawrence, Kansas, just south of 23rd Street. Haskell students frequently worked there.

20. Eric Wensman (Bird Creek Shawnee) explains, "Stomp Dances usually start around midnight and last until sunrise. The first four singers lead songs exclusively for tribal members who come from that dance ground. After the first set of men are done, guests are welcome to dance and lead and they will be called out by a 'Stickman,' or *Pochili*, who acts as an arena director and who serves at the will of the chief. The Stickman's responsibilities include going to the various delegations from other tribes who are there to 'help out' and inviting them to lead a song. Once this request has been made, the song leader asks a female shell shakers to follow behind him and shake cans for him. It is her job to

keep in time with the leader's songs. Both the leader and the leading shell-shaker set the tempo for the song and bring their own spirit to the dance. Other men and women fall in behind them, alternating between women and men. The men answer the leader when he sings his song, the rest of the women stay in time with the song as well. Stomp dancers proclaim that the spirits hear the dancers in the wee hours of the morning and come to relieve you of your problems, your worries, your health issues as you become one with the fire and the purpose of the dance. You can feel your burdens lift and you are at peace with yourself and your surroundings. The purpose of the dance is to revive yourself spiritually. Shawnees call it *Nikanikawe*, leading dance."

21. Officially, most boarding schools accepted American Indian children with a one-quarter or greater blood quantum. Here Hoevet describes how a conflict between her relatives and the Indian agent at Neosho Agency, in Oklahoma, led officials at Haskell to "discover" that she was less than one-quarter blood quantum. As a result, they expelled her from the only school she could afford.

22. Bo did learn who his father was and has a close relationship with his brother, Luke Shelton, who lives in Oklahoma.

23. Elsie Mae Hoevet wrote this on February 1, 2000.

PART IV
EASTERN SHAWNEE
LIFE HISTORIES

Interview decisions are never easy. Chief Glenna Wallace and Eric Wensman worked with me (Stephen Warren) to decide whom to interview. We searched for a mix of elders who could speak to the dramatic changes the tribe has undergone since 1945, the period beyond the scope of our research grant. We also wanted tribal citizens who could demonstrate the complexity of Eastern Shawnee identities. Some Eastern Shawnees participate in powwows, while others prefer the rituals of the White Oak Ceremonial Ground. Some do both, while others worship at the many Christian churches in the region. Some Eastern Shawnees invest most of their time in the political and business aspects of the tribe. Five interviews will invariably fall short of the range and complexity of Eastern Shawnee citizenship, but it is a beginning.

As tribal citizens and long-term elected officials, Larry Kropp, Chief Wallace, and Norma Kraus have experienced the dramatic changes brought about by the Indian Gaming Regulatory Act, which became law on October 17, 1988. As a return migrant from Oregon, Norma Kraus moved from east to west and back again as one of many thousands of Native Oklahomans drawn to the western United States. In contrast, Larry Kropp and Chief Wallace grew up in Oklahoma, in and around their peoples' original reservation. Their firsthand experiences with life in the Four Corners region, and their roles as the de facto historians of the Eastern Shawnee Tribe, inspired our choice.

In contrast, Winifred "Winkie" Froman and her son, Brett, are Eastern Shawnee tribal citizens who are active members of the White Oak Ceremonial Ground, a ritual community that is primarily associated with the Eastern Shawnees' neighbors, the Shawnee Tribe, another of the three federally recognized Shawnee tribes. Winkie grew up in White Oak and bore witness to the out-migration from this ceremonial community after World War II. Her son, Brett, is an assistant general manager of the Indigo Sky Casino. Raised primarily in Quapaw, Brett's life is intertwined with the nine tribes of Ottawa County.

The following life histories were conducted from February 20 to 21, 2016, in Ottawa County, Oklahoma. Each interview lasted approximately an hour. Councilman Larry Kropp, Chief Wallace, and Ceremonial Chief Shawn King were interviewed at the Eastern Shawnee Tribe's cultural preservation building near Wyandotte, Oklahoma. Brett and Rhonda Barnes and Winkie Froman were interviewed at Brett's home in Quapaw, Oklahoma. Norma and Joe Kraus were interviewed at their home at the Woodlands Elder Complex, built by the Eastern Shawnee Tribe, near Wyandotte. Eric Wensman, who was then the research manager of the grant, "A Search for Eastern Shawnee History," joined me in conducting the interviews. Each interview was transcribed and then shared with the interviewees. Minor corrections for grammar, and larger corrections for either cultural or personal privacy were made, according to the requests of the people we interviewed.

In these oral histories, ellipses are used not to indicate omissions, but to indicate where speech is faltering or trailing off. Dashes indicate abrupt interruptions in sentences.

12

An Interview with
Chief Glenna J. Wallace

Stephen Warren: I'm Stephen Warren. I'm sitting here with Eric Wensman, the research manager on the ANA grant, and Chief Glenna Wallace of the Eastern Shawnee Tribe of Oklahoma. Could we start with biographical information, such as where you were born, when you were born, who your parents were, that sort of thing?

Glenna J. Wallace: My parents were Champ Enyart, and my mother's name was Virgie Ellen— She was a Captain and married . . . her mother married a Crain, so it was Virgie Ellen Crain was her name. There were five of us children, I am the middle child. I have an older sister, Gene, who is deceased. I have an older brother, Charles, who was chief for eight years of the tribe. I have a younger sister, Dixie, who married a Martin. And I have a younger brother, Bud, Buddy Jo. So I'm exactly in the middle, with a brother and sister older and a brother and sister younger. My older brother and sister where born at Pawnee, Oklahoma, at an Indian hospital, but I was born at home. Home, at that time, was a place you can no longer see, and a house that I haven't been to, and is probably possibly not in existence now.

All of us lived in the Eastside district, which is nine miles east of Miami, and that's where many, many of the allotments were made to the Captain family. So we grew up with an extended family in that area. Where I was born was just about a quarter of a mile on south of what is now Eastside Baptist Church, and then back probably a quarter of a mile, then west down by a creek . . . a spring that's in that area. There was a log house down there. So I was born in that log house on Thanksgiving Day, which was my older brother Charles's birthday, so we share the same day, November 24. It was Thanksgiving Day.

My parents never had money. We were always financially poor, but we lived in a time when everybody else was financially poor as well, so we didn't really realize it. Had a very happy childhood. Lived a great deal off of the land, meaning that my dad hunted, as did my grandfather, and as did even my grandmother, you know, on my dad's side. So we ate a lot of rabbit, ate a lot of squirrel. We always raised a pig or two, butchered our own. We had our own smokehouse that, I remember, was built just up off the ground on stilts, and had our bacon and cured ham and things like that in there. We always had a cow, always had milk, always had eggs, always had chickens.

We had dinner almost every Sunday with my dad's mother, and it was always fried chicken, platter after platter of fried chicken. I used to always joke that, at that time, men always went first when it was time to eat, women always went next, and children always went last. So there might have been three platters of chicken to start off with, but when it came time for us, there were backs, and there were necks, and there were gizzards. And that's all I ever knew that a chicken had. I longed for the day that I would become an adult, when I would know what the white meat would be. The world changed in that time. And now if you eat, the children go first, the men go next, and the women go last. And the only difference is there aren't necks and there aren't backs, because people don't clean their own chickens now, so you don't usually have those pieces of meat.

Eric Wensman: Would you say there was plenty of game in this area?

Wallace: There was, at that time, absolutely, yes. Mm-hm. My granddad, when he was going to hunt for—and again, he's my non-Native grandfather. He didn't even take a gun with him, he was so good with just a rock, and he would take a rock and throw it and kill a rabbit, yes.

Warren: What kind of gardens did they keep?

Wallace: My dad and mom always had large gardens, and we . . . that time, we lived at a place that we did not have running water. We always had to go and haul water by the milk-can load. Not a barrel, but milk cans that you used to have. Whenever Milnot was, and went around and picked up milk, they always had those milk cans.[1] We hauled water, and we had a very large garden. We would always plant lots of tomatoes, lots of potatoes, lots of onions, lots of green beans, lots of corn. Didn't do such things as kale or spinach or things like that, but the staples we definitely did. Sometimes we had sweet potatoes, but not . . . I don't really recall those very much. But dad—A very, very large garden. So when it was time to plant, we would take that milk can of water, and we would have a dipper, and one would plant the tomato plant in the ground, and another one would come by with a dipper of water, and put in there.

We hauled our water from the creek. Or my granddad lived not too far from us, and he did have a well. It was one of those with those long pipes, you know, that went down into those buckets, and we would go down, and had a rope, and dropped that down in, and bring it up, and then fill those water cans.

Wensman: Would your drinking water come from that creek as well?

Wallace: Yes.

Wensman: And which creek would that be? In this area?

Wallace: Well, the creek—As far as drinking, water would come from granddad's well. Yeah, or back from that spring that I talked about. And I think that was a spring; I don't know that it was actually a creek.

Wensman: And the reason why I bring that up, because I come across—There used to be a spring on the way back from our house that my uncle would stop and get his drinking water. And then I met an elderly lady in Cherokee country, and there was a spring there, where they got their water.

Wallace: That's where we did.

Wensman: So, those are very uncommon now, for people to stop and get fresh drinking water there. That's an interesting note for this county.

Wallace: Well, we even put groceries or things . . . like that's where we kept our milk cool and so forth, was put it down in the spring.

Warren: When your father farmed, where did he get his seeds? Did he save seeds every season and then plant over? Or did he share with neighbors, or—?

Wallace: Save some seeds. But no. Primarily went to Miami to a place there, where we took milk to sell and so forth, and so there was a . . . I don't know . . . There used to be even a feed store here in Seneca, where they did the same thing.

Wensman: I have another question, and this reminds me of my folks. They always had chicken on Sunday, and I'm like, Where did y'all get all the chickens at?

Wallace: We raised our chickens.

Wensman: I mean, you had enough rotation in the chickens to be eating them every Sunday?

Wallace: Yes.

Warren: You'd think there would be, yeah, that you would deplete them at some point.

Wensman: Yeah, deplete your source, because—And it's the same story with my mom. She was like, "I'll never eat fresh chicken again." She hated cleaning them, you know. I was wanting to do that one time, and she was like, "No, I hated it because I had to eat them all the time." But yeah, I would think there was not enough in the rotation, you know, to produce eggs and sustain them.

Wallace: One of the last chiefs that I covered [in chapter 8], and one that I had the most difficulty with, it was about my great-great-grandpa Captain. They raised chickens, and his wife was largely responsible, and they used them to sell and to make money. And she wouldn't let the family eat much chicken, because if they ate it, then they were eating the money. And she— There's an article where my aunt was reflecting upon her childhood and said that they had a pig that was bad about getting out, and would get to the chickens, and would eat a chicken, and that grandma saw a chicken, the pig heading toward a chicken, and that grandpa had time to stop, but chose not to because he wanted chicken to eat. So that was his excuse, how he was able to get fried chicken.

Warren: So your father worked in the mines?

Wallace: He did, he did. It was not a pleasant experience. Mining was probably about all that he ever knew. His dad died when he was six months old, and he had older brothers, and just everybody in the area worked in the mines. And miners would ride together, they would have carpools, so forth. And the negative part for us is that they were paid once a week, and they would always get paid on Fridays, and the whole carpool would stop at the local tavern. And dad never came home with a full paycheck. And many times didn't—He came home with a lot of it being gone. If it weren't for uncle Thomas's grocery store, where we could go and charge or so forth—We would run a monthly bill, and so if we ran out of food or something—And of course, with those large gardens, we always canned a tremendous amount. I can remember that we always wanted a hundred quarts of tomatoes, and we wanted a hundred quarts of green beans, and things like that. So we always had food that way. But, ultimately, that drink—My dad became an alcoholic. He was an alcoholic. And so, yes, that affected all of us.

Wensman: You said your older brother and sisters were born in Pawnee. Did your folks work in the oil fields over there in that area? Did they live in the oil field camps?

Wallace: My granddad did, but before my mother was married. My granddad lived in the Sperry area. His wife died—who would be my grandmother—when my mother was only seven years of age. And so, there were six other children. So granddad came in an old . . . he actually came in a covered wagon. My mother came in a covered wagon from Sperry. And I remember my mother talking about that. Granddad had one little colt that he was so proud of, and he loved that colt, but it had to walk the entire way. And when they got to Miami they had to put it down. And granddad was not able to make it, and he cried over that. My mother would've been something like fifteen at that age, so she came to what would be the Eastside community. And she and her two younger brothers, those three lived up here.

Wensman: Why were they living in Sperry?

Wallace: He was down by . . . he worked in the oil fields.

Wensman: So there was a huge camp there, in Sperry, which was right on Bird Creek, and it's called Gillespie camp. It's an oilfield camp. It was almost a town, and that's where they worked, and there was several oil field camps in that area, and so . . . and that camp was well known at one time, and it set right on Bird Creek.

Wallace: I don't know what camp it was.

Wensman: That would have been the only camp there, if he came from Sperry, because it was huge.

Wallace: One of those pictures that shows those four little girls with the bows in their hair, I've had that picture . . . A friend of mine took that picture and had it scanned into a computer and has generated it, and generated it in color, because all we've had is that little black-and-white. And there is the story that my granddad was going off to work one day, and what happened, I don't know, but he and my grandmother had, evidently, a fierce argument, and he left mad. And she stayed home mad. He did not like the color red, and my grandmother, even though she was ill, sewed dresses all day long. And when he came home from work that evening, he had those four little girls . . . she had those four little girls dressed in red dresses, with red ribbons in their hair, waiting at the front door for my granddad. So she was a determined-mindset person.

Warren: Sounds like the apple didn't fall far from the tree, Chief.

Wallace: I wasn't about to say that, but I've often wondered that. I've often been told that my grandmother did not want her children raised around her Indian family. Because of the alcohol, because of the, oftentimes, fighting that goes along with that. And so we did not come up . . . my granddad did not come up at first, when the allotments were made.

Warren: But as you yourself have pointed out, it was your father who was the alcoholic, and he was non-Native.

Wallace: He was. Exactly.

Warren: What explains the idea that somehow alcoholism is associated with your Native side?

Wallace: Well, I explain it because it was fairly prevalent. I mean, all we have to do is go back and read in history that even on the removal . . . that people, meaning non-Natives, waited on Natives to come by to sell them—Even on the removal march, you know. And so alcohol—
    I think that's one of the things, if you were to ask me in my lifetime what changes I've seen and what I think are positive trends. I never attended any powwows, or attended events in my youth, or even young adulthood, because alcohol was present. And because of my experience with my father. And let me say, my father did ultimately get over being an alcoholic, he did give up drinking in his later years. But he was probably sixty and over before he gave up that lifestyle. And the person my children know as their grandfather is not the person that I had as a father at all. And I'm very thankful for that, because they have nothing but wonderful memories of . . . they may have been simple memories, but they weren't alcohol memories, and that's . . . that's wonderful. But I didn't go. Because of the way I grew up, I didn't like being around people who had excess to drink, and that was oftentimes associated with powwows and get-togethers. Those things I'm not necessarily responsible for, that other people are. But we police our powwows, and we police our gatherings anymore. That's not a part of it. So our children don't have to stay away, or adults. So that's one of the positive changes that has happened.

Warren: Well, we are jumping ahead. I wanted you to tell the story about what happened when your father accepted a settlement from the mine, and your work in Oregon and Washington. What years would that have been? And can you say a little bit about that?

12.1. Four sisters in red dresses. *Left to right*: Pauline Crain Mitchell, Ruth Crain Huggins, Elsie Crain Huls, and Vergie Crain Enyart, c. 1920. Photo courtesy of Glenna Wallace.

Wallace: My younger brother was born, I think, in 1943, and he would probably have been four or five years of age. So it would be '48, probably, when we were there. And my father took a mining settlement. We weren't getting ahead; maybe a change. The grass is always greener on the other side, and my father took his mining settlement. He bought a big flatbed truck, and they put a tarpaulin over that flatbed truck, and that truck became our home for the next two or three years. The five of us children, my mother and father, and then my mother's brother, Uncle Junior, and his wife, Aunt Jewel, and their two children, Sonny and Shirley, making a total of eleven. We left and drove. We had a little two-burner gas stove, a kerosene stove, and we had an ironing board. And I remember we had a milk can full of walnuts and things like that. We took off, and we would stop in parks and fix breakfast or whatever. And we went to Oregon and California, and we stayed there for something like three years.

We were migrant workers. It was a good time for me, because I was young, as I've said, [I was] in the Huckleberry Finn/Tom Sawyer age, and so it didn't matter to me if I was barefoot, if I didn't have clothing. Those three years affected my life tremendously because we were migrant workers. We were hard workers, we were good workers. And my mother and father had the philosophy that each child had to contribute to the finances of the family. So every place we went, whatever product it was, whatever fruit it was that we picked, we had a quantity specified for us that we were to pick that day that went to the family. Anything that exceeded that, we were able to keep that money ourselves. And so it taught me at a very early age how to set goals, how to exceed goals, how to have expectations, to develop a work ethic. I watched other people who cheated and tried to fill their green-bean sacks a faster way, and I tried that once and was caught the first time, and so it taught me immediately that cheating and taking the shortcut is never the wise way. So it taught me to be open and honest and work hard.

In those three years, sometimes we lived in a house, sometimes we lived in a barn. If we drove into an agricultural barn [and] it was vacant, or that had a place that we could drive in, then we would have a roof over our head, and we would sleep on a . . . maybe a bale of hay or spread out some bales of hay. I'm the one that was lucky enough that I usually got the ironing board that was in the truck. And I slept on the ironing board, sometimes under the truck, sometimes other places. I can remember, when I referenced green beans, there had been a pig farm there, and they had the individual pigsties, and each of us had our own pigsty that we could—I remember sweeping that dirt until it would just shine, and then putting down a blanket or something, and so we slept in a pigsty for however long that was.

We went to several different schools. I was accepted well in some places, not accepted well in other places. It's the first place I've ever known prejudice, first place I've ever known bias, first place I—I determined early in life that I wanted to be a schoolteacher. And it was the first place that I was extremely disappointed in schoolteachers because there were . . . it was almost like racial profiling, incomes of family. They're from Oklahoma, that was considered to be an inferior location. They're Native Americans or Indians, which is considered to be a minority. And they are migrant workers. So do you expect them to be at the top of the class? No. We were automatically, or I was automatically, placed at the bottom. Records didn't go with us. Got new shots every time for health immunizations, etc.

Warren: But you rose to the top of every elementary school class, only to start it all over again when you went to a new farm, correct?

Wallace: Absolutely, which was a good . . . It's a good learning experience. I found out early how it feels to be . . . thought to be inferior.

Warren: Your family, the Captain family, travelled with the Dushane family out to Oregon and Washington. There had already been a large exodus of Shawnees to Oregon. Did you meet up with them?

Wallace: We never met up with any of them. We did meet up with some of my father's family. And again, remember, he's the non-Native, and so they were located at Eugene, Oregon. That's where we went first, and then from that point we were on our own.

Warren: Ok. And so you came back to [Oklahoma] from those journeys when you were about twelve?

Wallace: Something like that. We came back to the same place that we had left. When we came back my father had health problems. He had tuberculosis. My father had to have surgery fairly soon. We reentered District No. 5, Moccasin Bend schools. Even though we had missed quite a few days of formal education, we really hadn't missed that much of education, because whatever would have been covered in that time, the three oldest . . . four oldest of us—Moccasin Bend was always a very good rural school. We learned reading, we learned mathematics, drilled on that. We had a bookmobile. We didn't have a library, but we had a bookmobile that came every week. You could check out as many books as you wanted, and so all of us were good readers. And the years that we were gone would have been the years . . . The mathematics didn't hurt at all, because every type of crop that we were working with was a different type of weight or a different type of measurement. So we quickly learned by experience what pounds and ounces and lugs and baskets and quarts and pints and . . . the mathematics. "Five cents a quart is what I am going to get after I pick over fifty quarts. And so if I get a quarter today, and I do that five days, I have a dollar and a quarter." And that was a lot of money. So we learned mathematics naturally. We learned geography naturally because we were travelling on the West Coast, and we learned social studies naturally because at that time there were Mexicans, there were other nationalities,

12.2. Picking strawberries in Gresham, Oregon, c. 1950. *Left to right*: Vergie Crain Enyart, Buddy Joe Enyart, Shirley Crain, Dixie Enyart Martin, Jean Enyart Buxton, Jewel Dushane Crain, Sonny Crain, Charles Enyart, Glenna Enyart Wallace. Photo courtesy of Jean Enyart Buxton.

there were other minorities. So we did the social studies. I guess we were actually ahead in learning psychology by personal experience. So when we came back, our education wasn't the least bit affected. And Moccasin Bend was a small school, but when I graduated from there in the eighth grade I was valedictorian. So when I went to high school in Wyandotte, which was, for a small school, much, much larger . . . and in the ninth grade I graduated a salutatorian. So it didn't have a negative effect. It gave us experience, experience that others in that area didn't have.

Warren: And Moccasin Bend No. 5 was right beside Captain Grocery?

Wallace: Yes.

Warren: So it became a community center of sorts?

Wallace: Absolutely.

Warren: For the Eastern Shawnees, could you say a little bit about what tribal gatherings were like at that time?

Wallace: We didn't have any. The Eastern Shawnees, you know—I find it interesting, after having talked with people from Oregon, now, as an adult. Those who left and went to Oregon, Washington—We didn't talk about being Native American. We didn't talk about being Indian. We lived in a community, and we were all equals and friends and families and our—And again, my grandmother died when I was only . . . when my mother was only seven, so I never knew my Native American grandmother. But our . . . the people who had their Native grandparents, those grandparents truly believed that they shouldn't learn the language, that they shouldn't learn the customs, because they were going out of style and they would be keeping them from being successful in this new world . . . new lifestyle that we lived. Whereas it seems to me, the ones I have talked about [it] with in Oregon, those people talked to them about . . . their grandparents talked to them about being Native American, because they had left it all back here, and they were always told, "You are Eastern Shawnee, you are Eastern Shawnee." I was really not brought up being told. I mean, I knew, but it was just something, you know, "You're Eastern Shawnee, you're Eastern Shawnee." But [it] wasn't anything that you would list at the top of who are you and what are your credentials. We would have never have listed . . . If they asked race, it was always, you marked Caucasian. You wouldn't mark Native American because we didn't talk about those things.

Warren: Why was being Native American seen as an impediment in the 1940s?

Wallace: I think the people truly—Well, many other people prior to that had to go to boarding school. Many people felt that we had to have education, and we didn't have that before. I just think they thought that the Native American, particularly the language and the customs, was one lifestyle, which was not the same as the other. And when they went to boarding school, they had to give all of that up, were punished if they did maintain that. So we just didn't participate. Oftentimes I hear tribal members saying, even some of my own cousins, "Well, we were raised in California, and we never learned any of that. So teach us." And we're saying, "We were brought up back here, but we didn't learn any of that either. So we can't teach you those cultural ways, because we weren't brought up in the cultural way."

Warren: Did religion play a role in the discrimination? What was religion like in Ottawa County in your childhood? Could you say a little bit about the Christian landscape?

Wallace: My parents never went to church, but I went to church ever since I was a small child. I wasn't made to go. I think it was . . . there was a church right there in the community, and if you wanted a social life, there wasn't anything else to do. So if you wanted to get out of your house, you went to church. So I've . . . I personally chose to be in church my entire life.

I went to two different churches there in the community. One was an Assembly of God church, and one was a Baptist church. And so I went to the Assembly of God church when I was younger, because that's where some of the family went, and then I made my own choice to go to the Baptist later on. And so Christianity is . . . I've never had a conflict between what we refer to [as] spirituality in our, the American Indian or Native American church, and Christianity. I still don't have a conflict, no.

Warren: And how did you manage to go to high school in Miami, Oklahoma, at the age of sixteen? I'm hoping that you could tell that story.

Wallace: Uh, when I started high school at Wyandotte, Oklahoma, I started in the ninth grade. And I had two feed-sack skirts and one blouse. Um, we had no transportation to speak of. I think we had one old car. But Wyandotte High School would be something like eight miles from where we lived. So it was a matter of get on the school bus, go to school, return home on the school bus. And if you went anyplace else, you walked. I wanted more than two feed-sack skirts and a feed-sack blouse, and there was going to be no way of getting that from my parents. There was going to be no way of my being able to do that unless I left home. And so, with my parent's permission, I moved away from home for one full year and lived in Miami, Oklahoma, and went to school from eight in the morning until noon, and then I went to my cousin's restaurant and worked from noon till eight o'clock, nine o'clock at night. And I lived in an apartment of my own, and knew about paying bills and managing time, and was able to get another skirt that was not a feed-sack skirt. Able to get a blouse that was not a feed-sack blouse.

I don't know that I have talked about this here. My father had tuberculosis. And [when] we came back from Oregon and California he had to be operated upon, and it was then that I knew,

12.3. Glenna J. Enyart Wallace, senior picture, Wyandotte High School, Wyandotte, Oklahoma, 1956. Photo courtesy of Glenna Wallace.

financially, there was . . . there wasn't any silver lining. There wasn't going to be any present dropped to us or something. And if I ever had any different life at all, I was going to have to be the one to provide that life. So education became very important to me. While I was in Oregon and California, when we were picking produce and so forth, after we reached our quota for the day, whenever we exceeded that, we got to keep that money. I was able to buy some dresses. I remember a dress that cost four dollars and ninety-eight cents, and it was the most beautiful dress I had ever seen in my life. And I was able to save for it, and buy it, and knew that I had done that by my own labors. And it was just a good feeling. And so I knew that when I came back and started high school, if I was going to have anything, I had to do it. And so it was a simple choice.

Warren: You married when you were sixteen, correct?

Wallace: I was sixteen chronologically, but stop and think about the life that I had lived. Would you say that I was sixteen?

Warren: And how old were you when you had your first child?

Wallace: I didn't have my first child until I was eighteen. But I'd been married two years.

Warren: By the time you were in your early twenties, you had a master's degree and were on the way to the professorate.

Wallace: I started teaching college with a master's degree at age twenty-seven. So, the way that I did it, I wasn't much behind people who would have graduated with me in high school and going straight on to college. So, I was fortunate.

Warren: How did you do it?

Wallace: Well, I had a husband who was very supportive after two years. The first two years he was not supportive at all. And I think that was part of the time period we lived in. To him, that was a blow to the male ego . . . that there must have been some dissatisfaction with him on my part, and that wasn't so at all. When I stood in that hospital waiting room and saw my father after the surgery, and I looked at my mother . . . and my mother had five children. My mother hadn't finished high school. I knew that my mother had no options. So the word option became very important to me. Option has always been a word that was important to me, be it good or be it bad. I didn't choose to run for chief, even though I had been asked to for fifteen years, because I didn't have the option of having a retirement. And I could serve on the Business Committee and serve the tribe at the same time, but get my retirement locked in where I had [the] option. Because there is always turnover in elections. So options [have] always been very important to me.

And I was extremely fortunate that I guess I had that grandmother's make-your-red-dresses [disposition], you know. The first two years of going to school, my husband wasn't that support- ive. But, in fact, the day that I enrolled in college, my husband didn't know that I enrolled. And I went and wrote the check for my tuition and so forth without ever telling him. And I went . . . I was only going three days a week, and I was only going half-days, so he had already gone to work before I left, and I was home before he got home. And it was only after a week or two that I thought, "The checks are going to be coming in, and he's going to go through them and see this. I have to tell him." Because I knew he would say no, but if I was already started [I could say], "Look I have been here two weeks, [and] you haven't even noticed. You still have your meals. You still have . . . The laundry's done. The children are taken care of."

I was fortunate in the other way, also. My mom and dad . . . My dad was disabled, but they were both home. They weren't working, and so I chose to go to NEO [Northeastern Oklahoma A&M College] because I had to drive right past there, and so I could leave my children there in the daytime. So I had babysitting. Had it not been for them, I would not have been able to do that, because we couldn't afford that. And so my parents were a blessing by my being able to do that. I didn't graduate from NEO. It took sixty hours to graduate, and in that first semester I went part-time, because I wasn't sure I could handle all of that. So I was four hours shy of graduating. But it wasn't worth my time to come back for a complete semester there, when I could just transfer on up to Pittsburg [State University]. And I have to praise NEO. That many years ago, I didn't lose a single hour in transfer or anything. [Of] course, I had studied every- thing very carefully.

And when I went to Pittsburg . . . when fifteen hours was the normal load, I was taking nine- teen, twenty, twenty-one hours so that I could finish. And raising the children. But my husband was helping. He was helpful at that point. He had decided I was not going to give up, and now we had more invested in me than that. And so, when I finished my bachelor's, I was just fortu- nate enough that I applied for a scholarship to do my master's, and they did . . . I received that. And when I finished that, they had an opening at Crowder College, and I was contacted about that. I didn't apply there. A person there who was on the board of trustees, who lived in Seneca, knew that I had finished my master's, and they had a vacancy. She contacted me, and so it just all worked out.

Warren: And you had an amazing first dean at Crowder, did you not?

Wallace: I did.

Warren: He was a real mentor.

Wallace: He was. Dean Gibbons. I do not know why. I can't explain it. But also, I basically had two presidents while I was there, and both presidents were the same way. They saw something that I didn't know was within me. And he kept giving me opportunities that required me to grow. And so I . . . I took those opportunities, and I grew. And it always led to other opportunities.

Warren: And one of those opportunities that I'd like you to say a little bit about is the fact that you've visited seventy countries in your life. How did that come about?

Wallace: I started out in communications, and that was so long ago that they didn't even call it communications. It was just called an English major. So I was an English teacher, and—But the English department was in what would be the communications department, and ultimately would be the fine arts department. And so I was an instructor and started having these opportunities for other areas.

At that time, Newton County [Missouri] didn't even have a GED program. So if a person dropped out of school, their future was just sunk, because there was just no opportunity to do that. And so that was one of the things that they wanted to start, was a GED program. And so I was very active in that, and taught classes, and managed that, and then went on and we were able to get scholarships and for adults. And every time, it always led to something else. So by that time, then, because that GED program was successful, I was promoted to the department chair. And the department grew, and I was then promoted to the division chair, and the division chair included all the fine arts. And certainly fine arts is not, was not, my background. And McDonald County, particularly, was a very rural, backward county.[2] And to try to bring fine arts and fine art programs in was very difficult. Until it occurred to me that first they have to . . . witness and experience some of those fine arts. So I started a travel program.

At first we started taking them to places like Broadway, or places where they could see fine drama, or we would take them to operas and so forth. Did that three or four years. We couldn't afford to pay their way, but we could keep it as cheap as possible. We weren't in it for profit or anything. And it occurred to me, it was much easier to sell trips to Paris than it was to sell trips to Broadway every single year. So I quickly began offering trips abroad, and that grew and grew, and that led into working with developing exchange programs. So, exchange programs for students, exchange programs for faculty . . . and that led into my being able to go to England, and being able to spend almost a year in Australia, teaching at three different institutions there, and that grew into being director of international travel. And all of that while I was still teaching, and still me being a division chair, or working with many of these other programs.

Warren: It seems as if the two characteristics of your life are that you are a workaholic who is very entrepreneurial.

Wallace: I guess I plead guilty.

Warren: You had mentioned earlier that your grandmother did not want you to be raised Shawnee, or in any Indian way. When did your Indian identity come back to you? When did you decide that you really wanted to become involved in the life of your tribe again?

Wallace: I really didn't make that decision. It was the entrepreneurial . . . and it was also the family connection. I really had not been involved in the tribe very much at all until my mother ultimately became involved. My mother became secretary, and because of seeing my mother, I attended a few meetings. But I still didn't become that involved until gaming started. And in 1984, when they opened a bingo hall, my older sister contracted for the concession stand. And my older sister asked me, because I had always worked two or three jobs those last three years of my education. I had to take out student loans and so forth, and I wanted those paid off, and I wanted a cash basis for my own children to be able to go to college. So when she was going to contract and take the concession stand, I agreed to work weekends, so Friday, Saturday, and Sunday, and they were open only four days. She would be in charge of the kitchen, and I would be in the . . . the front. I was always good at mathematics and computing things in my head, and so we didn't have fancy machines or cash registers or anything, so I was in charge of the front and handled all the orders. So then I became involved in the tribe. And I might not have become so involved even then, except my husband, unfortunately, had heart problems and had a series of heart attacks, and he passed away in 1988. So when you think of 1984 to 1988 . . . After he passed away, then I had more free time and began to attend some Business Committee meetings, and felt that I had as much to offer as other candidates. So that's when I became involved.

Warren: Okay, and I've read elsewhere that when your mother was [tribal] secretary, the budget of the Eastern Shawnee Tribe was approximately fifty dollars a year.

Wallace: Fifty dollars a year, exactly. When they wanted to notify tribal members that they were having an extra meeting or something, they didn't even have money for stamps to mail. So they would go to somebody's house that might have a phone or something and try to call people, or—And if they had any money left over from that fifty dollars, they had to return it to the government. Yes.

Warren: You've witnessed such a remarkable change in your tribe over the years. Now your budgets run into the tens of millions of dollars.

Wallace: Absolutely.

Warren: What impresses you about that? About the changes that have occurred?

Wallace: Well, first, I'm extremely proud. I use the example of a sculpture up at Indigo Sky that has two females there. One's a female elder, and one's a younger female, and they are standing on a boulder. I think the rest of the world has almost defined Native Americans by male warriors in the past, and absolutely, our history had male warriors, and absolutely, it was a vital part of our history. But rarely, [if] ever, do you see anything else. Even when they want to honor . . . If a city wants to honor Native Americans, they still honor with a statue of Little Turtle, or they still honor with a statue of Tecumseh, or they still honor with some other male warrior. Our culture shouldn't be restricted to that. And our culture, this tribe . . . We were removed from Ohio in 1832. We were with another tribe. We were approximately 250 people total, with both tribes together. We came to Indian Territory, [and] were even placed on the wrong land, and so here we have travelled this far and didn't even have a homeland. And it's been a struggle. Through this research—I just showed you a document where an Indian agent was writing and saying that in that particular document we were down to only eighty-three people. We actually got down [to] less than that, but eighty-three people. And he says in there, there are only seven or eight males who are over the age of twenty-one. It truly was an example of almost total successful genocide. We came that close. And we've had to struggle and struggle and struggle. And that boulder at Indigo Sky is split, and a little sapling, a little tree, has burst through there, and just keeps forcing its way to greater growth and strength. And I use that as parallel for the Eastern Shawnee Tribe. I think that's been our struggle. And it's just like we would not be denied our birth . . . our birthright.

Warren: You are the also the first female chief in the history of the Eastern Shawnee Tribe.

Wallace: That's correct, and I don't understand that. When I go back and read in 1893 that there were only seven or eight males, I guess I don't understand why a female didn't come forward. I mean there are eighty-three, and if there are only seven or eight males over the age of twenty-one, and we're told that our culture, that in the Shawnee [culture], females were strong in the past, and they had a peace council—I'm sorry, maybe that's just the difference in our personalities or something, but when there's a problem, I don't think of being male or female. I think, There's a problem, and somebody needs to work on it. I don't understand how that happened.

Warren: Well, certainly in Shawnee Bread dances, there are female chiefs.

Wallace: Absolutely.

Warren: *Hokimawiiqa.*

Wallace: Absolutely.

Warren: And so you must be very proud of breaking the political barrier?

Wallace: I'm just thankful that, at least from my vantage point, the tribe has succeeded. The tribe has grown. The tribe has prospered. And it's not necessarily because of me. Everybody has come forth and worked.

Warren: I want to ask you a couple additional questions. First, I'd like for you to say a little bit about your pioneering work in Ohio, and in returning to Ohio. And what motivated you to do that?

Wallace: I became interested in our tribe's history, again, because of my education. When I returned from Australia in 2000, just as I had an academic dean who always encouraged me to grow, I also had a president who did the same, and his name is Kent Farnsworth. Kent Farnsworth was the chairman of the Missouri Humanities Council. And in 2000 they were looking forward, looking ahead, and they knew that the Lewis and Clark Bicentennial was going to be approaching. He had a chairman of the Missouri Humanities who was adamant that the Native Americans would be included in this bicentennial. That the original Lewis and Clark expedition had basically been a loss for Indians and for Native Americans, and he wanted to make sure—this was Michael Bouman—wanted to make sure that the Native Americans would be included and would have a major voice, at least in the state of Missouri. That's all he could speak for. And he [Michael Bouman] began early recruiting, and the president of my college was, as I say, the chair of that Humanities Council. And when he asked, "Do you know any Native Americans whose tribes were involved?" And before they reached Saint Louis, Lewis and Clark were over in what would be Shawnee Territory—Apple Creek, Cape Girardeau—and the Shawnees are definitely mentioned in those journals. So the Shawnee was the first tribe mentioned in the Lewis and Clark [journals]. So my president was asked, "Do you know a Shawnee?" And my president said, "Well, yes, I do." And, "Well, do you know a Shawnee that lives in Missouri?" And I lived within two miles of this complex, but I'm on the Missouri side, and my president said, "Yes, I do." And the chairman said, "Is this person able to speak?" And my president laughed and said, "Yes, she is."

Warren: She might be able to speak a little bit.

Wallace: "She gives speeches for us all the time." And so my president, the chairman of the Missouri Humanities Council, came down to see me and asked me to do programs, and I said I have no problem speaking, [but] I have to be honest with you, I don't know my tribe's history. I don't know of anybody who knows my tribe's history. And so he said, "Well this is your opportunity to correct that." And I said, "That's a project that I'm going to do after I retire." And he said, "Well, I would prefer that to be a project that you undertake now." And my president came and said, "You can do this, Glenna." And so I began researching.

So that's how I actually began. And in researching my tribe's history, I couldn't find out that much about my tribe. Most of the things that had been written were written about Shawnees. But if they were written about two tribes, they were primarily the Absentee [Shawnee] Tribe and the—at that time—the Loyal Tribe . . . Loyal Shawnee Tribe. And so I kind of put on the red dress and said, "Well, I'm going to do something about this." So in the summertime, for the next six years, I travelled with various Chautauqua programs. And often in there—not all of them, but often—some of them were indeed about . . . certainly the two years with Lewis and Clark. So that's where I came to know my history. And [I] realized then that all of our sites were back in Ohio, and we as a tribe had not been there. And so, when I became chief, we went back to Ohio. And trying to arrange places to go, I had to contact Ohio Historical Society. They didn't return telephone calls. They weren't too receptive. I was just determined that we were going to go to some places. I just kept calling, and kept knocking on doors, and I guess they decided I wasn't going to stop. And so they began to return my calls, and that led into a closer relationship. We went into Wapatomica that first year. And Wapatomica . . . when we went there, that was the first time Shawnees had been on Wapatomica for more than two hundred years. We went there, and every one of us cried, as well as the people from Ohio Historical Society. And I have to say, they didn't always know who they were talking with, whether it was a federally recognized tribe, or a claimant group, or whatever. So I can see their reluctance. But they didn't have to be that reluctant. So it was about like a boulder with that little tree, up there at Indigo Sky, that had to break through that. And that has totally changed now, not only for our tribe, but for all federally recognized tribes, because there are many people in this area who now have contact and association and a close relationship with Ohio Historical—They've changed that name to Ohio History Connection now. And even in this grant they're a partner, and that would have never been the situation years ago. So I have to admit, yes, I'm proud of that.

Warren: What has going back to Ohio meant to you as a Shawnee person? What have you learned from it? Could you say a little bit more about Ohio's place in your mind now?

Wallace: Well, first let me emphasize that Oklahoma is our home now and will always be our home. So, it's not that I want to leave Oklahoma or change any of that. It's simply every piece of our history . . . well, not every piece, but so much of our history occurred in Ohio. I want to make sure those places are preserved, are protected. And we're not able to do that here in Oklahoma. So it's . . . they're the conduit. And I've had people that helped me grow. So, if I can help them to grow, or be the impetus that causes them to realize what they really have there, and that they should take care of it, and that they should be working with federally recognized tribes to maintain that history and those places, then so be it. I don't want to. I don't like going back and having people play golf on the mounds.[3] That's a sacred place. That should be changed. And if somebody has to point the finger or raise the voice and say, "This is not as it should be," that doesn't mean that everything we do is correct. But somebody has to start that somewhere, and I just don't think that's right.

Warren: What is your vision for the tribe, for your grandchildren and perhaps even their grandchildren? What would you want for them as Shawnee people?

Wallace: You know, it's probably been said many, many times in Native American worlds. We say that when we make decisions, we should make decisions knowing it's going to impact seven generations from now. And I quite often absolutely say, when we're making decisions, "I want you to think, I'm going to die, you're going to die, and these people around us are going to die, but the tribe is not." So when we make decisions, it shouldn't be a decision for me. It's a decision to make this tribe sustainable and to continue. I've had many things that I'm proud of that I think have happened and advanced while I [have been] chief. Part of that being that now, when we have all of our services and our benefits, they're available to tribal citizens everywhere. It doesn't matter whether they live in Oregon, or whether they're in Alaska, or whether they are in Hawaii or Ohio. That wasn't the case when I became chief. So I've worked to try to bring an awareness that we're all Eastern Shawnee. And there are many times that other people have had to show me that vision, rather than my showing them the vision. And so I would hope that we would still be a tribe that people will be proud of, that our citizens will be proud of, and that it gives them a pride in wanting to say that they're a part of the . . . that they are an Eastern Shawnee tribal citizen. And I would hope it would be a pride that they want to help advance the tribe in some way, wherever they are. Anybody could research. They don't have to live back here in Ottawa County to research and be able to find some of these missing links. And that they would be able to say so. In this age, this technological age, there [are] many ways that people could help. It's just raising that awareness. And so I hope all of us, generation after generation, continue to develop that awareness and continue to make a tribe that they're proud of.

NOTES

1. By the 1930s, the Milnot Company sold milk byproducts in cans. In 1948 the company opened a large plant in Seneca, Missouri.

2. Newton County, where Crowder College is located in Neosho, Missouri, and McDonald County, just south of Newton, both border northeast Oklahoma.

3. There are at least two golf courses, Moundbuilders Country Club in Newark and Mound Gold Club in Miamisburg, that are built on Hopewell and Adena mound complexes.

13

An Interview with
Larry Kropp, First Council

Stephen Warren: I'm sitting here with Larry Kropp, who's an Eastern Shawnee tribal citizen and a member of the Business Committee of the Eastern Shawnee Tribe of Oklahoma [and Eric Wensman, the research manager of the ANA grant]. And Larry, before we get into the nitty-gritty, I was wondering if you could just tell us when and where you were born.

Larry Kropp: Well, I was born in 1948, July 21. I was born in Joplin, Missouri. I tell everybody my first ride was in a hearse and my last ride is going to be in a hearse.

Warren: They brought a baby home in a hearse?

Kropp: In a hearse. I was born in Joplin, Missouri, in a hospital. We were good friends with the undertaker in Baxter Springs, Kansas, and Mom had a little [bit of a] difficult time, and at that period of time they used the hearse for an ambulance as well as for a hearse. And he sent the hearse up with the ambulance bed in it to bring Mom and I back from the hospital to home. That's the reason why I say my first ride was in a hearse and my last ride will be in a hearse.

Warren: What a great story. But you were raised primarily in Quapaw.

Kropp: Yes.

Warren: And you went to Lincolnville Elementary School, correct?

Kropp: Yes. Lincolnville, it was just a rural school, two-room school, and actually it was a four-room school till 1907. Then a tornado came through and took the top floor off of it. And they rebuilt the roof on it and reduced it down to just a one-story building; it was two rooms. As far as the comparison, we always thought Quapaw was the big city, far as that goes. We enjoyed the pie suppers, and yeah, the community gatherings all happened at the school and everything. It was a pretty enjoyable time. [I] went there till I was in the sixth grade, and in the sixth grade they consolidated the schools and sent me to the big city of Quapaw then.

Warren: Quapaw was pretty much an Indian town, was it not?

Kropp: Yeah, you didn't realize it at the time. I said there was no distinction made between the Indians and non-Indians. Everybody played together and got along together. I said it was big-time Indians, I guess now.

Warren: Given that there was no distinction, I wonder what your earliest memory is of being Indian. Where you thought, "Oh wow, I am a Quapaw" or "I am a Shawnee." When did it first occur to you?

Kropp: I never really gave it much consideration. That's just the way we were raised, you know. Nobody ever made a distinction out of being either Quapaw or Shawnee, you know. Everybody got along together. As far as pointing it out, I didn't really point it out till I got in the service, when I was nineteen years old, and they found out I was Native American. Of course, Native American and everybody start calling ya Chief. I didn't think anything about it.

Warren: You joined the military when you were nineteen. What branch were you in?

Kropp: I was in the air force.

Warren: Did you serve in Vietnam?

Kropp: I served *over* Vietnam. I was a crew chief on the KC-135, and we done air-fueling and supportive combat missions. And several times, I said, we used to refuel the bombers and fighters as well as [do] surveillance [on] all their planes.

I was based . . . My home base was Little Rock Air Force Base, [where I was] on [the] B-58, and then I went on to Fairchild Air Force Base, [where I was] on [the] KC-135, which is in Washington State. But I made it around the world about a dozen times on TDYs [temporary duties], so Okinawa, Guam, Alaska, where else, Spain. Made the rounds quite a bit.

Warren: When were you discharged from the military?

Kropp: February '72. I think I was what about twenty-two or twenty-three, somewhere around there. I figured I made it four years without getting shot at—knowingly get shot at—so I figured it was time to get out. I came back home like everybody else at that time. People kind of treated you differently than they do military people now. Back during that period of time, I said, you were required to fly with your military uniform on, and I was . . . just recall going through the airport in Chicago one time in my dress blues. People were spitting on ya and calling ya a baby killer and everything else during that period of time. After you got out, there's kind of a tendency to put everything away and kind of forget about it and start looking for a job.

Warren: Right now you own a ranch?

Kropp: Well, a farm-ranch.

Warren: With fifty head of cattle?

Kropp: Yeah.

Warren: Have you always done that?

Kropp: Oh, I've always been involved in farming. That's all my dad done all his life was farm. No. I got out of the service, I drove a bulldozer for a while, worked in different odd jobs, to go work for a truck line, and drove a truck for thirty-one years, worked on a freight dock and drove a truck.

Warren: In addition to farming?

Kropp: Yeah, farming everything on the side.

Warren: How has farming changed over the years? I mean, from when you first started to today?

Kropp: Well, I think about when I was, oh, I guess probably maybe ten . . . and so we had an old grain truck; we were cutting wheat. And back then they used the old Alice Chalmers pull combine. It was a family affair. Same way, my dad, brothers, and nephews . . . they kind of farmed together and helped one another when it come to cutting wheat. They had the old, real tight pull combines, and each combine . . . the header on it to cut it with, well, one of them was five foot, and two of them was four foot. That's all you cut, was a swath four foot wide. And out of that four foot or five foot, you probably only used about three and a half foot because you didn't get full use of it. I can remember setting up. We had one field we were cutting up, and standing in the back of the truck, about half-full of wheat, and we always used to play in the grain truck, you know, standing up there, looking at those three tractors, those three combines out there, thinking, Man, this is how the big farmers do it. And now you have combines that cut thirty-two foot.

Warren: Yeah, and machines that cost more than half a million dollars.

Kropp: Oh yeah, just to get in a field with them would cost you every bit of half a million dollars to even turn around. We got all our farm ground leased out, and all we do is bail hay and feed the cows.

Warren: So what people probably don't know about you, Larry, is that you're the de facto tribal historian.

Kropp: Well, family historian. I don't know about tribal. Long difference there . . . a lot of difference there.

Warren: Well, we'll see. I wonder if you could just tell us about your respective family histories. And by that I mean the German, the Quapaw, and the Eastern Shawnee. We'd like to hear it all.

Kropp: Hear it all. Well, I was sitting here thinking of where to start at. I tell everybody . . . Well, while my dad's family was Quapaw in Arkansas, southern Arkansas, fighting against the French down there, my mom's family was in Ohio, fighting with the French against the British. They both were removed to Oklahoma, and that's how they came of me. No, it's pretty interesting. Of course, I don't know what to tell on something like that. No, the way things worked out, I guess Mom was raised down at [Moccasin Bend] No. 5. My dad moved around quite a bit in his younger years. One of the stories my mom told me was, when they went to No. 5 school, old Moccasin Bend schoolhouse, Mom was in the third grade and Dad was in the fifth grade, and he bribed my mom with a stick of gum to be his girlfriend. And so he went to school there for about a year and a half, and then he moved to another school, and they didn't have any contact till he . . . I guess he was seventeen years old. And he started writing letters. He had a car, and [he] started writing letters back to mom, and they got reacquainted, and just evolved from there. There again, I said, the families, you don't know, you always hear the stories about the in-laws and all this, but everybody got along pretty good, I guess.

Warren: And your line of [descent in] the Eastern Shawnee tribe is the Captain family?

Kropp: Yes. My grandfather was Tom Captain. That was Mom's side of the family.

Warren: I wondered if you could tell us about the stories about the Captain family name and how it was acquired.

Kropp: Well, I've heard three versions, and grandpa always laughed when he told his version of it. His was the third version. The first version I've heard people say is, well, he was well thought of, and he served as a marshal, and they gave him the title—as he helped the cavalry and was a scout—and gave him the title Captain. That was the first version. Second version was that which . . . I guess, in fact, he was in the military or helped there, and he helped dole out rations and everything when they were in Kansas, and on their way and the troops gave him . . . bestowed the title of Captain on him there. Now, Grandpa's version was, on the walk from Ohio to Oklahoma, that great-grandpa had pigs that he used to stick to [make them] walk along and keep the pigs under control, and the troops made comments about, "Well, we see how you captain your troops," which is, "You're in command of your troops." That's the way Grandpa's version was. He said that they commented about how he captain[ed] his troops, meaning marching the pigs along the walk, and they bestowed the name Captain on him. So who knows?

Warren: What was Quapaw like? You have also German ancestry. And they ran a blacksmith shop in Kansas?

Kropp: Well, originally, they ran a blacksmith shop on my dad's side of the family in Weir, Kansas. And they moved to Oklahoma, sold the shop, when him and Grandma got married and moved back to Quapaw, on her allotment, and got into the mining. Of course, a lot of the skills that [were] required running a blacksmith shop at the time were the same ones that applied in the machinery and everything in the mining operations. They were pretty successful as far as the mining ventures on the allotment. A lot of the Quapaws relied on the government and the BIA to dictate to them. And people taking advantage of them. Fortunately, Grandpa was smart enough in his business-mind not to allow the government to step in and other people to control his mining operations. He was able, and confidently enough, to do it himself. And it was pretty profitable for him.

Warren: So, your grandfather, his allotment was mined?

Kropp: Grandma's allotment was mined.

Warren: Grandma's allotment was mined. And they maintained control of that mine so it was Native-owned?

Kropp: Yes, Native-owned. Yes. Her grandma and her . . . she had two, three brothers, and all their allotments were right together, and they managed to control all of them.

Warren: How did they do it? Do you know much about the story of how they were able to keep white people from divesting them of their land?

Kropp: Grandpa carried a gun all the time, I can tell you that. I still have the gun. And grandma carried a gun. No, there was a lot of problems, 'course, then, during that era of the '20s and everything. There was a lot of people taking advantage, and there was a—Of course, they relied on the . . . I guess, the competency of allotted people. Because not knowing . . . not knowing how a lot of tribes had the same problem, not knowing how to manage their land and everything . . . And you had to keep your head in it. I know there was a strong sense of family and a strong sense of keeping . . . taking care of your own.

Warren: And those were lead and zinc mines?

Kropp: Yes.

Warren: And how were they mined at the time? I've heard stories about mules that went blind down in the shaft.

Kropp: Yep, they put them in the ground, and they stayed in the ground till they went blind. The allotments where my grandma and grandpa was, they had to sink shafts. And the lead ran out in drifts . . . what they called drifts, and they would follow a drift wherever it went, up and down, and open up caverns, and it was so extensive in that area. And these were mined prior to World War II. And during World War II, when the demand for the lead and the zinc were so great, they had to get as much out as fast as possible for the war effort. And so they . . . Man, they cut everything. [It's] what was referred to as high and wide. They [had] little regard for safety . . . They just wanted to get the lead out.

Warren: Do you have memories of men who were harmed or who had lung-related illnesses?

Kropp: Oh, yeah. At Quapaw, at that time, you always knew somebody that had cough, cancer, and everything in their lungs. They was always . . . Guy lost his leg in the mines, rocks fell on him or something. There was always people around that you knew that that's what happened, "Oh, they was hurt in the mines."

Warren: It was just commonplace?

Kropp: Yeah commonplace.

13.1. A typical day for many Shawnees in the lead and zinc mines of Ottawa County, Oklahoma, c. 1930. Photo courtesy of Larry Kropp.

Warren: What are your thoughts on it today, as you look back on the chat piles?

Kropp: Well, thank God we had it during World War II, but today's efforts—Now you're on the edge of a fifty-square-mile [area] of a hazard-waste site. They spent untold millions of dollars trying to clean up, and they're still cleaning it up. At the time, it served a purpose. I hated to see the land left in the condition it is in, but it served a purpose.

Warren: What's your Bonnie and Clyde story?

Kropp: Oh, Bonnie—Well, my grandpa, like I said, he was well known in the mining industry, and everybody said he had a big safe in his house. And everybody always thought he kept cash in it, which . . . the only thing he kept in it was mine records. Well, he had two individuals break in and hold him at gunpoint and tie him up and pistol-whip my grandpa, trying to get him to open up the safe, and he refused. Well, my dad's brother, my uncle, he got loose, and he slipped out an upstairs window and went to the mines after some of the miners to come back and take care of the incident. Well, by the time they got back, the old boys already took off. Well, my grandpa hired a night watchman to stay after that happened. And about a week after he hired him, the two guys showed up again, and they got into a gunfight, and the night watchman was shot. They took him to Picher, to the hospital overnight. The bill for the overnight—Grandpa hired him a private nurse, and care was thirty-six dollars for the overnight. The ole' boy, he passed on the next day. But that's when . . . I'd say [it] was a pretty rough area at that time. Everybody up there started carrying guns back then. I think that was about '20 . . . 1924 or 1925, if I remember right.

Warren: And what about Quapaw itself? I just wonder if you could share stories or memories of the Quapaw Powwow as a boy?

Kropp: Oh, the Quapaw Powwow, from my place, was only about a mile away . . . a little over a mile away. And we would go down there at the powwow, and everybody asked, "Well, did you dance when you was younger?" And no, my family didn't dance. We went to the powwow for two reasons: to eat and to visit, and that was it. It was like a homecoming. Eric's heard this before. Later on [in] life I went to powwow for another reason: to chase girls. But [I] wasn't very successful. No it was . . . The powwow used to be . . . you just met old friends you hadn't seen and visited. You'd go down there and sit all day long and renew your acquaintances and everything. It was good for that. A lot of people came in from long distances for powwow, [which was] where you got to see them.

Warren: So, they timed it with the Fourth of July?

Kropp: Yep. Timed it with the Fourth of July. They have a three-day holiday in there, one way or other.

Eric Wensman: Did you look forward to the powwow?

Kropp: Oh, yeah.

Wensman: The whole family?

Kropp: Yeah. Yeah, like I said, you'd get some good eats down there.

Warren: Were there other Indian events in the area that you remember attending or being part of?

Kropp: No, none that comes to mind right off. I'm sure there was later on. During the '60s there was . . . they had some different stuff sponsored by the college, and that's when White Oak was going on. We went down to White Oak once, I think.

Wensman: Would your dad be invited to a feast or a lot of funerals?

Kropp: Yeah, a lot of funerals and everything. Yeah, and they had the feast for the funerals and everything. And oh, yeah, I've got tons of . . . well, if I could find them . . . I've probably got the obituary for about half of the Quapaw Tribe [from] when Grandma was alive.

Wensman: Well, I know they have a memorial feast every year. Would y'all go to those as well?

Kropp: Yes. Yeah, later on, if it was somebody we were close with, we did. Yeah.

Wensman: So, I mean, you guys were pretty active with the folks around here?

Kropp: Oh, yeah. Involved with the tribe and everything. Well, of course, you didn't think of being involved, you were just—

Wensman: You were just in it?

Kropp: You were just in it. You didn't realize it was tribal involvement as much as you do a personal relationship. If you lose a friend, you have a memorial feast. You're going to go to the feast.

Warren: Everybody always talks about Moccasin Bend No. 5 school and the Captain Grocery. Could you say something about those places and why they are so important to the Eastern Shawnees?

Kropp: Back in the day, it was a gathering place. Everybody used to come down on Sunday afternoon. Grandma always had a pot of beans on, and it seemed like the more people that showed up, the more water she had to [add] to [the] beans, but everybody always ate. Everybody. Oh, on the east side of the old store was a carport built on. And everybody back then . . . You had your pop case to sit on, and that's where you sat out there and listened to stories. And everybody— Course, it was all family and neighbors and everything. Then, later on, there was a rodeo arena

13.2. Exterior of Captain's Grocery in Eastside community, c. 1952. *Left to right*: Florence Captain, Larry Kropp, T. A. Captain, Terry Kropp. Photo courtesy of Larry Kropp.

that grandpa got. And they had Saturday night ropings and Sunday afternoon ropings. Got rope calves. All the stories that went along with that, and everything so.

Wensman: Was that just another way for him to make money, having that?

Kropp: No. It was . . . Nobody else had one around. Grandpa used to be [a] horseman in his day, and he enjoyed watching.

Wensman: Did they have jackpots?

Kropp: Yeah, jackpots, more or less. We sat there and watched and visit[ed]. . . . Watched the cowboys rope. Jim Archer, one of the characters there, he used to come up there all the time. He was a quite the hand [at being a] cowboy. A lot of the old cowboys come up there all the time. Seen some good things happen up there.

Warren: I came across an oral history with Tom Captain from 1971. And in it he turns down the opportunity for the government to build a tribal council house.

Kropp: Well, that's depends on whose story you're listening to there.

Warren: Well, that's his story.

Kropp: Well, he was accused of stealing the money.

Warren: From the government?

Kropp: From the government. He was accused of stealing the money. What he done was actually—He was good friends with Bob Whitebird, who was chief of the Quapaws, the chairman of the Quapaws. And grandpa, at that time, said, "We don't have a place to build a place like that." So he actually contacted Bob and gave the money to the Quapaws to build their first longhouse with. But grandpa was accused by several people of stealing that money. So I never would've forget that. And grandpa never . . . as generous as he was . . . probably never had over a hundred dollars in the bank at one time in his life. Just a lot of hard feelings about that.

Warren: He alludes to that in the interview. Why do you think he turned it down and gave it to Mr. Whitebird?

Kropp: This piece of property right here? At that time, all it was, was farm ground and brush. You didn't have an actual place to put such a building in.[1] And the interest in the Eastern Shawnees at that time was very minimal. Well, they used to have the tribal meetings up at the Eastside Baptist Church, or Christian Church, at that time. And there [would] probably be maybe fifteen people. And the fifteen people that showed up out of ten, they was all mad and wanting money. And it was kind of a hard deal. I'm trying to think of the right words to put it in. There was no tradition . . . I guess would be . . . involved with the Eastern Shawnees at that time. Of course, I think Grandpa, he more or less felt like the way to survive [was] through assimilation, because of everything that he had seen in his day and the ways he had been treated and everything. So, I heard him speak Shawnee very little. Basically whenever him and Bob Whitebird would get together, they would make comparison about the Shawnee language and the Quapaw language, and there was a lot of words that would interchange in the two.

Warren: What were some of your grandfather's experiences with discrimination?

Kropp: Well, he was a—I'll probably step on somebodies toes. Grandpa despised the town of Seneca. The town of Seneca, in his day, all it had was bars lined up and down. They made their profit off of selling whiskey to the Indians, and every time the Indians would get a little bit of money [at] all—He called them whiskey drummers. They lined up and take all the money and everything they could get, just for whiskey. Grandpa had the experience one time . . . He played cards down at the bar down here all night long, and he thought he was good friends with the constable at the time. He stepped out about daylight, and the sun was coming up over the buildings on the east side of the road, and the constable walked up and said, "Tom, how'd you do last night?" Grandpa made the mistake of saying, "Well, I won a little bit." Next thing he knew, he was blackjacked and knocked out in the middle of the road and arrested, drug off to jail. And the fine was everything he had in his pocket. So there was a lot of—You get into the Modocs and ask them about Seneca.

The Modocs was ready to declare war on the city of Seneca at one time. There was a sixteen-year-old boy that bought a pair of boots on credit and with promise to pay when he got his check from the Quapaw Agency, which used to be down here. And he said when he got his money from them he would pay. Well, the ole boy that owned the store saw the boy on Friday morning—I believe it was Friday or Saturday morning—in the street, and he got his gun and took after him, shooting him. He shot at him three times in the street and chased him into a store across the street, and the boy was hiding behind a stove, and he shot him, point-blank range, and killed him. The Modocs were ready to declare war on the city of Seneca. It took the Indian agent all he could do just to settle them down.

Warren: Something that I have observed in the archival record that I'd like you to talk more about is just the geographic position of Eastern Shawnees. It's the very first tribe—that and the Quapaw, depending on where you are—that you encounter from either Missouri or Kansas. How did that border life shape both communities?

Kropp: Well, the Eastern Shawnees—I'm sure the Quapaws, when they moved in up here, were not allowed to leave the reservation. They were left on the reservation to starve to death. They . . . Some of the older people I've talked to talked about [how] their parents would actually cut wood and have to sneak into Baxter Springs to sell their wood and sneak back into Indian Territory or Quapaw Territory in order just to get by. And that's the reason the Quapaws . . . a lot of them are leaving their lands and going to the Osage, to live with the Osage. The Osage kind of provided for them. The Eastern Shawnee—I really see no difference. When they stuck them down here, the government put them down here to die. They didn't want to be bothered with [them]. They talk about a thorn in the flesh [of] Jesus. The Native Americans served as a thorn in the flesh to the government of the United States at that period in time. Andrew Jackson had no compassion for them. He said get them out of here, they're subhuman . . . a class too subhuman. Unfortunately, a few of those individuals they sent down here were able to survive and put us where we're at today. My personal feelings . . . I don't know how Eric [Wensman] feels about it. There was no love lost between . . . The same way with the Quapaws. They were leaving to go with the Osage. The white man was coming in on their territory, staking claims. They actually had to get troops from Fort Scott, spend two years [there], and run everybody back across [the state line] to allow the Quapaws to come back. That's when the Quapaws got in the process of getting allotments and everything else. Before the lead mines and everything.

Warren: What was Captain Grocery like? It almost sounds like it was the tribal headquarters.

Kropp: It was a gathering point. Grandpa . . . I can remember had all kinds of documents and everything he kept under the cash register. There's a stack of documents in there. But it was a gathering point. Anybody that knew Grandpa—It was just . . . basically, it was a three-room building. It had the store in front, a kitchen, and a bedroom. And anybody that had anything to say about the Eastern Shawnees would come, and they would sit and hash it out, either in the store part or back in the kitchen part. And that's where the old Indian agents used to come. I remember them com[ing] in there and asking Grandpa questions. Usually on the weekends, on Sundays. Grandma fed everybody that came. Usually all the kids, neighbors, and everybody else was there.

Wensman: Larry, you mentioned about your grandpa giving that money to Bob Whitebird. You think that is one of the reasons why—? In the spirit that they helped one another . . . that's why these tribes are still here today?

Kropp: Yeah, people don't realize that. I said used to. Well, like the gentleman I spoke to from the . . . oh, a tribe up in Kansas, I can't think of it now. He had a t-shirt on. Oh, "Pottawatomi Citizen Band, Pottawatomis BC," that's what his t-shirt said. And I was asking him, I said, "Are you on the Business Committee?" He laughed and he said, "No. BC. Citizen Band of Pottawatomi 'Before Casinos.'" But back in the day, before the tribes got where they had the . . . You didn't see any distinction. Everybody worked together. There was a great deal of respect between Bob and Grandpa both. They would sit and visit. And Grandpa, actually, when he was able to drive, he would drive to Quapaw and set and visit with Bob, and Bob would come down during the week and set there in the store and visit. There's a lot of respect, mutual respect, for one another. To me, that's what the tribes used to be. There wasn't the distinction [that is] made now, because "We have a bigger casino than you got," or "We got a little casino," [or] "We don't have a casino." You know, the tribes all worked together to survive.

Wensman: And then he had the same relationship with the other tribes? With Modocs and the Senecas and Peorias, those folks?

Kropp: Yeah, the Peorias, too. Grandpa got along good with all of them. He and the Modocs argued over property a couple times, I guess. And that's still occurring today. But, you know, I can't remember having any knock-down-drag-outs or any arguments with any of the other tribes. None of them had anything.

Wensman: Would you say that because of those relationships, that's why we are still here today?

Kropp: Oh, yeah. That's got a lot to do with it. They leaned on one another. We were talking, out in Oregon, about the commodity cheese. You said you never had commodity cheese?

Wensman: No, I've ate commodity cheese.

Kropp: Are you familiar with commodity cheese?

Warren: Mm-hm.

Kropp: It's kind of, everybody is in the same boat, let's put it that way. You wasn't rich, you wasn't poor. The commodity cheese was a trading item. We were raised on the farm. We had fruit trees, we had blackberries, we had beef, chickens, everything. We sold eggs. Somebody that didn't have eggs, you could always swap them eggs for something, for the commodity cheese. And, well, the commodity cheese was good, 'cause you could use it for macaroni and cheese, you could use it for grilled cheese sandwiches, you could use it for a number of things. And grandpa always . . . When he run the store, they . . . people would come in, and if the people didn't have certain groceries, he would trade. 'Course, that commodity cheese come in five-pound chunks. He would trade them groceries in the store for the commodity cheese. And he would keep the commodity cheese down in the cooler in the store. Well, the family in there, if we wanted cheese, we would go back there just to swap off something else [or] bring grandpa down some eggs. It was just a big trade. Commodity cheese used to be a pretty good joke around here.

Wensman: Did you all go to the dances at Seneca too?

Kropp: No, we never did. Nope, never did. We stayed up around Quapaw.

Wensman: Was that too far?

Kropp: We never had a vehicle that would make it that far. I guess the old cars you had . . . I think back in that period of time . . . We was up in teenage years before you got a good enough car to trust [to] get all over the country in. That used to be a good ways down there. I remember going down there, I think in '54 if I remember right. We went down there, that's when the lake went dry.

Wensman: Was there any racism in the town of Miami?

Kropp: Oh, [in] Miami there was, yeah.

Wensman: It was bad?

Kropp: Oh, yeah. Back then it was, yeah.

Warren: How did it manifest itself? I want to be able to see it and imagine it.

Kropp: There again, this is my opinion, and for all it's worth it might not be worth two cents. But a lot of the tribal people used to get a check every month. That was not only royalties, but through some other means . . . support. A lot of the Quapaw people had land and everything, so the BIA dubbed them as unable to handle their own finances. So they would just give them a check every month. During that first week or so after they got that check, my gosh, they had big parties, and half the city of Miami wine and dined them. But after that check was gone, they treated them like dogs. As long as they had money, they were good, but if they had no money, they didn't have nothing. I said it was one of them times whenever, if you could pass for white, you were white. I guess so you wouldn't get everybody [saying], "That's just a bunch of them dumb Indians out there."

Warren: But in Quapaw you didn't experience that.

Kropp: No, I didn't. Well everybody in there was Indian, I think.

Wensman: Only in Miami?

Kropp: Yeah, just in Miami.

Warren: And Seneca?

Kropp: Yeah, and the town of Seneca, yeah.

Wensman: How about these other little towns? Like, what's this little town, Peoria, over here?

Kropp: Peoria? Captains are related to half of Peoria at the time. Peoria . . . Everybody over at Peoria are mixed-bloods.

Wensman: So, when Miami had their fair, would it be hard for Natives to go to the fair?

Kropp: It wouldn't be hard to go. It would be hard to stay out of a fight. That's basically it. Back in the '50s and everything. There was no love lost between them.

Warren: And then, on a federal level, in the '50s, you know, you have that period of termination and relocation, and that's something that you probably knew something about, right? Because the Wyandottes and the Modocs . . . and I think there was one other tribe that was terminated.

Kropp: I remember Mom and Dad talking about it. Well, I remember Dad talking about it with Grandpa down there, and Grandpa's idea was to hang on as long as we could. There was not going to be any self-termination. If the government forces you into it, what are you going to do? But no. Grandpa . . . he fought to keep the tribe alive.

Warren: Why did he do that?

Kropp: I think it was a connection with the ancestors. Just because [of] the heritage that was passed down.

Warren: But given the fact that meetings devolved to fifteen people, that was quite a courageous act on his part.

Kropp: Yeah, they used to take up money to send letters to other tribal members. They didn't have enough money in the tribal funds to buy stamps or paper or anything. So they would take up money from everybody that was there for stamps, to send out letters or notices or anything.

Wensman: Did you ever know any Indians that didn't want to be Indian?

Kropp: Oh, yeah. Well, I told you, out there we used to play cowboys and Indians as kids, but nobody wanted to be the Indians. They got beat all the time. Oh, yeah, there was. Especially girls.

But now things have changed. I said a lot of girls I knew growing up and everything, you tell them they were Indian, they would be insulted. But now it's changed. My wife, she was raised in Tulsa, and her family has Cherokee in them, but they refused to be acknowledged as Cherokee, so they said they were black Dutch. There was a lot of stigma putting on the fact that you were Indian back then.

Wensman: But you think that's changed today?

Kropp: Yeah, I think . . . Well, look at the rolls. There again, before casinos and after casinos. When people realize you got a casino, it's not "I want to be Eastern Shawnee." It's "What can the Eastern Shawnee do for me?" It's sad, you know. I would love to see this BlueJacket building, where we have our meeting down here, to be filled with 150, two hundred people, just to show tribal interest. I think there's a renewal in the younger generation now. But even they're not going to start coming to the meetings and everything. That's the sad part about it. I keep telling all the kids, "It's going to take people a lot smarter than what I am, one of these days, to deal with the business of the tribe." I'm just in there trying to hold things together.

Wensman: Is there any particular thing you think that kids would like to see the tribe do?

Kropp: I think you guys are doing a good job as far as the resurrection of the language and everything. It's a lot easier to teach the kids the language. The younger minds are easier to talk than what us old hard-heads are. You guys are doing a good job as far as that goes. But they're going to have to have a desire to do it.

Warren: I was hoping that you would offer a vision of the future. Where would you like the tribe to be two generations from now?

Kropp: Two generations? Now, we are on an upward climb. Two generations from now I want to see that success of the Eastern Shawnee Tribe continue. I think that there's a world of potential out there, but it's going to take unity, and it's going to take education and unity for people out there. And to take advantage of opportunities.

Warren: What does success look like?

Kropp: Success looks like—Look on the hill [gestures toward the Indigo Sky Casino]. That's the start of success right there. The hardest thing I have done since I've been on [the Business Committee] . . . Well, that was hard up there. Whenever we agreed to build that, we had people that actually just wanted to construct a tin building out there and go from there. I said the hardest thing I've done is to approve the add-on to Indigo Sky. I know it's got to have confidence in the people that's up there and confidence in our employees and everything, to know it's going, but that's a pretty good step for a little tribe our size. You have people out here wanting benefits on one hand. Well, there again, this is my own two-cents' worth. I don't rely on the tribe for my existence. I'm appreciative for everything the tribe does for me, but my life is going on if the tribe didn't provide. I'm still going to be Eastern Shawnee if there was nothing here, you know. And there's so many people now that, like I said earlier, [say] "I'm Eastern Shawnee. What's in it for me?" And it really wouldn't bother me to stop all the benefits, personally, for me, and go on and apply that to the next two generations to ensure success in business and the tribe still being here. I know that the benefits . . . there's a lot of people needing them, but I don't want to create a dependency on them. It won't get me reelected I know.

Warren: Are there cultural things you'd like to see?

Kropp: Oh, these guys are doing a good job of renewing the culture. So much of the people don't understand. I said, "What's Eastern Shawnee culture?" But there is no specific Eastern Shawnee culture. There's *Shawnee* culture. But they want details of Eastern Shawnee culture. Is that the way you see it? There's Shawnee culture we draw from all three Shawnee tribes. Fortunately, we are starting to resurrect it, but the resurrection is occurring in association with the other two tribes. I think that's good.

Warren: How should you go about that, creating a cultural resurrection with the other two tribes? That's tricky work, is it not?

Kropp: Well, I know the . . . the Absentees. There are some of them that believe that what's ours is ours, and they don't want to share it. You get that feeling, too?

Wensman: Mm-hm.

Kropp: This is our culture. This is not the Eastern Shawnee culture. They don't want to share it. The ones I've had contact with are more than happy, and I think they are doing it by relationship forming between the tribes now. That they're realizing, we may not have the blood quantum or the skin tone of a lot of the Absentees, but a lot of the Absentees don't have the blood degree and the skin coloring now that their ancestors had. We're getting there; we're getting there.

Wensman: So, you would like to see more cooperation between the three to make us stronger as a people?

Kropp: Yeah. I think the only reason that the federal government chose to move the Shawnees down here in the different various fashions is because [of] their fear of the united Shawnee government within the state, or within Indian Territory. They thought, if they kept us divided up, we could never unite, because of the forces they had in Ohio and up through there. I think they were scared to death of the Shawnees.

Warren: In fact I've read Absentee Shawnee . . . an Absentee Shawnee woman from the 1870s who resisted allotment and dreamed of the reunification of the three tribes. And who has fought tooth and nail with the agent on that. We came across that on one of our trips to the National Archives.

Kropp: Is she the one that had the vision of the blonde-hair, blue-eyed Shawnees?

Warren: No, that would not be her.

People who are non-Native might not understand the subtle things you are saying about race. Non-Native people tend to think about Indians by phenotype, by appearance. But Larry, you've been very articulate about your own family background. I wonder how you think about identity. It isn't racial to you. When you see a Shawnee person, it isn't based on skin color.

Kropp: To me, as an Indian person, whether it be Shawnee—Or, I think you should present yourself in such a fashion that you have pride in your culture, you have pride in your ancestry, you may not be dark skinned, you may not be black haired. But you can go back. I coined the phrase one time and said, "We may be thin in blood, but strong in heart." To me, the Shawnee people need to devote that strength in their hearts and get away from the skin tone. I had an individual one time that worked at the casino, and he was receiving some pressure. The gentleman was gay, and he was receiving pressure at the casino about the way people was treating him. He called me up, and he was explaining his situation, and he said, "Mr. Kropp, I want you to know I'm gay." And I said, "Whoa, wait a minute. I don't care whether you're gay, straight, red, green, purple, black, or whatever. If you're doing your job and you're doing your job right, you won't have a bit of trouble." You have pride in your job. I feel the same way as far as the Native American ancestry. You take pride in that Native American ancestry. You live toward accomplishing something in your life, and not just take it for granted and stand there with your hand out.

Warren: So what should your grandchildren and their children do? What would you have them do? Do you have a vision?

Kropp: Kick their butts. [laughter] No, the same thing. I have mix-race grandchildren. I said my daughter and son were both adopted, and I have grandchildren that are Navajo–African American, and they're enrolled Navajo. I always kid with them, "Well, you have to have a card saying you're Navajo, but you don't have to have a card saying you're African American." It doesn't make a bit of sense to me. You know, just take pride in yourself. To me, that's the main thing. You got a lot of ancestors that have fought, as an example, both on the African American and the Native American side. You've got ancestors that fought to accomplish things throughout history. You need to draw from that the same thing with the Native Americans. Look at what your ancestors fought for, and you're still here. Take pride in the fact that you are Native American.

Warren: That's beautiful. Would you mind if we ended there?

Kropp: Good! I'll get talked out.

NOTE

1. The current tribal headquarters is on the site of what was then known as the Shawnee National Farm, just across the state line from Seneca, Missouri.

14

An Interview with Winifred "Winkie" Froman, Brett Barnes, and Rhonda Barnes

Stephen Warren: I'm Steve Warren, and I'm sitting here with Eric Wensman, Rhonda Barnes, Brett Barnes, and Wink, and I'm hoping that we can start off by just having you introduce yourselves, if you wouldn't mind telling us when you were born and where you were born.

Winkie Froman: Okay. My real name is Annie Winifred—Well, it used to be [Annie Winifred] Dick. Froman is my name now. But I grew up being called Winkie, or Wink. I was born in 1935 in White Oak, Oklahoma, in my grandma's place in the old homestead.

Oh, and this is kind of interesting: My uncle, Calvin (my dad was Lewis Dick and his brother Calvin was also staying with my grandma in this house out there), his wife was pregnant, too. So they went into Vinita for the doctor for my mother. The doctor was there when I was born. His name was Dr. Marx, and he looked at my Aunt Lib and said, "Oh, look, Cal! Looks like it won't be long before you'll be calling me." You know, she's standing there pregnant. And my grandma said, "I think before daylight." And he said, "Annie, if you're right on this, you can have my office in Vinita." Six hours and forty-five minutes later, she gave birth. So there was two babies born that night. My birthday's the 22nd, and hers is the 23rd because she came after me. So I heard that story all my life about there was six hours and forty-five minutes between me and Roberta.

Warren: You were born at home?

Froman: Mm-hm. So my grandma always liked to say, "So, that office up there's mine. Marx says it was mine." [laughter] She delivered a lot of babies. Lot of people didn't go in and get a doctor; they'd come after my grandma and she'd go with them.

Warren: So she was a midwife?

Froman: Mm-hm.

Warren: Did you ever learn any rules or protocols about homebirth, the Shawnee way?

Froman: Uh-uh, no. I didn't know where babies came from, either, and none of us did, I guess, because Freddy Halfmoon—I think it was him—he was out looking around because Grandma would come home and say, "Oh, so-and-so found a baby last night." You know, *found* a baby last night. So he was looking around out there, and I said, "What're you doing, Freddy?" And he said, "Looking for baby tracks." [laughter] He thought she'd just go find them and then go take them to this family.

Warren: What was White Oak like when you were growing up? Who lived there? How big of a community was it?

Froman: Oh, well, it was mostly Indians. I remember Pete White, who lived—how far would you say that place is, from Gram's place?—as the crow flies, a mile I guess, but if you went around the road . . . Anyway, he had a team wagon. If you wanted to go to White Oak to get groceries,

14.1. Traditional ceremonial regalia worn by Annie Winifred "Winkie" Froman and Ron Froman (past chief of the Peoria Tribe). Photo courtesy of Rhonda Barnes.

people would borrow his wagon to go get groceries, or sometimes we'd walk to Bowlin Spring. We'd walk there sometimes and get groceries. I remember a couple of my cousins was gonna carry my Gram across this creek. So they did this [gestures], you know, they had a thing with their arms and she sat there on them. They went across, and they started getting tickled, and she was getting scared they were gonna drop her in the water. But they got her across, and we walked on to Bowlin. So that was a treat. That's quite a ways to walk.

Brett Barnes: That's about two miles as the crow flies, isn't it?

Froman: Uh, I don't know. I'm not good at mileage.

Warren: And Bowlin Spring was an all-black town at the time, correct?

Froman: Mm-hm. And one time my Gram and them had pneumonia, I guess, or flu. Anyway, they were all sick, and Leonard Bowlin's dad—I didn't know him, I knew Leonard and Mary—but their parents was before I was born, I guess. Anyway, he happened by there and found them all sick in bed. He went home, got his wife, brought her back, and they stayed there and took care of them until they got well. So they were really good people.

Warren: It must have been odd to have an Indian town and a black town kind of beside [each other].

Froman: Well, they had a little Cherokee in them, I always heard. Good-looking family.

Warren: What were people doing for a living then? How did Shawnees and Cherokees and African Americans survive back in the '30s and '40s?

Froman: Gosh, I don't know. I know that's what happened to the population of the White Oak Hills, is it started moving away for work. Some of my cousins ended up in Tulsa and Wichita and a lot of different places because they had to go somewhere. This was like my [cousins], ones that's just barely older than me, you know? My generation had to leave there to make a living. So I don't know what the old folks did, because I just know my grandma didn't work. Well, I take that back. She worked like a slave at home, raising this big garden thing. But they would come up here, she and my auntie (one of her daughters), would come up to Quapaw and work for those rich Quapaws. They had money back then from the mines. So they'd come up and cook for them. Maybe if they were having a big deal, well, they'd come and get my grandma and my auntie, and they'd bring them up here, and they'd cook for them. And they'd get paid for that. But that would just be periodically, not all the time.

Warren: And you were saying earlier that you had not lived with a man in the house until you were married at the age of twenty-five.

Froman: Mm-hm. Well, my grandma didn't have a husband; he left her. She raised her kids by herself and ended up having to raise most of her grandkids because, you know, two wives passed away. Of course, when my mother passed away, she just left two kids, but when my uncle Frank's wife died, she left about seven kids. Of course, Gram couldn't keep them all in, so Uncle Frank took them to Seneca Boarding School. And they'd come in the summer and stay with us. Otherwise, it was just me and my grandma. When I moved into town, it was just me and my grandma. I never changed a baby's diaper. You know how girls babysat and stuff, or take care of younger? I never changed a diaper until I had my daughter.

Warren: Can you tell me more about your grandma's garden? And the sort of things that she grew?

Froman: I hate to talk about it, because I didn't help her, and I'll probably cry. [laughter] My auntie always said, "Your grandma just ruins you." I just remember she was working all the time, but the pole-bean thing just stuck in my mind. She planted Kentucky Wonder green beans, and she'd have her grandkids go out and cut pole for them, and they had to be as straight as they can be, and if they were too crooked she'd send them back until they could bring straighter ones in. She raised a lot of green beans, and sometimes she could send visitors home with a bushel of beans. She had enough to spare, so she shared them. And one uncle, well actually, by marriage, and he was a husband, his name was Clarence Secondine, I don't know. They were divorced, but he stayed out there at our house for a while, and he raised [a] lot of watermelons. And that was kind of a treat because we'd get a watermelon, and draw water out of the well, and put it in a tub . . . put the melon in the tub to kind of cool it, you know? Didn't have ice or anything. And we used to have to put cream or some milk in a jar, tie it with a rope, and put it down in the well to keep it cool. And that was our refrigerator.

Warren: What other vegetables did she grow? Besides Kentucky Wonder?

Froman: Well, potatoes. Then, I guess, tomatoes, too. I don't know how come the green beans just stuck in my mind. And corn, oh yeah. Lots of corn because, of course, we ate it while it was fresh, too. Corn on the cob. But we dried a lot of it. We'd just take it off the cob.

Warren: Do you know much about what kind of corn it was?

Froman: Indian corn. [laughter] Does it have another name? I don't know, either. Well, we had bred about three kinds. One, just cut it off the cob, and we had a screen porch, it was slanted just a little bit and was lower than the main house, and we'd spread sheets up there and we'd spread that corn up there. We had a ladder, and we'd have to climb up there as kids every once in a while and stir it around while it was drying. And then, that's the only way you could keep it, let it get good and dry, you know, and back it up and put it up all thin, and that was called *Wisko'pemi* [roasting ear corn]. And the *Nepen'takhwa* [sweet bread], we cut that off the cob, and then they had a big, long board, about like that [gestures], and they'd put holes in this tin, and they put this tin over it. It would be rounded over that board. And the rough would be up, and so it'd skin that, take the corn off by doing this [gestures]. And then bake this. It'd be juicy corn, you know, after skinning it. But that rough thing . . . might've been a name for it, I don't know. Anyway, bake it, and then cool that, and break it up, and it'd be the same thing. We'd dry it, too. Nowadays, my husband and I made some—Ron Froman—and we didn't have to dry it. We just get baggies and put it in the freezer after we'd bake it. That was really good stuff. When it just came out of the oven, you could just put either bacon grease on it or butter, and oh, it was good. Otherwise, when we'd cook it later, we'd put sugar in it and it was called sweetbread, *Nepen'takwha* in Shawnee. And then she made lye hominy, and that was *Sotewali* [sofke]. And she'd just cook a big ole pot of hominy in ashes and lye, skin it, and then rinse and rinse and rinse it. And then cook it and maybe put some pork with it or something and, oh, that was really good, too. So I know she made three kinds of things out of corn, so she raised a lot of corn. That was one of our main staples, I guess.

Warren: Was she responsible for growing the corn that was used in the White Oak Bread dances?

Froman: She probably took her corn down there. A lot of them then had gardens, you know, still lived out there back then. But it got where the more people moved away, and the few that was left hardly would have to get that corn from whoever we could. There was a family of Senecas—Nuckolls's family—and he helped us have corn. He gave us corn lots of times for our dance.

Eric Wensman: Is that Laura Nuckolls's daddy?

B. Barnes: Yes. Yeah, there's been several times we wouldn't have had enough corn to have our dance if it wasn't for Jeff Nuckolls. Jeff and Suzy were always good to us.

Wensman: And Jeff was what at the Seneca dance ground? Was he their chief?

Froman: No.

B. Barnes: No, because he's not Indian even.

Wensman: Oh, he's not?

B. Barnes: He's white man, but he knows more about it than most the Indians down there probably.

Wensman: And that's Laura's dad?

B. Barnes: Yeah.

Wensman: Okay.

Warren: Well Laura's mom is a pot hanger at Cowskin, right?

Froman: Mm-hm.

Warren: And so that's interesting. So, one of the ways that the tribes of northeastern Oklahoma help each other is through raising corn for each other, sharing corn, sharing seeds.

B. Barnes: Mm-hm.

Warren: What are some of your early memories of the White Oak Bread dances? And what was it like? And how has it changed over time?

Froman: Well, there were several years that I couldn't go there. My dad lived in Miami, and he got religion and got it bad; he was a fanatic about it. And he told me I wasn't to go down there. I wasn't to go to school dances. So there was a few years in there, my teenage years, that I couldn't go camp with my grandma. So I missed out on a lot then. I might've learned more if I could've been there. But, finally, he evened out, and he had a happy medium and realized that he could do both: he could go to his Baptist Church and he could also go to White Oak and enjoy people's company. So, it made me miss out on a few things. But I remember before all that happened, when I was just a kid, one of the funny things is we'd go hide, us kids would go hide when they were picking out dancers, because we didn't want to dance, because you had to sit there through that whole ceremony, you know. Dancing, that wasn't much fun for a kid. So we'd go hide so they wouldn't pick us. [laughter] But I remember I always got a new dress, too.

B. Barnes: So we still got some does that today. [laughter]

Froman: My grandma always made me a new dress for—we called it Main Day. I don't know why, but that was the name.

Warren: You called it Main Day?

Froman: We called it Main Day, the day we had the dance. Even though they was down there all week, but they were doing things to getting ready for that Main Day, making the bread and all that. And I always thought it was interesting when a dance *wasn't* going on, they would have football games and dances, just on a Saturday sometimes. Two of the guys would just walk all over the hills. They did a lot of walking, carrying a bet.

Warren: That bet string?

Froman: Mm-hm. All over, and everybody would meet down there at the stomp ground. Maybe take something to eat for after the ball game, because they'd just stay down there and have a dance that night. They took something, probably cold biscuits or something like that was all we had to take. Because they used to get mad at these kids when we went down, you know. We had to fill up a cooler with pop and cookies and everything. When I used to come down here, I had a cold biscuit. Lucky if I could've put some mustard on it. [laughter] Maybe a little salt meat. That was kind of neat, I thought, whoever would carry that bet all over the hills, and then go down and play, and then eat some kind of supper, and then dance that night.

Wensman: Would they dance all night?

Froman: Well, I don't remember. Probably.

B. Barnes: We'd go as long as we could.

Froman: I said to my grandma, "What'd you do with me?" She said, "Well, I'd make a pallet right behind me, behind the log where I was sitting, and it's where you'd sleep." And I told Ron that, because I couldn't even sleep down there after he built camp back up.

Wensman: So would there be a lot of Shawnees there?

Froman: Mm-hm. The hills were still full of Shawnees then. But they gradually, probably after the war [World War II], probably when the guys started getting home from the war, there was nothing for them to do, and they'd go off to . . . I know my favorite cousin, he ended up in . . . well, first it was Wichita. And he had learned—that was John Secondine's aunt—he had learned

14.2. Shawnees played games of chance long before casinos. *Shawnee Ribbon Bets*, 1948, Charles Banks Wilson, oil on canvas, GM 0127.1468, Gilcrease Museum, Tulsa, Oklahoma.

printing, like setting newspaper print. So, after he left Wichita, he moved to Saint Louis, and he worked for one of those . . . that big newspaper up there, setting print up there in Saint Louis.

B. Barnes: Boy, he was a good stomp dance leader.

Froman: Oh, he was one of our best leaders. He had a voice that just carried through those hills, it seems like. He was good. And he was like a big brother to me, actually. I was with Grams, say, my whole childhood, so it was like a lot of my cousins seemed closer to me, because when they'd come and see Gram, I was there, you know. So it was like I got to be around them more than anybody. My uncle John and them—the ones that got their house blown away in the storm—they used to come into town just about every Saturday. And I remember I was getting mad about it one time, because he'd just want to listen to baseball games on the radio. His wife and kids wanted to go downtown, and the kids probably wanted to go to the movies. (It cost a dime to go to a Western movie then. We had two theaters in Vinita. We were big time). Anyway, and I was wanting something; I was wanting to probably listen to music. By then—this was after, I think, I had a job, I was already through school—and he'd had maybe two ball games going on, and this was every Saturday. And I thought, "I'm getting tired of this, him taking up my Saturdays." So I kind of griped about it, and my grandma got kind of upset with me. But she never did spank me. Probably she should have. It's what your dad said.

B. Barnes: Mm-hm.

Warren: You know, everyone I've spoken to today has talked about their extended families, and how important they are, and I think non-Indians don't often understand that. Could you say a bit about this?

Froman: Yeah. If somebody came by, didn't have a home, she'd just let them stay there for a while. I remember this one kid, he was—What was his name? His mother's name was Nancy. David Six they called him, and he stayed there for quite a while. He didn't have any place to go, I guess. So she took him in.

B. Barnes: That's where we get it.

Rhonda Barnes: That's where *you* get it. [laughter] Not we, *you.*

Froman: Yeah he [Brett Barnes] was the only bail bondsman with a bed and breakfast. [laughter] That's what my husband said. If they didn't have a place to go, he'd bring them here, make Rhonda feed them, I guess, take care of them. Yeah, she didn't ever turn anybody away. Oh, what was we talking about?

Warren: I just wanted to learn more about the Bread dance and White Oak and what you learned from the Bread dances as a child.

Froman: Well, you can't learn much when you're hiding. [laughter] And I was too young then yet to pound corn. That was something to see. We had these round logs that they scooped out, you know. They were just *botakah.* And maybe sometimes it'd just be one, but sometimes it'd be two, one on each side. [gestures] Almost rhythmic, almost like they had music to it, pounding that corn. When Ron and I was making it, we had a food processor to grind up our corn. And it still was a lot of work. He grew it right over there, across the road from here, and you shuck it, and then you cut it off the cob, and that's almost a day's work right there. And then, you can just do so much in the food processor, you can't put it all in there, you know. A little at a time, little at a time. You do all that, and then bake it. It's a long process.

Wensman: Was you on roll [a citizen] with the Eastern Shawnees then?

Froman: Yes. My dad was born too late for that. All of them was on the Cherokee roll as adopted or something, Gram and all her kids. But my dad was—They closed the roll or something, the way I understood it. James Dick was on the Eastern Shawnee roll, so they put my dad on this roll up here, and he in turn put me and George on this roll where he was.

Warren: When you were a child, did everyone, in your immediate experience, look Indian, phenotypically?

Froman: Mm-hm.

Warren: Around White Oak?

Froman: At White Oak, yeah. Everybody did. We weren't as dark as a lot of tribes were, I didn't think. Because I've seen some Indians, a lot of them, that are way darker than our tribe. We got along with all the white people around us.

Wensman: When do you remember your grandma getting a car? When do you remember your first car?

Froman: Oh god, we never did have a car.

Wensman: You never did have one?

Froman: No. We was po' [poor].

Wensman: How did they get to Quapaw?

Froman: They'd come after them.

Wensman: Oh, those Quapaws would?

Froman: Yeah. They'd come after in a big truck and not just bring . . . and even Gram, but anybody that wanted to come up to their powwow.

Wensman: Oh, so they'd come get them for the dance?

Froman: Mm-hm. But they got them mostly to cook.

Wensman: Would they come get at you for anything else? Like any of their feasts or anything? To cook for them?

Froman: I don't know. I don't know what else they did.

Wensman: Did you get to go to the powwow with your grandma?

Froman: Well, I guess when I was little. She had to take me with her. But after I got to be a teenager and I could stay at home—

Wensman: You just stayed?

Froman: I stayed at home.

Wensman: Do you remember going to Seneca as a kid?

Froman: A few times.

Wensman: Somebody come by and get you all?

Froman: I don't know how they got to Seneca. Some of her kids probably had a car.

Wensman: They had a car by then?

Froman: Yeah. Oh, my grandma, she couldn't have drove. She couldn't read or write.

B. Barnes: When you say Seneca, you mean the Senecas' Green Corn dance?

Wensman: The dance ground, yeah.

Froman: Oh, I don't know how she got there.

Wensman: And what was your grandma's maiden name?

Froman: Carpenter. Ben Carpenter was her brother.

Wensman: Ben Carpenter was her brother?

Froman: Mm-hm. You know all those Carpenters, don't you?

Wensman: Yeah. And then she was married to—

Froman: James Dick.

Wensman: James Dick. My brother has a picture of all of them when they were young.

Froman: Really?

Wensman: Mm-hm.

B. Barnes: I'd like to see that.

Wensman: Ben and his three sisters. One married to a Daugherty, one married to a Secondine, one married to a Dick.

Froman: Cora was one.

Wensman: Cora. I forget the other two.

Froman: He, to my knowledge, never came to a White Oak dance.

Wensman: Who? The old man? Ben Carpenter?

Froman: Mm-hm.

Wensman: Really?

Froman: He was peyote [a believer in the Native American church].

Wensman: He was peyote all the way?

Froman: Mm-hm. And he had one son that wouldn't be caught dead out there at White Oak after the sun went down. I think it was Jocksey [George Carpenter].

Wensman: Why's that?

Froman: Scared.

Wensman: Jocksey was scared to go out there?

Froman: Mm-hm.

Wensman: But yet Ranny [Carpenter] was one of the leaders there?

Froman: Mm-hm.

Wensman: How about Kenneth and Leonard?

Froman: Kenneth used to come once in a while. And Leonard, he came, because I remember his wife playing football; she could really throw that ball far. What was her name? I can't remember. She was real dark. Don't know what tribe she was.

Wensman: I can't remember. They never had no kids. When you was young, who were some of the main people that was at the dance ground? Who were some of the leaders?

Froman: Well, Pete White, when I was a kid.

Wensman: He was the chief, right?

Froman: He was the head drummer. And I don't know when . . . let's see.

Wensman: Sam Perry, would he been one of them?

Froman: No. I don't remember him ever coming there. I was trying to think. Pete White, everybody called him Grandpa Pete. Bill Shawnee. There's a White Oak Bill Shawnee and a Tulsa Bill Shawnee.

Wensman: The White Oak Bill Shawnee was older.

Froman: Yeah. And I don't know when Tulsa Bill started coming there.

Wensman: Well, the White Oak Bill, he was your cousin, right? He was related to you?

Froman: I don't know. I'm trying to place him even. Bill Shawnee, he had a son named Bill and his daughter named Virgie. That's the one we used to have to go ask if we could bury somebody, because their father or grandfather, somebody, donated that land where our cemetery is.

B. Barnes: She's married to the Thompson guy.

Froman: Yeah, Vergie was. White guy. Anyway, we'd have to go—well, out of courtesy I think—we'd go ask them if we could bury somebody there. He gave it to us for the Shawnees.

B. Barnes: Yeah, I remember that white guy. Bob Thompson, isn't it?

Froman: Mm-hm.

B. Barnes: I could still remember him. Do you remember Grandpa Simpson Dushane ever being one of those singers down there?

Froman: I remember him, but I don't remember him singing. It could've been . . . Oh, William Elick, did he sing that, too? Now, he was Julie Dick's son. She had Mac Elick and William Elick, and then she had Jack Dick and Herman "Los" Dick. But William and Susie used to camp before they were where Julie Ann camps now. One time they were having their—what was it—their fiftieth wedding anniversary, William Elick and Susie Elick? And people started showing up at their camp, and Susie didn't know what was going on, and I guess somebody come up—She'd put another potato in the pot. And here they were coming for—They were gonna have a big deal about their anniversary, and it was a surprise. But I thought that was so funny. She said, "I'm just gonna put another potato in the pot."

B. Barnes: When I was little, and we lived in Quapaw, it was about two blocks from where William and Sue Elick lived. And I could remember asking, "Mom, can I go down to Sue Elick's and pick some cherry tomatoes?" So she said, "You better call her, see if she'll let you." So I called her up on the phone and said, "Sue Elick? This is Brett. Can I come down and pick some tomatoes?"

Froman: He couldn't just say Sue. He had to say her whole name.

B. Barnes: So I get there and she said, "Hello, Brett!" I said, "Hi, Sue Elick!" [laughter]

Warren: So, we haven't met you yet, Brett. Do you want to introduce yourself and tell us when you were born and where you're from?

B. Barnes: My name's Brett Barnes. I was born in Tulsa, they tell me. My mother's Winkie. My dad was Irvin Barnes. And I'm almost fifty years old.

Warren: I hear so much about Quapaw. I wonder if you all would want to say something about what Quapaw was like growing up. It was an "Indian town," that's what people say, and I would like to hear your definition of that.

B. Barnes: Well, I guess, I know from my observation throughout life, that's kind of where a lot of different tribes ended up. Probably originating from their relationship with those Quapaws. Just like mom said, a lot of the folks would go up there and had relationships with them, would work for them—because the Quapaws had money—and they'd help out other tribes by giving them opportunities to work. Relationships were built, and marriages were taking place, and a lot of intermarrying going on. We got a lot of relatives up there.

Warren: And is that where you used to stay a lot? With Viola [Dushane] and Evie, right?

B. Barnes: Well, Aunt Evie lived in Vinita, and mom and I'd go down with Sheila. We'd go down and spend the night with her. Sometimes she'd come up and stay with us. Aunt Rachel and Uncle Jess [Brown] come up and visit us, and they'd stay the night. When grandma Viola, my dad's mother—she was a Dushane, she married a Barnes and that's where the Barnes name came in, and she lived across town. I'd go stay with her some days, whenever mom and dad would leave

14.3. Mother and son, Annie Winifred "Winkie" Froman and Brett Barnes, 2016. Photo courtesy of Stephen Warren.

for work. I'd walk to school, and I decided about halfway there I didn't want to go, so I'd walk on over to Granny's house and act like I was sick, and she never would make me go to school, so she let me stay there.

Froman: How many times did this happen?

B. Barnes: Two or three, probably. [laughter]

Froman: Well, she babysat you when I went to work.

Warren: What was Viola Dushane like? I've always been so curious about her since Ben [Barnes] first told me about her.

Froman: She was a *huge* woman. I was kind of scared of her when I first met her. But she was good.

B. Barnes: She was good to me. Never did spank me, because I was a good kid.

Froman: Oh, I know it. His dad just walloped him good at the store one day, and we got home— but went by her house first, and I said, "Well, he got a whipping." Vi said, "I never have to whip him when we go to town." And Irv said, "That's because you let him do anything he wants to."

Wensman: Would you all have set up camp there at Quapaw Powwow?

B. Barnes: Yeah, she had a big camp.

Wensman: And that's who you stayed with?

B. Barnes: A long time ago, when we were little. That was before [we moved].

Froman: When we lived in Tulsa, we'd come up the weekend of the dance. And everybody would be at her camp. All the kids would be there. But after we moved to Quapaw, then we had our own camp.

Warren: And this is at Quapaw Powwow?

B. Barnes and **Froman:** Mm-hm.

Warren: Was that the biggest powwow in the region?

Froman: Mm-hm.

Warren: The Fourth of July powwow?

B. Barnes: Yep.

Warren: How long would it last?

Froman: It was the only one for a long, long time.

B. Barnes: Some years it would be three days, and some years it would be four days, depending on what day the holiday fell on, usually.

Warren: For those people who aren't familiar with powwows, what was distinctive about it— Quapaw Powwow? What set it apart from other powwows in the state or in the country?

Froman: Well, no, I never had been to another one.

Wensman: Probably because it was the only powwow around.

B. Barnes: For the longest time, yeah. All these other tribes didn't have powwows at that time.

Froman: Now when it . . . I don't know when it started, I can't remember when it started. Way before we moved up here. Who was that rich one's name? Alex Beaver? Alex Beaver, he put it on. And he had, like, maybe two places up there where he'd have cooks. They'd have long tables. They fed everybody that came. And eventually people started cooking at their own camp, probably after he died or whatever. Yeah, he furnished it. That's when they'd come up and get White Oak people to come up and dance and cook.

B. Barnes: Even years after that. And they may still do the rations. Somebody, the tribe, or him in his time . . . Somebody would buy all this beef, and I don't know what else they'd provide, but all the campers that were registered with their camps, they'd show up there with their camper sticker, and boy, they'd pack down just armloads of groceries and meats, pork and beef, to feed their families and feed their visitors. So, it was very well done.

Wensman: That's a longstanding tradition with the Quapaws is to feed all the camps.

B. Barnes: You bet.

Warren: And so Alex Beaver likely made his money through the lead mines.

Froman: Mm-hm.

Warren: And then used that money to start a powwow that was very well attended, am I understanding that correctly?

Froman: Mm-hm.

B. Barnes: To me, it just seems like that was a sign of hospitality. A sign of being able to value all those relationships between different families, between different tribes.

Froman: They weren't always as giving as he was, though.

Warren: What were the most common tribes at Quapaw Powwow? Who were the main allies of the Quapaw?

Froman: Poncas used to come up, didn't they? Lot of Poncas came up here.

B. Barnes: And, of course, there's a lot of Quapaws intermarried with Senecas. Lot of Quapaws intermarried with some Shawnees, and even some of these smaller tribes around here that didn't really have large populations. But a lot of them—like I say, with the Poncas and the Quapaws—there's a lot of them intermarried there.

Warren: That makes the Quapaw Powwow so interesting to me. That it's—You have these Siouan tribes interacting with Algonquians, these tribes that are native to Oklahoma hanging out with tribes that are removed to Oklahoma. It seems like quite an intercultural meeting ground.

Wensman: Well, I think all these tribes depended on the Quapaw, would that be honest to say?

B. Barnes: At least partially, yeah. In some part, yeah.

Froman: Oh, imagine, a lot of times we might've went hungry.

Wensman: If it wasn't for the Quapaws?

Froman: Yeah.

B. Barnes: Alex Beaver, I've been told, I've heard stories, how he'd own different properties, different homes, different houses, and there was different people that would be able to just go to him for help or in need. And he'd always help them out. In fact, the house that my dad and his family was raised in—you know, Ben's dad and my dad—they were raised out there in a home that he owned. They lived there all their childhood. I guess that's further evidence to what a generous man he was.

Froman: And it was haunted. [laughter]

Warren: Oh yeah?

Froman: That's what they told me.

Wensman: And the significance of the Fourth of July was [that was] when the Quapaws signed the treaty with the U.S. government. That's why they dance at the Fourth of July.

Warren: I was wondering about that. I thought, it can't be because of the Declaration of Independence.

Wensman: Well, that's what they say. And that's why they always gotta dance on the Fourth of July. Because they honor that treaty by dancing on the Fourth of July. Whatever day it falls on, they're going to dance. You understanding that, Wink?

Froman: I never heard that.

Wensman: But that's why they dance. And Red Lake dances at the same time, too, to honor that treaty on the Fourth of July.

Warren: An indigenous history of independence.

Wensman: Yeah. Which is kind of odd.

Warren: Yeah. Did you experience much discrimination growing up?

Froman: Never in my life. Never. When we left White Oak Hills . . . I was in the fourth grade when they moved us into town. Out there, everybody was related. All the Indian kids went to . . . Kelly School, it was called, just a little ways from the stomp ground. Now, I had a hard time when I moved in and had to go to school. That was hard for me because I looked so different. But I can't really remember. I just remember the kids staring at me, but I was fat, and I had braids, and I was dark. So they weren't used to that. I was the only one. And my grandma would walk me to school, and I'd follow her home, and I'd hide because I didn't want to be there. And made terrible grades, and that teacher passed me . . . was going to send me on to the fifth grade, which was going to be another school even. And when my dad found out about it—and he knew how bad I was doing my first year—so he told his wife to go up to that school and take me up there and tell her, when school started, that I needed to take that class over again, that I wasn't ready to go to the fifth grade. So she did, and so I spent another year. By then they were used to me. And by taking that, I was ready to go to the fifth then, after they got used to me and I got used to them. And I don't remember anybody ever making fun of me after that, or after I got out of school, wherever I went to work or applied for a job or anything.

I never, never was treated any different. And most of my friends were white after I moved into town. There was just one other Indian family there, I think. At that time, now, there was a lot of them that was part Indian that didn't own up to it back then. Because when I started I worked for the Bureau of Indian Affairs—I mean my job at the clinic was civil service—and all of a sudden all these people from Vinita was coming to the clinic, had Indian cards, and I said, "I went to school with all them kids. They didn't say they were Indian back then." There was just me and one other family that was Indian in Vinita, but half the town was coming to the clinic by then, when they dropped that one-fourth [policy]. You used to have to be a fourth [blood quantum on your Certificate Degree of Indian Blood (CDIB) card] to go get any.

Warren: To go get health services?

Froman: Yeah. And my gosh. Some of them—I don't know, I called them "three-digit Indians." I can't even think of some of numbers that they were.

Warren: "Three-digit Indians"?

Froman: Yeah, you know. When the fractions gets that low, how much Indian could they possibly be?

B. Barnes: We talking about the denominator?

Froman: Yeah. No, it's beyond that, over a hundred-and-something. Something over 128 and all kinds of stuff like that. Big numbers.

Warren: So many people first "discovered" their Indianness when the Indian Health Service changed its policies?

Froman: Yeah. When these tribes changed it, they found out they could get more money with more numbers, I guess. So they decided to let more people come in. And then it got where just everybody had a Cherokee princess in their family by then.

Wensman: When would you say that was?

Froman: I started to work at the clinic in 1978, I think. So it was, I guess, in the '70s. And when I started noticing all these people from Vinita showing up.

Wensman: Now, when you say, "in '78," was that when the clinic was in Miami? Are you going back as far as when the clinic was still down there at the foot of the hill, at the Seneca Indian School?

Froman: Well, we opened in '78, so I don't remember. Just when I had to go down to Wyandotte for a while, because the clinic wasn't finished yet. They were hiring us all, but our building wasn't ready. So some of them had to go to Jay and work, and I had to go to Wyandotte and work until it was open. And then we all go to work.

Wensman: Did most of the kids at White Oak—when you was young—did they go to boarding schools? Or did they just go to Kelly?

Froman: They went to White Oak, a lot of them.

Wensman: White Oak School?

Froman: Mm-hm.

Wensman: Now, Kelly School, that was on the ranch. The ranch had that school.

Froman: Yeah, it was right on the corner. When you're going to White Oak stomp ground, don't pull in there, just keep going until you get to the corner . . . until the mile corner. And there was a little schoolhouse building right there on the corner. That was called Kelly School, and that's where everybody went. They just went to eighth grade, and after that they went to White Oak School.

Wensman: Did Kelly Ranch fund that school?

Froman: I don't know.

Warren: I've never fully understood how some kids avoided boarding school and others didn't. How is it that White Oak kids were fortunate to be able to stay at home, whereas you also know children who went to Seneca? How did that work?

Froman: Well, the ones that I know that had to go was because their mother died, and the dad couldn't work and take care of them, too. And they couldn't expect the grandmother to raise all these kids, so they sent them to boarding school. But, you know, if they didn't have that hard luck, I guess they got to stay home then. Because a lot of them, like in my generation, they finished school at White Oak. Because Kelly closed long before. They didn't go too long. They had to close, so all of them had to go to White Oak anyway. But after eighth grade, they had to go to White Oak then.

Wensman: Do you remember Aunt Rachel [from] when you was a little girl?

Froman: Vaguely.

Warren: Who was Aunt Rachel, Eric?

Wensman: It would have been her aunt and my mom's aunt. My grandfather and her mother were—

B. Barnes: Brother and sister to Aunt Rachel?

Wensman: Yeah.

B. Barnes: Do you remember when Aunt Rachel and Uncle Jess moved back here from—what was it—North Carolina, or South Carolina?

Froman: South. Aiken, South Carolina, was where they lived. They lived in a lot of different places.

Wensman: So you didn't know any Washingtons when you were little?

Froman: No, I didn't. Anita [Valliere] did, more than me. But grandma and I, you know, we couldn't go anyplace unless somebody took us, because we didn't have a car. And I just don't, I was grown before I started meeting any of them.

Warren: Would you say a little bit about the importance of White Oak? And why it matters and what you've learned there over the years?

Froman: Well, it's hard for me to understand, but my grandma kept that dance going, back in the '50s, and probably '60s. Even though Rosie Dick Secondine was the head woman, but she didn't do anything when it was time to have the dance. I don't think it would have ever got started if my grandma didn't get it started. So she was the one that kept it going back when it was about to fizzle. And she just thought it was the most important thing in the world to her.

Warren: Is that because she kept gardens? Or why do you think that is?

Froman: I really don't know. When she would tell me anything, it would be, "That's just the way you do it. That's just the way they told me." Like her mother told her. She couldn't tell me why, a lot of times. Because I'd say, "Why?" There were so many bad signs. You just wouldn't believe some of the things she told me not to do because it was a bad sign. Just, to me, foolish little things, like moving a chair . . . standing there. And if I was talking and moving that chair, then she'd make me sit in it. And you weren't supposed to sweep after dark; you're supposed to do your sweeping during the daytime. I can't even think of some of them, there were so many it was hard to keep remembering all of them.

Wensman: You're not supposed to rock that chair.

Froman: No, no. If you do, you sit in it.

Wensman: Yeah, that was a big no-no.

Warren: Because you might be inviting the ancestors back?

Wensman: Yeah.

Froman: And if you heard this [tsk-tsk-tsk sound], you better quit doing whatever you're doing. I guess it was if you got people watching you, they wouldn't holler at you but they'd go [tsk-tsk-tsk sound] and that meant, "Stop, now." [Laughter]

Wensman: Why do you think the dance ground fizzled out, was close to fizzling out?

Froman: Well, I don't think it'd ever get started if my grandma didn't get things rolling. The one that's supposed to wasn't doing it.

Warren: So, after everybody started moving away, the dance ground really suffered?

Froman: Oh yeah. Oh yeah, it did. And I guess when everybody was out there, too, they could have things on the day they were supposed to. Like if the dogwood was blooming, you'd have your dance. It might be on Wednesday you could have Main Day. When people moved away, yeah, we'd have it on Saturday so people could come. Because there was just a few Indians out there then. So they had to change some rules.

B. Barnes: While ago, when she was talking about those football games, whenever we'd start that—ball season—would be at the spring Bread dance, and then there would be ball games. And on those weekends after that . . . at one time . . . even as recent enough for me to be able to remember it when I was a kid, we would have ball games down there. And then we'd have Memorial Day, play football on that day. And then, sometime, within a few weeks after that, we'd have last football game, and then we'd have to put that ball away for the season. But on all those nights, at one time, we used to dance more than what we do now. Because today, we just dance on the spring Bread dance in May, and then in August, our Green Corn dance, and then usually in October, our fall Bread dance. And then a Buffalo dance would fall in there somewhere, but we haven't done that in about twenty, fifteen years. But back in those days—when we'd still play those ball games—we'd dance those nights. And there's evidence of that right there between our camp and that northeast corner of that dance ground, where that walnut tree is growing out of that hump in the ground. That hump in the ground was the pile of ashes from all the fires that we danced around in that dance ground, back in those days when we danced more often. And so that's kind of a sad reminder, every time we're down there, when we look at that walnut tree coming out of that pile of ashes. And there's so many people alive today that don't even know what that hump is or how it originated. It's kind of a sad thing, but that's just a sign of the times, to where people had to move off to find work; people had to survive. And they'd come back, when and if they can, you know.

Wensman: Would you say they started dancing on the weekend in the '50s?

Froman: Probably so. Yeah, I think it'd been about, pretty much.

Wensman: Because one of the specific instances of that is like on Bird Creek. They used to have peyote meetings all the time, any time. It wasn't just on the weekends. So, I mean, they might have them through the week, go two, three nights in a row during the week. And then as time rolled on, they started doing it on the weekends.

Froman: So it affected that, too?

Wensman: It affected that as well. To me, that's a very interesting point, you know.

Froman: Yeah, they had to scatter. People had to scatter looking for work.

Warren: So much happened there, and you can almost date the problems tribes are having with the language to that time period as well. The people who know Shawnee tended to be those born before World War II, right? And after World War II, that's where you see a real split. Because that's when people began dispersing to large urban centers away from communities like White Oak Hills.

Wensman: Did almost everybody in the Hills talk Shawnee back then, when you was a girl?

Froman: Yeah, the old folks. Now, Rosie May Bob Peterson, she talked Shawnee nearly all the time. My grandma had to get modern, she talked English. The only time she'd talk Shawnee [was] when she got with all the old ladies and they'd talk, and I don't know what they were saying. As she got older, and she'd tell me something in Shawnee, and I'd just say, "Gram," and she'd say, "Oh, I forgot." Then she'd tell me. But I said, "If you talked to me when I was little, I'd know now." But she talked English to me. I can remember when we got a telephone. Way back then there was a lot of party lines, other people would be . . . several people would be on one line. If they were talking, you'd hang up, wait until they got through, and then you could talk. Well, you could hear if somebody picked up. So she'd be talking to somebody, a person, and she'd be talking Shawnee because she knew somebody was listening. [Laughter]

Warren: Like a different version of the code talkers?

Froman: I used to get so tickled. If someone was trying to listen, she'd switch over to Shawnee.

Warren: Could you say a bit about just the White Oak Ground and its importance? We didn't quite get to it, but I just think it's a remarkable tribute to the tenacity of the Shawnee people, that it's still in existence, and I wondered if you could say a little bit about that.

Froman: Well, like I said, it was really important to my grandma and to a lot of those old ladies. But it really got out of hand with drinking. And I'm really sorry about anything [my part in that]—But I mean, it started way before I grew up. But I wish—See, they've stopped it now. I just wish somebody could have stopped it when my grandma was still living because her—And I'm sure some of those other old ladies thought of it as their church. Well, didn't seem like much of a church, people being drunk. So I think she'd be really glad that they've stopped it. I don't know if they've stopped it completely, but it's pretty much stopped.

B. Barnes: I'm pretty confident in saying it's stopped. There's a few now that try to sneak in and bring a little bit, but they are very discreet. They hide it from us because they know all of us boys, we have come up there, and we've had them pour out their alcohol, and we've made them leave. Or we've given them the choice: pour it out or leave. And I think the word of that has spread to all those visitors. We got a few homeboys that still want to try to do that, but they know. They stay way back up at their camp because they can't get in breathing distance from us.

Warren: When did the no-alcohol policy begin to go into effect? When did it become such a concern that the ceremonial ground addressed it?

B. Barnes: It was as recent as—

Froman: About five years ago?

B. Barnes: Little longer than that, I'd say late '90s.

Wensman: Yeah, mid to late '90s.

B. Barnes: And you know, the old folks. I remember having a discussion about it down there with those old ladies and old men, and they'd say, "This time, we gotta put a stop to it. We gotta put a stop to it. So we offered our help, you know, the young guys. We said, "If you guys want to make that rule, we'll help enforce it." So, everybody pulling together, we decided. If there's any casualties that come about because of this, in the sense of losing members, because they can't set that aside for that one week . . .

Wensman: Would you say you lost members because of that?

B. Barnes: I think we kind of lost a couple, yeah.

R. Barnes: You've done that since I've been married to you.

B. Barnes: Yeah. So we've been together twenty-one years, so it's been within that twenty-one years. I don't know exactly when that was, I couldn't name the year.

Wensman: Kind of a strange dynamic, too, because it was old women and young guys enforcing it.

B. Barnes: Yeah.

Wensman: So it was kind of a weird power structure that made that happen. Didn't see a lot of the old men taking a firm stand on the issue. It's a lot of old women and all the young guys.

B. Barnes: Mm-hm.

Froman: When you talk about the importance of it, I can't know that. Because there's some things a woman don't know about the dance. I don't know why, really.

Warren: You could only speak to the women's role in the dance?

Froman: Yeah. My grandma'd go down there, work her fingers to the bone the whole week. She'd come home looking like leather from cooking on that fire, you know, cooking on the outside fire. She'd just be darker and her skin would just be tough looking. Of course, she did everything on that fire. She didn't have Crock-Pots like we do, slow cookers. But there's just some things that men do that we don't know anything about, not supposed to. So I can't really answer that. And then . . . I suppose . . . talk about it at all. So it's kind of hard to say, really, how it's important.

Warren: I know we're in the company of men, but are there things women learned through the Bread dance that are important?

Winkie: Well, yeah. They do things, like when they make that hoop. That's in the spring, isn't it? When they make that hoop with seeds on it? So I don't really know all the significance of it because, like I said, I didn't go a lot of times, like when I was a teenager. I had to become of age before I could go again. Or when my dad finally realized it was okay to go there. And when he finally realized he didn't have say-so over me anymore, too.

Wensman: Would you say that his religious practices were due to his wife?

Froman: No.

Wensman: Himself?

Froman: Just him. He was on the road to being an alcoholic. And he said if he hadn't got religion at that time, he would have been a full-blown alcoholic. So at least it did get him to stop drinking. And like I said, he did finally hit a happy medium where he leveled out and wasn't so rigid about it.

Warren: What's the future of the Shawnee Tribe, or just of the Shawnee people? I ask everyone what they would hope or wish for their grandchildren and their grandchildren's children.

Froman: The best way I can explain it is, when they were in school—probably can't mention any names—but there's a few people around that wanted them to be teaching some of the Indian ways at school. And you can't do that. I don't see how you could, when there's lots of different tribes. And to me . . . we learned that in our family. At school is to learn how to live in this world now, how to make a living. I said, some of them probably would've been mad at me. But the teacher really liked me because I didn't want my kids to learn how to weave a basket and set it out on the side of the road to sell baskets, for instance, that's just one. And there was a few people up here that . . . they thought they should probably be learning something like that at school, and I don't believe that way. It's my personal [belief]. I wanted them to know how to go out and make a living. But when the dance was going on, our dance, I wanted them to go to our dance and do that. Does that make sense?

Warren: That makes perfect sense.

B. Barnes: Can I add to that?

Warren: I would love that. I was just about to ask.

B. Barnes: I think that's—knowing how she feels—I know Dad felt the same way. And I think that's what has guided my opinion on that, too. Because we haven't had this conversation between us, that I could remember. But I know I've had this conversation with people at work, down there at the Eastern Shawnee Tribe. And a bunch of them have learned my opinion and thoughts on this. That it's important, to me, to survive and thrive in today's society, to be successful in the white man's world and play that game, too. But at the same time, I'm so proud of the fact that regardless, or despite, all the efforts taken, or measures taken, to try to put a stop to us observing our traditions and ceremonial ways, that we've managed to maintain it and still work and make a living, and then have to put in the extra time and effort and the ability to finance it out of our pocket to keep that going. To me, that's something to be proud of, because I'm one of those that am somewhat bitter about the relationship between Native American people and the U.S. government. So I'm proud of the fact that we can play their ball game and beat them at their game, and we can still say, "Na-na-na, we're still maintaining this, too, and we still know who we are, and we still have it, and it's still alive today." So I feel *very* strongly about that, and I'm proud of that.

15

An Interview with
Shawn King, Ceremonial Chief

Stephen Warren: All right, so I'm sitting here with Shawn King, the ceremonial chief of the Eastern Shawnee Tribe, and Eric Wensman, the research manager for the ANA grant administered by the Eastern Shawnee Tribe. And why don't we get started, Shawn, and just ask you to tell us a little bit about when you were born and where you were born.

Shawn King: I was born February 19, 1971. I was born in Miami, Oklahoma, at the Baptist Regional Hospital. I lived in Miami, oh, I think for about four years. We kind of moved around a lot. My dad was in the service in Vietnam. When he'd come home, we lived in Wyandotte for quite some time, and then shortly after that my mother and father divorced, and we kind of moved around a lot. We lived in Fairland, Oklahoma, for a little while, Welch, Oklahoma, and then we moved out to western Kansas, out to Cimarron, Kansas. We stayed out there for several years. Then we came back to Wyandotte, Oklahoma, where I lived with my grandmother and was raised . . . stayed with her till I was about twenty-one.

My mother was Barbara King, my dad was Larry King, and my grandmother was Bessie Goodeagle. She was full-blood Shawnee, Eastern Shawnee. Like I said, I stayed mainly with my grandma King—my dad's mother, Evelyn King—right there in the little town of Wyandotte.

Warren: What was it like growing up in the '70s? What was it like growing up Indian in this area of the world?

King: In the '70s I was really small, you know? Usually the highlight was the Quapaw Powwow. I used to love to go to that with my grandma, and then we'd go to Green Corn with my grandma, with the Seneca Cayugas, since I was little. But I had a lot of fun in the little town of Wyandotte. I lived about thirty steps from the school, so it was kind of hard for me to sneak off and hide. I got pretty good at it. I kind of had everything, you know, a kid could want right there. I had a bicycle, creek, you know, about a half a mile away from my grandmother's house. I could go fishing every day, and I utilized the school's playground, the basketball court, all kinds of stuff.

Warren: What was Quapaw Powwow like? Everyone we have talked with remembers Quapaw Powwow. What are some of your memories of it?

King: Oh, I just loved . . . I loved to watch the fancy dancers. I was amazed by them since I was a kid. Of course, everybody's probably told you about fry bread? I just . . . I always love to go down there. There was always lots of people, and [I] spent time with my aunt and my uncles, and we just sat around the camp, and I'd just play around with all the other kids that were there. We would go to . . . Trying to think of the name of that bridge. Was it Devil's Promenade? We'd go up there and throw stuff off and watch the fish go get it. Had an old man one time, took a beer tab, dropped it down on a hook, and caught a perch, so that was pretty cool.

Warren: Did you dance at the powwow?

15.1. Barbara Crawford King, mother of ceremonial chief Shawn King as well as daughters Donna King and Kelly Frantz. Photo courtesy of Shawn King.

King: No, I was too small. I didn't start dancing till 1991.

Warren: Ninety-one? What began or started your interest in powwow dancing?

King: Well, my grandmother, mainly. When I was smaller—Well, like I said, we would go to the Green Corn, and I was just amazed to sit there and watch them stomp dance. One day I . . . my grandmother . . . I turned around and looked at her and told her that "You know, one of these days, Grandma, I'm going to dance for you." And she just gave me a nod, and when I turned back around, the next thing I knew, I felt something push me and I was out there. She gave me a little boot.

    [This] was at the Green Corn. I didn't know what I was doing, but you know, people grabbed ahold of you, and put you right in line, and told you what to do, and what not to do. I just had a . . . I had quite a good time down there. Then my aunt Joann Morris, about in '91—you know, my grandmother, she died when I was eight—I kept telling my aunt that, and my aunt kind of helped me along. She helped me get my outfit and then—So that's reason. I really started dancing for my family. I wanted to dance for my grandma, and then—So that was my whole purpose for stepping in the arena. It was a really, kind of, spiritual thing for me. It helped me a lot. It kept me away from bad things, you know, that I could've gotten myself into.

Warren: Was it just the culture of the powwow that kept you away from it? Could you say something about what kept you on the right path with powwows?

King: Well, when I earn . . . When I earned my first eagle feather, I was sat down and I was told that, you know, you can't drink, you can't do drugs, you can't do these things and dance. Because you don't take that into that circle; it doesn't belong out there. You know, so it would

15.2. Bessie House-Crawford Goodeagle, grandmother of
ceremonial chief Shawn King. Photo courtesy of Shawn King.

be disrespectful for you to be doing that and be doing this at the same time. So I quit drinking, because I had drank for a little while before that, and that's what really helped me the most. It kept me . . . it kept me away from all that.

Warren: Who were some of your mentors when you were a young man just getting involved? Who conveyed that message to you?

King: Daniel Drew. He was a Cheyenne drum maker and a Sun dance painter. My uncle Jack King. Paul Bennet. Wiconi James and Hermus Lonedog also helped me a lot. Let's see, there's also John Bull Blalock. His son helped put my bustles together after we got it from the McClellan family. They made them for me, but I kept stringing them up backwards, and Clifford had to sit me down and show me how to do it. So, there was Jack Greenback. Those guys were really good to me. They just kind of sat me down and told me how I should be acting. What they expected,

15.3. Taking a break from fancy dancing, ceremonial chief Shawn King in his regalia. Photo courtesy of Shawn King.

you know, [how] to treat people. They taught me compassion, you know. They taught me how to be humble. They gave me lots of encouragement.

Warren: Was fancy dancing your first choice, or were you a grass dancer?

King: Fancy dancing.

Warren: It was fancy dancing all the way?

King: Yeah, it's been that way since I started. As a matter of fact, there was a couple of Eastern Shawnee elders that helped me. One of them was Florence Ruth. She helped me get my bustles. And then my grandmother got my roach, and my mother, she made my apron and things. Lamont Laird, he's the one that got me the goats that we wear around our ankles. And, as a matter of fact, that outfit, I still dance in it. I still have that same one, that very first one.

Eric Wensman: Did Frank McClellan make your bustles?

King: Uh-huh.

Wensman: Yeah, I mean, if you got a bustle set from Frank, that was pretty special.

Warren: Can you say a little bit about Frank?

King: He was a heck of a dancer, I'm telling you. The whole McClellan family was fancy dancers. You had Henry, Frank—

Wensman: Jeff, his son, is good. And then, I can't think of his brother, but if you had a set of their bustles, I mean that was like—They were powwow royalty. And so, yeah, to have that set, that's pretty cool, even today.

Warren: So, to walk into a powwow, people would know those McClellan bustles.

Wensman: They would know those bustles.

Warren: And they would know that this guy is legit because he has McClellan bustles.

King: One time, I was dancing, and one of—I believe it was Henry—come up, and just kind of touched me on the shoulder, and I turned around, and he said, "You know, my brother made those bustles for you." And I was like . . . it threw me in shock. And I looked at him. And they have a unique way they make their bustles. Signature on it. So, later—I want to say it was about '93 or '94—Ben McClellan and Linda, they adopted me. They took me in as one of theirs. So I got to meet all of the McClellan family, Frank Sr., Jr., then Henry, and I don't—I always just loved to watch Henry and them dance, 'cause I'm telling you, them guys could fly. They were fast. But I enjoyed, you know, fancy dancing. When I started I was dancing with people like R. G. Harris, Dwight White Buffalo. It's kind of changed over the years. I guess some of them moved on, and some of them may not still be here anymore.

Wensman: R. G. . . . R. G. was . . . Those guys were the big time. Like, if I was talking what I want my daughters to be like, they were the big time. And R. G. is still big time. Not so much a dancer, but he's moved on to be an emcee. They still call upon him all the time.

Warren: Ok, ok, what were the most important powwows you attended and you loved to participate in?

King: I liked . . . like I said, I liked going to Quapaw. We went to the Wyandottes', the Eastern Shawnees'. Went to the Tulsa IICOT [Intertribal Indian Club of Tulsa] powwow. There was a couple of them I went to. I went to one in Ohio. Then there's one in Kansas City. I can't remember what they called that one. My uncle, he had a Painted Horse War Dance Society, and I travelled with him quite a bit. We would go to schools and conventions and stuff like that.

Warren: What were some of the differences between those powwows, from an insider's perspective? Because to an outsider such as myself, it's harder to pick up on the differences that each powwow event offers in terms of culture. Could you say a little bit about these different venues and kind of what you would find there?

King: Quapaw was always kind of wild when I was young. I mean it was kind of . . . it was a blast down there, and they always shot the fireworks off.

Warren: Because it's held on the Fourth of July?

King: Yeah, because it was Fourth of July weekend. There were several of them. I'm trying to think of all of them I went to. There was Copan.

Wensman: Those were kind of it, though.

King: Yeah.

Wensman: And the Kansas City powwow was due to all those people moving to Kansas City to work. And they started their own club, just like Bill Blalock. The Blalocks moved up there, and Bruce Martin was one of them that come from that area, but it was from the families that moved to Kansas City to work.

Warren: Yeah, and so in Copan, you have a Delaware tribal powwow, and then in Quapaw, Quapaw Tribe Powwow, and in Kansas City, an urban Indian powwow, right? Does that change the experience of it, that context, or are they all the same?

King: Kind of different, now, to me . . . I don't know. You know, back in the '80s and the '90s . . . I guess maybe it was a generation thing. The younger kids today are a little bit different than we are, or I feel. In the contest powwows, they've kind of changed things a little bit. You know, because they got, like, a schedule they got to keep, and they got to keep everything on time. And you know, back in the '90s, I mean, they had contest powwows, but it just seemed like they were a little more relaxed. Just . . . they wasn't really worried about that time. I mean, sometimes we'd dance till one, two o'clock in the morning. Most of the time, now, they shut off about 10:30 P.M. anymore, eleven.

Warren: How has the Eastern Shawnee Powwow changed over time? I mean, we found a brochure from an early one that was from 1977. But then it must have gone dormant for a little bit, because you're on your twenty-fifth anniversary this year, right? And so you would have—You've been dancing for almost the entire length of the powwow, so what have you seen change in the Eastern Shawnee Powwow?

King: What I like about it the most is, like, everybody . . . it's just like a coming home, you know. You get to see tribal members that live way off. That, you know, you might have met ten years ago, or five years ago, or five minutes ago, you know. Then you're anxious to see them come back the next year, you know, and its really strange for me, 'cause when I started dancing, when I was young—And now I see all these children that were at my knees, now they are as tall as I am, and they got children at their knees. It's really been neat to watch these kids grow up. Its just like, there's just a bunch of them, you know. Like the Brock family, they have . . . I don't know, they got several grandkids, and now they all have children. It's just amazing how people travel, you know, and come to be here for three days, and then go back home. And you just wait till next year, where you get to see them again. You know, we've lost several along the way that are not here now, [from] when we first started it.

Warren: That's one thing the people forget about powwows, right? They also function as family reunions. Tribal ones, at least.

King: And now these young fancy dancers, boy, they get crazy now. They can do cartwheels, flips. 'Course, R. G. could probably always do that anyway. There's just so many, I mean. They have their own unique style now, these young guys now. They really tear it up out there.

Wensman: And I think Shawn's right, you know? This is the way Shawn seemed to grow up. There was people that he looked up to, and that's why he wanted to be in that circle. Because the families that he mentioned were very powerful powwow families. And to watch them, and you know, that's who you wanted to be. Just like an athlete, that's who you wanted to be like, that's who you wanted to dance like. You wanted his moves, you know, and to have those bustles that they make, and their outfits, 'cause they were the families that have come along for several generations that kept it going. And as a kid—I can relate to what he's saying, you know. That's what I was saying about my daughters. They see people out there that they want to be like, and all they're looking at is that circle, wouldn't you say?

King: Uh-huh.

Wensman: They're not looking [at] what's going on behind them, in the camps or whatever, the negative things. They're looking at that circle, and they want to be in that circle. So would you agree?

King: Yeah.

Wensman: That's what kept you there?

King: Uh-huh. It's kind of, like, a whole different—I know this is going to sound strange—kind of like a whole different world. Even though the powwow is a social dance, it's very spiritual in your heart, once you . . . once you take that first step out from underneath that arbor and step in there, and I don't know. It just, you know, I've been sick before. One time I was a headman dancer, and I had a fever of about 103. And my dad, he was like, "Well, you going to go home? What do you want to do?" And I said, "Well, I made a commitment." And the minute I stepped in that arena and started spinning and twirling, I don't know if I burnt the fever up or what, but I got to feeling better. There was a lot of people—like I mentioned Daniel Drew, you know—he'd come by, and they'd give you a little tap on the back or something and keep you moving and tell you, you know . . . I've had many of them tell me you can be healed out there in that center, if you stay out there, and if you pray while you're dancing. And it always seemed to work.

Warren: What was . . . What was Seneca Cowskin Ground like? Growing up, when you were visiting there? Did they still have the fair?

King: No, I didn't . . . When I was there, they were stomp dancing. My grandmother told me, you know, this is an actual ceremony. And so one of the first mistakes I made was climbing on the longhouse, and I had an elder grab me by the hips and kind of swat me on the tail, and she said, "You don't climb on that." And she explained to me what that building was. So, I don't know. But you always had kids running around, playing. We played ball. You know, one thing about it, when you're at powwow, or when you were at Green Corn, like, today it's so different. There, you don't feel scared, you don't feel that you're in an unsafe environment. Like, today, the way the world is changing, you know, you really have to keep an eye on your kids. You can't let them necessarily go places. The Green Corn or the powwows, I feel like my children are safe there. I don't know, there is just always a sense of security there, I guess.

Warren: How long have you been ceremonial chief?

King: Since 2010. I don't really feel the . . . you know . . . have any claim to that title that they put there. I was asked by the Captain family. I was about nineteen. What had happened was, I had attended several of our tribal funerals, and I asked our chief at that time—You know, Buck [Captain]. I asked him, "Buck, can I ask you kind of personal question?" He said, "Yeah." And I said, "How come you don't bury our people?" I noticed that the Ottawas or the Senecas, you know, they were always taking care of our funerals up here. Anyway, Buck said, "I don't think that that is what I should be doing." He said, "I am the chief and that's what I should take care of." I didn't mean any way disrespectful, I was just asking a question to him. And just about a few weeks later, his son Neil approached me, and he asked me if I would be interested in being taught to do that, you know, to take care of our own people. And, you know, immediately I told him, "No, I'm just a nineteen-year-old kid. I just was asking a question." And then, later on, they come back, as a father and a son, and they were both the chiefs—he was the second chief. And they asked me if I would do that. And they said, "It's about time that someone takes care of ours." So, at nineteen they sent me to Charlie Dawes, which was the Ottawa chief, and Charlie told me right off the bat, you know, when I sat down, he said, "Well, young man, this is kind of . . . I don't know how you go on about doing this, but I understand that your people have lost their culture, have lost their way. And I understand what they are wanting to do, so I will show you a universal, kind of like, a universal kind of—Where you're not stepping over things and stepping on things or doing things you shouldn't be doing."

And then it went from there to a Cheyenne elder that I spoke of. He was the one that actually gave me the rite. He did not give me a right to do it in the Cheyenne way, but he did give me a rite. There was a ceremony at his house that we went through together. Because I had to bury my little brother-in-law, he'd got shot. So it started from about nineteen on. But from about nineteen to about twenty-five, you know, I was with many different people, you know. I started helping my uncle dig graves, cover the graves, and then he just started calling on me to help him. I helped him till I was probably about, I don't know, twenty, twenty-five. Then, after that, I just started doing it. People called when they pass away, or things like that.

Warren: Your role has expanded far beyond funerals, though, correct?

King: Uh-huh. Well, when I started helping my uncle and these other gentlemen, you know, they always told me, when someone asked me to do something, you do it. You don't question it. If they need your help, you go and help where you can. So that entails, you know, a lot of times I'll go to the hospital to see someone who's sick, an elder or young person, sometimes they'll call and ask when a baby is about ready to be born. It's kind of, it's really expanded, you know. Bobby Bluejacket was the elder, you know. I was driving a truck, and Bobby Bluejacket came, and he said, "Son, we need to get you out of this truck." I said, "Well, I don't want to get out of this truck." He said, "Well, you need to be down here doing what you are supposed to be doing. It's too hard for you to do what you're doing and be in that truck at the same time."

So, the Business Committee at that time, they made a way for me to come here. And that's kind of how that got started. A tribal elder come and got me. Because I've been taking care of it for so long, but there was some conflicts, you know. I'd be out on the road, some five hundred miles away, and somebody would pass away. It would take me a couple days to get in, and it was kind of hard for the families, and got kind of hard for me and my employer, so the tribe made a way. I actually came here as an ICW [Indian Child Welfare] employee, and then that switched over, and basically kind of converted it all into one deal. Traveled to school to teach dance classes, kind of just go anywhere that I'm asked to go.

Warren: So you travel and do workshops at area schools?

King: Uh-huh. We teach them, you know, first the stuff about powwows. . . . We teach them how to—We usually take a group of children with us, and we'll teach one to two kids from each category of dance, you know, like jingle dress, fancy shawl, buckskin, traditional dancers, fancy dancers, grass dancers, and we just open them up to that. We always round dance well. The kids, you know, they are always afraid they are breaking a rule because they might not be Native. [I tell them,] "No, you can come out here! The round dance is social, so come on!"

Our main presentation . . . One of my greatest goals is to help stop suicide, you know, that's a passion. I lost my dad in 1995. He was a Vietnam vet, and he took his life, and ever since then, you know, when I hear that word or I see someone struggling, I want to do everything I can as a person to help. Because, you know, they don't realize it, once it's done, what gets left behind, you know? So that's part of doing what I do here. We've incorporated—We had a . . . from 2010 to 2012 we had about fourteen suicide attempts, and it just kept escalating and going and going, and this is not just Eastern Shawnee. This is just in general, you know. And they don't have to be Eastern Shawnee. But that number just kept growing and growing and getting extremely alarming. I went to the Business Committee, and I spoke to them, and what we needed to do, and they made a way to bring counselors here, so we actually have counselors on staff here at the tribe. It's also the drugs and alcohol. This is a husband-and-wife team of counselors, and that's kind of my main goal right now, is try to prevent that as much as possible.

Warren: Have you noticed a common pattern to the suicide attempts, or to the troubled people you've worked with? What's behind the increasing numbers?

King: Finances. It can be everything from substance abuse to financial, marriages coming apart. It kind of has a wide variety now. It has a wide span.

Warren: I wanted to ask you how the tribe has changed over the years. Many of the people we have spoken with have talked about the period before casinos and after casinos. I don't want to put any words in your mouth. But from 1971 to 2016, how has the tribe changed? How has your experience of being an Eastern Shawnee man changed? Can you help us understand differences over time?

King: Well, from—I came to work here when I was fifteen years old, on a summer youth program. This building was our bingo hall. That building next to it was the AOA [Administration on Aging], where we fed the elders, and the building right straight across from us was the administration building, the BlueJacket building. This was all a dirt parking lot, it was all gravel. And it's been pretty . . . pretty unique to sit around and watch all these things go up. You know, the things that were here. Like I said, I remember when this was all gravel, and sometimes summer youth kids would do donuts in it, when they'd come to work. But I just watched everything change, you know, as they've progressed. But, like, what we claim as our ceremonial grounds, down there across the creek, when we first started making that, there's some playground equipment down there, and I just happened to be driving around with one of our elders, and I said, "You know, Perry." I said, "When we get down here and get everything started, what're we going to do? Where you guys wanting me to put all this equipment, you know, this playground stuff? Do you want it over by the powwow grounds for the kids to use over there? Or what do you want to do?" He always called me Slim. And he said, "Slim, I've never asked you to do anything before that I can think of, and I'm going to ask you to leave it right where it's at, 'cause," he said, "you may not know where it came from." I asked him where did it come from, and it come from the Wyandotte Boarding School. He said, "Our elders told him that that was the only enjoyment they had, was that playground equipment. Some of them still recognize it. We have one that, you know, the minute he thought something was going to happen to it, he was like, "You leave that alone."

But, you know, the powwow ground was, like, a great experience for all of us, you know, when they built it.

Warren: When was it built?

King: It was built in '91. When they put it here, they—Might have been '92, it was . . . '91 or '92 . . . trying to remember. But when they, the elders—There were certain families that said, "Hey, lets go and ask the Business Committee if we can do this." 'Cause, you know, like I said, we had lost pretty much everything, and this was something that we could do that wouldn't be breaking any rules or anything. So that's how that come about, was, like, four of our elders went to the Business Committee and asked, you know. The chief at the time said, yeah, let's do it. And then it just started out that way, and we worked hours on end to build it. It was quite a task, but there were several times we were down there till two o'clock in the morning getting the ground ready, getting it all set up. That, kind of, was the thing that put everybody together. You know, it just drew everybody in, and then after that it just grew and grew and grew, and there were times it was just kind of quiet, and then it boomed again. I can't wait for the twenty-fifth [anniversary].

Warren: Do you have special events planned?

King: I don't know. I hope they do. I was kind of hoping that they'd go back and get the original people that were the head staff and bring them back. Because it was Robbie Blalock, Lynetta Blalock, Frank Wolf . . . now my memory is starting to slide. I can't remember them all, but I remember those guys. They'd come over here 'cause they were huge powwow families, and they basically took us by the hand and said, "This is how you do it. These are the dos and don'ts." And they, those particular families, helped us get it started. Billy Charles, all those. David Tyner, he'd come over and helped. But I remembered the Blalock family was a huge help to us. And then the McClellan family, they were here, they'd come and help.

Warren: So, for you it's not the casino that's the most significant event, it's the creation of the powwow?

King: Yeah, yeah the casino is very important to our people. I don't really pay that much attention to it. It just, you know, like I said, when I came here when I was fifteen, and you know, the tribe had a lot of little functions going on inside. They used to have . . . one of the things I miss the most . . . They had a group of ladies, and we just always called them the "beading ladies," 'cause they had their little projects, they had their own special little deal, and they'd say, "Hey, Shawn, we need this," and I'd run and get it. "Hey, Shawn, can you get that?" It is . . . was just . . . I don't know, I grew up watching, and that's where I met a lot of these elders we have today. That, you know, I've just sat back and grew up watching these guys, and enjoyed all of them.

Wensman: Do you still have those type people, the beading ladies? Or they can't bead no more?

King: Well, we've pretty much lost every one of them. They . . . My aunt would come down and helped quite a bit. Mrs. Captain, Madalyn [D.], Flora Beaty, there was just a little group of them there. And they were so fun to come in and hear them talking and get mad.

Wensman: So that was a big loss?

King: Yeah, I miss them, you know. It . . . it was so funny, because they'd have me go get them thread or something like that, because I could spin around pretty good. Then I was always moving cabinets for them, or [they'd ask,] "Shawn, where'd you put this? Shawn, where'd you put that?" [And I'd say,] "I didn't touch it."

Warren: Where do you see the tribe going? What's the future of the Eastern Shawnee Tribe? What would you like to see for your people?

King: I'd like to see them diversify their businesses a little bit. They're working on that. It is in process. They're in the process of doing that. I've always worried about the casino, you know. The way the economy is, and you know, things like the revenue dropping. I've always been concerned about that. So, you know . . . They're getting involved in trucking, they're getting involved in all kinds of other businesses now, and that's kind of made me relax. I used to sit on the Business Committee. I used to be first council. And it's just changing all the time because of the economy. You know, and that's a fast-paced world. I'd never want to work in a casino or anything like that, but I know the employees work their tail ends off. You know, they work hard up there. And you know, that's why we have what we do have, 'cause of the guys up there. If it wasn't for them, we really wouldn't have anything. But, you know, the tribe and the Business Committee, current Business Committee, they're working night and day to explore other businesses and get other things started, you know. To make sure that these benefits, you know, for our kids [to] go to school and take care of our elders and our houses and things.

Warren: Right! What about cultural aspirations? You have a vision of Shawnee culture for the future?

King: Well, I know that the chief and the Business Committee and, you know, this man here with us today [Wensman], there's several of them in the cultural department that are working very hard, you know, to help teach our people the language again, to teach us about all the Shawnee ways, part of the culture, and I'm very proud of that. It's been real neat to come up on these young boys, you know. I have some nephews that will come up and say something to me in Shawnee, and I might look at them kind of funny, and then they'll tell me what they're saying. And so it's been neat to hear them kind of converse back and forth, you know. And you know, I applaud everything that they're doing to help secure that in the future, so it doesn't get lost again, so to speak.

Warren: Is there something that I haven't emphasized, that you want to?

King: I'd like to see our people be more unified. You know a lot more unity in our people. You know, 'cause I see where tribal politics sometimes get in the way of that. And I just think that, you know, if we were more unified together as a whole, we'd go a lot further together. You know, these children, they need our help. Our tribal children, our tribal children neighbors, you know, the other tribes'. Because in this counseling, I have . . . I've had these young people tell me, "Well, we didn't know we could go there." And our tribe does this [at] absolutely no cost to a family, nothing. The Business Committee just absorbed it all. And I've had other tribes tell me, well, their tribe doesn't have that. And I said, well, you're welcome to come here. And then . . . Now, you see all these tribes getting involved here, wanting to put a stop to suicide and the substance abuse and the spousal abuse and things like that. We're all trying to work together now, to help kind of do what we can to prevent that as much as possible. That, I think, is the biggest thing I want to see, is the tribe be, you know more . . . more unity, all working together. 'Cause, like I said, a lot of the people, when I grew up, they're all gone now. But I still remember every one of them, just about everything they told me, just like that picture of that drum right there. That's . . . a Cheyenne was the one that made that. I can recognize that drum anywhere. It's sitting out in the lobby right now. Just . . . I don't know . . . just, I'd like to see the people get—I'd like to also see our leaders get more active, you know. But they got these rules as a Business Committee. They all can't be together at one time. And I'd just like to see us all get more active together. But they're growing in leaps and bounds.

Warren: Yes, sir, they are.

Wensman: I think once you . . . The impact that you had, like the . . . when you . . . just like your story, you're talking about being at dances, going to powwows and helping people, and I think that's a very important part to convey to the children, younger teenagers, teenage boys, that you're there to help. Just like I seen you, and I don't know who was with you that day, you brought some wood to White Oak when they was having their dance. And that type of leadership is something that you don't necessarily have to explain, but you know, taking some kids with you, and say like, "Hey we're taking some wood over there." And they see what you actually doing, and a lot of times kids just learn by watching. They don't have to hear . . . give them a speech . . . that we're going down there to help, but they see you doing it, and then they follow that role. And some of the things that you are doing, you know, I hope they are observing what you are doing. Just like this powwow. No one's touched on that, which I think is a big part of it. Just like how you went into that circle and what your thoughts were to that. That's something that needs to be conveyed to the kids, and I'm sure you're doing that on a continual basis. I mean, 'cause you do help a lot of people, and I guess to get the kids together, or young men, so they can just watch, not necessarily have to give them a speech about it, but just watch. And they'll ask you, "Why? Why do we do this?" And that gives you the opportunity to explain. I think it's great, your leadership, that you're showing with the kids. And I mean, that's going to be a major help in keeping things going, because after all, Shawnees do just help one another, and you don't have to necessarily explain. So, but yeah, I admire you for what you said about the dance ground.

And it's just like keeping a kid—One of the things that I did was . . . reason why I stayed in high school [was] 'cause I loved to play football, and I kept my grades up you know. They weren't the best grades, but I kept them up enough to play, and that's just like going up to dance. You want to dance, you know, and you see people out there, just like Shawn. He talked about all these people that are big-time powerful powwow people. And you look, and if you're a kid that's interested, and you're [in awe], you want to watch, especially with a fancy dance. "Hey, I want to watch this guy." And, as a kid, I remember doing that. You know, one of the guys that I liked to watch when I was a kid, and Sonny Glass was one of them. He was always walking around with a puppet, but you know, he was one of those big-time dancers. Or Larry Daylight, you know, everyone watched Larry Daylight. Or Johnny Whitecloud in the '70s, you know. It was like, "Hey, they're getting ready to dance." And you know, you was up there watching. So I love that story, what you just told, so we're—Just get the kids involved. And "Hey, look at these people. You want to be like them, you want to dance like them." 'Cause, you know, we all played football, you would want to run a move just like Billy Sims or somebody, Joe Washington when I was a kid. But I admire what you're doing with the tribe and the kids, and want things to continue to grow.

Warren: Thanks for your time.

King: You're welcome. *Niyaawe.*

16

An Interview with
Norma Kraus and Joe Kraus

Warren: It is February 21, 2016, and my name is Steve Warren, and I'm sitting here with Eric Wensman of the ANA grant, and I'm hoping that the people I'm interviewing can introduce themselves and tell me their names and where they were born.

N. Kraus: My name is Norma Kraus now, but I was born Norma Jean Strickland. In . . . I was born in Oklahoma. I was born at Claremore Indian hospital in 1938 and, what else do I tell? Anyway, I don't remember a lot when I was young. I remember some stories that mom told me, um, 'cause we moved to Oregon when I was six. I had started school at Wyandotte, and I been there for six weeks, and we went out to Oregon for a visit, and we just never came back. Like I said, I can remember a few things we did before . . . before we moved out there, but at six you don't remember a lot.

Warren: So you would've moved to Oregon in 1944?

N. Kraus: Yeah, it would have been.

Warren: What prompted your move?

N. Kraus: Dad was in the navy, and my grandpa and a couple of my aunts had moved out there. And so Mom took us kids on the train, and we went out there, and like I said we didn't come [back]. She liked it. Family was out there, so we stayed.

Warren: Did you all go to work in the shipyards?

N. Kraus: She did, she did. Like I said, dad was in the navy, and she, I don't know, I guess she had to work, I don't know. But she did.

Warren: Was it named the Kaiser shipyard?

N. Kraus: Uh, I don't know.

J. Kraus: Probably, that's where my dad worked.

N. Kraus: In Portland?

J. Kraus: In Vancouver. I don't know what they had before.

N. Kraus: Yeah, she worked in Portland.

J. Kraus: I'm not sure what it would be, then, if it was . . . if it was Kaiser or not.

Warren: Ok, ok. What sort of work was she doing in the shipyard?

N. Kraus: She started out, I think . . . She said she started out welding, and she was . . . she was young, you know. She had four of us kids already, but she was only like twenty-one, and raised back here. And so she wasn't very world-wise, you know. And she said the group that she worked with were very, um, used a lot of profanity, you know. And they could tell she was uncomfortable, so they asked the director or whatever to move her. So they moved her to another department.

Warren: Wow.

N. Kraus: Yeah. [Laughter]

Warren: So, did she migrate with several other Eastern Shawnee families?

N. Kraus: Well, with our immediate family, her sister. Yeah, there was one of her sisters that went out with us.

Warren: What were the names of those families in Oklahoma and in Oregon?

N. Kraus: Um, well, there was my aunt Vivian. She's the one . . . I think . . . she was the one that went out with us kids and mom. And she was married to Payton—Can't remember his last name. But anyway, he had passed away, and . . . and I think maybe that might have been partly why we went out there. Um, but then she came back, back out here, and then she ended up marrying Frank Gokey. And you've probably heard of him, too. They're, uh, they're Sac and Fox, so. And then there was my aunt Gladys and her family. They lived out there already. Two of my uncles had moved out there. They were young, and they'd gone out there when Grandpa went— and that was Virgil Millhollin—and I think Uncle Jap moved out there with them too—that was Jasper Millhollin. And then he later moved to Colorado. And who else went? Uncle Doe, Joshua. Sorry, all these nicknames. And I don't think any of the boys were married at that time. Uncle Johnny got married when we were out there. Who else was there?

J. Kraus: Virgil?

N. Kraus: I said Virgil, didn't I? Thought I did. But they were all pretty young at that time, you know.

Warren: Right, and so a bunch of Eastern Shawnees move out to Oregon, and there are Sac and Fox marriages and other Oklahoma marriages in Oregon, so what was the community like there that you found yourself in? It sounds like there are a bunch of Okies in Oregon.

N. Kraus: It was. Migrant, really, because you know, after the war [World War II] was over, and Dad came home and everything, what we did, mostly, was travel around and pick fruit and berries and stuff like that. He never was much of a worker, so he depended on us, all of the family, to keeping us going.

Warren: So you worked as a migrant laborer, too? What sort of crops did you follow? And what states did you work in?

N. Kraus: Uh, actually, Oregon was the only state we worked in. But we picked fruit—pears, apples, peaches, whatever—at Hood River mostly. And we picked berries, several types of berries. I know one time, the folks—this was after I wasn't at home anymore—they picked hops, and just everything, strawberries sometime mostly.

J. Kraus: Beans.

N. Kraus: Beans, yeah.

Warren: How old were you when you started? And when did you stop?

N. Kraus: Well, I think I was about . . . probably about eight when we started picking fruit and stuff, 'cause I was six when we moved out there, and dad was still in the navy for a while, and it wasn't until after he got out, and probably even a year after that, before we started picking fruit and stuff. So he was . . . he worked in a sawmill before that, and we lived up on the . . . we called it Squaw Mountain. And it was quite a ways from other people, but that's where the sawmill was. They had a big building. It was just three great big, long, narrow rooms, and one was, you know, like a living room. We had a stove in there, and mom and dad's bed, and then other one we used for, like, a kitchen. And then the other room was us kids' bedroom. So . . . and, you know, not much furnishings or anything like that, and this [was] before we started doing all the moving around and picking fruit and stuff. I remember, you know . . . the kids nowadays, they . . . Christmas is such a big thing to them, but you know, I remember when I was in the first grade, that we had Christmas at school, I didn't know what Christmas was. At that time, I had no idea what Christmas was. And my mom . . . We drew names, and my mom had gotten this pretty little doll for this girl, that I got her name, and I wanted it so bad, and I got it. But that was the first Christmas I can remember. And then, when we lived up there on Squaw Mountain, we had some Christmases, but you know the fire department, at that time, it took up used toys and stuff and repaired them and would take them out to different families that didn't have much. And we thought they were the best thing ever, you know. Things have changed so much; it's just unbelievable.

Warren: Do you have memories of discrimination, either as an Oklahoman or as a Native person in Oregon?

N. Kraus: Not really, I don't. I know some people say they did, but I didn't where we lived. Actually, where we lived, up there on Squaw Mountain, family lived up there, too. Or not always family, some of the Eastern Shawnees from here did, too.[1] The Brocks. So we grew up with them . . . those kids, too.

Warren: What did you know about being Shawnee in Oregon?

N. Kraus: I didn't, I didn't. When was I first aware of it? I guess when we got that payment in, what year was that?

J. Kraus: '64.

N. Kraus: '64.

Warren: What payment was that?

N. Kraus: It was just a payment to Eastern Shawnee, Absentee Shawnee, Cherokee . . . Cherokee Shawnees, I think they called them then.

J. Kraus: It was from 1938.

N. Kraus: And I think that was the first time that I even really knew anything about being Indian, other than, well, even then I didn't know. But my aunt did, because when she was . . . when I was going to school here in Wyandotte . . . Well, after I was born. I wasn't going to school yet. She was, and she asked to take me to school for show and tell, 'cause I was her little Indian niece. [Laughter]

Warren: So that was your first experience of being Indian.

N. Kraus: Yeah, but I don't remember it. That's just what my mom told me, you know. [Laughter] But, yeah, I think the first thing I knew was when we got that payment, and mom had us enrolled, you know, but I wasn't aware of it or anything.

Warren: So, I'm just puzzled by that. And I am wondering about your primary identity, given the fact that you were living among Eastern Shawnees, but you didn't speak necessarily about being Shawnee, living and marrying. A member of your family married a Sac and Fox person. But you weren't talking about it. Can you explore this with me?

N. Kraus: No, well, that was my aunt Viv. Not really, because we just didn't discuss being Indian or anything. We were just . . . just there.

Warren: Did you discuss Oklahoma at all?

N. Kraus: Not really. I think we were too involved with just living and getting by.

Warren: Ok.

Wensman: So you, as a child, picked for income?

N. Kraus: Oh yeah, yeah.

Wensman: How much would you say you was supposed to get? What was you making?

N. Kraus: I have no idea. Dad got it, took it all. And all I remember, actually, about it, it was hard work. It was fun, except that he would make us so mad because he would always carry on about how much more he could pick than we could. I mean, we were little kids, you know. He wasn't a nice man.

Wensman: But it was every day?

N. Kraus: Yeah.

Wensman: In the summertime? And did you go to school during the year?

N. Kraus: Winter, yeah. And we went to, sometimes, several schools in a year.

Wensman: In a year's time?

N. Kraus: Uh-huh, just from moving around to pick fruit, you know.

Warren: Did it ever normalize to a point where you could, say, graduate high school? Or what happened with your education?

N. Kraus: Oh, yeah, I graduated high school. When I was eleven—think I was eleven—I was taken away from the family and later adopted by some people by the name of Cap and Hettie Broyles. And then I just had a normal life. I mean, it was a life different than what I'd ever known. But it was a good life.

Warren: And they were non-Natives?

N. Kraus: Right.

Warren: Because this was before the Indian Child Welfare Act.[2]

N. Kraus: Right.

Warren: And so, then you were raised in Oregon? In Portland?

N. Kraus: Gresham. Well, they lived in Willamette, which is . . . I don't know how to explain it to you. Well, it's by Oregon City. You've heard of Oregon City, I'm sure.

J. Kraus: South of Portland.

N. Kraus: Yeah, it wasn't very far from there. And I finished eighth grade, I graduated eighth grade there, at Willamette School, and went to high school at West Linn, all four years.

16.1. Norma Strickland Kraus serving in the military. Photo courtesy of Norma Kraus.

Warren: And then after that you joined the military?

N. Kraus: After that I worked at the county library for a little over a year, I believe. And then I joined the service.

Warren: When and why did you decide to join the military? Was this somewhat unusual for that age?

N. Kraus: I wanted to get away. I had broken up with my boyfriend, or he broke up with me. We were engaged, but he broke up with me and . . . crazy, crazy . . . He didn't like girls that smoked, so after that I started smoking. Spiting him, you know? And then I went into the service just to get away, and partly to see some of the country.

Warren: And this was in 1959?

N. Kraus: Probably. I don't remember dates. I'm horrible with dates.

Warren: So what sort of things did you do in the military?

N. Kraus: I was a clerk-typist. I worked for a lieutenant, his office.

Wensman: Did you ever rank?

N. Kraus: I was a . . . when I got out I was a spec. four [specialist].

Wensman: A spec. four?

Warren: And for how long did you serve?

N. Kraus: Two years.

Warren: Ok, and what happened when you left?

N. Kraus: What happened when I left? Well, I had met another guy when I was in the service, and I ended up getting pregnant, and that's why I was only in two years. Actually, I signed up for three. And, of course, when I got pregnant, at that time they put you out. Now, you know, they let them stay in, but they didn't then. And so I went home, and I went back to my natural parents.

Warren: You did?

N. Kraus: Uh-huh.

Warren: So you stayed in contact with them after your adoption?

N. Kraus: I did, all the time. Uh-huh.

Warren: Oh, so it was an open adoption?

N. Kraus: Yeah, yeah. So, yeah, I was always in contact with my biological family.

Wensman: Was you very disappointed you had to get out of the service?

N. Kraus: Yes, I loved it. I probably would've made a career of it. They tried their best to get me to go to officer school. No, I don't want none of that. [Laughter]

Wensman: So women, they just kicked them out?

N. Kraus: If they were pregnant, yeah.

Wensman: If you'd been married would it have been a different story?

N. Kraus: No.

Wensman: Bottom line, you were gone.

N. Kraus: Uh-huh.

Warren and Wensman: Wow.

J. Kraus: Times have changed.

Warren: Yes, they have. Yes, sir, they have. This is a lot to take in, because so far we have an out-migration [to] Oregon at the age of six, working in fields by the age of eight, adopting out of the family at the age of eleven, joining the military, and then reuniting [with your birth family]. Throughout all this, I would like for the people reading this to know that we are [conducting this interview] in a retirement community run by the Eastern Shawnee Tribe, on what remains of Eastern Shawnee tribal land in northeastern Oklahoma [in Ottawa County]. So, at some point, Norma, you reconnected quite profoundly with your people.

N. Kraus: Yeah. Once I realized, you know, after we moved back here, then I really became interested in tribal affairs and stuff.

Warren: But your motivation for returning in 1972 was not tribally motivated.

N. Kraus: No, no. Dad was real bad sick. He had emphysema, and he told Mom that he wanted to die back here. And so she and my youngest brother and my sister and Dad moved back here. And as he got worse . . . 'course, she had to work . . . he would . . . he had never worked enough that he drew Social Security. All he had was a veteran's pension. Yeah, and it wasn't very much, and so she had to go to work, and she had nobody to take care of my dad, and he got to the point where he had to have care, you know. So we were talking about moving to Montana, and then when he got so bad we decided to come back here and help her out.

Warren: So you all [Joe and Norma] met in Oregon?

J. Kraus: Yeah.

N. Kraus: We grew up not too many miles apart out there.

Warren: Ok.

N. Kraus: It was crazy, and we didn't meet till after I was out of the service, he was out of the service, and one day—Anyway, his name is Joseph, Joe. And my brother kept saying I have this friend I want you to meet, and I said no. And he was working rotating shifts at the paper mill, and I was working evenings at the hospital, and so, anyway, I kept putting him off. And I don't know what Joe did or not, but it took us a while to meet each other. And finally in April—was it April?

J. Kraus: April, I think.

N. Kraus: Yeah, April, we finally had our first date.

Warren: Oh, ok.

N. Kraus: And my little girl, Teresa, was already calling him Daddy.

J. Kraus: I met . . . I come over to her folks' house, and—'cause I was running around with her brother—and so I met—

N. Kraus: Teresa.

J. Kraus: So, anyway then.

N. Kraus: She was just little, she was less than two years old, but she was talking, and she called him Daddy.

J. Kraus: We met in April and got married in June.

Wensman: Oh you met in April and married in June?
   [Laughter]

Kraus: And we've been married fifty-three years.

Wensman: Oh, wow.

Warren: Congratulations.

J. Kraus: So, anyway.

Warren: So you came back [to Oklahoma] to care for your father, and then, after that, something must have happened to interest you in the tribe?

N. Kraus: Well, after he died, Mom was working at the sewing factory in Miami.[3] And when he died, she just kind of . . . I don't know, lost interest in everything. And I kept trying to get her to go back to work, and she wouldn't, and finally I told Joe, I said, "I'm going to go get a job up there, and maybe she'll go back," and she did. And she came out of it, you know, ok. But I did not like that job, working in the sewing factory.

Warren: What sort of work were you doing?

N. Kraus: I liked to sew, but not that kind.

J. Kraus: Making jeans.

N. Kraus: Yeah, and doing the same thing over and over and over and over. And so I quit, and I went to work in a leather place, where they made holsters and stuff like that. And I worked what, three, four days?

J. Kraus: One day, I think. One or two days.

N. Kraus: I don't know. However, it wasn't many, and I got a call from Sears, 'cause I had applied there, and I worked there for, I don't know, two years? Two years.

J. Kraus: Two years, three years, something.

N. Kraus: And I had also, after that, applied for a job at the tribe.

Warren: Ok.

N. Kraus: And that's when I went to work for the tribe. And I went to work for the tribe as a receptionist.

Warren: Ok.

Wensman: And what year was that?

J. Kraus: '80, '81, I think. '80 or '81.

N. Kraus: Was it that late? I was going to look all that stuff up before you guys came, and I didn't. I don't remember . . . Anyway, I went to work for the tribe as a receptionist. And I had done jobs as bookkeeper, too. In fact, I went to school at H&R Block, and I did work for them for a couple years while we were in Oregon. So she was teaching me some of the bookkeeping for the tribe, and at that time there was her, Marilyn, Debbie, me, and Steve Abernathy, that was the only employees we had.

Wensman: But still, yet. That was a pretty big staff.

N. Kraus: At that time, it was a very big staff.

Wensman: How was it funded?

N. Kraus: Grants. We had a health grant and a bureau grant.

Warren: Because this would've been, if it was 1981, it would've been three years before the bingo hall was built.

N. Kraus: I think it was earlier than that, really, 'cause I think I had worked for [the] tribe longer than that before the bingo came in.

J. Kraus: Well, yeah, they—Well, they built that building, that industrial building for—

N. Kraus: That was built, though, long before I started working for them. Yeah, 'cause when I started working for them, we had that little building that you go into . . . the . . . have you been down there?

Warren: Yes.

N. Kraus: To Bordertown. Ok, as you first go in, the little building to the right.

J. Kraus: Gaming commission now.

N. Kraus: Yeah, that's gaming commission now, but that's where our offices were. And then we had an industrial building, and then we had a little building up at the park. And that's all the buildings we had. And industrial building was empty. After I had worked for the tribe for a while, we got an AOA [Administration on Aging] program, and we used the building up at the park for that. First off, we took meals out, and then we got . . . were feeding up there.[4]

Warren: What was the tribe like in . . . when you first started working for it? I mean, who were the regular people who would come to meetings?

N. Kraus: Um, Jim Greenfeather was the chief when we first moved out here. [At the] time I went to work for the tribe, Chief Captain was our chief. And I remember going to meetings when Jim was chief in Miami. And, uh, there would be my uncle, some of the Captains, and my mom and me, and probably about a dozen people.

Warren: Just a dozen people?

N. Kraus: Probably.

Warren: And where would you all meet?

N. Kraus: You know, I don't remember what building we was meeting in. Probably at the . . . I really don't remember where it was. Might have been one of the rooms at the bureau, I would assume, because that's where the office was at that time.

J. Kraus: In Miami, yeah.

Warren: And at that time, um, I've heard legendary stories about Floyd Leonard, the chief of the Miami Tribe, and Buck Captain, and the fact that they got a lot done together, that there were a lot of intertribal relationships at the time.

N. Kraus: I wasn't too familiar with the other tribes at that time. Not until I had worked for the tribe for a while, and you know, started having dealings with them. But at the time you are talking about, I didn't know much about them. And I didn't know much about Buck either, really.

Warren: What was he like?

N. Kraus: He was a good man. Good man.

Warren: What mattered to him as a leader?

N. Kraus: What mattered? The people, tribal members, he . . . really, he was a good chief. Um, a lot of stories about him cheating, you know, and taking money from the tribe and everything. No. Even my mother would say, "Oh he always sticks plenty in his pocket, how does he get his money otherwise?" And I'd say, "There's no way, Mom. I'm the bookkeeper out there and I know where every penny goes, and it does not go in his pocket." So, see, I was even hearing this stuff from my own family.

Warren: It's kind of a thankless position.

N. Kraus: Yes, it is. And I have always said that everybody in the tribe should sit on the Business Committee at some point in their life. 'Cause it is, it's hard. I did, I was on the Business Committee for a while. It's a hard job.

Warren: So, I told you that we'd talk about the period before casinos and after casinos. Would you like to say a few words about that transformation?

N. Kraus: Well, it started out with the bingo hall, and they opened up in the industrial building. But before we even did that, you know, we had our AOA program. We got, you know, where we fed the people and stuff. And that little building next to it there, that's where we fed them. So we had other things going, too, before we started the bingo. And we did, we started out with our bingo. We did very well, and then it got where we started making less and less money, and I don't know what was going on. It's hard to tell, but it did get to the point where we were making less and less. Finally they let that—I can't remember his name.

J. Kraus: I don't either.

N. Kraus: Anyway, it was the guy that opened up the bingo for us. He had been the manager out at—

J. Kraus: Oh, Allen. David Allen.

N. Kraus: David Allen, yeah. He was the one that started it for us. And it was on—He got a certain percentage, and I think somewhere along the line the percentage got twisted around. So anyway, they finally let him go, and we took it over ourself, and we always operated everything, from there on, ourselves, and done very well. Now, I didn't have much to do with, with any of the casino stuff or anything. I have worked at the casino, I worked in the gift shop and stuff, but as far as having anything to do with the operation of it or anything like that, I didn't. I just always worked in the administrative part of the tribe.

Wensman: Would you ever be on the Business Committee again?

N. Kraus: No.

Wensman: Don't need the headache?

N. Kraus: No, I'm seventy-seven years old. [Laughter] No. It's tough, it really is. I mean, you know, if you don't mind being called names and whatever, it's ok, I guess.

Warren: What are the tough parts of the job?

N. Kraus: Basically that, just having people, you know, just making remarks about you and saying things that are untrue and saying we aren't looking out for the tribe and, you know, most of us are. If we are on the Business Committee, we are. We've got a young man on there right now; I didn't want him on the Business Committee, but he's doing a good job. I mean, most of them, once they get on the Business Committee, they do a good job. They try, anyway. We have a few that don't, but most of them are concerned.

Wensman: Well, one of the things we ask everybody is what direction do you see the tribe going? And where would you like the tribe to be in ten, twenty more years?

N. Kraus: You know, I don't really know. Because, you know, as far as it's benefits for tribal members and stuff, my viewpoint on that has always been, it was our ancestors that had it tough. And they're the ones that deserved it, and they're the ones that didn't get it, and so what we're getting is just what they should've had and didn't have. Um, the tribal members have less and less blood—Indian blood—in them, all the time. I mean we're down to the nitty-gritty, you know, degrees now, so I think it's great, but still do we really deserve it?

Wensman: That's a good question.

N. Kraus: I just feel bad that it wasn't our ancestors that had this opportunity.

Wensman: That got the money. Well, I mean, you was basically in the same boat as they were growing up.

N. Kraus: Yeah, to a point, but I don't think we even had it as bad as they did. 'Cause I remember, when my mom was growing up, she lived in a one-room shack, no floor, cracks in the walls because all they used was slab wood to build it. And wintertime, they had snow, rain come in, you know, it was just a very rude shelter that they lived in. And even when I was little, and I remember this, we lived in a one-room house. We did have a floor, but Mom said when her and dad got married, they lived in a little chicken coop for a while.

Wensman: And where did they live?

N. Kraus: Out by Wyandotte. Over on Highway 10. We got . . . the tribe now has some land, and it was originally mom's family's land.

J. Kraus: You know where the Wayside Church is?

Wensman: Yes.

J. Kraus: Going on down Highway 10.

N. Kraus: Almost directly across from there.

J. Kraus: It was up about a half a mile from there, to a mile north of the church, they had property on the left and right side of that road.

N. Kraus: But now the tribe owns it. I think.

J. Kraus: The forty-five acres was sold to somebody else, wasn't it?

N. Kraus: Yeah, that land, that's where we lived. So I did live on Mom's allotted land for a while.

Wensman: Do you still have that land?

N. Kraus: No, that's what I was saying. That was sold. I believe it was the Senecas bought it. And now our tribe just bought it.

Wensman: Oh, ok.

N. Kraus: So it's now tribal land.

Wensman: Do you try to convey these stories to your children and grandchildren?

N. Kraus: Sometimes, yeah, I tell them stuff. And see, I got my daughter Melanie, you've met her I'm sure, she's assistant manager of the casino. I got a granddaughter that is a junior hostess, and I got a granddaughter that works there as well.

Wensman: Well did you ever—when y'all moved back, did you all go to Quapaw Powwow?

N. Kraus: Yeah.

J. Kraus: Oh, yeah.

N. Kraus: Yeah, we used to go all the time to the Quapaw Powwow.

Wensman: Was that an annual event for you?

N. Kraus: Yeah, pretty much. We went just about every year, didn't we?

J. Kraus: Yeah.

Wensman: Did you have friends that camped there and stuff, or relatives?

N. Kraus: No.

J. Kraus: No.

N. Kraus: People I knew, you know, but not really friends.

J. Kraus: Yeah.

Wensman: Would you spend all three days there?

N. Kraus: No.

Wensman: Just go one night or something?

N. Kraus: Yeah.

Wensman: And the kids loved to go?

N. Kraus: Yeah, they loved to do anything [where] they could run and chase and whatever.

Wensman: But they never danced or anything?

N. Kraus: Uh, no. No, not that I recall.

Wensman: Did they have shawls, where they would go out and dance?

N. Kraus: Not then, no. It wasn't until later, till we started having our powwows, that we got involved in any of that. Even me.

J. Kraus: Jennifer was a powwow princess one year, junior powwow princess, at our powwow [a] few years ago. I don't remember, it had to be at least ten years ago. I don't remember.

Wensman: [To Joe] Well, have you enjoyed living here? Now, you're from Portland, is that correct?

J. Kraus: Right. Basically, I was born in Montana, and my dad—little bit of quick history—he was a farmer in Montana. Well, during the war, there was no jobs for farmers in Montana during the war. So, they . . . he moved to the West Coast, to Vancouver, Washington, to work in the shipyards. Then he worked—my mom worked in the shipyards, too—at Vancouver. We lived in the housing projects. And in 1946 we moved to . . . when he got out of . . . when the war was over, they quit building ships. He got a job at Reynolds Metals there, at Troutdale, Oregon. And he worked there at Reynolds Metals, too, and this one here worked over twenty years—twenty-two or twenty-three years—at Reynolds Metal. And so, then, I just grew up out there, and then after I got out of . . . well, when I was in high school, I joined the marine corps. And I spent four years in the marine corps. And then I got out, and then I was working in a paper mill, and that's when I met Norma. And then we got married, and then we lived there at West Linn, across the river from Oregon City, for seven years, and then her dad got sick, and we just sold our house and just packed up and moved out here. Bought a little house, and she just . . . we lived about . . . not quite a half mile from where her mom lived. And she'd go down every day and stay with her dad, and get the kids off to school, and stay with her dad all day long while her mom worked. And did that for about a year and half before he passed. 'Cause the veterans said they couldn't do . . . for him, so either put him in the nursing home or take him home, and he wanted to die at home, so that was a choice they gave him. So that was back in '73, '74 . . . '72, '73, and so that . . . that's how we got out here.

Warren: Was 1992 the first annual powwow?

N. Kraus: 1992, the year of the Indian.

Warren: The year of the Indian. Yes, 1492 to 1992. Was the year of the Indian.

N. Kraus: We must of started them [our powwows] the same year we got our—No, we got our casino came in before that. Like I said.

Wensman: Was that a pretty exciting time for everybody?

N. Kraus: Oh yeah, yeah.

Wensman: It was an exciting time for everybody, all tribes, because they was able to get the bingo. I remember everybody—It was a big deal.

N. Kraus: Yeah. 'Course, Senecas and Quapaws had it before we did.

J. Kraus: Yeah, our daughter Melanie, she worked for bingo before they started the casino and . . . a long time.

Wensman: Did you go to Seneca Green Corn as well? Did you ever go there?

N. Kraus: We have, yeah. We've gone a couple times.

Wensman: How about to White Oak?

N. Kraus: I've been to White Oak, yeah.

Wensman: Did you go in the '60s, or when you first moved here?

N. Kraus: No, no, it was after I was working for the tribe when I went. Um, our grandson—his dad is a Seneca-Cayuga—and he's one you should probably talk to, but he's at Harvard.

Wensman: Oh, he's at school at Harvard.

N. Kraus: Yeah, he . . . he's really into our tribal history.

Warren: What is his full name?

N. Kraus: Caden Thomas Chase.

J. Kraus: He . . . he's trying to get the young people involved in the culture, and that's great, you know . . . I think that it's just, when we was young and stuff, there wasn't no culture where we lived at, you know. We'd go see her uncles and cousins and stuff like that all the time. And go on picnics and stuff.

N. Kraus: It wasn't Indian type stuff.

J. Kraus: Then we'd come out here, we'd go to the . . . and start eating the uh . . . the uh, onions.

Wensman: Wild onions.

J. Kraus: The wild onions and stuff like that. I remember right after we moved out here, her and her mom went down to a spring, digging up onions, and they come back, and they was just full of chiggers. [Laughter]

N. Kraus: That wasn't too long after we moved out here. He had to take my dad down to Muskogee to the hospital, and he was upset because he didn't get to go on the picnic with us. When he got back, he was happy he hadn't gone. We fought chiggers for over a week, and that was horrible.

Wensman: What did y'all do for medical care, the Eastern Shawnees, back in the '60s and '70s here? Did you go to Claremore?

N. Kraus: Here? We didn't move out here till '72.

Wensman: Well after that, I mean. Did you go to Claremore? Or was—

N. Kraus: We had a clinic in . . . Where was that clinic at?

Joe and **N. Kraus:** In Wyandotte.

N. Kraus: Yeah.

Wensman: Oh, the Wyandottes had one?

N. Kraus: Yeah. And I think it was the Senecas that ran it, but it was at Wyandotte.

Wensman: But if you had to go to the hospital, would you—?

N. Kraus: Claremore.

Wensman: You went to Claremore? To the old hospital?

N. Kraus: Yeah.

Wensman: Was any of your children born there?

N. Kraus: Um, not ours, no. But some of our grandkids have been.

Wensman: Ok.

J. Kraus: Yeah, our kids was all born in Oregon.

Wensman: Ok.

J. Kraus: Yeah, so . . . yeah, our youngest was, I think four years old . . . four or five years old when we moved out here.

Wensman: How tough was it to pack up and move from Oregon? Financially and, you know, roads weren't that great then.

N. Kraus: It wasn't too bad then.

J. Kraus: Well, you know, the thing about it is, Oregon was so far more advanced in roads and stuff than what Oklahoma was, and the jobs, too. I went from what $4.75 an hour to two dollars an hour when I moved back out here. I mean it was just that much difference.

N. Kraus: Can you imagine how many years ago that was?

Wensman: That was in '73, something like that?

J. Kraus: '72, yeah. Two dollars and a half, an hour, yeah.

Wensman: Did you ever feel like you made a mistake when you got here?

J. Kraus: No, I love this place.

N. Kraus: No.

J. Kraus: No, it . . . because you're going to spend what you make. I mean, it was tough. We had four kids, but we got by, you know. And I guess that's the attitude that all the elders always had. That they always got by.

N. Kraus: Yeah, make sure your kids are fed, and life went on.

J. Kraus: You had a car that smoked, so what?

N. Kraus: You know, I don't think life was so tough that people . . . That's basically what they did, they just went from day to day, you know, just survive. And they got it, was just a mindset thing, this is what we have to do, and they just did it.

Wensman: Well, Norma, is there anything you would like to tell us about the tribe that you'd like to see the tribe do? Or anything that you want us to know about you before we come to an end on the interview?

N. Kraus: I'd like to see them get more housing for the tribal members. More of these duplexes, more regular housing for the tribal members. I'd like to see them build us a real community building. You know, where if we wanted to have a party or something with our families, or whatever, we could do it and, you know, like Wyandotte has a community building, plus they have a playground and stuff, and it's really nice. That's where we had that birthday party for Boston yesterday. I'd like to see something like that. Um, gosh, they've got so much going already, you know, much more than I'd ever dreamed they'd get.

J. Kraus: Yeah they've done marvelous, you know. When we moved out here, when she first worked for the tribe, they didn't have a maintenance crew, any mowing, or anything. It was all volunteer.

N. Kraus: So the people that worked there, it . . . families that volunteered with the lawn and stuff like that.

J. Kraus: Any upkeep and stuff like that.

N. Kraus: Yeah, our tribe was pretty poor when I started working for them. We had fifty-six dollars in the bank. We had the grants, you know, but as far as tribal, a fund, that's what we had was fifty-six dollars.

N. Kraus: We have good employees, very good employees, but going to get some bad ones . . . bad ones along the way, always . . . but overall, I think the tribe has done fantastic. I think Glenna is the absolute best. She is a . . . I said . . . if for no other reason than this: she is a fantastic public relations person. And she has gotten us more money because of that, even from other tribes, you know. She's fantastic. Her whole family are . . . they're great people. But then, I like just about everybody, so. But she is, she's great. Charles Enyart is great. He was a good chief.

Wensman: Ok.

Warren: Well, thank you. *Niyaawe.*

NOTES

1. Squaw Mountain is forty-three miles southeast of Portland in the foothills of Oregon's Cascade Mountains.

2. In 1978 Congress passed the Indian Child Welfare Act (ICWA). Prior to this date, American Indian children were frequently removed from their traditional homes and placed with non-Native parents. Since then, federally recognized tribes have had jurisdiction over their tribal citizens' children.

3. Here she refers to Oklahoma Leather/Burlington Manufacturing, Inc., which specialized in jeans and jackets.

4. Since 1978 the Administration on Aging has been providing grants to tribal communities to provide better nutrition and support services for the elderly.

Bibliography

MANUSCRIPT AND ARCHIVAL SOURCES

Cass, Lewis, Papers. William Clements Library. University of Michigan. Ann Arbor.

Documents Relating to Indian Affairs. History Collection. University of Wisconsin Digital Collections.

  Documents Relating to the Negotiation of Ratified and Unratified Treaties With Various Indian Tribes, 1801–1869

  Office of Indian Affairs, Annual Report of the Commissioner of Indian Affairs

Draper Manuscripts. State Historical Society of Wisconsin, Madison.

  Harrison, William Henry, Papers

  Tecumseh Papers

Eastern Shawnee Tribe of Oklahoma Digital Collection, *Ohio Memory*, www.ohiomemory.org/cdm /landingpage/collection/p16007coll27.

Great Lakes and Ohio Valley Ethnohistory Collection. Glenn A. Black Laboratory of Archaeology. Indiana University Bloomington.

  Shawnee File

  Wyandot File

Harrison, William Henry, Papers. Indiana Historical Society.

Library and Archives Canada. Ottawa.

  British Military and Naval Records (Record Group 8), C Series

  Indian Affairs (Record Group 10)

McArthur, Duncan, Papers. Library of Congress. Washington, D.C.

Missouri Historical Society. St. Louis.

  Forsyth, Thomas, Papers

  Graham, Richard, Papers

National Anthropological Archives. Smithsonian Institution.

  American Society for Ethnohistory Papers

  Gatschet, Albert, Manuscripts

Political Papers. Ohio History Connection Archives. Ohio History Center. Columbus.

  Meigs, Return J., Papers

  Worthington, Thomas, Papers

Record Group 75, Records of the Bureau of Indian Affairs. National Archives and Records Administration.

  General Records of the Bureau of Indian Affairs

  Records of the Michigan Superintendency

  Records of the Quapaw Agency

Record Group 107, Records of the Office of the Secretary of War. National Archives and Records Administration.

Western History Collections and Digital Collections. University of Oklahoma. Norman.

  Doris Duke Duke Collection of American Indian Oral History

  Indian-Pioneer Papers Collection

NEWSPAPERS

Evening Gazette (Xenia, Ohio)
Miami Record-Herald
National Intelligencer
Niles' Register
Neosho (Mo.) Daily News
Sandusky (Ohio) Register
Shooting Star (Wyandotte, Oklahoma)

PUBLISHED SOURCES

Abel, Annie H. *The American Indians and the End of the Confederacy, 1863–1866.* 1925. Reprint, Lincoln: University of Nebraska Press, 1993.

Adams, John Quincy. *Memoirs of John Quincy Adams: Comprising Portions of His Diary from 1795 to 1848.* Edited by Charles Francis Adams. Philadelphia: J. B. Lippincott, 1875.

Alder, Henry Clay. *A History of Jonathan Alder: His Life and Captivity among the Indians.* Akron, Ohio: University of Akron Press, 2002.

American State Papers: Documents, Legislative and Executive, of the Congress of the United States. Class II, *Indian Affairs.* Edited by Walter Lowrie, Matthew St. Clair Clarke, and Walter S. Franklin. 2 Vols. Washington, D.C.: Gales and Seaton, 1832–34.

Anaya, S. James. *International Human Rights and Indigenous Peoples.* New York: Wolters Kluwer, 2009.

Anderson, Gary Clayton. *Ethnic Cleansing and the Indian: The Crime That Should Haunt America.* Norman: University of Oklahoma Press, 2014.

Bader, Anne Tobbe. "Evidence of Ritualized Mortuary Behavior at the Meyer Site: An Inadvertent Discovery in Spencer County, Indiana." *Indiana Archaeology* 5, no. 2 (2010/11): 10–49.

Badger, Joseph A. *A Memoir of Joseph Badger.* Hudson, Ohio: Ingersoll, 1851.

Baird, W. David. *The Quapaw Indians: A History of the Downstream People.* Norman: University of Oklahoma Press, 1979.

Banks, Dean. "Civil War Refugees from Indian Territory, in the North, 1861–1864." *The Chronicles of Oklahoma* 41, no. 3 (Fall 1963).

Barnes, Lela, ed. "An Editor Looks at Early-Day Kansas: The Letters of Charles Monroe Chase, the Letters of 1873." *The Kansas Quarterly* 26, no. 3 (Autumn 1960).

Barry, Louise, ed. "William Clark's Diary: May 1826–February, 1831." *Kansas Historical Quarterly* 16 (February 1948).

Bass, Randy. "Disrupting Ourselves: The Problem of Learning in Higher Education" *Educause Review* 47, no. 2 (March/April 2012).

Bauer, William J., Jr. *We Were All Like Migrant Workers Here: Work, Community, and Memory on California's Round Valley Reservation, 1850–1941.* Chapel Hill: University of North Carolina Press, 2009.

Bearss, Edwin C. "The Civil War in Indian Territory and the Fort Smith Council: Transcript of Keynote Address." In *Proceedings: War and Reconstruction in Indian Territory: A History Conference in Observance of the 130th Anniversary of the Fort Smith Council,* edited by Juliet L. Galonska. Fort Smith, Arkansas: National Park Service, 1995.

Beatty, James K. "Interpreting the Shawnee Sun: Literacy and Cultural Persistence in Indian Country, 1833–1841." *Kansas History* 31, no. 4 (Winter 2008).

Bergmann, William H. *The American National State and the Early West.* New York: Cambridge University Press, 2012.

Bernholz, Charles D., Laura K. Weakly, Brian L. Pytlik Zillig, and Karin Dalziel, eds. *As Long as Grass Shall Grow and Water Run: The Treaties Formed by the Confederate States of America and the Tribes in Indian Territory, 1861.* Center for Digital Research in the Humanities, University of Nebraska, Lincoln. http://csaindiantreaties.unl.edu/.

Bickham, Troy O. "Blackfish (1729?–1779)." *Oxford Dictionary of National Biography.* Oxford University Press, 2004. www.oxforddnb.com/view/article/74802.

Blackman, Jon S. *Oklahoma's Indian New Deal.* Norman: University of Oklahoma Press, 2013.

Bledsoe, S. T. *Indian Land Laws.* 2nd edition. Kansas City: Vernon Law Books, 1913.

Bonnin, Gertrude. *Oklahoma's Poor Rich Indians: An Orgy of Graft and Exploitation of the Five Civilized Tribes—Legalized Robbery.* Philadelphia: Indian Rights Association, 1924.

Bowes, John P. *Exiles and Pioneers: Eastern Indians in the Trans-Mississippi West.* New York: Cambridge University Press, 2007.

Buchman, Randall. *A Sorrowful Journey.* Defiance, Ohio: Defiance College Press, 2007.

Bureau of Indian Affairs. "Indian Entities Recognized and Eligible to Receive Services from the United States Bureau of Indian Affairs." *Federal Register* 81, no. 19 (January 29, 2016).

Burton, Jeffrey. *Indian Territory and the United States, 1866–1906.* Norman: University of Oklahoma Press: 1995.

Caldwell, Martha B. *Annals of Shawnee Methodist Mission and Indian Manual Labor School.* Topeka: Kansas State Historical Society, 1977.

Calhoun, John C. *The Papers of John C. Calhoun.* Edited by W. Edwin Hemphill. 27 vols. Columbia: University of South Carolina Press, 1959–2003.

Callender, Charles. "Shawnee." In *Handbook of North American Indians,* edited by William C. Sturtevant and Bruce G. Trigger. Washington, D.C.: Smithsonian Institution, 1978.

Calloway, Colin. *The American Revolution in Indian Country: Crisis and Diversity in Native American Communities.* New York: Cambridge University Press, 1995.

———. *Pen and Ink Witchcraft: Treaties and Treaty Making in American Indian History.* New York: Oxford University Press, 2013.

———. *The Shawnees and the War for America.* New York: Viking, 2008.

Canby, William C., Jr. *American Indian Law in a Nutshell.* 5th ed. St. Paul, Minn.: West Academic Publishing, 2009.

Carlson, Keith Thor. *The Power of Place, The Problem of Time: Aboriginal Identity and Historical Consciousness in the Cauldron of Colonialism.* Toronto: University of Toronto Press, 2011.

Carter, Clarence E., ed. *Territorial Papers of the United States.* 27 Vols. Washington, D.C.: Government Printing Office, 1934–75.

Carter, Harvey Lewis. *The Life and Times of Little Turtle.* Urbana: University of Illinois Press, 1987.

Cayton, Andrew R. L. *Ohio: A History of a People.* Columbus: Ohio State University Press, 2002.

Chang, David A. *The Color of the Land: Race, Nation, and the Politics of Land Ownership in Oklahoma, 1832–1929.* Chapel Hill: University of North Carolina Press, 2010.

Clark, Blue. "Ottawa." In *Indian Tribes of Oklahoma: A Guide.* Norman: University of Oklahoma Press, 2009.

Clark, Jerry E. *The Shawnee.* Lexington: University Press of Kentucky, 1993.

Clinton, Robert N. "Treaties with Native Nations: Iconic Historical Relic or Modern Necessity?" In *Nation to Nation: Treaties Between the United States & American Indian Nations,* edited by Suzan Shown Harjo. Washington, D.C.: National Museum of the American Indian, 2014.

Cochran, Thomas C., ed. *The New American State Papers: 1789–1860: Indian Affairs.* Wilmington, Del.: Scholarly Resources, 1972.

Cohen, Fay G. *Treaties on Trial: The Continuing Controversy over Northwest Indian Fishing Rights.* Seattle: University of Washington Press, 1986.

Cohen, Felix S. *Felix S. Cohen's Handbook of Federal Indian Law.* San Francisco: Lexis Law Publisher, 1982.

Debo, Angie. *And Still the Waters Run: The Betrayal of the Five Civilized Tribes.* Princeton, N.J.: Princeton University Press, 1940.

Deloria, Vine, Jr., and Raymond DeMallie. *Documents of American Indian Diplomacy: Treaties, Agreements, and Conventions 1775–1979.* Norman: University of Oklahoma Press, 1999.

Denson, Andrew. *Demanding the Cherokee Nation: Indian Autonomy and American Culture, 1830–1900.* Lincoln: University of Nebraska Press, 2004.

De Puy, Henry F. *A Bibliography of the English Colonial Treaties with the American Indians: Including a Synopsis of each Treaty.* Union, N.J.: Lawbook Exchange, 2001.

Dowd, Gregory Evans. *War Under Heaven: Pontiac, the Indian Nations, and the British Empire.* Baltimore: Johns Hopkins University Press, 2004.

Edmunds, R. David. "Edmunds—Tecumseh." *Indians of the Midwest.* Video. 11:32. 2009. http://publications.newberry.org/indiansofthemidwest/indian-imagery/how-we-know/. Transcript available at http://publications.newberry.org/indiansofthemidwest/indian-imagery/how-we-know/video-transcript-tecumseh-imagery/.

———, ed. *Enduring Nations: Native Americans in the Midwest.* Urbana: University of Illinois Press, 2008.

———. "'Evil Men Who Add to Our Difficulties': Shawnees, Quakers, and William Wells, 1807–1808." *American Indian Culture and Research Journal* 14, no. 4 (1990).

———. "Main Poc: Potawatomi Wabeno." *American Indian Quarterly* 9, no. 3 (Summer 1985).

———. "Native Americans, New Voices: American Indian History, 1895–1995." *American Historical Review* 100, no. 3 (June 1995).

———. *The Potawatomis: Keepers of the Fire.* Norman: University of Oklahoma Press, 1978.

———. *The Shawnee Prophet.* Lincoln: University of Nebraska Press, 1983.

———. *Tecumseh and the Quest for Indian Leadership.* Boston: Little, Brown, 1984.

———. "A Watchful Safeguard to Our Habitations: Black Hoof and the Loyal Shawnees." In *Native Americans in the New Republic,* edited by Frederick E. Hoxie, Ronald Hoffman, and Peter J. Albert. Charlottesville: University Press of Virginia, 1999.

Esaray, Logan, ed. *Messages and Letters of William Henry Harrison.* 2 vols. New York: Arno Press, 1975.

Faulk, Odie B. *The Modoc People.* Phoenix: Indian Tribal Series, 1976.

Fisher, Andrew H. *Shadow Tribe: The Making of Columbia River Indian Identity.* Seattle: Center for the Study of the Pacific Northwest/University of Washington Press, 2010.

Fischer, LeRoy H., ed. *The Civil War Era in Indian Territory.* Los Angeles: Lorrin L. Morrison, 1974.

Foreman, Carolyn Thomas. "The Armstrongs of Indian Territory, Part II: William Armstrong." *The Chronicles of Oklahoma* 30, no. 4 (Fall 1952).

Foreman, Grant. *The Five Civilized Tribes.* Norman: University of Oklahoma Press, 1934.

———. *Indians and Pioneers: The Story of the American Southwest before 1830.* Norman: University of Oklahoma Press, 1930.

———. *Last Trek of the Indians.* Chicago: University of Chicago Press, 1946.

———. "The Life of Montfort Stokes in the Indian Territory." *The North Carolina Historical Review* 16, no. 4 (October 1939).

Foster, William Omer. "The Career of Montfort Stokes in Oklahoma." *The Chronicles of Oklahoma* 18, no. 1 (March 1940).

Franklin, Benjamin. *Pennsylvania, and the First Nations: The Treaties of 1736–62.* Edited by Susan Kalter. Chicago: University of Illinois Press, 2006.

Galloway, William Albert, and Charles Burleigh Galbreath. *Old Chillicothe: Shawnee and Pioneer History, Conflicts and Romance in the Northwest Territories.* Xenia, Ohio: Buckeye Press, 1934.

Gannett, Henry. "A Gazetteer of Indian Territory." United States Geological Survey, Bulletin No. 248, Washington, D.C.: Government Printing Office, 190.

Genetin-Pilawa, C. Joseph. *Crooked Paths to Allotment: The Fight over Federal Indian Policy after the Civil War.* Chapel Hill: University of North Carolina Press, 2012.

Getches, David H., Charles F. Wilkinson, Robert A. Williams, and Matthew L. M. Fletcher. *Federal Indian Law.* 6th ed. St. Paul, Minn.: West Academic Publishing, 2011.

Gibson, Arrell Morgan. "America's Exiles." *The Chronicles of Oklahoma* 54, no. 1 (Spring 1976).

———. "Wyandotte Mission: The Early Years, 1871–1900." *The Chronicles of Oklahoma* 36, no. 2 (Summer 1958).

Gideon, D. C. *Indian Territory: Descriptive Biographical and Genealogical Including the Landed Estates, County Seats Etc., Etc. with a General History of the Territory.* New York: Lewis Publishing, 1901.

Gilley, Brian Joseph. *A Longhouse Fragmented: Ohio Iroquois Autonomy in the Nineteenth Century.* Albany: State University of New York Press, 2015.

Gilpin, Alec. *The War of 1812 in the Old Northwest.* East Lansing: Michigan State University Press, 1958.

Glover, Jeffrey. *Paper Sovereigns: Anglo-Native Treaties and the Law of Nations, 1604–1664.* Philadelphia: University of Pennsylvania Press, 2014.

Green, Michael D. "Small Indian Tracts in Northeastern Indian Territory." In *Historical Atlas of Oklahoma*, edited by Charles Robert Goins and Danney Goble. Norman: University of Oklahoma Press, 2006.

Greene, Don. *Shawnee Heritage 1: Shawnee Genealogy and Family History.* Oregon: Vision ePublications, 2008.

Hagan, William T. *Indian Police and Judges: Experiments in Acculturation and Control.* New Haven, Conn.: Yale University Press, 1966.

Hamill, James F. *Going Indian.* Urbana: University of Illinois Press, 2006.

Hancks, Larry K. *The Emigrant Tribes: Wyandot, Delaware & Shawnee, a Chronology.* Kansas City, Kan.: Larry K. Hancks, 2003.

Harris, Frank H. "The Seneca Sub-agency, 1832–1838." *The Chronicles of Oklahoma* 42, no. 2 (Summer 1964).

Harvey, Henry. *History of the Shawnee Indians, from the Year 1681 to 1854.* Cincinnati: E. Morgan and Sons, 1855.

Hauptman, Laurence M. *The Iroquois in the Civil War: From Battlefield to Reservation.* Syracuse, N.Y.: Syracuse University Press, 1993.

Hayden, Robert M. "Schindler's Fate: Genocide, Ethnic Cleansing, and Population Transfers." *Slavic Review* 55, no. 4 (1996): 727–48.

Hecker, Lisa. "Homestead Act." *Kansapedia.* Kansas Historical Society. Created 2010. Modified 2013. Available at www.kshs.org/kansapedia/homestead-act/15142.

Hill, Leonard U. *John Johnston and the Indians in the Land of the Three Miamis.* Columbus, Ohio: Stoneman, 1957.

Hixson, Walter, *American Foreign Relations: A New Diplomatic History.* New York: Routledge, 2015.

Hoover, Elizabeth. "Cultural and Health Implications of Fish Advisories in a Native American Community." *Ecological Processes* 2, no. 4 (2013).

Howard, James H. "Pan-Indian Culture of Oklahoma." *Scientific Monthly* 18, no. 5 (November 1955).

———. *Shawnee!: The Ceremonialism of a Native Indian Tribe and Its Cultural Background.* Athens: Ohio University Press, 1981.

Howe, Henry. *Historical Collections of Ohio.* Vol. 1. Cincinnati: C. J. Krehbiel, 1904.

Hoxie, Frederick E. *A Final Promise: The Campaign to Assimilate the Indians, 1880–1920.* Lincoln: University of Nebraska Press, 2001.

Indian Treaties, and Laws and Regulation Relating to Indian Affairs. Washington City: Way and Gideon, 1826.

Iverson, Peter. *"We Are Still Here": American Indians in the Twentieth Century.* Wheeling, Mich.: Harlan Davidson, 1998.

Jackson, Jason Baird. "The Opposite of Powwow: Ignoring and Incorporating the Intertribal War Dance in the Oklahoma Stomp Dance Community." *Plains Anthropologist* 48 (2003).

Jefferson, Thomas. *The Papers of Thomas Jefferson.* 39 vols. Edited by Barbara B. Oberg. Princeton, N.J.: Princeton University Press, 1950–2012.

Jennings, Francis. *The Ambiguous Iroquois Empire: The Covenant Chain Confederation of Indian Tribes with English Colonies from Its beginnings to the Lancaster Treaty of 1744.* New York: W. W. Norton, 1984.

———. *The History and Culture of Iroquois Diplomacy: An Interdisciplinary Guide to the Treaties of the Six Nations and Their League.* Syracuse, N.Y.: Syracuse University Press, 1985.

Jones, Dorothy V. *License for Empire: Colonialism by Treaty in Early America.* Chicago: University of Chicago Press, 1982.

Jortner, Adam. *The Gods of Prophetstown: The Battle of Tippecanoe and the Holy War for the American Frontier.* New York: Oxford University Press, 2012.

"Journal of the Indian Territory." *The Chronicles of Oklahoma* 3, no. 1 (March 1925).

Journal of the General Council of the Indian Territory [1870]. . . . Lawrence: Excelsior Book and Job Printing Office, 1871. Reprint, Wilmington, Delaware and London: Scholarly Resources, 1975.

Journal of the General Council of the Indian Territory, 1871–75. Lawrence, Kans.: Journal Book and Job Printing House, 1872. Topeka: Kansas State Historical Society, 1959. University of Oklahoma Microfilm 160.

Kan, Sergei, ed. *Sharing Our Knowledge: The Tlingit and Their Coastal Neighbors.* Lincoln: University of Nebraska Press, 2015.

Kappler, Charles J., ed. *Indian Affairs: Laws and Treaties.* Vols. 1–2. Washington, D.C.: Government Printing Office, 1904.

———, comp. and ed. *Indian Treaties, 1778–1883.* New York: Ameron House, 1972.

Keefe, James F., and Lynn Morrow, eds. *The White River Chronicles of S. C. Turnbo.* Fayetteville: University of Arkansas Press, 1994.

Kidwell, Clara Sue. *The Choctaws in Oklahoma: From Tribe to Nation, 1855–1970.* Norman: University of Oklahoma Press, 2008.

Kievet, Joyce Ann. *Trail of Tears to Veil of Tears: The Impact of Removal on Reconstruction.* Ph.D. diss., University of Houston, 2002.

King, Joseph B. "The Ottawa Indians in Kansas and Oklahoma." In *Collections of the Kansas State Historical Society, 1913–1914, Together with Addresses at Annual Meetings, Memorials, and Miscellaneous Papers.* Vol. 13. Edited by William E. Connelley. Topeka: Kansas State Printing Plant, W. R. Smith, 1915.

Klopfenstein, Carl G. "Westward Ho! The Removal of the Ohio Shawnees, 1832–1833." *Bulletin of the Historical and Philosophical Society of Ohio* 15, no. 1 (1957).

Kohn, Rita, and William Lynwood Montell, eds. *Always a People: Oral Histories of Contemporary Woodland Indians.* Indianapolis: Indiana Historical Society, 1996.

Lakomäki, Sami. *Gathering Together: The Shawnee People through Diaspora and Nationhood, 1600–1870.* New Haven, Conn.: Yale University Press, 2014.

———. "'Our Line': The Shawnees, the United States, and Competing Borders on the Great Lakes 'Borderlands,' 1795–1832." *Journal of the Early Republic* 34 (2014).

Lankford, George. "Shawnee Convergence: Immigrant Indians in the Ozarks." *The Arkansas Historical Quarterly* 59 (Winter 1999).

LaVere, David. *Contrary Neighbors: Southern Plains and Removed Indians in Indian Territory.* Norman: University of Oklahoma Press, 2001.

Lipscomb, Andrew A., and Albert Ellery Bergh, eds. *The Writings of Thomas Jefferson.* Washington D.C.: Government Printing Office, 1903.

Littlefield, Daniel F. "The Treaties of 1866: Reconstruction or Re-Destruction?" In *Proceedings: War and Reconstruction in Indian Territory: A History Conference in Observance of the 130th Anniversary of the Fort Smith Council,* edited by Juliet L. Galonska. Fort Smith, Ark.: National Park Service, 1995.

Llewellyn, Karl N., and E. Adamson Hoebel. *The Cheyenne Way: Conflict and Case Law in Primitive Jurisprudence.* 1941. Reprint, Getzville, New York: W. S. Hein, 1967.

Lossing, Benson J. *Pictorial Fieldbook of the War of 1812.* New York: Harper and Brothers, 1868.

Martin, Lucille J. "A History of the Modoc Indians: An Acculturation Study." *The Chronicles of Oklahoma* 47, no. 4 (Winter 1969–70).

Matthews, John Joseph. *The Osages: Children of the Middle Waters.* Norman: University of Oklahoma Press, 1961.

McAfee, Robert Breckinridge. *History of the Late War in the Western Country.* Lexington, Ky.: Worsley and Smite, 1816.

McCoy, Isaac. *History of Baptist Indian Missions.* Washington, D.C.: William M. Morrison, 1840.

McKenney, Thomas L., and James Hall. *History of the Indian Tribes of North America, with Biographical Sketches and Anecdotes of the Principal Chiefs.* 3 vols. 1855; reprint. Edinburgh: John Grant, 1933.

McLoughlin, William. *After the Trail of Tears: The Cherokees' Struggle for Sovereignty, 1839–1880.* Chapel Hill: University of North Carolina Press, 1994.

McMurray, William J. *History of Auglaize County, Ohio.* 2 vols. Indianapolis: Indiana Historical Publishing, 1923.

McNeil, Kenneth. "Confederate Treaties with the Tribes of Indian Territory." *The Chronicles of Oklahoma* 42, no. 4 (Winter 1964–1965).

Meriam, Lewis. *Report: The Problem of Indian Administration.* Baltimore: Johns Hopkins Press, 1928.

Meserve, John Bartlett. "Governor Montfort Stokes." *The Chronicles of Oklahoma* 13, no. 3 (September 1935).

Michigan Pioneer and Historical Society. *Collections of the Michigan Pioneer and Historical Society.* Vol. 40. Lansing: Michigan Historical Commission, 1929.

Miles, Tiya. *The House on Diamond Hill: A Cherokee Plantation Story.* Chapel Hill: University of North Carolina Press, 2010.

Milk, Theresa. *Haskell Institute: 19th Century Stories of Sacrifice and Survival.* Lawrence, Kans.: Mammoth Publications, 2007.

Miller, Robert J. "American Indian Constitutions and Their Influence on the United States Constitution." *Proceedings of the American Philosophical Society* 159, no. 1 (2015).

———. "American Indian Influence on the United States Constitution and Its Framers." *American Indian Law Review* 18, no. 1 (1993).

———. "Economic Development in Indian Country: Will Capitalism or Socialism Succeed?" *Oregon Law Review* 80 (2002).

———. "Exercising Cultural Self-Determination: The Makah Indian Tribe Goes Whaling." *American Indian Law Review* 25, no. 2 (2001).

———. "The International Law of Colonialism: A Comparative Analysis." *Lewis and Clark Law Review* 15, no. 4 (2012).

———. *Native America, Discovered and Conquered: Thomas Jefferson, Lewis & Clark, and Manifest Destiny.* Westport, Conn.: Praeger Publishers, 2006.

————. "Speaking with Forked Tongues: Indian Treaties, Salmon, and the Endangered Species Act." *Oregon Law Review* 70, no. 3 (1991).

Miller, Robert J., and Maril Hazlett. "The 'Drunken Indian'—Myth Distilled into Reality through Federal Indian Alcohol Policy." *Arizona State Law Journal* 28, no. 1 (1996).

Miner, H. Craig. *The Corporation and the Indian: Tribal Sovereignty and Industrial Civilization in Indian Territory, 1865–1907.* Columbia: University of Missouri Press, 1976.

————. *The St. Louis–San Francisco Transcontinental Railroad: The Thirty-fifth Parallel Project, 1853–1890.* Lawrence: University Press of Kansas, 1972.

Moreton-Robinson, Aileen. *The White Possessive: Property, Power, and Indigenous Sovereignty.* Minneapolis: University of Minnesota Press, 2015.

Morton, Ohland. "Reconstruction in the Creek Nation." *The Chronicles of Oklahoma* 9, no. 2 (June 1931).

Moundbuilders Country Club. "The Golf Course." Moundbuilders Country Club History. Accessed February 22, 2016. www.moundbuilderscc.com/files/The%20Golf%20Course.pdf/.

National Park Service. *A Brief History of the Modoc War.* www.nps.gov/labe/planyourvisit/upload/MODOC%20WAR.pdf.

Nieberding, Welma. *The History of Ottawa County.* Marceline, Mo.: Walsworth Publishing, 1983.

Nolen, Curtis L. "The Okmulgee Constitution: A Step towards Indian Self-Determination." *The Chronicles of Oklahoma* 58, no. 3 (Fall 1980).

Oklahoma Tourism and Recreation Department. *Oklahoma Indian Country Guide.* Oklahoma City: Oklahoma Tourism and Recreation Department, 2010.

"Okmulgee Constitution (Several Indian Nations in Indian Territory, 1870)." In *Documents of Native American Political Development: 1500s to 1933*, edited by David E. Wilkins. New York: Oxford University Press, 2009.

Oregon Historical Society. "Modoc War." *The Oregon Encyclopedia.* www.oregonencyclopedia.org/articles/modoc_war/#.VnNfx5VIiUk.

Osborne-Gowey, Cathleen M. "'No One Cared We Was Just Indian Women': Plants as a Catalyst to Eastern Shawnee Women's Identity Change." Maaster's thesis, Oregon State University, 2002.

Parker, Linda. "Indian Colonization in Northeastern and Central Indian Territory." In *America's Exiles: Indian Colonization in Oklahoma*, edited by Arrell Morgan Gibson. Oklahoma City: Oklahoma Historical Society Press, 1976.

Peake, Ora B. *A History of the United States Factory System, 1795–1822.* Denver: Sage Books, 1954.

Perdue, Theda. *The Cherokee Nation and the Trail of Tears.* New York: Penguin, 2007.

————. *Cherokee Women.* Lincoln: University of Nebraska Press, 1998.

————. *Nations Remembered: An Oral History of the Cherokee, Chickasaws, Creeks, and Seminoles in Oklahoma, 1865–1907.* Norman: University of Oklahoma Press, 1993.

Perrin, W. H., and J. H. Both. *History of Logan County and Ohio.* Chicago: O. L. Baskin, 1880.

Public Statutes at Large of the United States. Edited by Richard Peters. Vol. 7. Boston: Charles C. Little and James Brown, 1846.

Philp, Kenneth R. *John Collier's Crusade for Indian Reform: 1920–1954.* Tucson: University of Arizona Press, 1977.

————. "Termination: A Legacy of the New Deal." *Western Historical Quarterly* 14, no. 2 (April 1983).

Pipestem, F. Browning, and G. William Rice. "The Mythology of the Oklahoma Indians: A Survey of the Legal Status of Indian Tribes in Oklahoma." *American Indian Law Review* 6, no. 2 (1978).

Pratt, Richard Henry. *Battlefield and Classroom; An Autobiography by Richard Henry Pratt.* Edited by Robert N. Utley. Norman: University of Oklahoma Press, 2003.

Prucha, Francis Paul. *American Indian Treaties: The History of a Political Anomaly.* Berkeley: University of California Press, 1994.

————, ed. *Documents of United States Indian Policy*. 3rd ed. Lincoln: University of Nebraska Press, 2000.

————. *The Great Father: The United States Government and the American Indians*. 2 vols. Lincoln: University of Nebraska Press, 1984.

Quaife, Milo Milton, ed. *War on the Detroit: The Chronicles of Thomas Verchers de Boucherville and the Capitulation by an Ohio Volunteer*. Chicago: Lakeside Press, 1940.

Rammage, Stuart A. *The Militia Stood Alone: Malcolm's Mills, 6 November 1814*. Summerland, B.C.: Valley Publishing, 2000.

"Removal of Indians from Ohio: Dunihue Correspondence of 1832." *Indiana Magazine of History* 35, no. 4 (1939).

Richardson, James D., ed. *A Compilation of Messages and Papers of the Presidents 1777–78*. Washington, D.C.: Government Printing Office, 1910.

Rollins, Willard H. *The Osage: An Ethnohistorical Study of Hegemony on the Prairie-Plains*. Columbia: University of Missouri Press, 1984.

Roosevelt, Theodore. "First Annual Message." December 3, 1901. *The American Presidency Project*, edited by Gerhard Peters and John T. Woolley. www.presidency.ucsb.edu.

Rosenthal, H. D. *Their Day in Court: A History of the Indian Claims Commission*. New York: Garland Publishing, 1990.

Rossiter, Clinton L., ed. *The Federalist Papers*. New York: New American Library, 1961.

Royster, Judith V. *Native American Natural Resources Law*. 3rd ed. Durham, N.C.: Carolina Academic Press, 2013.

Scherer, Mark R. "Dawes Act." In *Encyclopedia of the Great Plains*, edited by David J. Wishart. Lincoln: University of Nebraska Press, 2004.

Shetrone, Henry C., and Emerson F. Greenman. "Explorations of the Seip Group Of Pre-Historic Earthworks." *Ohio History Journal* 40, no. 3 (July 1931).

Smith, Roberta White, and Ruby White Sequichie. *A Brief History of the Seneca-Cayuga Tribe*. Wyandotte, Okla.: Gregath Publishing, 2000.

Smith, Robert E. "A Life for a Pair of Boots: The Murder of Shepalina." *The Chronicles of Oklahoma* 71, no. 1 (Spring 1991).

Spencer, Joab. "Interview with Robert Sidney Douglas." In *History of Southeast Missouri: A Narrative of its Historical Progress, Its People, and Its Principle Interest*. Chicago: Lewis Publishing, 1912.

Stark, Heidi Kiiwetinepinesiik. "Nenabozho's Smart Berries: Rethinking Tribal Sovereignty and Accountability." *Michigan State Law Review* 2013, no. 2 (2013).

Steffen, Jerome O. "Stokes Commission." *Encyclopedia of Oklahoma History and Culture*. www.okhistory.org/publications/enc/entry.php?entry=ST040.

St. Jean, Wendy. *Remaining Chickasaw in Indian Territory, 1830s–1907*. Tuscaloosa: University of Alabama Press, 2011.

Stockwell, Mary. *The Other Trail of Tears: The Removal of the Ohio Indians*. Yardley, Penn.: Westholme, 2014.

Strickland, Rennard. *The Indians in Oklahoma*. Norman: University of Oklahoma Press, 1980.

————. *Fire and the Spirits: Cherokee Law from Clan to Court*. Norman: University of Oklahoma Press, 1976.

Sugden, John. *Blue Jacket: Warrior of the Shawnees*. Lincoln: University of Nebraska Press, 2000.

————. *Tecumseh: A Life*. New York: Holt, 1997.

Tanner, Helen Hornbeck. *Atlas of Great Lakes Indian History*. Norman: University of Oklahoma Press, 1987.

————. "The Glaize in 1792: A Composite Indian Community." In *American Encounters: Natives and Newcomers from European Contact to Indian Removal, 1500–1850*, edited by Peter C. Mancall and James H. Merrell. New York: Routledge Press, 2000.

United Nations. *United Nations Declaration on the Rights of Indigenous Peoples.* A/Res/61/295. Sept. 13, 2007.

United Nations Security Council. "Final Report of the Commission of Experts Established Pursuant to United Nations Security Council Resolution 780 (1992)." May 27, 1994.

United States. *Document 512: Correspondence on the Subject of the Emigration of Indians, between the 30th November, 1831, and the 27th December, 1833.* 5 vols. Washington, D.C.: Duff Green, 1834–35.

United States Government Accountability Office. *Indian Issues, Federal Funding for Non-Federally Recognized Tribes.* Edited by Anu K. Mittal et al. (Washington D.C.: Government Accountability Office, 2012).

United States President. "Modoc Reservation." *Executive Orders Relating to Indian Reservations, May 14, 1855–July 1, 1912* (Washington, D.C.: Government Printing Office, 1912).

Viola, Herman J. *The Indian Legacy of Charles Bird King.* Washington, D.C.: Smithsonian Institution Press, 1976.

Vizenor, Gerald, and Jill Doerfler. *The White Earth Nation: Ratification of a Native Democratic Constitution.* Lincoln: University of Nebraska Press, 2012.

Wallace, Anthony F. C. *The Death and Rebirth of the Seneca.* New York: Random House, 1969.

———. *Jefferson and the Indians: The Tragic Fate of the First Americans.* Cambridge, Mass.: Belknap, Harvard University Press, 1999.

Warren, Stephen. "The Ohio Shawnees' Struggle against Removal, 1814–30." In *Enduring Nations: Native Americans in the Midwest,* edited by R. David Edmunds. Urbana: University of Illinois Press, 2008.

———. *The Shawnees and Their Neighbors, 1795–1870.* Urbana: University of Illinois Press, 2007.

———. *The Worlds the Shawnees Made: Migration and Violence in Early America.* Chapel Hill: University of North Carolina Press, 2014.

Wheeler-Voegelin, Erminie. "Shawnee Musical Instruments." *American Anthropologist* 44, no. 3 (1942).

Wilkins, David E. *Tribes, Treaties, and Constitutional Tribulations.* Austin: University of Texas Press, 1999.

Wilkinson, Charles F. *American Indians, Time, and the Law.* New Haven, Conn.: Yale University Press, 1987.

Wilkinson, Charles F., and John M. Volkman. "Judicial Review of Indian Treaty Abrogation: 'As Long as Water Flows, or Grass Grows Upon the Earth'—How Long a Time Is That?" *California Law Review* 63, no. 3 (1975).

Wilson, Charles Banks. *Indians of Eastern Oklahoma Including Quapaw Agency Indians.* Afton, Okla.: Buffalo Publishing, 1947–56.

Wright, Muriel H. *A Guide to the Indian Tribes of Oklahoma.* Norman: University of Oklahoma Press, 1951.

———. "A Report to The General Council of the Indian Territory Meeting at Okmulgee in 1873." *The Chronicles of Oklahoma* 34, no. 1 (Spring 1956).

Contributors

Benjamin J. Barnes lives in Miami, Oklahoma, where he is currently serving a four-year term as the second chief of the Shawnee Tribe. He is vigorously involved in language and cultural preservation and has worked on numerous language and cultural preservation projects with colleagues from institutions such as Indiana University's Glenn A. Black Laboratory of Archaeology and the Ohio History Connection in Columbus, Ohio.

Brett Barnes is the assistant general manager of the Indigo Sky Casino and a citizen of the Eastern Shawnee Tribe of Oklahoma. He is an active member of the White Oak Stomp Ground, where he occupies a ceremonial position. He currently resides in Miami, Oklahoma, with his wife, Rhonda.

Rhonda Barnes has been married to Brett Barnes for twenty-one years. They have five children and three grandchildren. Rhonda is an employee of the Eastern Shawnee Tribe of Oklahoma and resides in Miami, Oklahoma.

Amy Dianne Bergseth is a doctoral candidate in the History Department at the University of Oklahoma. She received her B.A. from Miami University in Oxford, Ohio. Her master's thesis is entitled "'Our Claims Rights Means Nothing': Causes of Myaamia (Miami Indian) Removal from Kansas to Oklahoma," and her doctoral dissertation explores nation building and tribal interactions among the nine northeastern Oklahoma Indian nations from the mid-nineteenth century into the twentieth.

John P. Bowes lives in Lexington, Kentucky, with his wife, Sarah, and two daughters, Callie and Reese. He is a professor of history at Eastern Kentucky University. He holds a B.A. from Yale University and a Ph.D. from the University of California, Los Angeles. He is author of *Exiles and Pioneers: Eastern Indians and the Trans-Mississippi West* and *Land Too Good for Indians: Northern Indian Removal*.

Robert "Bobby" BlueJacket, Eastern Shawnee Tribal Elder, was born February 23, 1930, on his grandmother Carrie BlueJacket's allotment. His parents were Clyde Leroy BlueJacket (the youngest son of Charles and Carrie BlueJacket) and Ethel Lucille Welch. His father was Chief of the Eastern Shawnee Tribe of Oklahoma from 1970 to 1974. Bobby is a World War II veteran from the China-Burma-India theater. He spent the majority of his life in the truck tire, tire-casing, and recycling business. His children are Dennis W., Erin Lee, Lindy Renee, and Patrick C. BlueJacket. He also raised Kelly Lee and Julie Kathleen Barkhuff BlueJacket as well as Jennifer, Jessica, and Samantha BlueJacket.

Robin Dushane serves the Eastern Shawnee people as the Tribal Historic Preservation Officer. In this capacity she manages consultations with various municipalities and state and federal agencies in regard to federal projects involving ground-disturbing activities throughout the Shawnee historical lands. She advocates for the protection of cultural and historical village sites, including sacred sites and ancestral burial sites as necessary. She also oversees the production of cultural events, Shawnee language revitalization, tribal museum development, and grant management.

R. David Edmunds is retired as the Watson Professor of American History at the University of Texas at Dallas. He received his Ph.D. from the University of Oklahoma and has held fellowships from the Ford Foundation, the Newberry Library, and the Guggenheim Foundation. The past president of both the Western History Association and the American Society for Ethnohistory, Edmunds has been honored with the Award of Merit by the American Indian Historians Association. He has received teaching awards from four separate universities and is the author or editor of ten books and more than a hundred articles or essays.

Winifred "Winkie" Froman was born in White Oak, Oklahoma, and raised in the nearby town of Vinita. She worked for the Indian Health Service. Winkie is an Eastern Shawnee tribal citizen and one of the oldest members of the White Oak Stomp Ground.

Elsie Mae "Sis" Captain Vivier Hoevet's sons, Frank Eugene "Bo" Hoevet and Douglas D. "DeeDee" Vivier, wish to say, "Our Mother decided at one time that she should write a story of her life to pass on to her children and grandchildren so they would know what it was like growing up in Oklahoma as an Indian child of the Eastern Shawnee Tribe. We are happy to share her story and wish to say that there may be a few mistakes as far as names are concerned, as all family members had their given names and nicknames. (This part of history still continues with the family to this day.) We hope you enjoy the story of her life as much as we did. We think she did an awesome job!"

Shawn King was raised in Wyandotte, Oklahoma, where he graduated from high school in 1989. He is married to Melva King. They reside in Tiff City, Missouri, and have seven children. He has been ceremonial chief since April 7, 2010.

Norma Jean Strickland Kraus was born June 11, 1938. When she was six her family moved to Oregon, where she was later adopted by Cap and Hettie Broyles. After serving in the Women's Army Corp, she married Joseph Kraus June 5, 1962, and had four children. In 1972 they moved to Oklahoma to care for her ailing father. In 1980 she went to work for the Eastern Shawnee Tribe as the secretary and roll clerk, then later worked in accounting and eventually became the assistant business manager and served on the Business Committee. She continues to volunteer for the tribe and is currently chairperson of the election board.

Joseph Kraus was born in Montana, but his family migrated in search of work to Washington, and ultimately to Oregon. A veteran of the United States Marine Corps, Joe worked most of his life as a welder.

Larry Kropp, a citizen of the Eastern Shawnee Tribe of Oklahoma, is currently serving his third term as first council of the Business Committee. Larry is a graduate of Northeastern Oklahoma A&M College and a veteran of the Vietnam War, during which he served in the U.S. Air Force. Larry learned tribal traditions from his grandfather, Chief Thomas Captain, at the Captain Grocery, the heart of the Eastside Community and makeshift tribal center. After retiring as a driver for Yellow Freight, his service to the tribe began as chairman of the election board. Over the past fifteen years he has served on many committees: NAGPRA, the Board of Directors for Redstone Construction (from its beginning until it was sold), and the Board of Directors for People's Bank of Seneca. He attends Indian gaming conferences as tribal representative to the Oklahoma Gaming Commission, and he has made numerous trips to Ohio and Washington, D.C., on the tribe's behalf. Larry and his family reside in rural Quapaw, Oklahoma, where he actively maintains the family farm in partnership with his brother, raising beef cattle and hay.

Sami Lakomäki is a lecturer of cultural anthropology at the University of Oulu, Finland. His first book, *Gathering Together: The Shawnee People through Diaspora and Nationhood, 1600–1870,* won the 2015 Erminie Wheeler-Voegelin Book Award, given by the American Society for Ethnohistory. Currently he is working on a comparative project exploring indigenous status and the relations between Native peoples and colonial states in eastern North America and northern Scandinavia during the seventeenth and eighteenth centuries.

Sarah Mohawk Dushane Longbone was born in 1887 to John Mohawk (Eastern Shawnee, 1855–1929) and Jane Pipe (Wyandotte, 1868–1889). She was raised by her Wyandotte grandparents, Winfield S. Pipe and Susan Splitlog. She attended Seneca Indian School for a short time and Haskell Institute from ages twelve to twenty-one. She spoke the Seneca, Wyandotte, and Shawnee languages and served as a professional interpreter. She was the mother of ten children and raised several grandchildren. Nancy Dushane Gallenkamp, one of her daughters, went on to serve as one of the first women on the Eastern Shawnee Business Committee as tribal secretary.

Robert J. Miller is a professor at Arizona State University College of Law. He is a justice on the Grand Ronde Tribe Court of Appeals and is a member of the Navajo Nation Council of Economic Advisors. He was elected to the American Law Institute in 2012 and to the American Philosophical Society in 2014. He is the author of *Discovering Indigenous Lands: The Doctrine of Discovery in the English Colonies*, *Reservation Capitalism: Economic Development in Indian Country*, and *Native America, Discovered and Conquered: Thomas Jefferson, Lewis and Clark and Manifest Destiny*. He is a citizen of the Eastern Shawnee Tribe of Oklahoma.

Cathleen "Cat" Osborne-Gowey is an instructor in the Women, Gender, and Sexuality Departments for both Oregon State University and Utah State University. Ms. Osborne-Gowey is the creator, administrative consultant, and out-of-state advocate for the Eastern Shawnee Family Violence Prevention Program. Cat has nearly fifteen years of experience working, researching, and writing on issues related not only to domestic violence and sexual assault in tribal communities but also to traditional uses of plants and language preservation and assisting the King Island Inupiaq community in the documentation of the culture, ethnobotany, and geography of King Island, Alaska.

Glenna J. Wallace was first elected chief of the Eastern Shawnee Tribe in 2006. She was born in Ottawa County, Oklahoma, and has lived within fifteen miles of her birthplace her entire life, except for three years when she and her family were migrant workers on the West Coast. She served as instructor, department chair, division chair, director of travel, and interim academic dean at Crowder College in Neosho, Missouri, where she taught approximately 25,000 students. A dedicated community servant, she has served on countless committees and boards and has been honored with numerous awards.

Stephen Warren is associate professor of history and American studies at the University of Iowa. His research has been supported by grants from the American Philosophical Society, the Colonial Williamsburg Foundation, and the Newberry Library. He is the author of *The Shawnees and their Neighbors, 1795-1870* and *The Worlds the Shawnees Made: Migration and Violence in Early America*, the latter of which was named a 2015 Choice Outstanding Title. In 2009, he appeared in the WGBH/American Experience documentary, *Tecumseh's Vision*.

Eric Wensman is a Bird Creek Shawnee from Sperry, Oklahoma. An active member of the Native American Church, Eric works tirelessly on behalf of language preservation. In the third year of the project, Eric worked as the research manager for the grant "A Search for Eastern Shawnee History." He currently teaches language classes for the Shawnee Tribe.

Index

Page references in *italics* denote illustrations; references ending in *t* refer to tables.

CPSIA information can be obtained
at www.ICGtesting.com
Printed in the USA
LVHW020052030623
748752LV00006B/573

9 780806 192208